P9-EMM-772

A CRITICAL INTRODUCTION

THIRD EDITION

MARIA PRAMAGGIORE & TOM WALLIS

Allyn & Bacon

Editor in Chief: Karon Bowers
Senior Acquisitions Editor: Jeanne Zalesky
Associate Editor: Angela Pickard
Editorial Assistant: Stephanie Chaisson
Executive Marketing Manager: Wendy Gordon

For related titles and support materials, visit our online catalog at www.ablongman.com

Copyright © 2011, 2008, 2005 Laurence King Publishing Ltd

All rights reserved. No part of the material protected by this copyright notice may be reproduced or utilized in any form or by any means, electronic or mechanical, including photocopying, recording, or by any information storage and retrieval system, without written permission from the copyright owner.

To obtain permission(s) to use material from this work, please submit a written request to Allyn and Bacon, Permissions Department, 75 Arlington Street, Boston, MA 02116, or fax your request to 617-848-7320.

Library of Congress Cataloging-in-Publication Data

Pramaggiore, Maria, 1960-
    Film : a critical introduction / Maria Pramaggiore, Tom Wallis. -- 3rd ed.
        p. cm.
    Includes bibliographical references and index.
    ISBN-13: 978-0-205-77077-9 (pbk. : alk. paper)
    ISBN-10: 0-205-77077-0 (pbk. : alk. paper)
    1. Motion pictures. 2. Cinematography. 3. Film criticism. I. Wallis, Tom. II. Title.
    PN1994.P663 2011
    809.2'3--dc22

                                    2010036088

This book was designed and produced by
Laurence King Publishing Ltd
361–373 City Road
London EC1V 1LR
United Kingdom
www.laurenceking.com

LAURENCE KING

Printed in China

10 9 8 7 6 5 4

Senior Editor: Clare Double
Design: www.blokgraphic.com
Picture Researcher: Evi Peroulaki

Front cover: Above, *A Bout de Souffle*, Interfoto/Alamy;
Below, *Avatar*, Twentieth Century-Fox Film Corporation/
The Kobal Collection.

Frontispiece: Ofelia is enthralled by the mysterious faun
in *Pan's Labyrinth*. © Moviestore collection Ltd/Alamy.

Allyn & Bacon
is an imprint of

Why you need this new edition

Film is a constantly evolving art form, affected and inspired by aesthetic ambitions, technology, economics, and history. This new edition of *Film: A Critical Introduction* will provide you with the skills needed to successfully critique and analyze film. Its approach will enhance your appreciation of the cinema and introduce you to the most contemporary issues in the field of film studies Using both classic and current examples, this book teaches you strategies for translating your ideas about film into written criticism and analysis. Woven throughout the text are intricate discussions of the current issues in film theory, covering subjects from sound production to documentary. This updated coverage will keep your perspective on film fresh and informed. Below are some of the key updates in this new edition.

- Every chapter has been revised to incorporate **new films and approaches in film studies scholarship**. These updates will allow you to explore the connections between and among canonical titles and popular, contemporary films. Having the ability to recognize and make these connections will **strengthen your writing skills and enhance your ability to participate in provocative class discussions.**

- New, in-depth Film Analysis essays on *No Country for Old Men*, *Pan's Labyrinth*, *Slumdog Millionaire*, and *Ratcatcher* have been added to the text. These **contemporary examples illustrate the book's core concepts** and demonstrate how to **apply what you learn** in class to the films you watch on your own.

After studying this book, you will watch every film with a far more critically engaged eye.

- Enhanced Study Notes accompanying the Film Analysis essays provide you with **guidance on how to write cogent, well-developed essays for an academic audience**. This material takes you through the stages of the writing process, providing pointers on taking notes, organizing ideas, incorporating research, shaping paragraph structure, composing introductions and conclusions, and fine tuning prose on the sentence-level.

- New, **contextualized readings** have been incorporated into this edition, including: *Avatar* and genre hybridity, *Diva* and theories of film sound, *Inglourious Basterds* and intertexuality, *District 9* and genre revision, *Knocked Up* and the ideology of the Bromance, and *Wall-E* and the representation of gender, *The Wrestler* and star persona. These readings will ease you into more **complex, theoretical approaches to film studies**. Drawing on examples taken from contemporary cinema, this edition makes film theory **relevant to you** while broadening your understanding of what it means to interpret a film.

- Major updates reflect the **latest developments in production and exhibition, including Mumblecore, digital technologies, and 3D** These updates illustrate how technological advances influence filmmaking practices in every arena, from the blockbuster (*Avatar*) to the low budget indie film (*Funny Ha Ha*).

Contents

Preface

We strongly believe that cinema is both an art form and a unique social institution: while moving pictures provide hours of pleasure and entertainment, they also deserve serious intellectual consideration. *Film: A Critical Introduction* is aimed at both college students and general readers who love movies, but who may not possess all the tools necessary for analyzing films and creating interpretive arguments.

Learning about film is more exciting than ever. New technologies make movies—and information and opinions about them—readily available on many different platforms. The internet and mobile devices have enhanced our fascination with the medium, moving many of us beyond the multiplex movie theater and the feature length fiction film. We can stream short films on Ubu, watch high-definition Blu-ray discs with special features and commentary tracks, and seek out, and contribute to, online fan and expert communities (often the same thing). YouTube and Vimeo provide exhibition outlets for budding filmmakers. Most film enthusiasts want to learn how to describe the cinematic techniques used by their favorite directors and to be able to place those aspects of a film in aesthetic, historical and social contexts. Not surprisingly, film studies programs are growing at every educational level.

This textbook is designed for readers who possess a broad range of information but may not have the tools and framework for conceiving of cinema as both an aesthetic and cultural institution. The book provides those resources by focusing on careful analysis and logical argumentation, practices that are critical to an intellectual engagement with the medium. The material helps readers to master film techniques and terminology. It highlights research skills and rhetorical strategies, enabling students to build comprehensive, thoughtful interpretations of films. And rather than limiting a discussion of writing to a single chapter, it encourages readers to build their interpretive skills at the same time that they enhance their knowledge of form, visual style, and sound.

What's New in this Edition

In this new third edition of *Film: A Critical Introduction*, we have revised each chapter by adding discussions of major contemporary films, addressing current research in film studies, and acknowledging important changes taking place within the film industry. Many end-of-chapter Film Analysis essays have been replaced and we've added new readings of classic and contemporary films. In addition, throughout the text, we have threaded intricate discussions of the current issues in film theory, from sound production to documentaries. Part Three has specifically undergone major revisions so that the entire section clearly frames the debates around ideological criticism, national and transnational cinema, and genre and *auteur* theory that animate contemporary film scholarship. We hope that these changes initiate excitement in the classroom and enhance film scholarship and criticism. We made adjustments to this new edition specifically to improve one of the central features of this book: its emphasis on helping students translate their ideas about film into written criticism and analysis. Below are some of the key updates to this new third edition of *Film: A Critical Introduction*.

- Every chapter has been revised to incorporate new films and film studies scholarship in an effort to highlight that film studies is more than a celebration of classic texts; it is a vibrant and growing field. Discussions of new films invite students to explore the connections between and among canonical titles and popular, contemporary films.

- New, in-depth Film Analysis essays on *No Country for Old Men*, *Pan's Labyrinth*, *Slumdog Millionaire*, and *Ratcatcher* demonstrate the relevance of each chapter's core concepts to the study and appreciation of "modern classics." We hope that this will motivate students to become more critically engaged viewers when they watch movies outside the classroom.

- Enhanced Study Notes with Film Analysis essays provide guidance on how to write cogent, well-developed essays for an academic audience. These tips take readers through the writing process, providing pointers on taking notes, organizing ideas, incorporating research, shaping paragraph structure, composing introductions and conclusions, and fine tuning prose on the sentence-level.

- A new annotated student essay on *Let the Right One In* serves as a guide for conducting academic research and as an example of peer work. This essay demonstrates how conducting research can expand one's understanding of and appreciation for a wildly popular genre: the vampire film. In addition, the revamped instruction on how to write a research paper includes an updated and expanded list of web resources.

- New, contextualized readings have been incorporated into this edition, including: *Avatar* and genre hybridity, *Diva* and theories of film sound, *Inglourious Basterds* and intertexuality, *District 9* and genre revision, *Knocked Up* and the ideology of the Bromance, *Wall-E* and the representation of gender, *The Wrestler* and star persona. These readings ease students into more complex, theoretical approaches to film studies. Drawing on examples taken from contemporary cinema, this edition makes film theory relevant to students while broadening their understanding of what it means to interpret a film.

- Major updates reflect the latest developments in production and exhibition, including Mumblecore, digital technologies, and 3D. These updates illustrate how technological advances influence filmmaking practices in every arena, from the blockbuster (*Avatar*) to the low budget indie film (*Funny Ha Ha*).

The Structure of this Book

The book is divided into three parts. Part One introduces the importance of film analysis, offering helpful strategies for discerning the ways in which films produce meaning. The final chapter in Part One formally establishes a key aspect of the book's overall focus: the importance of developing interpretive and evaluative skills by constructing written arguments.

In Part Two, individual chapters examine the fundamental elements of film, including narrative form, *mise en scène*, cinematography, editing, sound, and alternatives to narrative cinema. Each chapter introduces terms, techniques, and concepts, then goes further, helping readers to use this information to interpret films. In Chapters 4–9, Techniques in Practice sections model the way that specific skills (for example, the choice of a lens) can be used as the basis for interpreting a scene or film. In addition, end-of-chapter Film Analysis essays address one of that chapter's major topics in relation to a specific film, such as *Slumdog Millionaire*, *Ratcatcher*, and *Meshes of the Afternoon*.

Part Three introduces critical frameworks that help us to examine cinema as a social and cultural institution. We open Part Three with a discussion of film and ideology in order to emphasize that, regardless of the context, filmmaking is a social institution that can embody, enact, or reject a culture's belief system. We focus on Hollywood in its role as the American national cinema, probing the way mainstream films reflect and sometimes reject American values and beliefs. In Chapter 11, we examine diverse national and international contexts in which cinema flourishes and include a section on theories and practices of national and transnational cinemas. In Chapter 14, we have expanded our readings in *auteur* criticism to help students understand the way scholars who study individual directors conduct their research and writing. Overall, Part Three moves the reader beyond textual analysis of individual films to consider the way film scholars approach various relationships between films and their social contexts.

Special Features

Techniques in Practice sections in Chapters 4–9 use key concepts and film techniques to analyze and interpret a scene, a film, or several films. These sections reinforce the idea that the ultimate goal of mastering definitions and concepts, and paying close attention to details, is to formulate rich interpretations.

Inset boxes in Chapters 2–8 help students understand the filmmaking process, including industry personnel and trades.

Film Analysis essays in Chapters 2 and 4–9 address a major topic area covered in the chapter (for example, setting) in a carefully developed discussion of one or two films. *Sidebars* containing Study Notes draw attention to rhetorical strategies, clarifying the process by which writers move from the basics, such as gathering details, to conceptual tasks such as generating ideas and organizing an argument.

Samples of film scholarship and criticism throughout Part Three illustrate important modes of inquiry in film studies (for example, genre criticism) and familiarize readers with the conceptual and rhetorical diversity of writing about film.

Works consulted lists at the ends of chapters point students to possibilities for further research.

Relevant examples from a wide variety of films engage the reader's interest without sacrificing intellectual rigor. While the book focuses on narrative filmmaking, it also offers in-depth discussions and analyses of avant-garde and documentary films, and features a number of important films made outside Hollywood.

An extensive glossary defines the terms discussed in each chapter.

Online Resources

For instructors:
Instructor's Manual and Test Bank
The Instructor's Manual provides a Chapter-at-a-Glance grid, Chapter Overview of key concepts, Learning Objectives, Lecture Launchers and In-Class Activities for each chapter of the book. The Test Bank includes a wide variety of question formats, including true/false, multiple choice, fill-in-the-blank, short answer, and short essay. Rather than categorizing these questions according to format, we have arranged them according to the organizational logic of the book. Available for download at www.pearsonhighered.com/irc (access code required).

MyTest (Instructor Supplement)
This flexible, online test generating software includes all questions found in the Test Bank section of the Classroom Kits, allowing instructors to create their own personalized exams. Instructors can also edit any of the existing test questions and even add new questions. Other special features of this program include random generation of test questions, creation of alternate versions of the same test, scrambling of question sequence, and test preview before printing. Available at www.pearson-mytest.com (access code required).

PowerPoint™ Presentation Package
This text-specific package, prepared by William Christy at Ohio University, provides a basis for your lecture with PowerPoint™ slides for each chapter of the book. Available for download at www.pearsonhighered.com/irc (access code required).

For students: Pearson Allyn & Bacon Film Study Site
This open access study tool helps students explore the theory and industry of film. The study site includes learning objectives, web links, and practice tests organized by major topics in the film studies course. Available at www.abfilmstudies.com.

For instructors and students: MyCommunicationKit
MyCommunicationKit is an online supplement that offers book-specific learning objectives, chapter summaries, web links, flashcards and practice tests as well as video clips and activities to aid student learning and comprehension. New to MyCommunicationKit is Pearson's MediaShare, a video upload tool that allows students to upload video clips for their instructor and classmates to watch (whether face-to-face or online) and provide online feedback and comments. Structured much like a social networking site, MediaShare can help promote a sense of community among students. Also included in MyCommunicationKit is Pearson's MySearchLab™, a valuable tool to help students conduct online research. Available at www.mycommunicationkit.com (access code required).

Acknowledgments

Writing this book would have been impossible without the support, input, and energy of many, many people. We are grateful for the collegial spirit of our film studies mentors and friends, especially Joe Gomez, Jim Morrison, Andrea Mensch, Marsha and Devin Orgeron, Ora Gelley, Jans Wager, Tom Gunning, Robin Blaetz, Guo-Juin Hong, Nora Alter, Diane Negra, and Krin Gabbard.

We were lucky to work with supportive editors at Laurence King Publishing and Allyn and Bacon for this third edition, especially Philip Cooper, Clare Double, Sarah Batten, Jeanne Zalesky, and Stephanie Chaisson. Allan Sommerville transformed our prosaic text and images into an aesthetically pleasing whole. Thanks again to Lee Greenfield, Richard Mason, Karon Bowers, Jenny Lupica, Karen Dubno, Matthew Taylor, Molly Taylor, Michael Kish, Suzanne Stradley and Tim Nicholson for helping to usher in the earlier editions of this textbook.

To Todd Platt: Thank you yet again for sharing your ever-expanding DVD library. To Beth Hardin and Chris Barrett: Thank you for all of your tech (and emotional) support. To Stephanie, Sadie and the Full Frame gang: your enthusiasm and ideas have kept us going. To Amanda Roop, Dawn Ferguson, Steve Luyendyk, Todd Morgan, and Richard Nicholl: your friendship and spiritual support sustained us while writing this edition. Thanks especially to Anne Pramaggiore, Melissa Shaheen, and Millie, Frank S. and Charles Wallis. We would also like to honor the continuing influence of Frank J. Wallis, and Alfred and Jeanne Pramaggiore; thank you for sharing your love for the magical world of the cinema in our youth, and thank you being pillars of wisdom and strength as we grew into adulthood.

Finally, we would like to thank the readers whose constructive feedback was invaluable as we revised this book: Mary Healey Jamiel, University of Rhode Island; Chris Cagle, Temple University; Leon Lewis, Appalachian State University; Therese Grisham, DePaul University.

Maria Pramaggiore and Tom Wallis
September 2010

Introduction to Film Analysis

Adolescent angst in *Let the Right One In.*

Film is a complex art form and cultural institution whose influence spans the twentieth century and transcends it. In its infancy, film depended on the technology of the industrial revolution and the business model associated with the penny arcade. In its maturity, the cinema emerged as a global entertainment industry, instigating and taking advantage of technological developments in photography, sound recording, and, eventually, electronic and digital imaging. The cinema not only contributed to a mass culture of entertainment and celebrity; it also provided a forum for education and critique through the tradition of social documentary, and served as a medium of personal expression in the form of avant-garde films and home movies.

Many film lovers value movie spectacles that transport them to a magical world of romance, drama, and adventure. Others seek out challenging films that provide a rigorous intellectual and aesthetic experience. This book contends that these two desires are not mutually exclusive: the most profound moments of immersion in cinema art also invite audiences to ponder social, aesthetic, moral, and intellectual questions.

In Part One, Chapter 1 provides an overview of the book's approach. Chapter 2 introduces the foundation of film interpretation. It helps readers to develop strategies for critical reading and analysis so that they may better understand the way films build meaning through the systematic use of details. It also lays out the goal of film analysis: the clear and convincing description, evaluation, and interpretation of films. Chapter 3 takes film analysis to the next stage: developing, organizing, and writing thoughtful interpretations.

Introduction

CHAPTER ONE

Last night I was in the Kingdom of Shadows.

Maxim Gorky, on attending his first film screening

Watching a movie takes most viewers out of their everyday lives and transports them to a different world, a realm that Russian writer Maxim Gorky called "the Kingdom of Shadows." When 35 mm films are projected in a movie theater, a powerful beam of light passes through translucent celluloid to produce those "shadows," the larger-than-life images on the big screen. Whether people watch a film in a movie theater or the digitized version at home on Blu-ray, they continue to visit Gorky's kingdom (fig. **1.1**). They immerse themselves in the lives of fictional characters, develop opinions about historical events, and become captivated by artistic combinations of color, light, and sound. Because films engage viewers on an emotional level, some people criticize the cinema as escapist entertainment. Yet others praise it as an imaginative art form that allows people to realize their dreams and fantasies. The reality is that films do both of these things, and more.

1.1 Film viewers lose themselves in what Gorky called "the Kingdom of Shadows."

Watching films can be both emotionally satisfying and intellectually stimulating. This book offers essential tools for developing a critical approach to the film medium, based on knowledge about the way films are made and the way they can be interpreted in aesthetic, technological, and cultural contexts. One premise of this book is that moviegoers who learn to analyze films and to build thoughtful interpretations will enhance their experience (and enjoyment) of the cinema. This book is not intended to turn every reader into a professional critic or scholar. But it does emphasize that training in film helps viewers to understand and enjoy their experiences of film. The more viewers know about how films are made, why certain films have been celebrated and others ridiculed, and how movies contribute to culture, the better they are able to understand and interpret the films they see.

One of this book's major concerns is film analysis, and one of its central aims is to help readers identify the major elements of film art and recognize the way those elements work together to produce meaning. It emphasizes the value of critical reading, which means putting those analytical skills to use by examining and questioning a film's organization and visual style.

The book also encourages students to develop the skills necessary to build sound written interpretations. The writing process helps to clarify thoughts and organize ideas. By focusing on writing skills, the book emphasizes the importance of constructing thoughtful interpretations.

Cinema: A Confluence of Artistry, Industry, and Technology

The most recognizable image of the cinema as an art form and a cultural institution may be that of an audience of individuals sitting in a darkened theater watching larger-than-life images on a screen, as depicted in figure 1.1. But that combination of machinery (35 mm projectors), material (reels of cellulose acetate), venue (a commercial movie theater), and form (feature-length narrative film) represents only one moment in a long and varied history of film production and reception. This manifestation of film art was the result of the interaction of technological developments, economic structures and opportunities, and aesthetic experimentation. The golden age of the movie palace does not represent the inevitable evolution of moving picture art, nor does that model of spectatorship circumscribe the ways that films can enrich our lives. The history of film production and exhibition merges social and economic factors as well as innovations in technology and aesthetics.

During the late nineteenth century, technological advances in photography established the basis for recording moving images on film. Experiments conducted by Eadweard Muybridge and Étienne-Jules Marey moved still photography in the direction of motion pictures. Muybridge and Marey's experiments in serial photography had as much to do with scientific discovery as they did with film as an art form. Muybridge's famous photographs of horses in motion (1878) were inspired by a question that Leland Stanford (later Governor of California) hired Muybridge to answer: do horses lift all four feet off the ground when running? (The answer was yes.) Muybridge set up a bank of still cameras, each of which captured a shot of the horse as it moved by. These sequences of still shots offered insight into the details of human and animal movement (fig. **1.2**).

By 1888 inventor Thomas Edison and his assistant William Dickson began to focus on motion picture technology and developed the Kinetograph, a camera that recorded motion pictures on rolls of film, and the Kinetoscope, a machine with a peep-hole viewer that an individual looked through to see those films (fig. **1.3**). Film rapidly became a popular mass-market entertainment medium. Then, as now, there were a variety of ways to see films: Louis and August Lumière traveled the world filming *actualités* (the earliest documentary films) and screening them for audiences in theaters they opened in European cities and in New York. In American cities, neighborhood theaters called nickelodeons charged 5 cents for admission and presented diverse programs of short films of 15–20 minutes in length.

During the 1910s and the 1920s the narrative feature film began to eclipse other types of movies as filmmakers began to develop cinema's narrative potential and as U.S. industry leaders sought to compete with French and German cinemas. The organization of the U.S. film industry into corporate entities produced the **star system** and the movie mogul, and instigated the migration from New York to southern California to evade competitors' restrictive patents and to take advantage of better weather and cheap real estate. It also consolidated the notion of films as commercial products. The studio system established in Hollywood—often referred to as an "assembly line" model of industrial production—became the dominant filmmaking practice, both in economic and aesthetic terms, in the United States and around the world.

Alternative modes of filmmaking and spectatorship have always existed alongside the commercial industry, however, including independent art cinema, experimental films, and documentaries. Economic and technological factors influence the production and the viewing of these types of films as well. For example, the advent of broadcast and cable television, and, more recently, the internet, has meant that more people have greater access to all kinds of films.

The contemporary history of cinema is, in part, a history of attempts to stave off the competition from newer entertainment technologies such as television. Television, often called the "small screen," emerged during the middle of the twentieth century as Americans moved out of urban centers into suburbs and began to reap the benefits of rising disposable income and leisure time by purchasing individual television sets. By the 1970s video technology made it

1.2 Series photography suggests movement.

1.3 Edison's Kinetoscope.

possible for people to watch feature films at home, which, in turn, changed the dynamics of the film industry. Home viewing has changed the social aspect of film spectatorship as people watch films of their choosing on sophisticated theater systems at home.

Digital technologies have had an enormous impact on both the economics and aesthetics of cinema. They have affected the way filmmakers make movies and the way fans consume them. The influence of the digital revolution can be felt in the way that filmmaking technologies, such as digital video cameras and editing software, are increasingly within the financial reach of most consumers. Aspiring film directors can shoot a film on an affordable digital camera or even with a cell-phone camera, mixing images and sound using software. YouTube, Vimeo, and atom.com invite budding *cineastes* to post their films for instantaneous, global distribution.

At the loftiest levels of commercial filmmaking, many major, big-budget studio productions, including *Avatar* (James Cameron 2009), *Public Enemies* (Michael Mann 2009), and *Sherlock Holmes* (Guy Ritchie 2009), were shot on digital formats rather than on film. With the advent of digital cinematography has come the resurgence of **3D**, which, until recently, was considered a quaint, outmoded technology from the 1950s. In 2010 the president of the Motion Picture Association of America (MPAA) predicted that, "together, digital presentation and 3D hold the promise of a dramatic game change in moviemaking and moviegoing" ("Worldwide Box Office").

The film industry has emphasized these exciting new technological developments in part because it becomes more and more difficult with each passing year to lure customers into movie theaters. Why? We can watch films in the comfort of our homes, with DVDs, Blu-ray discs or streaming video, or catch the latest flick on a computer or cell phone.

During the first decade of the millennium, consumers became accustomed to watching moving images on smaller, mobile screens, which poses challenges to both filmmaker and film exhibitors. Perhaps the most important point is that creative users of new technologies—much like Muybridge, Marey, Edison and Dickson—explore new aesthetic possibilities and challenge limitations. Cell phone images are no exception: cell phone imagemakers are developing aesthetic principles, namely, the frequent use of close-ups and extremely slow movements so as to eliminate blur.

The experience of film has never been limited to viewing feature-length narrative films on the big screen. Film, as an art form, a technological apparatus, and an industry, is intertwined with society, and more specifically with the image culture that permeates contemporary life. Artists and entrepreneurs, driven by aesthetic and/or economic motivations, continue to develop ways to encourage people to interact creatively with images.

How This Book is Organized

The book's introductory section, Part One, continues with Chapter 2, which offers strategies for embarking on film analysis. First, it considers the kinds of expectations that viewers bring to a film and then asks whether or not the film satisfies those expectations. Second, it looks at how a film's use of details and repetition can give clues about its underlying structure and meaning. As an example of film analysis in action, Chapter 2 concludes with a short essay on how the careful orchestration of detail creates meaning in Guillermo del Toro's *Pan's Labyrinth* (2006). This is the first in a series of end-of-chapter Film Analysis essays that the reader will find in Chapters 4 through 9. Part One concludes with Chapter 3, which focuses on writing about film. The chapter presents some ground rules for interpreting films in four contexts: the scene analysis, the film analysis paper, the research paper, and the film review. It prepares readers to write a textual analysis of an individual film that describes, evaluates, and interprets the film's formal mode of organization, sound, and visual style.

Part Two introduces the basic tools for performing film analysis. Chapters 4 through 9 lay out the characteristics of a film's formal mode of organization, visual style, and sound. These chapters help readers recognize film techniques, describe these techniques using film studies terminology, and understand the part each of them plays in the film's overall organization. Each chapter ends with a Film Analysis essay exploring one of the chapter's topics in relation to a specific film. The Study Notes that accompany each essay identify rhetorical techniques the writer has used to organize and develop ideas and emphasize major points.

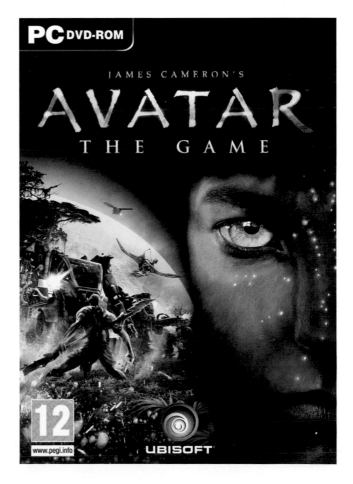

1.4 Industry convergence: *Avatar*, the video game.

The Study Notes establish a logical approach to writing. The first stage of writing involves brainstorming and writing a rough draft, including the following tasks: taking notes, creating the structural logic of an argument, explaining the thought process that connects details to controlling ideas, and conducting further research to supplement original ideas. Once the rough draft has been completed, the revision stage begins: tightening organization on the paragraph level and crafting an effective introduction and conclusion. Polishing sentence-level problems should be the last step in the writing process.

Part Three moves from the textual analysis of individual films to examine cinema more broadly as a cultural institution, discussing in Chapters 10 through 12 subjects such as the connection between movies and ideology, the relationship between social context and film style, and phenomena such as the star system. Chapters 13 and 14 investigate the relationship between films and two other important cultural institutions: popular structures for storytelling (genres) and the social and aesthetic role of the filmmaker, or *auteur* (a **director** whose *oeuvre* reveals a consistent artistic vision). Part Three concludes with Chapter 15, which discusses film as an industry, focusing on new technologies and industry convergence—a term that refers to the economic and technological blending of cinema with other entertainment industries (fig. **1.4**).

By the time readers have completed Part Three, they will be ready to formulate questions related to cinema as a cultural institution and to conduct independent research on film studies topics. Together, Parts Two and Three help readers develop the analytical, critical reading, and rhetorical skills to describe, interpret, and evaluate a film at the textual level and to engage current issues in film and media studies by moving beyond the individual text to consider film's broader cultural significance.

Technical Tips

- Although interpreting films requires knowledge of visual principles and sound design as well as narrative form, the discipline of film studies has adopted some of the terminology of literary studies, for example, describing films as "texts" and interpretations as "readings."
- The first time a technical term is used, it appears in boldface. All boldface terms are defined in the glossary.
- At the end of every chapter, a Works Consulted list provides references to material consulted for the chapter and for the Film Analysis.
- A summary in the form of a bulleted list appears at the end of Chapter 2 and Chapters 4 through 9.
- Chapters 2 through 8 contain inset boxes on various topics, including the terms that describe film production and personnel.
- The first time a film is mentioned, its title is accompanied by the name of the director and the release date. Titles of most foreign-language films appear in English first, then in the original language (or as a transliteration). Subsequent references are in English only. If a film is more generally known by its original-language title, the English translation is given in parentheses the first time the film is mentioned.
- Asian names appear according to the name under which the director's work has become known: Akira Kurosawa (surname second) and Wong Kar Wai (surname first). When conducting research on film directors, readers should consider the fact that book and journal publishers, DVD and Blu-ray manufacturers, and webmasters may use both systems.

Works Consulted

Gorky, Maxim. "The Kingdom of Shadows," in Gilbert Adair, *Movies*, pp. 10–13. London and New York: Penguin, 1999.

"Worldwide Box Office Continues to Soar; U.S. Admissions on the Rise." MPAA Press Release. March 10, 2010. www.mpaa.org.

An Approach to Film Analysis

CHAPTER TWO

How can you still enjoy movies, I am often asked [...],
when you spend all your time analyzing them and researching
them? All I can say in response is that I enjoy movies more
than ever, but admittedly, in a very different way from
my very first excursions into the illuminated darkness.

Andrew Sarris

When a college student tells a friend about seeing Stanley Kubrick's *Dr. Strangelove* (1964; fig. **2.2**), a black comedy about nuclear deterrence, what information does he convey? When a film reviewer writes about that film, does she present the same ideas as the friends who informally share their opinions? And when a film scholar writes an essay about that film, would he adopt the same approach as the casual viewer or the popular critic?

It seems likely that these three viewers would discuss the same film in different ways. Is one of them "right"? Casual viewers might focus on whether they formed a personal connection to characters or enjoyed a particular performance, such as Slim Pickens's comic turn. Were the special effects exciting? If so, they may decide to see more Kubrick films. By contrast, critics and scholars place their observations in a specialized framework. They use their knowledge of film

2.1 The arrangement of characters becomes a motif in *Slumdog Millionaire*.

2.2 Slim Pickens adds humor in Kubrick's black comedy *Dr. Strangelove*.

to formulate interpretations about what the film means, on the level of the story and on broader cultural and aesthetic levels.

A film critic would evaluate the film using criteria such as story coherence, technical innovations, and notable performances, perhaps comparing this film to other work by the same director. (Even film critics will differ in their approaches: a film critic writing in 2011 would probably use different evaluative criteria from one writing the year the film was released, because *Dr. Strangelove* has come to be recognized as an important classic.) A film scholar might write an essay arguing that *Dr. Strangelove* represents an important moment in cinema history when independent film production blossomed as the Hollywood studio system declined.

Any viewer's ability to find meaning in a film is based on knowledge, cultural experiences, preferences, formal training, and expectations. But the significance a viewer derives from a film also depends upon the choices the filmmaker has made. The more practiced the spectator is at recognizing artistic choices, the more he will understand and appreciate the film.

This chapter introduces two ideas that are essential to film analysis. The first one is that expectations influence filmmakers' choices and viewers' experiences of films. Those expectations involve many aspects of a film, including its formal mode of organization, genre, stars, and director. The second idea is that filmmakers present information, elicit emotions, and suggest ideas by orchestrating details in a systematic way. A close analysis of the way such details are used can therefore provide clues about the film's underlying structure and themes. Another way for a filmmaker to create meaning is through references to people, events, or issues outside the film itself, and this chapter also looks at how these references work. The chapter ends with a look at how an understanding of a film's structure and themes can form the basis for making different sorts of statements about it, and, in particular, for making interpretive claims about it.

Understanding Audience Expectations

All film viewers bring expectations to their experiences of film. Someone who goes to a Judd Apatow film for a laugh brings vastly different expectations from someone attending an Ingmar Bergman retrospective hoping to be challenged intellectually. Viewers form expectations about movies by learning about and experiencing film, visual art, and culture.

Expectations may be based on labels that film critics or the general public give to films such as "art cinema," "pure entertainment," or "chick flick." Labels that make a sharp distinction between art and entertainment miss the point that art films entertain because they are challenging, and that even an accessible action film requires visual artistry to produce stunning effects. In short, the distinction between art and entertainment is an artificial one, which wrongly suggests that only art films (which many people assume must be dull and academic affairs) are worthy of serious analysis. Nothing could be further from the truth.

Most viewers form expectations about the *kind* of film they plan to see. Will it tell a story or present an argument, or will it consist of abstract images set to a soundtrack? In narrative fiction films, viewers expect to see stories about human characters whose circumstances produce comedy or tragedy, or both. If these viewers planned to see a documentary instead, they would expect the film to present real-world events, and they might expect to be given factual information about a historical or contemporary situation. If these viewers saw an **avant-garde film**, they might not expect to see a story at all, since avant-garde film-makers see film as a visual art form rather than a storytelling medium.

If viewers expect all films to tell stories, they may be disappointed or confused by documentaries and avant-garde films. As film scholar Scott MacDonald points out, "by the time most people see their first avant-garde film, they have already seen hundreds of films in commercial theaters and on television and their sense of what a movie is has been almost indelibly imprinted in their conscious and unconscious minds." (MacDonald, p. 1) This doesn't mean, however, that audiences can't learn to value other types of cinematic experiences. Sometimes when viewers connect with an experimental film, the experience can be a life-changing event, one that opens up new ways for appreciating the cinema's expressive potential. What's most important, however, is to recognize that, despite their differences, each mode of organization provides viewers with profound and enjoyable experiences, and each type is amenable to analysis and interpretation using the tools provided in this book.

Expectations and Modes of Organization

Narrative fiction films are organized by the cause and effect logic of storytelling: they present characters who encounter obstacles as they attempt to achieve their goals. Viewers identify with characters and understand the choices they make, even if they themselves wouldn't make the same ones. In the Austin Powers films (Jay Roach 1997, 1999, 2002), a 1960s British spy is resurrected and must learn how to navigate the post-Cold War era while foiling the dastardly plans of his nemesis, Dr. Evil. Powers is motivated by pride in his image as a successful, swinging, James Bond type. The fact that he dresses and behaves according to the values and sartorial style of the 1960s creates obstacles for him and comic moments for the audience (see figs. 5.26, 5.27).

Most filmgoers expect to encounter characters such as Austin Powers whose motivations are clear. But filmmakers may flout the rules, and this may enhance or detract from the viewer's enjoyment. For example, a director may present a character with unclear motivations.

Characters with unclear motivations might seem strange to unsuspecting viewers, but they can be intriguing. In Michelangelo Antonioni's mystery *Blow-Up* (1966), the audience never learns why Jane (Vanessa Redgrave) was involved in a murder, or why the victim was killed. That missing information is consistent with the film's focus on a self-absorbed photographer (David Hemmings) who must learn that his camera does not help him see, understand,

2.3 An abstract image from Brakhage's *Black Ice*.

and control reality. Viewers who wish to be challenged appreciate the way films like this vary standard patterns of character development.

Viewers generally expect a narrative film to offer a conclusion that resolves conflicts. Some directors work against the traditional happy ending. The Coen brothers' crime-thriller *No Country for Old Men* (2007) follows a Texas sheriff as he pursues a deranged killer across the state. But the film concludes before the sheriff even meets the killer, much less brings him to justice. Audiences expecting order to be restored might feel as if the movie just stops short, because none of its conflicts get resolved. Such an open-ended conclusion may frustrate audiences, leaving them with lingering questions, not **closure**.

Some documentary films tell stories, although the stories originate in real-world events. These films may satisfy many of the expectations regarding characters, conflicts, and resolution that viewers bring to narrative fiction films. *The Cove* (Louie Psihoyos 2009) follows several environmental activists, led by dolphin trainer Ric O'Barry, as they carry out a covert operation to secure footage of Japanese fishermen capturing and killing dolphins. The film follows a very conventional and engaging narrative arc. Information about O'Barry's experience training dolphins for the television show *Flipper* appears early in the film to help audiences connect emotionally with O'Barry and to understand why he became a passionate animal rights activist. The film follows O'Barry as he assembles his team and designs a plan to infiltrate the restricted cove where fishermen slaughter the dolphins. The film resolves narrative tensions when the team manages to obtain the sought-after footage and initiates a campaign to bring this information to the public's attention. In short, *The Cove* allows ideas about animal rights and environmental protection to emerge from a story connected to a compelling individual who invites the viewer's identification just as a hero in a fictional story might do.

Other documentaries explore their subject matter through a less direct approach. *Winged Migration* ("*Le Peuple migrateur*"; Jacques Cluzaud and Michel Debats 2001) observes a real-world phenomenon—the migration of birds—without appearing to persuade the audience to accept an explicit message. Even so, the film contains an implicit idea: that birds are a unique and interesting life form and may be threatened by human activities such as hunting and industrial pollution.

Avant-garde films move even farther away from the conventions of narrative film. Avant-garde filmmakers explore the aesthetic capabilities of the film medium itself, seeing it as similar to painting, sculpture, or dance. They rarely tell stories or present arguments and, instead, make meaning through symbols and metaphors. A viewer of avant-garde films would expect that basic visual elements of the film medium, such as **composition** (the arrangement of visual elements in the frame) and editing patterns, will carry great significance, while characters or events are given less importance. Film enthusiasts who are open to a non-narrative exploration of sound and vision may enjoy the experimental works of filmmakers such as Stan Brakhage, whose mesmerizing short film *Black Ice* (1993; fig. **2.3**) consists of nothing but abstract, pulsating images.

Whether a filmmaker creates a narrative, documentary, or avant-garde film, he or she is aware of audience expectations. For their part, viewers bring expectations about the type of film they are seeing and may be delighted or disturbed by a filmmaker's choices.

Expectations about Genres, Stars, and Directors

When viewers plan to see a narrative fiction film, they probably arrive with specific expectations based on their knowledge of film genres, movie stars, and directors. Filmmakers anticipate that viewers have expectations, and they may or may not choose to fulfill them. Director Clint Eastwood satisfies viewers expecting classical Westerns when, at the conclusion of *Unforgiven* (1990), he stages a dramatic, revenge-driven shootout in which the film's hero uses his skill with a gun to subdue an entire town. Giving audiences what they expect may please them, but it also has the potential to bore them, so directors also thwart expectations, as Robert Altman does in *McCabe and Mrs. Miller* (1971), when he suggests that large industrial corporations, not individual pioneers, controlled the Wild West. The film's setting in the muddy and snowy northwest defies the look of the traditional Western, and the shootout at the film's conclusion does not glorify the hero's gunslinging prowess.

John Carney's *Once* (2006) charmed audiences by breaking the rules of the musical: rather than highlighting the glitzy song and dance numbers associated with the genre, it used non-professional actors and location shooting to create a realist film with a mature, down to earth sensibility (fig **2.4**).

Another important influence on expectations is the star system, a marketing process that studios, talent agencies, and the press use to transform actors into brand name products. Viewer expectations come into play because fans enjoy seeing their favorite actors in the same kind of roles again and again. Actors may be associated with genres: A movie starring Tom Cruise elicits expectations of an

2.4 *Once* challenges the conventions of the musical with its down-to-earth setting and characters.

action-packed extravaganza, whereas viewers might expect a film featuring Denzel Washington to be a character drama involving suspense and action (fig. **2.5**). John Wayne is linked to Westerns (fig. **2.6**), Judy Garland to musicals, and Humphrey Bogart to detective films. A typical Julia Roberts film revolves around romance and women's empowerment, whereas a film featuring Will Smith typically involves comedy and action.

The public forms expectations about directors as well. Alfred Hitchcock is known as the master of

2.5 *(left)* Denzel Washington plays a cop in the suspenseful drama *Inside Man*.

2.6 *(right)* John Wayne in *Stagecoach*: Hollywood's quintessential cowboy.

suspense, whereas Woody Allen films are associated with New York City settings, neurotic characters, and self-deprecating jokes. The name Busby Berkeley conjures up images of elaborate musicals, and John Ford is synonymous with the Western. James Cameron, David Fincher, and Kathryn Bigelow are known for action-oriented films, while Sam Mendes is respected for his character-driven dramas.

In order to analyze a film, one must consider viewer expectations and take note of which expectations are met and which ones are modified or rejected. If there are modifications, what are the effects of those choices?

In order to answer questions such as these, the viewer must take note of the seemingly minor details that are critical for conveying meaning. Paying close attention to the careful arrangement of detail is one way to identify a film's themes and structure. Just as classical music, a temporal art form, is organized by the repetition of musical phrases, so films use visual and sound details to organize the flow of information.

The Orchestration of Detail

Certain details seem to demand the viewer's attention. Those details may relate to a storyline or characters, or they may arise from the visual or sound aspects of the film. Usually, details claim attention because they are prominent. One way for a filmmaker to assure that audience attention will be focused on a detail is to repeat it. Christopher Nolan has developed a reputation for action films with mindbending psychological twists and fragmented narratives (*Following* [1998]; *Memento* [2000]; *Inception* [2010]).

Motifs

When any detail takes on significance through repetition, it is called a **motif**. Film-makers may employ any film element to develop a motif, including (among others) lines of dialogue, gestures, costumes, locations, props, music, color, and composition.

Motifs have a variety of functions. They can provide information about characters and reinforce the significance of an idea. In *Citizen Kane* (Orson Welles 1941), the last word spoken by newspaper magnate Charles Foster Kane (Orson Welles)—"rosebud"—serves as a motif. The fact that nobody knows what Kane meant by the word motivates Mr. Thompson (William Alland) to interview Kane's friends, ex-wife, and business associates. The repetition of "rosebud" unifies stories that five different narrators tell about Kane's life. Finally, the physical object the word refers to sheds light on Kane's hidden desires (fig. **2.7**).

Motifs often encourage spectators to compare and contrast moments over the course of a film. When an eerie black monolith appears in a prehistoric sequence and returns in the second and fourth parts of *2001: A Space Odyssey* (Stanley Kubrick 1968), viewers compare those moments in space and time. The eerie humming sound that accompanies the monolith each time it appears reinforces its mysterious nature and its importance to the film. The film questions whether humankind has made progress over the span of recorded time, and the recurring image of the mysterious monolith acts as a concrete object to use as a point of comparison and a potent symbol for generating interpretations.

Once established, motifs may evolve, suggesting change and development in a character or situation. In Alfred Hitchcock's *Notorious* (1946), Alicia Huberman (Ingrid Bergman) is introduced as a party girl. Hitchcock shows Alicia drinking to excess in an early scene at her Florida home. When she falls in love with T. R. Devlin (Cary Grant), she attempts to change her ways. Having a drink at a café with Devlin, she declines a second round. But Devlin ridicules her, doubting her ability to leave the past behind. So Alicia changes her mind and orders a double. Throughout the film, Devlin and Alicia both question whether she can change. The drinking motif, which evolves over the course of the film, helps to develop this theme.

2.7 Kane's hidden desires lost in his junk, in *Citizen Kane*.

A film need not limit its use of motifs to objects within the frame. An analysis of *Slumdog Millionaire* (Danny Boyle and Loveleen Tandan 2008) illustrates how filmmakers repeat a visual composition as a way of forwarding important ideas. In the film, two brothers, Jamal (Tanay Chheda) and Salim (Ashutosh Gajiwala), flee the slums of Mumbai where they were born. In their wandering, they accidentally stumble across the Taj Majal. Having been raised in abject poverty, Jamal and Salim have never even heard of the ornate mausoleum, even though it is India's most renowned landmark. To capture the boys' awe, Boyle and Tandan position them in the foreground looking toward the magnificent structure, which is cloaked in mist, in the distant background (fig. **2.1**). Boyle and

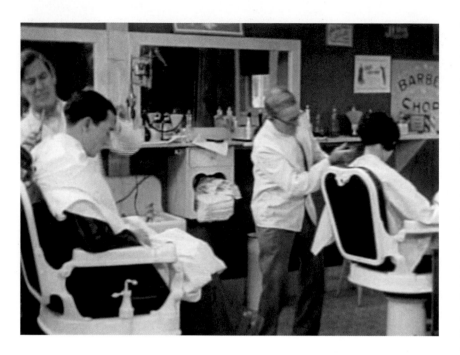

2.8 Identical haircuts in *Steamboat Bill, Jr.*

Tandan repeat this careful arrangement several times in the film to evoke the boys' experience of excited discovery and their simultaneous feelings of cultural alienation. Because of their poverty, Jamal and Salim are outsiders in their own country, far removed from the majestic treasures it has to offer wealthy tourists.

Repetition can also serve an important function in documentary films. Documentary filmmakers may repeat images to highlight their significance, as Albert and David Maysles do in *Gimme Shelter* (1970), a documentary about the Rolling Stones' American tour in 1969. The filmmakers repeat scenes that show a man being attacked near the stage during the Altamont concert. The first time, the viewer sees the images as part of the performance. But the images reappear in the next scene, where the filmmakers and band members watch the concert footage on an editing table. This repetition emphasizes the significance of the tragic incident and provides viewers with access to the band's reactions to the event.

Repetition can also create meaning in avant-garde films. Hollis Frampton's *Nostalgia* (1967) is based on the repetition of a simple, disjointed act: while the camera is trained on a photograph, a **voice-over** describes an image. Over time, it becomes apparent that the voice-over does not describe the image it accompanies but, rather, the next photograph in the series. At the end of each description, the photograph is burned. The burning motif signals the transition to a new combination of words and image but also comments on the ephemeral nature of photographic images and memories.

Parallels

Filmmakers sometimes use the repetition of details to create **parallels.** A parallel arises when two characters, events, or locations are compared through the use of a narrative element or visual or sound device. When this happens, viewers are encouraged to consider the similarities and differences. In *Steamboat Bill, Jr.* (Charles Reisner and Buster Keaton 1928), Bill Jr. (Buster Keaton) goes to have his hair cut. At the barbershop, a friend of his from college is also having her hair styled. A profile shot of Keaton and the woman with the same haircut draws a parallel between the two characters (fig. **2.8**). The joke is meant to suggest that Bill is not manly, a fear his father harbors because Bill is a college boy. The comic parallel of the haircut seems to confirm his father's suspicion. This being a Buster Keaton comedy, Bill ultimately gets the girl, despite (or perhaps because of) their identical haircuts.

Parallels can also play an important role in non-narrative films. In Walter Ruttmann's *Berlin, Symphony of a Great City* ("*Berlin, die Sinfonie der Groß-stadt*"; 1927), a quick **cut** between shots of dolls in a store window and pedestrians suggests their common physical posture and makes a humorous comment on the behavior of the frenzied populace (figs. **2.9**, **2.10**).

In avant-garde films, parallels may work as metaphors, suggesting the common characteristics of two images. *Un Chien Andalou* ("*An Andalusian Dog*"; Luis Buñuel and Salvador Dalí 1929) compares a shot of clouds slicing across the moon with one depicting the filmmaker Luis Buñuel slicing an eye (figs. **2.11**, **2.12**). The shift from beauty to horror functions as a metaphor for the way the movie intends to assault its viewers, and the film certainly did shock contemporary audiences with its irrational, anti-narrative structure.

Repeated details form patterns that contribute to a film's meaning. In a narrative fiction film, these elements may explain a character's motivation, present themes, and contribute to the overall flow of the story. In documentaries, they may encourage viewers to make connections between ideas or to reconsider their initial thoughts about an event. In avant-garde films, repetition can organize

2.9 *(left)* Dolls with sore feet …

2.10 *(right)* … seem to mock pedestrians who scurry across the street in *Berlin, Symphony of a Great City*.

2.11 *(left)* Clouds slicing across the moon in *Un Chien Andalou* ("*An Andalusian Dog*").

2.12 *(right)* An eye being sliced in *Un Chien Andalou*.

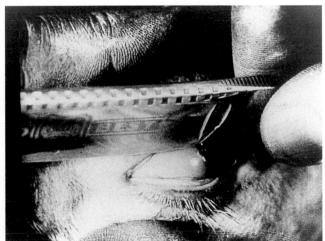

the flow of images and sound, and may create connections between seemingly dissimilar images. As a result, paying attention to repetition, motifs, and parallels can help viewers to recognize a film's deeper structure.

Details and Structure

One way to create a framework for meaning is to pay attention to the way a film begins and ends, and the way it unfolds in sections. Each section forms a part of the underlying structure of a film. A full analysis of the film reunites the parts and considers the way they interact to produce meaning.

Parallels and Structure

Parallels that invite viewers to compare the beginning and end of a film provide information about its overall structure. In Jafar Panahi's *The Circle* ("*Dayereh*"; 2000), the opening and closing shots are eerily similar, suggesting that events have gone full circle. The effort that several characters have expended over the course of the film may have been in vain. In *Winged Migration*, the filmmaker begins and ends with scenes of birds in the same location, emphasizing the cyclical, endlessly repeated pattern of migration. *Rear Window* (Alfred Hitchcock 1954) begins and ends in the same location, but the differences between the two scenes convey a great deal about the changes the two main characters have undergone. Identifying turning points will help the viewer grasp how and why characters undergo such dramatic changes.

Turning Points

Just as popular songs conform to a familiar pattern—the alternation between verse and chorus—so narrative feature films tend to flow according to a standard structure. Analyzing a narrative film involves dividing the story into beginning, middle, and end and tracking important **turning points**. Even before mastering the complexities of narrative form (the subject of Chapter 4), it is possible to recognize turning points that signal the end of one section of the film and the beginning of another.

Directors signal important moments such as these through camerawork, editing, and sound as well as through dialogue and action. The camera may linger on a shot to suggest its importance, or dramatic music may underscore a particularly significant action.

In *The 40 Year Old Virgin* (Judd Apatow 2005), Andy (Steve Carrell), a shy and reclusive person who does not drink, agrees to go out after work with his co-workers. As the camaraderie of the group makes him more

2.13 The group focuses on Andy as he lifts his glass in *The 40 Year Old Virgin*.

comfortable, Andy begins to open up, divulging personal information. He also drinks beer with his new friends, an act that signifies the step that he has taken into adult masculinity. The director calls attention to this moment by framing the scene to emphasize that Andy is now a member of the group (fig. **2.13**). Becoming attuned to significant turning points such as this one, and to how they are created, helps viewers gain a better understanding of a film's structure.

Tonal shifts can convey changes over time as well. Jeremiah Zagar's documentary *In a Dream* (2008) follows his family during a tumultuous period. Early in the film, Zagar's mother, Julia, recounts the early days of her marriage to Isaiah. She singles out the moment he discovered the art of making mosaics as a highlight of their early years together; suddenly Isaiah felt as if he had "found his life," she says. While Julia describes Isaiah's period of intense self-discovery, the audience sees contemporary footage in which the camera **tracks** behind her husband as he saunters down a hallway whose walls are completely covered by his mosaic work (fig. **2.14**). His slow, graceful movement through the kaleidoscopic array of colors and out through a doorway into the bright sunlight beyond captures the youthful optimism and the transcendent feeling of self-realization Julia recounts. Isaiah's family and career continue to blossom.

2.14 *(above)* Vibrant colors capture the magic of self-discovery in *In a Dream*.

2.15 *(below)* Muted lighting and dark colors indicate a mood shift in *In a Dream*.

But personal problems eventually threaten the sense of optimism and togetherness. The family falls into disarray, in part because Isaiah becomes romantically involved with another woman. When Julia describes this period of collapse, we see Isaiah walking through one of his mosaics once again, but here the lighting is dim and the pieces of vibrantly colored glass are barely visible (fig. **2.15**). Instead of moving, the camera remains still, suggesting how stasis has replaced progress at this point in the family's life together. This parallel use of space invites the audience to compare these two moments in Isaiah's life. The tonal shift contrasts the vitality of Isaiah's early self-discovery with this contemporary moment of self-doubt.

As the above discussion makes clear, all films are structured through turning points and repetition. Turning points and motifs help organize documentaries and experimental films as well as fiction films.

Repetition and Non-chronological Structure

In a documentary, a turning point may be based on a change from one topic to another. Alternatively, documentaries may be structured according to the various points of view brought to bear on an issue: the arguments for going to war could be positioned before or after the arguments for avoiding war. One of the most famous documentaries about the Holocaust, Alain Resnais's *Night and Fog*

("*Nuit et Brouillard*"; 1955) can be divided into parts according to certain visual attributes. The events occurring in Nazi Germany before and during World War II are depicted in black and white, while postwar images are filmed in color. Rather than presenting a straightforward chronology, Resnais interweaves the troubling events of the past and the apparent tranquility of the present, creating a strong visual contrast that also suggests that the past lives on.

Avant-garde films can be divided into sections as well. The turning points may be subtle, however, signaled by changes in the photographic properties of images, in the way the images and sound relate to one another, or in editing patterns that alter the film's rhythm or pace. Yoko Ono's *No. 4 (Bottoms)* (1966) is an 80-minute film entirely composed of images of rear ends walking away from the camera. At a certain point, Ono repeats some images, changing the viewer's relationship to them. Scott MacDonald argues that "once the film develops this mystery of whether a particular bottom has been seen before, the viewer's relationship with the bottoms becomes more personal: we look not to see a new bottom but to see if we 'know' a particular bottom already." (MacDonald, p. 26)

The goal of examining the relationship between details and structure is to arrive at a comprehensive analysis that takes into account the way seemingly minor elements combine to produce the overall design of a film. Viewers also must consider the details filmmakers include when they make references to people or events outside the film. Recognizing the importance of these references deepens the audience's understanding of the work.

Creating Meaning Through the World Beyond the Film

Films can also convey meaning by making reference to people and events that exist outside the world of the film. Viewers may understand plot details, character motivation, or themes better because of references to historical events, to other films, and to works of art. In some cases, those references are crucial to the audience's full understanding of the film, but in others, references may function simply as inside jokes.

Historical Events and Cultural Attitudes

Narrative films convey fictional stories, yet they frequently make reference to actual historical events. A film set in a particular era, for example the U.S. Civil War, will more than likely include well-known events such as the burning of Atlanta (depicted in *Gone with the Wind*; Victor Fleming 1939) or the battle at Petersburg (in *Cold Mountain*; Anthony Minghella 2003).

Audiences should not assume that historical references in period pieces (films set in the past) function only to establish the story's time and place. Many films use such references to develop important themes as well. One shot in *Inglourious Basterds* (Quentin Tarantino 2009) emphasizes a theater marquee emblazoned with the name of German film actress and director Leni Riefenstahl (fig. **2.16**). On the most basic level, this reference helps establish the historical context

for the events that unfold: the story takes place in Nazi-occupied France, and the marquee captures the Franco-German milieu. But this reference also helps develop the film's interest in how the cinema functions as a tool for nationalist propaganda. After starring as the athletic heroine in a series of mountaineer adventure films, Riefenstahl moved into directing. She had developed such a name for herself that Adolf Hitler commissioned her to film the Nazi party's 1934 rally at Nuremberg. The resulting film, *Triumph of the Will* (1934), presents Hitler as an exalted leader who will bring unity and discipline to the German people. Consequently, critics and scholars widely condemned Riefenstahl's film as propaganda for the Fascist regime. Therefore, this Riefenstahl reference also resonates with the propaganda film within Tarantino's film in which one lone and highly-disciplined German sniper manages to fend off the Allied advance … all while carving a perfectly ornate swastika in his perch using a cruddy pocket knife.

Historical references do not necessarily establish a film's setting in the historical past. While *Avatar* (Cameron 2009) is set on a distant planet in the future, key lines of dialogue reference current events. The plot involves a joint venture between the American military and a corporation, who both want to retrieve valuable energy resources from the planet Pandora. When Pandora's natives resist the occupation and the destruction of their sacred land, the menacing Col. Quaritch (Stephen Lang) vows to "fight terror with terror" and to retaliate with "shock and awe." These lines (and many others) specifically evoke President George W. Bush and the language his administration used to describe the United States' wars in Afghanistan and Iraq, prompting many critics to praise the film and just as many others to condemn it for equating the slaughter of the Na'vi on Pandora with U.S. military pursuits.

Stars and Public Figures as References

Films also make references through movie stars. Chapter 12 examines the star system, so it's sufficient for this discussion to observe that actors often repeat and reprise roles and that directors may expect audiences to make connections with those previous roles. Casting Al Pacino as Big Boy in *Dick Tracy* (Warren Beatty 1990; fig. **2.17**) was doubly comical, first because of Pacino's over-the-top

2.17 *(above)* Al Pacino as Big Boy in *Dick Tracy*.

2.18 *(below)* Mike Tyson plays himself in *The Hangover*.

performance, but second, because he parodied his performances as gangsters and undercover cops in previous films, including *The Godfather* films (1972, 1974, 1990), *Serpico* (Sidney Lumet 1973), and *Scarface* (Brian De Palma 1983). Wes Anderson's casting of George Clooney to be the voice for the crafty Mr. Fox in *The Fantastic Mr. Fox* (2009) may remind viewers of Clooney's earlier roles as Danny Ocean in *Ocean's Eleven* (Steven Soderbergh 2001) and its sequels. Like master criminal Ocean, Mr. Fox enjoys nothing more than planning elaborate heists (though Ocean has considerably more luck pulling his plans off).

Films can also make reference to public figures. Like other references, these figures may resonate with other details in the film and so they shouldn't just be taken at face value.

Professional boxer Mike Tyson appears as himself in *The Hangover* (Todd Phillips 2009), and his presence adds to the increasing madness that follows three groomsmen over the course of a night long bachelor party in Las Vegas (fig. **2.18**). During his reign in the 80s and early 90s, Tyson was notorious for his erratic and violent behavior both in and out of the ring; during one especially infamous bout, he literally bit off his opponent's ear. In the film, the drunken and drugged revelers are so intoxicated, they decide to take on Tyson, urinating in his pool and stealing his pet tiger. Casting Tyson was an especially effective choice, contributing to the comic premise of a night spiraling out of control as drugs and alcohol inhibit the characters' capacity to fully comprehend the ramifications of their increasingly outrageous actions.

Intertextual References

Films also make **intertextual references**, or references to other films or works of art. *Run Lola Run* ("*Lola rennt*"; Tom Tykwer 1999) makes a pointed visual reference to Alfred Hitchcock's *Vertigo* (1958). In a scene where Lola (Franka Potente) gambles at a casino to earn the money her boyfriend needs, the camera comes to rest on a painting of a woman. The shot resembles a scene in Hitchcock's film where a blonde Madeleine Elster (Kim Novak) sits before a portrait of the raven-haired Carlotta Valdez (figs. **2.19**, **2.20**). The woman's hairstyle—a spiral

French twist—is a prominent detail that may help viewers to connect the two films.

It's reasonable to ask whether this, or any, intertextual reference functions merely as a visual trick, designed to gratify viewers who recognize the portrait and distinctive hairstyle. In this case, the reference to *Vertigo* offers several interpretations that make it meaningful. The hairstyle contributes to a visual motif in the film involving a spiral pattern. As she hurries down the stairs of her apartment building and through the Berlin streets, Lola's path creates spirals (fig. **2.23**). Furthermore, the film's structure resembles a spi-

2.19 *(above)* Kim Novak and the portrait in *Vertigo*.

2.20 *(below)* The portrait in *Run Lola Run* references Hitchcock's *Vertigo*.

ral. Physically, Lola begins at the same point in each of the film's segments, performs the same actions, but always ends up at a different point, which suggests the idea of a slightly imperfect circle, or spiral. In some segments, Lola and her boyfriend are killed, but they return to life when the story begins again. The spiral motif and bringing characters back to life link the film to *Vertigo*, which has a repetitive structure in which characters seem to die and come back to life.

Avant-garde films also make references to the world outside films and to other films. Bruce Conner's *A Movie* (1958) and Chick Strand's *Cartoon la Mousse* (1979) are **compilation films** composed of scenes from other films (see figs. 9.36, 9.37). Each "borrowed" shot contributes meaning based on its look, its original content and context, and the way it is juxtaposed with other images.

FILM STYLE

For film critics who distinguish content from style, style is defined as the way the content of a film is presented to the audience. A romance story can be presented as a heartbreaking, melodramatic ordeal, with scenes of crashing ocean waves set to classical music, or as a whimsical romp that involves rides on Ferris wheels and 1960s pop music. For many filmmakers and critics, however, the story is inseparable from the way it is told, and style cannot be easily disengaged from subject matter.

Film scholars have long divided narrative fiction films into three stylistic categories: **classical**, **realist**, and **formalist**. The classical style includes the type of films made under the Hollywood studio system, in which the story is paramount. The various elements of film art (including lighting, editing, and sound) do not call attention to themselves as aesthetic devices: instead, they contribute unobtrusively to the smooth flow of the story. The goal is to invite viewers to become absorbed in the story, not to remind them that they are watching a film. Most commercial releases adopt a classical style, seeking to entertain audiences by immersing them in a fictional world.

Realist films reject some of the rules of classical narrative in terms of characters, stories, and structure. Films made in a realist style do not privilege the story at the expense of details that evoke characters, places, and eras. Their stories generally involve average, everyday people. Their plots may seem to digress, as filmmakers strive for spontaneity and immediacy rather than a highly crafted structure. In Vittorio De Sica's *Umberto D* (1952), an Italian neorealist film that chronicles the everyday lives of ordinary Italians after World War II, a well-known scene involves a maid going through her morning routine (fig. **2.21**). Her actions have no real consequences for the story; so, in a classical film that scene would be "wasted time." In this film, the scene establishes the texture of this minor character's daily life. Ironically, a realist style may be experienced as a more obtrusive style because it allows character and environment to take precedence over storytelling. Despite its name, realism is not reality. Like classicism, it is a style produced by a combination of techniques. Realist films may adopt a different approach than classical films, but they do not necessarily present a "truer" vision of reality. A case in point is the Jules Dassin

2.21 *(above)* In *Umberto D*, De Sica captures everyday life without obvious intervention on the part of the filmmaker.

2.22 *(below)* Formalism calls attention to artifice. In *Synecdoche, New York*, actors are cast to play the film's main characters, then another set of actors playing them.

film *Naked City*. Hailed for its gritty realism when it was released in 1947, audiences sixty years later can't help but notice the artificiality of the talky voice-over.

Formalist films are self-consciously interventionist. They explore abstract ideas through stories and characters. As such, these films generally rely on unusual visual techniques that call attention to themselves as artistic exploration. Formalist films such as Resnais's *Last Year at Marienbad* ("*L'année dernière à Marienbad*"; 1961), Andrej Tarkovsky's *Solaris* (1968), and *American Splendor* (Shari Springer Berman and Robert Pulcini 2003) self-consciously distance viewers from characters and plot. They raise philosophical questions about the nature of identity and reality.

One recent example of a formalist film—one whose story and style are highly self-conscious—is Charlie Kaufman's *Synecdoche, New York* (2008). Moderately successful and slightly neurotic playwright Caden Cotard (Philip Seymour Hoffman) goes about his everyday life in Schenectady in a slightly desultory way. He is estranged from his wife and daughter and begins to become obsessed with his own mortality. When he learns he has won a prestigious McArthur Grant, Cotard embarks on the project that will consume the rest of his life. He moves to New York City to mount his next production, in which he literally stages his own life, hiring actors to play himself, his now ex-wife Adele (Catherine Keener), his second wife Claire (Michelle Williams), who is also an actress, and Hazel (Samantha Morton), another woman at the theater with whom he becomes involved.

Once in Manhattan, Cotard rents a warehouse, constructs a replica of his Manhattan neighborhood within it, and begins rehearsing actors, coaching them to attend to the mundane and the everyday. The film becomes increasingly obscure: narrative chronology becomes difficult to follow as the mirror images of the main characters—their doubles— begin to assume as much importance as the central characters. Decades of Cotard's life are compressed into fleeting scenes, for example, when he visits his wife in Berlin, or has an argument with his father (Albert Finney). Pivotal emotional encounters get played out over and over again by the cast, which keeps multiplying because Cotard casts another set of actors to play the actors playing the central characters (fig. **2.22**). Cotard's play, and real life are now inseparable, not only for the director, but for all the actors and technical support crew who are living their lives inside the Manhattan warehouse. The dizzying circularity of the story gives rise to confusion as well as delight: some of the encounters between and among actors who play one another are absurdly hilarious. In his review of the film, Roger Ebert claims that viewers need to see this film twice: "I watched it the first time and knew it was a great film and that I had not mastered it."

Synecdoche, New York demonstrates the way that a film can integrate techniques associated with several aesthetic approaches. For example, the film's visual style is a disorienting blend of formalism and realism. On the one hand, the setting is overtly presented as artifice: viewers are constantly reminded that the world in which the characters live is a set, built by the theater's carpenters (in fig. 2.22, the curved roof of the warehouse is visible behind the characters). This formalism is countered, however, by Cotard's desire to meticulously re-create the details of his life: this translates into a highly detailed, realist depiction of the interiors and street scenes, many of which Kaufman shot on location in New York, helping to confound the viewer's sense of the real and the constructed.

The title alone points to the self-referential exploration of art's relationship to life, a theme that preoccupies formalist filmmakers. Grammatically, a synecdoche is a stand in—a part for a whole (using "wheels" to refer to a car) or a whole for a part ("the law" for a police officer). The title also functions as a pun and a near-homonym for Schenectady, the city in upstate New York where the film begins. The title speaks of the way that supposedly artificial performances such as that of Cotard's can stand in for "real" life, and vice versa. Kaufman's emphasis on this abstract relationship, which takes place at the expense of an easily understood plot, lends a degree of abstraction to *Synecdoche, New York*. This is often the case in formalist films, where ideas take precedence over plot, action, and character. What is particularly striking about Kaufman's film is the way he is able to fuse formalism and realism through a theatrical metaphor that's at least as old as Shakespeare, who wrote that all the world's a stage.

As this discussion makes clear, classical, realist and formalist approaches to film style should not be understood as three rigidly defined categories, but rather as a spectrum of aesthetic choices.

In one sense, all documentaries make reference to the world beyond film because they are based on historical events. Michael Moore's *Roger and Me* (1989) documents the closing of a GM plant in Flint, Michigan. Errol Morris's *Standard Operating Procedure* (2008) looks at the Abu Ghraib controversy. *Rock Hudson's Home Movies* (Mark Rappaport 1993) looks at cinema culture by examining

2.23 A spiral staircase provides another reference to *Vertigo*.

Rock Hudson's Hollywood career and his gay identity. The filmmaker suggests that Hudson's success depended on the public's ignorance about his sexuality whereas gay viewers saw Hudson as a gay icon from his earliest screen roles.

Meaningful References with Objects

Films also refer to specific real-world objects. Characters may drive a particular kind of vehicle, wear clothing made by a designer, and consume popular brands of beer and soft drinks. Often these references are the result of lucrative business deals called **product placement**. Corporations agree to pay film studios a fee to feature products in a film. In Steven Spielberg's *E.T: The Extra-Terrestrial* (1980), the script called for the alien to become hooked on M&Ms. But the Mars corporation was anxious about linking its product to a repulsive alien, so the production company turned to the makers of a new product, Reese's Pieces. *E.T.* caused a tremendous sensation, sending the demand for Reese's Pieces soaring and paving the way for a wave of product placement agreements (Monaco, p. 589).

The important question to ask is whether or not familiar products serve a purpose in terms of the film's meaning: do they help to form motifs, do they add significance? References to name-brand products should not be rejected out of hand as meaningless; they may serve a function in terms of character and story. The Coca-Cola company plays a role in creating satire in Kubrick's *Dr. Strangelove*, when an army colonel refuses to steal the machine's change for another officer to make a pay telephone call to the U.S. President to avert a nuclear disaster (fig. **2.24**). He is reluctant to raid the coin box because the machine is the property of an American corporation. Protecting the profits of a familiar name brand is more important than preserving life on earth.

The Goal of Film Analysis: Articulating Meaning

The purpose of film analysis—breaking a film down into component parts to see how it is put together—is to make statements about a film's themes and meaning. Those statements take three different forms, each one related to a different level of meaning. The first type of statement is descriptive: a **descriptive claim** is a neutral account of the basic characteristics of the film. Most descriptions of narrative fiction films involve plot events: "Set during the waning days of World War II, *Inglourious Basterds* follows two divergent plotlines that eventually intersect. In one, a young Shoshanna Dreyfus witnesses a Nazi Colonel Hans Landa (Christoph Waltz) brutally slaughter her family. She survives, but vows to get revenge. In the other, American Lt. Aldo Raine (Brad Pitt) and his ragtag company of allied soldiers plan to infiltrate the premiere of a Nazi propaganda film in an effort to assassinate Adolf Hitler. Unbeknownst to them, Shoshanna (Mélanie Laurent) has grown up, changed her name, and inherited the theater that is slated to host the screening, and she too has hatched a plan to destroy the venue…along with everyone in it." By stringing together a series of descriptive claims, this viewer has arrived at a **plot summary**—a sequential account of the important events in a film. Descriptive statements may also illustrate specific details about the film's visual or audio style: "In one shot, an ax juts out of a stump in the foreground of the frame while a man walks to his house in the background" (fig. **2.25**). Descriptive claims might also go beyond events and details and refer to intertextual connections and genre: "This composition resembles a similar shot (fig. **2.26**) from the Western *Shane* (George Stevens 1953)," or "*Inglourious Basterds* uses bits and pieces of composer Ennio Morricone's scores throughout."

An **interpretive claim** involves a more complex intellectual response than a descriptive claim. Interpretive claims present an argument about a film's meaning and significance. These claims address a film's themes and abstract ideas. They do more than simply identify a film's subject matter; they go further, making an argument about what the film does with this subject matter. Violence on the battlefield is the subject of every war movie, but an interpretive claim about a war film would identify what specifically the movie has to say about war and its causes or effects. For example, a spectator might notice that *Inglourious Basterds* focuses on the connections between and among cinema, propaganda, and warfare. An interpretive claim will make an argument about how Tarantino treats this subject matter: "*Inglourious Basterds* draws attention to the cinema's ability to manipulate audience emotion; by linking the American Western to the Nazi propaganda machine (and Tarantino's own wish-fulfillment fantasy in which Hitler gets his come-uppance), the film implies that the cinema is *always* prop-

2.24 A Coke machine as social satire in *Dr. Strangelove*.

aganda, luring audiences into a compelling, if overly simplistic (and sometimes disturbing), worldview."

These sentences make an argument that takes into consideration the careful orchestration of scenes throughout the film. In order to support such an overarching argument, the viewer would need to construct a logical thread of more narrowly focused interpretive claims about how individual scenes, motifs, parallels, turning points, and the like, all cohere. For example, a thorough treatment of the interpretive claim above might begin by describing how the film's **exposition** makes reference to classic Westerns. Its visual style recalls *Shane*, *The Searchers* (John Ford 1956), and *Once Upon a Time in the West* (Sergio Leone 1968), while at the same time Tarantino uses music by composer Ennio Morricone, famous for his work on "spa-

ghetti Westerns." In doing so, Tarantino equates this opening standoff between a French dairy farmer and an unrelenting German officer with the long history of cowboy pictures in the cinema. The film thus makes it clear that it is not interested in creating an authentic portrait of life during World War II. Instead, its self-conscious formalist approach draws attention to the cinematic lineage that connects *Inglourious Basterds* to a long tradition of films that reduce the complexity of the human experience to an overly-simplistic world in which good justifiably uses violence to vanquish evil.

2.25 *(above)* An intertextual reference to *Shane* in *Inglourious Basterds*.

2.26 *(below)* A dramatic composition in *Shane*.

This reading might go on to discuss the ironic implications of depicting an episode in the Holocaust while simultaneously referencing a Hollywood genre that, for much of its history, celebrated the eradication of Native Americans. This irony comes to a head when Tarantino explicitly depicts a theater full of Nazi officers reveling at the sight of a German sniper heroically picking off Allied soldiers. Tarantino puts the shoe on the other foot, so to speak, by showing American viewers of his film a mirror image of themselves cheering at the sight of violence enacted in the name of cultural retribution.

Further complicating matters is the fact that Aldo Raine and his band terrorize German soldiers by scalping them, a detail linking the ostensible "good guys" to classical Westerns' representation of Indians, who were typically portrayed as savages who threaten civilization. In short, Tarantino draws attention to and also complicates the way the cinema fosters nationalistic sentiment by maligning cultural and ethnic outsiders, a strategy that aligns Hollywood with the Nazi political propaganda within the film.

Such a reading might also take notice of how Raine's plot to kill Hitler coincides with Dreyfus's plan to co-opt the Nazi film with counter-propaganda before igniting the screen itself (using canisters of highly-flammable nitrate film stock) and burning down the theater full of trapped patrons. As such, *Inglourious Basterds* is as much about imagining the destruction of cinema itself as it is a fantasy about assassinating Hitler.

Of course, these statements are by no means the only interpretive claims someone might make about *Inglourious Basterds*. There can be many interpretations of any one film. Audiences who don't notice the cinematic references Tarantino heaps onto his film might be more interested in its depiction of the psychology of resistance: *"Inglourious Basterds* is about resisting oppression by instilling fear in those in power."

How should audiences determine which interpretation is correct? Although films support multiple interpretations, they do not generally support diametrically opposed claims; for example, if *Inglourious Basterds* is about legitimizing the use of terror to fight oppression, it can't simultaneously be about the value of engaging in non-violent resistance. Some claims have greater validity than others. To be convincing, an interpretive claim must be well supported by details from the film. Constructing valid interpretive claims is not a simple matter: a serious interpretation demands a thorough consideration of all aspects of the film.

An **evaluative claim** expresses the author's belief that the film is good, bad, or mediocre. In popular media outlets, film critics often rely on a shorthand mechanism for measuring a film's worth. One critic may give it a grade of "A," "F" or "C," for example, while other critics might employ a derivation of the "two thumbs up" formula made famous by Roger Ebert and Gene Siskel. This is the most basic example of an evaluative claim: "*Inglourious Basterds* is a great film." But this, in and of itself, is a weak argument, which probably wouldn't convince anyone to see the film because the speaker has not established any criteria for the evaluation. The listener simply does not know why the speaker thinks *Inglourious Basterds* is great.

A stronger evaluative claim includes the reasons why the evaluation is positive or negative: "*Inglourious Basterds* is great because its macabre sense of humor rarely appears in movies about World War II." This statement is more convincing than the first because it articulates the basis for judgment. Evaluative claims are always based on the evaluator's standards of what makes a movie worthwhile or not, and here the reviewer shares that information with his readers. Obviously, these standards will differ from person to person. But because this writer explicitly states why he liked the film, readers can gauge whether or not they are likely to agree with the reviewer's opinion. For example, someone who doesn't like traumatic historical events to be treated flippantly will know right away to avoid Tarantino's film based on the assertion above.

On the surface it would appear that making an evaluative claim is much simpler than making an interpretive claim; after all, to make an evaluative claim, one merely needs to express an opinion, correct? In reality, of the three types of claims, the evaluative claim is the most sophisticated argument to make because it relies on the speaker's ability to describe details from the film accurately and then to interpret what the film is trying to accomplish using these details. The film critic must take all of this into consideration before evaluating whether or not the film succeeds. This is why a single film can elicit so many provocative and, apparently, contradictory responses from serious film critics.

Inglourious Basterds prompted a wide array of passionate responses from critics: some praised and others loathed the film's irreverent treatment of history. *Newsweek*'s David Mendelsohn criticized the film's "turning Jews into Nazis" because, he argued, the film's fantasy of violent retribution stirs up emotions that "are precisely what lurk beneath the possibility that [another Holocaust] will happen." Stephanie Zacharek of *Salon.com*, on the other hand, praised the film. She argued that the violence was less central than Tarantino's use of intertextual references and retro look, which made the cinema's vintage style fashionable again: "*Inglourious Basterds* was shot the old-fashioned way: The camera is stationary throughout rather than held by hand – huzzah! [...] Tarantino pays careful attention not just to framing shots in a cool way, but also to orchestrating movement within the frame." As divergent as these opinions are, notice that neither critic settles for a discussion about whether or not audiences will be entertained. Rather, they both grapple with ideas Tarantino explores and the techniques he uses. In each case, the evaluation of the film's artistic merit follows careful interpretation.

The Importance of Developing Interpretive Claims

One of the most challenging and rewarding aspects of studying film is developing interpretive claims. Whereas a brief description may be helpful when deciding whether or not to see a film, interpretive claims move the conversation to a new level. Interpretation takes into account the complexity of films, capturing the way films affect viewers long after they have left the theater or turned off their Blu-ray player. Because interpretive claims grow out of description and analysis, they take account of the way that stories, characters, camera angles, sound effects, and other elements of film art interact to produce intense emotional and thought-provoking experiences.

Interpreting films also helps to develop logical thinking and writing skills, which Chapter 3 examines more fully. Making an interpretive claim about a favorite film is fun, but it also demands organization and keen insight. Finally, interpretations link films to larger issues. For example, the question implicit in the two conflicting critical interpretations of *Inglourious Basterds*—where one critic points to the ruinous social implications of revenge fantasies and the other focuses more narrowly on trends in film aesthetics—ought to generate provocative discussions about subjects that are important to the world outside the movie theater.

Summary

- Viewer expectations about formal organization, stars, directors, and genre influence their experience of films.
- Filmmakers anticipate expectations and may satisfy some expectations and offer novel approaches to others.
- Paying careful attention to repeated details helps to uncover important aspects of character, story, and structure.
- Motifs (any significant repeated element) and parallels (which ask viewers to compare and contrast two distinct characters, situations, or locations) are particularly important instances of repetition that, among other things, signal turning points and overall structure.
- Films produce meaning by making reference to history, to real-world locations, objects, or people, to other art forms, and to other films.

- Film style emerges from the interaction of a film's formal mode of organization, its subject matter, and its visual and sound elements. Three styles are differentiated according to specific traits: classical (invested in clear storytelling), realist (interested in exploring characters and capturing life), and formalist (overt intervention that calls attention to the process of representation).
- Three types of written statements provide information about a film's meaning: descriptive, evaluative, and interpretive statements.

Works Consulted

Cook, David. *A History of Narrative Film,* 3rd edn. New York: Norton, 1996.

Ebert, Roger. "*Synecdoche, New York.*" *Chicago Sun Times.* November 5, 2008. **rogerebert.suntimes.com**.

MacDonald, Scott. *Avant Garde Film: Motion Studies*. Cambridge: Cambridge University Press, 1993.

Mendelsohn, Daniel. "*Inglourious Basterds*: When Jews Attack." *Newsweek.* August 31, 2009. **http://www.newsweek.com/id/212016/page/2**.

Monaco, James. *How to Read a Film*, 3rd edn. New York and Oxford: Oxford University Press, 2000.

Rosenbaum, Jonathan. "The World According to Harvey and Bob," in *Movies as Politics*, pp. 159–65. Berkeley and Los Angeles, CA: University of California Press, 1997.

Sarris, Andrew. *The Primal Screen*. New York: Simon and Schuster, 1973.

Zacharek, Stephanie. "*Inglourious Basterds.*" *Salon.com.* August 21, 2009. **www.salon.com**.

FILM ANALYSIS

Reading Significant Details

To analyze a film, viewers must be active, which means paying attention to details, asking questions, and not taking anything for granted. If possible, viewers should watch a film twice before analyzing it in writing or in discussion, using the first viewing to simply watch the film and taking notes the second time through. If only one screening is possible, take notes during the first screening and watch a scene or listen to an exchange of dialogue more than once if it seems significant. Develop a system to chart the way motifs are established and developed.

The essay below looks at the ways that Guillermo Del Toro's *Pan's Labyrinth* uses motifs and parallels to add significance to a story about a girl's excursions into a fantasy world. To comprehend the significance of details in a film, viewers must first take note of them and then follow up by looking for patterns in the way a director repeats and modifies motifs.

Study notes offer tips about note-taking and paying attention to details.

The Orchestration of Detail in *Pan's Labyrinth*

In *Pan's Labyrinth* ("*El Labertino del Fauno*"; Guillermo del Toro 2006), the two main characters seek the promise of eternal life via radically different means. In the waning days of World War II, young Ofelia (Ivana Baquero)

2.27 (above) The Captain inhabits a world of straight lines in *Pan's Labyrinth*.

2.28 (above center) Ofelia is associated with circles in *Pan's Labyrinth*.

2.29 (below center) The Captain hosts the banquet in *Pan's Labyrinth*.

2.30 (below) A visual parallel in *Pan's Labyrinth*.

1 Film scholars need to tackle the tricky task of taking notes in the dark while watching movies. We suggest that you buy a lighted pen, or get comfortable dashing down shorthand notations, which you can later translate into more formal notes. See p. 47 for a list of acronyms that will help you speedily jot down descriptions of visual detail.

2 The purpose of collecting specific details from individual scenes is to provide evidence to support your interpretive claims. Notice that this paragraph thoroughly describes a specific moment in the film to illustrate an idea.

3 Notice that the authors provide context for most of their examples. On some occasions it might be appropriate to allude to details without helping the reader to situate these examples in a specific scene (see the end of paragraph 2, for example). But usually providing narrative context strengthens an argument because suggesting when something appears helps the reader perceive the careful *orchestration* of detail.

4 The most engaging film analysis will pay careful attention to subtle details. A casual viewer might overlook this less obvious variation in the watch motif, but this analysis demonstrates a thoughtful, critically engaged relationship with the text.

leaves her home to live with her new stepfather, the menacing captain of a fascist military outpost in the forests of Spain's northern Navarro mountains. Seeking to escape from this oppressive new environment via flights of fantasy, Ofelia meets a Faun in a mysterious underworld who promises the young girl an eternity of wonderment if she can complete three tasks to prove she's the reincarnation of a long-lost princess from a fabled magical kingdom. Her stepfather, the evil Captain Vidal (Sergi López) seeks a different kind of immortality; as an officer in General Francisco Franco's Fascist regime, he uses the threat of violence to impose his monomaniacal will, commanding the obedience of his family, his soldiers, and the citizenry rather than earning their respect.[1] Vidal is on a quest to etch his name into eternity by evoking fear in the memories of the generations who will follow him. Del Toro's brutal fairy tale makes it clear that, while Ofelia's ambitions in her fantasy world parallel Vidal's own efforts to reign in the physical realm, ultimately she chooses a path that adheres to her democratic principles instead of resorting to Vidal's totalitarian worldview. By drawing parallels between the Faun and the Captain, and between the imaginary and the real world, *Pan's Labyrinth* presents a moral perspective in which eternity is earned through self-sacrifice in the name of justice and equality, not the acceptance and exploitation of fascism's hierarchical structure for self-aggrandizement.

Del Toro helps establish both the Captain's goals and his psychological motivation by repeatedly drawing attention to watches and timepieces, turning time into an important motif. When Captain Vidal first appears, he is gazing anxiously at his pocket watch, obviously perturbed by the fact that his new bride Carmen (Ariadna Gil) and her daughter Ofelia are a few minutes late arriving at their new home. Thus, the opening scenes establish a pattern of repetition, which reflects Vidal's obsession with maintaining order and control irrespective of people's physical or emotional needs, much less their limitations (Carmen's entourage had to stop along the way because her pregnancy had made her nauseous). Throughout the film, Vidal gazes at his watch to ensure that his soldiers, staff, and family are all conforming to his strict schedule.[2]

The motif reappears in a subsequent scene, but the film varies the pattern of repetition. Rather than emphasizing the Captain's obsession with the timepiece, del Toro shows the Captain trying to distance himself from it. This variation in detail suggests *why* Vidal is so obsessed with time and order. When he hosts a dinner party for some of the military and cultural elites, one of the guests makes a casual comment about having heard a tale about Vidal's father, who, having been mortally wounded on the battlefield, smashed his pocket watch so that others would remember the exact moment he died. The gesture is a testament to the elder's courageous ability to maintain some kind of agency even in the face of his own death. Vidal refutes the story, but the camera's subtle, methodical track toward the Captain while he is listening to the guest relate the legend exposes the story's truth even while Vidal vehemently denies it.

Shortly after the dinner party scene, the watch reappears in a way that makes it clear that Vidal's lies about his father reveal an unspoken anxiety of having to live up to his father's legacy. Vidal retreats to the seclusion of his quarters and stands at his wash basin shaving (the Captain's impeccable dedication to grooming is another motif that suggests his fascistic obsession with order). When he looks down to rinse off his blade, he inadvertently spots the watch. Immediately his gloomy gaze returns to his own image in the mirror. Vidal stares blankly at his own visage, clearly lost in thoughts inspired by seeing the watch. Suddenly, he draws his straight razor up to the mirror and slashes his reflection across the neck.[3] By paying attention to the contexts in which the watch appears and reappears—the obsessive monitoring of others, the battlefield legend, the Captain's private quarters—the audience can see that the motif is, paradoxically, an emblem of both Vidal's insistence on maintaining control and his sense of weakness in the face of his father's legacy. In other words, the patterned repetition of shots involving the watch suggests that Vidal denies the legend not because it didn't happen, but because he feels insecure about his ability to live up to it. His suicidal gesture in the mirror is a sign of the self-loathing that is the by-product of his feelings of powerlessness. Not only does the shot sequence emphasize the motif, but so does the setting. The Captain's quarters are located in an old mill, and gears and cogs loom in the background as if he were literally trapped inside the machinery of a gigantic timepiece.[4] By orchestrating detail so that the suicidal gesture takes place in this environment, the film emphasizes the setting's metaphorical significance: the Captain is trapped by the watch and all that it represents.

Blind allegiance to rigid hierarchy governs the Captain's life; he feels compelled to follow his father's example and overcompensates for his feelings of inadequacy by demanding utter obedience from everyone around him. Ofelia, on the other hand, resists authority from the film's outset. When she first meets her stepfather, Ofelia offers him her left hand—"the wrong hand"—to shake as a greeting. Repeatedly, she challenges his power over her by refusing to acknowledge Vidal as her legal guardian, coldly referring to him as "the Captain" instead of her father. Furthermore, the film associates the Captain with spaces full of straight, orderly lines, whereas it links Ofelia

to circles, which suggest her more adaptable personality (Director's Commentary) (figs **2.27**, **2.28**). Most obviously, Ofelia sojourns in the fantasy worlds her books and her imagination have to offer, much to the consternation of Carmen and the Captain, who feel that these excursions are a waste of time. Quite simply, she isn't restricted by the rationality or rules associated with the "real world."

Paradoxically, while Ofelia is drawn to the fantasy world as an escape, what she finds is that the underworld offers her only twisted variations on the horrors that surround her in reality. Ofelia's struggle to navigate between myth and reality is set against the backdrop of the lingering conflict between Franco's recently instituted regime and the stalwart *Maquis* guerillas, who, in the 1940s, valiantly resisted Spain's turn toward ultra-nationalism. The rebels' struggle with the Captain is an important **plotline** that parallels and comments on Ofelia's quest. In one scene, the rebels excitedly follow news of the American assault on German forces on the beaches of Normandy. The brief historical reference succinctly links the motley band of warriors to the Allied democratic struggle against Fascism.

Del Toro repeatedly draws attention to the parallels between this organized and armed political resistance in the name of democracy and Ofelia's position with respect to the Captain. For example, for her first task, the Faun charges Ofelia with retrieving a magical key from a grotesque, over-sized, slimy toad. The mission equates Ofelia with Mercedes, a spy for the underground movement who has infiltrated Vidal's stronghold by working as his personal servant. Just as Ofelia wrests control of the key from the toad, Mercedes steals the key to the Captain's storeroom so the guerillas can pilfer vital supplies for their movement. This key motif draws a specific parallel between Ofelia's tasks in this fantasy world with the historical political resistance.

The film's second (and creepiest!) fantasy sequence makes these political implications even more explicit. The Faun sends Ofelia, armed with the magical key, into the lair of the sinewy, grotesque "Pale Man" in order to retrieve a magical dagger. Before sending the girl on her mission, the Faun instructs Ofelia not to eat anything off the Pale Man's banquet table, lest she awaken the beast and wind up becoming the meal herself. When Ofelia encounters the Pale Man, snoozing away, oblivious to her presence, Del Toro momentarily takes the camera's attention away from Ofelia and reveals a pile of shoes—gruesome evidence of all the victims the Pale Man has consumed—in the foreground, while flames roar in a large fireplace in the background. These small, but not insignificant, details allude to Nazi Germany's concentration camps, a historical reference that links the Pale Man to the atrocious horrors of an ideology to which Captain Vidal subscribes (Director's Commentary).

The fact that the Pale Man hoards food further underscores the parallel with Vidal, who also stingily controls the distribution of resources: he brutally executes a father and son for hunting rabbits near the camp, and he stores the region's vital rations behind lock and key. While Vidal doles out meager portions to the locals, he holds magnificent feasts for himself and his colleagues. In fact, the positioning of the Pale Man at the head of the lengthy banquet table, his back to a roaring fire, explicitly parallels the image of Vidal as the host of the party of privileged elites earlier in the film (figs **2.29**, **2.30**).[5] The systematic repetition of detail makes it clear that this fantasy is a metaphor for Ofelia's need to reject the Captain and his values.

When Ofelia succumbs to temptation and grabs a morsel off the Pale Man's table, she is acting out against Vidal's system of maintaining power by controlling the country's vital resources. Again, Ofelia's gesture links her to Mercedes and the resistance fighters who will soon "liberate" the goods stashed in Vidal's storehouse. Each of the fantasy sequences reinforces Ofelia's innate understanding of the importance of resisting rules that are unjust and oppressive. With each trip into the bizarre fantasies, Ofelia's relationships with Vidal and to authority in general grow more and more strained.

In fact, while the Faun initially appears to be a benevolent, avuncular figure in Ofelia's world, increasingly he reveals himself to be no more nurturing than Vidal. The parallel between these male authority figures becomes apparent as the film progresses and the Faun's kindly requests start to sound more and more like Vidal's impatient demands. And just as Vidal and the Pale Man hoard victuals, the Faun too appears in one scene munching on plump grapes, stingily doling a few bites out to the fairies at his service. Del Toro even casts the same actor (Doug Jones) to play the part of the Faun and the Pale Man, a choice that subtly underscores the implicit similarities between the two figures. So, although Ofelia almost instinctively questions her stepfather's unjust demands from the opening of the film, she eventually learns she must also challenge the authority of the one male figure she *wants* to trust.

This crisis of trust culminates in the film's climactic struggle over control of Ofelia's half-brother, who is also Vidal's son. This infant is a continuation of yet another important motif: father/son relationships. For Vidal, the birth of his heir is an all-important symbol of his family's legacy. The infant is the embodiment of Vidal's quest to build a reputation that will transcend time, because he will repeat the generational charge to live up to the family's narcissistic code of honor. Ofelia's final task is to abduct the infant and deliver him to the Faun, who waits in the center of his otherworldly labyrinth. Ironically, as the film draws to a close, the similarities between the Captain's and Ofelia's ambitions become apparent. While Ofelia desires eternal life in a magical land where she will reign as princess, Vidal seeks to secure a legacy that will remain omnipotent long after his death. In both cases, the infant is the secret to securing immortality.

But when Ofelia discovers that the Faun wants to use the infant as a sacrificial totem—only the blood of an innocent will open up the gateway to the magical kingdom—she suddenly understands that realizing her dream will come at another's expense. Offering the child would make her just like

5 The keener the attention to detail, the better the analysis.

Vidal, willing to sacrifice the lives of others for her own advantage. This is an option she refuses to accept, choosing instead to return the boy to his drunken, furious father, the Captain, who proceeds to shoot Ofelia for her disobedience. Quite literally, she sacrifices herself to save the life of another. Then, a miracle happens. As her blood drips into the well in the center of the Faun's labyrinth, it opens up the passageway to the magical kingdom. *She* was the innocent all along. Ofelia finds herself in an opulent room before her parents, an empty throne waiting for her. Curiously, she is wearing ruby red slippers, an intertextual reference to *The Wizard of Oz* that conjures up that film's exploration of the relationship between dreams and reality.[6] But instead of finding herself happy to return to the normalcy of the "real" world, as Dorothy does, Ofelia has finally transcended the horrors of Fascist Spain. The reward for her resistance to an unjust authority is an eternity in the magical world she has sought all along. The Faun reappears and explains to her that, in refusing to give up her brother, Ofelia had passed the real test: in choosing to reject an unjust social hierarchy and sacrificing herself for a greater cause, she had guaranteed her own immortality.

In contrast, as Vidal leaves the labyrinth carrying his son, he encounters the band of resistance fighters, who have overthrown the Fascist encampment. Sensing his impending death, Vidal makes one request: that the rebels tell the infant who his father was. Vidal's request is one final plea for immortality...to guarantee that his legend lives on, if only in his son's memory. But Mercedes, standing at the forefront of the band of resistance fighters, denies his request, promising that the boy will never even know the Captain's name. At the moment when Vidal realizes his legacy has come to an end, he is unceremoniously executed. His reward for a lifetime of mercilessly exploiting others is the eternal nothingness of anonymity.

Works Cited (in the essay)
Del Toro, Guillermo. Director's Commentary. *Pan's Labyrinth*. New Line DVD, 2006.

6 Note the author's explication of an intertextual reference that holds relevance for the film's theme.

Writing About Film

///

CHAPTER THREE

The best critic is one who illuminates whole
provinces of an art that you could not see before.

Stanley Kauffmann

///

The proliferation of blogs, zines, and the varied assortment of film-related sites
on the internet, not to mention the continued prevalence of newspaper and magazine reviews, mean that casual and avid film buffs alike now have access to a
wide array of film writing on a daily basis. Reviews, biographies, box office
statistics, behind-the-scenes gossip, and production information are all readily
available in print and on-line. Even the descriptive blurbs on the back of jewel-
boxes are examples of film writing.

Clearly, reading about film is an indispensable part of film culture. But this
chapter builds on the assumption articulated in Chapter 1 that writing about cinema can profoundly enhance one's appreciation of it. When instructors ask students to write about film in an academic setting, they expect students to consider
how a film (or a group of films) functions as a complex artistic and cultural document, in the hope that students will more fully appreciate the medium's social
significance, artistic potential, and diversity of forms.

Writing assignments also prepare students to take their interpretive skills
beyond the classroom. The act of writing can transform the spectator from passive fan to actively engaged participant in the dialogue taking place among

3.1 Eli anguishes over her prey
in *Let the Right One In*.

cinephiles in academia, on the internet, in print media, and in liner notes.

Chapter 2 introduced basic strategies that filmmakers employ to create meaning in their work. The chapter concluded by arguing the importance of studying these strategies and formulating interpretive claims about films based on your observations. This chapter emphasizes the importance of pursuing the next logical step: getting those ideas down on paper.

It begins with a discussion of strategies for preparing to write. Then it explores the four most common genres of writing about film: the scene analysis, the film analysis, the research paper, and the popular review.

Getting Started

Keeping a Film Journal

The Study Notes accompanying Chapter 2's reading of *Pan's Labyrinth* discuss the importance of taking notes during screenings. This is the first step in any type of film writing, be it a popular review or critical analysis. Some film enthusiasts and scholars also find it helpful to keep a screening journal—a cinephile's version of a diary.

A typical journal entry should include the film's title and important production information: its release date and studio, its director, its cast, and a brief plot summary. Because journals explore an individual's response to films, entries tend to vary significantly from one film to the next. Some entries might make an evaluative claim and explain the reasons for it. Others could include interpretive observations, noting among other things a film's motifs and parallels, references to other films, or significant scenes. Some entries might document details of the filmgoing experience: did the spectator see the film in a new venue or while traveling? How did the audience respond to the film? Was going to the movie part of a memorable date?

Because they document a person's most (and least) enjoyable experiences at the movies, film journals provide opportunities for personal exploration and creative thinking and writing. Furthermore, keeping a journal helps film students study for exams (by providing detailed information that prods the memory) and generate ideas for papers.

Formulating a Thesis

Whereas film journals encourage the spontaneous flow of ideas, formal writing demands that authors stay focused on a central, clearly defined argument. Because it articulates a main point in a sentence or two, the thesis statement is the most crucial element in any written analysis of a film. Consequently, most writers try to develop a working thesis *before* they start to write. Writing a formal analysis of a film (as opposed to an informal, personal journal entry) requires multiple viewings of the film(s) under consideration. Defining the main idea of a paper before undertaking these repeated screenings imposes order on the process by helping clarify what to look for. Obviously the thesis can and will evolve over the course of several viewings of a film. Nevertheless, crafting a provisional thesis statement is a crucial first step in writing a strong essay.

Many writers assume that drafting a thesis is a daunting task. Often students do not know what constitutes a strong thesis, or what a particular instructor looks for in a thesis. While a plot summary is appropriate in newspaper blurbs announcing the movies playing at the local theater, thesis statements go beyond superficial descriptive claims. A strong thesis for an academic paper does more than simply stating what would be obvious to anyone who watched the film; it organizes and interprets the information gleaned from analysis. A strong thesis proposes a debatable argument about a film and reveals the writer's understanding of themes and appreciation of the way cinematic techniques coalesce into a coherent artistic expression.

In the table on the following page are five common types of thesis statements: each makes an interpretive claim about a single film (fig. **3.2**). The left-hand column briefly summarizes each rhetorical approach, while the right-hand column offers sample thesis statements. This list is far from exhaustive; in fact, sophisticated claims commonly fuse elements from two or more of these rhetorical approaches.

Managing Verb Tense

As a general rule, scholars use the present tense when describing a film. For example, in the essay at the end of Chapter 2, the author says, "Vidal stares blankly at his own visage, clearly lost in thoughts inspired by seeing the watch" instead of "Vidal *stared* blankly." The logic behind this convention is that details in a film exist in the present; even though the action in *Pan's Labyrinth* unfolds in the 1940s, the film itself is an artifact that exists, unchanging, in the here and now.

There are two common exceptions to this rule. First, if you are comparing two moments in time in a film, refer to early events using the past tense and later events using the present. Consider this example from the essay on *Pan's Labyrinth*: "The Faun reappears and explains to her that, in refusing to give up her brother, Ofelia had passed the real test." The author describes the climax using the present tense, but when he alludes to events from earlier in the film, he shifts to past tense.

A second exception occurs when you are discussing details about a film's production history: "To prepare himself to direct *Citizen Kane*, Orson Welles watched John Ford's *Stagecoach*." The same rule holds true if you mention a film's reception: "Thanks to William Randolph Hearst's efforts to suppress the film, *Citizen Kane* was a box office flop."

Four Types of Writing About Film

The Scene Analysis Paper

The scene analysis is designed to help students identify narrative, visual, and sound elements and to establish the link between minute details and broader patterns of development in a film. With this assignment, the film instructor asks

3.2 Common rhetorical approaches for writing on a single film.

Rhetorical Approach	Sample Thesis Statement
Explain the significance of a single scene within a film's overall design. Consider what this scene contributes to the film's narrative development and/or central theme.	In the scene in *Fight Club* (David Fincher 1999) when Jack discovers Tyler's affair with Marla, it becomes clear that he feels disturbed by a woman's presence. Marla threatens Jack's intimate relationship with Tyler and undermines the very thing "Fight Club" promises to the participants: the restoration of male power.
Illustrate how a character (or group of characters) undergoes physical and/or emotional changes to attain a goal.	In *Precious* (Lee Daniels 2009), the main character is inhibited by her own lack of self-esteem in two ways: she cannot express herself at school (or anywhere else) and she is unable to defend herself against her mother's abuse. When a caring teacher encourages Precious to express her feelings in writing, she learns to value herself and begins to focus on the goal of being a good mother to her second child, which also requires that she establish her independence from her own mother.
Explore how a character's psychological or emotional makeup defines the film's primary conflict.	In Kathryn Bigelow's *The Hurt Locker* (2008), Sergeant William James, a specialist at defusing bombs, flaunts his risk-taking, daredevil approach to his job, which raises concerns among his fellow soldiers. James's macho bravado is his way of dealing with his emotional disconnectedness. The film visually expresses the predicament of this rugged, yet highly vulnerable man, through the cumbersome gear he wears to disable bombs. That protective shell insulates him from the world, hiding the feelings he cannot acknowledge openly, but also weighs him down physically and emotionally.
Discuss how a film consistently employs a particular stylistic device to develop its story and themes.	In Roman Polanksi's *Ghost Writer* (2010), repeated close-ups of the "breaking news" ticker on television establish a parallel between the television news and the main character. He is an anonymous writer paid to craft phrases about someone else's life that he hopes will entertain the reading public. Just as the "ghost" (as he refers to himself) must fabricate a compelling, if partly fictionalized, biography from random details, the broadcast entertainment industry transforms private lives into public sensationalism on a daily basis.
Argue that a film explores a cultural phenomenon; consider whether or not the film adopts a position on this phenomenon.	*District 9* (Neill Blomkamp 2009) is an allegorical science fiction film that casts a disapproving eye on South African apartheid, and systems of racial segregation and discrimination everywhere. The alien "prawns" who arrive on Earth, but seem to pose no threat, are forced into shantytowns and treated as worse than second-class citizens. The film's pseudo-documentary style, which makes the story that much more realistic, emphasizes this film's pointed social critique.

students to analyze one scene from a film carefully, discussing the specific qualities of each individual shot.

The purpose of this assignment is academic, since it requires students to demonstrate that they can read significant details and describe them using the language of film studies. In most cases, evaluative claims are irrelevant in this assignment. Rather, the scene analysis relies heavily on descriptive statements. In fact, some instructors require students only to describe the details of each shot's setting, cinematography, editing, and sound. Others ask students to develop interpretive claims, by analyzing how the scene contributes to motifs and themes developed over the course of the entire film.

The essay below forwards an interpretive claim about a scene from Fritz Lang's *The Big Heat* (1953), a particularly brutal *film noir*. *Film noir*, a French term meaning "dark film," describes a genre of American films with a downbeat tone that emerged in the 1940s. These films focused on social outcasts—criminals, private detectives, and losers—trapped in violent circumstances. Because this essay addresses an audience of film scholars, it relies on the vocabulary filmmakers and academics use to describe cinematic techniques. These terms may be unfamiliar to many readers, but they will be discussed in context in Part Two. All of the specialized film terms in bold are also defined in the Glossary.

"The Divided Human Spirit in Fritz Lang's *The Big Heat*"

Like many examples of *film noir*, Fritz Lang's *The Big Heat* focuses on an urban criminal underworld in order to explore the darker side of human existence. In the film, Detective Bannion (Glenn Ford) is an honest, hard-working cop investigating the mysterious suicide of one of his colleagues. As he delves into the case, he discovers a connection between the local crime syndicate and high-ranking members of his own police force. When a bomb meant for Bannion kills his wife instead, Bannion quits the force in a fit of anger and becomes a brooding, increasingly violent vigilante. During the course of his investigation, Bannion finds an unlikely compatriot in Debbie Marsh (Gloria Grahame), a gangster's moll brutalized and betrayed by her lover, Vince Stone (Lee Marvin). In one critical scene, Debbie commits murder to help Bannion. This scene is especially important because it underscores the duality of human nature. In the twisted moral logic of this *noir* world, an upstanding member of society reveals herself to be a moral reprobate, and a woman of questionable values redeems herself via an act of murder.[1]

Recognizing the scene's positioning within the film's overall narrative structure is critical for understanding what motivates Debbie. Before this scene, the film has emphasized Bannion's willingness to rely on violence in his quest for revenge. He is investigating Bertha Duncan (Jeanette Nolan), the widow of Bannion's dead colleague, and discovers that Bertha's husband had written a confessional letter prior to his suicide, detailing the connection between the police force and the crime syndicate. Bertha, who is using the letter to extort money from the syndicate, refuses to give the information to Bannion. In his frustration, Bannion begins to strangle Bertha and nearly kills her, but he is stopped by two police officers. Bannion has grown bitter over the course of his investigation and there is very little that distinguishes him from the gangsters he is investigating.

In a subsequent scene, Bannion tells Debbie about his investigation, complaining that Bertha's stubbornness has effectively put a halt to his pursuit of justice. At one point he confesses, "I almost killed her an hour ago. I should've." To this Debbie replies, "If you had, there wouldn't be much difference between you and Vince Stone." Herein lies the motivation for the scene at hand: Debbie kills Bertha to prevent Bannion from becoming like Vince Stone. In doing so, she redeems herself.[2]

The scene begins with an **establishing shot** of Bertha walking down the stairs as the doorbell rings. The **long shot** captures Bertha's flowing mink coat as well as the spaciousness of the house in general. Together these two elements establish that Bertha Duncan is wealthy; her ill-gotten wealth provides her a lavish lifestyle that the honest Bannion has never been able to afford. The camera **pans** right as Bertha answers the door, further underscoring the size of her house.

Lang cuts to a **medium close-up** of Debbie's profile. This shot simulates Bertha's point of view as she looks through the window in the door to see half

1 This introduction includes a brief plot summary and concludes with a thesis statement that argues why this scene is important to the film. Notice that the plot summary isn't merely filler. It establishes the thematic context for the scene by emphasizing Bannion's transition from honest cop to "brooding" outlaw. Focusing on these details paves the way for the thesis statement's claim about the duality, or two-sided nature, of the characters. For more advice on writing introductions, refer to the Study Notes that accompany the Film Analysis essay in Chapter 8.

2 At first glance these paragraphs seem like another detailed plot summary. But the author is making an interpretive point about the film's narrative. The paragraph begins with a claim about the importance of noticing when this scene occurs. The details that follow illustrate that studying the sequence of events is crucial to understanding character behavior. For more advice on organizing paragraphs, refer to the sidebar notes that accompany the Film Analysis essay in Chapter 7.

of Debbie's face. Debbie's face is the most important element of the *mise en scène*, as half of it appears normal, but the other half is covered with gauze. Earlier in the film, Vince Stone had thrown a pot of boiling coffee at Debbie in a fit of rage, scalding the left side of her face. Debbie's face is literally two-sided, becoming a visual representation of duality. Half of Debbie's personality has enjoyed the wealth and glamor afforded by her participation in the gangster lifestyle, but the other half—the pure, untainted half—befriends Bannion and acknowledges the immorality of Vince Stone's world. In this shot, Debbie's "good half" shows. Her scars are turned away from the camera, suggesting her desire to renounce her scarred past.[3]

Lang cuts to a **medium long shot** as Bertha opens the door and invites Debbie inside. Hard lighting emanating from the streetlights outside casts shadows on the wall, contributing to the film's dreadful *noir* atmosphere. Debbie enters the house, and, as the two walk side by side in a medium long shot, an obvious parallel develops: both Debbie and Bertha wear long mink coats (fig. **3.3**). Debbie's dialogue confirms the similarities apparent in the *mise en scène*: "I've been thinking about you and me . . . how much alike we are. The mink-coated girls." Her words reveal Debbie's regret that she, like Bertha, has led an immoral life, pursuing material wealth via corrupt means. Bertha is clearly frustrated by Debbie's opaque pronouncements, and she demands that Debbie explain herself more clearly. She takes an aggressive step toward her visitor. Lang cuts to a medium close-up of Debbie to emphasize the importance of her words: "We should use first names. We're sisters under the mink." Again, Debbie's words reveal her own recognition that she has led a corrupt life just like Bertha's.

A **reverse shot** reveals Bertha's increasing ire in a medium close-up, as she accuses Debbie of not making any sense. The camera pans to the right to follow Bertha as she moves to the desk on the other side of the room. Ironically, it was at this desk that Bertha's husband shot himself, plagued by guilt and shame. Now Bertha, perturbed and perhaps frightened by Debbie's presence, uses the phone on the desk to call Vince Stone. Her use of the desk expresses her complete indifference to her husband's death and her calculated refusal to sever the mob ties that killed him. Bertha stands behind the desk in a medium long shot and, as she picks up the phone, she tells Debbie, "You're not well."

The cut to a medium close-up of Debbie emphasizes the power of her reply: "I've never felt better in my life." Her hands fumble for something in her coat. She draws a gun and fires at Bertha. Crucially, this medium close-up includes Debbie, but the gun remains offscreen. Had the image been a medium or long shot, some attention would have been drawn to it. Instead,

3 This essay combines descriptive claims with interpretive claims. Where in this paragraph does the author link description to an interpretive idea? Which phrases make the connection between description and analysis clear?

3.3 "Sisters under the mink" in *The Big Heat.*

Lang keeps the camera's attention on Debbie's face so that the audience focuses on Debbie's self-proclaimed moral redemption rather than on the act of violence she is committing in Bannion's name.[4]

The final shot of the scene is a medium long shot of Bertha, wincing as the still unseen gun fires. She starts to slump, and the camera **tilts** down, following her collapse to the floor. Debbie has done Bannion's dirty work for him. She preserves what is left of his moral rectitude by killing Bertha. She also helps him with his investigation: now Bertha's husband's letter will be made public, and the thugs responsible for Bannion's wife's death will be arrested. In performing such a selfless act, Debbie—who earlier had no moral qualms about using mob money to supply herself with fancy clothes and a penthouse—redeems herself. When she kills Bertha, her sister under the mink, Debbie destroys the vanity and selfishness in herself that Bertha represents.

At the end of the shot, the gun falls into the frame. The framing distances Debbie from the violence she has just committed. However, Debbie makes no attempt to hide the gun or her fingerprints; she accepts her guilt and, consequently, confirms her redemption.

Because of her actions, Bannion rids himself of the anger and resentment festering inside him. In the film's resolution, he rejoins the police force, no longer needing to stand apart from society's rules and obligations. Still, the resolution's optimism is qualified by Debbie's death during a climactic shootout and complicated by Bannion's use of violence to seek vengeance. Yes, Debbie and Bannion redeem themselves. But Lang's film suggests that redemption may be a temporary state of being, because even the most honorable men and women are capable of committing horrific acts when they are pushed far enough.[5]

4 Here, an analysis of dialogue supports the main idea in this analysis. To extend the analysis of film sound, compare the voices of Gloria Grahame (Debbie) and Jeanette Nolan (Bertha) in this exchange. Do vocal differences suggest differences in character?

5 The essay's conclusion indicates the importance of the scene under discussion to later events in the film.

The Film Analysis

Like the scene analysis, the film analysis is a form of academic writing. This assignment demands that students trace an idea as it develops over the course of an entire film. Unlike the scene analysis, the film analysis doesn't require students to analyze every single shot—otherwise, the paper might be hundreds of pages long. Instead, this assignment requires students to develop a thesis about a film and then isolate passages from the film that illustrate that thesis.

In most cases, evaluative claims are irrelevant or inappropriate for this assignment. Usually instructors want students to focus on an interpretive claim. As with the scene analysis, the film analysis should utilize the vocabulary of film studies.

This essay explores how Buster Keaton's *Steamboat Bill Jr.* links questions about Bill's masculinity to two important themes: the conflict between father and son and Bill Sr.'s unwillingness to accept change.

The only plot summary occurs in the introduction. The summary consists of just a few sentences and functions solely to prod the memory of the reader who has not seen the film recently.

The author develops her ideas not through the detailed analysis of any one scene, but by revealing the patterns evident in four scenes from the film: the opening shot, Bill Jr.'s arrival, the barbershop scene, and the climax. These discussions function as the structural foundation of the essay—they illustrate the most crucial ideas the author wants to convey. The author refers to a number of minute details scattered throughout the film that supplement the essay's claims about how the characters develop in these four scenes.

"The Anxieties of Modernity in *Steamboat Bill Jr.*"

Buster Keaton's last great comedy, *Steamboat Bill Jr.* (1928), might at first glance appear to be a variation on Shakespeare's *Romeo and Juliet*. But in fact, the film is more interested in the troubled relationship between father and son. Bill Jr. (Keaton) visits his estranged father (Ernest Torrence) in a small Southern town. Coincidentally, Bill Jr. bumps into a college sweetheart, Marion (Marion Byron). Unfortunately their romance is temporarily put on hold when they discover that their fathers are business rivals and mortal enemies. The film's primary conflict—and the source of tension between Bill Jr. and his father that also keeps the lovers apart—is Bill Sr.'s fear of modernity. For Bill Sr., his son's longing for the daughter of the local business magnate represents the boy's abandonment of traditional values and his failure to be a real man. However, by the end of the film, Bill Sr. learns to accept that his son lives in the modern world and to recognize that it has some advantages.[1]

The first image in the film establishes the film's concern with the inevitable passage of time. A **high-angle** long shot of two fishermen in a canoe on the Mississippi River opens the film. The pastoral image at first appears to be a romantic depiction of the pre-industrial South. But the camera pans left, past a stand of trees, and finds the dogleg of the river. Here a modern riverboat, not a canoe, belches smoke as it moves upstream. The *mise en scène* and the camera movement in this **establishing shot** suggest the film's dominant theme: the conflict between past (the canoe) and present (the mechanized boat).

As the scene cuts to closer shots of individual characters, it becomes apparent that past and present are embodied by Bill Canfield (Torrence) and his rival J.J. King (Tom McGuire). Bill is stuck in the past. He wears a ratty sailor's uniform, smokes a corncob pipe, and his ship is called the *Stonewall Jackson*, all signifying his connection to the nineteenth century, to the Civil War, and the heyday of riverboat navigation. Furthermore, he suffers from an inability to adapt. His boat, as the rest of the film will make clear, is a decrepit relic that is slowly falling apart. Bill has not amassed the wealth he needs to compete with his rival in the steamboat business.

King, on the other hand, has his eyes set on the future. In contrast to Bill, whose attire links him to a rustic past, he wears a shiny top hat and black tuxedo. His fashionable clothing indicates that he is a modern man of wealth—wealth earned not in the field or on the river, like Bill's, but in the city. The film makes this point clear several times, as it emphasizes that King has his hand in many of the town's business operations. He is a modern entrepreneur who doesn't specialize in any one field. Instead, he has invested in everything. At one point in the film, King is seen operating a newspaper stand selling "out of town papers." This detail emphasizes how he is not established in town. He is more cosmopolitan, and represents a world where people, goods, and capital can move across an entire nation quickly and efficiently.[2]

1 Notice that this essay, like the previous scene analysis, is structured around an interpretive claim. The thesis does not simply describe Keaton's film, nor does it evaluate it.

2 Each of these paragraphs includes plenty of descriptive detail. But the author uses these details to illustrate an interpretive claim, which in turn supports the essay's central thesis. In this specific paragraph she describes the details associated with J.J. King and argues that these details link him to contemporary culture.

Despite Bill's stubborn adherence to the past, the rest of his family subscribes to King's modern approach. When Bill receives a telegram from his son, who is coming to visit during his vacation from college, the audience realizes that Bill Sr. is estranged from his family. In fact, the Canfields haven't lived together since Bill Jr. was a boy. When the family does communicate, the interaction is made possible by the very technology that Bill seems to fear: the telegram and the railroad, symbols of America's movement into the modern era.

Once father and son meet, the two begin to act out the conflict between past and present, usurping the Canfield–King conflict. Bill Sr. is displeased with his son's all-too-cozy connection to the modern world. Bill

3.4 Bill Jr. dwarfed by his father in *Steamboat Bill Jr.*

Jr. is the antithesis of his father. His attending college in Boston clearly goes against his father's stubborn idealization of the rural Southern lifestyle. As the two interact, it's evident that Bill Sr. thinks all of his son's so-called "book smarts" have prevented him from learning any real skills, such as running a steam engine or punching a man out. Much of the film's humor derives from Bill Jr.'s awkwardness on board his father's ship. He wears a formal sailor's uniform, much to his father's displeasure; he repeatedly runs into the ship's guidelines; he knocks the life-preserver into the water below (where it promptly sinks); and he accidentally hits a lever that engages the paddle and drives the boat into King's. Bill Jr. is clearly out of his element.

The film repeatedly draws attention to Keaton's small stature to emphasize Bill Jr.'s sense of displacement. He is dwarfed by the engine and by the numerous coils of wires and ropes. And, in one telling shot, Bill Jr. stands between his father and an engineer. He is dwarfed by the two hulking men, illustrating how, from his father's perspective, the boy is hopelessly ineffectual (fig. **3.4**).

The scene in the barbershop emphasizes Bill Jr.'s supposed lack of masculinity. Instead of lathering Bill Jr.'s entire face, the barber disdainfully dabs just a little bit of shaving cream onto the minuscule display of facial hair. He removes the mustache with two quick swipes of the razor blade, and then yanks out one remaining hair with a pair of tweezers, as if plucking a woman's eyebrows. The scene then cuts to a long shot of the establishment's two chairs. Bill Jr. is in one, and a woman (who will later turn out to be Marion) is in the other (see fig. 2.8). The *mise en scène* establishes a parallel between the two, clearly suggesting that Bill Jr. is effeminate: both face screen right; both have their head bowed at the same angle; and both wear similar styles of black hair. The parallel is underscored when the two look up and recognize one another from Boston. The fact

3 A strong essay will develop its thesis
using a few emphatically stated
supporting ideas. This sentence marks
the beginning of this paper's third and
final point. In this case the author argues
that, at the climax of the film, significant
motifs change. These changes, in turn,
signal important developments in the
characters. Can you identify the other
two central supporting points stated
earlier in this essay?

that Bill Jr.'s sweetheart is J.J. King's daughter infuriates Bill Sr., confirming his assumption that his long-lost son has been corrupted by his urban education.

But Bill Sr. comes to realize that his son's embrace of the modern does not necessarily mean a rejection of the father and his old-fashioned values; nor does it mean that his son lacks bravery and mechanical know-how.[3] After catching his son trying to arrange a midnight rendezvous with Marion, Bill Sr. gives up trying to rehabilitate his son and abruptly sends the boy back to Boston. Immediately afterwards, Bill Sr. is arrested when he gets into a fight with King. Bill Jr. hears that his father is in jail and vows to help him escape; rather than bearing a grudge against the man who disowned him, Bill Jr. remains committed to the family.

Despite his mousy demeanor and small stature, Bill Jr. proves to his father that being an intellectual doesn't mean he can't throw a wallop of a punch. After his initial escape plans fail (he bakes a file into a loaf of bread), Bill Jr. surprises his father and himself when he punches the prison guard and knocks him unconscious. The father's pride in his son is evident later when, after having escaped from prison, he returns to defend his son's honor. He winds up back in jail, thus sacrificing himself for the boy he had previously rejected.

During the climactic moments of the film, Bill Jr. also shows his father that his education (and the modern world that it represents) doesn't mean he is incapable of operating machinery. In fact, Bill Jr. proves to have an even greater capacity with machinery than his father. When a giant cyclone levels the town (and King's boat), Bill Jr. is the only man able to rescue his father, who is stuck inside his prison cell as the entire jail floats down the gushing Mississippi. Bill Jr. takes charge of the *Stonewall Jackson*, stepping into his father's shoes. Because there are no engineers around, he concocts a comically elaborate device for operating the boat. Using a convoluted web of ropes and levers, Bill Jr. is able to control the boat's speed and steer simultaneously. Through his ingenuity, Bill is able to rescue both his father and King.

To his father, Bill Jr. represents the threat of modernity. But his clever use of ropes seems to define modernity as a more sophisticated and refined use of machinery, not the useless or abstract knowledge that Bill fears. Bill Jr. embodies the idea that the conflict between past and present is predicated on a false dichotomy. Even King's entrepreneurial gumption doesn't negate Bill Sr.'s unrefined machinery—it depends on it. The film ends on a suitably romantic note, as the two fathers share a laugh on the deck of the *Stonewall Jackson* while Bill Jr. rescues a preacher, who will, of course, perform an *ad hoc* wedding ceremony. In establishing a union between Bill Jr. and Marion, the film's romantic conclusion also unites symbols of the past and present, and of the agrarian South and the industrial North.

The Research Paper

Unlike the scene analysis or the film analysis, whose primary function is to show that the author has mastered the materials in a professor's course, the research paper is designed to teach students important academic skills. The assignment asks students to read beyond assigned materials to broaden intellectual horizons and generate new ideas; to summarize and synthesize others' ideas to support their own; to acknowledge perspectives that contradict their own; and to argue against these perspectives with intellectual integrity and respect.

When a professor asks students to write a research paper, she wants them to participate in an ongoing scholarly conversation about the subject matter. The research paper requires the writer to draw ideas from a broad array of materials, including original documents, scholarly books and articles, newspapers, magazines, and websites.

A good research paper does not merely collect and repeat the information contained in these sources. Serious research involves a process whereby the writer gathers information and ideas that may support and contest the working thesis; the writer then reassesses the persuasive power of his working thesis in light of the evidence gathered.

Topics for research papers vary widely. A research paper might make an argument about the importance of an individual film's production history or remarkable style. It might analyze one film in relation to other films of the same genre. Some research papers might connect films to other cultural phenomena, or discuss a film in relation to the director's *oeuvre*. Scholars can easily incorporate research to help support an argument that uses any of these approaches and those outlined in fig. 3.2. Figure **3.5** outlines several approaches writers use when they pursue research and synthesize ideas taken from multiple texts (including more than one film, book, article, etc.).

The sample research paper on page 49 discusses the vampire film *Let the*

TAKING NOTES

After establishing a working thesis, writers should gather details and examples to support the main point. For film scholars, this means watching a movie several times, taking note of how narrative, *mise en scène*, cinematography, editing, and sound contribute to, complicate, or contradict the ideas associated with the working thesis.

Most film scholars rely on a shorthand system as they take notes during screenings. Developing a series of abbreviations helps viewers quickly note the basics of a shot's visual details without taking their eyes off the screen. Consider using the list of common abbreviations below:

Camera placement:
   ls = long shot
   ms = medium shot
   cu = close-up
   xcu = extreme close-up
   ha = high-angle
   la = low-angle

Camera movement:
   ts = tracking shot
   t = tilt
   ps = pan shot
   cr = crane
   hh = handheld
   z = zoom
   sl = screen left
   sr = screen right
   hkl and lkl = high-key lighting and low-key lighting

Editing:
   diss. = dissolve
   s/rs = shot/reverse shot
   ct. = cut
   fi/fo = fade-in/fade-out
   w = wipe

Right One In ("*Låt den rätte komma in*"; Tomas Alfredson 2008) within the context of the horror film tradition. It argues that this film's attitude toward the monster differs from classic depictions of horror. The author assumes that by comparing and contrasting *Let the Right One In* with other notable horror films, readers will gain a better understanding of what distinguishes this film from its predecessors.

Notice the sources this essay relies on. The author cites academic journals and books published by university presses, not popular magazines or books published at popular presses. An academic journal decides to accept (or reject) articles on the basis of the peer review, a professional selection process. One or two scholars in the field read and evaluate the integrity and sophistication of an essay submitted for publication. University presses use the same process, approving a manuscript for publication only after several readers have considered its intellectual merit. Manuscripts are generally chosen for publication based on their originality and intellectual rigor. While popular criticism has its place in film scholarship, rarely do successful research papers rely solely on popular materials such as popular books, newspapers, magazines, and websites.

In general, websites receive even less editorial scrutiny than magazines and newspapers. Much of the web's original content consists of self-published blogs, fan summaries, or reviews. Consequently, serious scholars should be wary of relying on the web. This is not to say that the internet cannot be a valuable tool. Major newspapers and scholarly journals are available electronically. In short, writers who want to take advantage of the web must evaluate the intellectual integrity of electronic sources.

A simple litmus test to evaluate the intellectual rigor of a website involves three steps. First, determine whether or not the website is affiliated with a

3.5 Common rhetorical approaches for papers involving research.

Rhetorical Approach	Sample Thesis Statement
Compare and contrast two films that explore a similar subject matter. What factors might account for their similarities or differences? The historical and cultural circumstances of production? The artists responsible for their production? Different source materials?	Both *Mean Streets* (1973) and *The Godfather* (1972) explore life in the mob, but where the former focuses on the daily routines of small-time hoods passing time, the latter focuses on the grandeur of mafia bosses and their attempts to sustain power. The rough-hewn, independent approach of *Mean Streets* is the result of director Martin Scorsese's quest to make a personal film about a lifestyle he witnessed growing up in the streets of New York City, whereas *The Godfather*'s more classic narrative results from a major studio's quest to produce a popular epic film by adapting an already popular novel.
Situate a film within a larger group of films, such as a genre (horror), historical movement (the French New Wave) or a director's *oeuvre*. How does the film compare to the other films in this grouping in terms of its themes and style?	Many scholars have argued that Stanley Kubrick's last film, *Eyes Wide Shut* (1999), with its focus on contemporary urban married life, represents a departure from his previous work. But analysis of the film in relation to the director's *oeuvre* reveals that his satirical view of human beings and the systems they design is in full evidence in this film.
Research the production history of a film. What obstacles did the filmmakers have to overcome to produce their movie? How did these obstacles influence the final film?	Francis Ford Coppola encountered so many difficulties when making *Apocalypse Now* (1979) that the production nearly collapsed on itself. Nevertheless, the director trudged onward, risking financial and mental ruin in an obsessive quest that closely resembled the war story he was filming.

university (a sign that the material has serious scholastic credentials), a professional film association (such as the Society for Cinema and Media Studies), or a reputable press or publication. Second, notice if the source provides details about the professional background of its authors; are they legitimate authorities on film and film culture? Third, determine when the website was last updated. A website that has not been updated for months or years may lack technical, editorial, and financial support, which should make scholars cautious.

This sample research paper, written by an undergraduate film major, begins by referring to published scholarship on the horror film. The rest of the essay uses this scholarly writing about the historical development of the genre to help interpret *Let the Right One In* in relation to other horror films. This is a common and effective rhetorical strategy in research papers because it guides the reader into the topic. Put another way, it mirrors the way one might be inspired to reflect on a film after having read someone else's perspective. Research often begins with casual reading. In this case, the author explored her interest in horror films, and that process enabled her to situate a hauntingly atypical vampire film within the genre as a whole.

Conducting research is comparable to listening in and joining an ongoing public dialogue. This essay doesn't just rehash claims others have made about horror. Instead, the author summarizes pertinent points and then develops and adds to them.

The New Vampire as Sympathetic Gothic Heroine In Tomas Alfredson's *Let the Right One In* (2008) By Cassandra Pope

Since the 1960s the horror film has deviated from classical horror, which was filled with gothic themes, to a new, postmodern horror, which emphasizes the disintegration of all boundaries. In classical horror films such as *Frankenstein* (James Whale 1931) or *Nosferatu* (F.W. Murnau 1922), the "enemy is readily identifiable and vulnerable to the efforts of the cooperative community," whereas the monster within postmodern horror is usually at first indistinguishable from so-called normal people (Piñedo, p. 103).[1] As Isabel Piñedo explains in her careful analysis, "The universe of the contemporary horror film is an uncertain one in which good and evil, normality and abnormality, reality and illusion become virtually indistinguishable" (p. 85). In other words, what makes the postmodern horror film terrifying is that audiences must face a killer that is hard to distinguish from normal people rather than a grotesque monster that is easily recognized (p. 85). Seen in this light, *Let the Right One In* is a postmodern revitalization of vampire lore precisely because it suggests that the humans are no less scary than vampires; what makes Alfredson's film so haunting is the fact that very little distinguishes the vampire Eli from Oskar, the vulnerable boy she befriends.

For contemporary fans of the genre, Mary Harron's notorious *American Psycho* (2000) is a textbook example of Piñedo's theory of postmodern horror. In the film, Patrick Bateman (Christian Bale) is the epitome of human physical perfection; far from suffering from the unmanageable curse of a mysterious bite or being condemned to survive as strange monster in a hostile, human environ-

1 The introduction begins by using research to help define a particular type of horror film. The rest of the essay measures *Let the Right One In* against the criteria for classical and postmodern horror films spelled out here.

RESOURCES FOR FILM SCHOLARSHIP

Libraries and the internet now contain a wealth of resources for film scholars. Here is a selective bibliography that includes some of the materials that may prove helpful to begin a research project.

Bibliographical resources:

Academic Search Premier: An electronic database that indexes articles from over 3,100 scholarly journals.

The Film Literature Index. Indexes academic and popular articles written on film since 1973.

MLA Bibliography. Indexes academic articles written on literature and film since 1964. Available in an electronic version.

Film & Television Literature Index: An electronic database that indexes articles from more than 600 journals and magazines.

JSTOR: An electronic database of scholarly journals, including several important film journals.

New York Times Film Reviews. Collection of the newspaper's popular reviews from 1913–68.

Project Muse. Electronic index of scholarly journals in the humanities since 1993.

Scholarly journals:

Cahiers du Cinéma (in French)
Camera Obscura
Cineaste
Cinefex
Cinema Journal
Film Comment
Film Quarterly
Journal of Film and Video
Literature/Film Quarterly
Screen
Sight and Sound
Velvet Light Trap

Popular and industry magazines:

American Cinematographer
Entertainment Weekly
Photoplay (a Hollywood fan magazine, no longer published)
Variety

Online resources:

The Internet Movie Database (imdb.com)
Bright Lights Film Journal (brightlightsfilm.com)
Jump Cut (ejumpcut.com)
Senses of Cinema (sensesofcinema.com)
FilmSound (filmsound.org)
Film Soundtrack Reviews (filmtracks.com)

---

ment, Bateman is in complete control and maintains an outward appearance that leads the rest of the world to believe he is without flaws. From the opening scene the audience quickly identifies Bateman and his colleagues as successful businessmen. Spectators relate to and may even envy these young men at first and it is not until the following scene in a nightclub where Bateman's inner sadistic nature becomes apparent. After being denied the use of a drink stamp by a waitress, the camera cuts to a medium shot of Bateman viciously telling the waitress that he wants to "stab [her] to death and play with [her] blood" (fig. **3.6**). While this would be frightening enough, Harron disorients the audience by cutting to reveal a reflection of Bateman's image in the bar mirror. It becomes apparent that Bateman was merely exclaiming these things to himself, within his mind. The suggestion that this man, one whom the audience identified with only minutes earlier, is internally unstable, is terrifying. The monster can reside within anyone, which is the essential idea of postmodern horror.

In contrast, the vampire, a figure easily associated with classical gothic horror, is usually clearly identifiable as a monster. Dark, brooding creatures of the night who feed upon human blood, the traditional vampire looks like the quintessential "bad guy". And yet, this gothic creature has continued to play a role within contemporary horror films. Rather than fading away, the vampire is still a well-known and increasingly popular monster, as evidenced by the rabid following cultivated by the *True Blood* television series and the hot-blooded teen vampires in the *Twilight* (Catherine Hardwicke 2008) books and films. However, rather than remain the easily identifiable gothic monster, the vampire has instead become a way for contemporary directors to create "postmodern horror films which retain characteristics of [the] classical genre" (Piñedo, p. 102).[2]

Tomas Alfredson's *Let the Right One In* is a hybrid horror film that combines the characteristics of the classical and postmodern horror film in its attempt to portray the vampire, Eli (Line Leandersson), as a sympathetic monster rather than a fearful one. As Milly Williamson writes in her book *The Lure of the Vampire*, "otherness returns in the vampires of the twentieth century as a source of empathy and identification" resulting in their "no longer [being] figures of fear, but figures of sympathy" instead (Williamson, p. 29). Gothic themes remain visible in Alfredson's work, such as the threatening presence of a supernatural creature (Eli), the uncanny, and the hostile location (the deserted, cold, and desolate world of Sweden in the 1980s). However, these elements are combined with a postmodern sensibility so that the very notion of what exactly is the real threat remains ambiguous, and the ultimate outcome of the film remains uncertain. The combination of the classical and the postmodern horror within *Let the Right One In* makes Eli an eerily compelling example of the "new vampire" of the twentieth century.

Eli, cursed with the immortality of vampirism, must travel from city to city with her sole accomplice Hakan (Per Ragner), in an effort to avoid revealing her monstrosity. Forced to live in constant isolation, Eli is an outsider whom viewers sympathize with rather than fear, for her inability to become a part of her surrounding culture is a characteristic that is all too human. Her "painful awareness of [her own] outsiderdom," is suggested when she tells Oskar (Kare Hedebrandt) "we cannot be friends" despite the fact that she clearly desires some kind of connection with the lonely student (Williamson, p. 24). This reveals Eli to be a conflicted character who is conscious of the fact that, because of her vampire nature,

2 The Study Notes that accompany the Film Analysis essay in Chapter 2 discussed the importance of gathering evidence drawn from a film to make convincing points. Research papers also gather evidence from films, but supplement this information with material drawn from other sources. The author does not treat this analysis of horror films as an end in itself, nor does she use this research to "fill up space" in her paper. Instead, this quote helps her develop her own ideas about how the monster Eli compares to her predecessors.

3.6 Fantasies of aggression: Patrick Bateman in *American Psycho*.

3.7 An uncanny image of childhood in *Let the Right One In*.

3 When conducting research, writers don't limit themselves to looking for sources that explicitly discuss the specific film under consideration. Essays that theorize film history, genre, or historical context might all provide fruitful material, which can help interpret your primary source. In fact, here the author goes outside the discipline of Film Studies altogether and uses psychoanalytic theories to help understand characters and settings.

she will remain an outcast in society forever. Eli's desire to blend in and be immersed within human culture becomes visible when she is unable to heed her own cautious reluctance and allows her relationship with Oskar to grow because she connects with his own feeling of being isolated from society.

Alfredson's unique intertwining of the classical and the postmodern becomes visible in the first meeting between Eli and Oskar. Here, Alfredson capitalizes on classical horror films' most integral gothic characteristic: the uncanny. The German word for uncanny, *unheimlich*, is literally defined as "the opposite of *heimlich*," which means familiar, or belonging to the home (Freud, p. 124).[3] Thus, the term uncanny refers to that which is terrifying because it is something or someone that was once recognizable to the viewers. By introducing the vampire Eli in the jungle gym within the center of an apartment complex's courtyard, Alfredson transforms this once familiar children's setting into something strange and uncanny. Adding to this sense of something familiar made strange is the fact that, later, Oskar expresses his interest in Eli by giving her his Rubik's Cube. Quite simply, two images closely associated with childhood become menacing (fig. **3.7**).

Alfredson's careful orchestration of camera placement and movement adds to the sense that an environment that should represent childhood innocence has become frightening. As Oskar leaves his building to enter the courtyard, rather than follow him from behind, the camera captures his entrance to the meeting place from a position in front of him. As a result, viewers are only allowed to speculate as to what Oskar sees before stepping outside. By preventing the audience from sharing Oskar's point of view, Alfredson leaves us feeling afraid and hesitant about entering a space that should feel comfortable. A medium shot reveals Oskar reaching into his coat to retrieve his pocketknife. The camera then tilts up to follow the knife, and ends in a shot showing Oskar's face as he scrutinizes his weapon. Because we are already aware of Oskar's keen interest in crimes, murders, and violent movies like *Deliverance* and *Taxi Driver*, this shot contributes to our sense of his weird fascination with death. The usually welcoming feelings associated with playgrounds and public courtyards is lost upon the audience, not just because Oskar twiddles with his knife, but also because this playground is eerily empty, since it is nighttime and most children are inside the warmth of their houses and getting ready for bed. Rather than accentuating the warm yellow and orange hues typically associated with playgrounds, daytime, and children, the scene remains cloaked in the bluish artificial lighting cast by the streetlamps. This unnatural lighting causes the scene to appear gothic. And although industrialized Sweden isn't an otherworldly fictitious setting, the anonymous city in *Let the Right One In* seems strangely cut off from the rest of the world and immersed within snowy silence. Its frigid temperatures make it appear uninhabitable to most audiences. This silence muffles all surrounding sounds, connoting feelings of being submerged, which awakens uncanny feelings which recall "the helplessness we experience in certain dream-states." (Freud, p. 144)[4]

But if Alfredson's use of the uncanny is in keeping with traditional horror films, this scene also confounds the gothic traditions of the vampire tale. For one thing, it's not entirely clear who is more menacing: the human or the vampire. As Oskar approaches the courtyard, he walks down a path that is directly in the center of the screen, suggesting that perhaps he aims for the "straight and narrow" path within life, one which remains morally correct, however, the camera pans slowly towards the left just as Oskar begins to stray off the path to head towards the tree where we are confronted with his inner wish to harm the children at school who have been bullying him. His obsession with death directly contrasts with Eli's wish to come into contact with life. Captured in a medium close-up, Oskar threatens the tree in the same manner in which the boys at school threaten him. He and the tree remain in focus in the foreground of the shot, while the buildings and snow within the background become blurry, suggesting his immersion within his fantasy of harming his torturers.

When Eli finally does appear, she embodies the idea of the uncanny, but her appearance is actually no more threatening than the image of Oskar beating up the tree. Her shabby appearance, animal-like stance, silence and warm weather clothes all alert the viewer that something is odd or amiss about her character. Tilting her head in the way that a predator would to observe its prey, Eli remains elevated in the scene, verifying her higher standing in the food chain. Eli's face remains darkened and obscured in the background, adding to the feelings of uncertainty and fear in connection with her role. Eli jumps down to the ground, leveling herself with Oskar, as if she is about to attack. Instead she tells Oskar, "I can't be friends with you" and turns to walk away.[5] Because she says this without first being approached by Oskar, Eli's comment seems to be directed towards herself rather than him in an effort to remind herself of her inability to interact socially with other human beings. A shift occurs as the audience becomes aware of Eli's understanding that she is an outcast, and as we view her restraint in harming another as a sacrifice, we empathize with Eli. Eli's painful self-sacrifice turns her into a character "like the heroine of the gothic novel [who] suffers from circumstances [she] didn't choose even if at times, [she] revels in [her] outsiderdom" as later scenes suggest (Williamson, p. 39).

4 The name and page number in parenthesis is one accepted method for documenting words and ideas taken from other sources. This refers the reader to the "Works Cited" page at the end of the essay. Here readers can find complete bibliographical information. Entries in the Works Cited page are ordered alphabetically by authors' last names. For more information on citing sources, refer to the Study Notes that accompany the Film Analysis essay in Chapter 6.

5 When writers quote dialogue from a film (the primary source), they do not need to include an in-text citation or a works cited entry. Such documentation is only required for secondary sources (i.e, published reviews, scholarly essays, and commentary tracks).

The film continues to complicate the audience's response to Eli by linking her to uncanny elements while simultaneously capitalizing on her vulnerability. For instance, Eli and Oskar return to the courtyard later in the film and the two of them bond over a toy Rubik's cube; she is a monster taken with the joys of brightly colored plastic. Though Eli seems to long for a release from her "vampiric malady" through her attempts within the film to directly avoid killing others in the quenching of her thirst, "the pull of vampirism is too powerful for [her] to resist and [she] reverts to [her] vampiric ways" multiple times in order to survive (Williamson, p. 32). The film finally undercuts Eli's innocence in the scene in which she makes her first kill onscreen by luring her victim using her childlike voice and appearance. The scene is strangely gothic as it takes place beneath a bridge in almost absolute darkness. In a long shot, the space directly under the bridge where Eli hides is pitch black, causing the appearance of a separate and unsafe world within the frame. The entire scene seems to hearken back to the popular fairy tale "The Three Billy Goats Gruff." And yet the Swedish setting is perfectly everyday and less imaginary than the world of the fairy tale. At first the man appears to be perfectly safe as long as he continues to stand outside of the dark shadows under the bridge and remain in the light cast by the streetlamp. But in the top of the frame there are steel railings, giving the appearance of a cage-like structure, which again alludes to the solitary confinement of this utterly ordinary city.

Crucially, the camera placement during the attack undercuts the horror of the event and allows the audience to sympathize with the perpetrator of the crime. The camera remains positioned to view the action under the bridge in a long shot, keeping the audience distanced during the entire sequence in which Eli attacks the man. We see her vampire nature, but Eli is nearly unrecognizable within the depths of the shadows. While still draining her victim of his blood, the camera captures Eli in another long shot in which the screen is obscured by many fences and railings both in the foreground and background, all creating a scene suggesting Eli's entrapment in her life as a vampire. Light cast upon Eli and her victim comes from another off-screen source causing the entire image to be caught in a ghostly glow again, connoting the gothic characteristics of classical horror films (fig. **3.1**). It is only when Eli kneels upon her victim's chest and begins to cry that the camera cuts to a medium close up, emphasizing her obvious remorse and guilt in having to kill a human for her own survival. Although filmed within strangely gothic settings, Eli's emotional outburst embodies the "new vampire" Williamson describes within her essay:

> Its unwanted vampirism is the violation it has suffered, it is expelled from humanity, is misrecognized as evil by a world to which it does not belong and its innocence and virtue are obfuscated by its very ontology, until we the readers or viewers come to understand the vampire's predicament (and therefore innocence), even if the world at large does not. (Williamson, pp. 43–44)

In short, Alfredson films the attack not to provide the customary chills and thrills we associate with horror films, but to stir up the audience's sympathy for the alienated creature.

3.8 Gothic doubles in *Let the Right One In*.

The blurred boundary between good and evil with regard to Eli's struggles against her animalistic nature becomes even more interesting when Alfredson presents us with yet another twist on the classical horror film: the gothic double. A staple of literature and film, the gothic double is an antagonistic character who is often the mutilated or twisted version of the innocent protagonist. In traditional horror films, the monstrous double typically acts out the repressed feelings and desires of the humans it pursues. But, by emphasizing Eli's purity and desire to be human, Alfredson suggests that Oskar may in fact be *Eli's* haunted gothic double. Although the audience most likely mistrusts Eli, *Let the Right One In* expresses its postmodern sensibility by suggesting that she is no more monstrous than the everyday human: Oskar.

Alfredson hints at this relationship several times throughout the film. Perhaps most prominent is the scene following Eli's first kill when we are first presented with the possibility that she is indeed innocent due to her struggles to resist her vampiric nature in an effort to become a part of the community in which she lives. The scene opens with a static shot of both Eli and Oskar's bedroom windows on exact opposite sides of the screen, split only by a slightly visible black pipe down the center (fig. **3.8**). Their bedroom windows seem to represent the similar and yet opposite natures of the two children. Although both children and their rooms are visible, Eli's room seems to cast off a more unnatural feel, a clear sign that she is Oskar's gothic double. While surrounded in the yellow hue within his room, suggesting warmth and life, Oskar's outline is much more clear and distinct than Eli, who is completely blurred and hidden in shadows cast by the blue light coming from her window. The blue tones suggest a much colder atmosphere as well as connoting images of death. Considered in isolation, these details evoke the traditional notion of the gothic double: Eli appears to be Oskar's deathly shadow. But the composition emphasizes the similarities between the two children. Oskar's curtains create strong vertical lines while Eli's shades create horizontal lines, and both suggest feelings of entrapment; both children experience feelings of claustrophobia emphasized by the tight framing of their windows.

Oskar is a living, breathing child who appears to fit in with his community, thus leaving Eli as the traditional gothic double as she is a vampire child who must isolate herself from the community because of her monstrous associations and who only emerges in the dark. Yet if Eli is the emblem "of misrecognized and persecuted innocence," she is perhaps more sympathetic than Oskar in the eyes of the viewers (Williamson, p. 40). Thus, Oskar becomes her gothic double, for while he appears to live the life of a normal child, his inability to fit into the community of his peers at school and his fantasies of causing harm to those who ridicule him make him appear as uncanny inwardly as Eli appears uncanny on the outside. Alfredson explains that "Eli is all that violence that [Oskar] feels inside but can't let out because he's too weak" ("Behind the Scenes"). Crucially, Oskar doesn't stifle his violent urges because he's morally superior. He does so because he's too afraid to act them out.

Oskar's questionable morals come in to play in a later scene in which he provokes Eli to enter his apartment without giving her permission to cross the threshold, causing her to bleed from bodily orifices before he ends her suffering. Rather than trusting Eli, Oskar risks her life and her vampire "rules" for his own twisted pleasure in seeing what the consequences will be. In short, in mirroring Oskar, Eli's presence is in keeping with the tradition of the gothic double in classic horror. However, in the classic manifestation, the gothic double is a dark, unsympathetic, repulsive perversion of the protagonist. In a postmodern twist, *Let the Right One In* upends this distinction, making it unclear which character is the twisted perversion.

At the film's conclusion, after Eli saves Oskar's life by murdering three of his classmates, they both must flee. This ending typifies postmodern horror in that the future of both children and the question of whether justice has been served remain open and ambiguous. Although some might argue for the innocence of the boys Eli kills, their constant desire to torment Oskar also confirms their innate evil. Having witnessed the bullies' increasingly violent assaults, surely the audience hopes Eli will indeed act on Oskar's desire to exact revenge. This moral ambiguity is part and parcel of postmodern horror. And while the viewers may find Eli sympathetic and inherently benevolent, the two children still remain in a society in which others are not able to accept Eli. Indeed, the film's last scene depicts the two lighting out for a new life together elsewhere. But right before this resolution, Alfredson repeats the exact same shot of falling snow against a black sky seen in the opening credits of the film, suggesting that the events within the film have come full circle, and while they have escaped one city, Oskar and Eli will only go to another in which similar events will take place. Inevitably, they will be cast out from society as well.

Oskar's role in the end of the film as Eli's friend is not entirely promising either, for he seems to take on the role of Hakan, Eli's previous father figure and "hunter." Because we are never told how that relationship began, we can only assume that his relationship with Eli followed the same trajectory as Oskar's. Oskar does indeed take on Hakan's role as guardian, and consequently he will someday come to the same demise. According to Alfredson, this ending can be interpreted as a happy one, since the two "children" have found one another.

But, he explains, the ending simultaneously has an ominous undertone "if you see [Oskar] as the next killer" (Behind the Scenes). The film's postmodern tack denies any comfortable understanding of what is monstrous and what is normal, and provides the audience with no firm sense of closure.

Throughout *Let the Right One In*, Tomas Alfredson's unique combination of the classical and the postmodern reflects the modern vampire's ambiguity. The vampire, once endowed with repulsive qualities in such classics as *Nosferatu*, is instead presented as the "new" vampire Milly Williamson addresses in her book *The Lure of the Vampire*. This new vampire is inflicted with "the struggle for innocence to be acknowledged and virtue to be recognized" (Williamson p. 44). Far more than a repugnant creature of the night, Eli is vulnerable and empathetic—well, she might be.

Works Cited (in the research paper)[6]

"Behind the Scenes." Producers: Gary Purviance, et. al. *Let the Right One In* DVD. Magnolia, 2009.

Freud, Sigmund. *The Uncanny*. New York: Penguin Books, 2003.

Piñedo, Isabel. "Postmodern Elements of the Contemporary Horror Film." *The Horror Film*, ed. Stephen Prince. New Brunswick, NJ: Rutgers University Press, 2004, pp. 85–117.

Williamson, Milly. *The Lure of the Vampire*. London: Wallflower Press, 2005.

6 Works Cited pages aren't merely a formality to give writers credit for their ideas. Scholars inevitably use these pages to help find sources that will be helpful in their own research. If you find a thorough bibliography, your research is halfway complete!

Conducting Archival Research

The research in the essay above is culled exclusively from published scholarship, or secondary sources. But film scholars also seek out primary sources such as a director's notes, internal studio memos, contemporary press materials, or private correspondence. Such archival materials can illustrate how a film was made, or explain what circumstances determined the final look of a film. Finding these rare materials can be a challenge, however, since scholars may need to obtain special permission to use the archives and must travel to film studios and collections. Below is a list of some major film archives:

- Black Film Archive at Indiana University (http://www.indiana.edu/~bfca/)
- British Film Institute (BFI) National Film and Television Archive (http://www.bfi.org.uk/nftva/)
- George Eastman House (http://www.eastmanhouse.org)
- Library of Congress Motion Picture and Television Reading Room (http://www.loc.gov/rr/mopic/)
- Margaret Herrick Library at the Academy of Motion Picture Arts and Sciences (http://www.oscars.org/mhl/index.html)
- The Museum of Modern Art (http://www.moma.org)
- National Center for Film and Video Presentation (The American Film Institute) (http://www.afi.com)
- The New York Public Library (http://www.nypl.org/branch/collections/dmc.html)
- Pacific Film Archive (http://www.bampfa.berkeley.edu/)
- University of California at Los Angeles (UCLA) (www.cinema.ucla.edu/)
- University of Southern California (USC) (http://www.usc.edu/libraries/subjects/cinema/)

- Wisconsin Center for Film and Theater Research
  (http://www.wisconsinhistory.org/wcftr/)

A more complete list of archives can be found at the Library of Congress Listing of Public Moving Image Archives and Research Centers (http://www.loc.gov/film/arch.html).

Scholars wanting to do research at an archive should first check its website, for two reasons. First, some materials may be available online. Second, many archives require researchers to make reservations to see materials in advance and do not allow walk-ins.

The Popular Review

Of the genres of film writing that students are commonly asked to read and/or write, the popular review is the one that is not strictly academic. Even the most casual film buffs actively seek out and read popular reviews as they determine which movie they should go see over the weekend.

The primary function of the popular review is to encourage audiences to see a particular film ... or to stay away at all costs. At its simplest, the essence of any popular review is one of two evaluative claims: "This is a good movie," or "this is a bad movie." More than just rating the entertainment value of movies, film critics also participate in public discourse on film and culture. By debating the relative worth of individual films in widely read publications, critics raise their readers' awareness of film as a serious art form worthy of careful consideration. This tradition has thrived on a diversity of opinions, including those of such notable figures as James Agee (*The Nation*), Edith Oliver (*The New Yorker*), Andrew Sarris (*The Village Voice*), Pauline Kael (*The New Yorker*), Stanley Kauffmann (*The New Republic*), Richard Schickel (*Time*), Peter Travers (*Rolling Stone*), and Cynthia Fuchs (PopMatters.com).

To support a claim, the popular reviewer must measure the film against a set of standards, or criteria. Effective reviewers are conscious of what criteria they use to evaluate films, and they make these criteria clear to their readers. In other words, readers should understand why a reviewer liked a film, so they can determine whether or not to trust the reviewer's judgement. In turn, a reviewer must carefully consider whom she is addressing, and evaluate a film using criteria her audience will recognize and might accept. Reviews in *Rolling Stone* magazine, for example, target the magazine's primary readership: males in their late teens and early twenties. In contrast, readers of *The New Yorker* tend to be older, middle-class intellectuals, and the magazine's film reviews generally address the values of that specific audience. Reviews in political magazines such as *The Weekly Standard* or *The Nation* evaluate films in large part based on their political values.

The reasons for liking or disliking a film have to be considered carefully. Anyone who has had the experience of liking a film only after a second viewing understands that one cannot always trust an initial response. Any number of factors may limit a viewer's ability to appreciate a movie after just one viewing. Perhaps the theater's environment or other patrons inhibited enjoyment; perhaps the film was simply too complex to comprehend fully after just one screening. When writing a review, try to avoid knee-jerk reactions. Instead, begin by considering what a film is trying to accomplish and how it tries to accomplish these things. The most convincing *evaluative* claims follow careful *interpretive* analysis.

While most popular reviews are easier to read than academic papers, they are not necessarily easier to write. In fact, since effective popular reviews usually take into account a film's thematic concerns and its aesthetic techniques without assuming that the reader has any formal training in film aesthetics, the popular review can be more difficult to write than an academic argument.

Consider the following review of the cult science fiction film *District 9* (Neill Blomkamp 2009), written by Scott Foundas. Notice how the review begins by situating the film within the tradition of science fiction and arguing that *District 9* is doing something fresh in a well-established genre. These paragraphs establish a central premise Foundas will use throughout his review. While this review doesn't have a formally declared thesis statement, as you would expect to find in a formal piece of academic writing, it does have a focus. In the opening, Foundas establishes the importance of prejudice and apartheid as a theme in the film, and this idea continues to inform his brief plot summary and his subsequent evaluation of *District 9*.

Unlike formal academic writing, journalistic film reviews often feature more playful, informal language. Notice the metaphors Foundas uses to help the reader imagine what the film looks like: aliens look like "cockroaches" and they wait for the "intergalactic AAA" to give their ship a jumpstart. In the first sentence, Foundas compares the stranded aliens to "huddled masses." This is an especially effective example of how good writers can make use of intertextual references. Foundas lifts this phrase from the inscription on the Statue of Liberty, which says "Give me your tired, your poor, your huddled masses yearning to breathe free." The film isn't set in the United States; nevertheless this reference helps Foundas establish the film's themes of immigration and prejudice (fig. **3.9**).

Finally, notice how Foundas interweaves a wide range of references and information to help his readers imagine a film they very likely haven't seen yet, and to help develop his evaluative logic: vintage films, contemporary films, historical details, television shows, and director Neill Blomkamp's production budget.

Aliens as Apartheid Metaphor in *District 9*
By Scott Foundas August 11, 2009
Reprinted with the permission of *The Village Voice*

The aliens have been with us for 20 years already at the start of South African director Neill Blomkamp's fast and furiously inventive *District 9*, their huddled masses long ago extracted from their broken-down mothership and deposited in the titular housing slum on the outskirts of Johannesburg. Unlike the space invaders of most science fiction, these six-foot-tall E.T.s (pejoratively nicknamed "prawns," but more closely resembling the love child of a cockroach and the Creature From the Black Lagoon) come neither in peace nor in malice. They are, we are told, the worker bees of whatever galaxy they hail from, accustomed to following orders rather than giving them. And so they find themselves dazed and confused in

3.9 Aliens as impoverished immigrants in *District 9*.

1 Like most reviews, this article begins with a short section that establishes the general tone. Foundas links *District 9* to a specific genre and identifies the film's historical allusions. But other reviews might begin by describing an especially evocative moment in the film, alluding to a relevant piece of production history, referring to past works by a director or star, or discussing a salient current event.

2 As with more formal modes of writing, the review requires the writer to gather "evidence" to describe and comment on the film. In most cases, the film reviewer faces inflexible word count limits, so this detail is used sparingly. Pay attention to how Foundas focuses his attention on the details that help him capture the film's critique of social oppression, which he alludes to in the opening paragraphs.

3 Foundas's review employs a three-part structure common to popular film criticism. The first section pithily evokes the author's opinion—it sets the mood, so to speak. The second section offers a succinct plot summary—just enough to give the reader an impression of the film without spoiling it. The third section goes into more detail about why the reviewer praises or condemns the film. Foundas begins the third section of his review here. Notice how he pulls various strands of thought together, linking his appreciation of the film's unusual visual style with its interest in the politics of intergalactic apartheid.

their new home, while their flying saucer still hovers inertly over the skyline, as if waiting for a jump-start from an intergalactic AAA.[1]

A high-end commercials director making his feature debut, Blomkamp (who also co-wrote the script with Terri Tatchell) milks his ostensibly fantastic scenario for all its allegorical worth. With its corrugated tin sheds and abject poverty, District 9 stands in for the township settlements where more than a million South African blacks still live without basic human services, two decades after the end of apartheid. But you don't have to squint too hard to also see the itinerant community as an all-purpose analog for the ghettos of Nazi Germany, America's inner cities, and all of those other places where unwanted, powerless peoples have been herded off, far from the backyards of the ruling class. Blomkamp's touch, however, is anything but heavy, and for most of its run time, *District 9* whizzes by with a resourcefulness and mordant wit nearly worthy of its obvious influences: *Invasion of the Body Snatchers*, *Dawn of the Dead*, and *Starship Troopers*.

As the movie begins, a wave of violent prawn unrest—not unlike the one that rocked South Africa's real townships only last month—has prompted the good people of Jo'burg to crave even greater distance from their sub-human neighbors, and a forced relocation of all alien residents to a Guantánamo-style tent city known as District 10 has become law.[2] Enter Multi-National United, a smarmy private military contractor that places the relocation in the hands of one Wikus van der Merwe (Sharlto Copley), a not very bright corporate lackey who also happens to be married to the boss's daughter. While MNU tries to decipher the aliens' advanced weapons technology (leading to one disturbing scene set in a research lab that Dr. Mengele would have loved), affable but clueless Wikus yearns to surmount claims of nepotism. Then everything goes haywire, with the oppressor getting a crash course in what it feels like to be the oppressed.

District 9 is never better than in its first 45 minutes, as Blomkamp maps out the film's social and economic realities via a grab bag of news reports, corporate videos, and CCTV cameras.[3] The aliens, we learn, can understand English, but speak in their own indigenous language of guttural grunts and clicks (making this one of two major releases this month, along with Quentin Tarantino's *Inglourious Basterds*, to predominantly feature subtitled dialogue). Meanwhile, inside the boundaries of District 9 itself, a cadre of Nigerian gangsters exploit the prawns by charging them exorbitant prices for

Chapter 3: Writing About Film

black-market goods (including the canned cat food the aliens regard as a culinary delicacy). Eventually, Blomkamp adds some straight dramatic scenes to the mix, around the point that the movie itself evolves into a somewhat more straightforward pursuit thriller—albeit one in which Wikus is both Dr. Richard Kimble and the one-armed man. Taking refuge in the very community he is supposed to be uprooting, the middle manager finds himself forming a tentative alliance with a science-geek prawn known by the anglicized name of Christopher Johnson (played by actor Jason Cope, with the aid of a few CGI enhancements), who may be his people's only hope for a better life and who turns out to be the most humane, compassionate character in the *District 9* landscape.

Even in the movie's most conventional stretches, Blomkamp puts things across with terrific verve, using action and computer effects to enhance rather than trump story and character.[4] *District 9* was produced, with help from *The Lord of the Rings* honcho Peter Jackson, for all of $30 million (about the average advertising budget on a standard Hollywood production) after plans for Jackson and Blomkamp to collaborate on a much larger-scale adaptation of the Halo video-game franchise fell apart, and the entire project seems carried along by the scrappy energy of a bright, young filmmaker working far away from Hollywood's prying, homogenizing eyes. Probably only with an advocate like Jackson to run interference for him could Blomkamp have gotten away with a lot of it—the Johannesburg setting (aren't alien invasions only supposed to happen in New York, L.A., or D.C.?), the dweeby hero, the thick South African accents, the subtitles. I can't wait to see what Blomkamp does next, and I very much hope he gets even less money to do it.[5]

4 A film critic should be able to pinpoint his criteria for evaluation. What ingredients must a film have to warrant a positive review? Earlier, for example, Foundas singles out the film's ability to connect a science fiction tale to current social realities. Clearly, Foundas appreciates films that offer social commentary. Here, Foundas describes *District 9*'s action set pieces. Does he appear to like explosions just for the sake of seeing a "cool" explosion, or is there something specific about the way the film makes use of pyrotechnics that's especially effective?

5 Foundas ends with a paragraph that discusses the film's relatively miniscule budget. Why does he conclude by hoping Blomkamp gets an even smaller budget for his next film? How does Foundas manage to connect this discussion of finances to his central focus on *District 9*'s sophisticated themes?

This chapter concludes Part One of this book. Chapter 1 explained the connection between film analysis and film appreciation, and Chapter 2 introduced strategies for taking the first steps toward film analysis. This chapter has shown how interpretation and writing go hand in hand, and both are activities that engage scholars and film enthusiasts alike. Despite the obvious differences between formal academic analysis and popular film reviews, both approaches demand an appreciation of how films systematically use narrative, visual, and sound details to evoke characters, themes, and abstract ideas. They also demand that attention be paid to the writing genre and its audience.

Part Two of this book builds on the materials covered in the first three chapters by providing the vocabulary and intellectual tools needed to describe cinematic techniques, beginning with a discussion of narrative form, and moving through visual elements and sound. Developing the ability to notice—and the vocabulary to describe—specific visual, sound, and storytelling techniques and their potential effects on viewers is critical to constructing clear and thoughtful interpretive claims. By the end of Part Two, readers should be able to write in each of the four modes outlined in Chapter 3, using the proper terminology to construct cogent arguments about cinema.

Film Analysis

Predator becomes prey in *No Country for Old Men*.

Part Two provides readers with the analytical tools needed to interpret films. These tools include identifying the elements of film art and the terminology that film scholars and filmmakers use to describe film techniques. Part Two also helps readers to develop the skills necessary to write a comprehensive textual analysis.

Chapters 4 through 8 offer readers a thorough understanding of five components of film: narrative form (the way the story is structured), *mise en scène* (or cinematic staging), cinematography, editing, and sound. These chapters explore a wide variety of films, yet they all emphasize narrative as a mode of organizing visual and sound elements. Chapter 9 focuses specific attention on documentary and avant-garde films, emphasizing the fact that these films, even if they do not tell a story, also orchestrate visual and sound details to produce meaning according to definable organizing principles.

Part Two also offers several opportunities for readers to build on the writing skills developed in Chapter 3. Film analyses at the end of Chapters 4 through 9 offer examples of film writing and provide useful tips on topics such as logic and organization and incorporating outside research.

Narrative Form

//

CHAPTER FOUR

One should not tell stories as straightline narratives.
There are so many other possibilities, and film would
only enrich them.

Peter Greenaway

//

The opening scenes of the animated feature *Finding Nemo* (Andrew Stanton and
Lee Unkrich 2003; fig. **4.1**) depict a devoted pair of clownfish named Marlin and
Coral. Marlin persuades Coral to lay their eggs in an underwater cave that is both
beautiful and dangerous. Its proximity to a drop-off makes the clownfish vulnerable to the larger fish from deeper waters that prey on them. Sadly, a tragedy
occurs when an ocean predator consumes Coral along with the entire collection

4.1 Marlin and Dory navigate through a dangerous jellyfish colony in *Finding Nemo*.

of unhatched eggs, except for one, whom Marlin names Nemo. As Nemo grows up, Marlin becomes an overprotective father, sure that, because one of his fins is damaged, Nemo cannot survive without constant care. When Nemo rebels and ventures out past the drop-off, he is captured by humans who transport him to an aquarium in a dentist's office in Australia. The remainder of the film is devoted to Marlin's quest to rescue Nemo from these dangerous humans.

The events that take place in the opening moments of the film are critical to the viewer's understanding of the characters. In particular, Marlin's fears about the drop-off and his insistence that Nemo play it safe are **motivated**. That is, Marlin's behavior is shaped by his earlier experiences. Marlin was not born a killjoy, taking pleasure in squelching everyone's fun: to the contrary, in the opening scenes with Coral he is ebullient and daring. The attack has taught Marlin to be wary of the world, so, as a way of keeping him safe, he impresses on his son that untold dangers lurk beyond the drop-off.

If the filmmakers had not chosen to present Marlin's predicament in the **exposition**—the opening scenes of a film, during which a great deal of information about the characters and situation is imparted—then viewers might find him an unsympathetic character and might question why he won't allow Nemo to have any fun. This story is about Marlin learning to enjoy life again as much as it is about Nemo discovering his own abilities; therefore it is important that viewers connect emotionally with both father and son. One way to encourage audiences to warm up to characters who have limitations and quirks is to use the exposition to show that there is a reason for their idiosyncrasies. Another is to imply subtly that a character has faced difficulties in the past—in his or her **backstory**, the story events that take place before the film begins—and suggest that those experiences continue to shape that character's behavior. Choices regarding how and when to present information contribute to the overall storytelling framework of the film. That organizing framework is called a film's **narrative form**.

Becoming familiar with the role of narrative as a structuring device allows viewers to grasp character change and development, to recognize parallels and motifs and, most importantly, to synthesize these details to build an interpretation of a film's themes.

Although most feature films are organized according to principles of narrative form, there are other types of films which are organized differently. Chapter 9 examines some alternatives to narrative fiction film. This chapter offers a definition of narrative and looks at some of the key concepts employed when analyzing narrative form. It then goes on to examine the structure that most conventional narrative films take and some alternatives to that structure. The chapter ends by looking at some of the perspectives from which a film can be narrated, or appear to be narrated.

Defining Narrative

A narrative is an account of a string of events occurring in space and time. Not merely a cluster of random elements, a narrative presents an ordered series of events connected by the logic of cause and effect. Narratives piece events together in a linear fashion that clearly shows the audience the reasons for, and the consequences of, character behavior. Marlin is overprotective because of his heartache, and this in turn makes Nemo crave adventure. This logic of cause and effect ties together character traits, goals, obstacles, and actions.

Narrative films generally focus on human characters and their struggles. Characters possess traits, face conflicts, perform actions, and undergo changes that enable or hinder their pursuit of a specific goal. The goal may be concrete or abstract, lofty or banal: in some cases it may be finding love; in others it may be saving humanity or arriving safely at a destination. Russian narrative theorist Tzvetlan Todorov argued that all narratives involve the disruption of a stable situation, which makes restoration of equilibrium an important goal. Chances are good that characters attain stability only after undergoing important changes: for example, after reconsidering goals and the means of attaining them and facing down internal demons or external challenges.

Characters encounter obstacles to attaining goals: these obstacles arise from within, from other characters, from non-human characters (in horror and science fiction), and from forces of nature. They may be concrete physical challenges (scaling a mountain), the actions and desires of others (a lover's rejection), or internal psychological or emotional issues (fear of commitment). In some cases the characters may not achieve the goal they are pursuing: events, or their own failings, may conspire against them.

Many narrative films involve characters overcoming obstacles on more than one level. The *Lord of the Rings* trilogy (Peter Jackson 2001, 2002, 2003) offers an example. The primary obstacle the Fellowship faces is the physical challenge posed by the Dark Lord Sauron and his Orcs, yet each character also faces internal challenges as the group moves toward its collective goal. Frodo, for example, must resist the lure of the ring.

Filmmakers orchestrate story details in a systematic way to produce a meaningful and enjoyable experience for the audience. They establish and explore characters and their conflicts using the panoply of cinematic techniques available, including dialogue, music, visual effects, locations, costumes, colors, and editing. This chapter focuses specifically on the narrative choices available to screenwriters and film directors and helps readers to recognize the conventions of classical narrative form as well as alternatives to those conventions. The next section discusses how filmmakers often combine elements that do not exist in the story world with their fictional narratives.

Framing the Fictional World: Diegetic and Non-diegetic Elements

Narrative films often include elements that exist outside the fictional world of the story—such as the opening or closing credits, or background music. The implied world of the story, including settings, characters, sounds, and events, is the **diegesis**. Elements that exist outside the diegesis are called **non-diegetic** or **extradiegetic** devices. The audience is aware of these non-diegetic components of the film, but the characters, of course, are not.

▪▪

THE SCREENPLAY

The process of making a feature film begins with an original or an adapted **screenplay**, written by a screenwriter, based on fictional events or non-fiction source material. A screenplay that has not been commissioned—one that a screenwriter submits for consideration—is called a **spec script**. Screenplays usually go through a number of revisions, modified by script doctors, who are specialists in a particular area, such as dialogue. During **pre-production**, the director adds information (numbering scenes, determining camera placement, cuts, and sound cues) to produce the **shooting script**, which is the day-to-day guide the director and cinematographer use during production. After each day of shooting, the script supervisor maintains a detailed log of the scenes filmed that day.

Filmmakers use non-diegetic elements for several reasons: they may draw attention to aspects of the narrative from a position outside the story, they communicate with the audience directly, and they engage viewers on an emotional level.

Most narrative films tell a story by simply showing a sequence of actions, but others include a narrator, who may or may not be one of the characters in the film. A non-diegetic narrator, one who is not a character in the story, may not seem to have a vested interest in explaining events a certain way and thus may appear to be objective. Non-diegetic narrators address the audience in *Band of Outsiders* (*Bande à part*, Jean-Luc Godard 1964), *Dogville* (Lars Von Trier 2003), and *Inglourious Basterds*.

A non-diegetic **voice-over** narrates *The Royal Tenenbaums* (Wes Anderson 2001). In the same film, a non-diegetic visual device creates an analogy between the narration and the act of reading stories aloud to children. A large printed page opens new "chapters" of the film (fig. **4.2**).

Narration by a character from the fictional world, such as Holly (Sissy Spacek) in *Badlands* (Terrence Malick 1974) or Lovelace (Robin Williams) in *Happy Feet* (George Miller 2006) is a diegetic element, even if the character narrates from a point in time that is earlier or later than the events depicted. (A full treatment of this diegetic technique appears in the discussion of character subjectivity later in this chapter.)

Music may function as a diegetic or a non-diegetic element. Often filmmakers use non-diegetic music (that is, music without a source in the story world) to accompany action or romantic scenes. The music communicates directly to viewers on an emotional level, enhancing the actions depicted.

Non-diegetic narration and music accomplish several things: they frame the diegesis (providing information from a vantage point unavailable within the story world), interrupt the diegesis (distancing viewers or creating humor), and enhance the mood of the diegesis (reinforcing moments of danger or romance).

4.2 The book device in *The Royal Tenenbaums*.

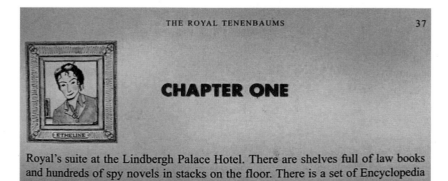

THE ROYAL TENENBAUMS   37

CHAPTER ONE

ETHELINE

Royal's suite at the Lindbergh Palace Hotel. There are shelves full of law books and hundreds of spy novels in stacks on the floor. There is a set of Encyclopedia

Within the Diegesis: Selecting and Organizing Events

Feature films typically have a **running time,** or **screen time** of between 90 and 180 minutes. But the stories they tell rarely take place in that amount of time. "Real time" films such as Hitchcock's *Rope* (1948), in which the events take exactly as long as the film's running time to unfold, are rare exceptions to this rule.

How do filmmakers tell stories that span entire lives in this short period of time? Buck Henry, screenwriter of *The Graduate* (Mike Nichols 1967) and *To Die For* (Gus Van Sant 1995), explains: "the secret of a film script is compression" (Peacock, p. 111). That is, films do not depict every moment of their characters' lives; in fact, they omit a great deal. Days, months, or even years may pass in the blink of an eye, or during a **fade-out**.

Simply put, filmmakers choose to present certain events and leave others out. This seemingly obvious principle of storytelling is so important to narrative form that Russian literary theorists created two terms to describe the fact that a writer (or, in this case, a screenwriter) transforms a complete, chronological story (the *fabula*) into an abbreviated, reorganized version of events that plays out on screen for the audience (the *syuzhet*).

The *syuzhet* refers to the selection and ordering of the actions explicitly presented on screen. The *fabula* is the chronological narrative, in its entirety, that implicitly stands behind the events depicted. The *fabula* includes events that take place during the span of time of the *syuzhet* that are implied but not overtly represented. The *fabula* also incorporates a character's backstory (a character's formative experiences before the beginning of the *syuzhet*). Some film scholars prefer the terms plot (*syuzhet*) and story (*fabula*). But, because viewers typically use "plot" and "story" indiscriminately to mean "narrative," these admittedly unusual Russian terms are better suited to the precise terminology of film analysis.

The significance of the difference between *fabula* and *syuzhet* is not simply that events are left out. Instead, the important question is: what is the effect of these choices? Does it change a viewer's perception of a character or the flow of action that certain events are represented while others are not?

The *syuzhet* entails more than simply eliminating events from the *fabula*—it also involves re-ordering events. The *syuzhet* can begin at any point within the *fabula*, including the end. *Citizen Kane* and *The Prestige* (Christopher Nolan 2006) begin at the end of the *fabula* and move backward in time. Filmmakers may use **flashbacks** and **flashforwards**, scenes from the past or future that interrupt the film's present tense, to rearrange the chronology of the *fabula*.

Repositioning events influences the way the audience understands them. In *Out of the Past* (Jacques Tourneur 1947), Jeff (Robert Mitchum) tells his fiancée, Ann (Rhonda Fleming), about his former life of crime in several long flashbacks. Those flashbacks appear after the film's opening scenes have presented Jeff as an ordinary man living in a small town. By manipulating the order of events— showing his present life first and then showing his past—the *syuzhet* encourages viewers to sympathize with Jeff. They see him as an upstanding citizen before they learn he once worked for a criminal.

The flashbacks emphasize the fact that Jeff's past intrudes into his current life. The re-emergence of his past disrupts Jeff's equilibrium, and he takes action to prevent his former associates from coming back into his life. But no matter how hard he tries, Jeff cannot escape the consequences of his past. In this example, the screenwriter reorders the *fabula* in order to influence viewers' engagement with the main character. It also leads viewers to the central theme of the film, which is signified by the title and underscored by the flashback structure. The notion that Jeff cannot escape his criminal past marks this film as a *film noir*.

Fabula events that are omitted from the *syuzhet* may have a strong bearing on the way the audience interprets the narrative. In Orson Welles's *Touch of Evil* (1958), a late *film noir*, a criminal suspect finally confesses to a crime. Prior to the confession, he had maintained his innocence, even though police captain Hank Quinlan (Orson Welles) had framed him for the crime. The confession is not presented in the *syuzhet* but is mentioned in an aside to Mike Vargas (Charlton Heston), another official who opposes Quinlan and his corrupt methods. Oddly enough, the confession vindicates Quinlan. True, he violates ethical principles and breaks laws by framing suspects. Yet, after the suspect confesses, Quinlan's repeated claim that he only frames the guilty rings true.

What might have been the consequences of including the confession in the *syuzhet*? Would giving that moment dramatic emphasis cause the audience to admire Quinlan's flawed approach? By leaving the confession out of the *syuzhet*, the film balances the discovery of the truth with Quinlan's violation of laws and procedures. Quinlan is not applauded for having the right instincts about the suspect. The tension between following procedures (associated with Vargas) and doing whatever is necessary to apprehend criminals (Quinlan's approach) is a central conflict in the film. The decision to leave the confession out of the *syuzhet* contributes to the ambiguous nature of the conflict.

The *syuzhet* may also manipulate the frequency of events (how many times an act occurs). A single *fabula* event may be depicted more than once, sometimes from the perspective of several characters, as with Susan Alexander's opera debut in *Citizen Kane*. The film presents the debut twice, once from Susan's perspective and once from Jed Leland's.

The distinction between the *fabula* and *syuzhet* makes clear that each event represented in a film has been selected and ordered systematically—there are no accidents. The *syuzhet* may distill, condense, and expand on *fabula* events, giving writers and directors great latitude in portraying characters and events. The *syuzhet* need not chronicle every moment in the *fabula*, and it usually emphasizes the importance of some moments relative to others. When analyzing a narrative film, take note of the *fabula* events that have been left out of the *syuzhet*, changes in chronology, and events that may occur more than once; they often reveal important aspects of structure, character, and theme.

Narrative Structure

The standard pattern that shapes narrative films is the **three-act structure**. Act One introduces characters, goals, and conflict(s) and ends with a first turning point, which causes a shift to Act Two. A turning point, which may be signaled through dialogue, setting, or other visual or sound techniques, represents a moment when an important change has occurred that affects a character or situation. Generally, at this point the main character (the **protagonist**) modifies the methods by which she plans to attain her goals, or changes those goals altogether. In Act Two, the protagonist meets obstacles, possibly arising from the actions of another central figure who opposes her, called the **antagonist**. The conflicts increase in number and complexity, leading to a major turning point, referred to as the climax. Act Three presents the **dénouement**, a series of events that resolves the conflicts that have arisen—not always happily. When the concluding moments of the film tie up all the loose strands, leaving no unanswered questions, the film is said to provide **closure**.

Film scholar Kristin Thompson has recently argued that both classical and contemporary Hollywood films actually exhibit a **four-part structure** (fig. **4.3**). The parts, which are of roughly equal length, are demarcated by turning points linked to character goals. The main difference between the three-act model and Thompson's four-part structure is that she locates a critical turning point at the midway point—the "dead center" of the film.

In the four-part structure, the introduction leads to an initial turning point, which is followed by a complicating action. This leads in turn to the central turning point at the halfway mark. After that shift, a period of development takes place; this is where the protagonist clearly struggles toward goals. That struggle leads to the climax, followed by the resolution and epilogue.

At the beginning of a film, audiences find themselves thrust into a fictional world of characters and actions they cannot fully understand. To help orient viewers at the opening of a film, filmmakers often impart a great deal of information in a relatively short period of screen time. The very opening of the film, dense with narrative details, is called the exposition. The exposition brings viewers "up to speed" on place, time, characters, and circumstances. The exposition is not synonymous with the first act, however. The first act includes the exposition but generally is longer, because it also sets up the film's primary conflict.

The exposition of *Rear Window* introduces the audience to a group of people living in the New York apartment building where protagonist L.B. Jeffries (Jimmy Stewart) lives. The cast of characters includes a dancer, a sculptor, a couple with a dog, a composer, and some sunbathers. After panning across the courtyard, taking note of these neighbors through Jeffries's open window, the camera cuts

4.3 Three- and four-part narrative structures.

Three-Act Structure	Four-Part Structure (Thompson)
Act One: Exposition leads to turning point	1. Exposition leads to turning point
Act Two: Complications lead to climax	2. Complicating action leads to major turning point at halfway mark
	3. Development: struggle toward goal leads to climax
Act Three: Action leading to resolution	4. Epilogue

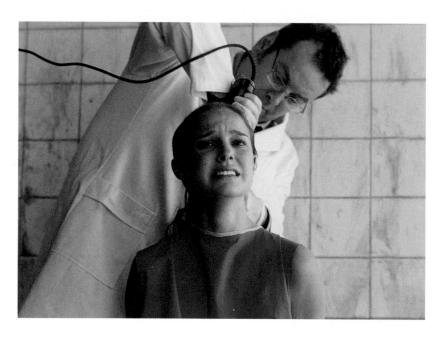

4.4 A visible change in Evey's physical form signals the beginning of her internal change in *V for Vendetta*.

to a large thermometer and then tracks backward into Jeffries's apartment. The camera sweeps through the interior, as if examining its contents with curiosity. In a brief amount of screen time, Hitchcock conveys a good deal of information: Jeffries's name (written on his leg cast), his profession (adventure photographer), his physical state (explained by the photograph of an automobile accident), and his ambivalence about romance (the positive and negative photograph of a glamorous woman).

Spectators may absorb some of this information without even being aware of doing so. This dialogue-free exposition—Jeffries is asleep—lays the groundwork for all the events that occur in the film. It introduces Jeffries's physical predicament, his voyeuristic tendencies, and the stifling summer temperatures which bring people and their secrets out into the courtyard. Introducing details in the exposition and exploiting them later is an example of the conscious placement and repetition of information.

After noticing important details in the exposition, scholars should be careful to recognize when characters and their traits undergo important changes, and how these changes correspond to the three- (or four-) act structure. Typically, critical transitions between acts are marked by lines of dialogue, changes in setting, or major events that suggest a shift in character or circumstance. In *The Wizard of Oz* (Victor Fleming 1939), Dorothy's now legendary line "We're not in Kansas any more" draws attention to the dramatic shift in her circumstances at the end of Act One, after the cyclone has carried her to the land of Oz. In *V for Vendetta* (James McTeigue 2005), after Evey Hammond (Natalie Portman) is arrested, her captor shears her hair completely (fig. **4.4**). This physical transformation is a turning point that signifies the beginning of a process of internal change, as Evey rejects the authoritarian culture in which she lives and joins an underground resistance movement.

Alternatives to Conventional Narrative Structure

Not all narrative films conform to a three-act or four-part structure. Remaining attentive to narrative, visual, and sound details that signal turning points makes it possible to discern alternative narrative structures. Even in unconventional narratives, turning points signal structural shifts.

In *Full Metal Jacket* (Stanley Kubrick 1987), a two-part structure is reinforced by a change in setting and a parallel. An abrupt transition from training camp to combat takes place when, after a fade, the film moves the action from Parris Island, South Carolina, to Da Nang, Vietnam. The geographical shift represents an important change in the protagonist's goal: in the first half of the film, Joker (Matthew Modine) must learn how to survive marine training camp both mentally and physically. In the second, he must learn how to survive his tour of duty in Vietnam. Several parallels signal the two-part structure: each segment begins with a popular song and ends with a protracted scene of violent death.

Another variation on structure is the use of **frame narration**. This technique, used in *The Cabinet of Dr. Caligari* ("*Das Kabinett des Dr. Caligari*"; Robert Wiene 1919), consists of a character who narrates an embedded tale to onscreen or implied listeners. This allows for the creation of two distinct diegeses, and there may be complicated interactions between the two. The narrator may or may not be a character within the embedded tale, and may or may not appraise the events with objectivity.

In *Caligari*, Francis (Friedrich Feher) tells a rapt listener the fantastic tale of the mysterious Dr. Caligari (Werner Krauss), a man who travels with a somnambulist (sleepwalker), whose mind he controls. Under Caligari's spell the sleepwalker, Cesare (Conrad Veidt), terrorizes an entire town, killing Francis's best friend and kidnapping his fiancée. As Francis narrates this bizarre story, the embedded tale unfolds in flashbacks. The film's shocking conclusion returns to the circumstances of Francis's narration and casts doubt on his reliability: he is a paranoid madman living in a mental institution. Caligari is actually the benevolent hospital director.

Another important alternative is the **episodic** narrative. In episodic narratives, events are not tightly connected in a cause-and-effect sequence and characters do not focus on a single goal. Character actions may appear to be unmotivated, with hours or days unfolding in a spontaneous flow, and the movie may seem to digress. These films are sometimes referred to as "a day in the life of ...," which suggests the way they equalize the importance of many events, rather than singling out dramatic turning points and climaxes. An episodic structure emphasizes the repetition of everyday events rather than the dramatic accu-

4.5 A ride to nowhere: the carnival centrifuge in *The 400 Blows*.

mulation of tension toward a moment of crisis. Some episodic narratives conclude without resolving the conflicts; if this is the case, the film is said to be **open-ended.**

The 400 Blows ("Les Quatre Cents Coups "; François Truffaut 1959) is an episodic film that revolves around the daily experiences of a young boy named Antoine Doinel (Jean-Pierre Léaud). The boy's daily routine is elaborated in scenes depicting him at school, at home, and with friends. Although a conflict exists between Antoine and his parents, Antoine's goals are unclear.

Instead of setting up the characters and conflicts, the film's exposition establishes a state of mind. It shows schoolboys passing around a provocative calendar of women, establishing Antoine's age—somewhere within the traumatic stage of life known as puberty—and his boredom and restlessness at school. The film chronicles Antoine's daily life without highlighting important events. He goes to school, he does chores at home, he runs errands, overhears a conversation about the horrors of childbirth, and gets ready for bed. The next day he does not go to school, an obvious break in his routine that acts as a turning point, although the reasons for it are obscure. Antoine wanders aimlessly with his friend René (Patrick Auffray), riding a carnival centrifuge, seeing a film, and playing pinball (fig. **4.5**).

TECHNIQUES IN PRACTICE

Narrative Structure in *Stagecoach*

John Ford's *Stagecoach* (1939) is an example of a film with a conventional narrative structure. Based on "Stage to Lordsburg," an Ernest Haycox short story published in *Collier's* magazine in 1937, the film's three-act structure is marked by events and shifts in geographical setting. The film follows a group of people traveling by stagecoach from the town of Tonto to Lordsburg. The *syuzhet* contains several **lines of action** (or **plotlines**) that converge. Many conventional narrative films combine two narrative paths, with one involving romance and the other concerned with a professional goal, a civic duty, or the attainment of a long-held dream. Here, the two lines of action that assume prominence are the stagecoach journey and Ringo Kid's quest for revenge.

The exposition introduces eight residents of Tonto as they prepare for the journey. Director John Ford makes it clear that each one of this diverse group of stagecoach passengers has an individual motivation for the trip. Dallas (Claire Trevor) is a prostitute who has been expelled from Tonto by the self-righteous Law and Order League. The pregnant Lucy Mallory (Louise Platt) intends to join her husband, a cavalry soldier, while Gatewood (Berton Churchill), a banker, has stolen money from his bank and is using the trip to make his getaway. The gambler Hatfield (John Carradine) has a personal reason for making the trip: his chivalric code demands that he go along to protect Lucy Mallory. Doc Boone (Thomas Mitchell), an amiable drunkard, has been evicted by his landlady.

Although each character has a specific motivation for going, they all share the goal of reaching Lordsburg. The central conflict facing the travelers emerges when a cavalry report comes in that Geronimo has been active in the area. The threat of hostile Indians—a stereotype and staple of the classical Western—represents an external obstacle to the achievement of that goal.

The first act concludes with an important turning point. Ringo Kid flags the stagecoach down after it has left Tonto. He wants to ride to Lordsburg to find the Plummer brothers and avenge the deaths of his brother and father. Although he appears later than the other characters, Ringo's desire for revenge becomes a central line of action. (In fact, Sheriff Curly Wilcox anticipated Ringo's appearance early in the first act, when he tells coach driver Buck that, because Ringo broke out of jail and might be looking for the Plummers, the Sheriff must accompany the stage.) Curly, who sympathizes with Ringo because he knew his father, takes Ringo into "custody." Ringo's goal is clear, and his obstacles are external (Sheriff Curly, the Plummer brothers, the law). Goals and conflicts are well established as the stage heads toward Dry Fork, the first stop on the journey.

The second act involves complications within both lines of action. The geographical journey west is complicated by the Indian threat and clashes among the travelers. At the first stop in Dry Fork, Lucy Mallory, Hatfield, and Gatewood make their distaste for Dallas apparent. Furthermore, the travelers are divided as to whether or not they should forge ahead to Lordsburg, given the threat of attack. They travel to Apache Wells, where, with the help of Doc Boone and Dallas, Lucy Mallory gives birth. The baby's arrival is an added complication, but the event forces Ringo to acknowledge his feelings for Dallas. After leaving Apache Wells, the stagecoach must ford a river because Geronimo and his men have ransacked the next town, Lee's Ferry. Reminding them of their vulnerability, the event tests their physical ability and builds tension around the increased possibility of an attack.

Throughout the second act, Ringo encounters an internal obstacle because he develops romantic feelings for Dallas. Their relationship threatens to interfere with his plan for revenge and introduces suspense: can Ringo still carry out his plans, or will he run away with Dallas? If he goes after the Plummers and survives, what kind of future could Ringo and Dallas have if he is arrested?

The climax occurs when Geronimo attacks the stagecoach between Lee's Ferry and Lordsburg (fig. **4.6**). The passengers ward off the Indians just long enough for the cavalry to rescue them. This resolves the line of action associated with the stagecoach journey: the dénouement traces the arrival of the stage in Lordsburg as various characters meet their fates. Hatfield has been killed in the

4.6 The climax of *Stagecoach*: Geronimo's attack.

4.7 *(left)* Gatewood is arrested near the end of *Stagecoach*: justice is served.

4.8 *(right)* Ringo and Dallas head for the border, providing closure.

attack, Lucy and her baby will be reunited with her husband, and Gatewood is arrested (fig. **4.7**). But director John Ford defers the climax of the second line of action, which involves Ringo's revenge. In Lordsburg, Ringo faces down the Plummers and kills them. The conclusion offers closure on all levels: Ringo exacts his revenge, and then he and Dallas (with the help of Doc Boone and Sheriff Curly) escape to his ranch in Mexico (fig. **4.8**).

Stagecoach may be examined in terms of Thompson's four-part structure. The primary difference lies in the analysis of Act Two. After the exposition, the first turning point (Ringo's arrival) signals the start of the complicating action for both lines of action. What event marks the major turning point halfway through the film? What goals do the characters dedicate themselves to achieving after that turning point, in the section Thompson calls development? How are the lines of action resolved?

While out in the city, Antoine sees his mother kissing a stranger, a shocking moment whose significance is not immediately clear. Nothing in Antoine's life changes overtly because of this act, though a conventionally structured film might emphasize this traumatic moment as an important turning point through camera or sound techniques, which Truffaut avoids. In a conversation shortly afterward, Mme. Doinel speaks to Antoine about keeping secrets from his father, and offers him money should he do well in school. He labors over an essay but is accused of plagiarism and suspended. Antoine moves into René's apartment and the boys' high jinks ultimately land Antoine in jail.

Although cause-and-effect relations are in evidence in this sequence of events—Antoine's misbehavior has consequences—the protagonist's motivations and goals are not clear. He is inarticulate and engages in bad behavior without a specific target; when he does have a target, it seems inappropriate. For example, he steals a typewriter from his father's workplace, even though his father has played a benign and positive role in his life.

Sent to an observation center for juvenile delinquents, Antoine opens up to the psychologist, revealing an underlying emotional conflict that explains, in retrospect, much of his anti-social behavior. His parents married because his mother was pregnant, and Antoine learned from his grandmother that his mother wanted to have an abortion. When Antoine defies the family code of secrecy and writes a letter home that contains the truth about the kiss he witnessed, his mother visits him and informs him that he will be sent to Labor Detention (a boot camp). Antoine runs away, but officials pursue him. At the film's conclusion, Antoine finds himself at the beach, making an earlier line of dialogue significant in retrospect. Antoine had told René he would like to join the navy so he could see the ocean. Another case where dialogue is significant only in retrospect is the conversation Antoine overhears about childbirth.

The 400 Blows defies conventional narrative form in a number of ways. The film focuses on Antoine's relationships rather than his actions. Scenes do not build conflict, but defuse it. Antoine does not respond to the illicit kiss he witnesses, but avoids the matter.

Antoine's carnival ride suggests the cyclical character of Antoine's life: little forward progress is made. When he finally does name the conflict within his family, the information only retrospectively explains the tension between Antoine and his mother. Finally, while the events of the conclusion are clear—his parents assert their authority to send him away and Antoine escapes—their significance is not. Antoine resists the imposition of parental and governmental authority and runs away. At the end of the film, his future is uncertain (see fig. 5.14).

Variations on Narrative Conventions: Beyond Structure

The two-part, frame/embedded tale, and episodic structures of *Full Metal Jacket*, *Dr. Caligari*, and *The 400 Blows* offer alternatives to standard narrative construction. But there are a number of other ways films resist and rewrite the rules of narrative.

The principles of narrative that govern most commercial feature films emerged from the practices and preferences of Hollywood filmmakers in the early part of the twentieth century. Commercial Hollywood studios established a formula for making popular films and refined these rules over several decades. The "rules" for classical Hollywood narrative film include:

- Clarity. Viewers should not be confused about setting, time, events, or character motivations.
- Unity. Connections between cause and effect must be direct and complete.
- Characters. They should invite viewer identification, be active, and seek goals.
- Closure. Third acts and epilogues should tie up loose ends and answer all questions.

- "Unobtrusive craftsmanship" (Thompson 1991, p. 11). Stories are told in a manner that draws viewers into the diegesis and does not call attention to the storytelling process.

A number of narrative filmmaking traditions have modified or rejected the rules of the dominant Hollywood method of storytelling. Art films, independent films, non-Western films, and unconventional Hollywood films represent alternatives to the standard form, to the delight of many and the dismay of others. The ways that they challenge convention are suggested below. Any film may exhibit one or more of these features, and may do so in a subtle or dramatic way.

- Lack of clarity. Multiple, conflicting lines of action, inconsistent characters, extreme degree of character subjectivity. Examples: *Citizen Kane*, *The Conversation*, *Mystery Train*, *Rashômon* (Akira Kurosawa 1950), *Run Lola Run*, *The Thin Red Line* (Terrence Malick 1998), *Fight Club* (Fincher 1998), *Donnie Darko* (Richard Kelly 2001), *I'm Not There* (Todd Haynes 2007)
- Lack of unity. Broken chain of cause and effect. Examples: *Last Year at Marienbad*, *Memento*, *Mulholland Drive* (David Lynch 2001), *Reservoir Dogs* (Quentin Tarantino 1992)
- Open-endedness. Questions are left unanswered or conflicts unresolved. Examples: *The 400 Blows*, *L'avventura* ("*The Adventure*"; Michelangelo Antonioni 1960), *The Italian Job* (Peter Collinson 1969), *Blow-Up*, *The Break-Up* (Peyton Reed 2006), *White Ribbon* (Michael Haneke 2009)
- Unconventional characterizations.
  - Audience is distanced from characters rather than invited to identify. Examples: *Badlands*, *The Conversation*, *Dead Man* (Jim Jarmusch 1996); *Persona* (Ingmar Bergman 1966), *There Will Be Blood*
  - Characters contemplate or talk about action rather than taking action. Examples: *Cleo from 5 to 7*, *My Dinner with André* (Louis Malle 1981), *Stranger than Paradise* (Jim Jarmusch 1983), *A Scanner Darkly* (Richard Linklater 2006)
  - Character goals are unclear. Examples: *The Graduate*, *The 400 Blows*
  - Narrators may be unreliable. Examples: *Dr. Caligari*, *Rashômon*, *The Usual Suspects*
- Intrusions, direct address to the audience and other devices call attention to narrative as a process. Examples: *American Splendor* (Shari Springer Berman and Robert Pulcini 2003), *Just Another Girl on the IRT* (Leslie Harris 1993), *The Nasty Girl* ("*Das schreckliche Mädchen*"; Paul Verhoeven 1990), *Dogville*, *Persona* (Ingmar Bergman 1966), *The Usual Suspects*, *Natural Born Killers* (Oliver Stone 1994), *Stranger Than Fiction* (Marc Foster 2006), *Synechdoche, New York*

Perspective and Meaning

A narrator can play a crucial role in novels and short stories. By establishing a position or angle of vision on the story events—a perspective—the narrator determines whether the reader has access to the same information that characters possess. Stories narrated in the **first person** use the pronoun "I" and limit readers to a single character's knowledge and understanding of events. **Third-person** narration conveys the story from a position outside any single character's experiences. In literature, the use of "he" and "she" signals the narrator's third-person perspective. A third-person narration can be relatively limited—where the reader's access to information is limited to that of a few characters—or **omniscient** ("all-knowing"), where the reader has more information than any character.

Films treat narration differently. Although characters occasionally address the audience using the first person "I" in a voice-over, films rarely use a first-person narration throughout an entire film. *Cloverfield* (Matt Reeves 2008) experimented with a postmodern take on first-person narration. The events in this film are told almost entirely from the perspective of an obsessive videographer who can't seem to put down his camera, even while reptilian beasts from outer space decimate New York (fig. **4.9**). The camera literally points at everything the protagonist sees, but the viewer's inability to see the main character inhibits identification.

Most films employ a system of **restricted narration**, which conveys external events as well as the knowledge, thoughts, and feelings of one or two major characters without the intervention of an explicit narrator. The story seems to unfold rather than to be narrated to the audience. Viewers experience the story from the perspective(s) of a few major characters. They become aligned with those characters because the film imparts the information, knowledge, and experiences that those characters have.

Within an overall framework of restricted narration, directors sometimes provide viewers with information that main characters do not possess. These selective moments of omniscience—where viewers gain more knowledge than major characters—usually occur in scenes that do not include the protagonist(s). Viewers consider the story details presented in such scenes as well as the significance of the uneven distribution of information among the characters in their understanding of the narrative.

Filmmakers may shift away from restricted narration to omniscience within a film for several reasons: to explain story events of which the character is unaware, to align viewers with other important characters, and to create suspense.

The fact that the audience has more information than Alicia Huberman (Ingrid Bergman) and T.R. Devlin (Cary Grant) in *Notorious* (1946) is critical to building the suspense of the film's second half. Over the course of several scenes, viewers learn that Alex Sebastian (Claude Rains) and Mrs. Sebastian (Madame Konstantin)— Alicia's husband and mother-in-law and the targets of her investigation—have dis-

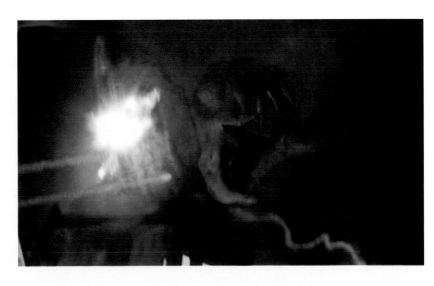

4.9 First-person camerawork in *Cloverfield*.

4.10 A moment of omniscience: Alex and Mrs. Sebastian discuss Alicia in *Notorious*.

covered that Alicia is a government agent and have begun poisoning her (fig. **4.10**). Neither Alicia nor Devlin (her supervisor and love interest) suspects her cover has been blown, so they are unaware of any danger. The audience may despair of Alicia making it out alive and wonder whether Devlin will catch on in time to save her. If Hitchcock had limited the viewer to Alicia's perspective, the audience would be just as unaware of the danger as she is and the suspense would have been eliminated.

Furthermore, by providing the audience with more information than his two protagonists possess, Hitchcock ties the spy and the romance plotlines together. Viewers are likely to become frustrated when the lovers clash over Alicia's illness, which affects their relationship as well as their mission. Devlin misinterprets Alicia's sickness as a hangover, thinking she has reverted to her old drinking ways. Alicia responds rebelliously; she encourages him in his misperception, angry that he refuses to see that she has changed. Because the omniscient perspective makes the audience aware of the actual jeopardy that Alicia faces, it casts a different light on Devlin's treatment of Alicia. Not only is he petty and unfair, but his inability to control his personal feelings seems likely to cost Alicia her life. By manipulating perspective, Hitchcock lays the emotional groundwork that prepares the audience for Devlin's final confrontation with the Sebastians and his reconciliation with Alicia (fig. **4.11**).

Character Subjectivity

"Point of view" is a term sometimes used in a literary context to describe the overall system of narration in a novel, poem, or short story. But in film, the term designates a very specific and limited use of camera to indicate perspective. A **point-of-view shot** occurs when the audience temporarily shares the visual perspective of a character or a group of characters. Simply put, the camera points in the direction that the character looks, simulating her field of vision.

Point-of-view shots do not necessarily result in the audience understanding or sympathizing with a character. Emotional engagement may result from a simple point-of-view shot, but usually a deeper connection is accomplished through a pattern of shots or a combination of narrative, visual, and sound elements.

Point-of-view shots can, but don't always, align viewers with characters. They help to explain the way characters experience the world, validate characters' interpretations of events, and provide information about motivation. In *Broken*

Blossoms (D.W. Griffith 1919), shots from the point of view of Lucy (Lillian Gish) communicate the young girl's fear of men. The camera adopts the girl's point of view when she is about to be kissed by Cheng (Richard Barthelmess), who loves her and has saved her life, but Lucy nevertheless rejects him. The reason becomes clear later, when the camera once again adopts Lucy's point of view as her abusive father, Battling (Donald Crisp), who has repeatedly beaten her, approaches her in a sexually menacing manner. In addition to point-of-view shots, the director uses the actors and setting to create a physical parallel between the two men (figs. **4.12**, **4.13**), thus suggesting that Lucy's fear of Cheng is the result of years of parental abuse.

Diegetic sound techniques such as voice-over narration or a character's **direct address** to the camera can be used to place audiences more firmly within a character's subjectivity. Voice-overs, when characters step outside the flow of events to talk to themselves, to an implied listener, or to the audience, expose audiences to a character's thoughts. Voice-overs are a distinctive characteristic of *film noir*, and are featured in *The Big Sleep* (Howard Hawks 1946) and *Lady from Shanghai* (Orson Welles 1947). Voice-overs allow characters to reflect back on their lives in *Badlands*, *Goodfellas* (Martin Scorsese 1990), and *Fight Club*.

In *Just Another Girl on the IRT*, Chantel (Ariyan Johnson 1992) tells the

4.11 Devlin rescues Alicia in *Notorious*.

4.12 *(left)* Battling approaches Lucy in *Broken Blossoms*.

4.13 *(right)* Cheng approaching Lucy in *Broken Blossoms* visually recalls the earlier scene.

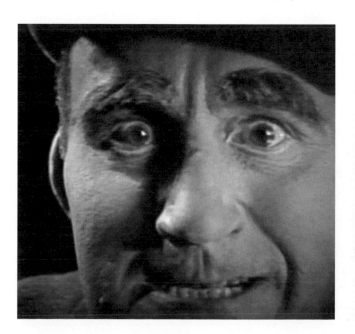

Noticing Shifts in Narration

Some films, such as Hitchcock's *Psycho*, contain significant shifts in narration. These shifts do not necessarily move in a single direction, from restricted to omniscient or vice versa. Throughout a film like *Psycho*, moments of omniscience may reveal an important piece of information, after which the narration will return to a restricted level.

Psycho's early scenes focus on Marion Crane (Janet Leigh), her relationship with Sam (John Gavin), and her theft of $40,000 from her employer. Marion's importance as a character is reinforced when she encounters a Highway Patrol Officer. The scene, composed of several point-of-view shots, emphasizes that the film is primarily concerned with Marion's thoughts and actions. In fact, in the scene where Marion leaves Phoenix, Hitchcock allows viewers to share Marion's subjectivity, as her imagined thoughts of what her co-workers and Sam will say when they learn of her perfidy play out inside her head, and on the soundtrack.

Viewers soon learn that, had Hitchcock continued to employ this level of restricted narration, which constrains our knowledge to what Marion thinks and does, we would no longer be engaged with the film at all, since Marion is murdered quite early on. (This shocked audiences at the time of *Psycho*'s

4.14 *(above left)* Norman spies on Marion in *Psycho*.

4.15 *(above right)* A point-of-view shot reveals what Norman sees.

4.16 *(below left)* Marion's car slowly sinks, seen from Norman's point of view.

4.17 *(below right)* A close-up of Norman watching anxiously.

release; rare is the film in which the protagonist is killed, much less a third of the way into the film).

Although Marion's death is quite shocking, the shift to a more omniscient narration that allows viewers to continue to share in the story line occurs several scenes before the infamous shower scene where Marion dies. In fact, the camera begins to acknowledge Norman Bates's (Anthony Perkins) point of view in scenes where Marion does not appear. When Norman reads Marion's pseudonym in the hotel register, the audience shares his point of view and understands that Norman knows Marion lied to him. When Norman spies on Marion as she undresses, looking through a hole in the wall, the audience also shares his point of view (figs. **4.14** and **4.15**).

After Marion's death, when Norman hides the evidence, point of view shots may evoke audience sympathy for him. The scene alternates between point of view shots that align the audience with Norman as he watches Marion's car stubbornly refusing to sink in the pond (fig. **4.16**) and close ups of Norman, at first worried (fig. **4.17**) and then, when the car finally goes under, relieved.

In this section of the film, the audience is treated to a restricted narration that limits our knowledge of events to what Norman experiences. However, the remainder of the film moves toward greater omniscience and departs from this exclusive focus on Norman to incorporate the thoughts and actions of Sam, Lila (Vera Miles), Marion's sister who has come to investigate her disappearance, and Mr. Arbogast (Martin Balsalm), a private investigator. By this point, the film's shifting narration has encouraged viewers to accept some dramatic shifts in character alignment from Marion, to Norman, to Lila.

To close the film with a twist, Hitchcock makes masterful use of a narration that may seem fully omniscient, but in fact is not. He prevents the audience from learning one critical aspect of Norman's story—the true nature of his relationship with his mother—until the end of the film.

4.18 Chantel addresses the audience directly in *Just Another Girl on the IRT*.

audience in no uncertain terms who she is and what she stands for, speaking directly to the camera as she would to one of her friends (fig. **4.18**). The direct address also serves a thematic purpose, because Chantel wants to tell her story in order to counteract the culture's stereotyped images of young African-American women.

Sound may also align viewers with a character at a less conscious level than point-of-view shots. In the opening shot of *The Conversation*, viewers hear odd, scrambled sounds that do not correspond to the images in front of them, which depict a crowd in San Francisco's Union Square. Several moments into the scene, it becomes clear that the sounds are distortions produced by recording equipment. They are diegetic sounds, but they are heard only by the characters taping the conversation of two characters in the square.

Truly inventive filmmakers like John Waters can come up with unusual ways of connecting audiences with a character's subjectivity, When *Polyester* (1981) was released in theaters, spectators were given an Odorama card. At designated moments during the film, they could scratch off part of the card and experience the fragrant and foul aromas encountered by the film's protagonist, Francine Fishpaw (Divine), who suffers from having a too-keen sense of smell. Beyond its sheer fun and novelty, this device asks the film spectator to use more than merely two senses (sight and hearing).

Figure **4.19** summarizes the elements of narrative form covered in this chapter. Like all narrative art forms, narrative films depend on characters, conflicts, and cause-and-effect logic. Unlike stories, novels and plays, films uniquely depend on sound and visual elements to establish place and time, develop characters, suggest ideas, and create mood. The next chapter examines the integrated program of visual design that determines the overall "look" of a film, a complex element of cinema art referred to as *mise en scène*.

4.19 Narrative Form.

Elements of narrative	Characters, actions, time, place, causality
Selection and ordering of narrative elements	*Syuzhet*: events selected, arranged, and presented on screen; *fabula*: all events that explicitly and implicitly underlie the *syuzhet*, in chronological order
Presentation of the fictional world	Diegetic: part of the implied story world; non-diegetic: exists outside story world
Structure	Three-act, four-part, frame/embedded, episodic
Narration	Omniscient, restricted, subjective

Summary

- The diegesis consists of the world of the story. Non-diegetic elements allow the filmmaker to communicate with the audience directly, rather than through characters or other aspects of the fictional world.
- The distinction between the *syuzhet* and the *fabula* is critical for understanding the significance of the order and selection of events. The *syuzhet* contains all represented events whereas the *fabula* consists of a complete and chronological accounting of all represented and implied events.
- Many narrative films conform to a three-act or four-part structure. Alternatives to this model include two-part structures, frame/embedded tale, and episodic narratives.
- Some films adopt, and others discard, conventions of narrative form, such as unity, clarity, sympathetic, action-oriented characters, closure, and unobtrusive craftsmanship.

- Most narrative films use restricted narration, but may shift to omniscient narration at key moments. When viewers know more than the characters do about an event, that knowledge affects their response to the character and may generate suspense.
- Point-of-view shots may or may not align viewers with characters. They may encourage viewers to understand and sympathize with characters, as do character voice-overs and direct address (both diegetic elements).

Works Consulted

Barbarow, George. "*Rashômon* and the Fifth Witness," in *"Rashômon": Akira Kurosawa, Director*. New Brunswick and London: Rutgers University Press, 1987, pp. 145–8.

Buscombe, Edward. *Stagecoach*. London: British Film Institute, 1992.

Gras, Vernon and Marguerite, eds. *Interviews: Peter Greenaway*. Jackson, MI: University of Mississippi Press, 2000.

Peacock, Richard. *The Art of Moviemaking: Script to Screen*. Upper Saddle River, NJ: Prentice-Hall, 2001.

Richie, Donald, ed. *"Rashômon": Akira Kurosawa, Director*. New Brunswick and London: Rutgers University Press, 1987.

Richie, Donald, ed. *Focus on "Rashômon"*. Englewood Cliffs: Prentice-Hall, 1972.

Thompson, Kristin. *Storytelling in the New Hollywood*. Cambridge: Harvard University Press, 1999.

Thompson, Kristin. *Storytelling in Film and Television*. Cambridge: Harvard University Press, 2003.

Zunser, Jesse. Review of *Rashômon*, in *Focus on "Rashômon."* Englewood Cliffs: Prentice-Hall, 1972, pp. 37–8.

FILM ANALYSIS

Analyzing Narrative Structure

The essay below analyzes narrative form in *Slumdog Millionaire* (Danny Boyle and Loveleen Tandan 2008). According to the author, even though *Slumdog* was adapted from the novel *Q&A* by Indian writer Vikas Swaroop, was set in Mumbai, and is organized by a flashback structure, its narrative system conforms to that of a traditional Hollywood film.

Before beginning any type of writing project, it's a good idea to make an outline. An outline is a blueprint: it contains your main idea and lays out a logical progression for the ideas that support that main point. Use this process to begin to sketch out specific details from the film to use as examples to illustrate and develop your claims. Remain flexible to new ideas at this stage of the process: you may need to reconsider, eliminate, or reorder your ideas and examples to achieve clarity and coherence.

The outline below identifies the thesis statement and establishes this writer's organizational logic. Be aware that there is no set formula for organizing an essay: in fact, writers often outline more than one approach and then eliminate those that fail to come together. The structure of an essay depends upon what the writer believes to be the most important assertions; how she connects those ideas to details from the film (and to other concepts); and how she organizes sentences and paragraphs so that each claim is fully developed. An essay should build a meaningful argument, not simply list loosely connected observations about the film.

Thesis: *Slumdog Millionaire* appears to depart from the conventions of narrative cinema because of its pronounced use of flashbacks and its Indian characters and setting. But in fact, the film obeys fairly strictly the conventions of the classical Hollywood model in terms of its structure, characters, and plot line.

Outline

I. Flashback Structure

A. *Slumdog* is composed of a frame story (the game show) and an embedded tale (Jamal's life story), which unfolds through numerous flashbacks. The film appears to possess a non-traditional structure, similar to that of *Citizen Kane* and *Rashômon*—films that use flashbacks to challenge classical narrative conventions.

B. The *syuzhet* reorders the chronological events of the *fabula* by alternating past and present. Yet the flashbacks follow a clear chronology. Also, each flashback is motivated by and, in turn, explains events in the frame story.

C. Flashbacks can disrupt the viewer's sense of sequence and cause and effect (use quote from film scholar to support this point). The film does not exploit the potential disruptiveness of flashbacks.

D. The primary purpose of the flashbacks is to present Jamal's life story, creating tight connections between cause and effect, which is associated with classical Hollywood storytelling. The film differs from *Citizen Kane* and *Rashômon* because they use flashbacks to introduce ambiguity and uncertainty.

II. Characters and Setting

A. Identify the three main characters: Jamal, Salim, and Latika.

B. Define characters in classical films: goal seeking and oriented toward taking action.

C. Jamal, as the main character, pursues specific goals and has an action orientation.

  1. He seeks to escape his slumdog youth—which Boyle visually represents as the dead-end quality of the slums themselves, and the way some people are able to move through and out of the slums in cars or on trains.

  2. He seeks to reunite with Latika, which is the reason he goes on the game show in the first place; she is an avid fan.

III. Strong Closure and Double Plot Lines

A. Like classical films, *Slumdog* has strong closure and two plot lines.

B. The use of the deadline for the climax is a feature of classical cinema.

C. One classical plotline involves heterosexual romance: Jamal reunites with Latika.

D. The other classical plotline is related to work, war, a quest or mission: Jamal wins the prize on the game show.

E. The film has strong closure, much more so than the two films used as comparison/contrast.

As you read the essay below, notice how it follows the outline, transforming numbered sections into carefully structured supporting arguments.

Slumdog Millionaire (2008), a modestly budgeted $15 million British production, nearly became a straight to DVD release after Warner Brothers' Studios, which owned the distribution rights, expressed serious doubts about its commercial potential. Released theatrically by Fox Searchlight and Warner Brothers, the film achieved box office success, taking in more than $150 million, and earned high critical praise, garnering four Golden Globes, seven BAFTA awards, and eight Academy Awards. With a screenplay adapted from the novel *Q&A* by Vikus Swarup about a poor, uneducated young man from the slums of Mumbai who becomes a contestant on a television game show, the film's flashback-riddled narrative seems to draw heavily upon the popular song and dance-driven Hindi cinema (also referred to as Bollywood), although it is translated through the kinetically charged visual style of director Danny Boyle (*Trainspotting* [1996], *28 Days Later* [2002], *Sunshine* [2007]). In fact, Boyle used several Bollywood films as models (Kumar). A close analysis of *Slumdog Millionaire*'s narrative elements—in particular, its numerous flashbacks, and its Indian characters, plot, and cultural milieu—reveals a highly conventional treatment of chronology, character, and plot that conforms to classical Hollywood narrative patterns. Film scholar David Bordwell has argued "[t]he classical tradition has become a default framework for international cinematic expression, a point of departure for nearly every filmmaker" (Bordwell 2006, p. 12) and *Slumdog Millionaire* is no exception.

What appears to be *Slumdog Millionaire*'s most striking departure from standard cinematic storytelling practices is its extensive use of flashbacks. Hollywood narratives typically present stories through a three-act structure enacted in the present tense, where each act offers a clear beginning, middle, and end. In contrast, *Slumdog* seems to dwell on the past; the *syuzhet* reorders the chronological story (the *fabula*) by continually moving back and forth between the present and the past. Like the novel *Q&A*, from which it was adapted, *Slumdog* is organized by a frame story depicting Jamal Malik's (Dev Patel) participation in *Who Wants to Be a Millionaire?* and his temporary detention by the police on suspicion of cheating. This frame story is continually interrupted by flashback sequences relating his harrowing childhood experiences. This frame story and embedded tale structure resembles well known films such as *Citizen Kane* and *Rashômon*, which challenge the classical storytelling structures through multiple flashbacks that introduce ambiguity and provide contradictory information.

Boyle employs flashbacks that reveal the hardships Jamal and his brother Salim (Sarfaraz Khan) faced as orphans after their mother is killed during anti-Muslim riots. Unlike the flashbacks in *Citizen Kane* and *Rashômon*, these do not introduce contradictions or ambiguity. Instead, they are clearly motivated and explained by the frame story of the game show. After

4.20 The game show in *Slumdog Millionaire*'s frame story.

each question is posed to Jamal—by both the game show host Prem Kapur (Anil Kapoor) and the police who interrogate him because they suspect him of cheating—he remembers experiences that provide the information he needs to answer the question (fig. **4.20**)

The tight cause-and-effect logic underlying the use of flashbacks undercuts the potential narrative disruptiveness of the flashbacks. Maureen Turim writes that flashbacks are "manipulations of narrative temporality" (p. 16) that can be used to call attention to the fabricated nature of storytelling and to point to the potentially unreliable aspects of memory, as is the case with flashbacks in *Citizen Kane* and *Rashômon*. On the other hand, Turim notes, directorial choices can "naturalize these temporal manipulations, such as locating [flashbacks] in the psyche or the storytelling capacity of a character within the fiction" (Turim, p. 16). This is precisely the case in *Slumdog Millionaire*: Jamal's flashbacks are clearly located within his psyche. The use of a **wipe** as a visual transition into his memories confirms the fact that the flashback sequences are located in Jamal's mind: Jamal's face and the past events briefly share the same frame (fig. **4.21**) The audience has no reason to doubt the veracity of his memories or experience the flashbacks as a disruption to the flow of the frame story. His memories have the authority of fact. Moreover, they fully explain the conflict in the frame story: the dispute over his ability to answer the questions without resorting to cheating.

This close linkage between the past and the present—the fact that Jamal's early years eventually explain everything about his presence on the television show and his ability to answer the questions—conforms to a classical Hollywood storytelling model where "[c]ausality is the prime unifying principle." (Bordwell 1986, p. 19) Certainly, the flashbacks in *Slumdog* serve several functions: they provide suspenseful moments when the audience waits to learn if Jamal can answer the next question; they simulate a quiz show experience for viewers who may be trying to figure out how a particular flashback will give rise to a correct answer; and they resemble the way Hindi cinema uses song and dance sequences as "telescoped narratives" that deepen the emotional texture of the story (Gopal and Moorti, p. 5). However, the flashbacks ultimately present a chronological story of Jamal's life without introducing uncertainty or disturbing temporal relations or cause-effect linkages.

Jamal, his older brother Salim, and his love interest Latika (Freida Pinto) are the central characters in this story (although some critics rightly point to the vital role played by the city of Mumbai itself). Like characters in classical films, they have defined psychological traits, they are goal oriented and they must overcome obstacles to achieve their goals. The story

traces the way that these three individuals, and especially Jamal, attempt to achieve goals: they seek
to rise above poverty, earn respect
in the rapidly changing social and
economic setting of Mumbai, and
find love and acceptance. Visually,
Boyle depicts the slums as a space
that others move through on their
way to better places: the gangster
Javed drives through in his white
Mercedes as the boys scamper
through the streets to elude the police. The train passes close by the
slum, but never stops to transport
the slum dwellers to another location (fig. **4.22**). This motif helps
to crystallize one of Jamal's goals:
to escape the slums. In fact, train
travel itself forms a larger motif in
the film, as Jamal and Salim jump
trains to escape their predicament
on several occasions.

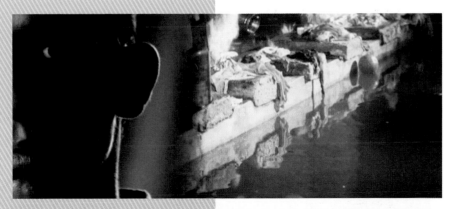

4.21 (above) A wipe in *Slumdog Millionaire*.

4.22 (below) The slums, where the train
never stops—*Slumdog Millionaire*.

As Jamal's flashbacks unfold,
viewers learn that Jamal earned his surprising toughness (which allows him
to withstand torture at the hands of the police) the hard way: as a poor,
Muslim orphan, he is an outsider in his own culture and hence he knows
whose picture graces a $100 bill (given to him by wealthy tourists), but does
not know the phrase on the Indian national seal. He is exploited along with
numerous other children, and his brother betrays him on more than one occasion. In the most dramatic example, in one flashback scene, Salim coerces
Latika into a sexual relationship and then abandons Jamal. These flashbacks
present the reasons why Jamal has become who he is: they explain why
his goals are to prove himself to be more than merely a "chaiwala" and to
reunite with Latika (who is an avid fan of *Who Wants to be A Millionaire?*).

The climax of *Slumdog Millionaire* occurs when Jamal re-establishes contact with Latika (his primary goal) and then takes a guess at the last question, upon which rides 20 million rupees. The **parallel editing** in the scenes
leading up to this suspenseful moment decisively shift the narrative focus
to the story's present tense and away from the past: time is running out for
Jamal on the television show; time is also running out for Salim, who helps
Latika to engineer her escape from Javed and pays the ultimate price. In the
orchestration of the climax as a time limited event, the film again obeys the
rules of conventional Hollywood storytelling: "That the climax of a classical
film is often a deadline shows the structural power of defining dramatic du-

ration as the time it takes to achieve or to fail to achieve a goal." (Bordwell 1986, p. 19)

Furthermore, the climactic moment in this film lays bare the double plotlines that have structured the film throughout: the unrequited love between Jamal and Latika, and Jamal's struggle to break free of the oppressive circumstances of his upbringing. This two-pronged approach is also reminiscent of classical films, which generally have two related plotlines, one involving heterosexual romance and the other related to work, war, a quest or mission (Bordwell 1986, p. 19).

Slumdog Millionaire's narrative provides strong closure, as Jamal moves from despised slumdog to national hero and wins the love of his life, and Salim willingly pays for his life of bad choices and criminal behavior. Returning to the earlier comparison with two films that make extensive use of flashbacks, *Citizen Kane* and *Rashōmon*, reveals that Boyle has made a conscious choice not to use flashbacks to create multiple perspectives or to leave any ambiguity at the film's conclusion.

Despite *Slumdog Millionaire*'s numerous flashbacks and its Indian characters, setting, and story depicting a young man's struggles with dire poverty, Hindu nationalism, and Mumbai globalization, the film's overall narrative structure adheres to the classical storytelling practices of Hollywood cinema during the Studio Era and afterward.

Works Cited (in the essay)

Bordwell, David. *The Way Hollywood Tells It: Story and Style in Modern Movies*. Berkeley: University of California Press, 2006.

_____. "Classical Hollywood Cinema: Narrational principles and procedures." In *Narrative, Apparatus, Ideology*, ed. Philip Rosen, pp. 17–34. New York: Columbia University Press, 1986.

Desai, Radhika. "Imagi Nation: The reconfiguration of national Identity in Bombay Cinema in the 1990s." In *Once upon a time in Bollywood: the global swing in Hindi cinema*, ed. Gurbir Jolly, Zenia Wadhwani and Deborah Barretto, pp. 43–60. Toronto: TSAR, 2007.

Dwyer, Rachel and Divia Patel. *Cinema India: the visual culture of Hindi film*. New Brunswick: Rutgers University Press, 2002.

Flaherty, Mike. "Fox, WB to share *Slumdog* distribution." *Variety*. August 20, 2008. www.variety.com

Gopal, Sagita and Sujata Moorti. "Introduction: Travels of Hindi Song and Dance." In *Global Bollywood: Travels of Hindi Song and Dance*, eds. Gopal and Moorti, pp. 1–60. Minneapolis: University of Minnesota Press, 2008.

Kumar, Avitata. "Slumdog's Bollywood Ancestors." *Vanity Fair*. December 23, 2008. www.vanityfair.com

Mishra, Vijay. *Bollywood Cinema: Temples of Desire*. New York: Routledge, 2002.

Nandy, Ashis. "Indian Popular Cinema as a Slum's Eye View of Politics." In *The Bollywood Reader*, eds. Rajinder Dudrah and Jigna Desai, pp. 73–84. New York: Open University Press, 2008.

O' Hehir, Andrew. "Thrill ride through a 'maximum city'." *Salon.com*. Nov 12, 2008. www.salon.com

Raghavendra, M.K. *Seduced by the Familiar: Narration and Meaning in Indian Popular Cinema*. Delhi and Oxford: Oxford University Press, 2008.

Turim, Maureen. *Flashbacks in Film: Memory and History*. New York and London: Routledge, 1989.

Mise en Scène

CHAPTER FIVE

What matters is the way space is cut up, the precision
of what happens within the magical space of the frame,
where I refuse to allow the smallest clumsiness.

Federico Fellini

Francis Ford Coppola's *The Godfather* (1972) opens with a wedding. Connie
(Talia Shire), the daughter of Don Vito Corleone (Marlon Brando), marries Carlo
Rizzi (Gianni Russo) at the Corleone estate outside New York City. About halfway through the film, Vito's son Michael (Al Pacino), who is hiding from enemies in Sicily, marries a young woman named Apollonia in the small town of

5.1 Connie's lavish wedding
in *The Godfather*.

5.2 Michael's humble village wedding in *The Godfather*.

Corleone. Although both scenes depict Corleone family weddings, they look very different. The first scene is a lavish reception held on the lawn of the imposing Corleone mansion. Connie wears an extravagant wedding gown (fig. **5.1**) while hundreds of guests drink copiously and feast on lasagne.

By contrast, in the scene of Michael and Apollonia's wedding, the actual ceremony is shown at the small village church (fig. **5.2**). The wedding party parades through the dusty streets of the rustic countryside. The bride and groom circulate among their guests, serving them candy, before dancing together in the town square. This comparison raises a question related to the use of visual details: what significance can be derived from the fact that these two weddings look so different?

Narrative and visual elements work together to establish differences between the two Corleone weddings. Connie's wedding emphasizes the secular (non-religious) aspects of the event. First, the scene does not depict the marriage ceremony itself. Also, Vito takes care of business matters during the reception, as well-wishers ask him for favors. Costumes and props—including the fancy automobiles parked nearby—tell viewers that the guests are affluent. By contrast, the scene of Michael's wedding foregrounds the marriage by showing the priest blessing the couple in the doorway of the church. A small number of people attend their reception. Everyone is dressed simply, including the groom, who wears a black suit instead of a tuxedo. As they serve their guests, the wedding couple, not the ostentatious display of wealth, takes center stage. These details of setting, costume, and props imply that, in America, wealth and business take precedence over family and community. This conflict between business and family assumes great significance over the course of the *Godfather* trilogy, becoming one of its major themes.

This chapter explores the way filmmakers carefully orchestrate visual details such as these to develop characters, support themes, and create mood. Settings and costumes, like those in *The Godfather*, are just two elements within an integrated design program called *mise en scène*, which has four major components: setting, the human figure, lighting, and composition. It then looks at two specific styles of *mise en scène*: that associated with German Expressionist cinema of the 1920s and the French style of the 1930s known as Poetic Realism. These distinctive approaches suggest different ways that *mise en scène* creates fictional worlds that viewers find compelling.

The term *mise en scène* (pronounced "meez ahn sen") originated in the theater and literally means staging a scene through the artful arrangement of actors, scenery, lighting, and props—everything that the audience sees. In a film,

DESIGNING THE LOOK OF THE FILM

The *mise en scène* is determined during pre-production and production and involves the work of many people. The production designer's careful planning contributes greatly to the coherence of the *mise en scène*. The director and production designer make decisions about how the story world will look well before principal photography begins. The art director supervises the construction of scale models and computer graphics to preview possibilities. Location scouts travel to find locations. A construction coordinator directs carpenters who build sets according to the specifications in blueprints drawn up by set designers; set decorators find the appropriate materials to make the space a plausible environment and translate the production designer's themes into visual details. Set dressers work during shooting, arranging the items on the set.

Casting directors audition actors and extras. Costume designers present sketches to the director for approval, and wardrobe supervisors acquire and manage costumes. Make-up artists and hairdressers work with actors to achieve the desired physical appearance for the characters. The property master is responsible for finding and maintaining props. The director runs rehearsals with actors before shooting begins, working on **blocking** (the plan for actors' movements), choreography (in action sequences or song and dance numbers), and the subtleties of each actor's performance.

the *mise en scène* is the province of the production designer, who works in collaboration with the film director. In a narrative film, *mise en scène* creates the look of the story world. In documentary films, directors do not usually control their environment, but they can choose which elements to focus on. Avant-garde filmmakers may dispense with a story altogether, yet they still arrange the elements in the frame according to aesthetic principles described in this chapter.

Each element of the *mise en scène*—the setting, the human figure, lighting, and composition—influences the viewer's experience of the story, characters, space, and time. Filmmakers use details in a systematic manner not only to create a world on screen, but also to indicate character development, present motifs, amplify themes, and establish mood.

Setting

Setting refers to the places where the film's action unfolds. These places may be general or specific locations, real or imaginary places. In *Notorious*, events occur in two cities: Miami, Florida, and Rio de Janeiro, Brazil. In each city there are a number of specific locations as well: the Miami County Courthouse, Alicia Huberman's house, and, in Rio, Alicia's apartment, the race track, the government offices, and Alex Sebastian's house. The change in setting from Miami to Rio marks a turning point in the narrative when Alicia commits to changing her life by becoming a government agent.

Alicia's apartment and Alex's house are sets built on a studio soundstage, a large, warehouse-like structure that houses sets and provides optimum control over lighting and sound when filming. Constructing a set provides filmmakers with the maximum degree of control over their shooting environment. On an indoor set, directors and cinematographers do not have to contend with bad weather, noise, and unreliable lighting conditions. These are precisely the conditions that pose challenges to documentary filmmakers.

A constructed set can be built to the filmmaker's precise specifications. For Marcel Carné's *Children of Paradise* ("*Les Enfants du Paradis* "; 1945), an outdoor set was constructed on a studio back lot to simulate a nineteenth-century Paris street. In order to use the small space to convey the feel of a bustling city block, the builders constructed a line of two-story buildings that diminished in size from the foreground to the background (fig. **5.3**). To maintain proportions, Carné had small-scale carriages built and employed dwarves as extras in the distant areas of the shot. This production technique is called **forced perspective**: filmmakers construct and arrange buildings and objects on the set so that they diminish in size dramatically from foreground to background. Because the human eye uses the relative size of objects as a gauge of depth, the large disparity in size between foreground and background objects creates the illusion of greater depth.

Most commercial films today contain scenes shot on location; for example, in Ridley Scott's *Blade Runner* (1982) the Bradbury building grounds the film's futuristic Los Angeles setting in a familiar, present-day structure. Locations may contain recognizable physical landmarks, such as the Grand Canyon in *Thelma & Louise* (Ridley Scott 1991). Shooting on location does not necessarily mean filming where the story is set. Francis Ford Coppola filmed his Vietnam War epic *Apocalypse Now* in the Philippine rainforest.

5.3 Constructed set of a city street, from *Children of Paradise*.

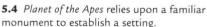
5.4 *Planet of the Apes* relies upon a familiar monument to establish a setting.

Whether shooting on a soundstage or on location, filmmakers may carefully craft a recognizable story world. They can make reference to familiar, human-made objects to convey the significance of place. One example is director Franklin Schaffner's use of the Statue of Liberty in *Planet of the Apes* (1968; fig. **5.4**) to reveal for the protagonist George Taylor (Charlton Heston) the fact that human civilization has been eclipsed by the society of the apes. The destruction of this statue, and all it symbolizes, drives home the grim reality of this futuristic dystopia, where human liberty has been buried.

Filmmakers also use **computer-generated imagery** (CGI) to create settings. In *Alice* (Tim Burton 2010), a contemporary sequel to the Lewis Carroll stories, "Underland" was generated with the help of computer graphics. Deciding whether to construct sets, to use locations, and/or to take advantage of newer computer technologies is part of the creative challenge of filmmaking. These decisions also relate to the business of filmmaking, as location shooting is often complex, time-consuming, unpredictable, and more expensive than shooting on a set.

Describing Setting: Visual and Spatial Attributes

The visual characteristics of a setting evoke responses from the audience. Do events take place inside buildings or outdoors? Are settings living spaces, work places, or public spaces? Are they spacious or cramped, sunny and bright, or dim and shadowy? Are they full of bits and pieces or empty?

At first glance, an open, bright, exterior setting might suggest limitless possibilities, as in rock climbing scenes in *North Face* ("*Nordwand*" Philipp Stölzl 2010), whereas a dark, cramped interior, like that in the opening of *Memento*, may connote entrapment. But open space can also serve as the site of banality or dread, or both, as it does in the rural Kansas setting of *Capote*, where writer Truman Capote investigates a shocking murder (fig. **5.5**). The *contextual* use of setting is important to interpreting *mise en scène*. The context for interpretation includes the actions taking place there as well as the way the setting relates to other settings used throughout the film.

The director or location scout chooses particular spaces for their visual and spatial attributes. Those qualities inevitably transmit cultural meanings as well as emotional implications. The stately but hollow beach house in *Interiors* (Woody Allen 1978) reflects material wealth and emotional distance. The nondescript apartments in *Office Space* (Mike Judge 1999) convey the central characters' sterile, homogeneous home environments, which mirror their gray work cubicles. Settings need not be ornately decorated or breathtakingly beautiful to offer insight into the lives of characters.

5.5 In *Capote*, the barren, ominous Kansas landscape contrasts sharply with lively scenes set in New York.

Setting

95

5.6 Dancing in the streets in *Billy Elliot*.

5.7 The unspecified city in *Sunrise*.

The Functions of Setting

The primary functions of setting are to establish time and place, to introduce ideas and themes, and to create mood. In a period film, the setting recreates a place and time; visual details are especially important when the time period is essential to the film's story and themes. Historical research contributed to the meticulous depiction of New York City in the 1870s in Martin Scorsese's *The Age of Innocence* (1993), a film about the struggle between love and obligation in high society. The settings, which speak of the ritualized behavior of this group of people, were integral to the representation of the protagonist's decision to remain with his wife and suppress his passionate love for another woman—a choice that might be difficult for contemporary audiences to understand. Director Scorsese said, "the setting's important only to show why this love is impossible" (Cocks and Scorsese, p. vii). Even the most "accurate" representations are subject to creative license. In the case of *The Age of Innocence*, the city of Troy, New York, was used as an exterior location for action set in Manhattan.

Certain genres are linked to settings and time periods. Westerns are set in the American West in the late nineteenth century, whereas gangster films typically take place in a modern, urban environment. Other genres, such as romantic comedies, are less dependent on geography or historical period.

As with any element of filmmaking, directors sometimes choose to use settings that work against expectations. Although musicals can take place anywhere, the singing and dancing that define the genre often take place in stylized, theatrical settings. But musicals such as *Dancer in the Dark* (Lars von Trier 2000) and *Billy Elliot* (Stephen Daldry 2000) contain numbers choreographed amid urban neighborhoods (fig. **5.6**), factories, and prisons. These films inventively test the genre's boundaries by emphasizing the incongruity of bleak settings as the backdrop for musical extravaganzas.

Settings need not refer to existing locations or actual historical periods: instead they may evoke a generic sense of place or stand for implicit ideas. The large, bustling, but unspecified city in F.W. Murnau's *Sunrise* (1927) is important mainly because it provides a contrast to the bucolic countryside where the main characters live (fig. **5.7**). The city is never named. In this film, it is less important to know the specific location of the city than to recognize it as a source of excitement that ultimately allows a husband and wife to rediscover their love for one another.

Settings help to determine the mood of a scene or an entire film. In *Crash*, a film about the damaging effects of racism in the United States, dusty roads and car-clogged freeways set the stage for numerous hostile interactions among residents of Los Angeles (see fig. 6.20). Settings also offer opportunities for creating motifs.

The Human Figure

As the above examples suggest, actors' performances contribute a great deal to a film's meaning. Most narrative feature films tell stories about human beings and the conflicts they face. Casting (the selection of actors), acting style, and the placement and movement of figures influence the viewer's response to fictional characters, their strengths and weaknesses, and their hopes and fears.

Casting

Choosing actors is one of the most important decisions a director can make. Usually a casting director organizes auditions, but "A-list" actors are generally cast without the indignity of an audition. Their agents negotiate with directors

TECHNIQUES IN PRACTICE

Same Film, Different Settings

The significance of any setting derives not only from its visual and spatial qualities, but also from the way it functions in relation to other settings in the film. In *Full Metal Jacket*, the dramatic contrast between the film's two primary settings generates ideas and develops themes. In the first section, the rigid order of the Parris Island, South Carolina, marine training camp is emphasized by geometrical compositions, including the precise right angles formed by the men when they run in formation by the vertical columns in the barracks. The columns look rigid, upright, and homogeneous—mirroring the appearance of the two lines of men standing in front of them, all wearing identical white underwear (fig. **5.8**). This physical parallel compares the men with architecture and suggests at least two ideas. The first is that these men form the structural support of the entire military organization. A second idea hints at the purpose of the rigorous and dehumanizing training: like the blank, faceless columns, the men must sacrifice their individuality to become marines.

This ordered setting contrasts sharply with the settings in Vietnam. The latter suggest the breakdown of military discipline and social order. As the marines move into Hue City, the men are neither geometrical nor precise: they amble in ragged clusters, moving haphazardly, not in straight lines (fig. **5.9**). The frame is full of diverse objects arranged in a random fashion: soldiers, tanks, trash, and

5.8 Columns visually reinforce the lines of men in *Full Metal Jacket*.

5.9 *(left)* In combat, the marines fall into disarray.

5.10 *(right)* Lines suggest a temporary restoration of order.

hollowed-out burning buildings. The buildings stand in direct contrast to the pristine interior and supporting columns of the Parris Island barracks. Under fire, in the field, the hierarchical chain of command breaks down, and the marines take actions and make decisions in the heat of the moment. The changing *mise en scène* reflects and enhances the shifts between order and chaos.

After the battle, the film's final scene shows the soldiers marching toward the river, singing the *Mickey Mouse* theme song. Private Joker's voice-over tells of his relief at being alive. These closing moments show the soldiers marching toward the same destination. They are not in perfect geometric formation, but they are moving in an orderly way in the same direction (fig. **5.10**). Because they are shown in silhouette, they all look the same. The men are anonymous, as they were in their underwear in the barracks. The sense of a temporary restoration of order comes not only from the voice-over and cessation of combat, but also from a *mise en scène* that subtly reintroduces some visual attributes from the first half of the film.

TECHNIQUES IN PRACTICE

Same Setting, Different Film

Another way to interpret settings is to consider the way that one setting is used to achieve different effects in different movies. Ideas and feelings that viewers associate with a setting in the abstract may not apply to any specific film's use of that setting. For example, the beach may spur associations of light-heartedness, leisure, and freedom. But the significance of that environment in a film depends on the way it functions in the narrative and relates to other visual and sound elements in the film. Beach settings have played important yet very different roles in the follow-ing films, to name only a few: *From Here to Eternity* (Fred Zinnemann 1953), *10* (Blake Edwards 1979), *Chariots of Fire* (Hugh Hudson 1981), *Local Hero* (Bill Forsyth 1983), *Glory* (Edward Zwick 1989), *Cast Away* (Robert Zemeckis 2000), *Whale Rider* (Niki Caro 2002), and *Troy* (Wolfgang Peterson 2004). The following examples illustrate the importance of using context when interpreting the role of setting.

In *The Piano* (Jane Campion 1993) Scottish settler Stewart (Sam Neill) leaves the piano that his mail-bride Ada (Holly Hunter) has brought with her from Scotland behind on the New Zealand beach after she arrives there with her belong-ings. When she returns to that spot with Mr. Baines (Harvey Keitel) and her daughter Flora (Anna Pacquin), her joy at being reunited with her beloved instrument is enhanced by the setting (fig. **5.11**). The beach's bright open space offers a visual contrast to the dense, green forest and the dim, wood-walled interiors of the settlers' homes (fig. **5.12**). Ada smiles and moves fluidly as she plays the piano and Flora dances wildly to the music. Ada and Flora's movements and smil-ing facial expressions underscore feelings of openness and provide insight into their emotions. In this film, the beach represents, among other things, the intense pleasure of crea-tive self-expression.

Bhaji on the Beach (Gurinder Chadha 1994) also features a beach setting. Its inclusion in the film's title signals its central importance. The story fol-lows a diverse group of South Asian women as they take a day trip to Bris-tol, England. In comparison to the cramped bus ride in the opening of the film, the beach offers freedom of movement and privacy (fig. **5.13**). These are thematically important because the mature women in the group, who adhere to Indian traditions, often disapprove of the younger women, who have grown up in Britain and have adopted Western behavior.

But the beach is not a space of vast, wild, unspoiled beauty as it is in *The Piano*; alongside expanses of sand, fast food restaurants and a strip club appear. The women exhibit various levels of comfort with the informality of the beach and its tourist attractions, highlighting the theme of the generational and cultural differences that divide the women.

The final scene of *The 400 Blows* finds the troubled young protagonist, Antoine Doinel, running from a juvenile deten-tion center to the beach. The setting seems incongruous after the urban streets that have served as the character's usual environment. The beach does not promise the unfet-tered freedom conventionally associated with that setting. Instead, the slowness of Antoine's movements and a final

5.11 (*above*) Ada expresses herself by playing the piano on the beach in *The Piano*.

5.12 (*below*) The brown-toned interior of Baines's house in *The Piano*.

5.13 The beach provides a setting for a clash of generations in *Bhaji on the Beach*.

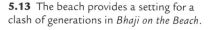

5.14 Antoine contemplates his future in *The 400 Blows*.

5.15 Diouana mopping the floor in *Black Girl*.

freeze frame render the scene ambiguous (fig. **5.14**). Will he escape to freedom? Does the ocean signify an opportunity for rebirth, or does it represent yet another boundary? The uncertainty of the final moment on the beach contributes to the film's non-traditional narrative structure.

In the opening scene of *Black Girl* ("*La Noire de...*"; Ousmane Sembene 1966), a young Senegalese woman named Diouana (Mbissine Thérèse Diop) leaves Senegal, a former French colony, and travels to France by ocean liner to work for a wealthy family. Once in Nice, however, she realizes that her function there is not to care for the children, as she had been told, but to serve as maid and cook. The family neglects to pay her salary and their constant demands make her a virtual prisoner in the stifling apartment (fig. **5.15**). She has few opportunities to leave the apartment, much less explore the beach. Depressed and desperate, Diouana decides to take her own life.

Under the circumstances, a beach scene depicting carefree vacationers who sun themselves and read newspapers (fig. **5.16**) must be interpreted ironically. Only the privileged are permitted to frolic on the beach; their servants remain inside. The scene of the beach highlights Diouana's exploitation and her invisibility.

In these examples, beach settings produce meaning within a specific context. In *Black Girl*, the beach represents a dead end rather than a site of transcendence, as it seems to be for Ada in *The Piano*. In *Black Girl* and *Bhaji on the Beach*, the beach setting highlights cultural conflicts. In *The 400 Blows*, the beach setting and the freeze frame raise more questions about where Antoine is headed than they answer.

5.16 Carefree vacationers on the beach in *Black Girl*.

and studio executives, sometimes discussing the star's wishes regarding the casting of other actors and desired changes in the script.

Well-known stars can earn more than $20 million per film, but they may be worth it because attaching a popular celebrity to a project helps to secure financing. In recent years, studios have moved from these astronomical salaries to a system called cash break zero, where stars earn smaller salaries up front, but share in the profits studios make after they break even on a film. Some prominent actors occasionally work "for scale" (the minimum wage for professional actors) if they like a particular script or because they enjoy the experience of making low-budget films.

Filmmakers may be limited in their casting choices for commercial reasons. Alfonso Cuarón—director of *Y Tu Mamá También* ("And Your Mother As Well" 2001)—was hired to direct the third *Harry Potter* film, *Prisoner of Azkaban* (2004), but was not permitted to hire different actors or alter the production design because that would have risked alienating the fans of the popular *Harry Potter* series.

The practice of **typecasting**—repeatedly casting an actor in the same kind of role—offers benefits to stars and studios. Stars sometimes prefer roles that will play to their strengths and reinforce their image. At the same time, because actors' fees represent a large percentage of production costs, and because audiences often go to movies to see favorite stars, studio executives prefer to minimize risk and to stick with a "sure thing" in terms of casting. So, for example, Harrison Ford developed his persona as an ironic swashbuckler in both the *Star Wars* and the *Indiana Jones* series in the late 1970s and early 1980s. This character type has sustained his career for four decades.

Sometimes actors deliberately choose roles that work against type. This can be a risky proposition, since fans may refuse to accept this shift from their familiar frame of reference. Seth Rogen became a household name portraying droll teddy-bear slackers with hearts of gold in *40 Year Old Virgin*, *Knocked Up* (Judd Apatow 2007), and *Pineapple Express* (David Gordon Green 2008). When Rogen chose to explore the obsessive and self-destructive dark side of this character in *Observe and Report* (Jody Hill 2009), fans weren't sure whether to laugh at, or be shocked by, the character's bizarre behavior (or Rogen's decision to play against type), so they mainly just stayed away from theaters. This is not to say that actors are incapable of moving beyond typecasting, but that commercial considerations may limit their opportunities to do so.

Acting Style

Actors may bring a public image and traces of their previous roles to each new character they play, but they also bring training in a particular acting style. In early cinema, stage acting techniques influenced film acting and a highly emotive, almost pantomime style prevailed. In silent films, exaggerated facial and bodily expressions were the primary means of conveying the story. In contemporary film, actors are more likely to subdue their expressiveness, as they know they can depend upon sound and visual technologies to capture the nuances of their performances.

5.17 James Dean, a leading exponent of "The Method."

Film scholar Barry King identifies several categories of actors, based on the way their performances are perceived by audiences. Impersonation describes the work of actors who seem to disappear into their roles: actors with this ability to transform themselves include Meryl Streep, Sean Penn, and Julianne Moore. Personification refers to the work of actors who remain themselves or always play themselves and may have scripts written specifically to exploit their particular attributes. Katharine Hepburn, Cary Grant, Reese Witherspoon, and Sandra Bullock belong in this category. Technical acting refers to the mastery of external details of a character such as an accent or physical trait, as evident in Peter Sellers' and Jim Carrey's work.

During the Hollywood studio era, personification was favored because actors who developed recognizable personas might also become stars. Repeating the same kind of characters over and over again brought paying fans back to the box office. Examples include Fred Astaire, Ginger Rogers, Humphrey Bogart, Henry Fonda, and Bette Davis. As the studio system began to break down, and as European styles of acting began to gain adherents in the U.S., **method acting** gained prominence on the stage, in Hollywood and, eventually, in independent film productions of the 1950s and 1960s. Method acting depends upon an actor's immersion in a character and can be linked to the mode of acting that King describes as impersonation.

5.18 *The Machinist*: this emaciated insomniac would soon bulk up to become Batman.

The most influential school of film acting is method acting, a style based on the theories of Russian theater director Constantin Stanislavski, who brought a new, psychological realism to character depiction in the early twentieth century. "The Method" was further developed by the Group Theatre of the 1930s, committed to presenting plays to promote social awareness and activism. Many Group Theatre practitioners went on to become stage and film actors and directors associated with the Actors' Studio, founded in New York in 1947 by Lee Strasberg. Method actors inhabit the psychological reality of their characters. They immerse themselves in the feelings of the character and then connect those emotions to their own experiences to realize the performance. Prominent method actors include Marlon Brando, James Dean (fig. **5.17**), Julie Harris, and Robert De Niro. Contemporary actors continue to use method acting techniques. In order to prepare for a role as a non-drinking cop in *L.A. Confidential* (Curtis Hanson 1997), notorious boozer Russell Crowe stopped drinking alcohol for six months. Christian Bale lost 63 pounds to play the role of a man who never sleeps in *The Machinist* (Brad Anderson 2004; fig. **5.18**), and Hilary Swank reportedly lived as a man to prepare for her role in *Boys Don't Cry* (Kimberly Peirce 1999).

Actors' performances also depend on the narrative: protagonists are presented in lead roles; their sidekicks, friends, and other lesser personages are played out in supporting roles. **Character actors** often play the same supporting roles in many films, but they generally do not achieve the widespread recognition enjoyed by lead actors. Examples of character actors include Franklin Pangborn, Steve Buscemi, Thelma Ritter, Phillip Seymour Hoffman, and Maggie Smith. **Extras** are hired to appear anonymously, often in crowd scenes (although computer graphics also allow special effects technicians to create crowd scenes in post-production). **Cameos** are brief appearances by well-known actors playing themselves. Ensemble acting is based on an equitable distribution of the work and the glory. Directors such as Robert Altman, Woody Allen, Mike Leigh, and Christopher Guest often collaborate with large ensemble casts.

Acting Brechtian: Distancing the Audience

An actor's skill in bringing a character to life—his ability to make audience members believe in the character—is essential to involving viewers in a realist film. But some filmmakers reject the conventions of realism. Directors such as Rainer Werner Fassbinder, Jean-Luc Godard, Alain Resnais, and Charlie Kaufman have explored the film medium as a process of representation. Uninterested in the psychological believability of characters, they draw on German dramatist Bertolt Brecht's ideas about acting, which emphasize the artifice, not the authenticity, of performance. Brecht's Epic Theater was an attempt to stimulate the audience's critical thought processes, as well as their emotions, by calling attention to the aesthetic and political frameworks that produce stories and characters. **Brechtian distanciation** refers to the destruction of the theatrical illusion for the purpose of eliciting an intellectual response in the audience.

An example of a Brechtian approach is David Lynch's *Mulholland Drive* (2001). The actors' performances are intentionally opaque: they do not reveal their characters' inner thoughts or emotions. Rita (Laura Harring) is a blank slate because a car accident has robbed her of her identity. Betty (Naomi Watts) assumes the role of a Nancy Drew detective to help Rita. Adam (Justin Theroux) acts the role of a film director as scripted by powerful movie moguls. Ironically, in the one scene where viewers might feel most connected to Betty, she is reading for a part in a film. In the audition—a performance—Betty expresses more emotion than she does in the rest of the film. Lynch's use of anti-realist acting, combined with a fragmented narrative that originates in one character's dreams,

5.19 In David Lynch's *Mulholland Drive*, all the world's a stage.

forces viewers to pull away from the story and constantly to ask questions about the "reality" of the characters and events. In this bizarre and self-reflexive film, even a simple home or office setting is treated like a theater stage (fig. **5.19**).

Actors' Bodies: Figure Placement

In rehearsal, directors work with the actors to block the action, establishing movements that change their physical relationships with other actors and with the camera. **Figure placement and movement**—what audiences see on screen—can produce artful compositions, provide information about characters and their relationships, develop motifs, and reinforce themes.

Directors treat actors' bodies as elements of the visual field. Figures who tower over other characters, for example, may dominate them in some other way in the film, whereas characters who meet each other on the same physical level (high/low) and plane of depth (foreground/background) may exhibit a more equitable relationship. Characters who occupy the foreground gain visual prominence through their apparent proximity to the viewer. They may assume a greater narrative importance as well. The analysis below looks at how figure placement in Orson Welles's *Citizen Kane* conveys the ongoing predicament of the film's central character.

TECHNIQUES IN PRACTICE

Figure Placement in *Citizen Kane*

A scene in *Citizen Kane* illustrates the way the careful positioning of actors produces meaning. In the Colorado boarding house scene, characters are positioned in ways that provide insight into their relationships and suggest Charles Foster Kane's motivations later in his life.

As the Kanes and Mr. Thatcher (George Coulouris) discuss Charles's future, Mary Kane (Agnes Moorehead) sits very close to the camera. The banker Thatcher is seated behind her, while her husband, Jim Kane (Harry Shannon), moves between the foreground and middle ground of the shot. Charles, who can be heard as he plays outside in the snow, is visible through the window. The prominence of Mary Kane underlines her position of authority. She makes the decision to send her son Charles away to grow up as Thatcher's ward, believing that she is acting in his best interests.

Mary and Jim Kane disagree about the decision. Their difference of opinion on this matter is signified by dialogue as well as figure placement. Moving around in the middle ground, Jim mutters his opposition to Mary's plan. After he learns that the agreement with the bank will provide him with a sum of money, however, he decisively walks away from Mary and Thatcher. He resigns himself to the decision Mary has made with the statement, "It's all for the best." His movement is closely linked to his self-serving line of dialogue. He closes the window, severing his relationship with his son Charles, who can no longer be heard.

Mary immediately stands up, moves to the window, and opens it. She calls to Charles as she tells no one in particular that she has had his trunk packed for a week. Opening the window reverses the action Jim has taken, suggesting the tension between them. Mary is troubled by her decision to send the boy away, a fact that becomes evident when she re-establishes the connection to her son. These movements and dialogue contradict her earlier stoicism, providing insight into her mixed feelings. The viewer gains access to Mary's emotions through her movement and proximity to the camera.

Similarly, Charles's movements compellingly narrate the early years of his life in visual terms. Even when Charles can be seen through the window, he is positioned between the other characters. When the scene moves outside the boarding house, he moves back and forth between the three adults as each one of them claims his attention (fig. **5.20**). Ultimately, after thrusting his sled at Thatcher (an act repeated symbolically throughout the film), Charles ends up in his mother's arms, but that protection will be short-lived. He will leave with Thatcher that afternoon.

The figure placement and movement convey the idea that Mary is the most powerful figure in the boy's life. As a child, he has no say in his own future. As an adult, Charles's desire for power and control is linked to his powerlessness in this life-changing moment. When Charles perceives that others are exerting control over him, he reacts strongly, as he does, for example, when political rival Jim Gettys (Ray Collins), his wife, Emily (Ruth Warrick), and his friend Susan Alexander (Dorothy Comingore) try to convince him to withdraw from the governor's race. Useful comparisons can be made between the figure placement in the two scenes, beginning with Charles's location in the depth of the frame, surrounded by others. Recurring patterns of figure placement visually convey one of the important questions concerning Charles Foster Kane: is he in charge of his life, or are other people making decisions for him?

5.20 The three adults vie for the young Charles's attention in *Citizen Kane*.

Actors' Bodies: Costumes and Props

In the Colorado boarding house scene, the clothing that Mary, Jim, Thatcher, and Charles wear helps to define each of them. There are obvious differences between Jim's homespun vest and trousers and Thatcher's formal attire and top hat. Costumes provide information about time and place, but, more importantly, they express social milieu and personal style.

Costumes cannot be simply taken at face value, but must be interpreted in the context of the film. Clothing is a highly personal matter. Characters wear their clothes on their bodies; they are literally attached to their wardrobe. In the modern gothic *Sunset Boulevard* (Billy Wilder 1950), down-and-out writer Joe Gillis (William Holden) undergoes a sartorial transformation when he meets the Hollywood has-been Norma Desmond (Gloria Swanson). Desmond still dresses the part of a glamorous film star and buys expensive suits for Joe so he can accompany her around Hollywood. Joe's apparent rise in status occurs at the expense of his integrity, however. His new clothes are a symbol of economic dependence. His costume transition indicates not a sudden stroke of good fortune but a loss of control over his own life. One store clerk treats Joe like a gigolo, snidely telling him to choose the more expensive coat, since the lady is paying for it (fig. **5.21**).

Finally, clothing (and the lack thereof) carries cultural implications. In *Bhaji on the Beach*, the older women wear traditional Indian dress and the younger women wear contemporary English garments; thus, clothing visually demarcates the generational divide (see fig. 5.13). Iranian director Tamineh Milani's films about the effects of the Islamic revolution of the late 1970s depict women wearing the veil (fig. **5.22**). While many women at that time wore the veil to show support for the Islamic cause, just as many women preferred to continue wearing Western-style clothing. But Milani could not depict the diversity of the era because government restrictions in place when she made her film prevented filmmakers from showing women without veils.

Like costumes, props establish character and hint at change and development. Props are moveable objects owned or used by characters and range from automobiles to a child's teddy bear. The degree of narrative or symbolic importance of props varies: six-shooters, parasols, and lassos are standard props for Western films, just as machine guns and getaway cars are central to the gangster genre. None of these items necessarily carries any symbolic weight. Some props are purely functional and do not enrich the exploration of character or contribute to a motif.

But sometimes a prop holds tremendous importance and may embody or reinforce a film's themes. In Vittorio

5.21 *(above)* Joe Gillis is fitted for an expensive suit in *Sunset Boulevard*.

5.22 *(below)* Veiled women in *The Hidden Half* (2002).

De Sica's *Bicycle Thieves* ("*Ladri di biciclette*"; 1948) (long mistranslated as *Bicycle Thief*), the bicycle is not only a means of transportation for Antonio Ricci (Lamberto Maggiorani), but also a symbol of the desperate situation facing the people of postwar Italy. When Ricci's bicycle is stolen, he loses his job. Similarly, in *The Station Agent* (Thomas McCarthy 2003), Fin's (Peter Dinklage) most prized possession—his pocket watch—represents more than simply a functional tool. It symbolizes his slightly old-fashioned affinity for trains as well as his desire for punctuality, predictability, and order (fig. **5.23**).

Actors' Bodies: Makeup

Makeup and hairstyles establish time period, reveal character traits, and signal changes in characters. Makeup was used in early cinema simply to make actors' faces visible. But improvements in film stock and lighting mean that makeup is now used to enhance or minimize an actor's prominent features or to simulate youth or advanced age.

Makeup and **prostheses** (three-dimensional makeup that is attached to actors' faces and bodies) can alter an actor's appearance so that he or she resembles a

5.23 In *The Station Agent*, Fin's formal attire distinguishes him from his friends.

5.24 (*left*) In *The Hours* a prosthetic nose changes Nicole Kidman's face.

5.25 (*right*) The novelist Virginia Woolf.

5.26 *(left)* Mike Myers as Austin Powers.

5.27 *(right)* Myers as Dr. Evil in *Austin Powers: International Man of Mystery*.

historical figure, enhancing a film's claim to historical accuracy. This was the case when Nicole Kidman played novelist Virginia Woolf in *The Hours* (Stephen Daldry 2002). Kidman was fitted with a prosthetic nose (fig. **5.24**) to evoke Woolf's unique facial characteristics. Woolf's face may be familiar to many viewers because photographs of the writer have been published in books she wrote as well as in books others have written about her (fig. **5.25**).

Makeup and prostheses may produce comical or frightening effects. In the *Austin Powers* films, Mike Myers plays several characters (Powers, Dr. Evil, and Fat Bastard) with the help of makeup, costumes, hairstyle, and prostheses (figs. **5.26**, **5.27**).

Horror film monsters and science fiction creatures pose great challenges for makeup artists and costume designers. To become the monster in *Frankenstein* (James Whale 1931), Boris Karloff sat for many hours while technicians applied layers of makeup and prostheses; his bulky costume included weights in his shoes, which helped him create the monster's distinctive shuffle (fig. 13.2).

Digital effects that are added in post-production also modify an actor's appearance. In *The Mask* (Charles Russell 1994), **morphing** accomplishes Jim Carrey's grotesque transformation. Images of actors may be altered in a variety of ways using computer graphics programs: for example, an image can be scanned into the computer and unwanted elements digitally "painted out" of the image or the background. In David Fincher's *The Curious Case of Benjamin Button* (2008) a combination of prosthetic and "digital makeup" was used to render the bizarre reverse aging process of the film's main character.

As the brief discussion of acting and the human body makes clear, playing a part requires an actor to transform himself. In a way, actors are shape shifters, losing their identities to the characters they portray. For many, Lon Chaney, Hollywood's "Man of a Thousand Faces" encapsulates the rigorous physical challenges all actors face when they get into character. Chaney earned his moniker (nickname) because of his expert use of makeup and prostheses in vintage horror films such as *The Hunchback of Notre Dame* (Wallace Worsley 1923) and *Phantom of the Opera* (Rupert Julian 1925), movies in which he played outcasts with disabilities. But Chaney didn't become famous just because he endured grueling hours applying his own makeup for each shot. Chaney was able to physically transform himself into a new character for every role he played, even when the part did not require elaborate makeup. As Alonzo in *The Unknown* (Tod Browning 1927), he pretends to be armless then has both of his arms amputated in a pitiful and unsuccessful attempt to win the love of a fellow circus performer (fig. **5.28**). Chaney makes this performance memorable not because he's buried underneath layers of makeup, but because he is the consummate master of his bodily and facial expressiveness.

5.28 *(above)* Lon Chaney's physical performance as Alonzo in *The Unknown*.

5.29 *(center)* Hard light captures the weariness of the character in *8½*.

5.30 *(below)* Soft light creates a romantic mood in *Forgetting Sarah Marshall*.

Lighting

Light is an essential requirement of filmmaking. Without light entering the camera lens, no image would be recorded. Lighting is an element of *mise en scène* because it illuminates the set and the actors and can be used to create certain moods and effects. But it is also related to issues of cinematography, since film stock, lenses and filters, and processing techniques all affect the look of a film. Lighting furthers the audience's understanding of characters, underscores particular actions, develops themes, and establishes mood.

Light exhibits three attributes: quality (hard or soft), placement (the direction from which the light strikes the subject), and contrast (high or low). **Hard light**, produced by a relatively small light source positioned close to the subject, tends to be unflattering because it creates deep shadows and emphasizes surface imperfections (fig. **5.29**). **Soft light**, from a larger source that is diffused (scattered) over a bigger area or reflected off a surface before it strikes the subject, minimizes facial details, including wrinkles (fig. **5.30**). Unless a character is intended to appear plain or unattractive, cinematographers use soft light so that the actors' faces appear in the most attractive way. Skilled Hollywood cinematographers produce flattering renderings

5.31 *(above)* Diffused lighting at the "magic hour" in *Days of Heaven*.

5.32 *(left)* Frontal lighting washes out facial detail from Greta Garbo in *Mata Hari* (1931).

of stars by taking special care with the quality and the positioning of light sources.

Available light (or **natural light**) from the sun can be hard or soft, depending on time of day, time of year, angle of the sun, cloud cover, and geographical location. It may also vary in color. According to Sandi Sissel, Director of Photography for Mira Nair's *Salaam Bombay!* (1988), "You can take a lens with absolutely no filtration and point it, and you'll get footage back from Moscow that will be grayish blue and you will get footage back from India that will be golden." (LoBrutto, p. 175)

One reason why early U.S. filmmakers settled in southern California in the 1910s was the golden-hued quality of the light there. Cinematographers generally agree that the most beautiful light falls during what cinematographer Nestor Almendros has called the "magic hour": just before sunrise and just after sunset, when the diffusion of the sun's light produces glowing images (fig. **5.31**).

The direction of light (or positioning of lighting sources) also produces a variety of different effects. A light source directly in front of the subject (frontal lighting) creates a flat effect, washing out facial detail and creating shadows directly behind the subject (fig. **5.32**). Lighting from either side of the subject produces a sculptural effect, rendering three dimensions by making volume and texture visible (fig. **5.33**). Lighting from behind separates the subject from the background (fig. **5.34**).

Most filmmakers supplement natural lighting with artificial light for greater control over the illumination of the image. Documentary and low-budget feature films, however, often favor natural light, their choices partly dictated by consideration of cost and limitations of the shooting environment (particularly important for documentary filmmakers who wish to minimize the disruptiveness of their presence). Independent filmmaker Lenny Lipton pithily sums up the commercial film industry's approach to lighting. He writes, "If you are interested in lighting a bottle of cola so that it glimmers and glistens, or if your concern is to light a starlet's face so that she looks fantastically like a piece of stone, you will go to very nearly insane lengths to control the lighting." (Lipton, p. 218)

In the Hollywood studio era, a system of lighting was developed that would allow cinematographers to do just that. **Three-point lighting** has remained a standard approach to lighting. The method is designed to ensure the appropriate level of illumination and to eliminate shadows (fig. **5.35**). The primary source of light is the key light, the frontal lighting source aimed at the subject from a range of positions. The key light can be set up next to the camera or moved away from it on either side, approaching a 45° angle on the camera–subject axis. The closer the key light gets to 45°, the more the subject will be illuminated from the side, which produces sculptural effects (fig. **5.36**).

The fill light is a light (or light-reflecting surface) positioned on the opposite side of the subject from the key light. Its purpose is to eliminate the shadows cast by the key light and to regulate the degree of contrast. The back light (aimed at the subject from behind and above) visually separates subject from background. When used with minimal key or fill lighting, the backlight produces a silhouette effect.

In addition to these three sources of light, eye lights are aimed directly into the

5.33 *(left)* Side lighting intensifies a moment of fierce anger in *The Cranes Are Flying*.

5.34 *(right)* Backlighting in *Batman Begins* (Christopher Nolan 2005) adds drama to Batman's descent down a spiral staircase.

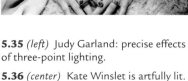

5.35 *(left)* Judy Garland: precise effects of three-point lighting.

5.36 *(center)* Kate Winslet is artfully lit.

5.37 *(right)* Vivien Leigh was known for her characteristic gleaming eyes.

eyes of an actor to produce a gleam in the eye (fig. **5.37**). These are also called obie lights, named for Merle Oberon, the actress for whom they were developed. Side lights or kicker lights model the subject in three dimensions by illuminating it from either side.

Image contrast—one of the most important factors in establishing mood—depends on the relative intensity of the key light to the fill light (key/fill), also known as the lighting ratio. **High-key lighting** refers to a lighting design in which the key to fill ratio is 2:1 or lower. In this configuration, the fill light is nearly as intense as the key light. Thus it eliminates virtually all of the shadows cast by the key light and provides an even illumination of the subject, with most facial details washed out (fig. **5.42**). High-key lighting tends to create a hopeful mood, appropriate for light comedies and for cheery scenes in musicals such as *The Sound of Music* (Robert Wise 1965). The scene when Maria (Julie Andrews)

5.38 High-key lighting in *The Sound of Music*.

confronts a group of disapproving Sisters (fig. **5.38**) shows how the use of high key lighting allows the walls in the background to have subtle shading without losing any detail. The set is evenly illuminated.

Natural-key lighting (or normal lighting) is produced with a ratio of key to fill light between 4:1 and 8:1. Here the key light is somewhat more intense than the fill light, so the fill is no longer able to eliminate every shadow (fig. **5.39**).

Low-key lighting is produced by increasing the intensity of the key light relative to the fill. In low-key lighting, the lighting ratio (key/fill) is between 16:1 and 32:1. The much greater intensity of the key light makes it impossible for the fill to eliminate shadows, producing an image with a number of shadows (often on characters' faces) and high contrast (many grades of lightness and darkness; fig. **5.40**).

Low-key lighting creates a somber or forbidding mood and is often used in crime dramas and *film noir*. It is also the favored lighting style for gothic horror films because it adds a sense of gloom to any setting (fig. **5.41**). Note that several lighting styles may be used in a single film: as the Von Trapp family escapes from the Nazis in *The Sound of Music*, low-key lighting helps shift the film's mood from the brighter scenes to signify the danger involved.

Notice that the terminology of high- and low-key lighting is counter-intuitive: a higher ratio of key to fill is in fact a low-key lighting set up.

5.39 *(left)* Natural-key lighting in Jim Jarmusch's *Broken Flowers* (2005).

5.40 *(right)* The somber tone of Clint Eastwood's *Million Dollar Baby* (2004) is reinforced by low-key lighting.

5.41 Low-key lighting often sets an ominous tone in horror films—*The Orphan* (Jaume Collet-Serra 2009).

Composition

The last aspect of *mise en scène* examined in this chapter is composition, defined as the visual arrangement of the objects, actors, and space within the frame. A filmmaker's treatment of composition may reiterate underlying themes and ideas, and may also produce a striking visual effect.

Balance and Symmetry

The space of the frame can be thought of as a two-dimensional space, where principles of visual art can be brought to bear. One important principle is to ensure there is balance or symmetry within the frame. The frame can be partitioned horizontally, on a left–right axis, and vertically, from top to bottom. A balanced composition has an equitable distribution of bright and dark areas, striking colors, objects and/or figures. In classical Hollywood films, symmetry was often achieved by centering actors in the shot (see fig. **5.42**).

In *Holiday*, the two figures on either side of Katharine Hepburn, as well as the play of light and dark, balance the frame and suggest both harmony and order.

Although the main character in *The Pianist* (fig. **5.43**) occupies the center of the frame in the scene in which he escapes from the Warsaw apartment where he has been hiding, the symmetrical composition does not imply harmony. In this case, parallel lines lead the viewer's eye into the depth of the frame to a vanishing point. The composition emphasizes the overwhelming immensity of the destruction of World War II.

By contrast, an unbalanced composition leads the viewer's eye in a particular direction by giving greater emphasis to a bright or dark area of the frame, to an object or actor, or to an area of color. Asymmetry may suggest a lack of equilibrium, but, as with all aspects of *mise en scène*, the composition must be interpreted in context.

The closing shot of Michelangelo Antonioni's *L'Avventura* (1960) divides the frame into two parts: on the right, a flat wall appears; on the left, a man and woman sit with their backs to the camera and stare into the distance, where a mountain appears (fig. **5.44**). This composition creates several contrasts: the wall seems to have only two dimensions, whereas the left side of the frame offers depth. The uniform texture of the wall is at odds with the way the couple's dense,

5.42 *(above)* Katharine Hepburn in the center of the frame in *Holiday*.

5.43 *(below)* In *The Pianist*, bombed-out buildings line the Warsaw streets, creating a symmetrical composition.

dark clothing distinguishes them from the horizon. The flat surface and right angles of the wall contrast with the diagonal formed by the seated man and the standing woman. These visual tensions result in the viewer repeatedly scanning the image without his eyes coming to rest in any one place, a form of visual open-endedness.

Lines and Diagonals

Graphic elements such as lines play a role in composition. The human eye tends to respond to diagonal lines, vertical lines, and horizontal lines in decreasing degrees of emphasis. All three may be used as compositional elements, but a diagonal line carries the most visual weight.

A startling diagonal composition opens Nicholas Ray's *Rebel without a Cause*. Jim (James Dean) lies sprawled on a street; the camera captures him dramatically at near-eye level (fig. **5.45**). Ray, who had studied with the architect Frank Lloyd Wright, drew on Impressionist painter Edouard Manet's *Le Toréro mort* ("Dead Bullfighter"; 1864) to create this intimate yet formally composed horizontal shot (fig. **5.46**). The painting resonates throughout the film on a thematic

5.44 *(above)* The closing shot of *L'Avventura*.

5.45 *(center)* James Dean resembles Manet's bullfighter in *Rebel without a Cause*.

5.46 *(below)* Edouard Manet: *Le Toréro mort* ("The Dead Bullfighter"), 1864.

level as well: Manet's sense of the bullfighter's romanticism is woven into Ray's portrayal of tempestuous and self-destructive youth. The complex references of this visually arresting shot underscore the fact that the opening and closing shots of a film carry tremendous significance.

In *Batman Begins*, the diagonal lines created by the building's support beams frame Batman (Christian Bale; fig. **5.47**). The composition emphasizes Batman's organic, rounded, asymmetrical form in the foreground, which opposes the regular, geometrical lines of the building's structure. This visual contrast reminds viewers that Batman is a primal force operating outside the norms of rational society: he draws on animalistic energies to carry out his death-defying acts.

When directors place actors in the frame, they make choices regarding the way those actors' bodies will be situated

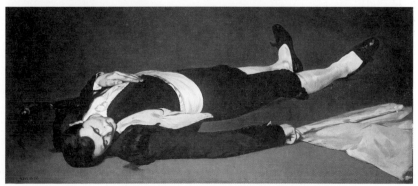

5.47 Batman's shape, color, and density contrast with the diagonal support beams in this composition.

5.48 *(left)* Loose framing emphasizes the open space in *Badlands*.

5.49 *(right)* Tight framing gives a sense of constricted space in *Red Desert*.

in space. **Loose framing** refers to shots in which figures have a great deal of open space around them—this may suggest freedom or isolation, depending on the narrative context and the other elements in the frame (fig. **5.48**). **Tight framing** describes an image in which the lack of space around the subject contributes to a sense of constriction. Tight framing in *Red Desert* ("*Il deserto rosso*"; Michelangelo Antonioni 1964) depicts physical and psychological confinement and suggests in visual terms the impossibility of escape (fig. **5.49**). But tight framing does not always imply entrapment. In *There Will Be Blood* (P.T. Anderson 2007), Daniel Plainview (Daniel Day Lewis) bonds with his adopted son, H.W. (Dillon Freasier). The tight framing, created by the bank on the left side of the frame and the trees on the right, suggests a moment of intimacy as the two share

5.50 *(above)* Tight framing creates intimacy in *There Will Be Blood*.

5.51 *(below)* Loose framing suggests the loss of a close connection in *There Will Be Blood*.

a moment of excitement being in the outdoors (fig. **5.50**). But this moment of intimacy disappears quickly when the oil magnate Daniel walks away to survey the land he wants to drill. As Daniel and H.W. look out over the plains, the camera cranes upwards to a loosely framed panoramic shot, suggesting how the father has abandoned a moment of intimacy to pursue his sweeping entrepreneurial vision (fig. **5.51**).

Foreground and Background

Directors distinguish between the frame's foreground and background. They may place objects or actors in the foreground in order to highlight their narrative significance—as Welles does with Mary Kane in the boarding house scene. They may also make it possible to distinguish important details in the background, another feature of the *Citizen Kane* boarding house scene. They may direct viewer's attention into the depth of the frame through the use of perspective, as Carné does in *Children of Paradise*.

In Alfred Hitchcock's *Notorious* (1946), Alicia's husband, Alex, and her mother-in-law discover she is spying on them and they begin to poison her. The poisoning becomes part of the film's drinking motif, which repeatedly shows Alicia (Ingrid Bergman) drinking substances that harm her (fig. **5.52**). The

5.52 The poisoned cup in the foreground dominates the frame in *Notorious*.

suspenseful series of scenes culminates in a shot whose composition emphasizes the poisoned coffee. Alicia's cup is granted an exaggerated visual importance in the foreground of the composition: its proximity to the camera and its size make it impossible for the viewer to ignore, although Alicia is still unaware of its danger.

Light and Dark

Arranging light and dark areas in the frame is an important aspect of composition. Using contrasting areas of lightness and darkness to create compositional effects is referred to as **chiaroscuro**, after a classical painting technique. In *The Third Man* (Carol Reed 1949), Harry Lime (Orson Welles) meets his fate in an artfully lit underground tunnel (fig. **5.53**).

Color

Production designers develop a color palette, or range of colors, appropriate to the subject matter or the mood of the film. In doing so, they take into account the way audiences respond to the properties of color. When white light is refracted, it produces colors along a spectrum from red to violet, each with a different wavelength. Because viewers perceive reds, yellows, and oranges as warm (vibrant with energy), and blues and greens as cool (relaxing rather than

5.53 Chiaroscuro evokes drama at the tense climax of *The Third Man*.

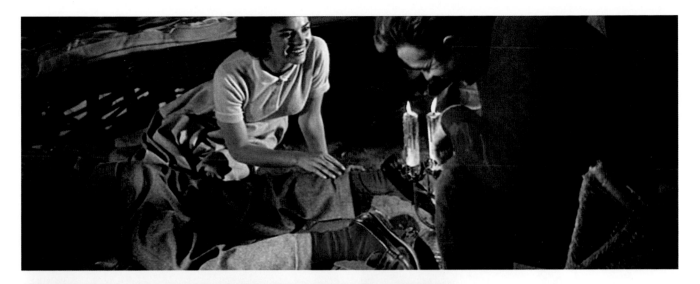

5.54 *(above)* The color red links characters in *Rebel without a Cause*.

5.55 *(left)* Reds emphasizes the summer heat in *Do the Right Thing*.

exciting), filmmakers choose to incorporate colors into sets, costumes, and props according to the effect they are seeking to create.

Like any other visual technique, color in the *mise en scène* may function as a motif. Nicholas Ray repeatedly uses the color red to suggest the fusion of existential anguish and sexual urges of the younger generation in *Rebel without a Cause*. Red appears in Jim's jacket, Judy's coat and lipstick, and in the simulated explosion of the galaxy at the Observatory. Later, Plato's (Sal Mineo) red sock (fig. **5.54**) links him to Judy and Jim. All three teenagers feel lonely and out of place, and they eventually find the companionship they lack at home in one another. In *Do the Right Thing* (Spike Lee 1989), the viewer is repeatedly reminded of the heat of the summer's day by the red and yellow in costumes and in the set (fig. **5.55**).

5.56 Desaturated color creates a washed-out look in *Dancer in the Dark*.

5.57 *(left)* Saturated color in *In the Mood for Love* evokes earlier Technicolor films about Asia.

5.58 *(above)* *The World of Suzie Wong* (1960), filmed in Technicolor.

Saturation refers to the strength of a **hue** (red, green, blue, yellow, etc.). **Desaturated** colors are less pure; they contain more white than saturated colors and thus they look grayish, pale or washed out. In Lars von Trier's *Dancer in the Dark* (2000), desaturated color establishes the dreariness of the characters' lives (fig. **5.56**).

Wong Kar Wai's *In the Mood for Love* ("*Fa yeung nin wa* "; 2000) uses saturated hues to depict the sensual, colorful dresses and neon lights of Hong Kong in the 1960s (fig. **5.57**). In using color this way, the film makes visual reference to American films about Asia set in that period and filmed in Technicolor, including *Love is a Many-Splendored Thing* (Henry King 1955) and *The World of Suzie Wong* (Richard Quine 1960; fig. **5.58**).

While conventional cultural associations may attach to certain colors that appear in the *mise en scène*—black for mourning, for example—it is important when forwarding interpretations to consider the contextual use of color in relation to cultural norms, narrative elements, and other visual techniques in the film under consideration.

Two Approaches to *Mise en Scène*

The Frame in Two Dimensions: *Mise en Scène* in German Expressionism

Several German films released in the decade immediately following World War I (1918–28) were so visually distinctive that contemporary critics lauded their merits, making the Weimar Republic's film industry one of the first internationally recognized national cinemas. Robert Wiene's horror classic *The Cabinet of Dr. Caligari* (1919) helped make the German film industry Hollywood's most serious competitor. French critics coined the term *Caligarisme* to describe films made in this style, but most film critics and scholars use the term **German Expressionism**, named for the Expressionist movement in painting and sculpture that began in Germany before World War I. Along with *The Golem* ("*Der Golem*"; Paul Wegener 1920), *Dr. Mabuse, The Gambler* ("*Dr Mabuse, der Spieler*"; Fritz Lang 1922), *Metropolis* (Fritz Lang 1926), *Nosferatu* (F.W. Murnau 1922), *The Last Laugh* ("*Der letzte Mann*"; F.W. Murnau 1922), and *Faust* (F.W. Murnau 1926), Wiene's film is recognized as one of the canonical examples of German Expressionist cinema.

Film scholars have debated whether the style was a reflection of German culture and psychology or simply a creative response to financial constraints. Lotte Eisner and Siegfried Kracauer argue that *Caligari* reflects German interests in mysticism and ominously foretells the coming of Hitler, whereas Thomas Elsaesser contends that the German film studio, Universum Film Aktiengesellschaft (UFA), was strapped for cash during production of *Caligari* and opted to build intentionally primitive sets. Some argue that the German film industry used stylized set designs and cinematography to distinguish German art films from more pedestrian Hollywood fare. What no one disputes, however, is that the dramatic use of *mise en scène* is one of the primary reasons German Expressionism was, and is, so visually distinctive and important to film history.

The film's macabre story (which involves a murderous madman and a sleepwalker), chiaroscuro lighting, diagonal lines, and bizarre, artificial sets give the film a distinctive look (fig. **5.59**). The combination of visual elements conveys a world out of balance and suggests extreme states of subjectivity—that is, states of feeling rather than being. The visual system externalizes characters' unbalanced perceptions of the world.

The sets in *Caligari* reflect contemporary experiments in the visual arts, namely the emphasis on distortion, jagged shapes, and irregularity in Expressionist painting, sculpture, and theater. Artists such as Ernst Ludwig Kirchner, Max Pechstein, and Käthe Kollwitz explored the ways distorted lines and shapes convey profound emotions in figurative paintings, lithographs, prints, and woodcuts. Hermann Warm, one of the three set designers on *Caligari* (all of whom were Expressionist artists), felt that "films must be drawings

5.59 Edgy angles and chiaroscuro lighting heighten the tension in *The Cabinet of Dr. Caligari*.

5.60 Francis's apocalyptic dream, from *The Butcher Boy*.

brought to life." (quoted in Ellis and Wexman, p. 54)

Since the 1920s, many filmmakers have used *mise en scène* to depict extreme states of subjectivity, including Neil Jordan, Terry Gilliam, Tim Burton, and Michel Gondry. Jordan's *The Butcher Boy* (1997) presents the disturbed inner world of Francis Brady, who grows up in a small town in post-World War II Ireland. In a dream, he witnesses the detonation of a nuclear bomb (whose mushroom cloud rises above a postcard-perfect image of rural Ireland), then roams the gray, charred landscape, encountering bizarre pig carcasses and space aliens. The *mise en scène* renders Francis's trauma with startling and surreal immediacy (fig. **5.60**). Cinematic expressionism is not always associated with a tragically disturbed psyche, however. In *Charlie and the Chocolate Factory* (2005), Tim Burton renders the fantastic and childlike world of Willie Wonka's candy factory through a prism of primary colors, whimsical costumes, and outlandish sets (fig. **5.61**).

Combining *Mise en Scène* and Camerawork: The Frame in Three Dimensions in French Poetic Realism

André Bazin, one of the co-founders of the influential French film journal *Cahiers du Cinéma* ("Cinema Notebooks"), celebrated films that made dramatic use of three-dimensional space. He described this approach as a *mise en scène* aesthetic—one that emphasized movement through choreography within the scene rather than through editing.

Although Bazin focused on the importance of *mise en scène*, he also discussed cinematography. His ideas show that elements of film are inevitably interrelated and that analysis and interpretation must take into account the fact that film techniques work together, combining to produce an overall experience for the viewer. Using Bazin's ideas to discuss the *mise en scène* aesthetic and French Poetic Realism thus serves as a conclusion to this chapter and an introduction to the next chapter on cinematography.

Bazin celebrated the films of French Poetic Realism because they emphasize the space of the story world: the setting and the arrangement of figures. The films of three of the most important directors of French cinema during the 1930s—Marcel Carné, Julien Duvivier, and Jean Renoir—emphasize the complex interplay between individuals and society. Whereas Hollywood favored stories about individuals transcending social limitations, French Poetic Realist films depicted characters whose fates are determined by their social milieu.

These filmmakers used *mise en scène* to illuminate the possibilities and limitations of characters trapped by social circumstance. In *Pépé le Moko* (Julien Duvivier 1937), the title character, a criminal, finds himself psychologically trapped in the sprawling casbah of Algiers, the very environment that affords him his freedom from the law. Pépé (Jean Gabin) has fallen in love with a traveling socialite; he sacrifices his freedom, and ultimately his life, when he leaves the casbah in order to be with her. A common feature of Poetic Realist films was the depiction of characters such as Pépé, whose desires are at odds with society.

Two visual characteristics of Poetic Realism convey the theme that one's social milieu determines one's fate: careful construction of the *mise en scène* and elaborate camera movement. Because these films explore how environment shapes human behavior and destiny, set designers paid attention to minute, yet meaningful, details. Unlike German Expressionism's self-consciously artificial *mise en scène*, that of Poetic Realism depicts realistic and identifiable environments. Poetic Realism's set designs are not distorted or artificial, yet they invest the image with atmosphere. In *The Rules of the Game* ("*La Règle du jeu* "; 1939), Renoir repeatedly emphasizes the intricately adorned rooms and hallways of a lavish French château (fig. **5.62**).

Bazin analyzed *The Grand Illusion* ("*La Grande Illusion*"; Jean Renoir 1937) in terms of its detailed *mise en scène*: "[The film's] realism is not the result of simple copying from life; rather, it is the product of a careful re-creation of character through the use of detail *which is not only accurate but meaningful as well.*" (Bazin, p. 63; emphasis added) Bazin's statement explains how Poetic Realism earned its name. The setting is realistic in that it reproduces the experience of the lived world, and it is poetic because the orchestration of visual techniques heightens the characters' psychological reality, making it tangible to viewers.

Technological factors played a role in determining the look of Poetic Realism. Given the movement's emphasis on detailed, realistic, and atmospheric settings, cinematographers were faced with the challenge of capturing the fine details of the *mise en scène* in three-dimensional space. In French films during the 1930s, camera mobility rapidly increased. In 1930, about one shot in ten involved a moving camera, whereas in 1935, one shot in three involved a moving rather than a stationary camera.

Camera movements combine with a carefully constructed set to produce emotional and intellectual depth in Jean Renoir's *The Crime of Monsieur Lange* ("*Le Crime de Monsieur Lange* "; 1935). Amédée Lange (René Lefèvre) works for a floundering publishing house, whose owner,

5.61 Willie Wonka (Johnny Depp) invites Charlie into a completely different world in *Charlie and the Chocolate Factory*.

5.62 A carefully orchestrated shot from Renoir's *The Rules of the Game*, an example of Poetic Realism.

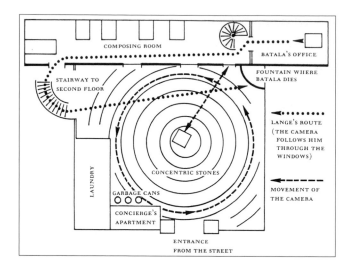

COMPOSING ROOM

BATALA'S OFFICE

STAIRWAY TO
SECOND FLOOR

FOUNTAIN WHERE
BATALA DIES

LANGE'S ROUTE
(THE CAMERA
FOLLOWS HIM
THROUGH THE
WINDOWS)

CONCENTRIC STONES

LAUNDRY

MOVEMENT OF
THE CAMERA

GARBAGE CANS

CONCIERGE'S
APARTMENT

ENTRANCE
FROM THE STREET

5.63 A sketch by André Bazin of the complex camera movement in *The Crime of Monsieur Lange*.

Batala (Jules Berry), callously seduces women and swindles his workers and investors. When Batala disappears and is presumed dead, Lange transforms the publishing company into a thriving cooperative that treats its workers, investors, and readers with respect. One night, in the midst of a celebratory staff party, Batala suddenly returns to stake his claim on the now prosperous company. Lange, unwilling to allow his former boss to ruin the cooperative spirit of the enterprise, shoots him.

What is most striking about the climactic scene is its choreography (fig. **5.63**). The episode begins with Batala trying to seduce Lange's new romantic interest, Valentine (Florelle), in a dark, cobble-stoned courtyard, while the staff revelry continues unabated across the way (only Lange and Valentine are aware of Batala's presence). As Batala corners Valentine, the camera cranes up to film Lange in the company office, two flights above the courtyard. He is stunned and distraught over Batala's demands. As Lange resolutely marches out of the office, the camera tracks his movement through the building and down the stairs. When Lange reaches the courtyard, he exits the frame at screen right, while the camera moves in the opposite direction, panning to the left. Instead of following Lange's movement, the camera pans across the courtyard, nearly completing a circle, until it finds Lange, Batala, and Valentine. Then Lange fires the gun.

The scene is a potent example of Poetic Realism's use of a mobile camera to explore the *mise en scène* in three dimensions and to establish emotional and psychological connections among people and events. The camera's careful attention to Lange's trek heightens the tension by postponing his inevitable confrontation with Batala. The camera's sweep of the courtyard symbolically collects the neighborhood's inhabitants, most notably the workers. This camera movement and the detailed set are crucial to the film's defense of Lange's character. He does not act out of self-interest—instead, Lange acts on behalf of all of his partners. Batala's murder becomes a communal act.

As this comparison of German Expressionism and French Poetic Realism suggests, analyzing a film's *mise en scène* can be a challenging enterprise, requiring attention to details of setting, figure placement, lighting, and composition as elements of the overall production design. Furthermore, these examples show that visual elements work in concert to produce meaning. Rich interpretations grow out of the serious contemplation of the interaction of aesthetic elements. The next chapter considers another important visual element: cinematography.

Summary

- *Mise en scène* (setting the scene or staging the action) is an integrated design program that establishes the "look" of a film.
- The setting refers to the location of the action, which can be shot on location or on an artificially constructed soundstage. Sets can be digitally enhanced.

The spatial attributes of settings contribute meaning, often by developing characters and their conflicts and suggesting themes.

- The human figure encompasses actors, including casting, acting style, figure placement and movement, and costumes, props, and makeup.
- Lighting can affect not only the look but also the mood of a film. Hollywood's standard three-point lighting produces bright, clear images with minimal shadows, whereas the low-key lighting characteristic of *film noir* makes use of shadows and contrast to convey intrigue and danger. The dramatic lighting schemes often used in horror films contribute to the audience's feelings of shock and unease.
- Composition is the art of using graphic elements such as balance, line, foreground and background, light and dark, and color to convey information, emotions, and meaning.
- German Expressionism and French Poetic Realism are different film styles that depend on a distinctive *mise en scène*.

Works Consulted

Arden, Darlene. "The Magic of ILM." **www.darlenearden.com/articleILM.htm**

Bazin, André. *Jean Renoir*. New York: Simon and Schuster, 1971. Trans. 1973.

Bizony, Piers. "Shipbuilding," in *The Making of "2001: A Space Odyssey."* New York: Random House, 2000, pp. 43–54.

"Brad Pitt goes to extremes in *Troy*." Reuters. May 13, 2004. **http:msnbc.msn.com/id/4953083. 6/20/2004**.

Cocks, Jay, and Martin Scorsese. *"The Age of Innocence": The Shooting Script*. New York: Newmarket Press, 1995.

Denby, David. Review of *Ali*. *The New Yorker*, January 28, 2002, p. 27.

Eisner, Lotte. *The Haunted Screen*. Berkeley, CA: University of California Press, 1952. Trans. 1969.

Ellis, Jack C., and Virginia Wright Wexman. *A History of Film*, 5th edn. Boston: Allyn and Bacon, 2002.

Elsaesser, Thomas. *Weimar Cinema and After: Germany's Historical Imaginary*. New York: Routledge, 2000.

Fellini, Federico. *Fellini on Fellini*, trans. Isabel Quigley. Cambridge and New York: Da Capo Press, 1996.

Gibson, Pamela Church. "Film Costume," in *The Oxford Guide to Film Studies*, ed. John Hill and Pamela Church Gibson. Oxford and New York: Oxford University Press, 1998, pp. 36–42.

Horn, John. "Producers Pursue a *Potter* with Pizzazz." *Raleigh News and Observer*, January 25, 2004, p. 3G.

Kelly, Mary Pat. *Martin Scorsese: A Journey*. New York: Thunder's Mouth Press, 1991.

King, Barry. "Articulating Stardom," *Screen*, 26/5, 1985, pp. 27–50.

Kracauer, Siegfried. *From "Caligari" to Hitler: A Psychological History of the German Film*. Princeton, NJ: Princeton University Press, 1971.

Lipton, Lenny. *Independent Filmmaking*. New York: Simon and Schuster, 1983.

LoBrutto, Vincent. *Principal Photography: Interviews with Feature Film Cinematographers*. London and Westport, CT: Praeger, 1999.

McDonald, Paul. "Film Acting," in *The Oxford Guide to Film Studies*, ed. John Hill and Pamela Church Gibson. Oxford and New York: Oxford University Press, 1998, pp. 30–6.

Mottram, James. *The Making of "Memento."* London: Faber and Faber, 2002.

Naremore, James. *Acting in the Cinema*. Berkeley, CA: University of California Press, 1990.

Scott, Walter. "Personality Parade." *Parade Magazine*, June 13, 2004, p. 1.

Sklar, Robert. *Film: An International History of the Medium*, 2nd edn. New York: Harry N. Abrams, 2002.

FILM ANALYSIS

The Functions of Space

This analysis focuses on the way a single aspect of *mise en scène* (the use of spatial oppositions) performs two functions: to develop characters and reinforce themes.

Learning how to describe specific details that support interpretive claims makes papers more engaging and convincing. These detailed descriptions must be clearly and logically linked to each of the paper's major ideas. Study Notes point out the way the author uses detailed descriptive claims to support interpretive claims.

Spatial Oppositions in *Thelma & Louise*

Ridley Scott's *Thelma & Louise* employs spatial oppositions to develop characters and to further one of the film's primary themes: the women's increasing independence. Initially, an opposition between settings highlights the differences between the two main characters. Over the course of the film, however, Thelma (Geena Davis) and Louise (Susan Sarandon) begin to share the same spaces as they drive into the open landscape of the Southwest. Their growing independence from the world they have left behind is made evident through contrasts between the settings they occupy and the settings inhabited by the men who pursue them. The film culminates in the two women's decision to keep going into an unconfined space rather than be imprisoned by the world they have left behind.[1]

The film opens with a contrast between the two protagonists, helping the audience to understand their personalities. Each woman appears in a kitchen. Louise, at work as a waitress in a bright, noisy, commercial kitchen at a diner, calls her friend Thelma. As she talks to Louise on the phone, Thelma paces back and forth in her kitchen at home: a dark, confining, and messy room in the home she shares with her husband, Darryl (Christopher McDonald). The fact that Louise works and Thelma stays at home is made clear in this spatial opposition and is reinforced by two other aspects of *mise en scène*: costumes and props. Thelma wears a sloppy bathrobe and eats a candy bar while Louise wears a white uniform. Louise is associated with hard work and discipline while Thelma is shown as childish and disorganized.[2]

The scene of the two women packing reinforces the contrast between them. The camera shows Thelma and Louise in their respective domestic spaces: Thelma dashes around the bedroom of her suburban house, packing everything she owns. Louise packs neatly in an apartment filled with light and mirrors, and free of the clutter that overwhelms Thelma's bedroom (figs. **5.64**, **5.65**).

When the women head out to spend the weekend at the hunting cabin of Louise's friend, the spaces they inhabit change a great deal. They stop at the Silver Bullet, a Country and Western bar. After Louise shoots and kills

1 This introductory paragraph covers the entirety of the film. Because of this, the reader expects the author to provide detailed descriptions of scenes throughout the film to support the claim that spatial oppositions develop characters and underscore themes.

2 The author carefully describes two spaces that provide information about the characters in them. The author establishes a context for the comparison (film opening, two characters) and provides useful details such as the candy bar and the uniform.

3 Here the author draws a contrast between early and late scenes in the film, using specific visual evidence to argue that the use of space changes over time. Without describing the difference in context (for example, when the details appear in the narrative), the claim could not be supported.

Harlan (Timothy Carhart), they stop at coffee shops and gas stations and stay in a series of anonymous hotel rooms. These settings are facsimiles of the domestic spaces they left behind (kitchens and bedrooms), but they are also public spaces. They measure the women's gradual move toward independence: even though Thelma and Louise have left their homes, they still haven't completely let go of the notion that, because they are women, society expects them to occupy domestic environments. Importantly, however, Thelma and Louise share these spaces, which they did not do in the film's opening scenes. They are becoming a team, and eventually make their stand against male authority together.[3]

As the film progresses, the women spend more of their time together in the car, a space that at first differentiates the women but later unites them. In the early scenes of the film, Louise always drives, while Thelma is content to ride in the passenger seat and put her feet up on the dashboard. After the shooting, Thelma drives the car wildly until Louise asks her to pull over. Louise does not trust Thelma with her car. Gradually, however, Thelma assumes more of the driving duties, taking some control over the shared space and the direction of their journey. The moment when Thelma begins to drive occurs just after J.D. (Brad Pitt) robs them; Thelma takes responsibility by dragging Louise into the car and driving away.[4] In other words, the car motif emphasizes how, as Thelma moves further away from her husband Darryl's control, she becomes more independent and less childlike.

As the film progresses, Thelma and Louise spend almost all of their time in the car, the vehicle that both symbolizes and helps them to enact their independence.

Late in the film, the women no longer bother to stop in hotels. They venture into the uninhabited areas of the desert Southwest (fig. **5.66**). The open landscape replaces diners and hotel rooms. This shift becomes most apparent after they stop in the middle of the night. Louise walks away from the car to take in the panorama of the rock formations in the empty desert landscape; the loose framing shows that she is surrounded by emptiness.[5] The women spend the night on the road, having freed themselves from the confines of

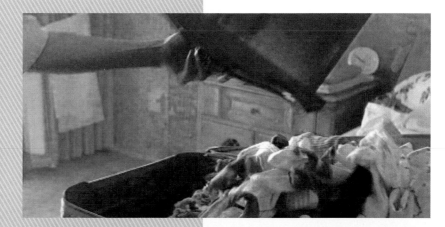

5.64 *(above)* Thelma's room is full of clutter at the beginning of *Thelma & Louise*.

5.65 *(below)* Louise packs neatly in *Thelma & Louise*.

4 The author cites a specific moment and visual detail to establish the turning point where the use of the space of the car changes dramatically.

5 Note how the author describes what this looks like, rather than simply tells the reader the women spend more time outside.

5.66 Thelma and Louise are surrounded by space in the empty desert landscape in *Thelma & Louise*.

6 The author shifts to another claim, focusing attention on the difference between the women and men. This is the moment where the essay begins to present evidence that the spaces men and women occupy differ more and more as the film progresses.

their homes and hotel rooms.

As the women move away from Arkansas geographically and psychologically, the men who pursue them become more confined in terms of the spaces they occupy.[6] The spatial opposition between Thelma and Louise has disappeared, and a new one takes its place: the opposition between the two women on the one hand and the Arkansas State Police/FBI and the men in their lives—Darryl and Jimmy (Michael Madsen)—on the other. The men are increasingly shown in offices and domestic spaces. Detective Hal Slocum (Harvey Keitel) first appears outside in the parking lot at the Silver Bullet. His second scene finds him at the office. Eventually, he moves into Darryl and Thelma's house, along with FBI agents who have set up shop in Darryl and Thelma's home, tapping the phone and watching videos (fig. **5.67**). Intermittent rainstorms emphasize the crowded and confining environs of the household. The increasing control and freedom the women exercise in relation to the bright, open desert landscape contrasts with the men who are tracking them—they move from police stations and offices into the tightly framed space of the Dickinson home.

The final scene uses the Grand Canyon to suggest the independence and freedom the women have attained. Rather than go to prison, or even return to the homes, apartments, workplaces, or hotel rooms they have left behind, they choose to keep driving into the open space. Whether or not viewers understand or agree with the women's decision, the logic of their flight into the canyon is unassailable, given the pattern of spatial opposition developed throughout the film.

5.67 FBI men tightly framed at Darryl's house in *Thelma & Louise*.

Cinematography

The history of light is the history of life,
and the human eye was the first camera.

Josef Von Sternberg

In *Pan's Labyrinth*, when young Ofelia arrives at her new home, she finds an environment that is as off-putting as her stepfather's personality: he is a Captain in Spain's fascist regime, and Ofelia's new domicile is a military outpost in the middle of a deep, dark forest. Director Guillermo del Toro casts this world in a blue sheen to emphasize just how inhospitable it is. Ofelia soon escapes into a series of fantasies, which take her into a strange new underworld that offers a brief reprieve from life with her evil stepfather. To accentuate how these fantasies take Ofelia into an inviting and welcoming realm, del Toro highlights golden, orange, and reddish hues—warm colors that stand in stark contrast to the cold, blue-grey tint of Captain Vidal's environment (fig. **6.1**).

In her adventures, Ofelia must navigate a third environment as well: that of the mysterious faun, who resides underneath the estate's labyrinthine hedges. As the essay at the end of Chapter 2 explains, this faun—who at first appears to

6.1 The warm gold and orange hues of the fantasy world in *Pan's Labyrinth*.

6.2 Filters and film stock accentuate the green colors in the Faun's realm in *Pan's Labyrinth*.

be benevolent—slowly begins to resemble the evil Captain Vidal. As del Toro explains, he bridges Ofelia's fantasy realm and her real life: "You have the blue outside world, you have the golden magical world, and then you have this netherworld [...] which technically belongs to both" (Director's Commentary). Del Toro differentiates this netherworld by emphasizing its greenish hue (fig. **6.2**).

Del Toro creates three different milieus, each with its own look. Achieving this varied color palette required more than just adjusting the *mise en scène*. Del Toro worked carefully with his art director *and* his cinematographer in a coordinated effort. By choosing film stock, manipulating the lighting, and using filters, del Toro enhanced the colors in the set and costumes (Calhoun). These aspects of filmmaking, which involve photographic or electronic aspects of producing images, fall under the general heading of cinematography.

Most audience members would be able to follow Ofelia's movements through these three worlds without the visual cues del Toro provides, so why would he go to such lengths? One answer is that cinematography can do more than support the narrative; it also contributes to the viewer's emotional response and aesthetic experience. As del Toro's cinematographer Guillermo Navarro explains, *Pan's Labyrinth* makes a powerful political statement without seeming didactic: "By creating parallel narratives of a fantasy world and a reality world, we could tell a political story without it coming across like a pamphlet" (quoted in Calhoun). Navarro's comment articulates the importance of using expressive cinematography and *mise en scène* to create a dramatic, emotional, yet subtle experience for the audience.

Cinematography techniques work in concert with a film's mode of organization, its *mise en scène* and editing, and its sound design to produce meaning. The most powerful uses of cinematography do more than simply display technical expertise: they provoke emotional, intellectual, and aesthetic responses.

Cinematographers "speak" to the audience in visual terms, using images the way writers use words. To grasp the full import of visual expression, viewers must move beyond selective vision, which is the tendency to notice only those things they want to see, they expect to see, and they are used to seeing. Veteran DP (Director of Photography) Edward Lachman observes, "We rely so heavily on the written word to translate an idea we don't trust how images can express an idea." (LoBrutto, p. 123) This statement defines the challenge of cinematography. Well-respected cinematographers such as Gregg Toland, Garrett Brown, Haskell Wexler, and Vince Pace have inventively experimented with the tools of cinematography. By constantly improving on the art and technology of image making, cinematographers expand the possibilities of cinema.

This chapter examines the ways filmmakers use cinematography to develop characters, tell a story, produce a distinctive look, suggest ideas, and evoke emotions. Although it addresses many technical aspects of filmmaking, the chapter is not designed to instruct would-be cinematographers in their craft. Interested readers are encouraged to consult *American Cinematographer* magazine and the *American Cinematographer's Manual* for instruction in filmmaking techniques.

In this chapter, the effects of a technique (that is, the way it works with other aspects of the film) are more important than the methods used to achieve it. When building an interpretive claim about a film, the first order of business is to identify a technique using the proper terminology. Second, the viewer moves beyond description, developing ideas about the technique as it works with other elements to produce meaning. Understanding how a technique emerged and developed, and how it has been used in various contexts, enhances interpretation, but is not central to it.

During the first 100 years of cinema, cinematography was synonymous with photography, a photochemical process. As electronic technologies such as **analog** and **digital video** recording have eclipsed traditional methods, cinematography has come to include many non-photographic processes such as **computer-generated imagery**, or CGI. Although digital technologies now augment photography-based processes and may replace them entirely, photography defined the visual language of film's first century. Therefore, this chapter examines photographic processes as well as digital technologies. The chapter discusses four elements of cinematography: camerawork (the operation, placement, and movement of the camera), **lenses** and **filters**, **film stock**, and **special visual effects**. Lastly, it looks at cinematographic effects made possible by digital film technology, and at the impact of that technology on film style.

FILM, VIDEO, AND DIGITAL TECHNOLOGIES: A COMPARISON

Capturing images on film involves photographic and chemical processes. Exposing film stock to light passing through a lens aperture (a circular opening of variable size) causes a chemical reaction in the light-sensitive silver halide particles in the film's **emulsion** (chemical layer). Developing exposed film in a chemical bath produces a **negative**: on black and white film, dark colors appear light and vice versa. With color film, a color will appear as its complement (red will appear green). The negative is printed to another roll of film to produce a **master positive**. Until the late 1920s, contact printing was used to make master positives: developed film was sandwiched between layers of raw film stock and light was aimed through the layers. The **optical printer**, developed in the late 1920s, projects the image onto raw film stock

(fig. **6.3**). This device was for many years the means of creating special effects. Copying a master negative onto reversal film produces a negative from which **release prints** are struck. These are the films exhibited in movie theaters.

In exhibition, projectors aim a beam of light through each frame of the release print as it advances mechanically. The light strikes a reflective screen on which the audience sees the images. A claw mechanism pulls each frame into place at a consistent speed of 24 frames per second (fps) but because projectors are equipped with two-bladed shutters, each frame flashes twice, and viewers actually see 48 fps (figs. **6.4**, **6.5**).

Film is prized for its high resolution—how much detail can be discerned in the image—and its potential for rendering

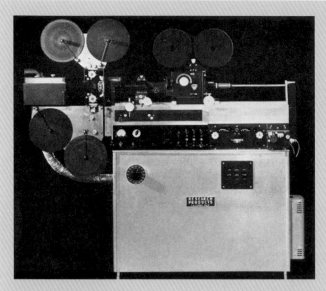

6.3 An optical printer.

beautiful, saturated color. Each frame of 35mm film contains approximately 18 million **pixels** (picture elements).

Instead of recording photographic images on film stock, video cameras capture images as an electronic signal and store them as waves (analog) or as a binary code of ones and zeros (digital). Video cameras capture images through **charge-coupled devices** (CCDs)—silicon chips whose sensors

convert light into an electric charge and, ultimately, into a signal. Most video cameras are equipped with CCDs that detect red, green, and blue. Digital video can be stored in a variety of formats, and the fact that image quality is not affected by successive generations of duplication makes video much less costly to use, but also makes digital images much easier to pirate.

Video monitors (including televisions) have three electron beams (red, green, and blue) housed in a cathode ray tube. In response to an input signal, each beam scans the image across the screen horizontally, one line at a time, illuminating light-emitting phosphors. The frequency of the scan makes it look like an integrated image. With **progressive scanning**, each frame is treated as a single field (older **interlaced scanning** systems treated images as two different fields of odd and even numbered lines).

The standard video format in the U.S. is NTSC (National Television Standards Committee); it yields 525 scan lines and a scanning rate of 29.97 fps. PAL, the format used in Europe, produces 625 lines at 25 fps. To convert film to NTSC the conversion process, called a 3:2 pull down, involves slowing the film down to 23.976 fps as it is run through a **telecine** machine, which creates one extra frame. The digital heir to the telecine is the film scanner; these machines scan individual film frames, and store the

6.4 A release print.

6.5 35 mm film projectors.

images on a digital intermediate, if the film will be edited in digital format. The images are then converted back to film for projection.

There are vocal and heart-felt debates within film studies about the relative merits of film and digital formats. For filmmakers, the advantages of digital video are many: while the equipment can be costly, capturing and storing digital images is far less expensive and cumbersome than using film. During production, cinematographers can see the images immediately, eliminating the waiting time and uncertainty associated with film processing. For exhibitors, the ease and cost savings of handling digital files rather than film reels is compelling, although converting theaters to digital projection systems requires a major investment. European movie chains have been the keenest to convert: the number of digital screens increased by 200% in Europe in 2009.

Historically, the drawbacks associated with digital image capture relative to film include lower resolution and less control over **depth of field**. But 4K digital cameras can reproduce the resolution of 35mm film well enough that the human eye cannot notice a difference. A variable frame rate capability and smaller CCDs mean they can better simulate the look of film (Wheeler, p. 60).

For budding cineastes, the benefits of digital video seem persuasive. It is far cheaper and easier to purchase digital video filmmaking equipment than it is to rent or buy film equipment. There are no processing costs, and the formats are extremely portable. It is quite difficult to purchase and maintain the equipment for projecting films.

The Camera in Time and Space

Creating Meaning in Time: The Shot

Cinematography involves both the spatial characteristics of the frame and the temporal, or time-dependent, character of the film medium. Narrative films tell stories, documentaries recount and observe events, avant-garde films create new combinations of image and sounds; all of these types of films unfold in space and time.

The **shot**, a single uninterrupted series of frames, is film's basic unit of expression: an image whose meaning unfolds through time. Shots vary in length from the briefest exposure of a single film frame to the uninterrupted exposure of a full roll of motion picture film. In Hitchcock's *Rope* (1948), the exposure of a roll of film without cuts yielded shots of about eight minutes in length. Editing several shots together produces a **scene**, which is a coherent unit: one that has its own beginning, middle, and end.

In order to use time on the set efficiently, directors and cinematographers generally plan each shot ahead of time. One method for planning shots is the **storyboard**—a series of drawings that lays out the film sequentially (fig. **6.6**). Some directors, such as Brian De Palma, use photographs as storyboards. Others, such as Jim Jarmusch, reject storyboards and even shot lists, preferring to improvise ("Interview" 2004). The DP designs **set-ups**, positioning actors, the camera, and lighting arrangement for each shot.

Films are generally not shot in chronological order, and, except on very low-budget productions, every shot is filmed more than once. Each version is called a **take**. In post-production, the editor and director choose which takes will appear in the film. Rejected takes are called **out-takes**.

Uninterrupted shots of more than one minute are called **long takes**. Orson Welles's *Touch of Evil* is renowned for its opening shot, a long take that follows

6.6 *(above)* A series of storyboards from *Gladiator* (Ridley Scott 2000).

6.7 *(right)* The celebrated crane shot at the beginning of *Touch of Evil*.

the movements of a couple on foot and a car with a bomb in its trunk as they both cross the Mexico–U.S. border (fig. **6.7**). The long take creates tension as two lines of action merge on narrative and visual levels. Robert Altman's *The Player* (1992) pays its respects to Welles with an inside joke: a continuous shot of eight minutes in length that opens the film. The camera sweeps by characters on a Hollywood studio back lot who reverently describe Welles's feat in *Touch of Evil*. Long takes build dramatic tension, emphasize the continuity of time and space, and allow directors to focus on the movement of actors in the space of the *mise en scène*.

Martin Scorsese is known for dramatic long takes. One celebrated example from *Goodfellas* depicts the courtship of a young couple. As Henry (Ray Liotta) and Karen (Lorraine Bracco) enter the famous New York nightclub the Copacabana, the camera moves fluidly, following them into the pandemonium of the kitchen and through the labyrinthine passages of the building on their way to the packed club. The relentless continuity of the shot, which takes about three minutes, conveys Karen's confusion and exhilaration as she is unwittingly drawn into Henry's world of organized crime (fig. **6.8**). This long take exaggerates time and space. The rapid-fire sequence of greetings and continuous movement into the club dramatize what would otherwise be an unremarkable experience for the characters, heightening drama and marking this exciting moment.

Altering Time: Slow and Fast Motion

Cinematographers can manipulate the speed of filming to compress or expand time. Unless special effects are desired, the standard recording speed is 24 frames per second. By reducing or increasing the camera's recording speed, and then projecting the film at 24 frames per second, filmmakers can affect the viewer's perception of time.

To produce **slow motion**, the camera records images at a speed faster than that at which it is projected. When the film is projected at the standard rate, the action appears to be slowed down. One minute of film recorded at 36 fps has a greater number of frames than one minute of film recorded at 24 fps. When

Chapter 6: Cinematography

projected at 24 fps, the 36 fps footage will take longer than one minute to screen, drawing out the action. Slow motion lengthens the duration of an action and seems to break down human movement into its component parts. Although the terminology here refers to film, these principles apply to any image recording and projection devices involving sequenced images at a consistent frame rate, including digital video.

Slow motion has been used for both comic and dramatic purposes. In *Darjeeling Limited* (Wes Anderson 2007), Peter (Adrien Brody) and Bill Murray run to catch a train in slow motion; because they are strangers who share a brief moment with a common purpose, the slow motion exaggerates and mocks the competitive anonymity of travel. In contrast, Kathryn Bigelow's *The Hurt Locker* uses slow motion to bring dramatic emphasis to the danger soldiers face during their deployment in Iraq; their experiences defusing bombs resist any comparison to the normal rhythms of everyday life.

6.8 The camera follows Henry and Karen on their first date.

To produce **fast motion**, cinematographers record images at a slower speed than the speed of projection. Fewer frames are exposed in one minute when shooting at a speed of 16 fps than at a speed of 24 fps. When projected at 24 fps, that action takes less than a minute on screen and appears unnaturally rapid.

F. W. Murnau used fast motion in *Nosferatu* to indicate the supernatural speed with which the vampire Count Orlock (Max Schreck) loads a group of coffins onto a cart as he prepares to leave his castle for England. After Orlock climbs into one of the coffins, stop-motion photography is used to make it appear as though the coffin lid leaps to the top of the coffin. The technique involves photographing a scene one frame at a time and moving the model between each shot. The process was also used to animate the beasts in *King Kong* (Merian C. Cooper and Ernest B. Schoedsack 1933), *Clash of the Titans* (Desmond Davis 1981; special effects by Ray Harryhausen), and *Fantastic Mr. Fox* (Wes Anderson 2009). **Go-motion**, a technique developed by Industrial Light and Magic, builds movement into single frames. In this process, the puppet or model is motorized and moves when the camera's shutter is open, creating a sense of blur. The technique was used for the whales in *Star Trek IV: The Voyage Home* (Leonard Nimoy 1986).

Time-lapse photography is a process of recording a very small number of images over a long period of time—say, one frame per minute or per day. Time-lapse nature photography can present a slow process, such as a flower blooming, in a matter of seconds.

Contemporary filmmakers have developed sophisticated methods for manipulating time. An impressive effect developed during the 1990s is called a

FROM STOP MOTION TO ANIMATION

Stop-motion photography (pixilation) is the technique underlying all film **animation** (fig. **6.9**). As early as 1906–7, J. Stuart Blackton used stop motion to animate objects and hand drawings in one-reel films for Vitagraph, and French filmmaker Emile Cohl combined animation and live action (Crafton, p. 71; Cook, p. 52). Animators soon developed a process using transparent overlays called **cels** (for "celluloid") to separate moving figures from static backgrounds, which avoided the problem of drawing each frame individually. Cel animation is a labor-intensive and time-consuming process, and it remained the standard technique for animated films until the 1990s.

Animated short films were exhibited with newsreels and fiction features, providing "humor, slapstick spectacle, animal protagonists, and fantastic events" (Crafton, p. 72). Disney Studios developed the iconic figure of Mickey Mouse during the 1920s, and Warner Brothers created Porky Pig, Elmer Fudd, Daffy Duck, and Bugs Bunny in the 1930s and 1940s. Disney Studios achieved commercial success with animated features such as *Snow White and the Seven Dwarfs* (David Hand 1937), *Pinocchio* (Ben Sharpsteen and Hamilton Luske 1940), and *Fantasia* (Ben Sharpsteen 1940; fig. **6.10**).

Animation experienced a renaissance during the 1990s. When it was on the point of eliminating its animation division in the 1990s, Disney (having moved into live-action feature films) did an about-face and purchased Pixar Studios (originally the computer graphics division of LucasFilm). Pixar's success with *Toy Story* (John Lasseter 1995), the first

6.9 Stop-motion photography animates insects in *The Cameraman's Revenge* (Wladyslaw Starewicz 1912).

6.10 Animals as characters in *Fantasia*, one of Disney's most successful animated features.

6.11 Rotoscoping and computer graphics animate live action in *Waking Life*.

computer-animated feature, re-energized commercial animation. Since then, several such films have earned critical acclaim, including *Toy Story 2* (John Lasseter 1999) and *Wall-E* (Andrew Stanton 2008). The fact that *Toy Story* and *Shrek 2* (Andrew Adamson et. al 2004) were the highest grossing films in the years they were released is an indication of the ever-increasing audience for animated films. Further evidence that animation appeals to a broad audience is the popularity of the critically acclaimed *Up* (Pete Docker and Bob Peterson 2009), which depicts the adventures of an elderly man trying to avoid spending his last days in a retirement home. The film's skillful treatment of a potentially downbeat theme makes it clear that animation is no longer (if it ever was) the domain of children.

Perhaps one influence on the thematic sophistication of Hollywood's animated films is the popularity of a Japanese style of animation, called *anime*. This style grew out of the film and television work of Osamu Tezuka during the 1950s and 1960s, and has garnered international attention via the films of Hayao Miyazaki, such as *Princess Mononoke* ("*Mononoke Hime*" 1997) and *Spirited Away* ("*Sen to Chihiro no Kami-kakushi*" 2001). *Anime* is not aimed at young audiences. In addition to the influence of Japanese *anime*, comic books and graphic novels of all kinds have emerged as important sources for films. Some graphic novels become live action films (*A History of Violence* [David Cronenberg 2005]), while others combine live action and animation to produce a hybrid visual style (*Sin City* [Frank Miller and Robert Rodriguez 2005]).

As part of the revitalization of animation through computer graphics, Richard Linklater took the artistry of the **rotoscope** to a new level in *Waking Life* (2001) and *A Scanner Darkly* (2006). The rotoscope projects photographs or footage onto glass so that images can be traced by hand as templates for cartoon characters (Rickitt, p. 141). After Linklater shot and edited a live action version of *Waking Life* on digital video, a team of animators used a computer program to trace over and color the entire film on a computer monitor. Working with a variety of animators in this way meant that each of the different scenes in the film has its own visual style (fig. **6.11**).

frozen time moment, or a bullet-time moment. These terms refer to a shot where a single action is viewed simultaneously from multiple vantage points. The technique, first used in *Blade* (Stephen Norrington 1998), gained widespread popularity after it was adopted for the martial arts scenes in *The Matrix*. To create this effect, more than 122 still cameras were arranged around the action, timed and calibrated in order to capture still images of the action at the same instant. Those still images were then used as a blueprint in digital post-production, where technicians "interpolated" additional frames. They create additional

6.12 *(above)* An eye-level scene from *Mildred Pierce*.

6.13 *(below)* A very different eye-level scene from *Tokyo Story*.

images to simulate the motion that could occur in between the actual stills. Combining the stills with the interpolated frames extended the duration of the shot. The result is a "time-frozen subject seen from changing perspectives." (Martin, p. 70) *The Matrix* employed a crew of forty photographers, 4–5 computer graphics designers, and 95–100 digital effects artists. Note that this stunning effect was created by combining traditional photography with digital post-production technology.

The Camera and Space: Height, Angle, and Shot Distance

Whereas the length of a take and slow and fast motion influence the viewer's sense of time, the positioning and movement of the camera affect the viewer's understanding of space. Camera placement and movement determine the way viewers perceive characters, events, and objects in the world on screen. Viewers can be forced to adopt the perspective of a single character (Coppola's *The Conversation* [1974]), may be implicated in voyeurism (Hitchcock's *Rear Window*), and can be made to see the world through the eyes of a vicious killer (John Carpenter's *Halloween* [1978]).

Three important variables for any shot are camera height, angle on the action, and distance from the action. These choices convey information, form motifs, introduce ideas, and create mood. Michael Chapman, DP for Scorsese's *Taxi Driver* (1976) and *Raging Bull*, feels that "camera angles tell us emotional things in ways that are mysterious." (Schaefer and Salvato, p. 124) Camera placement may evoke a wide range of emotions: the position of the camera may compel intimacy or establish a sense of distance from characters and situations. It is also important to remember what the camera placement excludes: **offscreen space** refers to spaces within the world of the story that are temporarily or permanently excluded from the viewer's vision. Filmmakers can use character behavior, dialogue, and sound to remind viewers that off-screen spaces exist, without showing them explicitly.

Camera Height

The camera's height most frequently approximates an eye-level view of the action (fig. **6.12**), but **eye-level shots** are usually combined with shots from higher and lower vantage points. This height convention can assume a variety of forms. Japanese filmmaker Yasuhiro Ozu consistently places the camera at about three feet above the ground. For Western viewers, this vantage point may appear unusual, but this camera height is at the approximate eye level of the action taking place, as characters sit on the floor (fig. **6.13**). In Stanley Kubrick's *The Shining* (1980), DP Garrett Brown used a floor-level camera to follow a child,

Chapter 6: Cinematography

Danny Torrance (Danny Lloyd), as he rides around the interior of the sinister Overlook Hotel on his Big Wheel. Brown comments on the surreal effect: "The fact that we were below the kid and the vanishing point toward which we were moving was hidden behind him gave this whole sequence a fantastic quality." (LoBrutto, p. 149) By placing the camera at the child's eye-level, Brown helps the audience feel how Danny is overwhelmed by the imposing spaces of the haunted hotel.

6.14 *(left)* A high-angle shot suggests Alex's fear in *Notorious*.

6.15 *(right)* A high-angle shot captures Jack's casual demeanor in *Brokeback Mountain*.

Camera Angle

Another aspect of camera position is angle. In most shots, the camera is level. **High-angle shots**, where the camera is positioned above the action and aimed downward, tend to minimize the subject. One result can be that characters seem less powerful. In *Notorious*, when Alex Sebastian confides to his mother that he has married a spy, the camera adopts an extreme high angle in a close-up, emphasizing his panic (fig. **6.14**). But high angles don't always suggest disempowerment; in *Brokeback Mountain* (fig. **6.15**), a high angle on Jack allows the viewer to read his casual demeanor through his body language as he leans against his pickup truck, in a classic cowboy pose.

6.16 An interior shot in *Stagecoach* makes the ceiling visible.

Low-angle shots, which position the camera below the subject, aiming upward, often exaggerate the size and volume of the subject. Characters often appear more powerful, as they physically dominate the shot. If a ceiling is visible in an interior shot, as is common in the films of John Ford, the camera has probably been positioned at a slightly low angle (fig. **6.16**). In Sergio

MOVING PICTURES AND VISUAL PERCEPTION

The viewer's ability to perceive any rapid succession of images as continuous motion—whether the images are presented on film or digital video—was, for much of the 20th century, believed to derive from two properties of human vision: **persistence of vision** (this theory argues that the brain holds an image for a few second after it's gone) and the **phi phenomenon** (whereby the eye perceives two lights flashing on and off as a single light moving). Yet no scientific consensus exists, and these theories have been called into question by recent work in cognitive film studies that seems to suggest the human brain processes short-term apparent motion using the same cognitive processes it uses for real motion. "We rapidly sample the world around us, noting the things that change and the things that do not change." (Anderson and Anderson) This model suggests that film spectators are, on the cognitive level, actively seeking out meaning rather than passively absorbing visual information.

Leone's *For a Few Dollars More* ("*Per qualche dollaro in più* "; 1965), a gunfight early in the film uses the contrast between level shots, low-angle shots, and high-angle shots to distinguish between bounty hunter Colonel Mortimer (Lee Van Cleef) and the man he is hunting. Low-angle shots of Mortimer imply his mastery of the situation. Even from a distance, he looms large in the frame because of the low angle. Level shots from behind Mortimer approximate his perspective, and they neither minimize nor exaggerate the wanted man. Finally, high-angle shots of the man tumbling to the ground after Mortimer shoots him emphasize his defeat (figs. **6.17**, **6.18**, **6.19**).

6.17 *(right)* A level shot of Mortimer in *For a Few Dollars More*.

6.18 *(below left)* A low-angle shot of Mortimer in *For a Few Dollars More*.

6.19 *(below right)* A high-angle shot of Mortimer's victim in *For a Few Dollars More*.

A **canted** or **Dutch angle** leans to one side. Generally, the subject creates a diagonal line in the frame. A canted angle often signifies a moment of imbalance or loss of control. In a scene depicting an automobile accident in *Crash* (fig. **6.20**), a canted angle suggests a breakdown of order because geographical reference points—and, specifically, the horizon—shift.

An **overhead shot**, also called a bird's eye shot, gives a unique perspective on the action from above. Cinematographers rarely use the bird's eye view, and when they do, typically they are striving for a dramatic effect. In *Psycho*, an overhead shot startles viewers and maintains the secret regarding Mother's identity (see fig. 7.4).

6.20 A canted angle in *Crash*.

Overhead shots are not always explained by plot events, however. A director may include these shots in order to alienate the spectator from the characters or action. When film techniques encourage spectators to step back from the story or characters in terms of their emotional engagement, the effect is said to distance the viewer. After the final shootout in *Taxi Driver*, when police arrive at the apartment where Iris (Jodie Foster) lives, a cut to an overhead shot depicts the police and Travis Bickle (Robert De Niro) from above (fig. **6.21**). The overhead angle combines with the static *mise en scène*—even the actors are frozen—to distance viewers from the action. To realize this shot, Scorsese's crew cut a hole in the ceiling above the room where the action takes place and shot the scene through the opening.

Camera Distance

Camera distance refers to the space between the camera and its subject, which can determine how emotionally involved the audience becomes with characters. In an **extreme long shot** (XLS) the human subject is very small in relation to the surrounding environment (fig. **6.22**). In a **long shot** (LS) from Agnès Varda's *Cleo from 5 to 7*, the camera captures the figure of protagonist Cleo (Corinne Marchand) in its entirety. It is prominent because it occupies relatively more space in the frame, but is still

6.21 An overhead shot in *Taxi Driver*.

6.22 *(below)* An extreme long shot in *The Birds* (Alfred Hitchcock 1963).

6.23 *(right)* A long shot from *Cleo from 5 to 7.*

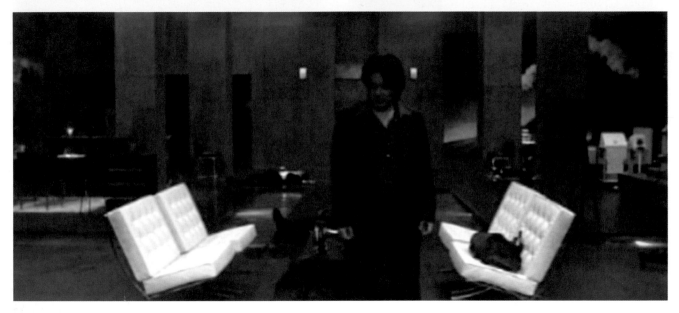

6.24 *(above)* A medium long shot from *Oldboy* (Chan-wook Park 2003)

6.25 *(below)* A medium shot from *Napoleon Dynamite* (Jared Hess 2004).

entirely within the frame (fig. **6.23**). A **medium long shot** (MLS) from *Oldboy* captures the human figure from the knees up (fig. **6.24**). A **medium shot** (MS) situates the human body in the frame from the waist up (fig. **6.25**); a **medium close-up** (MCU) from the chest up (fig. **6.27**). A close-up (CU) closes in on a section of the body, such as the face, torso, legs, or hands (fig. **6.26**). An **extreme close-up** (XCU) will depict only a body part such as an eye, ear, or finger (see fig. 7.25).

Medium shots and close-ups tend to produce a greater sense of intimacy by allowing viewers to focus on actors' faces and character emotions, whereas long shots tend to emphasize the environment and the space that surrounds the characters. However, the effect of any shot distance must be interpreted in context. Most filmmakers vary shot distance, not only to serve the needs of the narrative, but also to create patterns, develop motifs, and support themes.

Filmmakers can also use shot distance to convey abstract ideas. Carl Theodor Dreyer depends almost exclusively on close-ups and medium shots of Joan of Arc and her interrogators in *The Passion of Joan of Arc* ("*La Passion de Jeanne d'Arc*"; 1928). Joan's trial and this use of close-ups emphasize Joan's spiritual power, not her military prowess. Dreyer championed the close-up because he believed the soul is visible in the human face.

Ingmar Bergman's *Persona* uses close-ups of two characters to suggest the intensity of their relationship. Emotionally troubled actress Elisabeth Vogler (Liv Ullman) and her nurse Alma (Bibi Andersson) seem to trade and merge their identities through several of Bergman's visual motifs. The use of tightly framed **two-shots**—in which both women's faces are visible in close-up—creates a visual metaphor for that merging (fig. **6.28**).

In contrast, in *2001* Stanley Kubrick uses long shots to suggest the insignificance of human beings and their aspirations. Long shots of astronauts Dave Bowman (Keir Dullea) and Frank Poole (Gary Lockwood) show their insignificance in relation to the mechanical and computerized environment they have helped to create, especially in the context of the vast universe (fig. **6.29**). The final shots of the film, which involve extreme close-ups of a human figure, produce a startling counterpoint to Kubrick's consistent use of long shots. Close-ups of the star child suggest the human potential for rebirth.

6.26 A close-up in Gus Van Sant's *Mala Noche* (1985).

6.27 *(left)* A medium close-up emphasizes spiritual transcendence in *The Passion of Joan of Arc*.

6.28 *(right)* A two-shot of Alma and Elisabeth in *Persona*.

6.29 A long shot emphasizes the machine-filled universe in *2001: A Space Odyssey*.

Camera Movement: Exploring Space

In addition to height, angle, and shot distance, camera movement can affect the meaning of shots and scenes. A camera that remains in the same position may produce a sense of stagnation. In contrast, a moving camera may encourage viewers to become involved in a character's physical or psychological sensations, or may act as a counterpoint to the action. Shifting the camera's height, angle, or distance merely to account for changes in character position is called **reframing**.

Horizontal and Vertical Movement

Some camera movements are horizontal and vertical. A **pan** is the horizontal turning motion of a camera fixed to a tripod, a movement typically used to show an expanse of landscape, whether it be a vast canyon or a crowded city street. An important moment in film history occurred when Edwin Porter included a pan in *The Life of an American Fireman* (1903). Porter's camera pans to follow firefighters as they rush to a fire; the moving camera finally rests on the burning house (fig. **6.30**). This pan integrated camerawork and narrative development, as film historians Gerald Mast and Bruce Kawin explain:

6.30 The burning house in *The Life of an American Fireman*.

This was not a simple matter of panning to cover a wide subject, like a city skyline; what it did was discover the logic for the pan, making a camera movement part of the film's dramatic strategy—because it followed a moving object and because it kept the burning house out of the frame until the moment Porter chose to reveal it. (Mast and Kawin, p. 39)

A **swish pan** occurs when a pan is executed so quickly that it produces a blurred image, indicating rapid activity or, sometimes, the passage of time. In Spike Lee's *Do the Right Thing*, a swish pan adds to the tension between Mookie (Spike Lee) and his boss, Sal (Danny Aiello). Mookie confronts Sal with his suspicion that Sal is romantically interested in his sister Jaye (Joie Lee). The camera moves so quickly from one character to the other that the intermediate space

appears blurred (fig. **6.31**).

A **tilt** refers to the technique of tipping the camera vertically while it remains secured to a tripod. The movement can simulate a character looking up or down, or help to isolate or exaggerate the vertical dimension of an object or setting. In *Citizen Kane*, when Mr. Thatcher (George Coulouris) presents Charles with a sled for Christmas, the young boy unwraps the gift, and then looks up at his guardian. The camera tilts upward, revealing that Thatcher towers over the boy. This tilt contributes to a parallel between Charles and Thatcher. This early tilt shows that Thatcher dominates Charles during his childhood. Later in the film, low angles on Kane suggest that he dominates others in the same way.

Movement in Three Dimensions

To free the camera in space, cinematographers sometimes mount cameras on rolling platforms called **dollies**, which ensure fluid, controlled, motion. A **crab dolly** has wheels that rotate, so the dolly can change direction. Very low-budget filmmakers sometimes use shopping carts as dollies and stand or sit inside. A **tracking shot** is accomplished by moving the camera, on a dolly, along a specially built track (fig. **6.32**). Tracking shots can trace movement laterally (across the frame) or in and out of the depth of the frame. In Stanley Kubrick's *Paths of Glory* (1957), a tracking shot emphasizes the forward momentum of General Mireau (George Macready) as he strides through the trenches of World War I, about to order his troops into battle (fig. **6.65**). The soldiers stand still as he passes, which further emphasizes his dominance.

Cameras mounted on cranes create sweeping, three-dimensional movements (fig. **6.33**). The long takes that open *A Touch of Evil* and *The Player* are **crane shots**. A crane shot also takes

6.32 A tracking shot on location—*Let the Right One In.*

place near the conclusion of Ethan and Joel Coen's *O Brother, Where Art Thou?* (2000), when the three bumbling miscreants Everett (George Clooney), Pete (John Turturro), and Delmar (Tim Blake Nelson) are about to be hanged. As Everett drops to his knees to pray, the camera adopts a high-angle position above him and then pulls back and upward, as if his appeal to the almighty has taken flight (figs. **6.34**, **6.35**).

Aerial shots, taken from airplanes and helicopters, allow filmmakers to compose shots from great distances. As Thelma and Louise begin to experience the freedom of leaving their conventional lives behind as they head for Mexico, an aerial shot underscores the sense of openness and contributes to a motif of flight. By contrast, aerial shots in Werner Herzog's *Grizzly Man* (2005) create a sense of foreboding, emphasizing the isolation of the Alaskan wilderness where Timothy Treadwell lived with grizzly bears (fig. **6.36**).

In many instances, filmmakers want to capture intimate scenes with subtle camera movements. Conventional motion picture cameras are heavy, however; without a brace, all the motion of the camera operator will be translated into shaky images. By the late 1950s and early 1960s lightweight 35 mm cameras used for recording newsreel footage during the 1940s had found their way into independent filmmaking. The Éclair Cameflex was the favorite of French New

6.33 *(above)* A camera mounted on a crane.

6.34 *(center)* Everett drops to his knees in *O Brother, Where Art Thou?*

6.35 *(below)* The camera pulls back and upward, away from Everett in *O Brother, Where Art Thou?*

Wave filmmakers. In the 1960s, light-weight 16 mm cameras able to record synchronized sound led to a flowering of documentary filmmaking, and, particularly, the non-interventionist **direct cinema** of filmmakers such as Richard Leacock, D.A. Penne-baker, Albert and David Maysles, and Frederick Wiseman in the U.S. and Chris Marker in France. The sense of immediacy produced by **hand-held shots** is evident in narrative fic-tion films as well, including *Medium Cool* (Haskell Wexler 1969), *Reservoir Dogs* (Quentin Tarantino 1991), and *Cloverfield*.

6.36 An aerial shot from *Grizzly Man*.

Other innovations in camera technology included the small, lightweight, and quiet Panaflex camera, first used on Steven Spielberg's *Sugarland Express* (1974) to capture handheld shots with dialogue in a moving car. Cinematographer Garrett Brown developed a stabilizing device worn by the camera operator that he patented as the **Steadicam**, first used on *Rocky* (John Avildsen, 1976). The Steadicam permits fluid camera movement, allows greater mobility than tracking shots, and minimizes shakiness (fig. **6.37**). Brown describes the effect of his invention: "the moving camera lets you break into the medium itself—the screen stops being a wall and becomes a space you can play in." (LoBrutto, p. 139) Brown has gone on to develop other devices that allow filmmakers to incorpo-rate fluid movement, such as the underwater moby cam and the SkyCam, a sys-tem that involves suspending and moving cameras using cables and pulleys.

6.37 Garrett Brown using a Steadicam while shooting *The Shining*.

As this discussion suggests, discerning the significance of camera placement and movement requires careful consideration of a shot in context. Broadly speaking, camera move-ment can function in five ways. It may:

- reveal information in a dramatic fashion, as in *The Life of an American Fireman*.
- establish a character's perspective: the tilt in *Citizen Kane* aligns the viewer with the small boy.
- convey a sense of space: the aerial shot encompasses a vast wilderness in *Grizzly Man*.
- suggest mood, as in *Cloverfield*, where a handheld camera translates fear and conflict between characters into a visually upsetting experience.
- emphasize the continuity of time and space (*Goodfellas*) and expand time and space.

Lenses and Filters: The Frame in Depth

Although the camera seems to function like an eye as it records images, the camera does not see the world the way that the human eye does. Eyes and cameras both use lenses to focus rays of light. The rays converge, producing an image of the object being observed. The lens of the human eye focuses light rays that enter the pupil on the retina. In the camera, the lens focuses the light rays entering the **aperture** on the film stock. Camera lenses must be carefully calibrated to produce the desired image. On the set, the **focus puller** carefully measures the distance from the lens to the subject being photographed, then marks the focus ring with tape and moves the camera's focal ring to those marks during filming (focus is precisely determined by measurements, not by looking through the camera lens). Keeping images in focus would seem to be a rather basic element of filmmaking, but, in fact, DPs use lenses and filters not just to maintain proper focus, but also to shape the environment, create mood, and develop themes.

In *Elephant* (Gus Van Sant 2003), a motif involving **selective focus** suggests ways that the film's teenage characters fit into, or are alienated from, their suburban high school milieu. The film follows a number of students through their day, with numerous scenes where they pass one another in the hallway. In two of these scenes, Elias (Elias McConnell) and Michelle (Kristen Hicks) walk to class down the same hallway. Yet they interact with their environment very differently. In a shot of the popular student Elias, people and objects are in focus, suggesting his immersion in the world of high school and his greater sociability (fig. **6.38**). By contrast, a shot taken from over Michelle's shoulder emphasizes her disaffection and loneliness: the world around her seems an undifferentiated blur (fig. **6.39**).

The Visual Characteristics of Lenses: Depth of Field and Focal Length

Lenses allow filmmakers to shape the space of the story (or, in an avant-garde film, the visual field in which images take shape). Different lenses have different visual characteristics. Understanding the focal properties of lenses helps viewers

6.38 *(left)* Deeper focus in *Elephant*: Elias's perspective.

6.39 *(right)* Selective focus in *Elephant*: Michelle's isolated perspective.

to assess the frame as a visual field that serves as an environment for the action, that creates the texture of another reality, or externalizes a character's feelings. Most important is the **depth of field**, or the "range of acceptable sharpness before and behind the plane of focus" (*American Cinematographer's Manual*, p. 161). Depth of field describes the space in front of and behind the primary subject where objects remain in crisp focus.

Lenses may be **normal**, **wide-angle**, or **telephoto**. Each of these different lenses produces a distinctive look because the **focal length** of a lens (the measurement, in millimeters, of the distance from the surface of the lens to the surface of the film in the camera) in large part determines depth of field (figs. **6.40**, **6.41**, **6.42**). Given the same aperture and focus distance, a lens with a longer focal length will produce a shallower depth of field than a lens with a shorter focal length.

The normal lens (focal length: 27 to 75 mm) approximates the vision and perspective of the human eye. No spatial distortions are apparent. The wide angle lens, sometimes called a short lens because it has a focal length of less than 27 mm, produces a wider angle of view than the human eye and exaggerates the frame's depth. Characters (or objects) in the foreground appear larger than they are, and characters (or objects) in the background appear smaller than they are. The viewer reads this discrepancy as enhanced depth: the distance between foreground and background appears greater than it actually is. Also, movement toward the camera appears faster than it is: a character will appear to make more rapid progress through the depth of the frame toward the camera than if a normal lens were used. This lens also accelerates the convergence of parallel lines so they appear to bend more than they do when seen through a normal lens (Zettl, p. 153). This is why figures positioned close to the camera appear to bulge outward.

In *Fear and Loathing in Las Vegas* (1998), Terry Gilliam makes frequent use of wide-angle lenses to convey the drugged-out frenzy of the main characters,

6.40 *(top left)* A shot taken with a normal lens.

6.41 *(top right)* Wide angle lens: note the exaggerated sense of depth and deep focus.

6.42 *(above)* Telephoto lens: note the compression (flattening) of depth and selective focus.

Photographs by Pfeiffer Photos.
Artwork by Thomas Sayre, Clearscapes "Gyre"
Permanent collection of the North Carolina Museum of Art.

6.43 *(left)* The distortion of depth and size in *Fear and Loathing in Las Vegas*: the gun in the foreground appears unusually large.

6.44 *(right)* A wide-angle lens produces the pronounced curvature of Depp's face in *Fear and Loathing in Las Vegas*.

Hunter S. Thompson (Johnny Depp) and Dr. Gonzo (Benicio del Toro). One shot illustrates two characteristics of the wide-angle lens: exaggerated depth and wide peripheral vision (fig. **6.43**). Another shot captures the way the wide-angle distorts straight lines by making them appear to bend: note the rounded, bulbous appearance of actor Johnny Depp's face (fig. **6.44**).

An **extreme wide-angle** or **fish-eye lens** (focal length less than 17.5 mm)

TECHNIQUES IN PRACTICE

Patterns of Camera Placement and Movement

In Spike Lee's *Do the Right Thing*, patterns of camera placement and movement establish relationships between the characters. Canted angles, close-ups, and tracking shots communicate the rising tensions among residents of a Brooklyn city block on a summer day.

Lee and DP Ernest Dickerson use canted angles to emphasize conflict between characters. Canted angles define the confrontation early in the day when Mothersister (Ruby Dee) yells at Da Mayor (Ossie Davis) from her window. The second time these characters interact, Jaye (Joie Lee) is combing Mothersister's hair on the stoop and Da Mayor walks by. Once again, canted angles are used for both Mothersister and Da Mayor, suggesting they are at odds. Their differences are also evident in their contentious dialogue.

A shift in the relationship between these two characters is partially sug-

6.45 A canted angle close-up emphasizes the tension in this scene from *Do the Right Thing*.

Chapter 6: Cinematography

gested by a shift in camera angle. Late in the day, after Da Mayor has saved a child from being hit by a car, Mothersister praises his heroism. During this conversation, low camera angles on both characters hint that they have called a truce. By the end of the film, they have become friends.

Canted angles and close-ups visually define disputes between other characters. When Radio Raheem (Bill Nunn) buys batteries for his boom box from the Korean grocers, canted angles and close-ups indicate Raheem's impatience at having to repeat himself. Canted angles also show the Korean grocers' anger toward his superior attitude. The first time Raheem enters Sal's pizzeria, canted angles and close-ups emphasize the two men's anger as Sal (Danny Aiello) bellows at Raheem to turn his music down (fig. **6.45**). In the final scene of confrontation, extreme close-ups combine with loud music and raised voices to help viewers recognize that anger is spiraling out of control.

In addition to canted angles and close-ups, Lee uses tracking shots. In a startling sequence, Lee films Mookie, Pino, a Latino gang leader, a police officer, and the Korean grocer as they face the camera directly and spout racial epithets. As each character expresses these sentiments, the camera tracks in toward the character, ending the shot in a close-up. At the conclusion of this vignette, the camera remains immobile as the love-preaching DJ, Mr. Señor Love Daddy (Samuel Jackson), rolls toward it (figs. **6.46**, **6.47**). He delivers a very different message, asking everyone to "cool out." In this sequence, the shift from the camera tracking in toward unmoving characters to Señor Love Daddy moving toward the stationary camera, visually underscores the DJ's attempt to reverse the unrelenting messages of hate.

6.46 *(above)* Señor Love Daddy starts to move toward the camera in *Do the Right Thing.*

6.47 *(below)* Señor Love Daddy closes in on the camera in *Do the Right Thing.*

dramatically distorts images so that most straight lines appear to be curved. In Darren Aronofsky's *Requiem for a Dream* (2000), a fish-eye lens depicts a scene in which three friends, Harry (Jared Leto), Marion (Jennifer Connelly), and Tyrone (Marlon Wayans), take drugs. The visual distortion mimics the effects of the drugs (fig. **6.48**).

Telephoto lenses, sometimes called long lenses because their focal lengths range from 75 mm to 1000 mm, compress the distance between objects at different distances from the lens; that is, the distance between foreground and background appears to be less than it actually is. These lenses appear to slow down the motion of an object or character toward the camera. The telephoto lens also inhibits the convergence of parallel lines, so they will not appear to curve (Zettl, p. 153).

A telephoto lens is used in *Run Lola Run* as Lola desperately sprints to save her boyfriend's life (fig. **6.49**). She is in focus, but people and objects in the foreground and background are not. This shallow depth of field isolates her, separating the in-focus element from background and foreground. The moment underscores Lola's solitary quest to save her boyfriend; she is on her own. It offers a contrast to scenes depicting Lola's frenetic run through the streets of Berlin. There, a wide-angle lens enhances her movement from the background to the foreground, emphasizing her speed (fig. **6.50**).

Rack focus is a change of focus from one plane of depth to another. In Lynne Ramsay's *Ratcatcher* (1999), James Gillespie (William Eadie) watches as a hearse carrying the corpse of his friend passes him. When the hearse is in the frame, the background remains in focus (fig. **6.51**). But when the hearse exits the frame, rack focusing brings the foreground where James sits into sharp relief (fig. **6.52**).

Rack focus can create a dramatic visual effect by overtly withholding and then revealing information about narrative space. Another cinematographic technique reveals excess information about narrative space: **split screen** cinematography combines two or more images into a single frame, giving audiences multiple perspectives. The musical documentary *Woodstock* (Michael Wadleigh 1970) employed split-screen cinematography to capture the epic scope of this massive music festival. At some points in the film, Wadleigh reveals the performances and the audience reaction in the same frame. At other points, the split

6.48 *(above)* A fish-eye lens distorts the sense of space in *Requiem for a Dream*.

6.49 *(center)* A telephoto lens used in *Run Lola Run*.

6.50 *(below)* A wide-angle used in *Run Lola Run*.

Chapter 6: Cinematography

screen captures huge swaths of people while also granting the audience access to more intimate encounters (fig. **6.53**). Celebrating the forty-year anniversary of the historic event, Ang Lee's fiction film *Taking Woodstock* (2009) also employed the split-screen, stirring up the indelible memory of Wadleigh's documentary (fig. **6.54**).

The Zoom Lens

Zoom lenses have a variable focal length. Zooming changes the size of the filmed subject without changing the distance between the subject and the camera. By rotating the barrel of the lens, cinematographers move from wide-angle to telephoto (**zooming in**, which magnifies the subject) or from telephoto to wide-angle (**zooming out**, which makes the subject appear smaller). When zooming in or out, the subject remains in focus. The opening of Francis Ford Coppola's *The Conversation* makes use of an extended zoom from a position and angle high above the action. In keeping with the film's theme of surveillance, the slow zoom in magnifies the people congregating in San Francisco's Union Square. The telephoto lens's shallow depth of field helps to produce selective focus, singling out the couple engaged in the conversation that Harry Caul (Gene Hackman) has been hired to record (figs. **6.55**, **6.56**, **6.57**).

Distinguishing between a zoom in and a tracking shot that moves toward the subject can be a challenge. Viewers should keep in mind that zooming in (moving from a wide angle to a telephoto) will minimize depth perception; instead of sensing the camera moving toward the subject, viewers might feel instead that

6.51 *(left)* In *Ratcatcher*, the shot begins with the background in focus.

6.52 *(right)* Rack focus brings the foreground into focus.

6.53 *(above)* A split-screen image from *Woodstock*.

6.54 *(below)* Ang Lee pays homage to Woodstock's famous split-screen cinematography in *Taking Woodstock*.

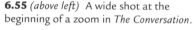

the subject is pulled toward the camera. Sometimes during a zoom in, objects in the foreground at the edge of the frame stay in place for much of the shot while objects in the distance get closer. This is a telltale sign that the camera isn't actually moving.

Combining Camera Movement and Lens Movement

Filmmakers sometimes combine camera movement and the zoom lens to create unusual shots. In *Vertigo*, Hitchcock created the **trombone shot**. Initially, the camera was trained on a model of a stairwell, with the zoom fully in so that the stairwell filled the frame. The camera tracked in toward the model as the lens zoomed out (figs. **6.58**, **6.59**). This combination produces an unsettling physical effect because the stairwell remains the same size (tracking toward it would make it larger, but zooming out counteracts the track), but the apparent depth of the stairs increases (the zoom-out increases the depth of field).

This dramatic shot translates a character's visceral, uncomfortable sensations to the viewer. The effect simulates panicky feelings of acrophobia (fear of heights) felt by Scottie Ferguson (James Stewart).

6.55 *(above left)* A wide shot at the beginning of a zoom in *The Conversation*.

6.56 *(above right)* A closer shot, later in the zoom in *The Conversation*.

6.57 *(center)* A telephoto shot picks out the couple talking in *The Conversation*. Note the diminished depth and selective focus.

6.58 *(below left)* The beginning of the trombone shot from *Vertigo*.

6.59 *(below right)* In the second part of the shot, the floor appears to fall away.

6.60 *(left)* A diffusion filter creates a romantic atmosphere in *The Sound of Music*.

6.61 *(center)* *Moulin Rouge* uses Technicolor, along with filters and smoke, to suggest a Toulouse-Lautrec painting.

6.62 *(below)* A painting by Toulouse-Lautrec—John Huston's visual source for his Technicolor musical.

Through the Lens: Filters and Diffusers

Filters change the quality of light entering the lens by absorbing light in different ways. They affect contrast, sharpness, color, and light intensity. **Neutral-density filters** absorb all wavelengths and permit less light overall to strike the film stock. **Polarizing filters** increase color saturation and contrast in outdoor shots.

Diffusion filters "bend" the light coming into the lens, blurring the image. Mesh, netting, and gauze (silk fabric), when placed over the lens, act as crude diffusion filters and reduce sharpness. These devices enhance the appearance of the human face (wrinkles and blemishes disappear). This is why filmmakers turn so readily to the diffusion filter to shoot love scenes. As the image from *The Sound of Music* demonstrates (fig. **6.60**), the diffusion filter softens the image and creates a dreamy, romantic look.

Fog filters have a glass surface with numerous etched spots that refract light, so they create the appearance of water droplets in the air. An image also can be "fogged" by applying substances such as petroleum jelly to a clear filter in front of the lens. **Star filters** create points of light that streak outward from a light source.

Color filters absorb certain wavelengths but leave others unaffected. On black-and-white film, color filters provide contrast control; they can lighten or darken tones. On color film, they can produce a range of effects. For *Moulin Rouge* (1952), director John Huston hired the still photographer Eliot Elisofon as a special color consultant. He and cinematographer Oswald Morris designed a system of shooting through fog filters, smoke, and colored lights to evoke the visual style of a painting by Henri Toulouse-Lautrec, the subject of the film (fig. **6.61**, **6.62**).

Day for night refers to the practice of shooting during the day but using filters and underexposure to create the illusion of nighttime. French cinema theorists call the technique *nuit Américain* (or "American night"). Day-for-night shooting is generally more successful on black-and-white film, using red or yellow filters to darken the blue sky. Still, contemporary filmmakers shooting on color film stock occasionally find the need to shoot day for night. While shooting *Pan's Labyrinth*'s exterior scenes on location, cinematographer Guillermo Navarro couldn't run electricity to light the forest after dark. Instead, he shot in daylight and underexposed his film. To create the effect of moonlight, he used reflectors to bounce sunlight off the leaves "so that when the sun hit the greens in the forest, they would pop" (quoted in Calhoun).

DEEP FOCUS CINEMATOGRAPHY

In the late 1930s, "fast" lenses and advances in lighting technology helped cinematographers such as Gregg Toland to perfect **deep-focus cinematography**, in which objects remain in focus from positions very near the camera to points at some distance from it. Working with William Wyler on films such as *Dead End* (1937) and *Wuthering Heights* (1939), Toland experimented with the techniques that later became well known as a result of his collaboration with Orson Welles on *Citizen Kane*. Toland used wide-angle lenses and stopped down the lens, making the aperture smaller to produce greater precision in focus. These wide-angle lenses, treated with a new anti-glare coating, were only one aspect of Toland's achievement however. He also used the fastest film stock available, Kodak XX, and employed large arc lamps that had been designed for shooting Technicolor. These lamps cast a more penetrating illumination needed to light the set with the lens aperture stopped down. Wyler, Welles, Jean Renoir, and John Ford, directors who choreographed actors and arranged sets with several planes of depth, are said to **compose in depth**. These directors accentuate the way the film frame can embody several levels of meaning.

When Orson Welles composes in depth, he creates spatial motifs. In *Citizen Kane*, Kane is routinely positioned between other people, who make decisions for him, as in the Colorado boarding house scene discussed in Chapter 4. But Kane also frequently occupies the background. In the scene where he signs over the management of his financial interests to Mr. Thatcher, Kane stands between Thatcher and Bernstein (Everett Sloane). Kane also stands near the back wall of the room (fig. **6.63**). His moving forward to sit at the table with the two men and sign the documents signals that he becomes resigned to his fate. Welles choreographs this scene in three dimensions; at first, Kane is trapped between his financial advisers, yet he also distances himself from their values. He moves forward in this scene, as in several others, to assert himself, although the outcome may be self-defeating. The complexity of the scene—and Welles's ability to develop this spatial motif—is crucially dependent upon Toland's mastery of deep-focus cinematography.

6.63 Deep focus keeps Kane visible in the background in *Citizen Kane*.

Film Stock

Another key factor that will influence the final look of the film is the choice of film stock, which will affect the color and depth of contrast of the images produced. Experienced cinematographers come to depend upon particular film stocks to help create the look of a film. As increasing numbers of filmmakers make the move to digital cinematography—in part because film is costly, cumbersome, and introduces delays and uncertainty as the film must be processed before the images can be deemed acceptable—the more important decision becomes which camera to use. Digital cameras are equipped with different types of CCDs (see p. 132); they differ in their response to light and, thus, produce different types of images.

Characteristics of Film Stock

Film stock is composed of two parts: the **emulsion**, a light-sensitive chemical layer in which the image is formed, and the **base**, the flexible support material for the emulsion. The base for the earliest films was cellulose nitrate, a highly flammable substance that was replaced in the 1950s by cellulose triacetate.

The attributes of film stock include gauge, speed, and grain. **Gauge** refers to the size of the film, measured horizontally across the film stock (fig. **6.68**). Standard feature films are projected on 35 mm film. This has an image area four times that of 16 mm film, which has traditionally been the province of documentary, experimental, and independent filmmakers because 16 mm offers lighter cameras and less expensive processing. Super 8 and Regular 8 film, developed in the 1950s, were used primarily for home movies. Since the advent of inexpensive digital video cameras, Super 8 is now the medium of choice only for experimental filmmakers.

TECHNIQUES IN PRACTICE

Lenses and the Creation of Space

Stanley Kubrick's *Paths of Glory* (1957) and Robert Altman's *M*A*S*H* (1970) chronicle human experiences of war, yet the two filmmakers adopt very different approaches to this subject. One technical feature that offers insight into their differences is the choice of lens. Kubrick uses a wide-angle lens and composes in depth to emphasize the hierarchical structure of the army and its vast reach. In contrast, Altman uses a telephoto lens and frequent zooms to emphasize the chaotic aspects of a military organization.

Paths of Glory concerns three French soldiers during World War I who are charged with cowardice, court-martialed, and executed by a firing squad. Kubrick and cinematographer George Krause frequently employ a wide-angle lens to depict the hypocritical and power-hungry officers as well as the powerless foot soldiers ordered to fight a losing battle. The wide-angle lens and composition in depth not only convey the different experiences of officers and soldiers, but also suggest what binds them together: the highly

6.64 Deep focus cinematography in *Paths of Glory* emphasizes the formal, ornate setting.

ordered military system.

The film's opening scene depicts several lines of soldiers marching around the grounds of the stately château that serves as the headquarters of General Mireau (George Macready). The wide-angle lens takes in the vast open space around the château. Because many planes of depth are in focus, the scene highlights the linear pattern formed by marching soldiers. This scene presents the first instance of a motif: lines of men whose lives are controlled by others. The calm, ordered emptiness of the space suggests the distance of the headquarters from the deadly trenches where the war is being fought.

The wide-angle lens also shapes the viewer's sense of the château's interior. As General Broulard (Adolphe Menjou) manipulates the ambitious Mireau into ordering an assault on a well-defended German position, the men occupy a room decorated with exquisite antiques and works of art. The details of the room are clear because the lens allows many planes to remain in focus at the same time (fig. **6.64**). In this scene, Mireau claims that he feels a sense of responsibility for the lives of 8,000 men, but agrees to order the attack after Broulard makes it clear he will earn a promotion if he succeeds. The elegant setting contrasts with the brutal deaths that will result from their plans and establishes the generals' hypocrisy.

The next scene takes place in the trenches, a space that is the polar opposite of the château. The trenches are long, snaking pits cluttered with equipment and lined with soldiers. What little sky is visible above is hazy with the dust and debris from artillery fire. This cramped space is very different from the château, yet the wide-angle lens is equally effective at presenting its characteristics. The motif of powerless men standing in line reappears as General Mireau marches through the trenches on his way to see Colonel Dax (Kirk Douglas) to order the attack (fig. **6.65**). As the pompous Mireau strides through the trenches (accompanied by a martial drumbeat), the lens enhances the General's vigorous movement forward. This movement contrasts with that of the soldiers he talks to along the way; they are exhausted and stand still.

When Colonel Dax orders his men into battle, a wide-angle lens and slow tracking shot depict the trenches as an unending series of maze-like passages crowded with men. Once again, the leader moves past men who stand still. However, Dax and Mireau are very different military leaders. Dax actually leads his men into "no man's land" between the French and German barbed wire. The futile attack on the German Ant Hill, however, results in the death of many soldiers.

After the failed attack, Colonel Dax valiantly attempts to save the lives of three soldiers in his unit who are accused of deserting. He defends them at their trial, held in a room similar to the room where Mireau and Broulard meet: it is enormous, very bright, and full of open space. The trial is arranged in a very orderly way, with the defense and prosecution on either side of the judges. The deep space and symmetrical composition reinforce the hierarchical military power structure and the entrapment of the ordinary man within that system. As each accused man steps forward to testify, Kubrick positions him very close to the camera (fig. **6.66**). The guards in the background aren't in sharp focus, yet the enhanced sense of depth makes it clear that Kubrick once again uses a wide angle lens in these shots. The spatial distortion singles out each defendant as an individual, yet each one is also overwhelmed by the rigidly ordered environment. Because they occupy the lowest position in the hierarchy, the ordinary soldiers are doomed to die as pawns in the game played by the generals, who plot strategy from the safety of the villa.

6.65 (*above*) A tracking shot through the trenches in *Paths of Glory*.

6.66 (*below*) A wide angle lens isolates a soldier on trial in *Paths of Glory*.

Robert Altman and cinematographer Harold Stine adopt a very different approach in their Korean war comedy *M*∗*A*∗*S*∗*H*, using telephoto and zoom lenses to create a sense of decentralization and chaos. The use of the zoom lens suggests that the army hospital unit is composed of numerous eccentric individuals and that no structure or hierarchy exists to control them. The telephoto lens also allows Altman to depict the intimacy among the characters, amidst the confusion of the hospital environment.

The zoom lens frequently singles out the one emblem of a central authority in the film: the camp's public broadcast system. Yet zooms into the loudspeakers turn out to be ironic. The supposedly important messages are retracted, corrected, or make no sense. For example, the loudspeaker announces that all personnel must provide urine samples, then states that no one must do so.

During the opening credits, repeated zooms isolate injured soldiers carried to 4077th Mobile Army Surgical Hospital by helicopters. The zooms permit the viewer a brief medium shot or close-up of each wounded man before he is whisked away to the hospital, then the camera zooms out and moves on to another wounded soldier. The zooms establish the way war threatens to dehumanize soldiers and the doctors. The quick, intrusive zooms act as a metaphor for the treatment of the wounded men. The doctors attend to their injuries, usually by cutting into their bodies and then sewing them up. Rarely do doctors and patients interact on a personal level because the soldiers who survive are sent home or back into combat.

The telephoto lens, however, allows Altman to suggest the distinctive individuality and diversity of the doctors and nurses. In typical Altman style, the cast works as an ensemble. Although Hawkeye Pierce (Donald Sutherland), Duke (Tom Skerritt), and Trapper John (Elliott Gould) occupy center stage, the audience also becomes familiar with a number of minor characters, such as "Painless" (John Shuck), Lieutenant "Dish" (Jo Ann Pflug), and

6.67 Henry and Painless are physically trapped by the helicopter in *M*A*S*H*.

"Radar" (Gary Burghoff). The telephoto lens singles characters out through tight close-ups.

The reliance on close-ups adds to the film's sense of decentralization and lack of hierarchy. Visually the film presents a world without an overarching organization. Aside from the early aerial shot of Duke and Hawkeye driving toward the camp, there are no long shots that establish the overall geography of the hospital. Instead, medium shots and close-ups present a disorganized shanty town. Through close-ups, space is broken down into small units that don't add up to a coherent whole. One scene depicts Henry Blake (Roger Bowen) and Painless (John Shuck) as they stand behind a helicopter: they can be viewed through the scaffolding of the helicopter's tail, which dominates the foreground (fig. **6.67**). Altman places visual impediments between the viewers and the actors, who are generally the focus of audience attention, to emphasize the way the space is divided and confusing. The telephoto lens compresses the distance between characters and the objects that share their space, subtly creating a sense of claustrophobia and entrapment.

These two directors and their cinematographers convey ideas and emotions visually through the choice of lenses. The wide-angle lens and compositions in depth in *Paths of Glory* heighten the contrast between generals, who are in control, and foot soldiers, who are at the mercy of the system. The zooms and telephoto lens in *M*A*S*H* suggest a lack of order and the difficulty of making connections in a chaotic, decentralized, and claustrophobic environment.

CINEMATOGRAPHY ON THE SET

For most films, the DP collaborates with the director and art director before and during principal photography to think systematically about creating expressive visual images. Prior to the production phase, the director and DP confer about camera angles and effects, using the script to map out the specific set-up for each shot. Often, they create storyboards, with drawings, photographs, or computer simulations. During principal photography, the DP is responsible for all aspects of the photographic process, including camera placement, movement, and lighting set-ups. The crew includes: the camera operator, responsible for the operation and maintenance of the camera; the focus puller, who measures, marks, and moves the focus ring on the camera lens; and an assistant camera operator, who records the details of shots; the **gaffer**, the chief electrician, the **best boy**, and assistant electricians are responsible for the lighting equipment.

A **second unit** may be used for filming at a remote location, or for **insert** shots. Directors shooting on film use a **video-assist**, a video monitor that records the action and allows them to see what the shot looks like on screen. The film footage exposed in a given day is often printed, and **dailies** are screened to determine whether changes are necessary. Digital cinematography offers one major advantage over film during shooting: directors and DPs can view footage immediately, saving time and money.

While the DP's job theoretically is complete at the end of shooting, often she will work with the editor during post-production to ensure that the desired look is achieved. Now that visual effects are contracted out to special effects companies, such as Double Negative, the visual effects supervisor often acts as a liaison between the director and DP and the company producing visual effects.

6.68 Different gauges of film: 8 mm, 16 mm, 35 mm, 70 mm (65 mm with soundtrack).

Speed is a measure of a film stock's sensitivity to light and is measured by an index called the ASA or DIN number. The higher the ASA or DIN number, the greater the film's sensitivity to light, and the "faster" the film. **Fast** film stocks require less light to produce an acceptable image. Thus, a fast film stock works well under conditions of low light. A documentary filmmaker who cannot control lighting conditions on the shoot might use fast film to make sure the images will register. Fast stocks, however, are prone to producing grainy images. **Slow** film stocks are relatively insensitive to light but produce high-quality images under optimal lighting conditions. If a filmmaker can exercise a great deal of control over the light, as is the case on a studio set, then slow film renders the sharp, fine-grained images associated with the high **production values** of commercial Hollywood films.

The **grain** refers to the suspended particles of silver or color-sensitive grains in the emulsion layer. After processing, the grains may become visible as dots. Finer-grained, slow film stock records more detail and renders sharp images with high resolution. Grainy film, with its lower resolution and fuzzier images, is typically associated with black-and-white **newsreel** and documentary films. But feature filmmakers may deliberately produce grainy images to create a documentary feel, as Welles does in the newsreel that opens *Citizen Kane*, as Woody Allen does in *Zelig* (1983), and as Robert Zemeckis does in *Forrest Gump* (1994).

6.69 Overexposure produces glaring light in *Insomnia*.

Light and Exposure

Exposure refers to the amount of light striking the emulsion layer of the film stock. When the **shutter** of the camera opens, light passes through the aperture and strikes the film. The aperture size can be varied to let in a greater or smaller amount of light.

"Appropriate" exposure captures sufficient detail in both bright and dark areas of the frame. **Overexposure** occurs when more light than is required to produce an image strikes the film stock; the resulting image is noticeable for its high contrast, glaring light, and washed-out shadows (fig. **6.69**). Erik Skjoldbjærg's *Insomnia* (1997) demonstrates the aesthetic impact of overexposure. The thriller is set in Norway during the summer, and follows police detective Jonas Engström (Stellan Skarsgård) as he juggles three challenges: trying to solve the case of a murdered teenage girl, covering up his accidental shooting of his partner, and his bout of insomnia. The film's harsh, glaring light suggests the hallucinatory effect of sleeplessness during the season when the sun never seems to set. **Underexposure** occurs when too little light strikes the emulsion. Dark areas in an underexposed image will appear very dense, and overall contrast will be less than a properly exposed image (fig. **6.70**).

6.70 Underexposure produces a dense, dark effect in *Psycho*.

Film Stock and Color

Directors and cinematographers choose their film stock according to the aesthetic effects they are seeking to achieve. Occasionally black-and-white and color film stock may be used in the same film, to contrast between past and present, perhaps, or between reality and fantasy. In *The Wizard of Oz*, black-and-white film depicts depression-era Kansas whereas Technicolor film characterizes the fantasy world of Oz. In *A Matter of Life and Death* (also known as *Stairway to Heaven*; Michael Powell and Emeric Pressburger 1946), Heaven appears in black-and-white and Earth in color (figs. **6.71**, **6.72**).

Filmmaking has always involved color, even before the development of color film stock. The black-and-white one-reelers of French film pioneer Georges Méliès and Pathé Frères were hand-painted (fig. **6.73**), a painstaking and expensive process of painting sections of each frame with one or more colors (Sklar, p. 41). By around 1910, most films used color. The most prevalent technique was **tinting**, which involved bathing lengths of developed film (typically one scene at a time) in dye. Conventions developed so that blue was used for night scenes, amber for candle-lit interiors, and magenta for scenes of romance. By the 1920s, more than 80 percent of film prints were tinted (Salt, p. 150), including D.W. Griffith's *The Birth of a Nation* (1915), Wiene's *The Cabinet of Dr. Caligari* (fig. **6.74**), and Murnau's *Nosferatu*. Another practice, called **toning**, replaced silver halide with colored metal salts so that the dark portions of the frame

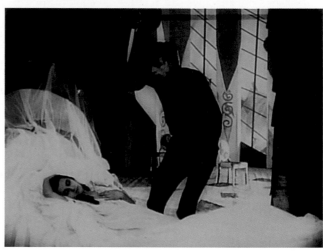

6.71 *(above left)* Earth appears in color in *A Matter of Life and Death*.

6.72 *(above right)* Heaven appears in black-and-white in *A Matter of Life and Death*.

6.73 *(below left)* A hand-painted scene from *The Life of Christ*.

6.74 *(below right)* An example of tinting from *The Cabinet of Dr. Caligari*.

appear in color rather than black. Mordanting involved developing the emulsion with a silver solution able to fix colored dyes (Usai, p. 9).

Even unadulterated black-and-white images vary in their tonal properties. First, black-and-white film stocks possess different properties: the earliest stocks were sensitive to blue and violet only. **Orthochromatic** film—sensitive to blue, violet, and green—was developed in the 1920s. Because it did not register the red tones of human faces, actors were required to wear heavy theatrical makeup. Black-and-white film stocks that were sensitive to all colors of the spectrum (called **panchromatic**) became the industry standard in the 1930s.

Second, filmmakers make different use of the same technologies. When Eastman Kodak and Agfa manufactured faster film stocks in the 1930s, movie studios responded to them differently, which resulted in distinctive visual styles. MGM overexposed the film, and then pulled (underdeveloped) the negative, creating a pearly gray look (fig. **6.75**). But at Twentieth Century Fox, the use of faster film meant DPs could stop down the lens (making the aperture smaller), increasing depth of field and contributing to deep-focus cinematography (Salt, p. 196). Fox thus became known for the clarity of its images (fig. **6.76**).

Although color film processes were developed in the 1930s, it wasn't until after World War II that color film developed into an industry standard. Color cinematography was a commercial and aesthetic enterprise: it was one way U.S. movie studios could compete with television, a black-and-white medium which, in the early 1950s, cost the film industry 500,000 tickets per week (Segrave, p. 5). Studios marketed their spectacles with the phrase "Glorious Technicolor." Between 1947 and 1954, the number of American films made in color rose from one in ten to one in two. By 1979, 96 percent of American films were made in color (Cook, pp. 462–3).

In 1922 the Technicolor Corporation developed a two-strip additive process. Two strips of negative film were exposed (using a beam splitter in the camera), printed separately on a red and a green layer of film stock, and cemented together for projection. The process was plagued by several problems: during screenings the cement melted under the high-intensity heat generated by projector lamps. Furthermore, the colors tended to fade to orange over time.

In 1928, Technicolor perfected a dye transfer process called imbibition printing, which became the basis for its three-color dye transfer process, the industry standard from 1935 until the mid-1950s. The process used three strips of negative film from which separate color matrices were made; then the color images were transferred onto a single print. The strengths of Technicolor were vibrant and stable colors that aged well. But Technicolor's *de facto* monopoly and the fact that the process used three times as much film stock as black-and-white cinematography meant that color films were costly to make. Film studios had to rent special equipment, use Technicolor labs to process the film, and pay for expertise directly from the Technicolor Corporation, in the form of **color consultants** to oversee the **color timing** (shot-to-shot color correction).

The development of Eastmancolor contributed to the widespread adoption of color cinematography. Eastmancolor uses a multilayered film stock. Each of the three layers of emulsion contains **dye couplers** sensitive to a different color: red, blue, and green. When developed, the grains to which the dyes have been coupled release the dye. This method produces sharper prints than the Technicolor process, but its colors are less saturated. The process became popular because film studios could use standard film cameras and process the film in their own labs, saving money. But the widespread use of Eastmancolor produced hidden, long-term costs. Prints made before 1983 are notorious for their unstable color; restoring these faded prints requires resources and technical expertise.

Color—as an element of *mise en scène* and cinematography—allows directors

6.75 *(above)* The characteristic pearly appearance of MGM films: *Queen Christina* (Rouben Mamoulian 1933).

6.76 *(below)* Twentieth Century Fox films from the 1930s were known for the clarity of the images: *Slave Ship* (Tay Garnett 1937).

6.77 *(above)* Saturated brown colors evoke an era in *The Godfather*.

6.78 *(below)* Harsh light and high contrast in *Salaam Bombay!*

to express ideas, themes, and mood. When cinematographers choose to shoot on color stock, they choose from a wide range of options. One factor that helps filmmakers decide from among these options is color quality; because the emulsion on different brands and types of film stocks varies, so does the color. Guillermo Navarro used three different types of Kodak film stock while shooting *Pan's Labyrinth*. The lyrical use of color in films from every cinematic tradition—from Coppola's *The Godfather* to Mira Nair's *Salaam Bombay!* (1988), from Jacques Demy's *The Umbrellas of Cherbourg* ("*Les parapluies de Cherbourg*"; 1964) to Zach Braff's *Garden State* (2004), and from Jason Reitman's *Juno* (2007) to Kurosawa's *Dreams* ("*Yume*"; 1990)—attests to the fact that color cinematography opened up an entirely new creative aspect of cinema (figs. **6.77**, **6.78**, **6.79**, **6.80**, **6.81**, **6.82**).

When analyzing the use of color in a film, attend to the specific ways color is used in relation to narrative, visual, and sound elements. Some questions to consider include:

- Are there strong areas of color or pronounced contrasts in the frame that demand attention?
- Are tones uniformly saturated or desaturated, producing a vibrant or somber mood? If so, do they act as complement or as counterpoint to the action?
- What are the effects of the *relative* saturation and warmth/coolness of colors in the *mise en scène*?
- Are color motifs developed, perhaps through *mise en scène* and/or cinematography techniques such as pushing, pulling, or flashing (see p. 171)?
- Do colors bear a particular cultural significance? Be sure to test initial associations against the full complement of elements at work in any film and to conduct research to make sure the cultural as well as narrative context is taken into account. Do not assume, for example, that red equals danger in every situation.

6.79 In *Juno*, primary colors capture adolescence: torn between childhood and adulthood.

6.80 An ashen gray is used for the apocalypse sequence in *Dreams*.

6.81 *(right)* Bright, otherworldly colors have a romantic effect in *The Umbrellas of Cherbourg*.

6.82 *(below)* Desaturated colors suggest alienation in *Garden State*.

Wide Film and Widescreen Formats

During the 1950s, U.S. movie studios developed **widescreen formats** as part of their campaign to compete with the popular new medium of television. These formats widened the traditional **aspect ratio** (a measure of the horizontal to the vertical dimension of the image) from the **Academy ratio** of 1.33:1 (also that of traditional television) to 1.85:1 or 2.35:1 (fig. **6.83**). Currently, U.S. movie theaters project films in those latter two aspect ratios. The aspect ratio for HDTV is 1.78:1 (also referred to as 16:9).

CinemaScope and Panavision use **anamorphic lens** attachments to create an aspect ratio of 2.35:1 with standard 35 mm film, cameras, and projectors. The anamorphic lens squeezes the image at a ratio of 2:1 horizontally onto a standard film frame. If the film were projected "as is," the image would look stretched from top to bottom and actors would look extremely tall and thin, but using anamorphic lenses on projectors unsqueezes the image (fig. **6.84 B**, **C**, and **D**). The first CinemaScope release was Twentieth Century Fox's *The Robe* (Henry Koster 1953).

Other widescreen processes involve changes in both cameras and film stock. **Cinerama** uses three cameras, three projectors, and a wide, curved screen. Viewers sitting in the "sweet spot" (in the center of the first ten rows) feel immersed in the image, which reaches past their peripheral vision on either side (fig. **6.85**). The technique was both novel and expensive; only a few films were made in the format, including *This is Cinerama* (Merian Cooper and Gunther von Fritsch 1952) and *How the West Was Won* (Henry Hathaway, John Ford, and George Marshall 1962).

One method for producing a wide screen image without using special lenses or equipment is **masking**. Cinematographers shoot a film using standard film stock at an aspect ratio of 1.33:1, but block out the top and bottom of the frame to achieve an aspect ratio of 1.85:1. Masking during shooting is rare because it is expensive to modify the camera, and this procedure sacrifices 36 percent of the image.

Wide film formats use a larger film stock than standard 35 mm stock. IMAX, Omnivax, and Showscan are shot on 70 mm film. The IMAX format grew in popularity the 1980s, particularly for nature documentaries. In this system, 65 mm film is run horizontally through the camera; its negative measures 70 mm × 49 mm (2.75 in × 1.90 in), which creates high-resolution images.

Vista Vision was an alternative to Cinemascope developed by Alfred Hitchcock that used standard 35 mm film stock but changed the orientation of the film so that the film moves through the camera horizontally instead of vertically. The larger image is of higher quality than standard processes. Abandoned in the 1940s, Vista Vision was resurrected for special effects work on *Star Wars*.

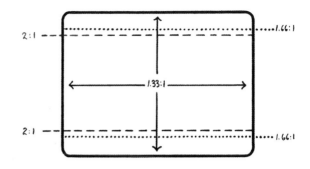

6.83 *(above)* A comparison of aspect ratios: Academy, 1.66:1, and 2:1.

6.84 *(below)* A squeezed image, created with an anamorphic lens.

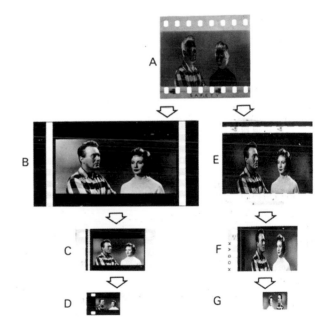

Stereoscopic 3D: Then and Now

The premise behind filmmaking in 3D (also called stereoscopic or S3D to distinguish it from 3D computer animation) is a very simple principle: humans see the world in three dimensions because of stereoscopic vision. Our two eyes, with their slightly different positioning, provide different visual information to the brain, which processes the discrepancy as depth.

Filmmakers have attempted to exploit opportunities for translating stereoscopic vision into 3D images since the 19th century. The first documented screening of a feature length 3D film was in 1922; according to *Moving Picture World* reviewer W.E. Keefe, *The Power of Love* was a six reel drama presented

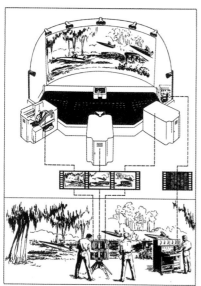

6.85 The Cinerama system.

"in full stereoscopic relief" to an audience at the Ambassador Hotel in Los Angeles (Keefe). Like movie audiences in the decades to come, those in attendance donned spectacles that held one blue and one red lens, known as anaglyph glasses.

The anaglyph method requires that in production, two film cameras shoot two completely different strips of film, one using a red color filter and the other cyan (blue-green). The two strips of film are projected together, with a slight offset. When screening the film, audience members wear the dual colored anaglyph glasses so that the red lens allows only the red part of the anaglyph image through to that eye, while the blue lens allows only the blue/green parts of the image through to the other eye. The brain interprets the differences in the images as distance, creating the perception of depth. Although this technology is closely associated with the decade of the 1950s, anaglyph 3D is still being used. In recent years, both *Spy Kids 3D: Game Over* (Robert Rodriguez 2003) and *Hannah Montana & Miley Cyrus: Best of Both Worlds Concert* (2008), were released on Blu-ray and DVD using red-cyan anaglyph technology.

Another 3D technology makes use of polarizing filters rather than color filters. Polarized lenses filter out light according to its direction rather than its color. When these 3D films are projected, viewers wear polarized lenses, which are grey in hue, like sunglasses. Like the anaglyphic system, the polarization of one lens permits only one image to enter that eye and cancels out the image viewed through the other eye, and vice versa.

In contrast to earlier 3D technologies, RealD Cinema, the most popular 3D format, uses circular rather than linear polarization. The two images are polarized in clockwise and counterclockwise directions, rather than in vertical and horizontal directions. RealD requires only one projector, which alternately projects right and left eye images. Read D Cinema was used for *Beowulf*, *My Bloody Valentine 3D* (Patrick Lussier 2009), *Coraline* (Henry Selick 2009), *Avatar*, *Alice in Wonderland*, and *Clash of the Titans* (Louis Leterrier 2010).

The 3D innovation widely credited to James Cameron and his DP Vince Pace on *Avatar* was the creation of a mobile stereoscopic camera outfit that used a computer to drive two lenses able to optically converge on objects as the angle of each lens changed independently. Using a beam splitter (a prism or mirror that splits a beam of light) rather than parallel cameras allowed Pace to reduce the distance between the focal points on the two lenses, better approximating the way human eyes work.

Despite the much-touted engineering advances the system represented, both Cameron and producer Jon Landau claim that these techniques were not designed to attract attention to themselves, but, instead, to involve viewers in the action to a much greater degree. "We see in depth all the time," Cameron

Chapter 6: Cinematography

remarked in an interview, "we kind of forget that we're wearing perpetual 3D glasses. So the movie works that way; you're just watching in 3D, just like real life" ("The Evolution of 3D").

Processing Film Stock

Once a film stock has been chosen and exposed, cinematographers can achieve unusual visual effects by making choices about processing methods. A number of specific techniques have been developed.

Scratching involves scraping the surface of the film to achieve the look of a home movie. Martin Scorsese's *Mean Streets* (1973) includes one of the characters' home movies, which the director shot and then scratched after processing. Quentin Tarantino scratched the negative for his contribution to *Grindhouse* (2007) to establish its B-movie credentials. Some avant-garde filmmakers scratch films to create patterns or to remind viewers of the material basis of the medium. Stan Brakhage scratched his name into film stock, signing his films the way painters do, only with motion.

Pushing a film (also known as overdevelopment) means allowing it a longer time in development, which increases contrast and density. **Pulling** a film negative (underdevelopment) reduces contrast. **Forced development** is a technique used when lighting levels are inadequate for normal exposures. Cinematographers deliberately underexpose the film and then overdevelop, or push, the film. This procedure affects contrast but not color.

Pre-fogging or **flashing** the negative desaturates color. Before, during, or after shooting, the film stock is exposed to a small amount of light, resulting in an image with reduced contrast. This technique was used for Altman's *McCabe and Mrs. Miller*, a film set at the turn of the twentieth century, to create the visual effect of an old photograph (see fig. **6.101**).

Bleach bypass printing is a process that involves leaving the silver grains in the emulsion layer rather than bleaching them out. This has the effect of desaturating the color because it is akin to adding a layer of black-and-white to a color negative. Steven Spielberg used bleach bypass in *Saving Private Ryan* (1998), where scenes of soldiers in combat during World War II are rendered in pale hues with silvery overtones. The desaturation of the color, combined with the khaki and brown palette of the settings and uniforms, recalls the sepia tones that are used in historical photographs and thus contributes to the film's emphasis on memory (fig. **6.86**).

6.86 Bleach bypass produces desaturated color in *Saving Private Ryan*.

Special Visual Effects

Although they are often associated with sci-fi or action films, special **visual effects** have been part of the film experience since the beginning of cinema and are used in all kinds of films. The earliest films, including Georges Méliès's

6.87 Some of the special effects journals and magazines available today.

A Trip to the Moon ("*Le voyage dans la lune*"; 1902) and Edwin Porter's *The Great Train Robbery* (1903) and *Dream of a Rarebit Fiend* (1906; see fig. 8.3), took advantage of the available technologies of multiple exposures, time-lapse photography, and hand painting to make moon-dwelling creatures appear and disappear or to enhance the impact of a safe full of cash that explodes during a train robbery. Special visual effects encompass painting, model building, prosthetics, photography, and computer graphics. In industry parlance, special (or mechanical) effects are created during production while visual effects (also called optical effects) are created in **post-production**, but the terms are often used interchangeably.

This section of the chapter presents commonly used visual effects and looks at how they are achieved and why they might be used. Digital visual effects are created with software programs, and practitioners in the field are constantly developing and perfecting new effects with every film project, so any discussion of techniques becomes out of date very quickly. The publications below explain traditional visual effects and track new developments:

> *American Cinematographer*
> *Cinefantastique*
> *Cinefex*
> *Digital Cinematography*
> *SMPTE Journal* (Society of Motion Picture and Television Engineers)
> *VFX World Magazine*

Describing these effects clearly and concisely, and addressing the way they support the narrative system, contributes to a thorough film analysis.

Manipulating the Image on the Set

Many visual effects are employed during principal photography to create optical illusions, including models, photo cutouts, makeup, prosthetics, front and rear projection, and matte paintings.

Models and miniatures are built for a variety of reasons: to create an object that does not exist—such as the ship in *Close Encounters of the Third Kind* (Steven Spielberg 1977)—or to destroy an object that does—such as the Capitol building in *Earth vs. the Flying Saucers* (Fred Sears, 1956; fig. **6.88**). Various models of the Titanic were built to recreate the historic vessel for James Cameron's *Titanic*: including a 1/20th-scale miniature, used for long shots, and a large-scale replica, used for tighter shots with actors on deck (fig. **6.89**).

6.88 *(above)* The Capitol under attack in *Earth vs. the Flying Saucers*.
6.89 *(below)* *Titanic* used a large-scale replica of the famous ship.

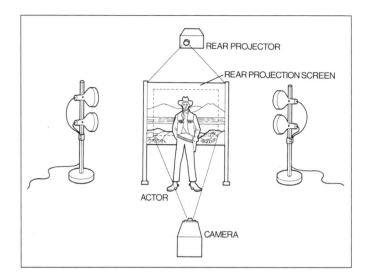

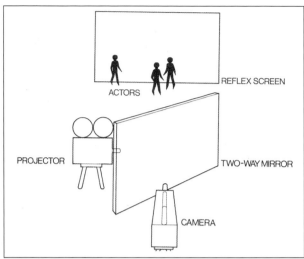

6.90 *(above left, right)* Rear and front projection systems.

6.91 *(below left)* Rear projection provides the background in *Marnie*.

6.92 *(below right)* Front projection in the ape sequence from *2001: A Space Odyssey*.

Common methods for projecting a background behind live actors during shooting are photo cutouts, and front and rear projection (fig. **6.90**). **Rear projection** (left) requires a projector to be placed behind a screen, onto which it projects an image. Actors stand in front of the screen and the camera records them in front of the projected background (fig. **6.91**). **Front projection** (see fig. 6.90, right) uses a half-silvered mirror in front of the camera. A projector aimed at the mirror projects the background, which the camera records as being projected behind the actors (fig. **6.92**).

Matte paintings are painted backdrops, typically used in establishing shots to convey a location. They are also used to extend the setting beyond the boundaries of the built set. They often incorporate optical illusions, such as forced perspective, in order to produce the appropriate sense of depth and atmosphere. Because they remain on screen for several seconds, they must be carefully planned.

Glass shots are a type of matte shot, created by positioning a pane of optically flawless glass with a painting on it between the camera and scene to be photographed. This combines the painting on the glass with the set or location—seen through the glass—behind it.

Traditional matte painting has now largely been replaced by digital matte painting, using software programs that allow artists to paint images in layers, and by **digital set extension**. For *The Truman Show* (Peter Weir 1998), Matte World Digital used computer graphics programs to create architectural extensions, adding several stories to existing buildings on location in Seaside, Florida, to produce the look of downtown Seahaven. But matte artist Chris Evans warns, "The computer can take many hours to calculate a realistic lighting effect that a good artist can achieve with a single dab of paint." (Rickitt, p. 209)

Creating Scene Transitions, Titles, and Credits: The Optical Printer

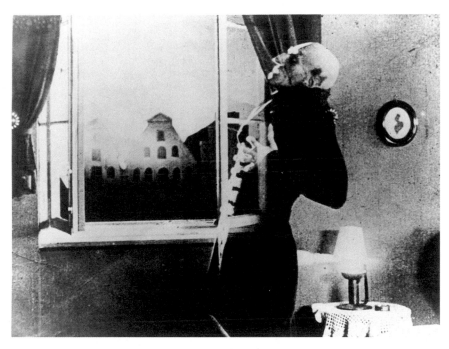

6.93 "Trick" photography: Orlock is exposed to the sun in a double exposure from *Nosferatu*.

An optical printer is a device that allows films to be re-photographed and has been used for numerous visual effects, including fades and dissolves (see fig. 6.3). For a **fade-out**, a scene is copied in the printer and near the end of the scene, the shutter is closed in increments, reducing the amount of light striking the copy. A **dissolve** results from copying a fade-out at the end of a scene onto the fade-in of the next scene (and is usually accomplished by rewinding the copied film and exposing it twice).

6.94 A skull is superimposed onto Norman's face in *Psycho*.

With the optical printer, technicians can create freeze frames such as the famous final shot of *Butch Cassidy and The Sundance Kid* (George Roy Hill 1969) by re-photographing a single frame many times over. **Double exposures** are achieved in camera by exposing film frames, then rewinding the film and exposing them again (fig. **6.93**, whereas optical printers are used to produce **superimpositions** such as the one at the conclusion of *Psycho* (fig. **6.94**).

Another use for the optical printer is to create split-screen effects, by exposing different areas of the frame at different times (figs. 6.53 and 6.54). Finally, optical printers are used to

6.95 *(left and right)* A matte shot dramatically alters the landscape.

create titles and credits by superimposing black-and-white film with title wording over live-action footage.

Optical and Digital Compositing: Assembling the Elements of the Shot

Compositing—also called a process shot—refers to the creation of a single image by combining elements filmed separately. Long the province of the optical printer, compositing is now largely accomplished digitally.

To combine an actor and a background filmed separately, filmmakers mask part of the frame during shooting, creating complementary **mattes** (sometimes called male and female). The matte allows the film to be exposed in one area only; the second, or counter, matte then masks the area the first had allowed to be exposed (fig. **6.95**). Mattes can be drawn by hand (and combined with countermatte footage in an optical printer) or created using computer programs.

Blue and **green screen** techniques refer to a compositing method that begins by shooting action against a blue or green background. This background is replaced with an image, called the background plate, through the use of a **traveling matte** (a mask used to cover portions of the image that move from frame to frame). As with most visual effects, compositing is now achieved digitally, by scanning the negative into a digital format, creating the composite on a computer, and scanning the images back out to film. The blue hue is used for optical compositing because there is so little blue in human skin that achieving the proper color balance for flesh tones in live action footage is easier. Green screens are used because they provide better resolution on video formats.

Digital compositing techniques, on the other hand, use any color background, and are used to blend live action footage with computer-generated images. In the closing scene of *The Matrix*, Neo and Morpheus hang from a rope dangling from a helicopter. The actors were shot hanging from a rope in the

Chapter 6: Cinematography

safety of a studio, and the cityscape of Sydney, Australia, was added later. Ropes and harnesses were digitally "erased" from the final print.

In the opening scene of *The Matrix*, effects artists used a technique that rearranged part of an actor's body. Trinity (Carrie-Anne Moss) flies through space in a corkscrew leap. During production, Moss was twirled around vertically in a rig that bound her feet and hands. In post-production, visual effects technicians "cut and pasted" her legs so they appear to kick. Effects supervisor John Gaeta called it "Frankensteining" her body—a reference to the classic horror story about animating a body composed of dead parts.

6.96 Using performance capture technology on the set of *Avatar*.

Performance Capture

The success of James Cameron's *Avatar* brought attention to the **performance capture** technology that Cameron used to create the Na'vi people of Pandora (who were based on actors) as well as the avatars—or doubles—of the human characters in the film, played by Sigourney Weaver and Sam Worthington. Robert Zemeckis had used this technology in *Polar Express* (2004), *Beowulf* (2007), and *A Christmas Carol* (2009), but with *Avatar* Cameron took the process to a new level, particularly with respect to capturing the subtle expressions on the actors' faces. In an interview, he says about the otherworldy Na'vi, "we don't have to necessarily believe that it's 100 percent photoreal [...] but we have to believe in them as emotional creatures, so we came up with the headrig," the apparatus that was responsible for capturing the actors' facial performances ("New Performance Capture").

The performance capture process for *Avatar* began with actors donning a full bodysuit studded with stripes and reference markers, and tightly fitting helmets (made from a cast of the actors' own heads) that aimed a digital camera at their faces and recorded expressions throughout the shoot. These cameras tracked dots of green ink that were distributed across the actors' faces to pick up subtle movements. Shooting took place in a CG environment dubbed "the volume" which was ringed by 120 digital cameras; data from these cameras were streamed into a software program that converted actors' movements into those of their CG characters for Cameron to view in real time (fig. **6.96**). Finally, the footage was sent to Weta Digital, the premier special effects house in New Zealand, for further fine tuning of facial expressions.

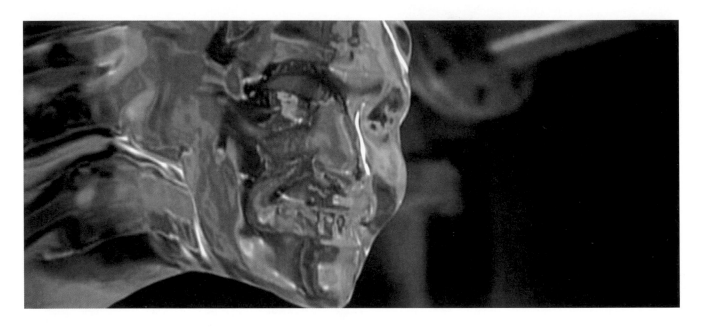

6.97 A morphing pseudopod in *The Abyss*.

Computer-Generated Images

Computer-generated imagery (CGI), made possible by the rapid development of powerful computers during the 1970s, was first used in a feature film in Disney's *Tron* (Steven Lisberger 1982) and first came to attention after it was used to create the watery pseudopod in *The Abyss* (Cameron 1989). CGI creates background images and objects using a three-part process: developing the spatial characteristics of an object through a 3D model (also called the **wireframe**), rendering (producing the finished image), and then animating the object and simulating camera movement (frame by frame).

6.98 The bullet-time special effect in *Blade II*.

Chapter 6: Cinematography

Adding and Subtracting Frames

Morphing is a process that involves the interpolation of frames using a computer program. The process begins with the creation of starting and ending images (say, a face before and after transformation), with specific areas within the images used as anchoring points (eyes, ears, and chin). The program then calculates the way the image must change in order for the first image to become the second over a series of frames (Rickitt, p. 86). The object appears to stretch as it metamorphoses into something else entirely (fig. **6.97**).

The special effects artists at work on *Blade* and later *The Matrix* and *Blade II* (Guillermo del Toro 2002) pioneered a slow-motion technique called by a number of names, including bullet-time and time slicing (fig. **6.98**). The shot is achieved by surrounding actors or objects with a ring of still cameras that trigger in sequence at a rapid rate (96 frames per second). When these shots are projected at a normal rate (24 frames per second)—in addition to adding and subtracting frames—the action appears to be slowed down or frozen, and may provide a 360° perspective.

Digital Cinema: Post-Production

The first uses of digital technology were in post-production, where filmmakers replaced chemical processing and optical printing with digital techniques. *O Brother, Where Art Thou?* was among the first major features to use "digital answer printing," now called digital intermediate, where the entire original film print was scanned into digital format, manipulated, and then reprinted on film stock for exhibition.

For *O Brother*, the digital manipulation mainly influenced the film's color design. Cinematographer Roger Deakins wanted to create a "dustbowl" effect to convey the depression-era 1930s South, with sepia and brown tones dominating. Through digital enhancement, bright green grass became amber. It is actually possible to compare the look of the film before and after digital processing by screening the **trailer** (the short advertising reel for the film) included on the

6.99 *(left)* A still from the trailer of *O Brother, Where Art Thou?*

6.100 *(right)* The same shot from the final cut of *O Brother, Where Art Thou?*

6.101 Vilmos Zsigmond's blue palette in *McCabe and Mrs. Miller*.

DVD. A difference in the tonal range and saturation of the colors is evident: in the trailer and out-takes, the grass is green and the sky is deep blue, whereas in the final cut of the film, the grass is brown and the sky is a faded gray (figs. **6.99**, **6.100**).

The same idea motivated Vilmos Zsigmond's cinematography for Robert Altman's *McCabe and Mrs. Miller*. Like Deakins, Zsigmond sought to create the look of a particular place and time through visual means. But he created a faded brown and blue palette and a filmy image texture through traditional photographic means, including filters and flashing (fig. **6.101**).

As with all new technologies, some visual effects artists use digital techniques imaginatively, pushing the envelope of film art; others use them to replace standard practices. Ultimately, digital processes have become integral to commercial filmmaking because they are less expensive than traditional methods and offer a director and art designer greater control. Improvements in computer graphics capabilities and an increasing number of trained personnel have made digital processes a significant part of commercial film production.

Digital Cinematography and Film Style

George Lucas, a pioneer in the development of special visual effects, shot *Star Wars Episode II: Attack of the Clones* (2002) digitally, but many theaters screened it through conventional film projection. In 2001 Lucas had planned to make and release the final Star Wars film, *Episode III: Revenge of the Sith*, using only digital formats (filming with digital cameras and delivering the film as a compressed file via DVD, satellite, or as a computer drive). But when the film was released in 2005, fewer than 100 movie screens in the U.S. (out of 35,000) could accommodate digital projection (Lieberman). Delays in moving to digital projection were related to disagreements within the entertainment industry over standards for digital projection (2K versus 4K), as well as the assumption of the cost of revamping movie theaters. By early 2006 major studios in the U.S. had settled on digital projection standards and signed an agreement with Access Integrated Technologies to use their digital system, paving the way for the industry-wide adoption of digital projection. The shift from film to digital images is motivated partly by a desire to improve on film images and also to take advantage of the flexibility of digital formats in production and exhibition.

One important question to ask is whether the digital revolution has changed the nature of film as a medium composed of expressive images that are, in narrative fiction films, linked to stories. Has an emphasis on special visual effects in *Lord of the Rings*, *Transformers*, and *Avatar* undercut the importance of character or theme? Is the industry using special effects to compete with sophisticated home viewing technologies (broadband cable, high-speed computer connections, and home theater systems) at the expense of thoughtful narratives? Film critic Gary Thompson writes that the latest advances in special effects leave audiences jaded, unable to be amazed by the magic of cinema (quoted in Pierson, p. 1). In 2004, critic David Denby wondered whether three directors whose work focuses on emotional connections (Sofia Coppola, Catherine Hardwicke, and Patty Jenkins) might "pull at least part of our movie culture away from frantic digital spectacle." (Denby, p. 86)

Certain trends in filmmaking—what Denby calls the "digital spectacle"—have emerged because of these technologies. One trend is the revival of the epic blockbuster, in the form of films like *300* and *Clash of the Titans*. CGI allows directors to create huge crowds through duplication, and digital compositing allows film makers to recreate historical eras, such as Victorian England in *Sherlock Holmes* (Guy Ritchie 2009).

Digital and 3D technologies undoubtedly will play an important role in international cinema in the future, as cinematographers and directors continue to explore their potential to dazzle. However, they will not supplant the human dramas that also appeal to so many moviegoers. In 2010, half of the ten films nominated for the Best Picture Academy Award were character-driven dramas: they were *Precious*, *An Education* (Lone Scherfig 2009), *Up in the Air* (Jason Reitman 2009), *A Serious Man* (Coen Brothers 2009) and *The Blind Side* (John Lee Hancock 2009). In fact, directors like Cameron and Spielberg say they have availed themselves of the latest sophisticated digital technologies in order to *retain* the human feel of their films.

To analyze and interpret individual films, viewers must consider what digital technologies contribute to the overall system of meaning. Shock, surprise, and delight at optical and digital tricks can make watching films fun. But to unearth a greater underlying significance, those effects must be read in relation to story, character, theme, tone, and style.

Cinematography is a powerful visual tool that has always depended on a mix of old and new technologies. Whether based on photochemical or electronic processes, cinematography works in concert with narrative elements, *mise en scène*, editing, and sound to produce an integrated aesthetic experience.

Summary

- The camera and time: The long take is a long uninterrupted shot that requires the choreography of actors and camera and produces continuity. By exposing more (or fewer) than 24 frames per second and projecting the footage at 24 fps, directors can create slow- and fast-motion effects, which can extend or shorten the apparent duration of events.
- The camera and space: by selecting camera height, angle, and distance, filmmakers present characters, actions, and locations from a particular visual perspective.
- Camera movement: choreographing camera movements, often with devices built expressly for this purpose, permits the camera to explore the frame in two and three dimensions, detaching the audience from the action or placing them in the midst of it.
- Lenses and filters: lenses affect the perception of the visual field, particularly in terms of depth. Wide-angle lenses increase the apparent space between objects in the foreground and background. Telephoto lenses do the opposite—they compress that visual distance. Normal lenses approximate human vision. Filters manipulate color and light.
- Film stock: gauge, grain, and speed affect the overall look of a film. Gauge refers to the size of the film format. Grain refers to the grains of silver halide in the film's emulsion. Fast film stocks are very sensitive to light, but may yield images with visible grain. Slow film stocks are relatively insensitive and produce high-quality images when light can be carefully controlled, as on a studio set.
- Special visual effects involve optical illusions and digital techniques used during principal photography and in post-production. This aspect of cinematography includes building models and miniatures, matte paintings or glass shots, or digitally enhancing built sets. It also encompasses optical and digital compositing, where several elements of the frame are produced separately and brought together using an optical printer or computer.
- While this chapter focuses on fiction films, cinematography also plays a role in documentary and avant-garde films.

Works Consulted

American Cinematographer's Manual. Hollywood, CA: ASC Press, 1993.

Anderson, Barbara and Joseph. "The Myth of Persistence of Vision Revisited." *Journal of Film and Video*, 45/1 (Spring 1993), pp. 3–12.

Arden, Darlene. "The Magic of ILM." **www.darlenearden.com/articleILM.htm**. 6/22/04.

Ascher, Steven, and Edward Pincus. *The Filmmaker's Handbook: A Comprehensive Guide for the Digital Age*. New York: Plume, 1999.

Barclay, Steven. *The Motion Picture Image: From Film to Digital*. Boston: Focal Press, 2000.

Calhoun, John. "Fear and Fantasy." *American Cinematographer*. (January 2007) **http://www. theasc.com/**

Cameron, James. "The Evolution of 3D Technology." Science Channel. **http://science.discovery. com/videos/**

————. "New Performance Capture Technology." Science Channel. **http://science.discovery. com/videos/**

Cook, David. *A History of Narrative Film*. New York: Norton, 1996.

Crafton, Donald. "Tricks and Animation," in *The Oxford History of World Cinema*, ed. Geoffrey Nowell-Smith. Oxford and New York: Oxford University Press, 1997, pp. 71–8.

Del Toro, Guillermo. Director's Commentary. *Pan's Labyrinth*. New Line DVD, 2006.

Denby, David. "Killer: Two Views of Aileen Wuornos," *The New Yorker*, January 26, 2004, pp. 84–6.

"Focus on Jim Jarmusch." Interview with Elvis Mitchell. Independent Film Channel, January 18, 2004.

Haines, Richard W. *Technicolor Movies: The History of Dye Transfer Printing*. Jefferson, NC: McFarland, 1993.

Handy, Bruce. "This is Cinerama." *Vanity Fair*, 488 (April 2001), pp. 258–74.

Hiltzik, Michael. "Digital Cinema Take 2." *Technology Review*, September 2002, pp. 36–44.

Keefe, W.E. "The Power of Love." *Moving Picture World*. October 21, 1922. **www.3dmovingpictures.com/pol.html**

Lieberman, David. "Digital Film Revolution Poised to Start Rolling." *USA Today*, May 17, 2005. **www.usatoday.com/money/media/2005-05-17-digital-cinema-usat_x.htm** September 23, 2006.

LoBrutto, Vincent. *Principal Photography; Interviews with Feature Film Cinematographers*. London and Westport, CT: Praeger, 1999.

Magid, Ron. "Vision Crew Unlimited's Artisans Lay Scale-model Keels for *Titanic*," *American Cinematographer*, 78/12 (December 1997), pp. 81–85.

Martin, Kevin H. "Jacking into the Matrix," *Cinefex*, 79 (October 1999), pp. 66–89.

Mast, Gerald, and Bruce Kawin. *A Short History of the Movies*, 6th edn. Boston and London: Allyn and Bacon, 1996.

Modleski, Tania. *The Women Who Knew Too Much: Hitchcock and Feminist Theory*. London and New York: Routledge, 1988.

Monaco, James. *How to Read a Film: Movies, Media, Multimedia*, 3rd edn. Oxford and New York: Oxford University Press, 2000.

Nowell-Smith, Geoffrey. *The Oxford History of World Cinema*. Oxford and New York: Oxford University Press, 1997.

Perisic, Zoran. *Visual Effects Cinematography*. Boston: Focal Press, 2000.

Pierson, Michele. *Special Effects: Still in Search of Wonder*. New York: Columbia University Press, 2002.

Rickitt, Richard. *Special Effects: The History and Technique*. London: Virgin Publishing, 2000.

Rogers, Pauline. *Contemporary Cinematographers on their Art*. Boston: Focal Press, 1998.

Rudolph, Eric. "This is your Life." *American Cinematographer*, 79/6 (June 1998), pp. 74–85.

Salt, Barry. *Film Style and Technology: History and Analysis*, 2nd edn. London: Starword, 1992.

Schaefer, Dennis, and Larry Salvato. *Masters of Light: Conversations with Contemporary Cinematographers*. Berkeley, CA: University of California Press, 1984.

Segrave, Kerry. *Movies at Home: How Hollywood came to Television*. Jefferson, NC: McFarland, 1999.

Sklar, Robert. *Film: An International History of the Medium*, 2nd edn. Upper Saddle River, NJ: Prentice-Hall and Harry N. Abrams, 2002.

Spoto, Donald. *The Art of Alfred Hitchcock: Fifty Years of His Motion Pictures*. New York: Doubleday, 1979.

Street, Rita. *Computer Animation: A Whole New World*. Gloucester, MA: Rockport Publishers, 1998.

Thompson, Anne. "Anatomy of a Motion Capture Scene in *Avatar*." *Popular Mechanics*. January 2010. **www.popularmechanics.com**

Usai, Paolo Chechi. "The Early Years," in *The Oxford History of World Cinema*. Oxford and New York: Oxford University Press, 1997, pp. 6–13.

Von Sternberg, Josef. *Fun in a Chinese Laundry*. New York: Macmillan, 1965.

Wheeler, Paul. *High Definition and 24p Cinematography*. Oxford: Focal Press, 2003.

Zettl, Herbert. *Sight, Sound, Motion: Applied Media Aesthetics*, 3rd edn. Belmont, CA: Wadsworth Publishing Co., 1999.

Cinematography as a Storytelling Device

This chapter has emphasized the way cinematography creates meaning in narrative fiction films. This sample essay puts these lessons into action, describing and analyzing the way cinematography can reveal a character's social circumstance, emotions, and thought process. While the emphasis here is cinematography, notice that the author also includes detailed descriptions of the *mise en scène*. Cinematic elements are intertwined, and thoughtful analysis usually requires careful attention to how a film combines details simultaneously.

Throughout the essay, the author uses facts and ideas gathered through research to illustrate and support critical points he makes. He paraphrases the work of others, and in some passages he relies on their words in direct quotations. Comments by the film's director and film scholars help to clarify descriptive statements about the film, provide historical context, and strengthen interpretative claims. Often scholars rely on research to help bolster ideas, but sometimes scholars use research to establish a contrasting position.

As this paper demonstrates, writers should make clear to their readers which ideas are original and which ideas are taken from other sources. That way, the reader knows who is responsible for the arguments and ideas. Study notes accompanying this essay offer pointers on how to use paraphrases and quotations, and how to document sources. Writers using a film as a primary text do not need to cite it in the bibliography, but they should be sure to acknowledge all other sources (books, journal articles, audio commentary tracks, or websites). Do not cite information that is considered common knowledge: cast and crew names, plot details, awards and release dates. Always ask your professor or publisher for the preferred method of documentation. In the humanities, you will usually be directed to *The Chicago Manual of Style* or *The MLA Handbook*.

Entrapment and Escape in *Ratcatcher*

When the Glasgow "dustmen" (sanitation workers) went on strike in 1976, the rapid accumulation of refuse transformed the city into a veritable wasteland. In *Ratcatcher* (1999), director Lynne Ramsay sets the fractured, episodic wanderings of protagonist James Gillespie against this historical backdrop, transforming a working class neighborhood's squalor into a central visual device that powerfully counters the cinema's tendency to idealize childhood. With its focus on a 12 year-old boy's struggle to come to terms with his position in society and his effort to find emotional intimacy, *Ratcatcher* has all the hallmarks of a coming of age tale. But whereas the typical coming of age tale celebrates the adolescent who gains wisdom, experience, and empathy during the transition from childhood to adulthood, *Ratcatcher* emphasizes James's tragic failure to complete the process. Overlooked by his family and by Scottish society at large, and plagued by his guilt over his friend Ryan's accidental death, James can neither find the guidance he needs to overcome the economic and social disadvantages he faces nor muster the courage to atone. Most coming of age tales embrace a character's movement into the next stage of life; by contrast, *Ratcatcher* traces the catastrophic consequences for an adolescent when he realizes there's nowhere for him to go.

From the film's outset, it is clear that James is anything but innocent. He steals; he breaks into homes; he silently watches as acquaintances sexually assault a neighborhood girl, and then he pursues a relationship with her himself. James is nevertheless a profoundly empathetic character. Ramsay tempers her portrait of James's hardscrabble life with a suggestion that vulnerability informs his behavior. His apparent deviance is a response to his fear, guilt, and powerlessness. "Children are brutal," says Ramsay, "They are incredibly brutal and then incredibly kind" (Interview).[1]

The opening shot establishes the complex approach the entire film will adopt as it represents the lives of children. A gauzy image slowly pulsates; the frame is so abstract that viewers might not fully be aware of what they are seeing (fig. **6.102**). A slow motion, medium close-up becomes the ethereal form of a child twisting himself in sheer curtains. The boy—Ryan Quinn—will be drowned in the nearby canal, making the first shot's visual poetry especially evocative. The opening image captures the bittersweet intricacies of the children Ramsay depicts. It is a playful moment that captures reckless abandon. But, paradoxically, it also hauntingly foreshadows Ryan's premature death, as the curtain sheer looks like a shroud (Interview).[2] Perhaps coincidentally, Ryan also looks like he's emerging from a cocoon, especially when Ramsay accelerates out of slow-motion midway through the shot. The effect suggests the passing of one phase of life and the arrival of another, as the boy slowly unravels and then blossoms into something different.

Ryan Quinn's death, which occurs in the next scene, is the dramatic event that animates the entire film. Having pushed his friend Ryan into the canal in a bout of innocent roughhousing, James is haunted by his friend's untimely death. The sequence that depicts Ryan's funeral procession emphasizes how James's apparent morose detachment from the rituals of mourning is actually the result of his emotional *over*investment in them. Taken alone, the *mise en scène* suggests a cold indifference to his friend's passing. James is absent from the first part of the scene, and when he does appear, he watches the proceedings from a distant vantage point instead of joining his

1 Direct quotations from dialogue or lyrics in a film used as a primary source do not have to be cited or documented in a bibliography. Include information on the director and year of release at the first mention of the film, as follows: (Lynne Ramsay 1999).

Here the writer quotes from a bonus feature included on the DVD. This is not the essay's primary source; it is research, so it needs to be documented. The citation at the end of the essay looks like this: Interview with Lynne Ramsay. *Ratcatcher*. The Criterion Collection DVD, 2002.

If the writer had cited a director's commentary track from a DVD, he would have needed to list the source in the bibliography as well.

2 Here the author chooses to paraphrases director Lynne Ramsay's idea. Reserve direct quotations for those passages where the original wording is important. In all other cases, summarize and paraphrase. By relating Ramsay's ideas about the opening shot, this paraphrase helps substantiate the author's own interpretation of the film's portrait of children.

6.102 Ryan Quinn in *Ratcatcher*—the curtain looks like a funeral shroud.

family. However, the cinematography makes evident the fact that James's tortured emotions are roiling under the surface. He appears in a medium shot, with his back to the camera, watching as the hearse slowly drives by in the background. Ramsay uses a telephoto lens so that, while the car is onscreen, the boy is centered in the frame, but appears blurry in the foreground. This divorces James from his surroundings. But the image also suggests that, even though James would like to avoid thinking about Ryan's death, the situation refuses to grant him that denial. In fact, he is utterly consumed by the guilty feelings he tries to repress; it is as if James's identity dissolves, as all of his (and most of our) attention is drawn toward the glossy black hearse in the background.

When the hearse exits the frame, taking Ryan's body with it, rack focusing brings James into clear view as he tries to distance himself even further from the funeral procession (figs. 6.51, 6.52). When he can no longer watch the car, James turns to face the camera and leaps off the wall on which he had been sitting, putting a substantial physical barrier between himself and Ryan. Ramsay's use of slow motion exaggerates this gesture, underscoring its central importance for understanding James's character. The slow motion transforms what would otherwise be understood as a purely incidental moment into an ethereal evocation of loss, as the camera cranes to follow his downward flight until he lands in a medium shot, trapped with his back against the wall, his eyes mournfully gazing at the ground.

A shared experience of mourning sets up an ominous parallel between James and Ryan. Longing for her missing son, Mrs. Quinn turns her affection toward James who, in her eyes, "is the double" of her Ryan. Mrs. Quinn's attempt to bond with her son's best friend is the first of many instances where dialogue and visual motifs suggest that James will literally and figuratively walk in the dead boy's shoes. Mrs. Quinn gives James the shoes she had purchased for Ryan before his death, using footwear in a failed attempt to revive her dead child. Further visual parallels between James and his dead friend amplify the feeling that James has traded his innocence for inevitable doom. As James lies on the kitchen table so his mother can pick the lice out of his hair, the camera situates him in a close-up whose composition matches an earlier shot of Ryan's face as he lay dead on the bank of the canal. And at one point, several neighborhood hoodlums threaten to toss James into the same canal where Ryan drowned and where, later, James's father prevents yet another boy from drowning. These moments suggest how these young boys—indeed, all of the children in the Maryhill neighborhood—are the powerless victims of a social system that has left them little hope of escaping their stinking, trash-filled slum.

Several features of the urban environment convey this sense of entrapment. The murky channel that took Ryan's life functions as a pivotal metaphor for James's captivity. It surrounds James and confronts him at every turn, evoking the seemingly inescapable forces stacked against him: the loss of his friend, poverty, his strained relationship with his alcoholic father, and his feelings of powerlessness. The canal's importance to the film is so critical that S.C. Aitken calls it a "place character," alluding to how the water's impact on James is as profound as any of the people in his life (Aitken, p. 78).[3] Like the canal, other architectural features of the city—as manifested in the tenement's walls, opaque windows, and vertiginous stairwells—also conspire to fence the residents in. Ramsay accentuates this detail by consistently using a telephoto lens to flatten James against walls, creating a claustrophobic environment. The heaps of garbage that multiply as the film progresses further constrict the environment, crowding out the people but providing ample space for rats to forage and multiply. Throughout, desaturated grays, greens, and browns dominate the frame, accentuating the neighborhood's squalor, and Ramsay's high angle long shots emphasize the residents' helplessness. Hemmed in by their own poverty, the people in Maryhill are little more than Glasgow's refuse. In fact, one interpretation of the film's obtuse title is that it refers to the neighborhood itself, a space capable of ensnaring and perhaps eradicating society's vermin.

A more typical coming of age narrative might revolve around the development of a central intimate relationship, which helps the protagonist cope with (if not rise above) hardship and gives him a sense of self worth. *Ratcatcher* invites audiences to maintain this expectation, as James's relationships with Kenny (a put upon, younger neighbor) and, especially, Anne Marie develop.

But Ramsay upsets expectations, making it clear that the budding romance is doomed because of the children's social and emotional circumstances. James and Anne Marie first meet when the thugs steal her glasses and callously toss them into the canal. Ramsay avoids using the conventional close-up to capture their growing intimacy, and instead focuses on James's hand as it tentatively caresses Margaret's wounded knee. After this moment of tenderness between them, James returns to the site where Anne Marie was first attacked and he stares at her spectacles resting in the muck. The scene implies that, because the glasses rest in the same waters where Ryan died, he is reluctant to wade in after them. James would like to retrieve the glasses, but he is too paralyzed by guilt and fear to help Anne Marie. Later, the two bond and James even professes his love for her. She becomes one of his few companions, prompting him to make a second effort rescuing her glasses. When he fails at this effort and then witnesses the gang of brutes molesting Anne Marie once again, he turns his back on her. His only mechanism for coping with his feelings of helplessness is to act as if he's coldly indifferent, if not hostile.

James's affinity for animals reflects how his insecurity leads to callousness. Early in the film, James plays with a rodent caught in a mousetrap. Instead of torturing it, he offers it food, a minute detail that points to his capacity for empathy. But after an especially nasty argument with his father, James runs out to the streets and starts stabbing at the rats crawling in the rubbish; Ramsay uses slow motion cinematography here to punctuate the

3 Notice that none of the paragraphs in this essay begin with a paraphrase or a quotation. In general, writers should always use research to help develop their own ideas. Paragraphs that begin with a quote subordinate a writer's original thought to material gleaned from research. Thus, you should open paragraphs with topic sentences that express the controlling idea in your own words, and then use cited material to reinforce this point.

6.103 *(above)* James savors a rare moment of escape.

6.104 *(below)* James, transfixed by the field outside the kitchen window.

event, drawing attention to the significance of this moment as a turning point, when James's nurturing disposition gives way to violence. In a sense, then, the film's title also refers to him. He becomes the "ratcatcher," turning against those who are even more vulnerable than he is.

If traditional ideas about coming of age tie the development of romantic intimacy with the adolescent's ability to rise above his circumstances, *Ratcatcher* links James's failure to rescue Anne Marie to his ultimate realization that there is no escape from his poverty. At one point, a short bus ride to a new housing development far removed from the urban blight offers James a reprieve from his angst, and Ramsay's camera placement, movement, and color palette underscore the freedom he feels in the strange utopia. The as-yet-to-be-finished apartments embody his family's hopes for a better future, as one of the film's subplots involves the father's (probably) doomed attempt to obtain financial assistance so they can move out of the city.

The setting itself has an almost mythical quality, as James's bus stops in the middle of a field; the boy literally gets off at the last stop. The wide-open space stands in stark contrast to the architectural elements of the city that surround and contain James: the canal, the walls, the stairwells, the windows. Immediately obvious is the contrast in color quality and camera placement between this scene in the suburbs and the scenes in the city. Desaturated hues give way to brilliant blue sky and warm, yellow tones. This is a magical place full of strange beauty and promise. Instead of relying on the slightly high angle shots and telephoto lenses that heretofore had flattened the boy against the immovable barriers of the city, Ramsay employs a rare dramatic low angle to film him playing on scaffolding (fig. **6.103**). The camera's position ensures that the blue sky is his only backdrop and thus captures the exuberance of an expansive space. Here, James is free to reinvent himself. There are no rats, no bullies, no unsupportive parents, no reminders of Ryan's tragic death.

Camera movement also reflects James's sense of freedom. The boy manages to find an unlocked door to an unfinished apartment—another barrier that gives way—and when he wanders into the kitchen, he is amazed by the experience of looking out a window and not seeing refuse, but instead golden fields of wheat. As James walks, awestruck, to the sill, the camera slowly tracks behind him and emphasizes this vision as, literally, a moment of transcendence. The camera follows him as he crosses the threshold, through the open window, into a world he's never seen before: the graceful glide of the tracking shot capturing the feeling of floating through space in dumbstruck amazement (fig. **6.104**). James's methodical inquisitiveness gives way to an explosion of energy when the boy starts to run through the fields, his exhilaration apparent in Ramsay's shift to frenzied handheld shots and rapid editing.

This scene has a dreamlike quality, making it clear that James's hopes of a better life are little more than a fantasy. Ramsay composes the image of James crawling through the window so that it would have a stylized quality: "I wanted [that shot] to look like a painting. I wanted it to be a frame within a frame" (Interview).[4] The beautiful artificiality of the image suggests how this moment isn't of this world. James's sense of liberation is a dream. Furthermore, as Jonathan Murray has observed, keeping in mind that *Ratcatcher* is set in the 1970s, audiences might recognize that the space that James visits is destined to become just another, newer version of the neighborhood where the Gillespie family now resides (Murray, p. 224).[5]

The impossibility of this dream becomes explicit when James returns to the same spot hoping to recapture those liberating feelings. Critical changes in the film's *mise en scène* and cinematography make his disappointment palpable. Instead of brilliant sunshine, the weather is dismal, and the open apartment is locked. Instead of placing the camera to emphasize James's

4 As a way of introducing Lynne Ramsay's words, this sentence paraphrases her point before providing the direct quotation. This is an effective way of ensuring that readers understand the significance of the quoted material.

6.105 *(above)* Locked out of the house he once fantasized about living in.

6.106 *(below)* The end of a dream: camera placement emphasizes James's sense of hopelessness.

5 Try to signal the beginning of paraphrased material. This helps the reader distinguish between your thoughts and ideas taken from research. This author signals the paraphrase with the words "as Jonathan Murray has observed" and ends the paraphrase with the page number. If your paraphrase is only one sentence long, the attributory phrase at the beginning isn't essential. But such a cue is imperative when summarized material is several sentences long. Murray, Jonathan. "Kids in America? Narratives of Transatlantic Influence in 1990s Scottish Cinema." *Screen*. Vol. 46, No. 2, 217–25, Summer 2005.

6 Quoted phrases should not stand by themselves. Incorporate quotes into original sentences. This is a sophisticated example of how to incorporate quoted material into a new sentence. Notice that this author doesn't quote an entire sentence. Instead, he singles out a critical passage and constructs a new sentence around those select words.

wonderment, Ramsay shoots this scene using eye-level and high angle shots that tightly frame the boy to reflect his sense of exclusion. Once again, Ramsay shoots out the kitchen window to look at the wheat field, but now the yellows are muted and cloaked by the gray rain clouds, and James is on the outside looking in (fig. **6.105**). In fact, he is too short to look through the glass, so he has to jump just to catch a glimpse of what he once thought could be his. His head repeatedly appears and disappears from the frame in a poignant image of a dream deferred, if not shattered. Eventually he gives up and begins the trek home. As James recedes from view, the shot negates the optimism of his first visit. A subsequent shot of him arriving in his neighborhood captures perfectly his sense of utter resignation and defeat: a high angle, extreme long shot finds him walking down his street, caught once again within the array of walls, fences, and cement (fig. **6.106**). Aitken observes how the shot is remarkable for its emptiness: "The garbage, the context of much of his social interaction, is gone." (p. 83)[6] The government cleans up the problem by bringing in military troops who incite the ire of the residents, which only adds to James's desolation.

Tragically, this coming of age tale doesn't conclude with the protagonist losing his innocence, gaining experience, and finding his station in life. Overwhelmed and alone, James's only recourse is suicide. In an ironic twist on the conventional wisdom that a child must confront his fears to become an adult, James faces his guilt but rejects adulthood. Rather than avoid the canal as he has tried to do the entire film, James hurls himself into the waters that took Ryan's life. Instead of experiencing a melodramatic, emotional catharsis that will allow him to live a richer and fuller life, he serenely floats to the bottom. While he sinks, he imagines his family reunited, walking together through the fields of wheat, carrying furnishings to their new home. This tragic ending alludes to a conventional happy ending of family reunion and social ascension. But this happy ending is only a fantasy: "The surreal double ending seems to promise family reconciliation on the one hand … and on the other hand, the swallowing release of death as James plunges into the canal." (Cullen). Yet neither promise is real. The parallel between Ryan and James is now complete, and the brutal Glasgow environment has claimed another victim.

Works Cited (in the essay)

Aitken, S.C. "Poetic Child Realism: Scottish Film and the Construction of Childhood." *Scottish Geographical Journal*. Vol. 123, No. 1, pp. 68–86, March 2007.

Cullen, Catherine. "Details Are Acoustical." *Afterimage*. Vol. 29, Issue I, July/August 2001. Online. Academic Search Premiere.

Interview with Lynne Ramsay. *Ratcatcher*. The Criterion Collection DVD, 2002.

Murray, Jonathan. "Kids in America? Narratives of Transatlantic Influence in 1990s Scottish Cinema." *Screen*. Vol. 46, No. 2, pp. 217–25, Summer 2005.

Editing

> One must learn to understand that editing is in
> actual fact a compulsory and deliberate guidance
> of the thoughts and associations of the spectator.
>
> V.I. Pudovkin

Throughout Peter Jackson's *Return of the King* (2003), the crusaders trying to
defeat the evil necromancer Sauron find themselves divided into multiple camps,
each isolated from the other. While Aragorn (Viggo Mortensen), Legolas (Orlando
Bloom), and Gandalf (Ian McKellen) each try to muster up the forces needed to
fight Sauron's army, Frodo (Elijah Wood) and Sam (Sean Astin) fend for themselves in their attempt to destroy the magical ring Sauron needs to consolidate
his evil powers. When Gandalf fears that Frodo and Sam's attempt has been
thwarted, audiences too would be left wondering whether or not the brave hob-
bits were still alive, were it not for Jackson's ability to reveal Frodo and Sam's
whereabouts.

Jackson's ability to move the audience back and forth among the various locations—the Path of the Dead in Rohan, the enclave of Minas Tirith, and the hills
of Mordor, where Frodo and Sam carry out their arduous task—is evidence of his
mastery of editing, the process of joining together two or more shots. Editing has
several practical functions: it makes the logistics of crafting feature-length films

7.1 An iris shot from *The Cabinet
of Dr. Caligari.*

(involving multiple lines of action) possible; it makes scenes easier to choreograph; and it cuts down on production costs.

Because a traditional motion picture camera magazine holds less than fifteen minutes' worth of film stock at a time, making a conventionally shot feature film would be impossible without editing multiple shots together. Only recently has the development of digital video and computer technology made the concept of a full-length, one-shot film possible, as demonstrated by Aleksandr Sokurov's *Russian Ark* (2002)—a celebration of the history of Russia's Hermitage Museum filmed in a single 96-minute shot.

Furthermore, editing allows filmmakers to simplify the choreography in each shot. Any continuous shot of more than a minute—called a long take—demands perfect choreography; actors and actresses must remember their lines of dialogue and blocking, while the camera operators must move the camera in perfect timing with the cast. If anyone on the set misses a cue, then the entire shot has to be redone, which can be time-consuming and expensive. Editing allows filmmakers to choose the best moments from various takes and combine them into one ideal scene—even if the decision is made out of necessity.

Editing also contributes to the aesthetic quality of a film. In contemporary films, rapid, purely kinetic cutting creates visual dynamism, drawing on the style of music videos. For instance, much of the momentum in Michael Mann's *Miami Vice* (2006) comes from extended meditations on the characters' movement from place to place in snazzy, super-charged vehicles. The editing in these passages complements the moody electronic score, stirring the audience's adrenaline with a cinematic evocation of speed and glamor.

But beyond its purely practical and aesthetic functions, editing can also convey important information. In narrative films, editing emphasizes character

THE KULESHOV EFFECT

One of the basic theoretical principles of editing is that the meaning produced by joining two shots together transcends the visual information contained in each individual shot. In other words, the meaning of a sequence of shots is more than the sum of its parts. In 1917, Soviet filmmaker Lev Kuleshov, a pioneer in editing techniques, began publishing articles on film as an art form. Eventually he established the "Kuleshov Workshop" to study the effects of editing on audiences. In one experiment, he cut back and forth between the same found footage of a man's (Ivan Mozhukhin) expressionless face and a succession of three other images: a bowl of soup, a woman's corpse in a coffin, and a young girl with a teddy bear. When he screened the sequence of shots for various audiences, they claimed that the man's facial expression registered an emotional response to each of the objects on screen. Kuleshov documented their comments:

> The public raved about the acting of the artist. They pointed out the heavy pensiveness of his mood over the forgotten soup, were touched and moved by the deep sorrow with which he looked on the dead woman, and admired the light, happy smile with which he surveyed the girl at play. But we knew that in all three cases the face was exactly the same. (quoted in Cook, p. 137)

His discovery illustrated that the meaning of a shot was determined not only by the material content of the shot, but also by its association with the preceding and succeeding shots. This general principle of editing is called the **Kuleshov effect**.

development and motivation, establishes motifs and parallels, and develops themes and ideas.

At its core, editing involves the manipulation of three things: the graphic qualities of two or more shots, the tempo at which these shots change, and the timing of each shot in relationship to other elements of the film. After examining each of these three elements of editing, this chapter looks first at how editing can be used in narrative films to construct the meaning of the story that the viewer sees unfolding on screen, and then at how editing can produce meaning at a more abstract level, by defying audience expectations and by creating visual associations.

The Attributes of Editing: Creating Meaning Through Collage, Tempo, and Timing

Joining Images: A Collage of Graphic Qualities

Editing forms a collage, an assortment of images joined together in a sequence. When images are joined, audiences formulate ideas and derive meaning by comparing the visual details of each shot. A comparison of two shots can reveal important changes in *mise en scène*, including setting. In Ernst Lubitsch's *Trouble in Paradise* (1932), for example, two thieves find true love when they meet one another, and skillful editing suggests the sexual tryst that unfolds on the night of their first encounter. In a two-shot, Gordon Monescu (Herbert Marshall) casually seduces Lily (Miriam Hopkins) while she reclines languorously on a couch (fig. **7.2**). In the following shot, the couch is empty (fig. **7.3**). The editing draws attention to important changes in the *mise en scène* to suggest that, as the evening wears on, the couple adjourn to the bedroom.

Editing can also encourage audiences to compare and contrast the cinematographic qualities of each shot. Consider the scene in *Psycho* when Mother murders the detective Arbogast (Martin Balsam). As the attack begins, audiences see an overhead shot of the detective reaching the top of the stairs and Mother running out to stab him (fig. **7.4**). Then there is a cut to a close-up of Arbogast's face (fig. **7.5**). According to director Hitchcock,

> the main reason for raising the camera [to an overhead shot] was to get the contrast between the long shot and the close-up of the big head as the knife came down on him. It was like music, you see, the high shot with the violins and suddenly the big head with the brass instruments clashing. (Truffaut, p. 276)

Hitchcock's quote suggests how the director was acutely aware of the way abrupt changes in camera positioning can evoke an emotional response.

7.2 *(above)* Monescu and Lily on the couch in *Trouble in Paradise*.

7.3 *(below)* The vacated couch: romance blooms by night's end.

7.4 *(left)* Arbogast and Mother on the stairwell in *Psycho*.

7.5 *(right)* A close-up of Arbogast suddenly facing terror.

7.6 *(above)* A medium close-up of Frodo in *Lord of the Rings: Return of the King*.

7.7 *(below)* A medium close-up of Gollum creates continuity in *Lord of the Rings: Return of the King*.

Of course, two juxtaposed shots do not have to be so dramatically different in order to be evocative. On the surface it may even appear as if a scene involving dialogue between two characters does not exploit changes in visual information from one shot to the next. In fact, such scenes commonly depict participants in a conversation from similar vantage points. In a fairly conventional scene from *Lord of the Rings: Return of the King*, the audience sees a medium close-up of Frodo as he addresses Gollum. In the next shot, audiences see Gollum in a medium close-up when he responds (figs. **7.6**, **7.7**). Because of the lack of graphic distinction between such shots, audiences tend to overlook how such combinations powerfully evoke the continuity of a conversation, even when the completed scene may be composed of many performances filmed over a period of time.

But careful attention to the editing in what appears to be a purely functional scene will demonstrate how many elements of the visual system a director can bring into play during a scene that revolves around the restrained dialogue between two characters. On the one hand, subtle differences in *mise en scène* and cinematography in these shots suggest Gollum's vulnerability in relation to Frodo: the creature is naked and quivering while the hobbit is clothed; the creature is filmed with a high-angle shot whereas Frodo appears in low-angle shots.

This example illustrates one of the basic principles of editing at work: editing is the combination of imagery, creating meaning by the play of one image against another. Editing complements dialogue by shaping visual information to evoke a response from the audience on emotional and intellectual levels.

Editing can also emphasize similarities between shots, establishing a point of comparison between two people, places, or things. A **graphic match** is when two shots are juxtaposed in a way that emphasizes their visual similarities. At the end of the first segment of *Run Lola Run*, Lola's boyfriend throws a red bag full of money up into the air (fig. **7.8**). This shot is followed by a shot of a red telephone receiver that Lola tosses upward each time she begins her run (fig. **7.9**). The graphic match establishes a visual connection between the two segments of the film.

Frodo's confrontation with Gollum illustrates how the technique can suggest complex ideas by suggesting parallels. The close camera proximity in each shot draws attention to both characters' fearful blue eyes, hinting at what might befall Frodo if he can't unburden himself of the ring's mysterious and destructive powers.

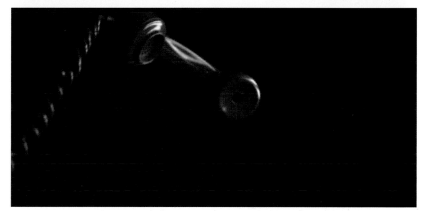

7.8 *(above)* Graphic match: the red bag full of money thrown into the air in *Run Lola Run*.

7.9 *(below)* The telephone receiver thrown in the air, from *Run Lola Run*.

Tempo

Filmmakers also encourage emotional and intellectual responses by adjusting tempo. The tempo in editing can be affected by two factors: the length of each shot and the type of shot transition—the visual effect used to move from one shot to the next.

Shot Length

The most obvious way that editors adjust tempo is by controlling the length of each shot: long takes tend to slow down the pace of a scene, while short takes quicken pace and intensity. Most movies combine long takes and short takes to allow for more variation and sophistication in the narrative pacing. Action scenes tend to rely on very short takes to convey excitement, while romantic scenes in the same movie unfold in longer takes at a more relaxed pace.

Scholars have studied the **average shot length** in films and discovered that the average shot in contemporary films is shorter than the average shot in older films. The difference between the rapid-fire editing of a modern action film such as *Sherlock Holmes* and a classic romance such as *Casablanca* (Michael Curtiz 1943) may seem obvious. But recent studies have shown that, with the advent of digital editing devices, shots are increasingly becoming shorter. According to film scholar Michael Brandt, "films cut traditionally [have] an average shot length of 5.15 seconds, compared to 4.75 seconds for the electronically cut films," a difference of almost 10%. Brandt goes on to suggest that editing at this rate allows audiences to respond only to rhythm, since the brevity of each shot does not allow audiences fully to comprehend the visual information before them:

> Other studies have shown that it takes an audience anywhere from 0.5 to 3 seconds to adjust to a new shot. If it takes the audience three seconds just to adjust to a cut to a shot, what happens when the average shot length is so short that the audience is never given a chance to catch up? (Brandt)

The tendency to rely on such rapid editing in recent films may explain why younger audiences are not initially receptive to older films: they seem slow-paced.

Shot Transitions

The second way in which filmmakers adjust the rhythm of editing is through **shot transitions**. A shot transition is the method of replacing one shot on screen with a second. The most common shot transition is the cut, when Shot A abruptly ends and Shot B immediately begins. A second common shot transition is the fade-out/fade-in, in which Shot A gradually darkens until the screen is completely black (or white, or red, or some other solid color) and then Shot B gradually appears. A third common shot transition is the **dissolve** (sometimes called overlapping, or lap dissolve), in which Shot A gradually disappears, while, simultaneously, Shot B gradually appears. Unlike fades, with a dissolve, the two shots will temporarily be superimposed. The viewer sees the two images overlapping one another (see fig. **7.19**).

Two other shot transitions are less common in contemporary films: the **wipe** and the **iris in/iris out**. A wipe is when Shot B appears to push Shot A off the screen; that is, a portion of Shot B will appear on one side of the screen and will move across the screen until Shot A disappears altogether. Unlike a dissolve, the two images do not overlap; instead the screen is divided, as in split-screen cinematography, and the second shot appears to expand to push the first shot out of the way (fig. **7.10**). An iris in/iris out occurs when a circular mask—a device placed over the lens of the camera that obscures part of the image—appears over Shot A. The circular mask gradually constricts around the image until the entire frame is black, at which point Shot B appears within a small circular mask. The circle, or iris, expands outward until Shot B takes up the entire screen. The iris in/iris out appears throughout *The Cabinet of Dr. Caligari* (fig. **7.1**). This technique functions in a similar way to the wipe and dissolve, in that iris shots are typically used as a transition from one scene to the next.

One function of these transitions is to help convey the passage of time, but they also affect the pacing of a scene. Cuts are almost invariably used within scenes because they connote an instantaneous change. They immediately alter the image, quickening the pace of the action. Even in a scene that relies primarily on long takes (and, hence, slow pacing), a cut often suggests a

7.10 A wipe in *Hidden Fortress*.

sudden change in mood or character dynamic. Such is the case in the scene from *Notorious* when Devlin returns to meet Alicia after learning that her assignment is to seduce a Nazi spy. While Alicia tries to make the evening romantic, the editing in the scene emphasizes how Devlin's seething jealousy contaminates the intimate mood. In a medium two-shot, Alicia embraces Devlin as she asks him why he is so distracted (fig. **7.11**). This long take contributes to the scene's relaxed pace and complements Alicia's casual playfulness as she questions him. But after Alicia jokingly suggests that Devlin must want to end their affair because he's secretly married, he replies bitterly, "I'll bet you've heard that line often enough," revealing his jealously over Alicia's sexual past. At this point, the scene cuts to a close-up of Alicia (fig. **7.12**). The abrupt change draws attention to the sudden shift in the emotional weight of the scene: Devlin's words have devastated Alicia.

Using shot transitions to join scenes affects the pace of a sequence or an entire movie. Fades can have an especially pronounced effect on the pace of a film because they give audiences a literal visual pause in the action. Jim Jarmusch's *Stranger than Paradise* (1984) is a pronounced example of how fades can slow the pace of a film. In order to evoke the lackadaisical, meandering lifestyle of his main characters, Jarmusch uses only fades to link each scene—to the point of frustration for some viewers. In contrast, Akira Kurosawa uses wipes throughout his samurai epic *Hidden Fortress* (1958; see fig. 7.10). Because wipes in the film move quickly across the screen, the editing maintains a visual dynamism, enhancing the film's lively action. Interestingly, *Hidden Fortress* had a profound influence on George Lucas's *Star Wars* (1977), right down to the use of wipes to build momentum.

Dissolves, fades, irises, and wipes rarely occur within scenes, since most scenes take place over an uninterrupted period of time. When they do occur within scenes, they usually introduce a memory or a fantasy. On rare occasions, these transitions are used within scenes without signaling a shift to a different

7.11 *(above)*, **7.12** *(below)* Cutting from a two shot to a close-up reveals romantic tension in *Notorious*.

7.13 Three attributes of editing in *Notorious*.

Attribute of Editing	Technique employed in *Notorious*
Collage (comparison/contrast of imagery)	Medium two-shot (romantic intimacy) vs. close-up (disappointment)
Tempo (shot length and transitions)	The cut abruptly changes the pace of the conversation. As Alicia and Devlin's words become more heated, the scene relies on shorter takes
Timing (coordinating cutting)	Cut to the close-up of Alicia coincides with Devlin's line, "I'll bet you've heard that line often enough"

time and place. When this occurs, the transitions dramatically slow down the pace of the scene.

A scene from *Fight Club* illustrates how fades suggest a more conspicuous protraction of time. When Tyler Durden (Brad Pitt) leaves the unnamed narrator (Edward Norton) after months of close friendship, his final words are presented in eight shots, the first four of which are connected by fades. Tyler wakes the narrator up in the middle of the night to deliver the news. After Tyler stands up to leave the room, the remaining shot transitions are cuts. The effect is hypnotic, conveying the narrator's dreamlike state of mind. Interestingly, the scene was originally edited using only cuts, but the filmmakers opted for the more narcotic feel of fades. The DVD includes both versions and allows audiences to compare them. The scene illustrates how the atypical use of fades within a scene slows the pace to suggest emotional detachment or a dreamy lack of engagement with the world.

Adjusting the Timing of Shot Transitions

The third way filmmakers use editing to produce meaning is by placing shot transitions so that they coincide with other visual and sound elements. The placement of shot transitions in relationship to these elements can punctuate the emotional and intellectual content of a scene. In narrative films, cutting within scenes tends to correspond to lines of dialogue. As in the balcony scene from *Notorious*, when a cut reveals how Alicia reacts to Devlin's prickly remarks, editing often corresponds to dialogue to highlight characters' responses.

In *The 400 Blows*, juvenile delinquent Antoine Doinel reads a passage from nineteenth-century French novelist Honoré de Balzac (fig. **7.14**). For most of the scene, Truffaut uses a long shot to show Antoine reclining on a couch, smoking. A voice-over reads Balzac's words, suggesting that the boy is so entranced with the book that he can literally hear the author's voice speaking to him. As the story moves to its climax and the tone of the voice-over intensifies, Truffaut cuts to a shot of the book itself from Antoine's point of view (fig. **7.15**). The editing underscores Antoine's passionate involvement with the story. As the narrator repeats the character's dying words (Archimedes' "Eureka! I have found it.") Truffaut cuts to a medium close-up of Antoine (fig. **7.16**). As he "hears" the words, his eyes lift to the sky in amazement. Cutting on a line of dialogue emphasizes the degree to which Balzac moves Antoine. The timing of the cut also adds a layer of meaning to the story's last line. Not only have Archimedes and the dying character "found it," but so

7.14 (*above*) Antoine reads in *The 400 Blows*.

7.15 (*center*) An eyeline match reveals Antoine's intense connection to the words.

7.16 (*below*) The words lead Antoine to a revelation.

Chapter 7: Editing

Using Contrasting Imagery and Timing to Romanticize the Outlaws in *Bonnie and Clyde*

Audiences in 1967 flocked to see Arthur Penn's new gangster film *Bonnie and Clyde.* Although the film was panned by a number of influential film critics, young viewers were drawn to the two characters. In retrospect, the popularity of the film isn't hard to explain, given the fact that in America the 1960s counter-culture youth movement was in full swing. The ad campaign said of Bonnie and Clyde, "They're young! They're in love! And they kill people!"

But the film's depiction of the two outlaws emphasizes their youth and romantic ideals far more than their violent acts. The film makes it clear that the gang of outlaws robs only from the wealthy banks that are foreclosing on poor farmers' properties. In contrast, the film's authority figures—bounty hunter Frank Hamer, Ivan Moss, and the banks—represent a stifling system that encourages ruthless self-interest. An analysis of two crucial scenes from the film illustrates how Penn uses editing to draw a contrast between the honesty, openness, and altruism of the outlaws and the dishonesty and hypocrisy of the establishment.

7.17 Two outlaws share a moment of tenderness in *Bonnie and Clyde.*

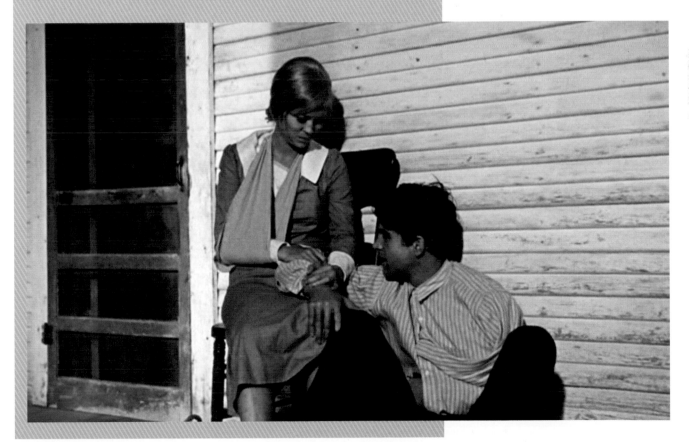

Late in *Bonnie and Clyde*, three remaining members of the gang of outlaws—Bonnie, Clyde, and C.W.—recuperate at C.W.'s father Ivan's house after being ambushed by the law. Bonnie (Faye Dunaway), Clyde (Warren Beatty), C.W. (Michael J. Pollard), and Ivan Moss sit on the porch discussing the newspaper's coverage of the police assault on the Barrow gang, which left Clyde's brother mortally wounded. As C.W. reads the paper, he asks why he is always listed as an "unidentified suspect." The scene cuts to a medium two-shot of Bonnie and Clyde, so that we see Clyde's response to C.W.'s question. He tells C.W. to be glad "that's all you are." While Clyde is still talking, the scene cuts to a medium close-up of Ivan. At this point the audience can see his devilish grin appear when he hears Clyde tell C.W., "as long as they don't know your last name." The timing of the cut emphasizes Ivan's realization that he can double-cross Bonnie and Clyde without jeopardizing his son. Ivan, at this point, becomes one of the many authority figures that the film condemns for being hypocritical.

A subsequent pairing of images underscores Ivan's duplicity. In one medium long shot, Bonnie and Clyde rest in one another's arms on the front porch, enjoying the peace, tranquility, and sunshine (fig. **7.17**). As the shot continues, C.W. and his father, Ivan, go inside to fix lunch; Ivan stops in the doorway and tells the young couple to stay as long as they want. Bonnie and Clyde sit for a few seconds longer in the sun. Then the scene abruptly cuts to a shot of the interior of the house, where Ivan is beating C.W. and berating his son for bringing such "trash" to his home (fig. **7.18**). The juxtaposition of the two shots is jolting. Penn uses the contrast between the two images (tranquility vs. violence; hospitality vs. condemnation; sunshine vs. a dingy interior) to emphasize Ivan's hypocrisy, and to distinguish his untrustworthiness from the young couple's loyalty to one another and their friends.

Throughout, *Bonnie and Clyde* underscores the integrity of the Barrow gang in contrast to the deceitfulness of the authority figures who pursue them. In linking the couple's innocence and moral integrity with images of tranquility and openness, the film romanticizes the two outlaws, who are ruthlessly gunned down by a corrupt establishment.

7.18 A sharply contrasting image from *Bonnie and Clyde*.

has the boy: he has discovered his love for art, which he mistakenly assumes will help him succeed in school.

Shot transitions may also correspond to visual cues. The first shot of *Citizen Kane*'s boarding house sequence is a long take from inside the room where Mrs. Kane signs the papers to send her son away. After she seals her son's fate, she walks to the window, which her husband has just closed (a symbolic gesture that reveals his willingness to relinquish ties to his own son). Mrs. Kane opens the window, and then the scene immediately cuts to the medium close-up of her in the foreground. These two shots demonstrate how editing can be timed to coincide with action; the cut places dramatic emphasis on Mrs. Kane's lifting the sash, encouraging audiences to see the emotional bond between mother and son. In short, editing can also correspond with an action, a character's gaze, a simple gesture, or lines of dialogue.

Careful analysis of editing demands consideration of how any single edit can exploit all three attributes of editing simultaneously for expressive purposes, as the balcony scene in *Notorious* demonstrates (see fig. **7.13**).

Story-Centered Editing and the Construction of Meaning

All films consisting of multiple shots, even those that do not tell stories, draw on the three attributes of editing discussed above. But almost all popular films revolve around a story, and, as Chapter 4 emphasizes, stories usually unfold over a period of time greater than the screen time and take place in a number of different spaces. In narrative films, editing's primary functions are to shape the audience's sense of time and to draw the audience's attention to important details of the story space.

Editing and Time

Narrative films tell stories by splicing (joining together) multiple shots to convey the cause-and-effect logic of the plot. The order in which an audience sees shots determines how the audience perceives the storyline. At the simplest level, as editors arrange shots within a scene, they have to create the illusion that the succession of shots depicts continuously flowing action. The arrangement of images to depict a unified story time is called **narrative sequencing**.

Out of Sight (Steven Soderbergh 1998) begins with Jack Foley walking out of a building and furiously throwing his necktie to the curb of a busy street. He then proceeds to cross the street to rob a bank. Despite the apparent simplicity of the sequence, Soderbergh actually used nine different shots (in 26 seconds) to document Jack's actions. Yet viewers of the film perceive the fragmented movement as one continuous action because the shots are joined.

In addition to creating the illusion of chronological time, narrative sequencing allows filmmakers to shape the audience's perception of time in three ways: to condense or expand time; to suggest the simultaneity of events happening in different settings; and to rearrange the order in which audiences see events.

Condensing and Expanding Time

The most obvious way narrative sequencing shapes how audiences perceive narrative time is by cutting out unnecessary events. The plot in most narrative films shows us only those actions and events that directly affect the outcome of the storyline. Billy Wilder's *Some Like it Hot* (1959) illustrates how narrative sequencing can simultaneously eliminate extraneous material, focus the audience's attention on the central conflict motivating the characters, and emphasize character development. Two musicians, Joe (Tony Curtis) and Jerry (Jack Lemmon), witness a mob hit. Fearing for their own lives because they are eyewitnesses, they don women's clothing and join an all-woman musical troupe that is leaving Chicago for Florida. When they call the agent in charge of hiring, we see and hear Joe adopting his best feminine voice as he inquires about the job. The shot dissolves into a close-up of four legs in high heels and stockings, clumsily walking down a train station's loading platform.

This example illustrates how narrative sequencing often achieves a purely functional purpose—it keeps the audience's attention from flagging. In just two shots, Wilder efficiently emphasizes how Joe and Jerry are going to get out of Chicago. He does not show the audience the two men scrambling for an entire wardrobe of women's clothing.

But in the process of manipulating time, narrative sequencing can also help a film develop emotional and/or intellectual intricacy. Changes in time and space invite audiences to make an immediate comparison between two distinct points in time. Changes in time may mark the presence of central conflicts or emphasize important stages in character development. More careful analysis of *Some Like it Hot* illustrates how an apparently simple shift in time yields important ideas about the film's character development and themes.

Wilder's use of editing emphasizes that this is a turning point for Joe and Jerry. Earlier scenes in the film depict them as conniving womanizers. Ironically, despite their sudden physical proximity to women (especially to Sugar, played by Marilyn Monroe), Joe and Jerry's masquerade makes it difficult for them to get physically intimate with them. From this point on, their characters evolve as they become more emotionally intimate with their fellow musicians.

Eliding time can also emphasize more abstract themes. In Ingmar Bergman's *The Seventh Seal* ("*Det sjunde inseglet* "; 1957), Death (Bengt Ekerot) comes to claim the life of a knight (Max von Sydow) who has just returned from the Crusades. But the knight convinces Death that the two should play a game of chess; the victor wins the knight's life. Early in the film, Bergman films a close-up of the chessboard the knight has set up on a rock near the ocean. A dissolve makes it appear as if the ocean's tide is washing away the chessboard. In narrative terms, the dissolve indicates the passage of time. The sun is setting on the horizon in the second shot, and clearly the knight has spent the entire day on the shoreline.

But the dissolve also carries with it a more profound symbolic meaning. Given the significance of the chessboard in the film, the editing emphasizes the frailty of life. Human life is as tenuous as chess pieces toppled by the sea. The editing's emphasis on the movement of the sun in this context also lends symbolic weight to the imagery; the end of the day clearly connotes the ending of life (fig. **7.19**).

Sometimes filmmakers use a **montage sequence** to indicate the passage of time. Instead of merely excising a period of time altogether via a dissolve or a fade-out, a montage sequence emphasizes the actual process of passing time (albeit in a condensed form). Montage sequences consist of several shots, each one occurring at a different point in time, and each joined together by an appropriate shot transition. A montage sequence can span hours, one day, a few months, or years.

In *Spider-Man*, a montage sequence depicts the hours that Peter Parker spends dreaming up the costume he will wear, which will complement his recently acquired powers. The film exploits the language of the montage sequence for comic effect when, after showing the amount of time Peter spends fantasizing about a sleek, form-fitting body-suit, the film reveals what he actually wears for his first public performance: a baggy red and blue sweatsuit and a ski mask.

7.19 A dissolve adds symbolic significance to *The Seventh Seal*.

In addition to condensing or eliminating time, editing also allows filmmakers to expand time by arranging multiple overlapping shots of a single action, so that portions of the action are repeated as it unfolds. In *Shoot the Piano Player* (*"Tirez sur le pianiste"*; François Truffaut 1960), amateur pianist Edouard Saroyan (Charles Aznavour) is invited to his first professional audition. When he arrives at the studio, he pauses nervously outside the door, and when he finally decides to ring the bell, the film presents his action in three consecutive and overlapping extreme close-up shots of his hand as it reaches for the button (fig. **7.20**). The editing effectively triples the amount of time it takes Saroyan to ring the doorbell and, by exaggerating a gesture that would otherwise be an inconsequential detail, suggests how much emotional investment he stakes in the audition.

Suggesting the Simultaneity of Events

Narrative sequencing also involves arranging the order in which audiences see events. For example, editing can suggest multiple lines of action unfolding simultaneously. **Parallel editing**, sometimes called cross-cutting, is when a film-maker cuts back and forth between two or more events occurring in different spaces, usually suggesting that these events are happening at the same time.

7.20 An extreme close-up of Saroyan's finger, from *Shoot the Piano Player*: editing exaggerates the gesture.

Often filmmakers use parallel editing to create suspense. Action films inevitably include parallel editing to suggest multiple lines of action that are converging on the same space, as in a car chase or rescue sequence. Sometimes a filmmaker uses parallel editing to compare two or more lines

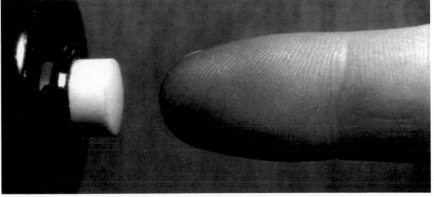

of action. In addition to suggesting that the depicted events are occurring simultaneously, such sequences also help develop themes. In *Billy Elliot*, Billy (Jamie Bell), the son of an out-of-work miner, develops a love for ballet, much to the dismay of his father, who has hopes that Billy might pursue boxing. At one point, a parallel editing sequence humorously suggests how Billy's entire family, with the notable exception of his father, expresses a love for music through movement. As the soundtrack plays T Rex's "Jitterbug Boogie," the sequence cross-cuts between four separate spaces: Billy practices his ballet routine in the local gym; his brother Tony listens to the same song and plays air-guitar in his bedroom; his grandmother practices long-forgotten ballet movements downstairs; and his father sits on the toilet gargling. The father's lack of engagement with the tune—and the fact that he sits on the commode, of all places, while everyone else dances—points to his preference for unrefined pursuits over the arts and helps explain his refusal to allow Billy to continue practicing ballet.

7.21 (*above*) The girl's eyes glaze over in *Walkabout*.

7.22 (*below*) Reality gives way to fantasy in *Walkabout*.

Arranging the Order of Events

Editing can also allow filmmakers to rearrange the sequence in which events are shown. Editing makes possible the expressive potential of those moments when a film's *syzuhet* reorders chronology to suggest a similarity between two points in time or a cause-and-effect relationship. The most common example of this is the flashback, when events taking place in the present are "interrupted" by images or scenes that have taken place in the past. Typically filmmakers give audiences a visual cue, such as a dissolve or a fade, to clarify that the narrative is making a sudden shift in chronology. Usually a flashback is motivated by the plot, as when a character—any of the narrators in *Citizen Kane*, for example—recalls a memory.

Flashbacks typically emphasize important causal factors in a film's *fabula*. As the end of chapter reading in Chapter 4 observes, *Slumdog Millionaire* uses wipes to transition between Jamal's childhood past and his present day game show quest. Doing so helps the audience understand why he is able to answer such diverse and difficult questions.

Editing also allows filmmakers to reveal a character's dreams or fantasies. Like a flashback, a dream is usually signaled by a shot transition that indicates the boundary between reality and fantasy. In *Walkabout* (Nicholas Roeg 1971), a teenage girl from the city and her young brother are stranded in the Australian outback. Eventually they are rescued by a young aboriginal male who guides them back to the industrialized world. Despite the mutual sexual attraction between the girl and her guide, they never overcome the cultural barriers that separate them; their desires remain unspoken. The film's resolution reveals that, on returning home, the girl has grown up and married a young professional. As he babbles on about his impending promotion, the camera slowly zooms in to her glazed eyes (fig. **7.21**). Then the scene dissolves into a shot of the aborigine, naked and diving into a lake in the outback. He swims over to a small island where the girl and her brother are sitting and laughing, also naked (fig. **7.22**).

The scene of the three characters frolicking together is clearly not a flashback, because the girl was never comfortable enough around her guide to express her affection for him, much less to take off her clothing in front of him. Instead, the scene is a fantasy, a longing for what could have been. Indeed, the editing in the remainder of the sequence emphasizes the sharp contrast between the happiness that she fantasizes about and the boredom of her daily routine. The jubilant laughter, unselfconscious nudity, and her playful demeanor are the antithesis of the dissatisfied gaze (complete with glassy eyes and blank expression), made-up face, and lack of interest with which she greets her husband. The idyllic landscape in her fantasy also contrasts with the blandness of her apartment in real life. The clash of the *mise en scène* in each shot indicates that she realizes she has sacrificed freedom and affection for sterile predictability.

On rare occasions, filmmakers will insert a flashforward, interrupting the events taking place in the present by images of events that will take place in the future. By their nature, flashforwards can be disorienting since they can only be understood as such after the "future" event occurs. Sometimes a flashforward may be logically explained by the narrative, as when a character has a premonition of upcoming events.

However, flashforwards are seldom logically justified in terms of the narrative; their significance is usually far more ambiguous. At one point in *Easy Rider* (Dennis Hopper 1969), Captain America (Peter Fonda) is interrupted as he talks by an inexplicable and brief shot of burning debris on the side of a road. Only later will viewers recognize that the debris they had seen earlier is the wreckage from Captain America's motorcycle crash, which occurs at the end of the film.

7.23 Chairs magically proliferate in this tableau shot from Georges Méliès's *The Black Imp* (1905).

Editing and Space

One of the many distinctions between film and theater is film's ability to draw audiences into the story space. When viewers see a play, their perspective is determined and limited by the distance between their seats and the stage. Early filmmakers relied largely on the **tableau shot**, a long shot in which the frame of the image resembles the proscenium arch of a stage (fig. **7.23**). The audience's perspective, in other words, is

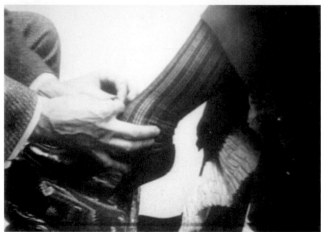

consistently distanced from the action onscreen, as it would be if they were watching a play.

Edwin S. Porter's *The Gay Shoe Clerk* (1903) demonstrates the remarkable storytelling potential filmmakers harnessed once they began experimenting with alternatives to the tableau shot. In the short comedy, a clerk helps a young woman try on shoes while her chaperone watches from the background. Eventually, the clerk's self-restraint crumbles, and he stands up to kiss the alluring customer. This infuriates the chaperone, who proceeds to bonk him over the head with an umbrella. The story is simple, but the film uses three shots instead of one to guarantee that the audience does not miss a key piece of narrative information. It begins with a standard tableau shot of all three characters sitting in the store (fig. **7.24**). But Porter cuts to a close-up—one of the first in cinema history—of the clerk's hands fitting a shoe onto his customer's foot. As he fumbles with the shoe, she raises her skirt, exposing her ankle … and then her calf (fig. **7.25**). The film then cuts back to the tableau shot, so audiences can see the riotous collapse of social decorum (fig. **7.26**). This famous close-up draws the viewer's attention to the most crucial information of the story space, encouraging empathy for a clerk enticed by a young woman whose provocations presumably go unnoticed by her chaperone.

Editing focuses the audience's attention on anything from the microscopic—as in *Three Kings* (David O. Russell 1999), which shows how muscle fiber reacts when a bullet enters the body—to the grand—as in *Return of the King*, when editing traces the lighting of pyres across a mountain range in a majestic call to arms. As filmmakers cut within scenes, they can draw the viewer's attention to a number of things, including the emotional tenor of a conversation, the objects of a character's gaze, important details in the *mise en scène*, and the group dynamics of a scene.

Shot/Reverse Shot

One of the most important editing techniques within a scene is the **shot/reverse shot**, a standard shot pattern that directors use to film conversations between two characters. This method dictates that a shot of a character speaking will be followed by a shot of another character's response, taken by a camera placed at the reverse angle of the first shot. The visual effect of this alternating camera placement is evident in shots from *Psycho* when Marion Crane and Norman Bates converse in his parlor (figs. **7.28**, **7.29**). Notice that neither character looks directly at the camera.

7.24 *(above)* *The Gay Shoe Clerk* begins with a tableau shot.

7.25 *(center)* One of the first close-ups in film history provides important information.

7.26 *(below)* The consequent collapse of social decorum occurs.

In general, actors avoid speaking directly to the viewer, because doing so acknowledges the audience's presence and destroys the illusion of a naturally unfolding story. Following standard practice for the shot/reverse shot, Hitchcock places the cameras slightly angled to the side rather than using point-of-view shots, as the overhead diagram of the scene illustrates (fig. **7.27**).

A more detailed analysis of the scene shows two specific ways this editing pattern defines the emotional dynamics of the scene. First, the timing of the cuts corresponds to the dialogue, guiding the audience's vantage point so that it remains focused on the characters' reactions to the spoken word. This editing pattern is so common in films that most viewers take its expressive power for granted.

The scene lasts for several minutes, and the camera largely volleys back and forth between two shots: an eye-level medium shot of Marion eating her sandwich and an eye-level medium shot of Norman reclining in a chair. The lack of exaggerated camera angles in these shots suggests the conversation has a pleasantly innocuous tenor. The editing emphasizes how each character responds to what the other has said. When Marion asks if Norman goes out with friends, the scene cuts to Norman so the audience can see his body's involuntary withdrawal as he offers his timid response that "a boy's best friend is his mother." When Marion says that she is looking for her "own private island" to escape to, the camera immediately cuts to Norman as he leans forward and asks, "what are you running away from?" His response marks a sudden shift in the dynamics of the conversation: now Marion is put into a defensive position, and Norman's leaning into the foreground offers a clear indication of his aggression, which is beginning to emerge. In other words, the timing of the cuts reveals which words affect him most and the specific physical and emotional responses he has to them.

A second way filmmakers can tap into the expressive potential of the shot/reverse shot is to orchestrate patterns of repetition and change. Typically, the alternating images in a shot/reverse shot sequence create a somewhat repetitious pattern. That is, when filmmakers return to a reverse angle, they often use a shot that is more or less consistent with the previous reverse-angle shot. However, editing can signal important shifts in the emotional dynamics of a scene by suddenly altering this pattern.

Through much of *Psycho*'s parlor scene, Hitchcock consistently employs the same eye-level medium shots of Marion and Norman. But when the undertone of the conversation becomes more loaded with Marion's and Norman's personal baggage, the editing emphasizes the (suddenly apparent) unspoken seriousness of the interchange. When Marion comments on overhearing Mother's

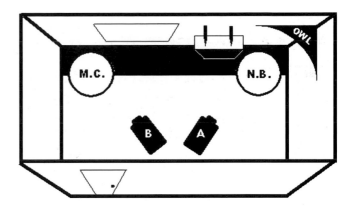

7.27 Camera placement in *Psycho* (image courtesy of artofallowance.com).

7.28 *(above)* Norman talks to Marion in the parlor in *Psycho*.

7.29 *(below)* A reverse shot of Marion in the same scene from *Psycho*.

7.30 The atmosphere changes in the parlor in *Psycho*.

7.31 *(above)* Mrs. Muir looks offscreen in *The Ghost and Mrs. Muir*.

7.32 *(below)* The eyeline match reveals the object of her gaze.

vicious critique of Norman, the reverse shot of Norman marks a radical departure from the pattern that has been established previously. Instead of shooting Norman from an eye-level medium shot, Hitchcock films him from a low-angle profile shot (fig. **7.30**). So, when Norman says he gets the urge to "leave her forever, or at least defy her," the audience sees him from a very disquieting vantage point. The sudden rupture in the shot/reverse shot sequence hints at the dark underside of Norman's submissive relationship with Mother, which Marion's inquisitiveness has just prodded. Moreover, the change in the camera's perspective positions Norman underneath a stuffed owl in the background, as if Norman were the bird's prey. The editing and the *mise en scène* coincide to create a visual metaphor for Norman's entrapment under Mother's watchful gaze.

The shift in the shot/reverse shot pattern allows Hitchcock to reframe the scene's physical space to illustrate disruptions in the scene's emotional space. In a sense, this scene paves the way for the more radical fissures in emotional space that will appear in the film's famous shower sequence.

Eyeline Match

A second key technique editors sometimes use to shape the audience's understanding of the geography of a scene is the **eyeline match**. This match cut uses a character's line of sight to motivate the cut. If a filmmaker wants to emphasize that a character is looking at a particular prop or another person, she will include a shot of the character looking offscreen, followed by a shot of the object or person that the character observes. This sequence of shots makes spatial relationships clear to the audience and guides viewers through a character's thought process. Sometimes the filmmaker will begin with the shot of the object or person, and then follow it with a shot of the character who is looking at it. In either case, the editing—via the eyeline match technique—allows audiences to understand what has captured the character's attention.

A scene from the classic romance *The Ghost and Mrs. Muir* (Joseph L. Mankiewicz 1947) shows how the eyeline match is a powerful storytelling device because it draws the audience into a character's thought process and emotional state. Just after Mrs. Muir meets the ghost of an old sea captain who haunts her new house, she goes to turn in for the evening. As she is undressing in her bedroom, something catches her eye and she turns to look offscreen (fig. **7.31**). An eyeline match reveals what has given her pause:

a portrait of the captain (fig. **7.32**). Taken together, these shots wordlessly evoke Mrs. Muir's sudden sense of reserve. Seeing the portrait of the man she has just met (in his ethereal form) makes her feel self-conscious about undressing, as if the picture itself could be watching her. After covering the portrait, she proceeds to undress. Later, in a comic and rather risqué revelation, the captain talks to her in bed—making it clear that he *was* watching her all along. Attentive viewers will notice the portrait in the reflection of the mirror in the first shot of the sequence, but the eyeline match guarantees that viewers don't miss it. This unusual maneuver encourages audiences to share Mrs. Muir's thought process. Like her, the viewer casually notices the portrait, but does not fully recognize its potential significance until a few seconds later.

Cutting to Emphasize Group Dynamics

In scenes involving more than one or two characters, filmmakers sometimes cut to specific areas of the *mise en scène* to help suggest complex group dynamics. This occurs frequently in scenes where the characters have conflicting goals and distinct character traits, where editing can help portray a complex interweaving of different emotions, types of behavior, and physical responses to stimuli.

One example is the scene in *Stagecoach* when the passengers gather around the table to have dinner in Dry Fork. As all the characters approach the table to find a seat, a medium long shot frames the three representatives of the American upper class: Gatewood, Lucy, and Hatfield. Ringo and Dallas—the outlaw and the prostitute—are noticeably absent. Then the scene cuts to a two-shot of them on the opposite side of the table as Ringo asks Dallas to have a seat facing Lucy (fig. **7.33**). The cut, in this context, isolates the two ostracized members of the group and establishes the class conflict that will govern the rest of the scene. Once Dallas accepts Ringo's offer, the reverse shot shows Gatewood's, Lucy's, Hatfield's, and even Doc Boone's shocked response (fig. **7.34**). The shot/reverse shot, in other words, makes palpable the disdain Gatewood, Lucy, and Hatfield feel for Dallas and Ringo.

7.33 *(above)* A two-shot of Ringo and Dallas in *Stagecoach* establishes them as outsiders.

7.34 *(below)* A reverse shot in *Stagecoach* reveals a shocked response.

Cutaways

Editing may also draw attention to non-human elements of the *mise en scène* that will influence the plot or help develop the theme of a film. Shots that focus the audience's attention on precise details are called **cutaways**. Unlike an eyeline match, a cutaway is not character-centered; the onscreen appearance of an object does not depend on a character having to "see it" in the previous shot.

In Dreyer's *The Passion of Joan of Arc*, an eyeline match reveals that Joan sees a shadow in the shape of a cross on the floor of her prison cell. She interprets the shadow as a sign from God. Later, Dreyer films a close-up shot once again, so that viewers see the feet of a church interrogator as he enters her cell and steps on the shadow. The imagery foreshadows how he will betray Joan's trust. For the second shot of the shadow, Dreyer uses a cutaway without an eyeline match, emphasizing that Joan does not see the interrogator tread on the shadow and so does not witness his defilement of her symbol of faith.

In short, editing offers filmmakers a powerful tool for drawing the audience's attention to what is important within the diegetic space. It allows filmmakers to bring the audience's perspective closer to (or further from) the action that unfolds in the story space and tells the audience what it should notice and when.

Beyond Narrative: Creating Meaning Outside the Story

So far this chapter has focused largely on the ways editing can generate story-centered meaning: how editing helps filmmakers indicate the passage of time and how editing emphasizes important narrative details in a scene. But there are two significant means by which editing can produce abstract ideas: it can defy audience expectations by departing from the "rules" of continuity editing, and it can associate two images with one another to produce meaning on the level of metaphor.

Continuity Editing: Conventional Patterns and "Bending the Rules"

Chapter 2 discussed how audiences carry with them certain expectations when they go to see movies: expectations based on the leading actor or actress in a movie, expectations shaped by marketing strategies, and expectations based on their assumptions of how a story should be told.

Audiences have expectations about how editing should function in a narrative film. Most importantly, audiences expect to see editing that is carefully calibrated with the action on screen. Most contemporary viewers might be put off by films that advance Bazin's *mise en scène* aesthetic (see pp. 122–4). Bazin advocated the use of long takes so that audiences experience an unmediated unfolding of reality. Some viewers may initially find the long take aesthetic tedious because they expect dramatic cutting to accentuate the emotional content of any given scene.

This point illustrates how Western audiences have very specific expectations about what editing should look like. These expectations are shaped by the Hollywood standard, which is called **continuity editing**, or invisible editing, because the cutting is so seamless from one shot to the next that audiences in the movie theater are not even aware that they are seeing an assembled sequence of images. In their attempt to "hide" the hundreds or thousands of shot transitions that make up an average feature film, continuity editors face two central challenges: to depict space with a coherent geography, and to create the illusion that narrative time unfolds in a linear fashion.

One major concern of continuity editing is to ensure that audiences have a clear sense of the geography of a scene. Because editing is a collage of collected images, changing shots can cause confusion. Any time a scene cuts to a new shot, the image becomes fragmented and the scene's coherence could potentially rupture. Continuity editing works to hide this fragmentation by employing two strategies: it relies on a systematic order for presenting shots and it maintains the consistency of direction on screen. These standard practices help ensure that audiences perceive the story space as unified and coherent.

Continuity and Space

To begin, editors usually rely on a **standard shot pattern**, which helps to orient audiences to the setting and spatial characteristics of a scene. Typically a scene begins with an **establishing shot**, which is usually (but not always) a long shot designed to clarify when and where the scene is taking place in relation to the previous scene and to provide an overview of the entire setting. Once the audience has a clear sense of where the characters are and how they are positioned in relation to one another, the filmmaker can cut to closer shots to emphasize important details. Continuity editing demands that filmmakers rely on standardized techniques—the shot/reverse shot and the eyeline match—to ensure that audiences understand why they are being shown this information. In other words, when Marilyn Monroe suddenly appears onscreen in *Some Like it Hot*, the use of the eyeline match justifies her presence: she has caught the eye of Joe and Jerry. As a scene ends, there is often a **re-establishing shot**, another long shot that reorients viewers to the environment, that offers closure to the scene, paving the way for the next scene. Longer scenes often include re-establishing shots midway through to reorient audiences when characters move about the setting.

In *High Noon* (Fred Zinnemann 1951), Marshal Will Kane (Gary Cooper) interrupts a church service to solicit the congregation's help in defending the community against Frank Miller (Ian MacDonald), a recently paroled outlaw who will arrive in town at noon. The scene begins with an establishing shot of the exterior of the church (fig. **7.35**). Kane walks into the frame and approaches the building. There is a cut to the interior of the church, a high-angle long shot of the congregation taken from behind the pulpit (fig. **7.36**). Kane enters the background of this shot.

After a cut to a medium shot of him addressing the man in the pulpit and an eyeline match that reveals Kane's view of the pulpit, the congre-

7.35 *(above)* An establishing shot of the church in *High Noon*.

7.36 *(above center)* A high-angle shot of the congregation inside the church focuses on the location of the action in *High Noon*.

7.37 *(below center)* Kane addresses the congregation in *High Noon*: tensions rise.

7.38 *(below)* A point-of-view shot from the pulpit in *High Noon*.

7.39 *(above)* The TV executive faces screen right in *Bamboozled*.

7.40 *(below)* In the next shot from *Bamboozled*, the TV executive faces screen left. Note the different backgrounds.

gation on either side of the aisle turns to gaze at the camera/Kane. The rest of the scene depicts the escalating tensions within the room when Kane addresses the parishioners via a series of shot/reverse shots and eyeline matches (figs. **7.37**, **7.38**). As is typical in continuity editing, the scene begins with the broadest details before it focuses on the more subtle interactions among the various characters involved.

Another way for filmmakers to ensure that audiences do not lose track of the setting's spatial arrangement as the scene moves from shot to shot, is to follow the **180-degree rule**. This rule dictates that, within a scene, once the camera starts filming on one side of the action, it will continue filming on that same side of the action for the rest of the scene unless there is a clearly articulated justification for crossing "the axis of action." As the overhead diagram of the parlor scene from *Psycho* illustrates (see fig. 7.27), Hitchcock films the entire scene from the same side of the set. His cameras never film from inside the shaded area—they do not cross the imaginary line running between Marion and Norman. Crossing the line would reverse the direction of the action so that suddenly the characters would be facing the opposite direction onscreen.

Another side effect of crossing the axis of action, or breaking the 180-degree rule, is that the background of the scene is suddenly changed. If Hitchcock had filmed Marion or Norman from inside the shaded area, the wall, which had heretofore been "invisible" in the scene, would have appeared in the background. Audiences might be confused if the window behind Marion suddenly turned into the threshold to the parlor. In short, the 180-degree rule helps maintain consistent screen direction and spatial unity. Within a scene, the axis of action may shift. If characters move, or if new characters enter the scene, the line adjusts accordingly, through reframing and, perhaps, a re-establishing shot. Still, most filmmakers conscientiously work to ensure that audiences perceive the direction of movement as consistent across shots. Spike Lee intentionally breaks the rule in *Bamboozled* (2000), during the scene in which a television executive (Michael Rapaport) berates his staff. One shot shows him sitting at the end of a conference table at screen left, facing right (fig. **7.39**), but the next shot is a close-up of him facing screen left (fig. **7.40**). The disorientation suggests confusion, and serves as a distancing device to undercut the authority of his words.

Continuity and Chronology

In addition to maintaining a coherent story space, continuity editing also regulates the audience's sense of linear time. Because editing is the art of joining images filmed at two or more distinct points in time, editing itself jeopardizes the illusion of chronological continuity. The best way to establish this illusion is to present events chronologically. As a rule, events appear onscreen in the order in

CONTINUITY EDITING

During principal photography, the **continuity editor** (or **script supervisor**) maintains a record of each shot to guarantee consistency from take to take. Her notes would specify each actor's costume and position, and the arrangement of the *mise en scène* in general at the end of each take. After the principal photography is completed, the **editor** works with the director to combine and cull the footage. To build a scene, directors and editors combine **master shots**—takes that cover the entire scene—with reaction shots, cutaways, and **B-roll** (secondary footage that may depart from the main subject of a scene, such as an exterior shot of the building where a scene takes place). For *Cold Mountain* (Anthony Minghella 2003), editor Walter Murch whittled 113 hours of material down to a two-and-a-half-hour film (Cellini, p. 3).

Because any single take may be filmed from multiple vantage points simultaneously, editors study footage on an editing deck that allows them to watch several takes at once before deciding which is the best one for the scene. Sometimes the editor will only use part of one take, selecting the best moments of an actor's performance from it.

An **assistant editor** catalogs all the takes, inspects the condition of the negative, and supervises the creation of optical effects (often contracted out). A **negative cutter** assembles the entire negative and cuts and splices it together, adhering to the editor's decisions. Positive prints are then made from the negative.

As digital post-production technologies have become the norm, the tools available to the editor have changed. Walter Murch cut *Cold Mountain* on Final Cut Pro, a professional editing software program which has become an industry standard. In an interview, he notes several differences using digital technology: he could show dailies to director Minghella on the set in Romania on a laptop and send a DVD of them to producer Sidney Pollock in Los Angeles. And the affordability of computer workstations relative to flatbed editing machines meant that he had four workstations functioning simultaneously rather than two. But Murch also acknowledges certain advantages of working with film. "When you actually had to make the cut physically on film, you naturally tended to think more about what you were about to do," Murch states, "which—in the right proportion—is a good thing to do." He misses the spontaneity of scanning through footage in search of a specific shot. "Inevitably before you got there, you found something that was better than what you had in mind. With random access, you immediately get what you want. Which may not be what you need." (Cellini)

which they occur in the *fabula*. Any exceptions to this principle are almost always motivated by narrative events. For example, *Citizen Kane*'s plot makes radical jumps back and forth in time, but this departure from chronological order is explained by the fact that Thompson is gathering the details about Kane's life from various narrators. So, even though Kane's life is presented "out of order," Thompson's quest is presented in chronological order.

Likewise, actions don't get repeated unless they happen more than once in the story, or the repetition is motivated (for example, a character has a flashback). In *Do the Right Thing*, Spike Lee breaks this rule twice for dramatic effect. When Mookie delivers a pizza to his girlfriend, Tina, he throws the pizza box down on the table and moves to embrace her—then the shot repeats itself. To unsophisticated viewers, it looks as if pizza boxes keep reappearing in Mookie's hands. Later, when Mookie throws the trashcan through Sal's window, an exterior shot shows the trashcan shattering the glass. Then Lee shows the same event from inside the pizzeria so that audiences see this pivotal moment from different vantage points. The unusual use of repetition becomes a motif of sorts, and reiterates the film's interest in the opposing forces of love (the embrace) and hate (the violence).

If the plot requires a flashback or dream sequence, to minimize disruption editors will include an appropriate shot transition, such as a fade or a dissolve. Such transitions ease audiences into the new location and time. An abrupt, inexplicable shift in the time and place of an action which is not "announced" by a transition results in a **jump cut**.

Consider, for example, the difference between two scenes in which characters drive a considerable distance in cars. In the classically edited *The Maltese Falcon* (John Huston 1941), Sam Spade (Humphrey Bogart) takes a taxi cab across town to investigate a mysterious address. In the first shot, Spade hires a cab to take him to the address. This shot dissolves to a close-up of a car wheel, which in turn dissolves into a shot of the cab pulling to the side of a curb in a dark San Francisco neighborhood (the address, it turns out, is a hoax). In three quick shots, Huston takes the action across town while maintaining the illusion of linear time. As Robert Ray points out, the dialogue complements the editing to help convey how much storytime is being depicted on screen: "Spade's question to the cabbie, 'You got plenty of gas?' tells the viewer that the forthcoming trip is a relatively long one" (Ray, p. 46).

By comparison, Jean-Luc Godard's *Breathless* ("*A Bout de Souffle*"; 1960) radically disrupts continuity in the scene when the thief Michel (Jean-Paul Belmondo)—who idolizes Humphrey Bogart—flees Marseilles in a car he has stolen. As Michel drives down the road, passing cars and talking to himself, several jump cuts disorient the viewer's sense of time and space, since there is no clear indication of how long he has been driving over the course of the sequence or how far he gets. Michel steals the car on a crowded street, and as he drives off, a jump cut suddenly places him in the outskirts of the city. Later, surrounding traffic suddenly disappears via jump cuts. The scene's depiction of time and space, in other words, is far more fragmented than Huston's in *The Maltese Falcon*.

Jump cuts can also occur within scenes taking place in a confined setting. To preserve visual continuity, filmmakers generally adhere to the **30-degree rule**, which dictates that the camera should move at least 30 degrees any time there is a cut within a scene. For example, if a scene calls for a cut from a medium shot to a close-up of the same actor for dramatic effect, the camera would need to move 30 degrees to either side. Moving the camera at least 30 degrees gives the cut dramatic purpose. Failure to do so gives the editing a feeling of unnecessary or random fragmentation.

Adding to the challenges of an editor working to maintain the illusion of linear time is the fact that he is invariably working with footage shot out of order and must choose from multiple takes of the same material. Most film crews contain at least one continuity editor (sometimes called the script supervisor), whose job is to maintain consistency of action from shot to shot. Shooting a single scene can take several days, and the production of an entire film can take months or years. To state the obvious, stars get out of char-

7.41 *(above)* A continuity error from *Seconds*: the stewardess has given Hudson a pillow.

7.42 *(below)* In this next shot from *Seconds* the pillow has mysteriously disappeared!

acter off camera; they change clothes, grow facial hair, and alter hairstyles … they gain weight. Continuity editors ensure that when actors get back into character, they resume the physical appearance they previously had. Any unintentional discrepancy from shot to shot—an inexplicable change in location, in costume, in posture, in hairstyle—is called a **continuity error**. In John Frankenheimer's *Seconds* (1966), "Tony" Wilson (Rock Hudson) receives a pillow from a flight attendant. The close-up of Hudson makes it clear that he places the pillow behind his head (fig. **7.41**). There is a cut to the reverse shot of the attendant, and then a cut back to Hudson—only now the pillow has disappeared (fig. **7.42**). After another reverse shot of the attendant, the scene cuts back to Hudson and the pillow is once again in place! Some viewers take great pleasure in finding continuity errors.

Continuity editors also ensure that cutting from shot to shot maintains a **match on action**. If a cut occurs while a character is in the midst of an action, the subsequent shot must begin so that audiences see the completion of that action, thus guaranteeing the illusion of fluid, continuous movement.

"Breaking the Rules": The French New Wave and its Influence

Because continuity editing is the norm, most film scholarship does not concern itself with discussing how a film adheres to the Hollywood standard. But critics and scholars do notice when a film departs from these conventions. Some films (such as *Seconds*) accidentally break the rules. But some filmmakers intentionally break them. Because audiences are used to seeing films that conform to the conventions of continuity editing, filmmakers like Spike Lee understand that intentionally upsetting these expectations can provoke emotional and intellectual responses. In fact, one of the most important movements in cinema history, the French New Wave (*Nouvelle Vague*), is important because it openly defied conventions of so-called "quality filmmaking" such as continuity editing.

In an era when audacious experimentation with editing is commonplace in the work of filmmakers such as Christopher Nolan or Darren Aronofsky, it may be difficult to imagine the initial shock audiences accustomed to classical filmmaking might have experienced seeing a film like *Cleo from 5 to 7* for the first time. The film begins with shots from the title character's point of view in color, intercut with reverse shots of her in black and white. In *Shoot the Piano Player*, a man promises that he's telling the truth by swearing on his mother's life; a startling cut shows an old woman clutching her heart and collapsing. This commitment to cinematic playfulness is one of the defining characteristics of the French New Wave. As the name implies, this movement—which lasted roughly from the late 1950s to the mid-1960s—rejected the staid traditions of French cinema. What united the most prominent directors of the New Wave—including François Truffaut, Jean Luc Godard, Agnès Varda, and Claude Chabrol—was a commitment to exploring the expressive promise of cinema and to tapping its potential to do more than simply adapt classic literature.

A willingness to challenge the conventions of editing is characteristic of the best films of the period. New Wave directors readily used wipes and irises—

7.43 *(above)* The teacher poses a question in *Band of Outsiders*.

7.44 *(below)* *Band of Outsiders* breaks the 180-degree rule.

transitions that were, by that point, considered crude relics of the silent era. The fact that New Wave directors flagrantly used these techniques announced their desire to investigate the language of the cinema, to experiment with storytelling, and to liberate the cinema from the constrictive conventions of the day. New Wave directors routinely discarded rules of continuity.

Godard's *Band of Outsiders* (1964) exemplifies much of what defines the New Wave. Like many films of the era, *Band of Outsiders* is an *hommage* to an American genre: the gangster heist film. Godard uses the heist scenario as a point of departure to reflect on the very nature of the cinema. In the film, Franz (Sami Frey) and Arthur (Claude Brasser) meet the beguiling Odile (Anna Karina) in an English class and convince her to participate in a second-rate robbery. Repeatedly, the young men re-enact famous Hollywood shootouts, a motif that suggests that the men are motivated primarily by their desire to emulate their favorite movies. In one famous scene, all three spontaneously perform a dance routine in a soda shop, transforming their daily routine into the stuff of a Hollywood musical. In short, the effects of cinema as a social and aesthetic phenomenon is one of the central themes of *Band of Outsiders*.

One scene in particular demonstrates the way the film breaks the rules of continuity editing to comment on the nature of the cinema. In English class the teacher asks a pupil to translate a phrase. Here the scene distinctly breaks two rules of continuity editing: the camera violates the 180-degree rule (as evident in the change in background and the reversed direction of the action), and we hear the student's response to the teacher's question twice (figs. **7.43**, **7.44**).

Immediately after affirming the student's response, the teacher directs the class's attention to the words of poet T.S. Eliot: "Everything that is new is automatically traditional." Eliot's quote comments on how any artistic expression, no matter how radical, becomes institutionalized. Initially this sentiment appears to contradict Godard's stylistic choice: in harking back to early experiments with film editing prior to the development of rules for continuity, Godard makes something old (and traditional) new. In particular, repeating details from different vantage points recalls early films such as Edwin Porter's *The Life of an American Fireman*. Godard's blatant borrowing creates a provocative new statement. Yet the juxtaposition of Eliot's quotation with Godard's startling appropriation of techniques from "primitive" cinema suggests that the act of creation is a cyclical process. Innovation inevitably becomes conventional, but the old can be made new again. Godard here acknowledges that his appropriation of early editing styles can create a "new wave" of films, and that *Band of Outsiders* (and French New Wave films in general) both contribute to and become part of a rich cinematic tradition.

Like 1970s punk rockers who appropriated the crude song structures of the 1950s and 1960s to reinvent popular music, and rap artists who sample beats and riffs from classic recordings (and even the snap and crackle of worn vinyl recordings), New Wave directors felt that returning to the medium's basic techniques and elements would propel film art forward. The classroom scene can be read as a call to arms of sorts—a defiant proposition that, to keep the medium alive and vibrant, filmmakers must be ready to deploy any and all expressive devices at their disposal.

The devil-may-care philosophy of the French New Wave has had a dramatic impact on American filmmaking since the 1960s, especially among independent directors. Godard's influence on independent figurehead Quentin Tarantino (*Pulp Fiction*, 1994; *Kill Bill*, 2003) is so pronounced that Tarantino named his production company after the French title for *Band of Outsiders* (*Bande à Part*).

Associational Editing: Editing and Metaphor

One of the great challenges of spoken language is finding a way to articulate abstract feelings or ideas. Writers run up against the limitations of the word when they are faced with having to describe something as basic, yet as abstruse, as romantic longing or fear. Authors use metaphors and similes to help their readers visualize what would otherwise be an indescribable feeling. Poet Robert Burns compares his love to "a red, red rose," and Lady Gaga compares the sensation of physical desire for a lover to a country: "hot like Mexico." Both examples describe the indescribable by associating it with something that is concrete and comprehensible. Editing also has the power to encourage audiences to meditate on equally abstract ideas.

In *Modern Times* (1936), with a simple cut, Charlie Chaplin implies that modern life breeds blind conformity; he juxtaposes a shot of sheep herded into a corral (toward their ultimate demise?) with throngs of frantic pedestrians during their morning commute to work. Hitchcock's *North by Northwest* concludes with a shot of Roger Thornhill helping his new bride, Eve, into their train berth, followed by a shot of a train entering into a tunnel. Taken together, the shots wryly suggest what censors wouldn't let Hitchcock explicitly show: the consummation of the couple's relationship. Both examples point to the power of associational editing—an approach favored by the Soviet filmmakers in the silent era.

Soviet Montage

Soviet montage is a style of editing built around the theory that editing should highlight the *differences* between shots to produce meaning. It was developed and perfected in Russia during the silent film era of the 1920s, when the Soviet regime had just come to power. Soviet leaders believed that film was an effective political tool, and filmmakers saw editing as the key to involving the audience in political and intellectual revolution. Exploiting the Kuleshov effect became the guiding principle of three of the major Soviet filmmakers in the 1920s: V.I. Pudovkin, Dziga Vertov (Denis Kaufman), and Sergei Eisenstein. These filmmakers studied D.W. Griffith's *Intolerance* (1916), a film that uses editing to establish thematic parallels between and among three unrelated narratives. All three directors experimented with the notion that, just as audiences could derive an emotional meaning from the juxtaposition of two completely unrelated shots, so, too, they could understand abstract political ideas.

7.45 *(left)* Faceless soldiers fire in *Battleship Potemkin.*

7.46 *(right)* Civilians scatter down the steps in *Battleship Potemkin.*

7.47 *(left)* Soldiers march down the steps in *Battleship Potemkin.*

7.48 *(right)* A mother clutches her son in *Battleship Potemkin.*

A careful analysis of four shots from the famous "Odessa Steps sequence" from Eisenstein's *Battleship Potemkin* illustrates how the intentionally jolting collision of images elicits both an emotional and an intellectual response. In this scene, set in Russia in 1905, the peaceful citizens of Odessa have gathered near the harbor to honor the mutinous sailors on board the battleship *Potemkin*. The sailors have revolted against their officers and, by extension, the Tsar. The Tsar sends troops to break up the congregation of citizens at the harbor. The troops fire on the civilians, and the peaceful protest turns into a massacre. Eisenstein based the scene on an actual historic event, which left seventy dead and 200 injured (Figes, p. 185). But rather than filming the sequence as an objective document of the event, Eisenstein's editing turns the conflict into a symbol of the oppression that only revolution can overturn. Throughout the sequence, Eisenstein uses editing to expand time, prolonging the impact of the Tsar's brutality by crosscutting among multiple lines of action and by showing pivotal moments of violence several times. When the troops begin to fire their guns, Eisenstein shows one

victim's head snapping backward with the force of the bullet. The same shot is repeated three times in rapid succession to underscore the horror of the moment.

Four shots appear midway through the sequence. In the first, a row of faceless soldiers fires down on the civilians, who are offscreen (fig. **7.45**). Next, a high-angle shot depicts throngs of civilians running scattershot down the steps, from screen left to screen right (fig. **7.46**). A third shot shows the soldiers progressing in a line down the steps (fig. **7.47**). The fourth shot is a medium close-up of a woman clutching her son to her chest and walking defiantly towards the soldiers (fig. **7.48**).

Eisenstein exploits visual opposition in these shots, as is evident in the character movement in each shot. While the soldiers march in unison, the crowd disperses chaotically. The contrast is equally apparent in the shot composition. The soldiers' boots create a rigid, seemingly impenetrable diagonal line, which sweeps across the screen with mechanical precision. The crowd, on the other hand, peppers the stairway at random as it scatters so that, instead of moving in unison, each civilian moves as an individual. This clash of opposing imagery suggests Eisenstein's main point: the troops represent a unified and oppressive force, lashing out at a disorganized array of ordinary citizens.

An abrupt contrast in shot distance also emphasizes the civilians' vulnerability. In the third shot, the soldiers are filmed with a long shot. The camera's perspective leaves them faceless, while the medium close-up of the woman in the fourth shot emphasizes her defiant facial expression and her son's drooping body (he has been trampled amid the confusion). In juxtaposing these shots, Eisenstein elicits an intellectual response: the troops represent a brutal, callous, and oppressive Tsarist regime which torments helpless individuals.

At the climax of the sequence, the eponymous battleship rises up in revolt and defends the citizens of Odessa. After the battleship fires on the Tsar's troops, Eisenstein adds three consecutive shots of statues of lions, each one in a different pose: one is asleep, the second has its head raised, and the third lion is standing up (figs. **7.49**, **7.50**, **7.51**). The effect is purely symbolic: the three shots create the effect of a sleeping lion (representing the people of Russia) awakening and rising up (against the Tsar).

Eisenstein's 1928 film *October* (*"Oktober"* or *Ten Days That Shook the World*) is even more bold in its use of editing to stimulate intellectual responses detached from any narrative cause-and-effect logic. The film depicts the period between the overthrow of the Tsar and the installation of the Leninist government. During this time, the moderate Kerensky established an interim government, which Eisenstein clearly depicts as obstructionist—a threat to the people's revolution. Eisenstein depicts Kerensky ordering the arrest of the revolution's leader Lenin and then confidently crossing his arms (fig. **7.52**). The scene then cuts to a shot of a statue of Napoleon, likewise represented with his arms crossed (fig. **7.53**). The clear implication is that Kerensky has become the new emperor; he is not a leader of the people but an egotistical despot. Instead of emphasizing narrative logic, the editing establishes a metaphor for Kerensky's dictatorial control.

Among the chief practitioners of montage editing there was some debate about how editing conveys ideas to the audience. Eisenstein's editing self-consciously created visual collisions. He advocated what he called a "dramatic

7.49 *(above)* The sleeping lion in *Battleship Potemkin*.

7.50 *(center)* The sleeping lion statue awakens in *Battleship Potemkin*.

7.51 *(below)* A statue of a lion with its head raised in *Battleship Potemkin*.

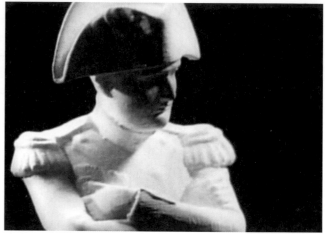

7.52 *(left)* Kerensky with arms crossed in *October*.

7.53 *(right)* The camera cuts to the statue of Napoleon in *October*.

principle" of editing, by which "montage is an idea that arises from the collision of independent shots—shots even opposite to one another." (Eisenstein, p. 49) Eisenstein described how Pudovkin, on the other hand, believed in an "epic principle," which held that "montage is the means of *unrolling* an idea with the help of single shots." (Eisenstein, p. 49) In other words, Pudovkin maintained that editing had the greatest power as an integral part in a series of narrative events.

Comparing the climactic sequence of Pudovkin's *Mother* ("*Mat*"; 1926) with the editing in *October* illustrates how his approach to editing differs from Eisenstein's. In *Mother*, Pavel (Nikolai Batalov), a man imprisoned for his revolutionary political beliefs, breaks out of his cell to join a parade of revolutionaries. During Pavel's escape, Pudovkin repeatedly cuts away to show images of ice breaking up on the river outside the prison. Like the juxtaposition of Kerensky with the statue in *October*, the cutting here conveys a metaphorical meaning; when combined with images of Pavel's escape, the break-up of the ice and the flow of the river come to symbolize the growing revolt and the dissolution of the Tsar's oppressive control. But unlike the shots in *October*, the imagery also has

7.54 Pavel on the ice in *Mother* ("*Mat*").

a narrative function: Pavel has to leap across the floes to join the protesters on the opposite side of the river (fig. **7.54**). The metaphorical power of the editing arises within the cause-and-effect logic of Pavel's story—not from the collision of two images with no narrative context.

As the Soviet practitioners understood, editing synthesizes the cinematography and *mise en scène* of individual shots into a series of images that, when taken as a whole, transcend the limitations of any one of the images in isolation.

Editing is the last of film's three visual elements described in this book. While this chapter has emphasized how a film creates meaning by combining images, the next chapter will explore how film creates meaning by combining those images with sound.

Summary

- This chapter has emphasized how all editing, even that used in completely abstract films, consists of three attributes: collage, tempo, and timing.
- In narrative films, editing helps shape the way audiences perceive time and space.
- Editing shapes the way time is presented onscreen in four ways: suggesting continuously flowing action; manipulating the duration of events; suggesting the simultaneity of events; and arranging the order of events.
- Editing can draw the audience's attention to important details of the narrative space by employing three different devices: the shot/reverse shot; the eyeline match; the cutaway.
- Many films follow the standards of continuity editing, a method for clearly presenting space and time.
- Editing can suggest more abstract ideas that transcend the literal scope of a film's narrative in two ways: by departing from the conventional rules of continuity editing and by employing associational editing.

Works Consulted

Bazin, André. "The Evolution of the Language of Cinema," in *Film Theory and Criticism*, ed. Gerald Mast *et al.*, 4th edn. New York: Oxford University Press, 1992, pp. 155–67.

Brandt, Michael. "Traditional Film Editing vs. Electronic Nonlinear Film Editing: A Comparison of Feature Films." *Nonlinear 4: The Website of Digital Video and Film Editing*. **http://www.nonlinear4.com/brandt.htm**. May 16, 2002.

Cellini, Joe. "An Interview with Walter Murch." **http://www.apple.com/pro/film/murch/ index.html**. June 16, 2004.

Cook, David. *A History of Narrative Film*. New York: Norton, 1996.

Dobbs, Lem. Commentary track. *The Limey* (DVD), dir. Steven Soderbergh. Artisan, 1999.

Eisenstein, Sergei. "A Dialectic Approach to Film Form." *Film Form*. San Diego, New York, and London: Harcourt Brace Jovanovich, 1949, pp. 45–63.

Ellis, Jack C., and Virginia Wright Wexman. *A History of Film*, 5th edn. Boston: Allyn and Bacon, 2002.

Figes, Orlando. *A People's Tragedy*. New York: Viking, 1997.

Kenez, Peter. *Cinema and Soviet Society: From the Revolution to the Death of Stalin*. New York: I.B. Tauris, 2001.

Leyda, Jay. *Kino: A History of the Russian and Soviet Film*. Princeton: Princeton University Press, 1960.

Neupert, Richard. *A History of the French New Wave Cinema*. Madison: University of Wisconsin Press, 2002.

Pudovkin, V.I. *Film Technique and Film Acting*. New York: Grove Press, 1970.

Ray, Robert. *A Certain Tendency of the Hollywood Cinema, 1930–1980*. Princeton: Princeton University Press, 1985.

Truffaut, François. *Hitchcock*, rev. edn. New York: Touchstone, 1993.

Tsivian, Yuri. "Dziga Vertov," in *The Oxford History of World Cinema*, ed. Geoffrey Nowell-Smith. Oxford and New York: Oxford University Press, 1996, pp. 92–3.

Soviet Montage Aesthetics in *The Godfather*

Soviet montage never caught on as a popular approach to filmmaking. It eventually fell out of favor under Stalin's regime, and even at the height of his productivity, Eisenstein's films weren't necessarily popular among audiences in the Soviet Union. Nevertheless, this aesthetic approach has had a lingering impact on other filmmakers. While Hollywood filmmaking is still largely wedded to the priority of telling a good, gripping story, some films incorporate Soviet montage as a means of offering shorthand commentary on characters, or of adding a layer of complexity to theme.

By and large, Francis Ford Coppola's *The Godfather* adheres to the standards of continuity editing. Nevertheless, the film provocatively combines continuity editing and montage editing to add layers of complexity to the story. In particular, Coppola uses montage editing to show that the Mafia justifies its dishonorable activities (murder) by linking them to honorable values (the importance of family and loyalty).

The film's opening dialogue establishes the film's principal theme: that the Corleone family uses violence to buttress the family. An undertaker explains how two men brought dishonor to his family when they raped and beat his daughter, leaving her permanently scarred. He asks powerful Mafia boss Don Vito Corleone (Marlon Brando) to deliver justice by killing the men. Corleone eventually agrees to help (though he refuses to have the men killed) as long as the undertaker pledges his loyalty to the godfather and promises to return the favor in the future.

The scene emphasizes the contradiction at the heart of Corleone's philosophy. He agrees to act on the undertaker's behalf only after the undertaker is brought into "the family." Only then can committing an act of violence become synonymous with honor and loyalty. Yet Corleone also wants to keep his business affairs and his own family life separate and believes he can do so. But, as this scene makes clear, violence and family honor are inextricably linked.

This contradiction is underlined by the editing. The cut from Don Corleone's office to the next scene draws attention to the connection between violent business and family life. After the undertaker leaves the room, the camera cuts to a medium close-up of Corleone as he says to the others in the dimly lit room, "We're not murderers, despite what this undertaker says." At this point there is a cut to an establishing shot of the next scene—the wedding of Corleone's daughter Connie, which is taking place at the same time the Don was meeting with the undertaker. The change of setting emphasizes contrast in a dramatic shift from darkened interior and hushed voices to the brightly lit exterior and noisy hubbub of the wedding. The visual contrast between the two images highlights the opposition between the activities taking place inside Corleone's office and those taking place outside.

The disparities between these shots suggest Corleone's attempt to keep family and business separate. But as the movie progresses, the two become increasingly indistinguishable from one another, as the wedding scene foreshadows. A wedding photographer tries to arrange a family portrait. Don Corleone refuses to let the picture be taken until his son Michael (Al Pacino) arrives. Michael is in the army, far removed from the Corleone business dealings. After his return, he is pulled into his father's "business" just as he is pulled into the wedding portrait. In the end the Don's attempt to keep family separate from business fails. Michael enters the picture, so to speak, and he becomes the new godfather.

The film's climax, an extended parallel editing sequence, juxtaposes images of another traditional ritual—a baptism—with images of multiple mob hits to suggest the final collapse of the boundary between the family and its business: violence. Michael has agreed to become the godfather of Connie's son, and simultaneously has ordered a series of murders to avenge those who have betrayed the Corleones. The acts confirm that he has replaced Vito as head of the family and the business. He is a new godfather in both senses of the word, but he is less successful than Vito at separating family and violence. Despite the apparent differences between the act of baptism and the act of murder, the parallel editing suggests an affinity between the honorable act of baptism and the dishonorable act of killing.

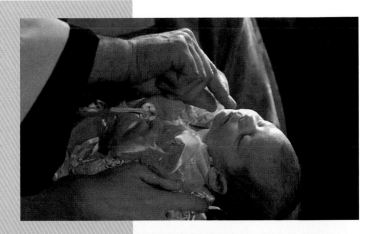

7.55 *(above)* The rituals of baptism in *The Godfather*.

7.56 *(below)* The rituals of killing in *The Godfather*.

As the infant's hood is removed, Coppola cuts to a close-up shot of a gun being taken out of its case. As the priest anoints the infant with oil, Coppola cuts to a barber applying shaving lotion to one of the hit men, grooming himself for his job. The editing continues to cross-cut between the baptism ceremony and the killers' preparation, suggesting the ritualistic qualities of both. Finally, the priest asks Michael, who holds the baby, if he renounces Satan. Coppola immediately cuts to a shot of the first hit being carried out. The scene then cuts back to a close-up of Michael as he responds, "I do." The scene then cuts to the murder of the second victim. Coppola continues to juxtapose Michael's renunciations of Satan with images of the hits that he has ordered (figs. **7.55**, **7.56**).

Like its opening, *The Godfather*'s climax illustrates how the boundary between family honor and corruption collapses. As the priest pours the holy water over the baby's head, the camera cuts to a series of shots that tallies up all the victims of Michael's orders. Just as Connie's son has been baptized with holy water, Michael has been baptized in blood.

Classical Editing

This essay analyzes a scene from Alfred Hitchcock's *Notorious*. It complements the brief analysis on page 197 of the patio scene, which explores how tempo can affect the emotional tenor of the scene. Notice that this analysis considers the way that all three attributes of editing—collage, tempo, and timing—contribute to the scene's expressiveness.

Study Notes accompanying the essay discuss strategies for writing effective paragraphs. When we begin to read and write, we learn that paragraphs are units of organization that play a pivotal role in helping readers discern major ideas and assimilate information. While there is no standard or ideal length for a paragraph (indeed, variation is an important writing strategy), longer paragraphs run the risk of incorporating too many ideas, which all struggle for attention at the same time. Shorter paragraphs, on the other hand, may introduce important ideas without offering enough discussion to develop those ideas or explain their significance.

For these reasons, good writers take great pains to organize paragraphs around a single idea. The sidebars stress how each paragraph is structured in order to foreground interpretive claims. This helps the reader follow the argument's main points.

Editing in *Notorious*

Ironically, the title of Alfred Hitchcock's *Notorious* doesn't refer to the film's devious antagonist Alex Sebastian (Claude Rains), the leader of a group of Nazis actively trying to develop nuclear technology in the years immediately after World War II. Instead, it refers to the film's heroic protagonist, Alicia Huberman (Ingrid Bergman). Society deems Alicia notorious for two reasons: her Nazi-sympathizing father has been convicted of treason, and she is a "party girl" who has been romantically involved with a number of men. But in the first act of the film, this supposedly wicked woman agrees to risk her life to infiltrate the ring of Nazis, a patriotic act she hopes will restore her tarnished reputation and earn the respect of the man she loves, American agent T.R. Devlin (Cary Grant). But when Alicia agrees to Devlin's request to go undercover—an assignment that requires her to rekindle a love affair with Alex Sebastian—Devlin repays her with cold resentment. Although Devlin loves Alicia, he mistrusts her because of her past, and he is overwhelmed by jealousy when she becomes involved with Alex. Oddly enough, he punishes her for doing the very thing he has asked her to do. Ultimately, Alicia becomes a pawn in a dangerous love triangle, with the two men vying for control. Editing in the famous horse track scene illustrates a pattern of behavior that repeats itself over the course of the film: whenever Alicia's masquerade of a relationship with Alex threatens Devlin's masculinity, he retaliates by impugning her reputation.[1]

During the scene, collage and timing emphasize how unguarded jealousy motivates Devlin to utter spiteful words that sting Alicia.[2] She has gone to the track with her new *faux* boyfriend, Alex, ostensibly to spend a romantic day at the races. But once at the track, she leaves his side and goes to the lower deck of the stadium, where she has secretly arranged to meet Devlin to discuss the case. As the two share information, the camera films them using a medium two-shot (fig. **7.57**). To be discreet, both smile gracefully and look offscreen, as if focusing on the race while exchanging pleasantries. As Alicia concludes her report, she reluctantly informs Devlin she has completed the first stage of the investigation by adding Alex to "her list of playmates." The scene cuts immediately to a medium close-up of Devlin, as he straightens his posture (as if he has been struck) and the smile on his face freezes. The collage—including both the change in Devlin's demeanor and facial expression and the transition from the two-shot to the emotionally freighted medium close-up—emphasizes a sudden shift in mood. Furthermore, the timing of the cut explains why Devlin's professionalism has given way to anger. He resents that Alicia has become sexually involved with someone else.[3]

Ingrid Bergman's performance makes it clear that Alicia's affair with Alex is the *last* thing she wants. She begins the affair not out of sexual desire, but because Devlin and her country have asked her to do so. Secretly she hopes that Devlin will ask her to quit the case. But Devlin is too self-absorbed to see her anguish, and, instead of releasing her from her obligation, he maliciously lashes out in the next exchange in this scene.

After Devlin has a chance to digest Alicia's news, he begins his attack. The editing captures his anger as well as Alicia's defensiveness. His first response is to proclaim wryly that she's made "pretty fast work"; the phrase serves to disparage her sexual ethics rather than to congratulate her on her skills at espionage. During the exchange of vicious barbs, the editing literally separates them by framing them individually. But when they try to speak amicably to one another—before and after the heated exchange—Hitchcock uses a two-shot in which they share the same space.

The editing's tempo also reflects the ebb and flow of emotions. When Alicia and Devlin try to act professionally and remain emotionally detached, Hitchcock relies on relatively long takes of the two-shot. But as tension escalates, the cutting speeds up considerably. When the two spies attempt to dial down their emotions and restore an air of professionalism, the tempo slows down via a longer take of the medium two-shot. But their efforts are short-lived. Devlin's jealousy and anger quickly resurface, and the rapid cutting from one medium close-up to another repeats itself.

The scene ensures that the audience's sympathy remains with Alicia and not Devlin. As the argument progresses, she pleads with him to understand her predicament: she has wanted to temper her "notorious" reputation as a party girl because she has fallen in love with him. Yet Alicia's assignment requires her to exploit the very reputation she's trying

1 Notice how the last sentence of the introductory paragraph announces the main idea that the rest of the essay will discuss. Everything else that follows this clearly demarcated thesis statement is subordinate to this main idea.

2 This sentence expresses the main idea of the paragraph. It functions much like a thesis statement for the rest of the paragraph. Such a sentence is called a "topic sentence." Topic sentences do not always have to be the first sentence of a paragraph; nor do they have to be limited to one sentence. But the strongest paragraphs in an academic essay will begin with a topic sentence or two. The reason why skimming an article or reviewing an assignment by reading the first sentence of each paragraph can be effective is that the most important ideas generally appear at the beginning. Can you understand how the argument of this essay progresses by reading the topic sentences?

3 Notice the overall structure of the paragraph up until this point. After the topic sentence, the author includes some descriptive sentences. This serves as evidence for the paragraph's main claim as articulated in the topic sentence. Here the author begins to analyze that evidence. Analysis explains the logical links between the evidence and the main claim. This is a standard organizational pattern in academic writing: claim, evidence, analysis.

7.57 Devlin and Alicia pretend to be casual acquaintances in *Notorious*.

4 Once again the paragraph begins with a claim and then offers evidence. Which sentences are descriptive, and which ones offer analysis of details? Look for phrases where the author briefly refers back to subjects described in more detail earlier. This is an effective strategy for emphasizing interpretive/analytical claims; it's a way to reiterate important details before explaining their significance.

7.58 (above) A medium close-up captures Alicia's anger in *Notorious*.

7.59 (center) Alicia's point of view in *Notorious*.

7.60 (below) A cut to a close-up emphasizes Alicia's pain in *Notorious*.

to shirk. Alicia is in a Catch-22 situation: she initially accepts the case out of a sense of patriotic duty, hoping to restore her reputation, but Devlin rejects her because, in his eyes, accepting the assignment only confirms that she is a woman of easy virtue.

Appropriately, the editing distances the audience from Devlin while simultaneously encouraging an emotional identification with Alicia. Repeatedly, Hitchcock uses an eyeline match to give viewers Alicia's point of view. The first shot in the pattern is the medium close-up of Alicia from the front as she turns to look at Devlin (fig. **7.58**). This is followed by a medium close-up profile shot of Devlin (fig. **7.59**). The contrast between the frontal shots of Alicia and the profile shots of Devlin allows the audience to see him from her perspective, both physically and emotionally. While she is emotionally open (the audience sees and can respond to her facial expression), he is cold and distant (the audience can only see half of his face, implying that he is trying to deny his feelings for her).

The audience's sympathetic identification with Alicia reaches its climax when Devlin tells her, "It wouldn't have been pretty if I had believed in you … if I had figured, 'She'd never be able to go through with it.'" Of all of Devlin's comments, these words have the greatest impact on Alicia, because Devlin is effectively saying that he's never loved her and that only an immoral woman could have accepted the case in the first place. In the middle of this line of dialogue, there is a cut from a medium close-up of Devlin to a *close-up* of Alicia, her eyes cast downward in dejection (fig. **7.60**). The timing of the cut draws attention to Alicia's pained reaction to Devlin's hateful words. Moreover, the juxtaposition of the (slightly) more distant shot of Devlin with the close-up of Alicia underscores the poignancy of the moment. As Devlin continues his diatribe, Hitchcock cuts back and forth between medium close-ups of Devlin and close-ups of Alicia, allowing the audience to witness the tears welling up in her eyes (a detail that otherwise might have been missed).[4]

The heated dialogue comes to an end when Devlin spies Alex approaching. Devlin and Alicia begin their affectless charade once again so as not to arouse Alex's suspicion, and once again the shift in tone is accompanied by a cut to a sustained medium two-shot. When Alex enters the frame, Devlin excuses himself, and Alex begins to interrogate Alicia. The end of the scene thus makes it clear that *both* men are monitoring Alicia for the same reason: jealousy. Alex has been watching Alicia to make sure she "behaves" properly. Crucially, Alex has no reason to suspect she is a spy. Rather, he is closely guarding her as his sexual property. This revelation establishes a parallel between the Nazi agent Alex and the American intelligence officer Devlin that will become more explicit as the film progresses. Both men claim to love Alicia, yet they physically and psychologically abuse her because neither fully trusts her romantic intentions.

Sound

///

CHAPTER EIGHT

> Audiovisual analysis must rely on words, and so we
> must take words seriously ... Why say "a sound" when
> we can say "crackling" or "rumbling" or "tremolo."
> Using more exact words allows us to confront and
> compare perceptions and to make progress in
> pinpointing and defining them.
>
> **Michael Chion**

///

In Terry Jones's comedic period film *Monty Python's Life of Brian* (1979), Roman
soldiers pursue Brian, a woebegone sad sack trying to shrug off claims that he's
a messiah. In an instant of poor judgment, Brian flees up a set of stairs, which
dead-ends at the top of a decrepit tower. Terrified, he falls from the top of the
tower. As he plunges toward his seemingly inevitable death, he falls into the seat
of a space ship, which is being pursued ... by another space ship. The chase
advances to outer space, and the squeal of tires on pavement rings out as the two
ships round sharp "corners" in the celestial chase scene (fig. **8.2**).

This wildly anachronistic, hilarious episode points to how integral sound is to
the construction of cinematic imagery. The scene parodies the way the sounds of
grinding gears and tires hitting the blacktop are as important in an action

8.1 Despite the explosive pyrotechnics,
the human voice remains audible in
Iron Man.

8.2 The comic space chase in *Monty Python's Life of Brian*.

sequence as the image of automobiles careening around corners. In this scene rubber does not literally touch asphalt, but Jones obliges—and ridicules—his audience's expectation that any good chase sequence will include the sound of roaring engines and squealing tires.

The film also illustrates how sound in a film does not always correspond to what's happening onscreen. It is an expressive element of film capable of operating independently from images. Often filmmakers encourage intellectual and emotional responses by including sounds that do not logically or literally correspond to the image. In this particular scene, Jones encourages laughter by exploiting the discrepancy between what the audience sees and what the audience hears.

But not all sounds differ so dramatically from the image being shown; nor do they all stimulate laughter. What emotional response does George Lucas encourage with the sound associated with the light sabers in *Star Wars* (1977)? What sound in this context might have produced laughter?

Though many film critics and scholars focus most of their attention on the narrative and visual elements of films, this chapter emphasizes how sound is an evocative element in its own right. As the above example suggests, sound plays a critical role in determining how audiences react to images, and so this chapter stresses the importance of learning how to think, talk, and write about sound, using concrete, analytical language.

This chapter begins with a brief history of the use of sound in films, followed by a discussion of the technical aspects of the **soundtrack**, which is generally created completely independently from the visual image. Then there is an examination of the different relationships that a filmmaker can create between sound and image. The last section looks at the three components of film sound in terms of the way filmmakers manipulate the relationship between sound and image.

A film soundtrack is composed of three elements: dialogue, music, and sound effects. These components are recorded separately from the images and from one another. **Mixing** is the process of combining the three elements of film sound into one soundtrack, which is added to the image track in post-production. Although the early years of cinema (1896–1927) are referred to as the silent era, the next section explains that films have always depended upon the relationship between image and sound, which involves aesthetic principles, technological innovations, and commercial considerations.

Film Sound: A Brief History

Contrary to popular assumption, movies were never "silent." In practice, a variety of sounds accompanied the exhibition of early films. A piano accompanied the first public film screenings on December 28, 1885, when the Lumière brothers projected their work at the Grand Café in Paris. In 1908 Camille Saint-Saëns composed the first film **score** (music specifically composed or arranged to accompany a film), but in general the musical accompaniment in the early days of the cinema was more off the cuff. Most films weren't scored, so musicians played whatever music they wanted to play, and "professionalism left much to be desired since, in many theaters, the orchestra would play through a certain number of compositions and then simply get up and leave the film and the audience." (Prendergast, p. 5) Nevertheless, music, live narration, and sound effects devices were all integral parts of the theater experience.

Cinema took a step toward industry-wide synchronization of sound and image in 1912, when Max Winkler devised a system of musical cue sheets that was subsequently adopted by the Universal Film Company. These cue sheets provided specific instructions on what musical pieces should be played during a screening and when. In contrast to this method of accompaniment, which was based on already existing compositions, big budget films such as D.W. Griffith's *The Birth of a Nation* (1915) had original scores. Exhibitors could hire entire orchestras for these films and transform screenings into elaborate galas. But this was not a uniform practice, since smaller theaters could not afford the large orchestras needed to perform such compositions. In the quest to help musicians coordinate their playing with the image, studios even briefly experimented with projecting the musical notes of the score with the film (similar to a subtitle), but audiences found this distracting (Prendergast, p. 13). Thus, from the earliest days of cinema, movies incorporated the three elements of film sound: dialogue, sound effects, and music.

Silent cinema, thus, was never silent. The distinction between early "silent" cinema and later sound cinema actually rests on the difference between live sound and recorded soundtracks that were affixed to the image track.

The idea of combining pre-recorded sound that could be synchronized with images motivated many early experiments with sound, but the process of developing a workable system for doing so spanned several decades.

An early system capable of synchronizing sound and image was Vitaphone's sound on disc system, where sound was recorded and played on separate discs. But it wasn't until 1927 that a group of exhibitors (Loew's, Universal, First National, Paramount, and Producers Distributing Corporation) signed the "Big Five Agreement," which stated that the signatories would jointly agree to adopt the single film sound system that they decided was the best one for the industry. Realizing that the introduction of several incompatible film sound systems would limit distribution and, ultimately, studio profits, they wanted to ensure technological standardization (Gomery, p. 13). As a result, by 1929, nearly 75 percent of Hollywood films included pre-recorded sound (Cook, p. 249).

By 1930 sound-on-film systems replaced sound on disc. Sound-on-film systems were based on the conversion of sound to electronic signals that were recorded as light impulses on film stock. These optical soundtracks appear as wavy lines along the edge of the film print. The sound information is read by a photoelectric cell on the projector as light from an exciter lamp passes through the soundtrack.

Critical Debates over Film Sound

One widely held misperception about early cinema was that the lack of pre-recorded sound crippled its expressive potential. For filmmakers at the time, the so-called silence was anything but a deficit. Edwin S. Porter's *Dream of a Rarebit Fiend* (1906), which uses **double-exposure** to capture the spatial disorientation that accompanies inebriation, demonstrates how, in its infancy, silent film made rapid advances in visual style (fig. **8.3**). By the time "talking pictures" arrived in 1927, the cinema had become a highly sophisticated visual medium.

Given the power of cinema's visual elements, the shift from live to recorded sound was not an unqualified step forward for the art. The need to record dialogue on the set affected the mobility of the camera, which, in turn, negatively impacted film style. Motion picture cameras had to be encased in soundproof booths so that microphones would not pick up the sound of their motors (fig. **8.4**). But, in the booth, the camera could pan only about 30 degrees to the right or left (Salt, p. 38). Marsha Kinder and Beverle Houston write, "the three elements that had been so crucial to the artistic development of the silent cinema—visual composition, camera movement, and editing—were severely restricted" (p. 52). The fact that early sound films were called "talking pictures" is revealing. No longer were they "moving pictures"; they were static images that "talked." The new sound technology sacrificed visual inventiveness and placed a high value on the novelty of hearing characters talk.

Murnau's first Hollywood film, *Sunrise* (1927), serves as a model of how cinema might have exploited sound technology differently, had dialogue not become the *raison d'être*. Produced on the cusp of the sound era, *Sunrise* was filmed silent, allowing the camera to perform wildly elaborate movements, including a famous tracking shot that follows the main character (George O'Brien) through a swamp as he trudges to meet his mistress. At one point the camera and the man's paths diverge, only to reunite when he meets his lover. Inventive choreography such as this, wherein the camera and the actor take separate paths, was not possible in the earliest talking pictures.

But *Sunrise* did reap the technological benefits of a pre-recorded musical soundtrack that allowed for the synchronization of sound and image. Thus, Hugo Riesenfeld was able to compose his original score *for* the image. The result is a dreamy fusion of sonic and visual expressionism. While there is no recorded dialogue, musical instruments occasionally stand in for the characters' voices, as when a French horn

8.3 Dramatic visual experimentation in *Dream of a Rarebit Fiend*.

mimics the sound of a husband's wail as he yells out for his wife (fig. **8.5**). In every way, the film is a visual *tour de force* that uses sound as a complementary element, not as a defining one. Today it is routinely heralded as one of the master-works of cinema. But when it was released in 1927, it was overshadowed by *The Jazz Singer* (Alan Crosland 1927)—the first *feature-length* film to include synchronized dialogue and musical numbers, whose success guaranteed the industry's shift to "talking pictures."

At the time, not everyone in the industry whole-heartedly embraced the new technologies of sound. French director René Clair argued that, with the development of talkies, "the screen has lost more than it has gained. It has conquered the world of voices, but it has lost the world of dreams" (Clair). Soviet filmmakers Sergei Eisenstein, V.I. Pudovkin, and Gregori Alexandrov feared that the use of sound technology would "proceed along the line of least resistance, i.e. along the line of satisfying simple curiosity" (Eisenstein). In their manifesto, these directors warned that, were filmmakers to rely on sound for conveying meaning, the cinema would be robbed of its visual energy and movies would be reduced to a medium for recording "'highly cultured dramas' and other photographed performances of a theatrical sort" (Eisenstein). Eventually, Clair, Eisenstein, Pudovkin, and Alexandrov all embraced sound technology. Clair and Eisenstein in particular directed films (for example, *Under the Roofs of Paris* [1930], *Alexander Nevsky* [1938]) that became influential precisely because of their creative use of synchronized sound. What these directors feared was the prospect of a cinema where sound—specifically talking—impeded the visual elements. In retrospect, the success of *The Jazz Singer* at the apparent expense of *Sunrise* confirms that, at least for a time, these fears were warranted.

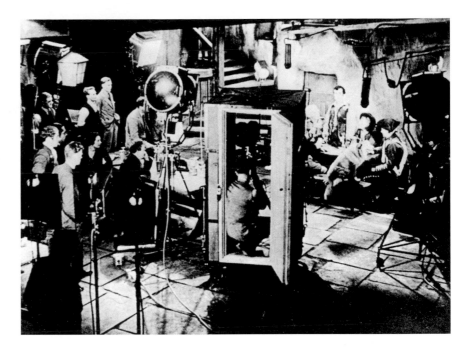

8.4 A camera in a soundproof booth.

8.5 Audiences hear the mournful wail of a French horn when they see this image in *Sunrise*.

The conversion to sound had more than an aesthetic impact on the film industry. The high costs of conversion to sound film hit independent producers particularly hard because it became more difficult to compete with better-financed, vertically integrated studios. Whereas African-American producers George and Noble Johnson of the Lincoln Motion Picture Company had lost their struggle to maintain their independence from Hollywood by the mid-1920s, Oscar Micheaux managed to continue making films into the 1930s and 1940s. Due in part to the cost of sound technology, Micheaux declared bankruptcy in 1928 but re-emerged with new investors in 1931 to make his first sound film. Jesse Algernon Rhines describes the sound films of Micheaux as "a miracle of entrepreneurial determination" although "they were not successful competitors with white productions even for an African-American audience." (Rhines, p. 31) Thus, while the advent of "talking pictures" fascinated audiences and promised to be a lucrative investment for Hollywood, some filmmakers questioned both the aesthetic and the economic consequences of the transition to sound.

In the late 1930s, the practice of re-recording, or post-synchronization, freed sound films from the idea that "everything seen on the screen must be heard on the soundtrack." (Cook, p. 271) The practice of re-recording allowed filmmakers to manipulate sound and to experiment with the relation of sound to image. Now almost all commercial films, even those whose aim is a realistic depiction of conversation, use dialogue recorded in post-production. The freedom engendered by post-synchronization has allowed filmmakers to transform film sound into a vital component of cinematic expression, completely independent of, and at times more weighty than, a film's visual information.

Repeatedly, advances in film sound technology have promised greater fidelity and a heightened sense of audio realism. In the 1950s (with the advent of magnetic tape recording), films began featuring multichannel soundtracks, which allowed filmmakers to add layers of sounds. Dolby and wireless eight-track recording contributed to the complex sound mixes of the Hollywood Renaissance filmmakers of the early 1970s. Multi-track recording and Dolby noise reduction produced sound with better definition and individuation, permitting a greater degree of detail. When *Star Wars*—one of the first major releases in Dolby—was in theaters, Dolby-equipped theaters earned more box office revenue than non-Dolby theaters (Shreger, p. 353). As a result, the industry responded: at the beginning of 1978 there were 700 Dolby-equipped theaters, but during that year the number grew at a rate of 500 per month (Shreger, p. 354). More recently filmmakers have shifted to digital sound reproduction in the form of THX, Dolby Digital, and DTS systems. This latest sound revolution extended to include products for the home theater, complete with sophisticated surround sound system.

Audiences' attraction to the recent proliferation of digital sound systems, which promise increased fidelity and more realistic sound, suggests a lingering, common misperception: that film sound should replicate the sounds one would experience in "real life." But film sound is an expressive element, as carefully composed as the image. Film sounds do not reproduce reality—they provide an aesthetic experience in conjunction with the images onscreen.

often appear onscreen talking. Audiences can hear their voices, but cannot understand their words, which compete with other sounds in the neighborhood: cars, music, and barking dogs. Hitchcock's use of sound demands that the audience share Jeffries's perspective. The audience can only speculate about what the other characters are saying, based on their tone of voice and their body movements.

These two examples illustrate how filmmakers carefully choose which sounds to include on the soundtrack, knowing that emphasizing a particular sound helps to shape the audience's perspective and to determine the emotional dynamics of a scene.

In addition to selecting what sounds an audience will hear, filmmakers also consider how these sounds will correspond to the imagery. Usually the soundtrack will offer an acoustic equivalent to the visual effect on the screen. For example, when the massive ship hits the iceberg in *Titanic*, the soundtrack conveys the sound of ice wrenching and tearing the ship's steel hull.

There are five ways that sound may differ from the imagery onscreen. Filmmakers can choose to create contrasts between:

- onscreen space and offscreen space
- objective images and subjective sound
- diegetic details and non-diegetic sound
- image time and sound time
- image mood and sound mood.

Emphasizing the Contrast between Onscreen and Offscreen Space

Sound is a powerful tool for helping filmmakers create the illusion that the world of the story extends beyond the boundaries of the frame. Sound often points to action that happens offscreen—details that are unseen, but which are important

8.7 Marion hears an argument taking place offscreen in *Psycho*.

factors shaping the storyline. After Marion Crane checks into her room at the Bates Motel in *Psycho*, she hears Mrs. Bates berating Norman (fig. **8.7**). While the audience never sees their argument, the soundtrack clarifies that mother and son are carrying out their squabble in the dark, gothic mansion on top of the hill. The fact that Mother's voice bleeds into Marion's room also reaffirms what the *mise en scène* has already suggested: that the eerie house and its inhabitant (Mother) pervade the hotel below. Crucially, audiences don't see Mother yelling at Norman; it's not the images that suggest her dominance, but the sound emanating from offscreen space.

Emphasizing the Difference between Objective Images and Subjective Sounds

Sound gives audiences access to what a character is thinking, even while the images continue to show what the character is doing or experiencing at an objective level. Sound can depict a character's subjectivity without the need to dissolve to a fantasy or flashback sequence. In *Psycho*, as Marion flees Phoenix with the $40,000 she has stolen, she imagines what others will say about her mysterious disappearance. Onscreen, Marion continues to drive her car, nervously but cautiously. But audiences hear, via the use of a voice-over, the voices she imagines, primarily those of her boss and the client from whom she's stolen. These voices do not exist in the external, objective world of the film. This use of sound to indicate character subjectivity is a motif running throughout the film, which suggests an important parallel between Norman and Marion. Audiences ultimately recognize that both characters act out their guilt in their minds. As the discussion of *Rear Window* above makes clear (p. 235), filmmakers can also emphasize subjective experience by *withholding* acoustic details.

Emphasizing the Difference between Diegetic Details and Non-diegetic Sound

Sound and image can differ in terms of their relationship to the story world. Using the terminology set out in Chapter 4, anything that the characters involved in the story can experience can be called diegetic sound, while anything outside the story space can be referred to as non-diegetic sound. By far the most common non-diegetic sound is music, but non-diegetic sound also includes, for example, sound effects that don't actually occur within the diegesis. In *Requiem for a Dream*, for example, a variety of sound effects simulate the experience of using drugs. In one montage sequence, the sound of a plane flying overhead accompanies fragmented images depicting the process of shooting heroin. While voice-overs are usually diegetic—examples include Martin Scorsese's *Goodfellas* and Lee Daniels's *Precious*—some films include a voice-over narration that is non-diegetic: that is, someone from outside the world of the story delivers the voice-over, as in *A.I.* (Steven Spielberg 2001) or *The Royal Tenenbaums*.

Non-diegetic sounds generally function as a form of direct address, wherein the filmmaker offers explicit commentary on the image. By noticing whether or not sounds are diegetic or non-diegetic, audiences can determine the degree to which the filmmaker is directly addressing them. In *Grosse Pointe Blank* (George Armitage 1997), when hired hit man Martin Q. Blank (John Cusack) goes to his high school reunion, he discovers that a cookie-cutter convenience store has been built where his parents' house used to stand. When he first realizes that his house is gone, audiences hear the chorus to the rock song "Live and Let Die" and recognize its dog-eat-dog philosophy. The music is non-diegetic: no visual cues indicate that Blank is listening to the song on a radio. His facial expression upon seeing the store registers his shock, however, and the music's lyrics and chords underscore his feelings of anger, cynicism, and dismay.

Diegetic sounds, on the other hand, help define an environment whose traits the characters must recognize to some degree. In the same film, when Blank enters the store, a silly muzak version of the same song plays over the tinny store speakers. This diegetic music helps to define the character of a store that has replaced a distinctive dwelling (Blank's home) with a bland, commercial setting and an array of cheap junk food.

Often diegetic music reveals character traits. When a character plays a song on a jukebox or listens to music on the radio, that music is an outward symbol of her taste or emotional state at a given point in time. In *Grosse Pointe Blank*, Blank's former girlfriend Debi Newberry (Minnie Driver), whom he jilted in high school, now works as a radio DJ. Throughout the film, she plays pop music from the 1980s in honor of the upcoming high school reunion—and nostalgically reminisces about her high school lover.

Emphasizing the Difference between Image Time and Sound Time

Combining sound and image allows filmmakers to present two different points in time simultaneously, as when a voice-over narration describes past events. In *Double Indemnity* (Billy Wilder 1944), the voice of Walter Neff (Fred MacMurray), speaking from the present, explains the visual images and actions of Neff's past. In *The Princess Bride* (Rob Reiner 1987), a grandfather (Peter Falk) narrates a story to his young grandson (Fred Savage). Falk's voice-over narration reminds viewers that the world onscreen is a fantasy, lovingly concocted by the interaction between the author, the storyteller, and the boy.

Discrepancies in sound and image time also occur during transitions between scenes. On occasion, the dominant sound at the end of one scene will carry over into the next scene, forming the aural equivalent of a dissolve called a **sound bridge**. Alternatively, some scenes end with the gradual emergence of the next scene's dominant sound. Such moments suggest the powerful aura of an event, as the sound acts as a reminder of its lingering presence or anticipates an event's arrival. In *Taxi Driver*, a pimp, Sport (Harvey Keitel), seduces Iris, a thirteen-year-old prostitute (Jodie Foster). He puts on soft music and whispers banal expressions of love, and slowly she succumbs to his overtures. Suddenly the audience hears the explosive roar of gunfire while Sport and Iris are still embracing onscreen. Then the film cuts to the man who will "rescue" Iris by the end of the film, Travis Bickle (Robert DeNiro), as he shoots in a firing range. The sound of Travis's gunplay seeps into the preceding scene, foreshadowing the climactic, bloody shootout between the two rivals for Iris's attention. On a thematic level, the fact that audiences hear a sound commonly associated with male aggression while seeing a distasteful seduction equates Sport's emotional manipulation with physical violence.

With a **lightning mix**, sound doesn't overlap from one scene into the next. Instead, filmmakers link scenes together by joining different sounds that have similar qualities. In *Citizen Kane*, Orson Welles, who had worked extensively in radio, pioneered the cinematic use of this technique. In a brief montage sequence depicting Kane's illicit affair with Susan Alexander and his short-lived political career, a lightning mix sonically links Kane's private and public lives. At the close of Susan's private recital for Kane, he claps his hands in appreciation. Several hands can be heard clapping as the sequence dissolves to a small gathering on a city street, where Jed Leland delivers a campaign speech for Kane. Leland's voice grows louder and more impassioned until the scene again dissolves to a huge political rally while the soundtrack shifts seamlessly to Kane's voice, which seems to take over where Leland's left off. Whereas a sound bridge allows a sound to extend beyond a scene, a lightning mix emphasizes sonic parallels in adjacent scenes.

Emphasizing Differences in Image Mood and Sound Mood

Finally, combining sound and image can produce a jolting contrast on an emotional level. While typically the soundtrack corresponds to the action and accentuates the mood evoked by visual details, sometimes filmmakers will pair an image with a sound that seems wildly inappropriate, producing a noticeable tension between aural and visual information. Such disjunctures can occur within the diegesis, as when Alex (Malcolm McDowell) sings "Singing In the Rain" while he rapes Mrs. Alexander in *A Clockwork Orange*, or when Jules (Samuel L. Jackson) talks about fast food before he assassinates a man in *Pulp Fiction*. In both cases, the conflict between comic or absurd sound and a disturbingly violent image suggests the perpetrator's indifference to his victim's plight.

Filmmakers may also choose non-diegetic sounds to work against the imagery. The result may be irony, as in the conclusion of *Dr. Strangelove*, when the soundtrack plays "We'll Meet Again," to images of nuclear annihilation. Told that a Doomsday device has destroyed the world, audiences must realize there is no possibility of what the song's lyrics promise: that two lovers will be able to meet again. The irony is a fitting conclusion to the film's repeated suggestion that the nuclear arms race is one expression of aggressive masculine sexuality.

Filmmakers can and do exploit all five variants of the relationship between sound and image. Sometimes the most creative use of film sound goes beyond simply trying to mirror the images onscreen or clarifying narrative events; the most profound examples of film sound often exploit the soundtrack's ability to add intellectual or emotional depth to the visual image. To develop valid interpretations of a film, viewers must be able first to define the relationship between sound and image and then describe its effect on the film's meaning.

Three Components of Film Sound

In narrative films, the words a screenwriter gives to his characters, the music they listen to, and the sounds in their environment all convey a wealth of information.

Dialogue

Dialogue forwards the narrative, giving voice to characters' aspirations, thoughts, and emotions, often making conflicts among characters evident in the process.

Text and Subtext

The primary function of spoken dialogue is to externalize a character's thoughts and feelings, bringing motivations, goals, plans, and conflicts to the surface. Screenwriters are careful to avoid dialogue that reiterates information already made clear by the image. Clunky dialogue that states the obvious is called **on-the-nose dialogue**.

The most effective dialogue works on several levels to suggest character motivations, even when characters are not fully aware of those feelings themselves. Dialogue makes meaning through the **text** (the words a characters says), the **line reading** (the way an actor says the line, including pauses, intonation, and emotion), and the **subtext** (the unstated meaning that underlies spoken words). Dialogue often works in a roundabout fashion and depends upon audiences to discern the subtext (what isn't stated directly) which eloquently reveals a character's complexity.

Although the dominant sound in most narrative films is that of the human voice, most viewers don't consider in specific terms what it is that allows the voice to convey so much information so quickly. Listening to dialogue involves more than noting what words are spoken. Characters in books "speak" as well— but films allow audiences actually to *hear* qualities of speech, making the experience far more dynamic than that of reading words printed on the page. Hearing the way an actor reads a line of dialogue can accentuate a sharp division between text and subtext.

Dialogue plays an important role in establishing character. It can also be used to emphasize setting, or a character's cultural background. It can define a character's relationship to others in terms of age, authority, or class. It can also reveal a character's level of education, or portray the level of a character's emotional and intellectual engagement with the story events. Finally, the voice can define a character's environment, and his relationship to that environment.

The human voice has four sonic attributes that invest words with emotional and intellectual depth: volume, pitch, vocal characteristics, and acoustic qualities. Each of these is examined below, along with one particular use of the voice that deserves special attention: the voice-over.

Volume

It almost goes without saying that volume reflects the level and the type of a person's engagement with her surroundings. Generally, the louder a person speaks, the greater the emotional intensity of her words. Sigourney Weaver's vocal performance as Ripley in *Alien* (Ridley Scott 1979) is restrained. Through much of the film, she delivers her lines softly, conveying her calm, rational demeanor. After the alien has killed the captain, leaving Ripley in charge, she meets with the remaining crew members to decide what they should do. Tempers flare, and for the first time in the film, Ripley raises her voice to command the others' attention. Once her authority is established and the others calm down, she lowers her voice again, conveying her methodical, carefully considered approach to solving the crew's dilemma. Only after the remainder of her crew is killed and she fails to stop the ship's self-destruct sequence does Ripley scream out in frustration, implying a momentary lapse in confidence and resolve.

Volume suggests the emotional vigor of dialogue. Loudness usually connotes a character experiencing intense emotion, such as anger, fear, or passion. Softness, on the other hand, usually connotes a more timid or carefully considered emotional response: tenderness, diffidence, sophistication, fear, or even guile.

Pitch

A sound's pitch refers to its frequency, or its position on a musical scale. In music, the lowest (or deepest) pitch is bass, and the highest pitch is soprano. While one immediately thinks of pitch as being a musical term, it can also be used to evaluate the quality of the speaking voice.

Typically, audiences associate deep voices (basses or baritones) with power or authority. Inspector Vargas (Charlton Heston) in *Touch of Evil*, Sean Connery's James Bond, and Marsellus Wallace (Ving Rhames) in *Pulp Fiction* are all characters whose deep voices convey dignity, restraint, and authority. However, deep voices can also be associated with evil or duplicity, such as the killer's menacing (and electronically altered) voice in the *Saw* series (2004–09).

Characters with high-pitched voices, on the other hand, are often associated with weakness. The difference between Charles Foster Kane's booming voice and Susan Alexander's piercing voice helps to define their relationship: Kane treats Susan like a little girl. In *Up*, the menace a Doberman is supposed to project is subverted by his high-pitched voice.

Speech Characteristics

The way a character speaks does more to define her individual persona than perhaps any other characteristic of the human voice. Her cultural background, her class, her interests, her aspirations, and even her limitations can all be revealed by subtle qualities of the voice such as accent, diction, and vocal tics.

A character's accent is a powerful indicator of background and social status. Through language, audiences readily recognize a character's nationality, for example. Meryl Streep has earned a reputation for her ability to adopt the accent of her characters, and the national identities of her broad array of roles include Italian American (*The Bridges of Madison County* [Clint Eastwood 1995]), Irish (*Dancing at Lughnasa* [Pat O'Connor 1998]), Polish (*Sophie's Choice* [Alan J. Pakula 1982]), and Danish (*Out of Africa* [Sydney Pollack 1985]). Some audiences may not initially recognize that, in *Dr. Strangelove*, Peter Sellers plays three different roles: Mandrake, a British officer; Muffley, the American president;

and the German scientist Dr. Strangelove. Sellers's stellar performance in the film relies on his ability to adopt three distinct accents so flawlessly. Frequently, actors train with dialect coaches to perfect their pronunciation.

But a character's accent usually contributes more to a film's storyline than just indicating where a person was raised. Often this background information plays a crucial role in helping audiences to understand a character's motivations or in helping a film explore broader themes. In British films, especially those about the effects of class-bound culture, such as *The Loneliness of the Long Distance Runner* (Tony Richardson 1962), *This Sporting Life* (Lindsay Anderson 1963), and *Sleuth* (Joseph L. Mankiewicz 1972), cockney accents are an immediate mark of the urban working class and a symbol of the characters' social and economic entrapment. In Wong Kar-Wai's *Chungking Express* ("*Chongqing Senlin*"; 1994), a lonely, heart-broken Cop 223 in Hong Kong tries desperately to start a conversation with a stranger in a bar. When she doesn't respond to his pick-up line, he repeats the same phrase in several different dialects, drawing attention to Hong Kong's multi-cultural makeup, which Cop 223 must negotiate if he is to establish an emotional connection.

American films frequently use accents to define characters according to regional background. In *Finding Nemo*, Crush (Andrew Stanton), a sea turtle, speaks with a Los Angeles Valley inflection that linguists call Valspeak that links him to the surfer lifestyle, contributing to the audience's perception of his laid-back persona. The linguistic marker works as a shorthand device for communicating information that helps audiences sense how and why his character differs from the uptight Marlin.

American movies rely on accents to link characters to specific locales across the U.S., from the Midwest (*Fargo*) to Louisiana (*Eve's Bayou* [Kasi Lemmons 1997]) to Boston (*The Departed* [Martin Scorsese]). Of course, when filmmakers rely on accents to flesh out two-dimensional, stock characters, they run the risk of perpetuating stereotypes, as when Southern accents are equated with a lack of intelligence and sophistication.

A character's diction—his choice of words—can also reveal his economic status or level of education. Consider how the foul language that spills out of the mouths of the thugs in Quentin Tarantino's *Reservoir Dogs* or *Pulp Fiction* distinguishes them from the more elite and sophisticated criminals (who rarely curse), such as Le Chiffre in *Casino Royale* (Martin Campbell 2006) or Thomas Crown in *The Thomas Crown Affair* (Norman Jewison 1968; John McTiernan 1999).

A character's inability to find the right words can also speak volumes. In Michael Cimino's Vietnam War epic *The Deer Hunter* (1978), a group of friends—all of them steelworkers in industrial Pennsylvania—go on one last hunting trip together before going off to war. When the careless Stanley (John Cazale) forgets his boots, the leader of the group, Michael (Robert De Niro), reprimands him for his irresponsibility. But words fail Michael as he tries to explain to Stanley the importance of responsibility. The only way he can impart his knowledge to Stanley is to hold up a bullet and say, "Stanley, see this? This is this. This ain't something else. This is this. From now on, you're on your own." Michael is unable to articulate his code of honor, which dictates that men have to take care of themselves. For him, actions are more important than words, partly because he lacks the formal education to express himself (which the film stereotypically associates with his working class background).

Finally, the human voice can be characterized by vocal tics particular to specific individuals. Marilyn Monroe, for example, is famous for her high, breathy voice, which audiences have associated with sensual fragility. In contrast, Katharine Hepburn in films such as *Holiday* (George Cukor 1938), *The African Queen* (John Huston 1951), *Rooster Cogburn* (Stuart Millar 1975), and *On Golden Pond* (Mark Rydell 1981) has a gravelly, quavering voice that helps to connote her characters' independence and strength.

Jimmy Stewart's voice is recognizable for its slow drawl, and its propensity to get higher in pitch as his characters become agitated. Stewart's unique voice complements his tendency to play characters notable for their humility and honor, as in *Mr. Smith Goes to Washington* (Frank Capra 1939), in which Stewart is an idealistic but naïve politician who combats corruption when he arrives in Washington. The contrast between Stewart's "aw-shucks" delivery and Grace Kelly's more crisp and refined voice helps suggest the class differences that divide the couple when they appear together in *Rear Window*.

In contrast, Humphrey Bogart tends to speak through his teeth and pursed lips without much modulation in his voice, contributing to the macho image that he projects in films such as *The Maltese Falcon*, *Casablanca* (Michael Curtiz 1942), *The Treasure of the Sierra Madre* (John Huston 1948), and *The African Queen*.

Some actors' voices are immediately recognizable for their rhythm. Jack Nicholson (*The Shining* [Stanley Kubrick 1980], *The Departed*) and Owen Wilson (*Meet the Parents* [Jay Roach 2000], *The Royal Tenenbaums*) speak in slow, fluid phrases. The carefully paced rhythm of their delivery often suggests quirkiness or lackadaisical menace. In contrast, Woody Allen (*Manhattan* [Woody Allen 1979]) and Ben Stiller (*Meet the Parents*, *The Royal Tenenbaums*) speak in quick bursts, suggesting their characters' hysterical anxiety. Bette Davis (*Jezebel* [William Wyler 1938], *Whatever Happened to Baby Jane?* [Robert Aldrich 1962]) is noted for the staccato or percussive quality of her voice, which often conveys overwrought emotions or maniacal hostility. Julia Roberts (*Eat Pray Love* [Ryan Murphy 2010]) is famous for a boisterous laugh that suggests her characters' self-confident love of life.

Acoustic Qualities

Manipulating the acoustic quality of the human voice can help filmmakers convey perspective and details about the surrounding environment. The way voices sound can suggest the distance between characters, or the mood, aura, or atmosphere of a place—its ambience. The quality of a sound's movement through a particular space—what might be called a sound's acoustic properties—can help determine whether that space feels cozy and intimate, or sterile and alienating.

Sound engineers can toy with the acoustic qualities of voices by adjusting microphones (for example, placing microphones away from an actress to suggest distance), and by making adjustments during mixing after the primary shooting is completed. At this point, the sound editor can freely manipulate the volume, balance (the relative volume coming from each speaker), and other acoustic properties of each sound, including the dialogue. When mixing the sound, the sound editor may add reverb (an echo) to the voices in a scene. This effect usually encourages audiences to imagine that the setting is expansive, and that the sounds are reverberating from some distant walls.

In *The Conversation*, Harry Caul (Gene Hackman) and Meredith (Elizabeth McRae) retreat from a group of revelers to have a one-on-one conversation. They wander into the middle of Caul's mammoth work-shop—a large, vacant warehouse. At first Caul is unable to overcome his reclusive tendencies, and he responds to Meredith's questions perfunctorily. The camera films them in a long shot

8.8 An echo establishes empty space in *The Conversation*.

(fig. **8.8**). Their voices echo, emphasizing the vast emptiness of the setting and the loneliness of Caul's self-imposed isolation. Soon Caul begins to open up to Meredith, and the scene cuts to a series of medium close-up tracking shots. As the scene becomes more intimate, sound engineer Walter Murch reduces the reverberation considerably, using the acoustic qualities of their voices to draw attention to the couple's temporary sense of physical and emotional closeness. When drunken revelers interrupt their conversation by revving a motor scooter, the scene cuts to a reverse tracking shot that ends on an extreme long shot of the couple and the circling scooter, suggesting the sudden loss of intimacy. As the camera moves away, the reverberation returns.

Through the mixing process, sound editors are able to conjure a broad array of audio illusions. By manipulating the acoustic characteristics of voices, a sound editor can create the effect of a character speaking from across a great distance, on the telephone, broadcasting via radio, speaking from behind a wall, and so on.

Addressing the Audience: the Voice-over

Because of its ability to encourage audience identification with characters onscreen, the voice-over deserves special attention. Diegetic voice-overs may function as a character's meditation on past events, as in Billy Wilder's *Sunset Boulevard*. Wilder's film begins with a third-person discussion about a corpse floating in a swimming pool. The film then launches into a flashback, at which point the voice-over switches to Joe Gillis's first-person account of the series of events that led to his own murder. Gillis's voice-over focuses the audience on him as the point of identification during the flashback. The film demonstrates how voice-overs can guide viewers through a series of events they might not otherwise understand.

Voice-overs can also allow audiences access to a character's immediate thoughts, as in *Mean Streets*, when audiences hear Charlie (Harvey Keitel) pray-ing in several voice-overs throughout the film. Again, such voice-overs allow audiences to experience a more profound level of engagement with that character.

Voice-overs aren't necessarily delivered by the central character, however.

Eddie Dupris (Morgan Freeman) narrates *Million Dollar Baby*, even though the tragic plot focuses on Frankie Dunn's (Clint Eastwood) relationship with boxer Maggie Fitzgerald (Hilary Swank). Eddie's voice-over provides audiences with a distanced, yet inexplicably omniscient vantage point on the events. (In fact, Eddie confesses he isn't quite sure what becomes of Frankie Dunn at the end of the film.) The voice-over allows audiences to have it both ways: they become intimately involved with Dunn's emotional collapse, yet in the end he remains the iconic image of the stoic American male, isolated and shrouded in mystery.

Narrators can be non-diegetic as well, offering what might seem to be an objective point of view. The post-production history of *March of the Penguins* (Luc Jacquet 2005) illustrates the fact that non-diegetic voice-overs shape the audience's response. The soundtrack to the French release featured voice-over dialogue "spoken" by the penguins themselves, accompanied by trendy Euro-pop music. Fearing that American audiences might not appreciate such a whimsical approach to a tale about life and death in the Antarctic, executives at Warner Brothers (the U.S. distributor) asked screenwriter Jordan Roberts to re-write the script with a more conventional approach to the voice-over. The American version features an academic voice-over, delivered by Morgan Freeman, which "explains" the birds' behavior, and includes an orchestral score by Alex Wurman. Though the two films contain more or less the same imagery, the French version is more akin to a family-oriented adventure film, while the U.S. version is a conventional documentary that presents the penguins' story from an overtly educational perspective.

In the poignant comedy, *Stranger than Fiction* (Marc Forster 2006), a voice-over narration is used to satirize the way audiences typically respond to this sound device, as we may implicitly trust any offscreen "voice of authority." IRS accountant Harold Crick (Will Ferrell) wakes up one day to a woman's voice-over narration that describes his every move and anticipates his thoughts. He consults a psychiatrist, who assures him that he is schizophrenic. However, a literary scholar who specializes in the phrase "little did he know" (played by Dustin Hoffman) informs him that he is a character in a story being authored by someone else. The latter scenario proves true, and Harold eventually meets the author Karen Eiffel (Emma Thompson) who unwittingly controls his fate. The voice-over in this film is a metaphorical device that provides both comedy—as Harold bristles under the control of an unseen figure—and tragedy—as Harold learns that, like all human beings, he is not fully in control of his destiny, and Karen learns that authors bear some responsibility for their literary creations.

Some filmmakers upset the audience's expectation that a voice-over will offer a stable point of identification. Terrence Malick's films, for example, tend to emphasize that the voice-over narration may not offer the most accurate or perceptive account of the events onscreen. In *Badlands*, Kit (Martin Sheen) and Holly (Sissy Spacek) go on a killing spree across the American Midwest. The film is narrated by Holly after her arrest, and her delivery of the lines is detached and riddled with romantic clichés. Their killing spree begins when Kit kills Holly's father. Holly expresses no real regret over her father's death. Instead, she tells the audience in a deadpan, affectless voice how she "sensed that her destiny now lay with Kit, for better or worse, and that it was better to spend a week with someone who loved [her] for what [she] was than years of loneliness." Rather than understanding and regretting the violence she has participated in, she sounds numb and ignorant.

Voice-over narration, whether diegetic or non-diegetic, can be unreliable. In Stanley Kubrick's picaresque *Barry Lyndon* (1975) a third-person narrator relates the tale of a wayward rogue's travels across Europe as he stumbles on adventure, romance, fortune, and, ultimately, a series of tragic reversals. Film scholar Mark Crispin Miller argues that, although Lyndon is a morally complex figure, the narration—which repeatedly passes judgment on the hero—is intentionally superficial. The narrator's "interpretations of his hero's motives are simple-minded, and his moral observations often jarringly intolerant." (Miller) The intentional discrepancy between sound and image contributes to a parallel between the intolerant narrator and viewers who "fail to watch closely and sympathetically." (Miller)

Malick's and Kubrick's experiments with sound demonstrate why viewers shouldn't assume that voice-overs promise the authoritative interpretation of events unfolding onscreen. Rather, audiences should recognize the often complex interplay between sound and image.

Sound Effects

Because dialogue is the element of film sound that usually receives the most emphasis onscreen (and in spectators' minds), some viewers may be tempted to think that sound effects are a minor, cosmetic component of a film's soundtrack. However, sound effects play an important role in shaping the audience's understanding of space.

Functions of Sound Effects

Sound effects can contribute to the emotional and intellectual depth of a scene in three ways: they can define a scene's location; they can lend a mood to the scene; and they can suggest the environment's impact on characters.

Define Location Sound effects play an important role in helping audiences understand the nature of the environment that surrounds the characters. From the beeping car horns of an urban thoroughfare in *Manhattan* to the swirling wind of a North African sandstorm in *The English Patient* (Anthony Minghella 1996), sound effects can suggest a wide array of environments.

Usually, sound effects define location rather generically. Urban films rely on the constant buzz of traffic in the background to evoke the hustle and bustle of the city, for example, while Westerns rely on the jangle of spurs and the howl of a coyote to connote the lonely, arid plains where the action will unfold.

In some films, however, sound effects define the setting more specifically, alluding to particular places at specific points in time. In *Raging Bull*, the pop of flashbulbs dominates the soundtrack, evoking an era when sports coverage was largely limited to newspapers rather than television. The sound of whirling helicopter rotors plays a crucial role in depicting the American conflict in Vietnam (*The Deer Hunter, Apocalypse Now, Platoon* [Oliver Stone 1986]) because the

8.9 The desolation of open space in *There Will Be Blood*.

war marked the first time that helicopters were used extensively in combat.

Sound effects can also evoke the vast emptiness of a setting. Silent moments in films are almost never silent; even when a character experiences solitude, audio details proliferate. Early in *There Will Be Blood*, prospector (and soon to be oil baron) Daniel Plainview sits alone on the western plains, listening only to the hiss of the bitter wind (fig. **8.9**). Over the course of the film's long, expository sequence there is very little to hear except the sound effects of a man toiling and then waiting in the elements. For several minutes, we learn nothing about Plainview, and this nothingness is all we need to know about Plainview: he is an empty man driven more by the desire to find riches buried in the land than to develop relationships with other people.

These examples of sound effects do not have an immediate bearing on the plot. They do, however, give audiences a greater sense of the physical environment and historical circumstances that surround the characters.

Lend Mood to an Environment As Chapter 5 explored, the visual attributes of a setting can create the emotional tenor of a scene. Sound effects can likewise contribute to the mood established by the *mise en scène*. Perhaps the most obvious examples of this effect can be found in horror films, where a common device for evoking fear is a pronounced clap of thunder. For example, in the scene in *Frankenstein* where Dr. Frankenstein creates life, his laboratory comes alive with crashes of thunder and the persistent buzz of electric transformers (fig. **8.10**). The justifiably famous sound effects in the scene help create an eerie atmosphere, and the parallel between the lightning and the electrical current in the machinery provides a potent symbol for the doctor's ability to harness nature in the name of science.

Of course, sound effects can produce a wide variety of moods. The persistent clinking of dishes and rattle of silverware in the exposition of *Thelma & Louise* evoke the hectic,

8.10 Sound effects add to the eerie atmosphere in *Frankenstein*.

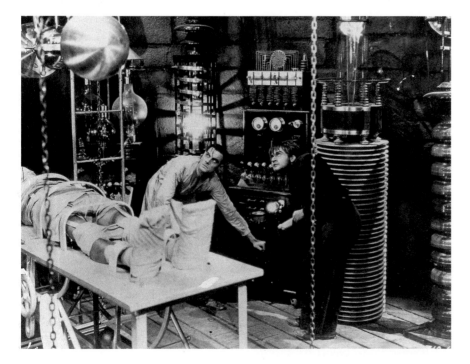

working-class environment of the diner where Louise works. The sound of the rushing elevated train in *The Godfather* suggests Michael's intensifying nervousness as he prepares to commit his first murder. The sounds of rustling wind and babbling brooks in *Brokeback Mountain* evoke an idyllic world far removed from the constraints of society. Sound effects can help to create a romantic environment or a terrifying one, establishing an intimate setting or an alienating one.

Portray the Environment's Impact on Characters Sound effects can help illustrate how the environment has a direct impact on characters. Action/adventure films, which typically feature characters being bombarded by explosions and gunfire, provide countless fruitful examples.

But this function of sound effects is certainly not limited to action films. In Antonioni's drama *Red Desert*, the sound of approaching boats is an important motif. The characters associate the sound with two potential threats that ocean liners present: disease (which the international ships transport, along with their cargo) and loneliness (the film implies that the male characters are frequently absent because of their business travel). This motif demonstrates the way sound effects are a powerful and sometimes subtle device for establishing how surroundings have a direct impact on people.

To suggest that sound effects have these three functions, however, is, in some cases, to impose an artificial distinction between the roles sound plays in films. Particularly expressive sound effects may serve all three functions simultaneously, defining location, creating mood, and portraying the environment's relation to characters.

Characteristics of Sound Effects

A crucial component of any analysis of a sound effect is a careful description of how that effect is created. Film scholars take particular note of four characteristics of sound effects: acoustic qualities, volume, regularity, and verisimilitude.

Acoustic Qualities In order to analyze sound effects it is important to be able to describe exactly what the audience hears, and to write about it with precision. As an example of subtly differing sound effects, consider the noises made by the opening and closing doors in *Alien* and the *Star Wars* series. When Captain Dallas (Tom Skerritt) pursues the alien in the former film, circular hatches close behind him one by one, sounding like sheets of grimy steel grating against one another. The clunky, mechanical sound effect befits the industrial aura of the starship *Nostromo*. In contrast,

8.11 A door closes on the Death Star in *Star Wars: Episode IV—A New Hope*.

The Human Voice as Aural Object

Some film theorists have argued that cinemagoers fail to recognize sound as a unique cinematic element, distinct from the visual image, with physical properties and aesthetic possibilities of its own. Sound waves do not seem to occupy a fixed location; they are not anchored by a screen the way visual images are. They move through space and enter the human body by causing vibrations in the tiny bones of the ear; thus they can envelop listeners with a greater degree of intimacy than visual images and, perhaps, elicit a different form of perceptual attention than the image demands. "The voice has greater command over space than the look," writes theorist Mary Ann Doane, "one can hear around corners, through walls." (p. 44) Doane argues for the primacy of aural over visual processing by taking note of the fact that, in humans, hearing develops prior to vision. "Space, for the child, is defined initially in terms of the audible, not the visible." (Doane, p. 44)

Despite the fact that sound possesses physical qualities and perceptual characteristics that are vastly different from those associated with the visual image, sound is frequently understood as a secondary feature of film, important only because it enhances or helps to make sense of the images onscreen. In the words of French film theorist Christian Metz, "the recognition of a sound leads directly to the question: a sound of what?" (Metz, p. 25) Metz argues that cinephiles and film scholars alike have ignored the unique properties of sound, which he termed, "the **aural object**"; one piece of evidence is that they describe sound using the attributes of visual images. "Sounds are more often classified according to the objects which transmit them than by their own characteristics," Metz writes (p. 25). One example that Metz cites is the familiar concept of offscreen sound: he points out that, while the source of a sound may be offscreen, the sound is continuing to issue forth from the soundtrack in the usual manner. The only difference is that the diegetic object that is ostensibly producing the sound is not made visible.

Filmmakers have also taken note of these displacements: respected sound designer and film editor Walter Murch (*The Conversation*; *Apocalypse Now*; *Jarhead*) concurs with Metz's view, stating "film sound is rarely appreciated for itself alone but functions largely as an enhancement of the visuals" ("Stretching Sound").

The human voice is one example of Metz's aural object; the voice is typically understood as a secondary attribute of the visual image, in large part because it is perceived in relation to a human body. Doane contends that voices in films are nearly always linked to bodies and that this is one way that the medium appears to offer unity, completeness, and realism, despite the fact that images, voices, and music are typically recorded at separate places and times. The primary purpose of the voice in film is to convey a character's attitudes and emotions through dialogue. Yet a voice can also assert its distinctiveness by contradicting the body it accompanies; a discrepancy between viewer expectations and the reality of a character's voice may produce incongruity, perhaps even comedy. In the Hollywood musical *Singin' in the Rain* (Stanley Donen and Gene Kelly 1952), popular silent film star Lina Lamont fails to make the transition to talking pictures because of her comically improper grammar and high-pitched, accented voice. (This very problem troubled the careers of silent stars such as Harold Lloyd and Norma Talmadge—one real world inspiration for Lamont).

In contrast to Doane, French film scholar Michel Chion is particularly interested in the *dis*embodied voice—that is, the human voice that is not attached to a visible character. He defines the **acousmetre** as the disembodied voice whose source is withheld from spectator completely or until late in the film (examples include Mother in Hitchcock's *Psycho*, the Wizard in *The Wizard of Oz* and the master criminal Dr. Mabuse in *The Testament of Dr. Mabuse* [Fritz Lang 1933]). According to Chion, withholding the source grants the voice a sense of mystery and power that is dispelled when the source becomes visible.

Embodied and disembodied voices serve as the focal point of Jean Jacques Beineix's 1982 cult classic, *Diva*. Several subplots revolve around the intrigue of the human voice in this offbeat film: in one, a moped-riding postman Jules (Frederic Andrei) is a passionate fan of renowned opera singer Cynthia Hawkins (played by soprano Wilhelmina Wiggins Fernandez). He makes a high quality recording of an aria she sings, steals her dress after the performance, and then fears the police are pursuing him because of his theft of her garment. In a related plot, Taiwanese businessmen seek to acquire and circulate Jules's pirated recording in order to pressure Hawkins into making a commercial recording, which she has never done. Hawkins has attempted to preserve her status as a vocal artist through live performances for devoted fans; she resists the pressure to record her voice and turn it into a purchasable commodity.

In yet another plotline, two police detectives attempt to identify and bring to justice the Antillais, a shadowy leader of an international drug and prostitution ring. This plotline revolves around another voice recording; that of Nadia, a dead prostitute and former girlfriend of the Antillais whose testimony has been recorded on a valuable but elusive cassette tape.

These diverse plotlines share a focus on the way that the human voice can be experienced live, as an attribute of the body that produces it, and also as an object that exists in its own right, detached from the body. Once recorded, Cynthia and Nadia's voices lose their connection to the singer or speaker that produced them. These voices are objects that can be possessed and replayed whenever the "owner" of the recording desires.

Diva's narrative forces viewers to pay attention to sound; yet director Beineix also uses the film's visual system to show that the human voice can move beyond its narrative function as a secondary attribute of character (in this case, Cynthia and Nadia). Beineix and cinematographer Philippe Rousselot use framing and camera movement to suggest the ways that Hawkins's aria

8.12 In *Diva*, camera movement suggests the way Cynthia's voice fills the space during her live performance.

8.13 The camera repeats its movement as Jules and Alba listen to Cynthia's recorded performance.

(and to a lesser extent, Nadia's testimony) take on lives of their own, and serve a purpose that sometimes rivals and overwhelms the images they "accompany."

In the film's opening scene, which depicts Cynthia's virtuoso performance of an aria from the opera "La Wally," the camera cranes above the stage, eventually moving into the auditorium seats to adopt the perspective of her audience, while also tracking around the oval amphitheater. This circular, floating camera movement visually characterizes the way that Cynthia's voice fills the space (fig. **8.12**). The camera recognizes Cynthia's aria as a moment of "pure voice," asking viewers to revel in its beauty and power rather than its connection to a character or narrative (the aria is not performed within the context of the full opera at this performance).

Diva traces the idea of pure voice through an aural and visual motif: Cynthia's aria is replayed at several points in the film and each time, the camera rises from the apparent source of the sound and rotates freely in space, repeating the camera movement in the first scene and mimicking the spatial expansiveness of Cynthia's voice. In one scene, Jules and his friend Alba listen to the "La Wally" recording through headphones, yet we hear Cynthia's voice on the soundtrack as it if were occupying the space of Jules's loft. The camera enhances this effect as it winds a circular path upward, as if imagining the meandering movement of Cynthia's voice, even though that sound is being transmitted through headphones (fig. **8.13**). The expressionist camera movement suggests that Cynthia's voice exists independently of her body, and of the recording devices that attempt to capture and objectify it.

By linking Cynthia's opera performance to this visual motif, Beineix asks viewers to recognize that the human voice is a critical element of the film's representational system, not merely a secondary aspect of character. Because he presents Nadia's posthumous testimony as an object of interest—her tape serves as a damning piece of evidence in the police investigation—Beineix also reminds us of the dangers of objectifying voices and bodies. Cynthia refuses to detach her voice from her body because she will lose control over it. Ironically, her attempt to maintain control seems to have failed when she learns that a recording has turned her voice into valuable property. But that object becomes a gift from Jules to the singer herself. This plotline parallels the prostitution subplot in which Nadia's testimony reveals the exploitive practices that are made possible when women's bodies are treated as commodities.

Through its narrative focus on women's voices and its striking cinematography, *Diva* directs our attention to the multifaceted nature of the voice and its relation to bodies and to visual images. In *Diva*, the distinction between the sound and its source is made clear, as the storyline and the cinematography endow the magnificent voice of the opera singer Cynthia Hawkins, and the recorded testimony of the murdered prostitute Nadia, with the status of aural objects.

when doorways open and close on the Death Star in *Star Wars*, the only sound is of decompressing air (fig. **8.11**). The hydraulic sound conveys the space station's efficient and sterile environment. Given the contexts in which these sounds appear, the difference between them is also entirely appropriate.

As they do with the human voice, sound editors can also adjust the acoustic qualities of a sound effect to help characterize the surrounding environment. For example, when the soldiers jump into the water as they assault the beach in *Saving Private Ryan*, a series of underwater shots combined with the muffled sound of explosions evokes the experience of being submerged. At one point the camera breaks the surface of the water and then goes under again (repeatedly), and the acoustic properties of the sound effects change accordingly. When the camera is above the surface, the sound effects are clear and piercing; when it is underwater, they are dampened. The result is to give the audience a vivid sense of the horror of having to struggle onto the beach at Normandy.

Volume Because dialogue tends to overwhelm sound effects, those rare moments when sound effects do compete with dialogue are particularly important. They suggest an environment that engulfs the characters within it.

Sometimes, however, filmmakers will diminish the volume of sound effects for expressive purposes. When Captain Miller (Tom Hanks) lands on the beach in *Saving Private Ryan*, the cacophony of explosions and shouting nearly disappears. The sonic frenzy is replaced by ominous white noise, which sounds like air blowing through an empty corridor. Because the shift in volume accompanies a medium close-up of Miller, audiences recognize that the soundtrack expresses the soldier's subjectivity. The horror of war has left him dazed. When one of Miller's subordinates asks him, "What do we do now sir?" audiences have to read the soldier's lips, because Miller does not hear the words. A whistle appears on the soundtrack. It grows louder and higher in pitch until it gives way to the sound effects of explosions and gunfire, and thus functions as an audio symbol of Miller's being "snapped back into reality." The experimentation with volume (which reappears in the climactic battle scene) develops the film's central theme: the importance of duty and self-sacrifice. Miller cannot let himself retreat from the horror he has witnessed; his subordinate's question reminds Miller that he has an obligation to guide the younger, inexperienced soldiers.

8.14 Dr. Frank Poole's haunting space walk in *2001*.

The expressive potential of adjusting the volume of sound effects goes well beyond war films, however. Kubrick's sci-fi epic *2001* employs restrained volume to suggest the emptiness of space, as when Dr. Frank Poole (Gary Lockwood) conducts a space walk and all the audience can hear is the sound of his breathing (fig. **8.14**). When the ship's computer cuts Poole's life support, the breathing suddenly gives way to a disturbing silence.

Regularity By and large, sound effects occur sporadically because in real life most sounds do not follow a set, repetitive pattern. Thus, when a sound effect does appear with rhythmic consistency, its persistence draws attention to a rigid order that runs counter to the more irregular rhythms of daily life. Consider how in films such as *Paths of Glory* the sound of soldiers' marching feet brings a mechanical precision that stands in contrast to the more random noises of combat later in the film.

Rosemary's Baby (Roman Polanski 1968) uses repetitive sound effects to suggest that the main character is suspended in time, unable to effect change. Indeed, the inexorable unfolding of time itself becomes a theme in the film. Rosemary (Mia Farrow) unwillingly becomes involved in a devious plot to deliver Satan's offspring to the world. Repeatedly, Polanski draws attention to the sound of a clock ticking mindlessly in the background. The sound effect complements other motifs involving the passage of time and natural cycles: Rosemary and others monitor her pregnancy; and the film emphasizes the changing seasons to draw attention to the passage of time.

8.15 Sound effects in *The Triplets of Belleville* equate fatigued cyclists with horses.

The film's emphasis on time wryly suggests that the delivery of Satan's child isn't supernatural. On the contrary, it is almost routine, and the ticking of the clock casually counts down the minutes until the end of the world. As with many sound effects that occur with regularity, the clock's rhythm emphasizes the contrast between the main character's hardship and the indifferent, business-as-usual mentality of her environment. In other contexts, however, repetitive sound effects may offer comfort.

Verisimilitude Typically Foley artists

and sound editors try to produce sounds with a high degree of verisimilitude. That is, audiences assume that the sounds that accompany images are true to life—that the creaking timbers in *Master and Commander: The Far Side of the World* (Peter Weir 2003) accurately represent the experience of life in the hull of a British frigate in the Napoleonic era, for example, or that the hexapede in *Avatar* sounds how a wild animal *would* sound in that faraway world. But on occasion, filmmakers will disregard verisimilitude altogether, and provide instead a sound that strives to be more expressive than representative.

In the animated film *The Triplets of Belleville* (*Belleville Rendez-vous* in the U.K.) (Sylvain Chomet 2003), exhausted cyclists in the Tour de France whinny like horses (fig. **8.15**). The joke reaches a gruesome conclusion when one rider, abducted by gangsters, gets murdered. The gangster pulls out his gun and then

TECHNIQUES IN PRACTICE

Sound Effects and the Construction of Class in *Days of Heaven*

American literature and film usually portray the plains of the Southwest as a rugged landscape that offers a liberating alternative to the Midwest's noisy, claustrophobic, and industrialized urban areas. In Terrence Malick's *Days of Heaven* (1978), lovers Bill (Richard Gere) and Abbey (Brooke Adams), along with Bill's younger sister (Linda Manz), flee Chicago. The three abandon the crowded city in favor of the spacious plains of the Texas panhandle, but they soon discover that the lush farmland too is industrialized. As in the city, Bill and Abbey find themselves at the very bottom of the class ladder. Rather than pastoral escape, the working-class lovers find only hard labor in the wheat fields of the Southwest.

The film's portrayal of industrialized spaces as noisome is apparent in the opening scene, in which Bill assaults his foreman at a Chicago foundry. The two men argue, but their dispute remains a mystery because the sound of pounding metal completely overwhelms their speech. The volume, acoustic characteristics, and regularity of the sound effects all work to convey the idea that Bill is consumed by this industrial space. The metal (an industrial material) clangs loudly and monotonously, evoking the maddening repetition associated with factory work. As the argument becomes more heated, the noise becomes louder, linking Bill's anger and frustration with mechanization. The pounding of steel also parallels the pounding of men's bodies in the fight, thus connecting the brutality of the argument with the brutality of the work space and the modern, industrialized world.

Later, when the three characters arrive in Texas, they find the migrant lifestyle anything but tranquil. One sequence depicting a day's work on the farm begins with the faint rustle of a breeze and the soft chirp of crickets. But the sound of a blacksmith banging a horseshoe soon disrupts the serenity. The rhythmic noise is a motif that establishes a parallel between the two spaces. Eventually the sound of the blacksmith gives way to the louder

8.16 *(left)* The start of the day on the farm in *Days of Heaven*.

8.17 *(right)* The Farmer takes it easy in *Days of Heaven*.

sound of the thrasher harvesting the wheat. Once again, the sound of machinery overwhelms the dialogue, and the characters are swallowed by their work environment (fig. **8.16**). Later, a close-up shot reveals a shovel feeding coal into the engine of the thrasher. This image mirrors an earlier shot in the foundry, confirming the parallel between Chicago and Texas.

By contrast, the unnamed Farmer (Sam Shepard) is associated with tranquility. His prosperity allows him the privilege of avoiding the industrial noise and spaces, thus establishing the class conflict that propels the film's main storyline. In one scene, the Farmer reclines on a divan in the middle of one of his fields while he listens to the foreman (Robert J. Wilke) tally up his profits (fig. **8.17**). The only sound effects in the scene are the faint rustle of wind through the wheat and the "ka-ching" sound of the adding machine. The sound of the machine situates the Farmer as part of the industrial system that engulfs Bill and Abbey, but the relative quiet clearly suggests his comfortable position in the upper class.

Both sound effects and images in *Days of Heaven* suggest that, by the turn of the century, the American West was already an industrialized region. While the Farmer can enjoy the privilege of a pastoral experience on his farm, Bill, Abbey, and the Girl remain trapped in their industrialized, working-class milieu.

the film cuts to an exterior hallway as audiences hear a shrill, startled neigh and the sound of a gunshot offscreen. The departure from verisimilitude—the substitution of a horse's neigh for a human shriek—introduces some black humor into the scene. The sound effect creates a metaphor equating the cyclists with animals: both are "disposed of" when they become injured and no longer useful.

Departures from verisimilitude have the potential to transcend representations of physical reality. They can allude to metaphorical or psychological truth rather than the sounds of everyday experience.

Music

On the set of *Lifeboat* (1944), Alfred Hitchcock questioned the logic of scoring a film set entirely on a lifeboat in World War II. Hitchcock wryly asked, "But where is the music supposed to come from out in the middle of the ocean?" Hearing of the director's reluctance to include a score, composer David Raksin suggested that Hitchcock should be asked "where the cameras come from." (quoted in Prendergast, pp. 222–3)

The exchange between Hitchcock and Raksin points to the central challenge film composers face. Most narrative films rely on music to engage the audience's attention, yet the same music threatens to make the artificiality of any film obvious. The composer's charge is to add soundtrack music that complements the imagery onscreen without calling attention to itself. In fact, film scholar Claudia Gorbman calls this music "unheard melodies" because audiences should not be *too* aware of the composer's work for fear of interfering with the story.

Functions of Film Music

In many cases, the only function of a score is to provide background music, which sustains audience attention and lends coherence to a scene as it moves from shot to shot. Composer Aaron Copland said that this music "helps to fill the empty spots between pauses in a conversation. ... [It] must weave its way underneath dialogue." (quoted in Prendergast, p. 218)

But, like the other elements of a film, music can develop systematically. It can establish motifs and parallels, and it can evolve with narrative context. In *The Lord of the Rings: The Fellowship of the Ring* (Peter Jackson 2001), when audiences first see Frodo Baggins (Elijah Wood), the soundtrack plays a faintly Gaelic tune, which represents the bucolic life in the Shire where Frodo lives. Later, when Frodo and Sam (Sean Astin) leave the Shire, Sam comments on how he will be going farther from home than he has ever gone before. While he talks, a melancholy French horn repeats the musical theme (a melody that becomes a motif), signaling their departure and Sam's impending homesickness. During the film's resolution, when Frodo and Sam agree to travel together on a quest to destroy the ring, a flute plays the theme. The instrumentation, with its Gaelic flair, conveys how the communal spirit of the Shire follows these two friends as they vow to work together to combat evil. Shore chose Celtic music, "one of the oldest [forms of] music in the world" to give the score "a feeling of antiquity" befitting the bygone era of the Shire (Otto and Spence).

Such systematic use of film music can contribute to the emotional and intellectual complexity of a film in five ways: it can establish the historical context for a scene; it can help depict a scene's geographical space; it can help define characters; it can help shape the emotional tenor of a scene; and it can provide a distanced or ironic commentary on a scene's visual information.

Establish Historical Context Music offers filmmakers an efficient means of defining a film's setting. Audiences should associate diegetic music with the story's time period, since, in the name of historical accuracy, most filmmakers will try to ensure that the music characters listen to would have been popular during the time when the story takes place. Throughout *The Last Picture Show* (Peter Bogdanovich 1971), the music of Hank Williams seeps out of car radios and jukeboxes, evoking the mood of a dying Texas town in the 1950s. The country music legend's lyrical emphasis on broken relationships and loneliness reflects the character's alienation. In *Saving Private Ryan*, the soldiers enjoy a brief respite from battle listening to the love songs of Edith Piaf. The choice of music is highly evocative of the story's setting in France, since Piaf had been an unofficial symbol of France and its resistance against Germany during World War II. The use of intentional anachronisms in *Marie Antoinette* (Sofia Coppola 2006), in which popular rock songs from the late twentieth century appear on the soundtrack even though the story is set in the eighteenth century, is rare in popular films, partly because music plays such an important role in situating the audience in the narrative's place and time.

Shaping Space Diegetic music can be used to help audiences perceive the geography of the setting. Consider how, in *Notorious*, Hitchcock underscores Alicia and Devlin's precarious situation as they investigate the wine cellar, spying on Alicia's suspicious husband. By lowering the volume of the party music on the soundtrack, the film emphasizes the cellar's proximity to the festivities upstairs. By using diegetic music to remind audiences of the geography of Sebastian's manor, Hitchcock invests the scene with a considerable amount of tension.

The loud dance music in a bar in *The 40 Year Old Virgin* emphasizes the crowded, boisterous singles scene that Andy Stitzer finds so daunting. In contrast, the soft music playing in the background through much of *Rear Window* contributes to the audience's understanding that Jeffries's open window looks out onto a busy courtyard. The barely perceptible music points to the fact that, although he is surrounded by neighbors, Jeffries is simultaneously cut off from them.

Music can even suggest the specific cultural makeup of a setting's location. The celebrated opening tracking shot in the re-released version of *Touch of Evil* contains an eclectic assortment of diegetic music, whereas the studio's original release included only a non-diegetic title song by Henry Mancini. An elaborate crane shot begins a tour of the streets of a town on the U.S.–Mexican border. As the camera passes various buildings, the soundtrack music changes, establishing that the town is full of bars playing loud music. Moreover, by having each bar play a different style of music, the soundtrack highlights the multicultural makeup of this border town.

Defining Character Just as many people express themselves through the music they listen to, so filmmakers use music to define characters. A particular song, artist, or type of music may function as a motif that informs audiences of a character's taste, demeanor, or attitude. In music terminology, the leitmotif (leading motif) was first used to describe the compositional strategies of Karl Maria von Weber and Richard Wagner, who used distinctive musical phrases and themes to define character and present ideas. Fritz Lang's thriller *M* (1931) offers one of cinema's first (and most disturbing) examples of how music can define a character. The child killer (Peter Lorre) whistles Edvard Grieg's sinister "In the Hall of the Mountain King" from *Peer Gynt*. In *Billy Elliot*, young Billy spends his days listening to the songs of the rock band T Rex while he fantasizes about becoming a ballet dancer. Given Billy's rejection of traditional gender roles and his ambiguous sexuality, T Rex is an appropriate choice, since the band's lead singer, Marc Bolan, was noted for his glam-rock androgyny.

Composers can also score non-diegetic musical motifs for specific characters. For *Once upon a Time in the West*, Ennio Morricone composed a haunting, almost tuneless song built around the lone wail of a harmonica. Throughout the film, this song is associated with the character called, appropriately enough, Harmonica (Charles Bronson). The theme is intimately connected to the character's personality. He plays the instrument himself, and a flashback eventually reveals that a harmonica played a pivotal role in a traumatic childhood event, which has haunted him ever since.

Harmonica's nemesis, Frank (Henry Fonda), is associated with an electric guitar that suggests the character's methodical menace. But submerged under the main melody of Frank's theme is the wail of the harmonica, suggesting the sadistic past these two men share. When the two characters finally meet for a climactic shootout, the two musical themes compete for audio space, representing the central conflict between two strong wills. While most scores are composed after shooting is completed, Morricone composed the score before shooting on the film began. Leone then played the score on the set during filming, so that each actor could move to the music. The unusual process Leone and Morricone adopted indicates how closely they tied the characters to the score's musical themes (Frayling, pp. 280–1).

Shaping Emotional Tenor Music plays an important role in helping audiences know how to interpret the mood of a scene. John Williams's score for *Jaws* (Steven Spielberg 1975) offers a good example of how music can help a filmmaker emphasize dramatic shifts in emotional tenor from scene to scene within a single film. The famous main theme—a sinister melody played primarily by low strings and based on an eerie, two-note progression—precedes each of the shark's attacks, and thus contributes to its horrific menace. But later, when Sheriff Brody (Roy Scheider) hits the high seas with two compatriots in pursuit of the shark, Williams's score is often more uptempo (fast) and lushly orchestrated to suggest the sheriff's sense of excitement and adventure.

Distancing the Audience Music sometimes exploits a contrast between sound and image. The effect of such a contrast is to distance the audience—to sever the connection between sound and image, so that the audience sees the images from a more critical perspective.

Sometimes, filmmakers use this technique to offer wry, satirical commentary. *Dr. Strangelove* begins with images of bomber planes refueling in mid-flight, a process that requires one plane to release fuel through a long tube into the tank of the bomber. Instead of using military music to accompany the image, Kubrick uses the airy, romantic tune "Try a Little Tenderness." The odd juxtaposition of sound and image transforms the military operation into a mechanical mating ritual, pointing to one of the film's central tenets: that weaponry is an absurd substitute phallus and that the arms race between the Soviet Union and the United States is a dangerous contest to see who has the biggest "equipment."

On other occasions, filmmakers exploit the juxtaposition of music and image to suggest the world's complete indifference to a character's plight. In *Face/Off* (John Woo 1997), a child listens to the song "Somewhere over the Rainbow" on headphones, oblivious to the bloody shootout taking place around him. At Club Silencio in *Mulholland Drive*, a torch singer collapses while performing a Spanish version of Roy Orbison's haunting ballad "Crying," but the vocals continue even while she lies on the stage unconscious. The strange discrepancy—whereby the music plays without regard to the singer's distress—makes it clear that the "live" performance wasn't what it initially appeared to be. The chanteuse was only lip-synching. In Sam Fuller's *Naked Kiss* (1964), a woman discovers her fiancé sexually molesting a child while a record of children singing a lullaby plays in the background. According to Claudia Gorbman, such instances "testify to the power of … music which blissfully lacks awareness or empathy; its very emotionlessness, juxtaposed with ensuing human catastrophe, is what provokes our emotional response." (Gorbman, p. 24) In other words, such blatant inappropriateness draws attention to the contrast between the music's complete lack of response and the audience's (hopefully) more empathetic response to these characters' predicaments.

Obviously, a piece of film music can carry out more than one of these functions simultaneously. To help recognize how a piece of music functions, audiences should train their ears to recognize five characteristics of film music.

Five Characteristics of Film Music

Film music is notoriously difficult to write about. Despite a song's uncanny ability to sweep audiences up into the romantic (or exciting, or tragic) sentiment unfolding onscreen, few people have the ability to describe how the music accomplishes this. Those who have formally studied music are perhaps best equipped to describe and analyze film music. For those who haven't spent years training their ears to dissect a tune into its individual components, the danger in trying to write about music is that the discussion will be too imprecise to inform or convince other readers. Vague adjectives such as "romantic" or "scary" are of little value when describing a melody.

Still, it is possible for non-musicians to talk and write concretely about film music. In order to think and write about it with specificity, begin by concentrating on these five attributes of film music: patterns of development; lyrical content; tempo and volume; instrumentation; and cultural significance.

Patterns of Development Like other elements of film, music develops systematically. Musical themes are often repeated, establishing motifs and parallels. And as musical motifs evolve, they signal important changes in the story. Consequently, perhaps the most important strategy for actively listening to and thinking about film music is to notice when a musical theme appears. Does the theme come to be associated with particular characters or settings? With particular emotions? With particular visual imagery?

In his score for *Star Wars*, John Williams developed two distinct melodies. The film's familiar main theme is associated with the idealism of the Rebel Alliance, whereas a more foreboding and militaristic theme (the tune is in a minor key and its plodding rhythm sounds like bootsteps) signals the presence of the evil Empire. In *He Got Game* (Spike Lee 1998), several montage sequences depicting basketball games are accompanied by Aaron Copland compositions, including "Appalachian Spring," and "Fanfare for the Common Man" from *Symphony No. 3*. The repetition of music and image elevates games of street ball to the status of high art. Copland's music famously refashioned "folk" melodies into high art just as Lee's film presents basketball as a vibrant urban art form. In both cases, the musical theme is repeatedly linked to a particular character, environment, or event.

Musical motifs can function in more abstract ways as well, helping viewers to draw parallels between characters, settings, or ideas. In *Jules and Jim*, the two title characters become fixated on a mysterious statue. When they see the statue for the first time, the sound of a melancholy flute accompanies the image. Later, when Jules (Oskar Werner) and Jim (Henri Serre) see Catherine (Jeanne Moreau) for the first time, the same tune plays in the background. The motif thus points to the mysterious opacity that Catherine shares with the statue, and which will fascinate the two men for twenty years.

Lyrical Content Since the late 1960s, soundtrack music has relied more on self-contained popular songs instead of scored material. Often (but not always) filmmakers choose songs whose lyrics are relevant to the image onscreen. Consequently, an analysis of film music should consider the possible significance of any lyrics.

Lyrics can be powerful indicators of mood or turning points in plot. In *Thelma & Louise*, after Thelma finally gathers the courage to ignore Darryl's orders and accompany Louise on a weekend getaway, the soundtrack plays Van Morrison's "Wild Night." The lyrics mirror Thelma and Louise's actions as each packs her bags in a parallel editing sequence:

> As you brush your shoes, you stand before your mirror
> And you comb your hair, grab your coat and hat

More importantly, the lyrics speak to the giddy anticipation both women feel over the prospect of escaping their humdrum daily routines:

> And everything looks so complete
> When you're walking down on the streets
> And the wind, it catches your feet
> Sets you flying, crying
> Ooh ooh-ooh wee, wild night, is calling *

©1971 WB Music Corp., and Caledonia Soul Music. All rights administered by WB Music Corp. All rights reserved. Used by permission of Alfred Publishing Co., Inc.

Interestingly, the soundtrack plays Martha Reeves's version of the song, emphasizing how this moment captures the excitement of the women's liberation.

Furthermore, the lyrics' emphasis on flying establishes one of the central motifs in the film: flight into open space as a metaphor for empowerment. In short, the use of the song effectively ends the film's exposition, as both women have made the first step away from their gender roles as housewife and waitress.

Tempo and Volume Tempo (speed) and volume are two attributes of music that are readily describable even to the untrained ear. They also play a significant role in determining the emotional intensity of a song (and, by extension, a scene).

Uptempo, or fast, melodies tend to convey frenetic energy and rapid movement. Chase scenes in action films, for example, usually rely on non-diegetic uptempo melodies. Slow melodies, on the other hand, suggest a more relaxed pace, or a lack of energy. Perhaps no scene exemplifies the distinction as effectively as when Benjamin hurries to prevent Elaine's marriage in *The Graduate*. As he drives from Berkeley to Santa Barbara—frantically stopping along the way to ask directions—a quickly strummed acoustic guitar corresponds to Benjamin's speed and anxiety. But soon the tempo of the music slows considerably, telling the audience exactly when Benjamin's car starts to run out of gas. Eventually the music putters out altogether, suggesting that his quest may be futile.

Like tempo, volume can also affect the intensity of a scene. But whereas tempo usually comments on a character's movement, volume usually characterizes the aura of the space surrounding characters. Loud music seems to swallow characters, whereas soft music connotes more intimacy.

One scene in *Apocalypse Now* exemplifies how altering volume can radically modulate the dynamics of a scene. A squadron of helicopters on a bombing raid approaches the target village, led by the demented racist Lt. Kilgore (Robert Duvall). The soldiers blast Wagner's "The Ride of the Valkyries" on an elaborate speaker system designed to terrify the enemy. The choice of music is an intertextual reference to *The Birth of a Nation*, whose original score featured Wagner's music accompanying the Ku Klux Klan's triumphant charge. Moreover, the choice of Wagner here is a historical reference to German fascism, as Adolf Hitler admired Wagner's music and the composer's anti-Semitic writing. The choice of music emphasizes Kilgore's racism and bigotry. Wagner dominates the mix on the soundtrack and offers audiences a sense of the soldiers' simultaneous fear and excitement. The music transforms what would otherwise be the confined space of a helicopter into a position of authority and dominance; the blaring music is an act of aggression that exceeds the physical space of the helicopter itself.

The sequence then cuts to the targeted village, whose silence is disrupted by the comparatively quiet ringing of a bell. Eventually Wagner's music can be heard on the soundtrack accompanying images of the village (fig. **8.18**). It gradually gets louder, culminating in the helicopters' attack. The abrupt movement from loud to soft shifts the audience's identification, so that the excitement audiences might otherwise share with the soldiers onscreen gives way to empathy for the villagers. Sound editor Walter Murch's manipulation of volume in this scene puts audiences in the position of the attacked, as well as the attacker.

The tempo and volume of non-diegetic music can also help paint internal

space. In *Psycho*, as Marion leaves Phoenix, the score is played quite loud and establishes her nervousness. Moreover, multiple melodic lines unfold in differing rhythms and suggest the dual facets of Marion's personality. At a lower pitch, the strings play a rapid progression of notes characterized by their sharp, distinct (staccato) sound. It is the dominant strain in the melody, which begins immediately after Marion's boss crosses the street in front of her car; his perplexed look makes it clear that he wonders why Marion is not home sick in bed, as she said she would be. As Marion continues her drive the next night, the plucking of the strings corresponds to the blinding rain and slashing windshield wipers, which clearly distract Marion, leading her to the Bates Motel. This line is clearly associated with Marion's fear as she leaves town and evades the law.

The second melodic line is higher pitched. The violins play a *legato* (notes that are smooth and connected) melody at half the speed of the lower notes. Given the narrative context, this upper melodic line seems to correspond with Marion's attempt to remain calm—or rather, to act calm when under the surface she is almost paralyzed with fear. In this regard, the two distinct melodic lines reflect one of the film's most important motifs: personalities torn asunder by conflicting desires. The volume and tempo of Bernard Herrmann's score are, in other words, a musical representation of psychosis.

Instrumentation It is not difficult to make generalizations about what instruments are used to perform a piece of music. Does an orchestra play the music? A brass ensemble? A string quartet? Do the musicians use electric or electronic instruments? Do the musicians sample and manipulate pre-recorded sounds? Bernard Herrmann's score for *Psycho* would have had a very different effect had he included brass instruments to temper the sound of the strings, especially during the piercing notes that accompany Marion's violent death. Different instruments create different moods, so the choice of instrumentation can play a dramatic role in creating an environment for a scene.

Instrumentation can suggest a film's time period and setting. For example, when Bill, Abbey, and the Girl flee Chicago at the beginning of *Days of Heaven*, an acoustic guitar accompanies images of the three riding southwest on a train. The instrument's association with folk music (and rural space) is an efficient way to emphasize the film's early twentieth-century time period and to signal the characters' movement from an urban to a rural locale. In contrast, Howard Shore's score for the opening credits of *Se7en* helps to establish the urban setting and grim tone by utilizing distorted electric and electronic instruments and sampled sound effects.

Some instruments may also portray more subtle emotional states. In Wong Kar-Wai's *In the Mood for Love* (2002), Su Li-zhen (Maggie Cheung) and Chow Mo-wan (Tony Leung) turn to one another for comfort after discovering their respective spouses are having an affair. On the verge of becoming romantically involved themselves, the would-be lovers separate, leaving their tentative love unrequited. Michael Galasso's score suggests the couple's unspoken longing for one another through the use of a cello "because it is such an evocative instrument, able to express strong emotions"; a low bass drum accompanies the cello, sounding like a "subliminal heartbeat" (Galasso, quoted in Lee).

Instrumentation can also suggest important character traits. John Carpenter's score for his slasher film *Halloween* (1978) is notable for its spare arrangement,

8.19 Harpo Marx is always associated with a horn or a harp.

revolving around the rapid repetition of two notes on the piano. The ominous simplicity reflects the terrifying incongruity that opens the film: the stalker/killer in the exposition is a child. The rudimentary piano sounds like a child doodling on the keyboard, but the staccato notes and rapid tempo suggests the character's violent, insistent energy.

Marx Brothers' films offer many comic examples of how instruments can be associated with a character. In these films, Harpo Marx never utters a word. His primary means of communication are his mischievous smile and an oversized bicycle horn, which he frequently honks in exclamation. Yet the chaotic frenzy of a Marx Brothers' film is always tempered by Harpo's romantic side, which appears when he tenderly serenades the audience with a harp (fig. **8.19**). The character's quirky humor arises from the bizarre juxtaposition of low-brow (the honking horn) and high-brow (the harp).

Cultural Significance Finally, filmmakers can add complexity to a film by using music that bears a specific cultural significance. A specific song or type of music may conjure up shared cultural knowledge, as in *Stagecoach*, when John Ford uses a familiar musical theme to tell audiences that Native Americans are near.

According to Claudia Gorbman, the film's "Indian music" produces meaning in part because of its "cultural-musical properties—[the] rhythmic repetition in groups of four with accented initial beat ... [which] *already* signify 'Indian' in the language of the American music industry" (Gorbman, p. 28).

Music that functions in this way often relies on stereotypes to produce meaning. The music in Ford's film is not authentic Apache music; it is a cliché that became a substitute for the authentic artifact because of its repetition in film, radio, and eventually TV.

In contrast, *Office Space* intentionally upsets cultural assumptions about music for comic effect. Throughout the film, three beleaguered office workers—Peter, Michael, and Samir (Ron Livingston, David Herman, and Ajay Naidu)—suffer through the mind-numbing tedium of their white collar jobs. Gangster rap by Canibus, Ice Cube, and the Geto Boys plays throughout the soundtrack, articulating the friends' growing frustration at work. The film trades on the irony that, while most viewers immediately associate rap with the so-called "urban experience," this trio of angry misfits is suburban and decidedly middle-class—quite the opposite of the gangsters romanticized in the lyrics. One riotous scene combines the Geto Boys' "Still" with the visual cues from gangster rap videos—canted, low-angle shots and slow motion—as the trio unleashes all its wrath on the company (fig. **8.20**). But instead of torturing some*body*, as celebrated in the lyrics, Peter, Michael, and Samir demolish the *thing* they hate most: the office printer. The ironic use of music, and the fact that it infiltrates the film's visual style as well, points to a larger theme in the film: how far removed these men are from the "street" problems described in the songs they worship. Yet it also evokes how rap's vitriolic expressions of disaffection transcend cultural, racial, and class barriers.

8.20 These office workers act out the lyrics of gangster rap in *Office Space*.

8.21 Music adds layers of meaning in *The Royal Tenenbaums*.

Filmmakers may also use songs whose production history holds some cultural significance. In *The Royal Tenenbaums*, after Richie Tenenbaum (Luke Wilson) unsuccessfully attempts to commit suicide, Nick Drake's recording of "Fly" plays softly in the background. The fact that Drake committed suicide adds poignancy to the scene beyond the melancholy of the actual tune itself (fig. **8.21**).

Film scholar Nora Alter explores the powerful role that non-diegetic music can play in the non-fiction essay film, a genre that may incorporate elements of documentary, fiction, and avant-garde films. "Critical attention is rarely focused on the soundtrack of the non-fiction essay film," she writes, "[a]nd yet, music is one of the most important and determining forces in this type of film. It structures the montage, shapes meaning, establishes tone, and encourages flights of fantasy." (Alter, p. 3) Alter offers a specific example of a musical composition that links two very different essay films together in compelling ways. A haunting Hanns Eichler score can be heard on the soundtrack of both Alain Resnais's *Night and Fog* (1955), a self-reflexive meditation on the death camps of World War II, and *Loin du Vietnam* (*Far from Vietnam*, 1967), an omnibus film about the Vietnam war made by Jean Luc Godard, Joris Ivens, William Klein, Claude Lelouch, Chris Marker, Resnais, and Agnes Varda. In 1967, it would have been extremely provocative to directly compare the U.S. prosecution of war in Southeast Asia to Hitler's genocidal practices, especially since the U.S. had been seen as a "savior from totalitarianism" in World War II (Alter, p. 4). However, Alter contends, Eisler's score connects these two catastrophic periods: "What could not be said or shown—and here it's important to recall that Resnais's films [...] were immediately censored by the French authorities—could be suggested through a musical composition." (p. 4) Even in non-fiction films, then, music "speaks" to audiences, but does so in an indirect way on what Alter calls a parallel track. In this instance, the musical score conveyed ideas about war, about

Bernard Herrmann's Score and Travis Bickle's Troubled Masculinity in *Taxi Driver*

In Martin Scorsese's *Taxi Driver*, Robert De Niro plays Travis Bickle, a lonely New York cab driver who is simultaneously sickened by the moral decay he sees everyday and obsessed with political campaigner Betsy (Cybill Shepherd). When his romance with Betsy fizzles out, Travis tries unsuccessfully to assassinate the political candidate Betsy works for. After he fails, Travis murders a pimp and several street hustlers in order to rescue the thirteen-year-old prostitute Iris (Jodie Foster). He becomes a local hero in the process. Travis's obsessions seem paradoxical: on one hand, he's a hopeless romantic, and on the other hand he's an explosive cynic who can only see the city's decay. But Bernard Herrmann's score emphasizes that Travis's romantic and violent sides are interrelated.

Herrmann's score for *Taxi Driver* (his last score in a career that began with *Citizen Kane* in 1941) introduces two dominant themes during the opening credits. The soundtrack alternates between the two, seemingly antithetical, non-diegetic themes. The first theme is spare and militaristic. It is built around two low, descending notes. Often the tonal progression is punctuated by the tapping of a snare drum, whose tempo gradually increases until the high note gives way to the low note. The second theme is a slow, lilting jazz tune played on a tenor saxophone. Onscreen, the image cuts back and forth between extreme close-ups of Travis's eyes and blurry, oversaturated point-of-view shots of New York City (fig. **8.22**). This suggests immediately that the music reflects two halves of his personality, and that Travis's perspective of the city is distorted.

Throughout the film, the militaristic theme is associated with Travis's seething anger. The foreboding theme, largely played on low brass instruments, reflects his military background in Vietnam, and his voice-over emphasizes that Travis will eventually use this background on the domestic front. As he contemplates how sordid the city has become, Travis's voice-over speaks of his hopes for a "real rain [to] come and wash all the scum off the streets." The militaristic theme typically accompanies these thoughts, suggesting that he, the lone stalwart against the "scum and the filth" of the city, might just be the "real rain" to clean up the street.

Yet, from the opening credits, the film clearly emphasizes that his condemnatory view of the city is a distorted and destructive one. Several scenes emphasize that Travis directs most of his hostility toward African Americans. Also, Travis repeatedly points weapons (or his fingers, as if

8.22 Travis's distorted point of view opens *Taxi Driver*.

they were a weapon) at innocent strangers: people walking on the streets, dancers on television, and women onscreen at the local porno theater.

Coming on the heels of Travis's fuming over the moral decay of the city, the romantic theme initially suggests that love could, perhaps, alleviate some of his anger and cynicism. It appears more frequently in the first half of the film, whenever Travis thinks longingly about Betsy. For example, when he sees Betsy for the first time, the music plays and Travis's voice-over explains, "She appeared like an angel out of this filthy mass." In his eyes, she stands apart from the rest of the city. Audiences may assume that her love, then, could save Travis from his anger. Once she rejects him, the theme is associated with Iris, suggesting that she becomes a substitute for Betsy.

But the film makes clear that Travis's psychotic ranting and his romantic longing, far from being opposites, are actually complementary. Travis's tirades against the city's culture, his love for Betsy, and his desire to rescue Iris are nothing more than means for him to prop up a wounded ego. What Travis really desires is to assert his dominance, by acting as the supreme moral force over an entire city and by protecting two women whom he sees as too helpless to defend themselves. His first thoughts of Betsy are notable for their misguided chivalry, and when he asks Betsy out, he promises to protect her. When Betsy rejects Travis, he turns his attention to Iris, someone who, he thinks, is in need of rescue. To underscore that Travis's motivations are selfish, the film depicts how Travis decides to rescue Iris only after he has failed to assassinate the politician Palantine—Travis's rival for Betsy's attention. Travis's attitude toward Betsy and Iris is rooted in insecurity and is thus closely linked to an undercurrent of male retribution and violence.

After the film's bloody shootout, the two musical themes fuse, drawing attention to this connection between romance and violence. As the camera slowly tracks down the hallway of the hotel, tallying up the carnage Travis has left in his wake, the non-diegetic romantic tune once associated with Betsy is played by low brass instruments and accentuated by pounding percussion. The romantic has combined with the militaristic. The film's producer, Michael Phillips, says that Herrmann "explained that the reason he did it was to show that this was where Travis's fantasies about women led him. ... His illusions, his self-perpetuating way of dealing with women had finally brought him to that bloody, violent outburst." (quoted in S. Smith, p. 15)

The film's score emphasizes that Travis's romantic longing for Betsy, his hatred for the city, and his rescue of Iris are all interrelated. His romantic ideals are essentially violent, since they require the subjugation of everyone's will to Travis's ego. The fact that the public lauds Travis as a hero at the end of the film is a crucial ironic twist. Scorsese suggests that Americans still valorize chivalry—a value system the film shows to be outdated, violent, self-serving, and destructive.

violent bloodshed, and about bearing witness, that were so politically sensitive that they could not be stated outright.

This discussion of sound concludes our book's coverage of the five technical aspects of film art (narrative, *mise en scène*, cinematography, editing, and sound). By and large this chapter (along with Chapters 4 through 7) has explored how these elements function in narrative films. Because sound lacks shape and form, writing about its use in cinema is in some ways more difficult than writing about narrative and visual content, but it is no less important.

Yet even films that don't tell stories can use sound to complement images onscreen, even when those images are abstract. While sound in such cases won't contribute narrative information such as historical context or a character's upbringing, the characteristics of the human voice, sound effects, and music will still be relevant. The next chapter takes up in more specific detail two such alternatives to narrative filmmaking: documentary and avant-garde cinema.

Summary

- The history of sound technology has seen several major developments, each one an attempt to provide higher fidelity.
- Because sound is added or altered during post-production, it is freed from the image.
- There are five common image–sound relationships: onscreen vs. offscreen sound; subjective vs. objective sound; diegetic vs. non-diegetic sound; image time vs. sound time; image mood vs. sound mood.
- The three components of film sound are: dialogue, sound effects, and music.
- In addition to the content of an actress's lines of dialogue, the four characteristics of her voice contribute to film's overall impact: volume, pitch, speech characteristics, and acoustic qualities.
- The voice-over is a powerful storytelling technique that can help maintain narrative coherence and provide a point of identification.
- Sound effects have three common functions in narrative films. They can define location, lend mood to an environment, and portray the environment's impact on characters.
- To be precise when describing sound effects, film scholars pay attention to four characteristics of sound effects: acoustic qualities; volume; regularity; verisimilitude.
- Five common functions of film music are: to establish historical context; to shape the audience's perception of space; to define character; to shape the emotional tenor of a scene; to distance the audience.
- It is possible to write concretely about music in film by noting these five characteristics: patterns of development; lyrics; tempo and volume; instrumentation; cultural significance.

Works Consulted

Alter, Nora. "Sound Thoughts: Hearing the Essay," *The Essay Film* ed. Sven Kramer and Thomas Tode. Konstanz: Konstanz University Press, forthcoming 2010, pp. 1–15.

Bordwell, David. *On the History of Film Style*. Cambridge, MA: Harvard University Press, 1997.

Carlsson, Sven. "Sound Design of *Star Wars*." Film Sound.org. **http://www.filmsound.org/ starwars/**. August 13, 2006.

Chion, Michel. *Audio-Vision: Sound on Screen*. New York: Columbia University Press, 1994.

————. *The Voice in Cinema*, trans Claudia Gorbman. NY: Columbia UP, 1999.

Clair, René. "The Art of Sound." *Film Sound.org*. **http://lavender.fortunecity.com/hawkslane/ 575/art-of-sound.htm**. August 11, 2006.

Cook, David. *A History of Narrative Film*. New York: Norton, 1996.

Doane, Mary Ann. "The Voice in the Cinema: the Articulation of Body and Space." *Yale French Studies* 60 (1980): pp. 33–50.

Eisenstein, S.M., V.I. Pudovkin, G.V. Alexandrov. "A Statement." *Film Sound.org*. **http://lavender. fortunecity.com/hawkslane/575/statement.htm**. August 11, 2006.

Festinger, Rob, and Todd Field. *In the Bedroom*. New York: Hyperion, 2002.

"Foley Artists at C5 Share Their Secrets." *C5, Inc. News*. **http://www.c5sound.com/newsroom/ secrets.php**. August 13, 2006.

Frayling, Christopher. *Sergio Leone: Something to Do with Death*. London: Faber, 2000.

Gomery, Douglas. "The Coming of Sound; Technological Change in the American Film Industry," in *Film Sound*, ed. Elizabeth Weis and John Belton. New York: Columbia University Press, 1985, pp. 5–24.

Gorbman, Claudia. *Unheard Melodies: Narrative Film Music*. Bloomington: Indiana University Press, 1987.

Grover-Friedlander, Michal. "*The Phantom of the Opera*: The lost voice of opera in silent film." *Cambridge Opera Journal* 11.2 (1999): pp. 179–92.

Kinder, Marsha, and Beverle Houston. *Close-Up: A Critical Perspective on Film*. New York: Harcourt, Brace, Jovanovich, 1972.

Lee, Joanna. "The Music of *In the Mood for Love*." *In the Mood for Love*. Dir. Wong Kar-Wai. DVD. USA/Criterion, 2002.

Leeper, Jill. "Crossing Borders: The Soundtrack for *Touch of Evil*," in *Soundtrack Available: Essays on Film and Popular Music*, ed. Pamela Robertson Wojcik and Arthur Knight. Durham, NC: Duke University Press, 2001, pp. 226–43.

LoBrutto, Vincent. *Sound on Film: Interviews with Creators of Film Sound*. Westport, CT: Praeger, 1994.

Metz, Christian. "Aural Objects," trans. Georgia Gurrieri. *Yale French Studies* 60 (1980): pp. 24–32.

Miller, Mark Crispin. "Barry Lyndon Reconsidered." *The Kubrick Site*. **http://www.visual-memory. co.uk/amk/doc/0086.html**. June 30, 2006. Originally published in *The Georgia Review*, 30/4 (1976).

Murch, Walter. "Stretching Sound to Help the Mind See." FilmSound.Org. **www.filmsound.org**. Adapted from "Sound Design: The Dancing Shadow" in *Projections 4: Film-makers on Film-making* (1995): pp. 237–51.

Otto, Jeff, and Spence D. "Howard Shore Interview." *ign.com*. (**http://music.ign.com/articles/ 446/446567pl.html**).

Prendergast, Roy M. *Film Music: A Neglected Art*, 2nd edn. New York: Norton, 1992.

Rhines, Jesse Algeron. *Black Films/White Money*. New Brunswick, NJ: Rutgers University Press, 1996.

Salt, Barry, "Film Style and Technology in the Thirties: Sound," in *Film Sound*, ed. Elizabeth Weis and John Belton. New York: Columbia University Press, 1985, pp. 37–43.

Shreger, Charles. "Altman, Dolby, and the Second Sound Revolution," in *Film Sound*, ed. Elizabeth Weis and John Belton. New York: Columbia University Press, 1985, pp. 348–55.

Smith, Jeff. *The Sound of Commerce*. New York: Columbia University Press, 1998.

Smith, Steven. "A Chorus of Isolation." *Taxi Driver*. Dir. Martin Scorsese. Laser Disc. Criterion/ Voyager Co. 1990.

Triggs, Jeffery Alan. "The Legacy of Babel: Language in Jean Renoir's *Grand Illusion*." *The New Orleans Review*, 15/2 (1988), pp. 70–4.

The Human Voice and Sound Effects

The essay below examines the way sound emphasizes that the gruesome violence in *No Country for Old Men* is in keeping with a long tradition of bloodshed.

The Study Notes that accompany this film analysis focus on strategies for writing introductions and conclusions. These paragraphs are notoriously difficult to write, largely because writers fear they may be redundant. However, introductions are important since they establish what the rest of the paper will cover, and conclusions often summarize the main argument. From the reader's perspective, these paragraphs aren't repetitive—they clarify. Introductions guide the reader into the argument, letting her know what main point(s) will be addressed in the body of the paper. Conclusions reiterate this main point in light of the ideas that have been developed throughout the paper.

Instructors look to introductions and conclusions to gauge how well students have synthesized their ideas. Researchers look to introductions and conclusions to help weed through piles of material quickly, since they offer a good indication of the scope of the essay. If a scholar doing research stumbles across a poorly written introduction or conclusion—one that fails clearly to delineate the specific issues covered in the article—there's a good chance he could ignore the whole piece, assuming that it doesn't address relevant topics. How does the introduction in this essay prepare the reader for the main argument that follows? How does the conclusion reiterate the logic that connects the essay's major claims?

Sound in *No Country for Old Men*: A Tradition of Violence

Set in 1980 in the midst of escalating drug wars in the United States, *No Country for Old Men* (Coen Bros. 2007), adapted from Cormac McCarthy's novel, begins with Sheriff Ed Bell's (Tommy Lee Jones) voice-over in which he describes his anxieties about an escalation of violent crime.[1] As he sees it, the era's brutality is beyond comprehension. Bell's nostalgic lament for better days coincides with footage of a deputy's arrest of Anton Chigurh (Javier Bardem), the calculating hired killer who *appears* to be the face of the modern violence Bell says he can't fathom: Chigurh soon kills the arresting officer and goes on a cross-country killing spree in search of stolen drug money. Bell is a relatively peripheral character in the narrative, which concentrates on the dangerous cat and mouse games between Chigurh and Llewelyn Moss (Josh Brolin), a welder who absconds with the drug money. Still, the sheriff's voice-over opens the film, and his dialogue will close the film, foregrounding his musings and focusing the film's thematic concerns on his emotional response to events he only observes from a distance. But careful study of the relationship between sound and image reveals Bell's condemnation of modern society to be off the mark.[2] This tension suggests that *No Country for Old Men* isn't exactly a social critique of changing times

1 Even though introductory paragraphs begin an essay, many authors actually write them after the body of the argument has been completed. This is because, during the writing process, a writer's argument usually evolves, or changes altogether, and it's difficult to introduce an argument that hasn't been completely formulated yet. So, many students find that, when they have difficulty getting started on a paper, the best strategy is to skip writing the introduction until a rough draft is finished.

2 Using a common rhetorical strategy, this author pulls the reader into his argument by focusing on one technique—the voice-over—to make a claim about the film as a whole. This author links this technique to the overall plot. Exploring the relationship between Bell's voice-over and the central plotline allows this author to home in on a central argument. Writers should minimize plot summary in introductions. Do not use the introduction as filler or merely to summarize the plot for readers who haven't seen the film. Use it instead to prepare the reader for the thesis, which follows.

3 Thesis statements almost always
conclude introductory paragraphs in
academic writing. Readers, at least in
Western cultures, are trained to look
for these all-important sentences at the
end of introductions. This is why it is
crucial for writers to spend so much
time crafting precise thesis statements
and to place these sentences at the end
of the introduction (not in the beginning,
and not in the middle). Be aware that
an introduction does not have to be
limited to one paragraph. In longer
papers, an introduction might be
several paragraphs—or even several
pages—long. But in general, short
papers (fifteen pages or less) require
short introductions.

and corroding values; rather, it is a psychological portrait of the aging sheriff's feelings of irrelevance and impotence as he tries to cope with his own mortality.[3]

Though Bell considers himself a wise, avuncular figure, his word choice and speech characteristics in his voice-over undercut his supposed authority. Most conventional voice-overs narrate directly to the audience from a point in time after the events depicted. That is, they speak to us from a vantage point that implicitly offers us the complete knowledge afforded by hindsight and experience. If the narrator is a character within the diegesis, he has already experienced the *fabula*'s events and is sharing his understanding of their ultimate significance with the audience. Quite simply, voice-overs usually work on the assumption that the narrator already knows where the story is headed. By contrast, Bell's voice-over contemplates the *present*. While he fondly describes decades past, he does so as a way of making sense of the world he occupies now: "You can't help but compare yourself against the old timers. You can't help but wonder how they'd've operated in these times." The fact that Bell casually rattles off the names of community figureheads as if we should know them ("Some of the old time sheriffs never even wore a gun. … Jim Scarborough never carried one. That's the younger Jim.") adds to the sense that his voice-over is conversational, not expository. The audience can't trust his narration to explain the events. Finally, Tommy Lee Jones's monotonous tone underscores the character's insecurity as opposed to highlighting his self-assured comprehension of the events he is describing. The voice-over invites us to consider whether his fears are based on well-earned objectivity, or perhaps come from a less reliable, emotionally inflected perspective.

Further complicating Bell's voice-over is the fact that the images contradict the sentiment he expresses. Although Bell invokes a modern world where crime is rampant, we don't see evidence of what he's talking about. Instead of showing streets crowded with junkies and thugs, the *mise en scène* fixes on wide swathes of the barren Texas plains, hemmed in by makeshift fence posts and barbed wire. The wind's persistent whirr emphasizes the essential emptiness of the setting. To be sure, the film includes more than its share of gruesome bloodshed. But the rustic Western setting and its historical and cinematic associations with genocide and marauding bandits suggest that the violence onscreen is anything but a symptom of twentieth-century American depravity. In fact, when Bell's deputy (Garret Dillahunt) shows Bell the corpses rotting in the backcountry—the victims of a drug war shootout—he refers to the site as the "O.K. Corral," a nod to 1881's famous shootout memorialized in countless history books and film. The reference makes clear that, while the motivations for violence might have evolved (from the conflicts between Native Americans and settlers, to ranchers and farmers, to warring drug factions), brutality has been an integral part of the American landscape for centuries.

To further emphasize that the area is steeped in violence, the film uses dialogue as well as visual techniques to draw repeated parallels between the more benevolent, folksy family man, Llewelyn, and Chigurh, the supposed face of irredeemable social decay. When Chigurh kills one man for his automobile, he politely asks the victim to "hold still" before murdering him (fig. **8.23**). In the very next scene, Llewelyn looks at wild game through the scope of his hunting rifle, and he too whispers to his prey to "hold still" (fig. **8.24**). The dialogue explicitly equates drug culture with another, culturally sanctioned blood ritual.

Sound designer Craig Berkey's sound effects in one of the film's action sequences develops the implications of this parallel even further. Sitting alone in the dark of his seedy hotel room, hiding from the mobsters who are pursuing him, Llewelyn discovers a tracking device hidden in the stolen briefcase full of cash. At the same instant, he hears a tell-tale thump reverberate down the hall. The Coen brothers generate suspense by relying solely on sound effects to hint at the doings offscreen. Another choice would have been to use parallel editing to grant the audience a moment of omniscience. Instead, the scene uses sound to put the viewer in Llewelyn's mindset, relying on hearing to surmise what is happening on the other side of the

door. His suspicions aroused, Llewelyn calls down to the front desk but gets no response. When Llewelyn had paid for his room, the desk clerk made it clear that he would be "on all night" and would let Llewelyn know if any other "swinging dick" came around, so the unanswered call means that the desk clerk has checked out early, so to speak. Moreover, the soundtrack emphasizes the eerie call and response between the ring on Llewelyn's earpiece and the distant rings from the front desk. The sound effects thus shape our perception of space. The hotel is so empty, there's no other noise to obscure the ringing sound from downstairs; Llewlyn is now alone with a killer. Furthermore, given that the hotel is small enough to hear what's going on at the desk, there's little room for evasive maneuvers. As he sits in his room strategizing, sound effects accentuate Llewelyn's building anxiety. Soon enough, he starts to hear the "beep beep beep" of the tracking device (which also recalls the sound of a heart monitor) and the sound of Chigurh's soft footsteps walking down the corridor. Both ominously grow louder as the killer approaches Llewelyn's door. The accelerating tempo of the rhythmic beeping makes it clear that the killer is getting closer...and that Llewelyn's heart is pounding faster.

More to the point, the use of sound in this scene contributes to the film's insistence (contrary to what Bell believes) that violence has been an attribute of this region for centuries. For one thing, the sonic emphasis on the intimacy of the hotel establishes a mood that's more in keeping with classic Western shootouts than urban crime films, an effect enhanced by the creaking

8.23 *(above)* Chigurh's unusual method of hunting in *No Country for Old Men*.

8.24 *(below)* Llewelyn—another hunter in *No Country for Old Men*.

floorboards that groan with every step the two men take. The sound effects that typically connote modern urban spaces are noticeably absent. There are no roaring engines, no screaming sirens, no pulsating rock tunes. The ambient sound is so minimal, that every move Llewelyn makes—from sitting on the bed to switching the light off—is, by comparison, a deafening and potentially deadly tip-off. At one point, Llewelyn lowers his head to the floor to peek under his door, and the airflow from the hallway whistles through the crevice, evoking the mood of a small, isolated place at night—an empty space that could just as easily be set in the early 1880s as the 1980s. The modern drug trade has drawn Llewelyn and Chigurh together, but sound makes it clear that this town is only a slightly updated reiteration of the "wild West."

Finally and perhaps most crucially, this undeniably tense encounter is laden with thematic significance because it offers parallels to the earlier scene of Llewelyn hunting in the backcountry. Earlier, when Llewelyn takes his shot, he wounds his prey rather than killing it, and so he must track the elk by following the trail of blood it leaves behind. In a reversal of fortune in the scene at the hotel, Llewelyn has become the prey stalked by a resourceful tracker. Though Chigurh has (minimal) technology at his disposal, the process of hunting and tracking is essentially the same. The parallel between the two scenes makes it clear that, contrary to Bell's wistful nostalgia for the good old days, the violence men involve themselves in isn't new: it's primal.

When Bell's efforts to stop the bloodshed prove to be futile, he commiserates with the sheriff in El Paso, the city where Mexican gang members finally gun Llewelyn down and kill him. Over dinner, the two elders repeat Bell's refrain, lamenting the changing times that have brought the "kids with green hair." In their minds, punk rock fashion is an apocalyptic sign of social decay. But, crucially, the film never shows a single punk rocker. Rather, most of the men sport very traditional duds: cowboy hats, boots, and jeans. Bell even singles out the youthful disregard for manners as a sure sign of the end times: "Once you quit hearing 'sir' or 'ma'am' the rest is soon to follow." Tellingly, when Chigurh breaks his arm in a freak car accident, two teenage boys stop to help him, repeatedly uttering, "Yes sir" and thus revealing their ingrained respect for all elders (even, unbeknownst to them, a brutal killer). Ironically, their respect for authority helps Chigurh evade the law. As Mary P. Nichols observes, this exchange belies Bell's fears: "The sheriff is wrong: the old forms are neither a protection for nor a sign of moral health." (Nichols, p. 211)

The unfounded anxieties Bell expresses in his opening voice-over essentially bookend the film. Instead of building to the expected confrontation between the forces of good and evil, the film seems to fizzle after Llewelyn meets his anticlimactic demise offscreen, ending with a protracted fourth act focusing on the sheriff's decision to retire. While the final scenes seem to deaden the brisk pace of a film that had become a nail-biting thriller, it's important to consider how the unusual anti-climax returns to and elaborates on Bell's fears. Bell's opening voice-over establishes his need to impose a sociological *raison d'être* upon violence. The film's conclusion explains the emotional motivation behind this need and points to the consequences that ensue when Bell acts on his faulty, overly personal logic.

In the final scene, Bell describes a dream to his accommodating wife, Loretta (Tess Harper). This moment makes explicit Bell's recognition that he grows closer to death by the day, which provides the psychological impetus behind his obsession with explaining the crimes he has failed to prevent. In this dream, Bell sees his father ride by on a horse. Bell knows that the patriarch is going ahead to start a fire and will be waiting for his son to arrive. The brief tale, infused with the sadness of a son missing his father, is clearly symbolic of Bell's subconscious meditation on the inevitability of aging and death. By reiterating the fact that he is already older than his father was when he died, Bell seems to understand that the place where his father waits is the afterlife: "I'm older now than he ever was by twenty years, so in a sense he's the younger man." But the afterlife Bell envisions isn't inviting. Rather, it is inhospitable and mysterious. Bell's voice breaks, revealing his profound vulnerability, as he remembers his father "fixin' to make a fire in all that dark, all that cold." Balancing Bell's meditation in the film's exposition with this melancholic vision, *No Country for Old Men* suggests that the sheriff's proclaimed fear of modern society represents an attempt to locate a logic behind the mysteries of life and death—to find a rationale that will reassure him in the face of his growing awareness that the odds of surviving are stacked against him. He acts on the false hope that quitting his job—withdrawing from a society he wants to believe has gone awry—will improve his odds. In fact, Bell's attempt to identify a contemporary sociological explanation for violence stands in stark contrast to Chigurh's use of the coin toss to decide if his victims live or die. The coin toss motif suggests how randomness, not logic, determines our fate. In other words, as Nichols points out, "The film is not about the world's injustice, but its unintelligibility." (p. 210)

The final scene, which depicts Bell trying to cope with life at home after retirement, makes it obvious that despite his choice to play it safe, Bell is still consumed by thoughts of death. In fact, in the midst of his retirement, Bell faces a more palpable kind of death: the premature decay of his sense of self-worth. The pleasantries of daily dialogue that Bell shares with Loretta when they sit down at the breakfast table make it obvious that he feels lost and alone now that he has nothing to do. When he asks if she approves of his plan to go horseback riding, she responds, "Well, I can't plan your day," her tone of voice sounding like an impatient parent imploring a child to take more responsibility. When he invites her to join him, she flatly responds, "Lord no, I'm not retired," the half-playful condescension in her voice obvious, as if to imply that she has *real* responsibilities to discharge. Though it's clear that there's still love between them, Bell's retirement has disrupted their domestic equilibrium and now they must struggle to find a new way to relate. Sound designer Craig Berkey amps up the everyday sound effects—the slurping lips sucking on coffee, the faint ring of fingertips dragging across the porcelain cups, the persistent breeze blowing outside—

4 Many writers find conclusions the most difficult part of the paper to write, because the purpose of the conclusion is to summarize the paper's main argument *without* sounding repetitious, being long-winded, or introducing a new idea altogether. Notice how this author discusses an element of the film heretofore ignored (its title) as a way of reiterating the main point. The author avoids using a self-announcing phrase, such as "In conclusion," to begin the paragraph. Such phrases are clunky and distracting.

5 In general, writers should avoid introducing new ideas or texts in the conclusion. But here the new idea encapsulates and reiterates the entire paper. Another option would be to provide a more straightforward summary. Yet another strategy some writers use to shape conclusions is to point to the need for further research on the topic at hand, or ask readers a provocative question designed to make them contemplate the ramifications of the main argument.

to emphasize the uncomfortable silences the couple now shares.

Put quite simply, now that Bell has quit law enforcement, he's left with nothing, and this leaves him plenty of time to sit and stew over his own mortality. When he begins to tell Loretta about his dreams, her flippant response speaks to Bell's sense of irrelevance: "Well, you got plenty of time for [dreams] now." Later, as he nears the end of his dream narration, the sound of his heavy, slightly-accelerated breathing implies that sadness burdens the former sheriff. He seems to struggle to hold back the tears brought on by his fears and sense of loss. "And then I woke up," he suddenly concludes. This afterlife was only a dream; it offers no succor for Bell's existential angst. The camera stares at Bell's weathered, worried face, the faint ticking of a clock audible on the soundtrack. Then the image cuts to black, leaving us with only the sound of the clock, counting down the remaining minutes in Bell's life and suggesting that time marches on, even when characters, dreams, lives, and narration die. The downbeat conclusion, with the image of nothingness juxtaposed with the sound of the clock, insinuates that time is the only thing that remains, and it moves on endlessly without us.

The film's title encapsulates the central idea discussed above.[4] At first glance, the viewer might mistakenly assume the phrase singles out a specific territory that is uniquely hostile, as if the title was actually [*This Is*] *No Country for Old Men*. But Cormac McCarthy took the title of his novel from the opening line of W. B. Yeats's poem "Sailing to Byzantium." Yeats's poem is a meditation on death's inevitability:

> That is no country for old men. The young
> In one another's arms, birds in the trees […]
> The salmon falls, the mackerel crowded seas, […]
> Whatever is begotten, born and dies.

In these lines, the speaker bemoans the fact that every living being is destined to die. But whereas Bell tries in vain to forestall his inexorable fate by retiring —not just from his job, but from life itself—Yeats's speaker proclaims that one's only hope for solace is to live boldly and deliberately in the face of death:

> An aged man is but a paltry thing,
> A tattered coat upon a stick, unless
> Soul clap its hands and sing, and louder sing

Ultimately, *No Country for Old Men* does not dwell on death as the source of profound sadness; appropriately enough, Llewelyn's and Carla Jean's deaths both occur *offscreen*. Rather, the tragic pathos rests in Bell's passive resignation. He is unable to live his life, and his soul can no longer manage to "clap its hands and sing, and louder sing."[5]

Works Cited (in the essay)

Nichols, Mary P. "Revisiting Heroism and Community in Contemporary Westerns: *No Country for Old Men* and *3:10 to Yuma*." *Perspectives on Political Science*, 37/4 (Fall 2008), pp. 207–15.
Yeats, W. B. "Sailing to Byzantium." *The Tower: A Facsimile Edition*. New York: Scribner, 2004, pp. 1–3.

Alternatives to Narrative Fiction Film: Documentary and Avant-garde Films

The logic of a work of art is the result of re-relating elements selected from reality into a new relationship so that a new reality is created which, in turn, endows the selected elements with a new value.

Maya Deren

Many moviegoers regard Hollywood films as the "real" cinema, much in the same way as an American tourist abroad might ask: "How much is this in *real* money?" (Stam, p. 5) But alternative filmmaking practices such as documentary and avant-garde cinemas are very real, and a sound grasp of their history and

9.1 *March of the Penguins*, one of the top grossing documentary films in history.

formal organization is crucial to understanding film art and culture. This chapter explores the formal characteristics of documentary and avant-garde films and emphasizes their particular histories and modes of organization.

Three Modes of Filmmaking: A Comparison

Documentary and avant-garde film depart from commercial fiction films in several ways, including their purpose, mode of production, exhibition venues, and their formal organization and visual style. Commercial films are based on fictional stories and designed to appeal to a mass audience in order to make profits for the companies that produce, distribute, and exhibit them. The parties involved—including writers, directors, actors, producers, studio executives, distributors, and exhibitors—treat films as products that entice the viewing public to spend money on films, concessions, and related toys and games. Not all commercial films turn out to be financially successful, but profitability is the primary goal of the large corporations that produce, distribute, and exhibit them.

Although some documentaries depict characters and stories, and some avant-garde films are interested in the way narratives work, neither type of film is *primarily* concerned with telling stories. Thus, they do not obey the rules of narrative form discussed in Chapter 4. Documentary films present contemporary or historical events rather than fictional stories. Documentary filmmakers may be motivated by reasons unrelated to profitability: they may be interested in educating viewers about a pressing social issue, in introducing viewers to extraordinary people and their achievements, in capturing the humor and pathos of everyday life, or in using the tools of their craft to create a profound experience. Most documentary filmmakers do not treat profits as a primary objective; usually they are pleased if they can just make a living!

The goals of avant-garde filmmakers, like those of documentary filmmakers, vary widely, but two principal concerns dominate. The first is the desire to explore the artistic and technological capabilities of the medium, usually by rejecting the conventional use to which film has been put: telling stories. Like many modern artists, avant-garde films highlight the medium's "materials" (film, light, sound); these films may also draw on connections to painting, sculpture, dance, music, and photography. The second major concern of many avant-garde filmmakers is to question orthodoxies beyond the realm of aesthetics. Avant-garde films often challenge conventional thinking about politics, culture, gender, race, and sexuality. These filmmakers use film as a means of personal expression to address important social issues and to expand the aesthetic vocabulary of film art.

Another way to differentiate commercial film from documentary and avant-garde film is to consider their methods of production and exhibition. Documentaries are not produced in the industrial context of Hollywood, where corporate executives, stars, management companies, guilds, and unions interact as part of a complex system. Instead, individuals or small groups of people work together, raising funds, renting equipment and space, and managing restrictive budgets. Documentary filmmakers spend weeks, months, or even years conducting research, doing interviews, and recording sound and images. Documentary films often have lower production values than commercial fiction films, owing in part to their smaller budgets. Also, unless a documentary filmmaker works exclusively with archival materials, the spontaneity of real-world events often prevents him from taking a "perfect" shot or recording flawless sound.

Typically, only a select few documentary films are granted theatrical release in art house cinemas or multiplexes or even make it onto DVD. Several international film festivals are devoted to documentaries, including the Full Frame Documentary Film Festival in Durham, North Carolina, and the IDFA in Amsterdam, the Netherlands. The peripheral status of documentary filmmaking relative to the Hollywood industry is reflected by the fact that there are just two Academy Awards for documentaries: one for short films and one for feature-length films.

In recent years, however, documentaries have gained ground, as mainstream audiences have flocked to movies from directors such as Errol Morris (*Standard Operating Procedure*), Michael Moore (*Capitalism: A Love Story* [2009]), Davis Guggenheim (*It Might Get Loud* [2008]), and Cynthia Wade (*Born Sweet* [2010]). The vigor with which audiences have embraced documentary filmmaking was evident in 2006, when *March of the Penguins* ("*Marche de l'empéreur*"; Luc Jacquet 2005) not only won the Academy Award for Best Documentary but also outgrossed each of the narrative feature films nominated for Best Picture.

As film exhibition moves further away from traditional theatrical venues to home viewing through cable and streaming video, documentary films will become even more accessible.

The popularity of two documentaries that deal with the natural environment, but which adopt radically different stylistic approaches, suggests that audiences now crave a wider array of documentary experiences. *March of the Penguins*

9.2 In *An Inconvenient Truth*, Al Gore presents facts, figures, and images related to global warming.

documents the death-defying acts of emperor penguins as they undertake their annual migration in order to mate (fig. **9.1**). *An Inconvenient Truth* (Davis Guggenheim 2006), which earned acclaim at the 2006 Cannes Film Festival, focuses on the devastating effects of global warming. The film is based on a series of public lectures given by former U.S. Vice-President Al Gore.

Both films address aspects of the natural world, but each has a slightly different approach. *March of the Penguins* offers a glimpse into a frozen world that most people will never see—Antarctica—while *An Inconvenient Truth* informs people about a reality that they may witness every day—the deleterious effects of the human reliance on fossil fuels on the environment. *March of the Penguins* uses actor Morgan Freeman's voice-over narration and breathtaking images of penguins' struggles for survival to enlighten and enchant audiences, whereas *An Inconvenient Truth* relies on Al Gore's direct narration, supplemented by photographs, scientific research, and statistical evidence, to inform viewers about human behavior, to assess its negative impact on the environment, and to issue a call to action (fig. **9.2**).

Interestingly, a third documentary film—one that did not garner a commercial release—also focuses on the natural world, but does so in a startlingly different way from these two films. *Site Specific: Las Vegas 05* (Olivo Barbieri 2005; see fig. **9.34**) is a short film that offers images of Las Vegas taken with a tilt and shift lens from a helicopter and edited with a soundtrack composed of the sounds of helicopter blades whirring and a water fountain spraying. This film invites viewers to take a closer look at the effects of human culture on the landscape. Ironically, the distance afforded by the helicopter shots renders the familiar details of cars and gambling casinos strangely haunting. Such creative experimentation suggests the vast possibilities of documentary filmmaking, although the public's continuing investment in feature-length films severely restricts the possibilities for seeing short documentary films.

In contrast to commercial feature films and documentaries, avant-garde films are made in an artisanal mode, often by just one person. Although many avant-garde filmmakers use technology in unconventional ways to produce new visual and sound experiences, the goal is not necessarily to make conventionally beautiful images, but, rather, to create thought-provoking sensual and aesthetic experiences. Experimental filmmakers may eschew synchronized soundtracks, sets, and even actors. The prospects for screening avant-garde films are very limited: their unusual subject matter, short length, and limited distribution channels mean they are only rarely screened in commercial movie theaters. Most experimental films are screened in art galleries, on university campuses, at cinemathèques, film clubs, and theaters devoted to art and avant-garde cinema (such as the now-defunct Cinema 16 in New York) and at film festivals such as MadCat in San Francisco and Flicker (an organization devoted to Super-8 filmmaking). Two important institutions that preserve and distribute experimental films are the Filmmakers' Cooperative in New York and Canyon Cinema in San Francisco. The website ubu (www.ubuweb.com) offers a comprehensive catalog of classic and more recent experimental films for online viewing.

Avant-garde films should not be confused with independent film, although filmmakers working in these modes tend to reject the commercial film production process. Independent feature filmmaking is not always synonymous with an anti-industry perspective, however, as avant-garde filmmaking almost always is. During the Hollywood studio era, independent producers such as Samuel Goldwyn and David O. Selznick circumvented the studio system and worked with directors such as Hitchcock, William Wyler, and William Wellman to make popular films. Many since then have made feature films without studio involvement, often by forming their own production companies. But these directors are not experimental filmmakers. Although they sometimes challenge Hollywood conventions, they produce feature-length narrative fiction films for wide distribution.

After looking at the history of documentary, the chapter turns to documentary form. It then discusses two theoretical aspects of documentary cinema: spectatorship and ethics. This is followed by a discussion of avant-garde cinema. Because documentary and avant-garde films have a lower commercial profile than mainstream narrative films, they can prove difficult to track down. The last section of this chapter provides some tips on research in this area.

Documentary Film: "The Creative Treatment of Actuality"

Most films made before 1907 were not narrative fiction films but short documentaries. These *actualités*, as they were known, were "shot around the world, nominally 'unstaged,' although many were documents of performances, dances, processions, and parades." (Russell, p. 52) Moments from daily life, as well as trips to foreign locales, were frequent subjects of the earliest films, including the works of Auguste and Louis Lumière. The novelty of moving images meant that simple vignettes of everyday activities such as a train leaving a station fascinated audiences.

9.3 Workers leaving a factory, an early Lumière brothers *actualité*.

As non-fiction films based on real world events, these *actualités* were precursors to the documentary film. Yet they vary in the way they present images: some early Lumière films record everyday acts, such as workers leaving a factory at the end of the day (fig. **9.3**). In others, subjects self-consciously acknowledge the camera, and the filmmakers develop rudimentary narratives. *The Waterer Gets Watered* ("*L'Arroseur arrosé*"; 1895) depicts the travails of a gardener attempting to do his job, while a young boy plays tricks on him (fig. **9.4**). The film has a beginning, middle, and end, and a comic twist. The legitimate question arises: at what point does a

9.4 A gardener is distracted by a young boy in *The Waterer Gets Watered*.

documentary film cease to be a document of reality and become instead a fictional creation?

The term "documentary" was coined by John Grierson, founder of the British documentary movement in the 1920s, who famously described documentary film as "the creative treatment of actuality." In his work for government agencies in Britain, Grierson argued that documentary film was superior to fiction film because it presented the real world, not a fantasy, but that it should do so with greater imagination than a standard newsreel. His deceptively simple phrase suggests the double-edged nature of documentary form. Filmmakers inventively shape the material of "real life" by selecting the subject matter, choosing angles and shots, making editing decisions, creating re-enactments, and adding music or voice-over narration. The outright scripting or staging of events during shooting is precluded. But a tension remains between an ideal—that documentaries capture unmediated reality—and the practical fact that making a film will influence the behavior of subjects and the outcome of events.

Documentary films engage viewers by showing them some aspect of the real world. A documentary filmmaker captures and organizes visual images and sound to convey that real world situation. Barbara Kopple's *Harlan County USA* (1977) depicts a struggle by coal miners who want to unionize and mine owners who oppose the union (fig. **9.5**). In one dramatic scene, Kopple captures the mine owner's agent driving through the picket line at night shooting at picketers. Without any commentary, the scene effectively makes the argument that the mine owners disregard the lives of the miners and explains why the miners need a union to protect themselves. Kopple captures and presents this moment of heightened reality in a way that encourages viewers to draw certain conclusions about the mine owners' unfair and dangerous labor practices. Kopple, whose many non-fiction films cover subjects from the U.S. labor movement to celebrities such as Woody Allen and the singing group The Dixie Chicks,

9.5 A mine owner's agent shoots at picketers in *Harlan County USA*.

received the American Film Institute's Lifetime Achievement Award in 2004.

As with fiction films, documentary filmmakers make choices involving structure, cinematography, sound, and editing. These choices influence how audiences interpret the events onscreen. In fact, documentary filmmakers may draw inspiration from their fictional counterparts. Jeremiah Zagar cites Lynne Ramsay's *Ratcatcher* as an important influence on his documentary *In a Dream*. He compares the ethereal shot following his father, an artist, through a kaleidoscopic hallway (fig. 2.14) to Ramsay's image of James crawling through the kitchen window (fig. 6.104):

She's showing the boy disappearing in the dream world, and we are showing that my father

Chapter 9: Alternatives to Narrative Fiction Film

disappeared into his own dream world. What Ramsay's film showed me is that you can film someone from behind and create a very emotional shot—it's the most emotional shot in the film, because you understand he is surrounded by his own dream. (Interview)

This cross-pollination makes it clear that visual choices in a documentary can be carefully designed for expressive effect. Documentary filmmakers may be primarily concerned with presenting the real world, but they also lure the audience into an absorbing emotional and aesthetic experience. In fact, some documentaries present ideas, information, and characters in story form.

Narrative Documentaries

Some documentaries trace the lives of individuals and, as a result, they resemble fiction films with characters, goals, and obstacles. "Working in documentary, I am innately dealing with real things happening in real time, and the question for me is how do I make them feel timeless?" says Zagar. "By using the fictional aesthetic within the documentary world."

Man on Wire (James Marsh 2008) tells the story of a man with a mission, and how he used his own mischievous brio, a well-crafted plan, and a team of dedicated accomplices to achieve his goal. Philippe Petit's aim was both simple and extraordinary: he wanted to perform his high wire act for the city of New York, and by extension, the whole world. He and his cohorts pulled off an amazing caper: in August 1974 they stretched his high wire between the two buildings at New York's World Trade Center that were, at the time, the tallest in the world. In what P.T. Barnum himself might have called a death defying stunt, Petit walked, sat, and balanced on the wire for 45 minutes, stunning an enrapt audience of casual onlookers 100 stories below (fig. **9.6**). Afterward, he was promptly arrested.

The documentary traces a precise narrative arc: the exposition introduces us to Petit's penchant for daring acrobatics in unexpected places, then the narrative follows Petit and his chums as they meticulously plan, execute, and celebrate their now world-famous stunt. Like many documentaries, *Man on Wire* makes use of archival footage from the historical period it covers, but it uses this material to shape a clear and dramatic narrative of aspirations, obstacles, and ultimate success. Elements of cause and effect come into play: in order to accomplish his goals, Petit must not only master his own body, he must also anticipate impediments that seem far beyond his control, including the weather, the laws of physics, and the law. With his remarkable self-possession, not to mention his boundless ambition, Petit may ultimately strike viewers of this film as more akin to a

9.6 Philippe Petit's bold stunt—*Man on Wire*.

fictional hero than an ordinary human being. More than that, this film may restore its viewers' faith in the human ability to dream big and live large.

Documentary Form

Film scholar Bill Nichols has developed a useful framework for evaluating a documentary's mode of organization. Nichols writes, "the logic organizing a documentary film supports an underlying argument, assertion, or claim about the historical world." (Nichols 2001, p. 27) The simplest argument a documentary film can make is that the images depicted in the film are real: that the film has captured some aspect of existence that is worthy of contemplation. Documentaries may also make other arguments: they may assert that the subject matter of the documentary is worthy of greater scrutiny (the issue has more sides than have been represented); that a social or economic practice has caused, or is causing, problems that need to be addressed; that a subculture is of interest because it resonates with culture at large (or, conversely, because it represents the profound diversity of humanity); that a forgotten but important cultural or historical figure needs to be given her due; that previous explanations of a historical event have not fully captured its complexity, or have deliberately ignored certain facts and some viewpoints.

Documentaries present this wide variety of arguments through rhetorical devices that appeal to logic, ethics, and emotions. Some documentaries use obvious strategies for argumentation, such as charts, facts, and expert witnesses. Others address viewers on an emotional level, encouraging them to see aspects of the world differently because they identify with a subject of the documentary. Some documentaries do both.

Viewers may be surprised to discover that even documentaries whose sole purpose seems to be light-hearted entertainment present arguments of some kind. The spirited energy of *Air Guitar Nation* (Alexander Lipsitz 2006) derives from the comic irony of seeing individuals perform rock music without an instrument as they compete for the honor of representing the U.S. in the Air Guitar World Championship in Finland (fig. **9.7**). Contestants assume bizarre alter egos—Björn Turoque, C-Diddy, and Red Plectrum—and go all out with costumes and wild stage antics to win the approval of the judges and audience members. On a deeper level, however, the film explores the power of rock music to bring together diverse groups of people and suggests that one crucial way that rock inspires such a devoted fan culture is by offering possibilities for fans to share their intensely personal identifications with rock stars by transforming mimicry into performance.

9.7 A different kind of "musical" performance on display in *Air Guitar Nation*.

Documentary filmmakers employ a number of rhetorical strategies to support their assertions. The rest of this section examines four strategies—the voice of authority, talking heads, direct cinema and *cinéma vérité*, and self-reflexivity. These rhetorical modes are mocked in the mockumentary, analyzed in the conclusion of this section.

Voice of Authority

One of the most basic strategies employed by documentary filmmakers is to combine voice-over narration with images in order to convince the audience of a particular claim about the world. Well-known political figures, respected celebrities, and actors with commanding vocal qualities may be employed to narrate these films in an authoritative style. Examples include Ken Burns's televized documentaries on baseball, jazz, and the U.S. Civil War. Burns gathers photographs, archival footage, and other visual evidence, sewing these images and sounds together with voice-over narration.

9.8 The *Why We Fight* series was highly influential during World War II.

Films that rely exclusively on this strategy include nature documentaries such as *March of the Penguins* and combat films in the *Why We Fight* series. Directed by Hollywood director Frank Capra during the 1940s, these newsreels offered American audiences images of World War II battles combined with scripted narration that persuaded Americans of the appropriateness of the military campaign (fig. **9.8**).

Films made with the sole intent of persuading viewers of the rightness of a single view are referred to as **propaganda films**. They promote a single position without any allowance for competing perspectives. Some documentary filmmakers attempt to offer a balanced perspective by including competing views, while others feel that their deeply held beliefs and research justify them in making the strongest argument possible for one point of view. In any event, it is important for viewers to consider the precise claim to authority represented by the narration. Is the author providing the textual information an expert on the subject, or is the narrator's commanding voice alone meant to convey authoritative knowledge?

Talking Heads and Director–Participant

A second rhetorical strategy combines images with verbal testimony from individuals affected by or knowledgeable about the subject matter of the documentary. This strategy allows real people, not a designated off-screen authority, to make assertions about the subject. Documentaries that rely exclusively on interviews are often called "talking heads" documentaries.

Interviews allow for a range of ideas to be presented and may convince the viewers that the reality the filmmaker has presented is complex. They may also capture the personal feelings of interview subjects, inviting viewer identification. *The Weather Underground* (Sam Green and Bill Siegel 2003) combines archival

9.9 The radical activist Bernardine Dohrn from *The Weather Underground*.

9.10 *(left)* Robot scientist voice-over in *Fast, Cheap, and Out of Control*: "Sometimes I feel like Yoda—I have to say 'I feel the force, don't try to control the robot.'"

9.11 *(right)* Mole-rat expert voice-over in *Fast, Cheap, and Out of Control*: "To me, it's this incredible mammal that breaks all the rules. A mammal with a queen, king, soldiers, workers, all playing roles."

footage from the 1960s and 1970s with contemporary interviews of Weather Underground radicals, along with activists who disagreed with their tactics, providing a contested vantage point from thirty years after the events (fig. **9.9**).

A documentary film director may edit images and sound to corroborate *or* to call into question the statements made by subjects. *Fast, Cheap, and Out of Control* (Errol Morris 1998) looks at four individuals and their work. Each of the four subjects works with animals or animal facsimiles: one is an animal trainer with the circus, another is a mole-rat expert, one is a topiary gardener who fashions enormous animals from shrubbery, and another is a scientist who creates robotic machines.

Morris adopts a bemused perspective on his subjects: his ironic distance is made evident through editing. He juxtaposes images of one subject with interviews with another, so it seems as if the people he interviews are making comments about the lives and work of other people. During shots of circus performers, the sound that accompanies the images comes from statements made by the mole-rat expert and robot scientist (figs. **9.10, 9.11**). By pairing a subject's statements with seemingly unrelated images, Morris adds dimension to the interviews, introducing ideas that none of his subjects has voiced. Morris gets at one truth by allowing the interviewees to tell their own stories, yet his editing encourages the audience to make unusual connections. For example, are human and mole-rat societies similar, because they both have sharply delineated roles such as king, queen, soldier, worker? Are circus performances akin to robotic movements? Are the robot scientist's concerns that he is too controlling relevant to other social contexts?

Unlike Morris, who presents complex ideas subtly, Michael Moore includes his own pointed commentary as well as interviews with others. Moore's controversial *Fahrenheit 9/11* (2004), which won the *Palme d'Or* at the 2004 Cannes Film Festival, is an unapologetic critique of American foreign policy since the terrorist attacks of September 11, 2001. In the film, Moore makes clear his feelings toward government leaders through antagonistic encounters with politicians. In one scene, he accosts members of Congress, asking them to volunteer their children for active duty in Iraq. His actions imply that politicians may find

it easy to pursue military options because they don't make the personal sacrifices that ordinary citizens make. Moore acts as narrator and participant, making his point of view clear to the audience (fig. **9.12**).

Super Size Me (2004) follows a similar strategy of directorial participation combined with interviews. Interested in dramatizing the health effects of fast food, director Morgan Spurlock meets with his doctors before embarking on a month of an all-McDonald's diet. Spurlock humorously narrates the changes in his body, interviews Big Mac addicts and his girlfriend, and returns to his doctors for periodic check-ups (fig. **9.13**). A little more than halfway through the month, he has grave concerns about the diet's health effects, which include weight gain, high cholesterol, elevated blood sugar, and liver distress. In this film, the director, his friends, and his doctors testify to the fact that fast food is unhealthy. The argument literally is presented through the director's body as well as in interviews and images.

Direct Cinema and *Cinéma Vérité*

A third rhetorical strategy in documentary represents a fairly radical shift from the talking heads mode, and especially from those films in which the director is a participant. This observational style is referred to as *cinéma vérité* (cinema of truth) or direct cinema. In the late 1950s and early 1960s, filmmakers in Canada, the U.S., and France all began to explore an intentionally unobtrusive type of documentary filmmaking that was enabled by the introduction of lightweight 16 mm cameras and the portable Nagra tape recorder, which helped record unfolding events with as little intervention as possible. In 1959, photographer and filmmaker Michael Brault of the National Film Board of Canada met Jean Rouch (who would later be dubbed the father of *cinéma vérité*) and collaborated on a film. Brault is recognized for having pioneered the handheld camera techniques so essential to the observational style. At the same time, in New York City, journalist Robert Drew founded Drew Associates with Richard Leacock, D.A. Pennebaker, and Albert and David Maysles. In less than a decade, they would change the look of documentary with powerful films on political and cultural subjects. They sought to record reality as it happened. The seminal works of this group include Drew's *Primary* (1960), the Maysles brothers' *Salesman* (1966), and Pennebaker's *Don't Look Back* (1967). While some use the terms direct cinema and *vérité* interchangeably, they can be distinguished from one another in terms of the way filmmakers understood "unfolding" reality. Robert Drew recounts a 1963 visit to France where he noted that *vérité* filmmakers had large crews and drew attention to themselves: "*Cinema vérité* filmmakers accost[ed] people on the street with a microphone. My goal was to capture real life without intruding. Between us there was a contradiction" (Zuber).

Two of direct cinema's visual techniques—the static camera and the long take—strongly connote the idea that viewers are invisible observers watching events unfold. The Maysles brothers' classic documentary *Salesman* uses long takes and a static camera to depict Bible salesmen in the Northeastern U.S. The

9.12 Michael Moore.

9.13 Spurlock prepares to conduct his experiment in *Super Size Me*.

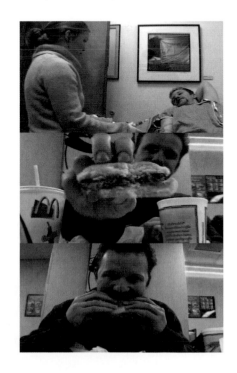

9.14 The district manager gives a pep talk in *Salesman*.

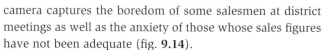

9.15 *(left)* Inmates perform in *Titicut Follies*.

9.16 *(right)* Staff members perform in *Titicut Follies*.

camera captures the boredom of some salesmen at district meetings as well as the anxiety of those whose sales figures have not been adequate (fig. **9.14**).

Even in direct cinema, directors make choices and employ techniques that convey ideas. Directors choose the subject matter, select the framing of shots, and juxtapose scenes through editing. In many regards, editing is the cinematic technique that offers the greatest influence over the material. In Fred Wiseman's controversial *Titicut Follies* (1967) the editing and framing make it difficult to distinguish between the staff and inmates at a mental institution (figs. **9.15**, **9.16**). Wiseman's camerawork and editing present a subtle argument that those deemed mentally unstable may not be so different from the rest of society, or that many social institutions force the sane and insane to behave the same way.

Self-reflexive Documentary

A fourth rhetorical strategy departs dramatically from direct cinema by including the process of filmmaking as part of the subject matter of the film. Bill Nichols calls this "self-reflexive documentary"; like formalist narrative films, these films refer to the process of making films and expose the way the medium constructs reality. They challenge audiences to consider the relationship between images and reality. Werner Herzog's *Grizzly Man* questions the nature of cinematic truth. Its subject is Timothy Treadwell, who spent thirteen summers in the Alaskan wilderness living with grizzly bears and who was ultimately killed by one of them. Herzog interviews people who knew Treadwell and makes liberal use of Treadwell's extensive video footage of himself (fig. **9.17**). Treadwell's numerous films and Herzog's implicit comparison between Treadwell and himself—both are obsessive individuals who take risks to capture what they love on film—present the audience with a dilemma. Can viewers accept at face value the

Chapter 9: Alternatives to Narrative Fiction Film

way Treadwell represents himself? If not, does that suggest that Herzog's own project of uncovering truth through cinema is doomed? The film's self-reflexivity—the way it refers to the film medium—is apparent in shots of Treadwell positioning his camera and in a scene where Herzog himself appears in the frame, listening to the audio tape that documents the death of Treadwell and his girlfriend.

9.17 Timothy Treadwell's films are a central focus of Herzog's *Grizzly Man*.

Keven McAlester's *You're Gonna Miss Me* (2008) traces the tragic consequences that ensued when rising musical sensation Roky Erickson had his budding career with the band the 13th Floor Elevators cut short by a drug arrest and subsequent incarceration in a mental institution in the 1970s. McAlester blends interviews with Roky, his brothers, and his mother, Evelyn (a recording artist in her own right), with the family's home movies, videotaped performances of Roky's band, and police surveillance films (which helped authorities wage the war on illegal drugs in the 1960s). In choosing to depict so much of Roky's story through films, McAlester injects self-reflexivity into the film. Viewers may question the motivations for filming Roky's live performances, for example, or marvel at the innocuous footage of young people dancing outdoors that was interpreted by the authorities as drug induced hysteria. Most crucially, the director's use of home movie footage of a coronation ceremony in which Evelyn crowns an adult Roky "king," suggests the way that Erikson family members define their identities through performance, and may have felt most themselves when they were performing (fig. **9.18**).

9.18 In Erikson family home movies, life becomes a performance.

The Mockumentary

Mockumentaries are not documentary films but fiction films that pose as documentaries by using familiar conventions. Comic examples include *This is Spinal Tap* (Rob Reiner 1984), *Fear of a Black Hat* (Rusty Cundieff 1994), *Best in Show* (Christopher Guest 2000), and *A Mighty Wind* (Christopher Guest 2003). These films adopt documentary strategies—primarily interview and *cinéma vérité* techniques—but their subject matter is fictional and their interviewees are characters played by actors. Humor

derives partly from strict attention to details: the filmmakers not only parody the documentary conventions precisely (as in the use of *faux* historical footage of the mock rock band Spinal Tap) but also capture the historical and cultural details of clothing, behavior, and musical styles (as in the fashions of *A Mighty Wind*).

Many narrative fiction films—comedies and dramas alike—employ this same strategy of hewing very closely to documentary conventions primarily to satirize a pressing social issue, and/or to poke fun at documentary filmmaking itself. Examples include *Punishment Park* (Peter Watkins 1971), *Brüno* (Larry Charles 2009), and *District 9*. A horror subgenre seems to be organizing around the same idea, and it includes *Cannibal Holocaust* (Ruggero Deodato 1980), *The Blair Witch Project, Paranormal Activity*, and *Cloverfield*.

Two Theoretical Questions

The conventional understanding of documentary films rests upon their status as documents, or records, of the real. Even the most stylistically innovative, thoughtful, and challenging documentaries of the past two decades, from *Crumb* (Terry Zwigoff 1994) and *Man on Wire*, to *Waltz with Bashir* (Ari Folman 2008) and *Restrepo* (Tim Hetherington and Sebastian Junger 2010) are, at the most fundamental level, concerned with presenting actual people, events, and social realities of one sort or another to viewers. It's easy to focus our attention on the many fascinating issues of ethics and aesthetics that arise when filmmakers attempt to tell stories, convey information, or create cinematic experiences that relate to real world subjects.

Documentary Spectatorship

One important topic that is often neglected within discussions of documentary form is the experience of spectatorship. Do we bring a different sort of thought process, or form of attention, to documentaries because they seek to represent reality? Do we possess expectations that we can satisfy with the specific experience of documentary films?

Documentary films speak to two potentially contradictory human impulses, according to Elizabeth Cowie. The first is a belief that reality is knowable, and that documentary films provide evidence that allows us to organize and interpret the world—even, or especially, a world we have not been exposed to—using rationality and logic. The second impulse seeks to engage with the real world as a spectacle, as a vision that exceeds even our wildest imaginations. Keith Beattie agrees with this line of thinking, observing that documentaries—from nature films to surf videos—offer the "cinema of attractions" that Sergei Eisenstein saw as critical to early cinema. Can desires for evidence and for spectacle be segregated into documentary and fiction film experiences? Cowie contends that this is a false distinction and that documentary films "involve us as desiring, as well as knowing, spectators." (Cowie, p. 20)

If we pursue this approach, and consider the nature of viewer involvement in documentary films rather than the textual characteristics of the films themselves, we might begin to look at documentary film not as an object—the movie we are watching—but as an experience of watching, as a mode of perceiving. Vivian Sobchack has written on documentary spectatorship in just this manner, using an approach derived from **phenomenology**, a field within philosophy that examines the content and processes of our conscious experiences.

For Sobchack, analyzing the structure, style, and subject matter of the film text itself only partly explains how documentary films function: we must also consider the spectator, who is an "active agent in constituting what counts as memory, fiction or document." (Sobchack, p. 253) Drawing on the work of Belgian psychologist Jean Pierre-Meunier, Sobchack discusses a continuum of film types—the home movie, the documentary, and the fiction film—to explain how the historical knowledge and personal memories that each viewer brings to a film influence her engagement with the scenarios depicted. We may think of home movies and videos as the most authentic, spontaneous, and unscripted of the three types (in part because they are made by amateurs). From a perceptual standpoint, viewers of their own home movies know more about the world depicted onscreen than the images portray, thus they can rely on their knowledge and memories to inform and enrich the world shown onscreen. This is less the case with documentaries, where a viewer's historical or personal knowledge of events may be nonexistent or spotty, and he therefore must rely on the film to provide most of the information about the world it is presenting. In fiction films, viewers rely to the greatest extent on the cues and clues that the film provides. We get our bearings in the fictional world mostly (but not entirely) though what the film depicts. When we watch *District 9*, for example, we depend upon the film to show us what an alien shantytown populated by "prawns" from outer space looks like. "Unlike our experience with the home movie or documentary," Sobchack writes, "the images of fiction are experienced as directly given to us and they exist not 'elsewhere' but 'here' in the virtual world that is 'there' before us." (p. 243) This progressively more "immersive" mode of attention (to use a term from gaming and virtual reality) partly defines the experience of watching a home movie, documentary, or fiction film.

But these rubrics of attention can become fluid, most obviously when motivated by something within the film text. An event in a fiction film may trigger viewers to move out of their immersion in the fiction. As an example of this shift, Sobchack discusses a scene in Renoir's *The Rules of the Game* in which a rabbit is shot and killed; she argues that our fictional consciousness may be transformed in moments such as these, when we consider the real rabbit whose life was ended. This migration of attention can occur without prompts. For example, we depend upon the fictional *mise en scène* in *District 9* to show us what the prawn ghetto looks like, yet we supplement this information with pre-existing knowledge of military maneuvers, scientific experimentation, and non-fiction filmmaking (since one of the fictional premises of the film is that it is a documentary). When we watch a fiction film set in a familiar city, we may find our attention turning to memories and experiences of that location, and this may affect the meaning of that location within the story. Documentary films may also give rise to similar shifts in our attention: rather than experiencing the documentary *Berkeley in the Sixties* (Mark Kitchell 1990) as a record of a historical era, viewers who lived there

9.19 Allakarillak feigns awe at the sight of the gramophone in *Nanook of the North*.

at that time might experience parts of the film as a home movie (Sobchack, p. 249).

These ideas about the fluidity of spectatorship encourage us to revisit the definition of documentary film. According to Sobchack, "a 'documentary' is not a thing but a subjective relationship [...] the viewer's consciousness determines what kind of cinematic object it is." (p. 251) This theoretical approach may inspire us to more thoughtfully consider our expectations about the nature of home movies, documentaries, and fiction films.

These ideas about documentary spectatorship underscore the fact that documentary films mediate reality, and that the documentary experience becomes a mutual construction of the filmmaker, the film, and the spectator.

Ethics and Ethnography

Unique ethical dilemmas arise within documentary filmmaking. Whose vision of reality is represented in a documentary film, and how can filmmakers ensure fairness and accuracy? Image ethicists encourage viewers to question the relationship between the filmmaker and the people whose lives are being represented. The **ethnographic films** of Robert Flaherty, one of the earliest and most influential documentary filmmakers, have been reconsidered in light of what is now known about Flaherty's methods.

Flaherty's *Nanook of the North* (1922), about the Inuit people in Canada, and *Man of Aran* (1937), about the Aran Islanders off the west coast of Ireland, are voice-of-authority documentaries organized by intertitles that explain the activities depicted. In his zeal to valorize what he considered the blissfully primitive cultures of the Inuit and the Aran islanders, however, Flaherty misrepresented the cultures he intended to document. In *Nanook Revisited* (1988), Inuit commentators point out that Flaherty gave the name Nanook (which means "bear" in Inkituk) to a man whose actual name was Allakarillak. Flaherty also clothed Allakarillak in polar bear leggings not typically worn by the Inuit, staged a seal hunt, and contrived a scene in which Allakarillak appeared to be ignorant about the new technology of the gramophone, although he was not (fig. **9.19**).

In *Man of Aran*, Flaherty staged a shark hunt and depicted the islanders gathering seaweed. Harry Watt, who worked with Flaherty on the film, stated:

> the film was a phoney [...] They hadn't caught those sharks for seventy-five years. They hardly ever took the seaweed up, and they took it up on donkeys; they didn't carry it on their backs [as the film depicted]. (Sussex, p. 31)

Flaherty's films capture a romantic idea of the Inuit and the Aran islanders rather than their reality in the 1920s and 1930s. They highlight the ethical complexities of documenting a culture, whether that culture is one to which the filmmaker belongs or one he visits.

Flaherty's filmmaking practices were extreme. Yet even filmmakers who take pains to avoid the staging of reality must recognize that their choices—including subject matter and style—imply underlying ethical principles related to the subjects filmed and the audience watching the film.

Some filmmakers use self-reflexive strategies to highlight the ethical dilemmas of documenting any culture and to make clear the director's role as observer–participant. For example, Minh-ha Trinh's *Surname Viet, Given Name Nam* (1989) questions the process of documenting exotic "others"—Vietnamese women—in political and philosophical terms. The first half of her film depicts women telling stories about their experiences of the war with the U.S. in the 1960s and 1970s. But the second half reveals that the subjects are not women in Vietnam telling their stories. Instead, they are Vietnamese-born women who live in the U.S. and agreed to act in the film. They have been reciting firsthand accounts written by other Vietnamese women. Trinh plays on audience expectations about the traditional characteristics of Vietnamese women. She also defies documentary conventions regarding the nature of testimony, because

9.20 Abstract images in *Surname Viet, Given Name Nam*.

she uses performers to tell other women's stories, then she asks the actors to comment on their role-playing. Who and where are the actual "subjects" and where is the truth? Trinh also tests the audience's willingness to consider film as a medium that constructs, rather than depicts, a reality by layering text with images and by incorporating poetry and abstract camerawork in the film (fig. **9.20**).

As these examples suggest, documentary filmmakers make creative use of reality for a number of purposes: to inform viewers about extraordinary or mundane aspects of reality, to encourage viewers to draw conclusions about world events, to change the audience's understanding of social issues, and to question the way the film medium constructs reality.

Avant-garde Film

Like documentary film, avant-garde film—called experimental film in the 1940s and 1950s and underground cinema during the 1960s and 1970s—represents an extraordinarily diverse array of filmmaking practices. Some avant-garde films tell bizarre stories, others focus on the abstract qualities of film images, while still others may choose to explore one particular technical aspect of film, such as slow motion, to exploit its effects to the full. Many avant-garde filmmakers have been associated with art and social change movements, including Surrealism, Minimalism, feminism, and gay and lesbian liberation.

If viewers think of cinema solely in terms of narrative film, then avant-garde films may put them off. These films require a different set of skills for interpretation. Scott MacDonald argues that avant-garde films evoke frustration because "they confront us with the necessity of redefining an experience we were sure we understood." (MacDonald, p. 2)

What kind of redefinition is MacDonald referring to? Avant-garde films rarely present straightforward stories or characters. Instead, they approach the medium as an aesthetic, philosophical, and/or political means of expression. They often isolate elements of film art—including cinematography, sound, and editing—and subject them to intense scrutiny. Avant-garde films often reject traditional methods for combining images and sound, startling the viewer with new possibilities. They may explore such things as: the way light achieves certain photographic effects; the influence of abstract shapes and color on emotions; how superimposition connects two images; how repetition inspires certain thoughts; how rapid editing overwhelms perceptual capacities; and whether an image means the same thing to viewers when it is paired with an unlikely soundtrack.

Avant-garde filmmakers break new ground in film aesthetics and cultural politics. The techniques experimental filmmakers use to challenge convention include time-lapse photography, fast, slow, and reverse motion, negative images, scratching and painting on the emulsion, superimposition, electronic soundtracks, and non-synchronized sound. Film scholar William Wees considers these devices "gestures of rebellion against the conventions of popular cinema [...] They confront the viewer with a more complex and dynamic experience of visual perception than is normally the case in film viewing." (Wees, p. 4) In other words, they ask viewers to pay close attention to images and sounds as sensual, emotional, and aesthetic experiences, meaningful on their own terms, not because they obey the logic of cause and effect.

The sections below examine several important styles and traditions in avant-garde filmmaking, including Surrealism, abstract film, the city symphony, structuralist film, and the compilation film. This examination is suggestive rather than comprehensive; an annotated list of resources for further research directs readers to sources for exploring the gamut of avant-garde filmmaking practices.

Surrealist Cinema

One film convention that early European avant-garde filmmakers rebelled against was narrative form. Surrealist film culture, centered in Paris, grew out of Dada and Surrealist currents in performance (Hugo Ball and Tristan Tzara), photography

9.21 *(left)* A ballerina becomes a man in *Entr'acte*.

9.22 *(right)* The fragmented perspective of a runaway hearse in *Entr'acte*.

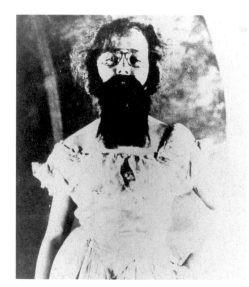

(Man Ray), and literature (André Breton). Surrealism explored the irrational, unconscious mind beneath the surface of reality.

Surrealist films are rife with humor, sexuality, and scandalous images. They reject conventional morality and poke fun at bourgeois values through form and content. *Un Chien andalou* (Luis Buñuel and Salvador Dalí 1929), *Entr'acte* (René Clair 1924), and *Ballet Mécanique* (Fernand Léger, Man Ray,

and Dudley Murphy 1924) are Surrealist films that subvert chronological time and narrative causality. In *Entr'acte* a series of loosely connected scenes includes a dancing ballerina who becomes a man (fig. **9.21**) and a runaway hearse that incites an absurd chase scene (fig. **9.22**). The chase uses familiar cinematic codes to comment on World War I as an out-of-control race toward death.

Un Chien andalou vigorously mocks narrative form as well. The sequence of events is not coherent; viewers cannot make sense of the film using cause-and-effect logic. Intertitles offer clichéd phrases apparently designed to orient viewers to a timeline, but the film renders the information useless. Although several intertitles announce that the action is moving backward or forward by years or hours, the events seem continuous. Unnamed characters have few goals or conflicts (although motifs include gender fluidity and sexual aggression). The soundtrack parodies the way non-diegetic music is used in narrative cinema to invoke emotions, pairing Wagner's *Tristan and Isolde* with bizarre vignettes that have little to do with romance. Slow motion is used merely for its own sake. One character shoots his double from across the room, and an inexplicable happy ending is tacked on at the conclusion, when a single cut permits a woman to move from an urban apartment location to the beach (figs. **9.23**, **9.24**). Surrealist films need not abandon narrative altogether. One of the most powerful early surrealist films was *The Fall of the House of Usher* (James Sibley Watson and Melville Usher 1928), which uses an Expressionist *mise en scène* and superimpositions to turn Edgar Allan Poe's story into a radical visual evocation of madness and decay (fig. **9.25**).

During World War II, a number of European artists and filmmakers left occupied Europe and came to the U.S., where an American avant-garde developed, particularly in New York and San Francisco. Within the American avant-garde, some filmmakers expanded on the Surrealist tradition, dismantling narrative and working in a poetic form. Maya Deren's 16-minute film *Meshes of the Afternoon* explores the dream state, suspending the notion of chronological time while relying on characters, settings, and the semblance of a narrative. Deren and her husband use domestic interiors as the nightmarish location for the

9.23 *(left)* A woman leaves her urban apartment in *Un Chien andalou.*

9.24 *(right)* The eyeline match renders story space illogical in *Un Chien andalou.*

9.25 A surreal evocation of madness in *The Fall of the House of Usher.*

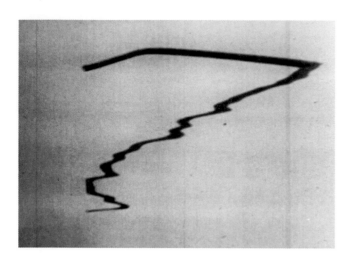

9.26 *H2O* captures the beauty of water in a linear composition.

dreamer's vivid and self-destructive imagination. (See Film Analysis, p. 303.) Another American avant-garde filmmaker whose work deals with trance-like states is Kenneth Anger, who describes cinema as "a magical weapon" (Le Cain). A child actor, Anger began making short experimental films at age seventeen, and his body of work, though small, has influenced filmmakers across avant-garde, underground, gay and lesbian, and mainstream cinemas. Anger's distinctive style relies on archetypes and symbols, on compilation soundtracks incorporating popular music (a technique that influenced Martin Scorsese), fragmentary narratives that focus on ritualized violence and eroticism (reflecting his interest in occult), and lovingly ironic treatments of popular culture. *Fireworks* (1947) and *Scorpio Rising* (1963) are two of his best-known works. In *Fireworks*, a man awakens from a dream in which he has seen himself in the arms of a sailor. He wanders in the night, is roughed up by a crowd of sailors, and ultimately finds his dream lover. When his lover unzips his pants, he pulls out a burning Roman candle. In 2010, Anger made a short film ad for the fashion house Missoni.

While contemporary filmmaker Sadie Benning does not focus on the dream state *per se*, her intensely autobiographical films depict everyday life as surreal. The meditative tone of many of her films reflects her isolation: one response to a world that is hostile to women and lesbians. In her earliest films, made at age fifteen, "her main subject was herself, coming to terms with a pervasive 1980s cultural of junk TV and mindless consumerism." (Morris) In *Flat is Beautiful* (1998), the actors all wear masks. The characters' "authentic feelings and desires continuously strain to break through these rigid, unforgiving, literally constructed identities." (Morris) Benning's work is notable because of her facility with the low-resolution Fisher Price Pixelvision camera (originally marketed as a toy for children), her complex examination of gender and sexuality, and her ability to integrate drawings, masks, video, and film in menacing and poetic ways.

Abstract Film

When the Surrealists were exploring irrationality, filmmakers such as Man Ray, Walter Ruttmann, and Hans Richter established a very different tradition, one of abstract filmmaking. Their films abandoned human figures altogether. *Opus I–IV* (Walter Ruttman 1921–5) and *Rhythmus 21* (Hans Richter 1921–4) pay attention to graphic form and rhythmic editing. Their animated, geometrical forms reflect their creators' idea that filmmaking was painting with motion. Man Ray's *Return to Reason* ("*Le Retour à la raison*"; 1923) made use of his signature technique, called rayography, which involved laying objects on unexposed film and exposing them to light briefly, creating contact images without the use of a camera.

Ralph Steiner's *H20* (1928), which comprises shots of water in a variety of manifestations, from raindrops to ocean waves, expresses the film medium's capacity for rendering movement both sensual and abstract (fig. **9.26**). At times the images of water appear to be two-dimensional compositions of light and shadow, formed by undulating lines.

Stan Brakhage made a number of abstract films that reflect his interest in the philosophy and physiology of vision. Brakhage sought to liberate human perception from a "'practical' view of experience in which the goal of amassing material wealth requires conformity in how we see and how we act." (MacDonald, p. 6) Abandoning goal-oriented perception in favor of "open, 'receptive' seeing," Brakhage painted on, bleached, and scraped the film surface to produce "closed-eye" vision; that is, the things people are capable of seeing when their eyes are closed (Wees, p. 126). Brakhage believed that the untutored eye absorbs and creates its own visual field before it learns to recognize familiar objects. Brakhage considered himself, "the most thorough documentary filmmaker in the world because I document the act of seeing as well as everything the light brings me." (quoted in Wees, p. 78)

Film scholar David Curtis wrote that Brakhage's films defy all conventional notions of filmmaking. They have "no story, no symbolism, no acting, no posed photographic beauty; the drama is [...] the drama of vision, a vision that implies a belief that the first priority is to see and record, the second to structure and interpret." (Curtis, p. 86) Although described within the abstract tradition here, Brakhage has been called a personal and visionary filmmaker because much of his work is both poetic and self-referential.

The City Symphony

Beginning in the 1920s, a number of filmmakers celebrated the vibrancy of the modern world with the **city symphony** film, a genre that combines documentary and experimental film. Walter Ruttmann's *Berlin, Symphony of a Great City* and

TECHNIQUES IN PRACTICE

Interpreting Abstract Films

Stan Brakhage's films can be challenging to interpret. But by attending to the principles that inform avant-garde filmmaking, and especially, the idea that avant-garde filmmakers often focus on the materials of the film medium, it's possible to gain a greater understanding of even the most abstract of his films. As with any analysis, the first step is simple description.

Two of Brakhage's later works call attention to basic elements of the film medium, namely, images and movement. Brakhage orchestrates color, light, movement, and tempo in different ways in *Black Ice* (1994) and *Dark Tower* (1999), inviting different aesthetic responses. In *Black Ice*, Brakhage creates the illusion of depth in order to convey a sense of unease, whereas in *Dark Tower* he develops a motif of conflict and opposition.

In *Black Ice*, splashes of red, white, green, blue, and yellow paint appear to advance toward the viewer as they revolve around the periphery of the frame (see fig. 2.3). Brakhage creates the illusion of movement—one of cinema's elemental functions—by subtly changing the size, shape, and hue of the paint from one frame to the next. Careful editing simulates shimmering movement.

9.27 Refracted light produces a stained-glass effect in *Dark Tower*, but an ominous black line looms over the dance of colors.

The division of the frame into sections of bright color and sections of blackness contributes to the illusion of depth. The color daubs at the outer areas of the frame create a bright foreground against the color-swallowing black in what appears to be the deeper center of the frame. Also, the splashes of paint that appear to move forward do so at a slower speed than the splotches rotating around the periphery. This discrepancy creates a sense of unease because it disrupts the viewer's spatial references and implies a kind of vertigo. Spectators may feel they are falling toward the screen. This sensory response can be related to the film's title—*Black Ice*—to suggest a tangible real world reference. Black ice, something that is both invisible and dangerous, causes people to lose their balance.

In *Dark Tower*, Brakhage also relies on film's basic elements—color and editing rhythms—but uses them to create different effects. This film unfolds in five distinct sequences: in the first section, a tapered dark shape occupies the center of the frame, with bright colors on either side. Those splashes of color become tinged with light in the second section of the film, creating a stained-glass effect. In the third section, the slices of light and color move against one another horizontally across the frame as if they are swords clashing. In the fourth section, a vertical strip of black dominates the center of the frame, repeating the pattern in the first section of the film but presenting a much bolder, towering central shape (fig. **9.27**). In the final moments of the film, the lines of color and light grow larger and give off white haloes.

Editing and composition in *Dark Tower* emphasize the division of frame into right and left, in contrast to the depth created in *Black Ice*. Again it's useful to consider the imagery in relation to the film's title. Brakhage's divided compositions and clashing colors are abstract versions of the medieval tower, a powerfully iconic structure that may be familiar from childhood fairly tales and contemporary films such as *The Lord of the Rings*. The editing emphasizes the physical clash of abstract entities, possibly connoting a mythic struggle between good and evil, darkness and light, or life and death.

Dziga Vertov and Boris Kaufman's *Man with a Movie Camera* ("*Chelovek s kinoapparatom*"; 1929) are organized by the chronological timeline of a single day. They open with images depicting early morning, and then proceed to document people as they work and carry out leisure activities before concluding in the darkness of the evening.

Ruttmann and Vertov's films present ideas through visual association: images produce meaning based on their visual attributes, not through the logic of cause and effect. Both filmmakers are fascinated by the movements of modern urban life and edit their films to establish visual comparisons. Ruttmann films a

sequence of blinds and store windows opening, marking the synchronicity of actions taken early in the day. At midday, he shows the way lunch interrupts the workday for both wealthy businessmen and factory workers.

Vertov's film reflects his utopian ideas about the machine age. His excitement about the modern industrial world can be inferred from his own assumed name, which means "spinning top." Sequences in *Man with a Movie Camera* transmit the aesthetic intoxication of machines in motion. One series of shots visually compares machines that rotate and spin, from the simple sewing machine to huge turbine engines (figs. **9.28**, **9.29**). The connection between the images lies in the similar circular motion.

Vertov also uses self-reflexive techniques to call attention to the process of making the film. At one point a woman gets out of bed and washes her face at a basin. She looks directly at the camera and blinks her eyes (fig. **9.30**). Vertov cuts to a shot of Venetian blinds opening and closing (fig. **9.31**). After cutting back and forth between the two images, he introduces a third: a close-up of a

9.28 *(left)* An image of rotation from *Man with a Movie Camera*: a sewing machine.

9.29 *(right)* Another image of rotation from *Man with a Movie Camera*: a turbine engine.

9.30 *(left)* Fluttering images of eyes in *Man with a Movie Camera*.

9.31 *(right)* Blinds in *Man with a Movie Camera*.

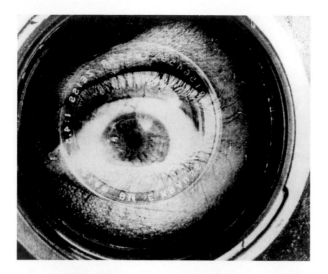

9.32 A camera-eye double exposure, from *Man with a Movie Camera*.

9.33 Superimposition creates an eerie and poetic cityscape in *Bridges Go Round*.

camera lens as its aperture opens and closes (fig. **9.32**). The editing invites spectators to contemplate the work of the film-maker as an observer of daily life and to note the parallels between the fluttering motion of the eyes, blinds, and the lens as they all let light in and out.

Vertov also includes images of a man with a movie camera traveling around the city and shows the editor (Kaufman's wife) selecting strips of film to splice together. The images she handles appear later in the film. Vertov believed that filmmaking should be a collaborative enterprise made by and for the mass public. For him, the ideal film would consist of many amateur artists shooting footage that would be assembled without regard to realism or continuity. Editors would create visual associations and metaphors that capture the underlying reality of the exciting modern world.

Two short experimental films of the 1950s that grow out of the city symphony tradition are Shirley Clarke's *Bridges Go Round* (1958) and Marie Mencken's *Go Go Go* (1963). Clarke's film offers an interesting lesson in the relationship between image and sound. In this non-narrative 3½-minute film, Clarke records the city skyline while driving across bridges, and then repeatedly superimposes the steel structures against the sky (fig. **9.33**). Clarke made two versions of the film. In one, a jazzy score by saxophone player and jazz producer Teo Macero accompanies the images; in the second, Bebe Barron's electronic score plays. Watching the two versions of Clarke's film can create vastly different impressions because each score emphasizes different elements of the images: the jazz score underlines the pace of editing and the camera movement, whereas the electronic score highlights the abstract futuristic patterns created by the images of bridges.

New York filmmaker, painter, and poet Marie Mencken made films that were an extension of her many talents. In them, surface, texture, and rhythm (including camera movement, editing, or fast motion) became central elements. *Go Go Go* uses a handheld camera and stop-motion photography to record activities of New Yorkers. Their speedy, repetitive movements suggest the irony of working so hard to accomplish anything: all activity is rendered useless in the long run. The experimental documentary *Site Specific: Las Vegas 05* contributes to the tradition of the city symphony by defamiliarizing the everyday experience of Las Vegas (fig. **9.34**).

One of the more recent entrants in the city symphony genre takes advantage of digital technology. Canadian artist Perry Bard has constructed "Man With A Movie Camera: Global Remake," a public art project that continually creates a remake of Vertov's classic film using uploaded images from around the world. Anyone who visits dziga.perrybard.net/ has the opportunity to match a shot from Vertov's film and thus become a part of Bard's ingenious tribute to Vertov's celebration of humans, technology, urban spaces, and the power of film editing.

Structuralist Film

In the 1960s, filmmakers, like painters and Conceptual artists, developed an interest in "a 'metaphysics' of the cinematic apparatus." (MacDonald, p. 37) Structuralist filmmakers explored strips of film, sound waves, cameras, and lenses.

In *Wavelength* (1967), Michael Snow manipulates a zoom lens in an attempt to examine film space and time. For Snow, "the camera is fixed in a mystical contemplation of a portion of space." (Sitney, p. 350) Throughout the film's 45-minute zoom, the shifting focal length reconfigures the space of a New York loft, from three-dimensional deep space to a two-dimensional flat surface. The shot slowly closes in on a photograph on the wall (fig. **9.35**). The soundtrack is a sine wave that rises in pitch, its own wavelengths shortening over the duration of the film.

9.34 Aerial cinematography (via an extremely long lens) transforms Las Vegas into a toy landscape in *Site Specific: Las Vegas 05*.

Wavelength is a reflection on cinematic form, not an exploration of character or action. Initially, the film appears to offer a narrative: women move a bookcase into an apartment; a man enters the room and falls down; a woman makes a telephone call to report the dead body to someone. But, finally, no story coalesces around these events. Instead, the film invites viewers to focus on the way their perception of time and space shifts as a result of cinematic acts of observation. Scott MacDonald calls the final irony the fact that the long, slow zoom ultimately delivers the viewer to "the absolute nemesis of the conventional cinema: to a still photograph viewed in silence for several minutes." (MacDonald, p. 36) In 2003, Michael Snow remade his own film, with an ironic twist that reflects contemporary realities. *WVLNT* (*Wavelength for Those Who Don't Have the Time*) is a 15-minute abbreviation of the original film that consists of the three original reels of *Wavelength* superimposed upon one another. This compressed remake acknowledges the fact that people can't invest 45 minutes to watch the original, and also puts an avant-garde spin on the notion of the director's cut.

9.35 A close-up of a photograph on the wall in *Wavelength*.

The Compilation Film

The compilation film reuses existing film footage in an entirely new context to generate innovative ideas. The use of found footage to stimulate new ideas recalls Marcel Duchamp's subversive aesthetic of ready-mades and *objets trouvés* ("found objects"). The compilation film offers opportunities for irony and invention: since the images all originate in another context, a compilation film can create the "new reality" described in the Deren quote that begins this chapter.

Bruce Conner's *Crossroads* (1976) is a prime example of the use of irony in compilation films. Conner, who had worked as a collage artist and sculptor before turning to film, drew the images from the film entirely from U.S. government footage of

a nuclear blast at the Bikini Atoll in July 1946. Working like a sculptor, Conner reshaped this raw material—re-editing the images (which were shot by 500 different cameras), orchestrating slow motion and adding sound elements—to make the film an awe-inspiring meditation on the sublime folly of weapons that have the capacity to destroy the planet. Because Conner turned these images of military might into art, many have criticized the film for aestheticizing violence.

In compilation films, themes and ideas can emerge from the careful sequencing and juxtaposition of vastly different images. Conner's *A Movie* (1958) exploits irony by juxtaposing shots of a submariner looking through a periscope (fig. **9.36**) with images of Marilyn Monroe (fig. **9.37**). The editing suggests the seaman sees the sexy images. When the submarine fires a torpedo, the explosion yields a mushroom cloud. The sequence turns on the humorous connection between war and sexual aggression but also offers sobering implications. In Chick Strand's *Cartoon La Mousse* (1979), footage from classic cartoons forms the centerpiece for an eerie meditation on romance and solitude.

A more recent compilation film, *Decasia* (Bill Morrison 2002), hypnotically juxtaposes decaying archival footage from *The Last Egyptian* (L. Frank Baum 1914), among many other sources, with an original symphonic score. The film evokes the cultural importance and neglect of the film medium as well as the ghostly beauty of degraded images.

9.36 *(above)* A submariner and periscope in *A Movie*.

9.37 *(below)* An image of Marilyn Monroe, from *A Movie*.

Conducting Research on Documentary and Avant-garde Films: Locating Sources

Locating avant-garde and documentary films may pose a challenge. Documentary and avant-garde films can be difficult to obtain; generally, most DVD outlets will offer a small selection at best. Some films are available only on film. Thus, the research process for scholars pursuing an interest in these films often begins with a detective story: finding film prints or locating an outlet to rent or purchase a DVD.

Conducting an online search for a director or film is one place to begin; but be aware that a great deal of information about alternative filmmaking, including articles and reviews, does not appear in online indexes. A university library may offer access to sources not readily available online. And a university reference librarian may be able to locate film, video, and digital materials through interlibrary loan.

The list below is another resource. Many of these sites and organizations make documentary or avant-garde films available through rental and purchase; in some cases, materials do not circulate but may be viewed on the premises.

1. Filmmakers' Cooperative: www.film-makerscoop.com
   Created by filmmakers in 1962, the Filmmakers' Coop is the largest
   archive and distributor of independent and avant-garde films in the world.

2. Anthology Film Archives: www.anthologyfilmarchives.org
   Established in 1970, Anthology Film Archives sponsors exhibits and
   screenings of important avant-garde films. In addition to its many public
   programs, the archive has a collection of films to serve the film student
   and film scholar. Use of this collection is by appointment only.

3. Women Make Movies: www.wmm.com
   Established in 1972, Women Make Movies is a multicultural, multiracial,
   non-profit media arts organization that facilitates the production,
   promotion, distribution, and exhibition of independent films and
   videotapes by and about women.

4. Canyon Cinema: www.canyoncinema.com
   Originally a San Francisco Bay Area cinemathèque, Canyon Cinema is
   one of the largest distributors of independent and experimental films from
   the early part of the twentieth century. Canyon also carries more than 100
   titles from new emerging filmmakers.

5. Ubu: ubuweb.com
   A website whose film and video section streams hundreds of historical
   and contemporary experimental films.

6. First Run Features: www.firstrunfeatures.com
   Distributes independent films and documentaries.

7. First Run/Icarus Films: www.frif.com
   A major distributor of documentary films.

8. DocuSeek: www.docuseek.com/startsearch.php
   "Film and video finder." A search site for documentary films that includes
   the collections of several large film distributors.

9. California Newsreel: www.newsreel.org
   Founded in 1968, California Newsreel is a center for documentary
   production and distribution. It has the largest North American holdings
   of films by and about Africa and African Americans.

Summary

- Documentary and avant-garde films differ from narrative fiction films in their
  purpose, mode of production, exhibition venue, and formal organization.
- While some documentaries and avant-garde films may use certain elements
  of narrative form, their primary purpose is not storytelling.
- Documentaries deal with some aspect of the real world, depicting or
  recreating historical or contemporary events.
- Documentaries can be grouped according to the following rhetorical
  strategies: a voice of authority approach; the talking heads approach;
  direct cinema; and self-reflexivity.
- Spectatorship practices offer one way to define the experience of
  documentary film.

- Ethical concerns including issues of balance and perspective are critical to documentary, whether a filmmaker is documenting the culture she lives in or a different culture.
- Avant-garde films (also called underground or experimental films) explore the aesthetic properties of the medium and often challenge aspects of the cultural and political status quo.
- Techniques commonly used in avant-garde films include: slow, fast, and reverse motion; superimposition; rapid editing; scratching or painting the surface of the film; and non-synchronized sound.
- Some traditions within avant-garde film include Surrealist, abstract films, city symphony, structural films, and compilation films.

Works Consulted

Beattie, Keith. *Documentary Display: Re-viewing Nonfiction Film and Video*. London and New York: Wallflower Press, 2009.

Brakhage, Stan. *Film at Wit's End: Eight Avant-garde Filmmakers*. New York: McPherson, 1989.

————. "Remarks." *By Brakhage: An Anthology*. Criterion Collection DVD, 2003.

Clark, VeVe, Millicent Hodson, and Catrina Neiman (ed.) *The Legend of Maya Deren*, vol. 1, part 2. New York: Anthology Film Archives/Film Culture, 1984.

Corner, John. *The Art of Record: A Critical Introduction to Documentary*. Manchester and NY: Manchester University Press, 1996.

————. *The Art of Record*. Manchester and New York: Manchester UP, 1996

Cowie, Elizabeth. "The Spectacle of Actuality." In *Collecting Visible Evidence*, edited by Jane Gaines and Michael Renov, pp. 19–45. Minneapolis: University of Minnesota Press, 1999.

Curtis, David. *Experimental Cinema: A Fifty Year Evolution*. New York: Dell, 1971.

Gidal, Peter. *Materialist Film*. London: Routledge, 1989.

Haller, Robert. "Kenneth Anger." Harvard Independent Film Group. February 1980. **www.geocities.com/Hollywood/Lot/1162/HCAngerBio_html.html** August 20, 2006.

Horak, Jan-Christopher. "The First American Avant-Garde, 1919–1945," in *Lovers of Cinema: The First American Film Avant-Garde 1919–45*, ed. Jan-Christopher Horak. Madison: University of Wisconsin Press, 1995, pp. 14–66.

James, David. *Allegories of Cinema: American Film in the 1960s*. Princeton: Princeton University Press, 1989.

Le Cain, Maximilian. "Kenneth Anger." Senses of Cinema. January 2003. **www.sensesofcinema.com/contents/directors/03/anger.html** September 15, 2006.

MacDonald, Scott. *Avant-Garde Film: Motion Studies*. Cambridge: Cambridge University Press, 1993.

Moritz, William. "Americans in Paris" in *Lovers of Cinema: The First American Film Avant-Garde 1919–45*, ed. Jan-Christopher Horak. Madison: University of Wisconsin Press, 1995, pp. 118–36.

Morris, Gary. "Behind the Mask: Sadie Benning's Pixel Pleasures." *Bright Lights Film Journal*, issue 24: April 1999. **www.brightlightsfilm.com/24/benning.html**. 2/17/04.

Nichols, Bill. *Introduction to Documentary*. Bloomington and Indianapolis: Indiana University Press, 2001.

————. *Representing Reality*. Bloomington and Indianapolis: Indiana University Press, 1991.

Peterson, James. *Dreams of Chaos, Visions of Order: Understanding the American Avant-Garde Cinema*. Detroit: Wayne State University Press, 1994.

Rees, A.L. *A History of Experimental Film and Video*. London: British Film Institute, 1999.

Rigney, Melissa. "Sadie Benning." *Senses of Cinema. Great Directors: A Critical Database*. **www.sensesofcinema.com/contents/directors/03/benning.html**. 2/17/04.

Rosen, Philip. "Document and Documentary: On the Persistence of Historical Concepts," in *Theorizing Documentary*, ed. Michael Renov. New York: Routledge, 1993.

Russell, Catherine. *Experimental Ethnography*. Durham, NC, and London: Duke University Press, 1999.

Sitney, P. Adams. *Visionary Film: The American Avant-Garde, 1943–1978*, 3rd edn. Oxford and New York: Oxford University Press, 2002.

Sobchack, Vivan. "Toward a Phenomenology of Nonfictional film experience." In *Collecting*

Visible Evidence, edited by Jane Gaines and Michael Renov, pp. 241–54. Minneapolis: University of Minnesota Press, 1999.

Stam, Robert. *Film Theory: An Introduction*. Malden, MA, and Oxford: Blackwell, 2000.

Sussex, Elizabeth. *The Rise and Fall of British Documentary*. Berkeley and Los Angeles: University of California Press, 1975.

Swann, Paul. *The British Documentary Film Movement, 1926–46*. Cambridge: Cambridge University Press, 1989.

Wees, William C. *Light Moving in Time: Studies in the Visual Aesthetics of Avant-Garde Film*. Berkeley: University of California Press, 1992.

Zagar, Jeremiah. Phone Interview. Conducted January 10, 2010.

Zuber, Sharon. "Robert Drew, Telephone Interview, June 4, 2003." *Re-Shaping Documentary Expectations: New Journalism and Direct Cinema*. Unpublished Dissertation. College of William and Mary, 2004.

FILM ANALYSIS

Interpreting Avant-garde Films

Maya Deren's haunting experimental films have had a visible influence on everything from music videos by Madonna and Milla Jovovich to contemporary films like *Inception* (Christopher Nolan 2010). In 1943 Deren's relationship with her husband, Alexander Hamid, was disintegrating. The couple made a film together that suggests their emotional turmoil, and the resulting *Meshes of the Afternoon* is surely one of the most important American Surrealist films. Some readers may assume avant-garde films defy any semblance of logic. But the analysis below illustrates that viewers can analyze and interpret experimental films using the terminology and approaches covered in Chapters 2 through 8.

The Study Notes point out strategies for constructing effective sentences. Current scholarship in rhetoric and composition recommends that polishing sentence-level problems should be the last step in the writing process. This chapter covers the last step in revision (excluding proofreading, of course): fine-tuning the prose. Many writers find that it's more efficient to worry about sentence-level problems after all their ideas are in place and in order.

Analyzing *Meshes of the Afternoon*

Maya Deren's short experimental film *Meshes of the Afternoon* (1943) depicts what would otherwise appear to be the most innocuous sequence of events. A woman returns home on a sunny afternoon, settles down to take a nap, and begins dreaming. But Deren's experimental visual techniques transform this everyday activity into a surreal, horrific event, allowing viewers to interpret the film as a meditation on the disintegration of her relationship with her husband, Alexander Hamid (who also helped shoot the film and who appears in the movie, along with Deren). Throughout the film, Deren's visual techniques transform tranquil images of domesticity into threatening portents of destruction, suggesting how the unnamed main character (Deren) feels trapped in a suffocating relationship.

The plot of the film simply repeats and expands on a woman's routine after returning home: as she walks up the sidewalk toward her house, she

1 Some students have difficulty incorporating film studies terminology into sentences. Most film terms are first and foremost nouns. Writers can use them anywhere they use nouns, so they can be the subject of the sentence. Prose gets unnecessarily wordy when writers only use people as the subject of a sentence. Instead of saying "Maya Deren constructs a plot that simply repeats ...," this author simplifies her prose by making film technique, the plot, the thing that *does the action*.

2 In most circumstances, people naturally speak in active voice; there is a subject that does an action to something or someone (that is, subject+verb+object): "the boy kicked the ball." *Passive voice* is when the object of the action becomes the subject of the sentence: "the ball was kicked by the boy." Notice that the passive voice makes the sentence sound clunky—unnecessarily wordy. There is nothing grammatically wrong with using the passive voice. In fact, several examples appear in this essay. But most writers try to avoid using it. How would this sentence sound in the passive voice? It would begin "Once the dream state is entered by the woman ..."

3 Plenty of sentences in this essay make Maya Deren, the film's director, the subject who is responsible for everything in the film. But are we really sure that Deren made all of these decisions? The film was a collaboration between two people. What if Alexander Hamid made some of the technical choices? These questions illustrate why it's important to practice using film studies terms as active agents in sentences; almost all films are collaborative efforts and assigning credit for each visual or sound effect to each individual would unnecessarily burden the writer. In this case, "Repeated eyeline matches" perform the action.

9.38 (*above*) The woman looks out of the window in *Meshes of the Afternoon*.

9.39 (*below*) The woman sees herself pursuing the shrouded figure in *Meshes of the Afternoon*.

sees a man in the distance.[1] She fumbles with her key and enters the house. After surveying the room (noticing several everyday domestic items: a record player, a telephone, a bread knife), she settles down for a nap in an easy chair, which allows her to look out a window and onto the sidewalk below. Once she falls asleep, this same routine is repeated in her dream state three times—with creative variation—suggesting how her subconscious is reflecting on and interpreting the psychological ramifications of this daily activity.

Once the woman enters her dream state, Deren exploits the conventions of continuity editing to undercut the apparent normalcy of the activities.[2] Each new cycle in the film's repetitive progression begins with an eyeline match of the woman looking out of her window to the image of herself below (fig. **9.38**). In other words, she sees herself running up the sidewalk after a mysterious, cloaked figure that resembles the Grim Reaper and which has "replaced" the anonymous male figure she saw at the beginning of the film (fig. **9.39**). At one point, the woman enters the house and, in another eyeline match, sees two other images of herself gathered around a table. Repeated eyeline matches create the illusion that the woman is looking at herself and emphasize how detached she is from her own identity.[3] In her dreams, she

sees herself in the third person repeating her daily activities, as if her domestic identity is disembodied from other aspects of her personality.

More dramatically, Deren's use of collage reveals how the woman's dream reinterprets tokens of domesticity as ominous portents of death and destruction. At one point in the film, three apparitions of the woman gather around a table and take turns picking up the key to the house from the center of the table. When the third figure picks up the key and turns her hand over, the key rests in her outstretched palm (fig. **9.40**). Deren then cuts to the same outstretched hand in the same position, but the palm holds a knife instead of the key (fig. **9.41**).[4] The editing makes it appear as if the key, a quintessential image of domesticity since it connotes a shared personal space, magically transforms into the knife, an image of violence. This graphic match equates marriage with violence or destruction.

This film's intimation of violence becomes much more explicit at this point, as the figure with the knife in her hand stands up from the table with the weapon drawn in attack mode. She approaches the reclining woman, and the film's use of eyeline match and point-of-view shots makes it clear that the standing woman is intent on stabbing her sleeping self-image. At this point, the editing's collage once again encourages viewers to associate domesticity with violence. One shot is a close-up profile of the reclining woman as the shiny knife blade slowly approaches her mouth.

Deren then cuts to an extreme close-up of the reclining woman's eyes as they open in shock; the glare of the knife blade is reflected in her face. The editing here makes it clear that the sleeping woman is about to be stabbed by the image of herself. But then Deren cuts to an extreme close-up of a man's face (presumably the husband, played by Hamid) retreating from the camera, suggesting that the shot is the woman's point of view of her husband, who has awakened her with a kiss.[5] More importantly, the sequence of shots draws a parallel between the imagined murder/suicide and the husband's tender kiss, once again associating domesticity with violence and destruction.

Some may be tempted to interpret the film as a depiction of domestic violence, but careful analysis of the imagery reveals that the film is really interested in the psychological trauma of marriage rather than physical abuse. After all, when the husband appears, he seems quite benevolent (carrying a flower, kissing the woman, tucking her into bed). Moreover, the figure that does appear threatening to the woman is herself. But Deren's use of an intentionally jolting collage of images transforms the couple's domesticated relationship and the husband's seemingly tender actions into harbingers of death. The suggestion is not that the woman in the film feels physically threatened by her husband, but that marriage itself has led to something just as terrifying: the loss of her identity.

9.40 (*above*) The symbolic key in *Meshes of the Afternoon*.

9.41 (*below*) A knife replaces the key in *Meshes of the Afternoon*.

4 While most of the terms in this book function as nouns, some can also function as verbs. For example, audiences can see "a zoom" (noun) onscreen, while a camera operator can "zoom in" (verb) on a face. Audiences can see "a dissolve" (noun), while image A "dissolves" (verb) to image B. Here the author uses editing terminology as a verb. How could the author rewrite the same sentence using "cut" as a noun? Writers should weigh a variety of approaches that express the same idea; this will introduce variety into the sentence structure, improving readability. Well-crafted prose develops a rhythm: notice, for example that the sentences in this paragraph vary in length from nine words in the final sentence to thirty-one words in the second sentence.

5 Because effective writers want to make their prose clear and concise, they avoid using modifiers that don't convey any information such as "very," "extremely," or "incredibly." Here the author uses "extreme" because it is a legitimate film term. But do you think "extremely interesting" offers greater precision than just saying "interesting"? Writers should use modifiers for poetic emphasis, but they also should try to avoid clichés. Would you rather see a movie about a "very interesting relationship" or an "exceptionally interesting relationship"? Perhaps you would be more intrigued if it were a "sadistic relationship"?

Cinema and Culture

Dressed for success: *Fantastic Mr. Fox.*

Part Three moves readers beyond a focus on textual analysis to consider the relationship between film and culture. These chapters present conceptual frameworks that approach cinema as a cultural, economic, and social institution. The topics of Chapters 10 through 15 do not exhaust potential areas of inquiry, but instead introduce several important fields within film studies. These chapters examine the relation between social context and film style, stardom, ideology, genre, *auteur* theory, and film as an industry. Each one explores ideas and questions that filmmakers, film enthusiasts, critics, and scholars contemplate when they investigate cinema's role in culture. Each chapter also includes examples of writing about cinema as a cultural institution.

By the time readers have completed Part Three, they will be prepared to formulate original questions related to cinema as a cultural institution and to conduct independent research on film studies topics.

Together, Parts Two and Three help readers develop the critical reading, analytical, and rhetorical skills to describe, interpret, and evaluate a film at the textual level and to engage current issues in film and media studies by moving beyond the individual text to consider the broader cultural significance of film.

Film and Ideology

///

CHAPTER TEN

Film drama is the opium of the people.

Dziga Vertov

///

Part Two of this textbook focuses primarily on learning how to read individual film texts, analyzing how films provoke emotional, intellectual, and aesthetic responses. This chapter broadens the scope for analysis by considering how films can be studied as the products of social and cultural environments, and thus can be more fully understood in relation to *other* cultural documents and practices. More specifically, it studies the way that films implicitly or overtly

10.1 As Mammy, Hattie McDaniel reluctantly does Scarlett's bidding in *Gone with the Wind*.

309

present ideologies, which are systems of beliefs, values, and opinions. As this chapter will explore, often we are unaware of how ideologies shape the way we perceive the world. To the uncritical eye, a film may appear to portray the world in a neutral fashion, when, in fact, its vision is based on underlying assumptions about the way things are or the way they should be. In other words, ideologies may be invisible, yet they shape the world in important ways by influencing the actions of individuals and groups. Among other things, they establish the parameters for what behavior and which identities are deemed normal and which ones are considered deviant.

Ideologies derive from deep-seated feelings about the world and about human society, and, therefore, they are not necessarily bound by the rules of logic. Those who fervently subscribe to a particular ideology may not be persuaded by scientific evidence that contradicts their views. Ideologies operate at an emotional level; they are formed and influenced by family and cultural background, personal experiences, education, and popular culture, including music, movies, magazines, television, and the internet.

Ideologies shape the relationship between an individual and culture, influencing her ideas about family structure, gender and sexuality, faith, the function of work, and the role of government, among other things. Those who advocate a particular ideology present it as "commonsensical" or "natural" and, therefore, not subject to question, yet ideologies depend on assumptions and assertions that remain open to debate. The distinction between what is natural versus what is unnatural can be a moving target. In general, what is considered "natural" is not a fixed point of reference but shifts radically from one culture to another, from one generation to the next, and from one group of people to another.

Ideologies provide the philosophical threads that weave a community together, guiding the actions of individuals, groups, and even entire societies. Yet they can also serve as the psychological and emotional justification for the differential treatment of some within a society, promoting the social dominance of one group over another. They have been used to rationalize oppression, violence, and genocide. One ideology that has held powerful sway for several centuries in North America, and that continues to influence American culture, is the notion of white supremacy, which casts the white race as superior to all others and which characterizes those who are not white as lesser beings or even as sub-human. Many used this ideology to attempt to justify the profitable system of enslaving Africans in the United States, the Caribbean, and elsewhere: scientific findings (based on now discredited racist classifications systems) and religious texts were used to defend the notion that slavery conformed to the natural order of things. Many white Europeans in the United States relied on this ideology to enrich themselves or simply to look the other way while the humanity of Africans and African Americans was denied. A similar system of racial classification—one based on the mythical notion of a superior Aryan race—was promulgated by the Nazi regime that rose to power in Germany prior to World War II (1939–45). Nazi ideology equated Jewish people with vermin: a plague to be eradicated. The ideology of Aryan supremacy was an important propaganda weapon that helped to secure popular support for Adolf Hitler's systematic attempt to obliterate all Jewish people in a Holocaust that ultimately claimed six million lives.

Ideology and Film Analysis

How is this discussion of ideologies relevant to the cinema? As the examples above might suggest, many ideologies don't appear in official state documents. Rather, they are widely held beliefs that are maintained subtly through everyday practices and conveyed through a variety of media, including film. A film presents an attitude toward its subject matter, and always reflects a particular perspective. Ideological film critics thus contend that even apparently apolitical films made purely to entertain are not free from ideology. The values that pervade a particular culture are inevitably embedded in the films made by the writers, directors, and producers who are part of that culture and who (in most cases) are hoping to attract audiences who make up that culture.

Judd Apatow's raunchy bromance *Knocked Up* (2007) offers a salient illustration of how the most popular of films open themselves up to ideological analysis. On the surface, the film's unending stream of profanity, its explicit sexuality, and its unabashed stoner comedy seem to confirm what culture warriors on the right charge when they complain about Hollywood's supposed sex-obsessed, anti-family liberalism.

However, the film provoked a healthy debate in which a number of conservatives praised its apparent embrace of traditional values while many progressives (including its star, Katherine Heigl) condemned it for forwarding a retrograde attitude toward women. Conservative critics specifically singled out *Knocked Up*'s (along with *Juno*'s) pro-life, pro-family sensibilities. When young television producer Alison Scott (Heigl) discovers she's pregnant after a one night stand with Ben Stone (Seth Rogen)—a lovable loser stuck in a state of perpetual, stoned adolescence with his male cohorts—Alison opts to have the baby, even though her decision threatens her career in the image-obsessed media. While her friends and family suggest that she consider terminating the pregnancy, she doesn't pursue that alternative. The film's unwavering embrace of Alison's decision to carry her pregnancy to term led *New York Times* columnist Ross Douthat to proclaim that, "by marrying raunch and moralism, Apatow's movies have done the near impossible: They've made an effectively conservative message about relationships and reproduction seem relatable, funny, down-to-earth and even sexy."

It's certainly overly simplistic to say the film condemns abortion. In fact, Alison's mother, whom the film clearly depicts as a level-headed, supportive maternal figure, tries to encourage her daughter to have one. But the film does imply that starting a family is the *best* choice. In doing so, *Knocked Up* reaffirms one of the most widely-embraced of American social ideologies: the nuclear family is the ideal for which we all should strive. Not only does the film's resolution show Ben and Alison optimistically riding home together to start their new family, but Apatow depicts every family relationship as essentially a positive force (fig. **10.2**).

While the choice to construct a happy ending around Ben and Alison's blossoming romance appears to be simply a matter of rudimentary storytelling, it's important to remember that it also caters to traditional attitudes. In the process of resolving narrative conflict in such a conventional way, *Knocked Up* implicitly

10.2 The creation of a new family in *Knocked Up*.

marginalizes alternative perspectives. Those critical of the film might argue that Alison doesn't need to fret about the social or economic difficulties of raising a child as a single mother. Unlike many women facing unwanted pregnancies, Alison is, conveniently, middle class with a secure job. In fact, her decision to have the child actually pays off professionally: by the resolution she is destined to start a family with the man she loves *and* her boss opts to give her even more time in front of the camera, because, he craftily observes, television audiences love pregnancy. In romanticizing Alison's decision, the film avoids presenting the very real complications that many women in her predicament might face and so, critics argue, it never treats abortion as a serious option for Alison. Other critics might argue that the film's tidy resolution reinforces the traditional notion that single women are less effective parents than married couples.

Film scholars don't have to limit their analysis of ideological content to hot button topics. While *Knocked Up* overtly tackles thorny issues like abortion rights and family structure, it is also informed by more broadly accepted ideologies in ways that the filmmakers might not self-consciously recognize. For example, Hollywood's stories typically embrace capitalism and individualism, the two central components of the American Dream, which hold that any hardworking individual will be able to rise above humble circumstances and become successful, perhaps even famous.

Knocked Up serves as an example of the way Hollywood reiterates this ideology in story form, presenting American society as a system in which even a disadvantaged underdog can pull himself up by his bootstraps and rise to the top. Ben isn't necessarily impoverished, but he is unemployed, motivated only by his desire to smoke a little weed throughout the day and to make a quick buck on an as-yet-to-be-finished web porn site. But when Alison ditches him for being so immature, Ben finally decides to get his life in order, and without too much effort, lands a comfortable job with a firm that pays him enough money to lease his own apartment and to support his budding family. The film's resolution thus reinforces the central tenets of the American Dream: anyone is capable of improving his social and economic situation by sheer determination, and those who do not succeed simply do not work hard enough.

An opposing view—one that emphasizes that there are destructive aspects to capitalism and individualism—treats the American Dream as a myth that disregards the limitations of a society that values competition more than communal responsibility, and one in which powerful interests threaten the ability of individuals to achieve success. From this critical perspective, *Knocked Up* and other films that validate the American Dream discourage any analysis of the forces that work against class mobility, such as the power of large corporations or government entities. Rejecting capitalist individualism, this alternative standpoint presents collective activity, including political and economic organization, as the only way to achieve lasting, democratic, social change that improves the lot of all economically disadvantaged people. Tellingly, the Soviet filmmakers during Lenin's rule often avoided valorizing characters acting in isolation. In keeping with Marxism's belief in communal action, Soviet directors such as Sergei Eisenstein and V. I. Pudovkin (see pp. 217–20) tended to deflate, or negate altogether, the importance of individual action.

As the brief discussion of *Knocked Up* makes clear, an ideology is a set of values that is not necessarily shared by all Americans or by people in other cultures. Yet these values shape the way individuals think about the world around them and thus can serve as a basis for stigmatizing those who do not share the same beliefs. Ideologies are implicated in practices of social power; they are rarely neutral. Instead, we use them to divide the world into us and them (or, self and other), into the normal (those who share our ideology) and the deviant (those who are unable or uninterested in pursuing the same goals and interests).

Because movies have such a profound impact on culture, scholars and critics who consider ideology an important aspect of any film see an inherent value in thinking critically about how they shape the way we perceive ourselves and others. Jonathan Rosenbaum, a film critic who regularly incorporates discussions of cultural ideologies in his writing, explains the approach: "What is designed to make people feel good at the movies has a profound relation to how and what they think and feel about the world around them." (Rosenbaum, p. 3) If the profit-driven film industry makes money by supplying viewers with films designed to make them feel good—rather than films designed to challenge their pre-existing beliefs—then popular formulas that work again and again may both shape and confirm the way people already think. Analyzing popular films in terms of their implicit ideologies can uncover the ideas and philosophies that shape culture.

In short, critics and scholars who approach the medium with an interest in ideology recognize that Hollywood films have an enormous impact on audiences in the United States. From the 1920s through the 1950s, movies were a major socializing force in American culture, influencing the way people looked, talked, and acted (Kellner, p. 128). Hollywood's lingering influence is readily apparent in the popular attitudes and expressions that have originated in Hollywood films. Consider two examples of how the popularity of a film can transform a line of dialogue into a popular catchphrase. During the 1980s, it was virtually impossible to avoid hearing people quoting Clint Eastwood's masculine taunt ("Go ahead… make my day") from *Sudden Impact* (Eastwood 1983), or mimicking Sean Penn's laid back surfer lingo ("Awesome dude!") from *Fast Times At Ridgemont High* (Heckerling 1982). Even President Ronald Reagan adopted Eastwood's line in 1985 when he threatened congress with a veto. The fact that these lines remain embedded in our national psyche nearly thirty years after the films first appeared points to the unshakable cultural impact the cinema can have.

But Hollywood's influence extends well beyond the United States. Film scholar Miriam Hansen has argued that Hollywood cinema provided the first "global vernacular"—an everyday language through which people all over the world grapple with the contradictory experiences of modernity (Hansen, p. 68). On the one hand, Hollywood has had a "leveling impact on indigenous cultures," neutralizing local culture in a wash of homogenized Americana. But on the other hand, it has been a modern force for progressive change, advancing the possibilities of democracy by challenging "prevailing social and sexual arrangements and advanc[ing] new possibilities of social identities and cultural styles." (p. 68) For this reason, Hollywood films offer scholars and critics a wealth of opportunities for studying the ways American cinema influences ideological perspectives in the U.S. and across the globe.

The Institutional Enforcement of Ideology: The Production Code and the Anti-Communist Witch Hunts

Audiences who have grown up watching films like *Knocked Up* might take its matter-of-fact treatment of sexuality for granted. But in the decades of the 1930s to the 1960s, filmmakers weren't permitted to even mention when characters were pregnant, much less depict lovers in the midst of heated passion. The birth of Little Coyote in *Stagecoach*, for example, comes as a shock to some viewers because, throughout the first two acts, the other passengers on board refer to Lucy Mallory as "ill" instead of stating what should be obvious: she needs to get to her husband quickly because she is about to give birth. Even as she goes into labor, none of the characters explicitly states what is happening. The audience must infer what has befallen Mrs. Mallory based on roundabout details: the drunken Doc must sober up in a hurry, other passengers start to prepare "lots of hot water," and there's mention of "the stork" having visited in the night.

This prohibition against direct reference to or representation of sexuality was articulated in Hollywood's Production Code. This practice of self-censorship offers a concrete example of how filmmakers and public interest groups, aware of the profound social influence of the cinema, monitored and molded the content of the movies in order to maintain what were perceived to be the United States' normative ideologies.

Ironically, the earliest Hollywood films weren't censored. Contemporary audiences might be shocked to see brief glimpses of nudity and risqué subject matter in early studio films. A 1916 Lois Weber film, *Where Are My Children*, for example, deals frankly with the taboo subjects of birth control and abortion. In fact, today, there are countless DVDs, film screenings, and cable network specials that titillate audiences with Pre-Code Hollywood films. But in the early 1920s, the industry found itself increasingly under attack from church groups and conservative publications, which denounced the industry because of scandals relating to sexual deviance, avarice, drugs, and alcohol. In 1915, the Supreme Court had ruled that motion pictures were not part of the press and therefore not constitutionally protected from censorship. As a result, the 1920s protests sparked industry-wide anxieties that movies would soon be subject to government censorship.

In response, Hollywood established the Motion Picture Producers and Distributors of America (MPPDA), an organization designed to help the industry regulate its own content. Former Postmaster General Will Hays—a conservative who, in his own words, put his "faith in God, in folks, in the nation, and in the Republican party"—headed the organization (quoted in Maltby, p. 238). While not the equivalent of a state censor, the MPPDA did ensure that the American film industry kept supposedly subversive content in check.

Initially the MPPDA offered little in the way of rules regarding appropriate and inappropriate content. In 1927, Hays drafted a list of "Don'ts and Be Carefuls" he expected studio filmmakers to consult as they developed and scripted their pictures. The "Don'ts"—subjects that Hays deemed unacceptable "irrespective of the manner in which they were treated"—included profanity, suggestive nudity, miscegenation (i.e., interracial relationships), scenes of childbirth, and ridicule of the clergy (quoted in Maltby, p. 239). Filmmakers were encouraged to "be careful" when depicting religious ceremonies, criminal behavior, the institution of marriage, and law enforcement.

The end of the 1920s saw another public backlash against Hollywood, in part because of celebrity scandals and the growing popularity of the gangster film. In 1933, The Catholic Legion of Decency was established to condemn and boycott immoral films. The MPPDA responded by turning its list of "Don'ts and Be Carefuls" into the Production Code, a list of rules prohibiting certain images and scenarios. (The entire text of the code can be found online at www.historymatters. gmu.edu/d/5099.) The most prominent addition to the original list was a preamble that read:

1. No picture shall be produced which will lower the moral standards of those who see it. Hence the sympathy of the audience shall never be thrown to the side of crime, wrongdoing, evil or sin.
2. Correct standards of life, subject only to the requirement of drama and entertainment, shall be presented.
3. Law, natural or human, shall not be ridiculed, nor shall sympathy be created for its violation. (quoted in Maltby, p. 242)

Implicit in the preamble is the assumption that any images outside of the dominant value system could have a negative impact on audiences. Crucially, the moral standards that films were supposed to uphold were defined by conservative groups, including members of the Catholic Church.

Increasingly challenged by directors such as Otto Preminger, who defied the code and released three films in the 1950s without certificates of approval, the Production Code ceased being enforced by the mid-1960s. In 1967, Jack Valenti, President of the Motion Picture Association of America, MPAA (as the MPPDA had been renamed), instituted the ratings system, which remains in effect today. This system solved some problems; for example, filmmakers now have much more freedom to portray a wide range of sexual and violent behavior. But the ratings system raises other issues, most notably what deserves an R or an NC-17 rating. Originally meant to distinguish films with challenging adult themes from pornographic films, NC-17 is effectively an economic kiss of death for any title bearing the rating, since many theaters and media outlets refuse to screen, rent, or sell films with this rating.

In the documentary *This Film is Not Yet Rated* (2006), Kirby Dick explores the secretive practices of the MPAA ratings board, and argues that the board wields tremendous power over the depiction of sexuality. He claims the board applies a different standard when it comes to violence and sexuality. First, scenes of graphic violence are less likely to garner NC-17 ratings than scenes of graphic sex. Second, "films with scenes of gay sex receive far more restrictive ratings than films with similarly shot scenes of straight sex," (Dick, p. 5) which, Dick contends, both reflects and contributes to anti-gay sentiments in American culture.

If the history of the Production Code offers an example of the way a film industry can self-consciously create films that propagate a value system, the case of the Hollywood Blacklist illustrates how powerful political interests attempted to intimidate those working in the film industry and to determine mainstream cinema's political content.

Anti-Communist Witch Hunts and Hollywood Cinema

One case study of the intersection of history, political ideology, and cinema was the investigation of the Hollywood film industry by the U.S. Congress's House Committee on Un-American Activities (HCUA), also known as HUAC, between 1947 and 1954. In 1947 the committee, established a decade earlier to investigate Nazi propaganda, began looking into charges that Communist propaganda was infiltrating Hollywood films. Members of the film community were called on to testify before the committee and to provide names of acquaintances and co-workers whom they believed to have been Communist sympathizers: some of the individuals named were never involved with the American Communist Party, others had been members decades earlier, still others were current members. Ten Hollywood writers and directors refused to answer questions about them-selves or their friends and co-workers, citing the First Amendment, which protects the right of American citizens to participate in political organizations without penalties or restrictions, regardless of their ideological bent. The committee charged those ten individuals, who became known as the **Hollywood Ten**, with contempt of Congress and they were sentenced to six months to a year in prison. They were: Alvah Bessie, Herbert Biberman, Lester Cole, Edward Dmytryk, Ring Lardner Jr., John Howard Lawson, Albert Maltz, Samuel Ornitz, Adrian Scott, and Dalton Trumbo (fig. **10.3**).

When the contempt citations were issued, forty-eight film industry executives (including Louis B. Mayer of MGM, Harry Cohn of Columbia, Dore Schary of RKO, and Samuel Goldwyn) met at the Waldorf Astoria hotel in New York. On November 25, 1947, Eric Johnston, the president of the MPAA, released

10.3 The Hollywood Ten.

the Waldorf Statement, which named more than 300 employees in the motion picture industry who supposedly were, or had been, Communist sympathizers. The list included Charlie Chaplin, Leonard Bernstein, John Garfield, Lee Grant, Lillian Hellman, Burl Ives, Dorothy Parker, Joseph Losey, Zero Mostel, Artie Shaw, Orson Welles, and Paul Robeson. The Waldorf statement also declared that each member of the Hollywood Ten would be discharged or suspended without pay and not re-hired until he was acquitted or had declared under oath that he was not a Communist. The group of individuals whose careers and lives were interrupted or ruined became known as the **Hollywood blacklist**, although the practices of blacklisting moved beyond the initial group of names. In the Waldorf statement, the leaders of the film industry announced: "We will not knowingly employ a Communist or a member of any party or group which advocates the overthrow of the government of the United States by force or by any illegal or unconstitutional methods." (Waldorf Statement) Allegations of leftist activities were enough to raise suspicions and might cost someone their job. Moreover, in many cases people unconnected to Communism *per se*, including labor union activists and gay men and lesbians, were targeted. The events mushroomed into what many historians describe as a witch hunt because the only way to clear one's name was to sully the reputation of a friend or colleague, whether or not such accusations had any foundation in reality.

The broader social context for these events was the shift in geopolitical power after World War II. Although the Soviet Union had been a U.S. ally during the war, the Soviet regime was increasingly viewed as a threat to U.S. interests when, during the late 1940s, the USSR blockaded West Berlin, installed puppet regimes in Eastern Europe, and tested a nuclear bomb. This climate of competition and mutual suspicion became known as the Cold War. Cold War ideologies played an important role in determining U.S. domestic policies well into the 1980s, when the Soviet Union disintegrated and ceased to be a superpower. Throughout the postwar era, some American politicians, foremost among them Senator Joseph McCarthy of Wisconsin, exploited the anxieties that the Cold War provoked to attack their political enemies and to suppress dissent within the country.

HUAC's practice of relying on unfounded accusation and innuendo to cast suspicion became known as McCarthyism because of McCarthy's relentless and unethical pursuit of supposed subversive elements. The fervor of McCarthy's anti-Communist rhetoric was matched by his ability to intimidate those who questioned his tactics or sought to expose the way he destroyed the lives of innocent individuals.

Along with many other important lessons, this historical episode suggests that the entertainment industry is hardly immune to politics. Filmmakers, stars, and producers have always been involved in politics and current events—from Frank Capra's *Why We Fight* newsreels during World War II to Jerry Bruckheimer's *Profiles from the Front Line* reality television series on the Afghanistan war (which aired in 2003). The powerful executives who control media corporations today have the same vested interest in protecting their brand name as those who signed the Waldorf Statement. They are eager to align themselves with popular, or at the very least, uncontroversial, political positions. These corporate executives not only depend on the general public to consume their products, but also answer to stockholders, Wall Street financial institutions, and government agencies that have the power to affect their job security and their studio's ability to do business.

Ideology and Film Spectatorship

A lively debate has been taking place for some time regarding ideology and film spectatorship. Are viewers simply held in thrall by a "message" that a filmmaker encodes in his or her film? Are all films the equivalent of propaganda, intentionally and systematically disseminating deceptive information in order to promote an idea or cause? Inspired by cultural critic Theodor Adorno and the Frankfurt School of critical theory (1930s–1960s), some ideological critics have argued that popular films are nothing more than vacuous products of a "culture industry." In this view, films transmit only those ideas that serve the hegemonic corporate and government interests that dominate society at large and the film industry in particular. During the late 1960s, with the increasingly public protests associated with civil rights, anti-Vietnam War, anti-colonial, student, and labor movements, critics associated with British film journal *Screen* began to question this all-encompassing view. They followed in the footsteps of Marxist theoretician Louis Althusser to argue that commercial cinema does not browbeat its viewers into submission, but, instead, compels individuals into compliance with existing economic and social arrangements. The cinema, along with other social institutions such as the media, education, and religion, **interpellate** members of society by defining what it means to be an individual. Films teach viewers how to be a man, woman, citizen, lover, worker, etc.

Another group of critics in this period, including Jean-Louis Baudry and Jean-Louis Comolli, argued that the film **apparatus** itself confers ideological effects. They pointed out that the cinema's physical and mechanical attributes produce a specific form of spectatorship. Individuals sit in a darkened room as images are projected; the physical apparatus provides spectators with an all-encompassing view of the world: that of the all-knowing, all-seeing, center of the universe. The camera's use of the rules of perspective contributes to this ideological effect because it creates a virtual position at the center of the story world for the spectator to occupy. In other words, what makes the cinema such a powerful tool for conveying ideology is the very pleasure we experience when we go to the movies: the feeling of being absorbed in a fictional world that is so utterly compelling that we don't think about it being a construction. Baudry and Comolli argued that this experience encourages the audience to be passive receptacles of the ideologies on display. They asked how it would be possible to counter the ideological effects of the apparatus, to break the spell of cinema's illusionism. Their solution was that films must lay bare the way the apparatus works, in self-reflexive films that constantly remind viewers they are watching films rather than allowing them to be caught up in the magical and mythical world of the narrative.

Other critics combine these apparatus arguments with psychoanalytic theories of the human subject to discuss the way the viewers respond to films on a psychological and emotional level. A prominent psychoanalytic film theorist, Christian Metz, drew on Sigmund Freud's theories regarding the critical importance of the sexual drives in human experience and Jacques Lacan's notion concerning the centrality of the gaze to the psychological development of the individual. Metz proposed that film spectatorship induces a regression to a near-infantile state and activates primal desires associated with narcissism (self-regard) and voyeurism (the desire for another, satisfied through looking). Feminist scholars Laura Mulvey and Teresa de Lauretis drew from apparatus, psychoanalytic, and Marxist film theorists to propose that the narrative structure of popular cinema itself, not merely its subject matter or the physical apparatus, reinforces a particular ideology: the male-dominated patriarchal system on which Western cultures are traditionally based. Mulvey argued that mainstream narrative cinema repeatedly places active male characters at the center of quest narratives in which they are rewarded for acting on their desires; by contrast, women characters are put on display as visual objects and they are punished for expressing their desires. For Mulvey, the cinema supplies the viewer with visual pleasure by providing opportunities for narcissistic identifications with the male protagonists, as well as satisfying voyeuristic desires with the spectacle of female bodies.

Since these lively debates of the 1970s, the range of topics in ideological criticism has expanded to include studies of race, sexuality, age, national identity, and disability, among other subjects. Film scholars no longer characterize the cinema as an agent of total repression and generally reject the idea that there is one identifiable "message" that emanates from popular films. Most critics agree that even a single film can incorporate contradictory ideologies.

Thus, scholars and critics don't just assume films reinforce dominant ideologies. They also analyze how some films go "against the grain," or, subtly question mainstream beliefs. For example, in an analysis of Billy Wilder's *Double Indemnity* (1944), James Naremore argues that, rather than contributing to the patriotic fervor of a country embroiled in World War II, this *film noir* actually presents a pessimistic view of American capitalism. The film concerns an insurance salesman, Walter Neff (Fred MacMurray), who participates in an ill-fated plot to help Phyllis Dietrichson (Barbara Stanwyck) murder her husband. Naremore discusses how Wilder's background as a German *émigré* influenced by Expressionism shaped the film's visual style and its critical perspective on the supposed advantages of modern American life, including the availability of manufactured consumer products. Wilder's take on America transforms the landscape of modern life into an alienating terrain, where the main characters' plan to murder a man to collect on his life insurance policy seems to reflect more broadly the life-numbing effects of an entire culture based on materialism:

> The theme of industrialized dehumanization is echoed in the relatively private offices on the second floor of the insurance company, which are almost interchangeable, decorated with nothing more than statistical charts and graphs. [...] The public world is equally massified: when Walter realizes that Phyllis wants to murder her husband,

he drinks a beer in his car at the drive-in restaurant; then he goes to the bowling alley at Third and Weston, where he bowls alone in an enormous room lined with identical lanes. (Naremore, p. 89)

Wilder's depiction of a supermarket—the epitome of a place where American goods are on display, readily available for mass consumption—shows it to be a space where products and people become anonymous (fig. **10.4**).

> Walter and Phyllis hold *sotto voce* conversations across aisles filled with baby food, beans, macaroni, tomatoes, and seemingly anything else that can be packaged and arranged in neat rows; they talk about murder in public, but the big store makes them anonymous, virtually invisible shoppers. (Naremore, p. 89)

Finally, Naremore points to the way Wilder's *mise en scène* likens the *femme fatale* to a manufactured product.

> [Phyllis] is blatantly provocative and visibly artificial; her ankle bracelet, her lacquered lipstick, her sunglasses, and above all her chromium hair give her a cheaply manufactured, metallic look. In keeping with this synthetic quality, her sex scenes are almost robotic, and she reacts to murder with icy calm. (Naremore, p. 89)

In his detailed analysis, Naremore studies how the cinematic elements of the film —specifically, the narrative, the sound, and the *mise en scène*—all coalesce to reflect an ideological position, which runs counter to America's dominant values.

Recent scholarly interest in spectatorship further complicates assumptions about the cinema being a monolithic tool of the power structure. Stuart Hall, Dick Hedbidge, Jacqueline Bobo, and Angela McRobbie, among others, have convincingly argued that film viewers are not passive receptacles but active participants who help to construct a film's meaning(s). Ideological critics may study the experiences of audience members, to the extent that those experiences are accessible through survey techniques or historical data. Reception studies research clearly shows that not every audience member responds to the same film in the same way. Viewers sometimes align themselves with the dominant cultural values expressed in a film, but in some circumstances they can and do question, resist, and reject those ideologies.

Following this tack, some critics study how films contain moments that appear to complicate inadvertently their central ideological thrust, leaving "fissures" for audiences to make alternative interpretations that undermine the film's otherwise apparent endorsement of dominant cultural beliefs.

Robin Wood performs this kind of analysis on Frank Capra's *It's a Wonderful Life* (1946), a film that, on the surface, reaffirms small town American

10.4 Planning murder amidst the supermarket's cornucopia in *Double Indemnity*.

values. In the film, George Bailey (James Stewart) spends his whole life sacrificing his dreams to help others. Despite his urge to travel the world, George marries, spends his life in his small home town of Bedford Falls, and runs his father's building and loan business. When he loses $8,000 because of an employee's forgetfulness and a rival banker's duplicity, he becomes despondent, resentful, and suicidal. A guardian angel intervenes and shows George what life in Bedford Falls would have been like without him. Run by the corrupt banker Potter, the town is full of vice, bars, and unhappiness. The angel Clarence inspires George to return to his family. On his return, he finds the entire community has pooled its resources to help replace the lost money.

On one level, the film emphasizes George's recommitment to family and middle-class values. Its wholesome evocation of the promise that American society can always overcome any snags in its capitalist economy is so emotionally resonant that *It's a Wonderful Life* has become an unavoidable staple of holiday season celebrations in the United States. But, Wood points out, by depicting an alternative, equally viable *film noir*-style Bedford Falls, the film exposes the unpleasant realities underneath the idealized small town world that George embraces in the conclusion.

> *It's a Wonderful Life* manages a convincing and moving
> affirmation of the values (and value) of bourgeois family life.
> Yet what is revealed, when disaster releases George's suppressed
> tensions, is the intensity of his resentment of the family and desire
> to destroy it—and with it, in significant relationship, his work (his
> culminating action is furiously to overthrow the drawing board with
> his plans for more small-town houses). [...] What is finally striking
> about the film's affirmation is the extreme precariousness of its
> basis [...]. [The film] may well be Capra's masterpiece, but it is
> more than that. Like all the greatest American films—fed by a com-
> plex generic tradition and, *beyond that, by the fears and aspirations
> of a whole culture—it at once transcends its director and would be
> inconceivable without him*. (Wood, pp. 295–6, emphasis added)

Wood ascribes a latent pessimism to the film's surface optimism. In other words, he reads the film as a critique of the American middle class because it draws attention to a whole culture's suppressed feelings of entrapment, paranoia, and dread that accompany the American Dream. Whereas James Naremore's analysis of *Double Indemnity* assumes a certain degree of intentionality on director Billy Wilder's part, Wood emphasizes that the critique embedded in *It's a Wonderful Life* is the product of cultural forces beyond Capra's control. The film embodies the anxieties of a culture that are provoked by its dominant ideology—ironically, an ideology the film intends to reinforce.

The discussions of film and ideology that make up the remainder of this chapter make specific reference to American cultural history. The scope of analysis is intentionally limited because ideologies tend to be culturally specific and it is usually inappropriate to generalize across such boundaries. Moreover, the discussions presented here are illustrative rather than exhaustive: readers are invited to explore additional topics for which ideological criticism is relevant.

Topics in Ideological Criticism

As the chapter thus far might indicate, approaching film using an ideological approach opens up many possibilities for analyzing what films make us think about, and how. What follows is a brief introduction to some fruitful topics in ideological criticism. By no means is this list exhaustive, but it does explore some important arenas in film studies.

One of the assumptions that unifies this seemingly disparate collection of topics—race, gender, sexuality, and disability in the cinema—is that filmmakers are inevitably faced with the need to represent characters from many different walks of life. Ideological critics often begin their analysis by studying how filmmakers represent characters with countervailing lifestyles and worldviews. For example, one way to identify ideologies is by investigating the way films rely on stereotypes to represent people and belief systems outside the mainstream. Stereotypes are oversimplified images that stimulate or reinforce beliefs about groups of people. These oversimplified representations reduce a wide range of differences among individuals to simplistic categorizations; they transform assumptions about groups of people into "realities"; they justify the position of those in power; and they perpetuate social prejudice and inequality. Furthermore, groups being stereotyped generally have little influence over the way various media represent them ("Media Stereotyping"). For example, Donald Bogle argues that the history of African-American characters in the cinema can be boiled down into a few choice stereotypes, including "Toms," "Coons," "Mammies," "Mulattoes," and "Bucks." Vito Russo's *The Celluloid Closet* does the same for gay men and lesbians, identifying Hollywood cinema's frequent depictions of gay men as effeminate and emotionally unstable sissies and of lesbians as predatory diesel dykes.

Frequently those outside the mainstream aren't stereotyped as much as they are ignored altogether. Often a film's ideology is made apparent by what's *not* in the film (i.e., what types of people are not represented) as by what is. As the following topics make clear, the long-running absence of particular types of characters reveals an unspoken, perhaps unselfconscious disregard for some groups' social value and importance.

Racial Ideology and American Cinema

In 2008, *Iron Man* (Jon Favreau) was the superhero of the summer. But in a blistering review, Cristobal Giraldez Catalan panned the film for taking the usual Hollywood tack: propping up the heroics of white, male characters, while simultaneously minimizing, belittling, or demonizing characters of color: "A black actor in a supporting role, ostensibly privileged as the high-ranking Colonel James, turns out to be [...] a tumor on Stark's persona to be subtly belittled and hushed throughout. [...] The Middle Eastern Doctor Yinsen (Shaun Toub), who thrice saves Stark's life, is the racial other, a shaking, hallowed other who also serves Stark's every request and demand." Catalan continues, arguing that in order to position the main character, Tony Stark (Robert Downey Jr) as its heroic center, *Iron Man* relies on a very conventional binary in which people of color are either vicious thugs or helpless primitives who rely on a white man ("even one who makes weapons of mass destruction") to rescue them (fig. **10.5**).

Catalan's compelling argument makes it clear that scholars and critics still interrogate how and what the cinema teaches its audiences about racial difference. This sort of interrogation reminds readers that America's attitudes about race have been informed by a long, vexed history of slavery and oppression.

10.5 White man as hero in *Iron Man*.

The ideology of white supremacy that underwrote chattel slavery and Jim Crow laws has been apparent in American films and in the Hollywood film industry throughout its history. Perhaps the most remarked-on example of a film that embodies racist ideologies is D.W. Griffith's *The Birth of a Nation*, a Civil War epic based on the *The Klansman* and *The Leopard's Spots*, written by Thomas Dixon.

While often studied as an important example of early narrative film because of Griffith's masterful grasp of storytelling techniques, this melodrama of two families' experiences during and after the Civil War concludes with a celebration of the establishment of the Ku Klux Klan by white Southerners during Reconstruction. The view that Griffith's family saga presents is that Klan violence is a necessary response to the growing social and political power of former slaves. The rule of law has supposedly begun to deteriorate as African Americans come to dominate the South Carolina legislature, visualized in a demeaning "historical tableau" that depicts the notion of black political efficacy as utterly inconceivable (fig. **10.6**). In Griffith's film, the threat of Klan violence—and, specifically, lynchings—is the only way to protect white Southern women from newly emboldened African-American men, who are invariably characterized as rapists. In general, Griffith's film depicts African-American characters as foolish, servile, or menacing, and the white characters, with a few exceptions, as noble and courageous. (The one ignoble white character in Griffith's film is a politician who advocates racial equality, but has ulterior motives for doing so.)

10.6 The demeaning tableau of the South Carolina legislature in *The Birth of a Nation*.

Owing to the racial segregation in the film industry at the time that *The Birth of a Nation* was filmed, most of the African-American characters—and all of those who would come into contact with white female actors— were played by white actors in blackface. The blackface minstrel tradition itself carries connotations of white supremacist ideology because minstrelsy involved the overt representation of blacks—played by white performers with black makeup on—as lazy and ignorant.

10.7 *(above)* The lynching of an innocent family in *Within Our Gates*.

10.8 *(below)* Threatening white male sexuality in *Within Our Gates*.

Many Hollywood films reinforce the idea of racial hierarchy in less obvious ways. First, most classical Hollywood films revolve exclusively around the concerns of white characters because their struggles are presumed to be both appealing and universally accessible to all audiences. Second, until the 1970s, the depiction of African Americans was compromised by racist stereotyping. Hattie McDaniel's roles in *The Little Colonel* (David Butler 1935) and *Gone With the Wind*, for example, reinforced one entrenched stereotype of black femininity: the nurturing but feisty Mammy, a caretaker who unselfishly ministers to the needs of white folks above all else (fig. **10.1**).

Griffith famously screened *The Birth of a Nation* for President Woodrow Wilson, a white Southerner who was reported to have praised the film's veracity, saying, "it is like writing history with lightning. And my only regret is that it is all so terribly true." (Recently scholars have asserted that Thomas Dixon fabricated the remark for publicity purposes.)

Griffith's "history" is an emotionally incendiary melodrama that ratified the belief that free African Americans posed a threat to the white population. Reaffirming the argument that ideologies in films have an impact on spectators, the 1915 release of *The Birth of a Nation* has been linked to a revival of the Ku Klux Klan organization, whose numbers had been languishing for more than a decade.

Griffith's film met with a cinematic rejoinder from an African-American perspective, however. The NAACP (National Association for the Advancement of Colored People) organized public protests. Oscar Micheaux, a former Pullman porter who became a novelist and filmmaker, wrote and directed *Within Our Gates* (1920). Micheaux had directed the first African-American feature film, *The Homesteader* (1919), and would go on to direct more than forty films between 1919 and 1948. *Within Our Gates* explicitly contradicts Griffith's history of the American South with a story of a young, educated African-American woman named Sylvia Landry (Evelyn Preer), who returns to her home in the South after a failed engagement, in order to help educate black children. Micheaux presents a world in which white power prevails, to the detriment of innocent African Americans. In one tragic scene, a white mob composed of men, women, and children celebrates the lynching of an innocent black man, woman, and child (fig. **10.7**). (The young son manages to escape the horrific fate of his parents.) The film not only depicts lynching in a distinctly non-heroic manner, but it also points to the threatening aspects of white male sexuality, as Sylvia is nearly raped by a white man who, unbeknownst to both of them at the time of the attack, turns out to be her father (fig. **10.8**).

Within Our Gates was shown to predominantly black audiences, often at white-owned theaters whose managers allowed Micheaux to screen films for black audiences at midnight; these events were called "midnight rambles." Independent films such as these, made by and for black audiences, came to be known as race films; they spanned a variety of genres and were produced until the 1950s. Race films provided black audiences with images of African-American experiences; they also had the goal of uplifting the race by countering the ideologies of white supremacy and its tangible effects. Yet, because many race films rely on Hollywood genres and character types, they are not always socially progressive, argues film scholar Jacqueline Stewart (Golus). In other words, the racist ideologies associated with American culture and mainstream cinema may even infiltrate films made by African Americans for African-American audiences—a point that becomes salient to the discussion below of the black action films of the 1970s.

In keeping with American culture's racial hierarchy, race films have not been valued by most film historians in the same way that films by white Hollywood directors have been. As Joseph Worrell writes, they are "difficult to situate in history, [so] it was convenient to ignore race filmmaking as an aesthetic or political practice." (Worrell) Most of Oscar Micheaux's films have been lost or destroyed; *Within Our Gates* was presumed to be lost until a copy was found in 1990 in the Filmoteca Español in Madrid, Spain, and was restored by the Library of Congress.

During the 1950s and 1960s, the era of the Civil Rights Movement, shifting ideologies of racial difference gradually made an impact on Hollywood cinema. Until the 1970s, the film industry denied African Americans membership in technical guilds and, as Melvin Donaldson notes, the lack of an economic base in the industry prevented African Americans from directing Hollywood films until the late 1960s (Donalson, p. 5). In Hollywood films, the first indication of changes in ideologies of race came about through the star system, as black actors and actresses began to achieve success in films made for white audiences.

During the 1960s, Sidney Poitier broke through the racial barrier in mainstream Hollywood films to become a huge star. He became the first African American man to win an Academy Award in a competitive category for his performance as Homer Smith, a wandering handyman who helps a small order of nuns build a chapel in *Lilies of the Field* (Ralph Nelson 1963).

The elegant Bahamian-raised Poitier's star persona developed across a series of subsequent films. He played educated, middle-class, upwardly mobile professionals in predominantly white cultural contexts in *A Patch of Blue* (Guy Green 1965), *To Sir With Love* (James Clavell 1967), *In the Heat of the Night* (Norman Jewison 1967), and *Guess Who's Coming to Dinner* (Stanley Kramer 1967). Kramer's award-winning drama, a social problem film depicting the liberal white parents' response to their daughter's interracial romance, epitomizes the way Hollywood directors represented Poitier in an idealized and often de-sexualized manner in order to ensure the acceptance of white audiences. Poitier plays Dr. John Wade Prentice, an accomplished medical doctor from Switzerland who has pioneered life-saving treatments in Africa and who convinces his fiancée Joey (Katherine Houghton) to wait until they are married to begin their sexual relationship (fig. **10.9**). Although the film's approach to its subject matter may seem tame by current standards, interracial marriage was illegal in seventeen U.S.

10.9 *Guess Who's Coming to Dinner*, one of many films that featured Sydney Poitier in an idealized way.

states until 1967, the year of the film's release, and the film's liberal perspective was controversial.

Whereas Poitier's sanitized characters represent an attempt on the part of major studios to endorse racial integration and to construct a version of black male sexuality that would be palatable for white audiences, Paula Massood points out that televized images of black resistance to police brutality during the Watts riots of 1965 "redefined the images of African Americans on screen for both blacks and whites." (Massood, p. 22) The response of African-American filmmakers to this development did anything but appease the sensibilities of white audiences. The popularity of Ossie Davis's *Cotton Comes to Harlem* (1970), which follows the exploits of rough and ready Harlem police officers named Gravedigger Jones and Coffin Ed Johnson, and Melvin Van Peebles's *Sweet Sweetback's Baadasssss Song* (1971), about a black hustler who becomes politicized and resists capture by a corrupt Los Angeles police force, ignited a cycle of action films featuring African-American characters with attitude, including *Shaft* (Gordon Parks 1971), *Superfly* (Gordon Parks Jr. 1972), *Coffy* (Jack Hill 1973), *Black Caesar* (Larry Cohen 1973), and *Foxy Brown* (Jack Hill 1974), among others.

These **blaxploitation** films—whose name indicates the combination of black characters and the low-budget action aesthetic of earlier exploitation cinemas—celebrated black power and resistance to dominant white culture rather than promoting the benefits of racial integration. In this way, the films echoed the political program of black activists of the era, including Malcolm X and the Black Panther Party. Films such as *Shaft* (fig. **10.10**) and *Superfly* depict thoughtful, sexually magnetic African-American men who use their wits and their physical prowess to outmaneuver their antagonists. Although blaxploitation grew out of the black independent filmmaking tradition, the popularity of these films attracted filmmakers whose primary interest was box office receipts. As a result, blaxploitation evolved into a series of formulaic films that seemed merely to reiterate stereotypes of black aggression. In a move that suggests the complexity of racial ideologies in cinema, the NAACP (which had, decades earlier, protested Griffith's *The Birth of a Nation*), combined with black civil rights groups like the Southern Christian Leadership Conference to form the Coalition Against Blaxploitation; the coalition protested the fact that these supposedly black-oriented films all too frequently reduced African Americans to outlaws, pimps, drug dealers, and prostitutes.

During the 1970s, a new generation of independent filmmakers, including Charles Burnett, Julie Dash, and Haile Gerima, focused explicitly on countering the ideological content of mainstream films. Collectively known as the L.A. School or the L.A. Rebellion, these directors "were interested in deconstructing Hollywood's ideological Prisonhouse," drawing on the Black Arts movement in the U.S. as well as various alternative filmmaking styles, including Italian neorealism, French New Wave cinema, Cuban Cinema, and Brazil's Cinema

Novo (Massood, p. 23). Their interest in experimenting with the traditional form of narrative fiction filmmaking—not merely the subject matter—reiterates the notion presented earlier that ideologies are perpetuated by the form as well as the content of narrative cinema. Throughout the 1980s, 1990s, and 2000s, African-American filmmakers have made further inroads into both mainstream and independent filmmaking, including Spike Lee, John Singleton, Albert and Allen Hughes, Reginald and Warrington Hudlin, Carl Franklin, and Tyler Perry. During the 1980s and 1990s, films focusing on inner city urban neighborhoods, including *Do the Right Thing*, *Boyz n the Hood* (John Singleton 1991), *New Jack City* (Mario van Peebles 1991), *Straight out of Brooklyn* (Matty Rich 1991), and *Menace to Society* (Albert and Allen Hughes 1993) once again ignited a debate about the impact of films that may unintentionally reiterate stereotypes of African American violence.

10.10 The quintessential 1970s black action hero: *Shaft*.

As this brief discussion suggests, historical practices of racial exclusion are important to consider when examining the way American films represent dominant culture and minority cultures. Ideological criticism now encompasses critiques of Hollywood's representation of African American, Latino/a, Asian-American and Native American people and their cultures. Furthermore, scholars have begun to address conventional representations of whiteness as well. A 2006 University of Minnesota study examining perceptions of racial identity revealed that white Americans are aware of their racial identity and are aware that it provides them with advantages relative to individuals of other racial groups. Film scholars Richard Dyer and Diane Negra, among others, have explored the way that whiteness has been constructed through films, marketing campaigns, and the development and promotion of star personas.

Gender and Cinema

Gender ideologies inform the operation of the industry and shape the kinds of stories that are told, and who gets to tell them.

The view that profound differences exist between men and women has influenced American culture for centuries, justifying laws and practices that have denied women autonomy and barred them from positions of social and economic power. Whereas some evolutionary biologists claim that males and females are not only different, but are the opposite of one another, in reality, men and women are more alike than they are different: they share 99 percent of the same DNA. Further, there is a great deal of variation within these two groups, not just between them.

Historically, the notion that men are superior to women, or that masculinity is normative and femininity is pathological, has prevailed in many societies. In patriarchies—societies whose laws and customs prohibit women from participating as full citizens—men exercise power and authority over all others. Women are prevented from exercising their rights to self-determination, often on the grounds that it is "unnatural" for them to do so. Patriarchal social practices range from women's exclusion from political life (women were not permitted to vote in the U.S. until 1918; in 2006, a record number of women served in the U.S. Congress, but accounted for less than 16 percent of the total), to economic inequities (women earned 77 percent of their male counterparts in 2005), to exclusion from civic activities (women were barred from serving in combat in the U.S. military until 1991), to the circulation of stereotypes (for example, the common but unsubstantiated claim that women are bad drivers).

The fact that women are underrepresented in Hollywood became a widespread topic of discussion after several studios hired women as executives in the early 2000s without a discernible increase in women's overall participation in the industry. In fact, women participated in filmmaking at much greater rates during the earliest years of cinema. More than 100 women directed films during the 1910s and 1920s; the most notable among them were Alice Guy Blachè, Lois Weber, and Mabel Normand. Yet only two women directors emerged during the Hollywood studio era: Dorothy Arzner and Ida Lupino. A study by Martha Lauzen of San Diego State University revealed that, in 2005, women made up only 7 percent of directors (a decline from a historical high of 11 percent in 2000) and 17 percent of directors, producers, screenwriters, cinematographers, and editors on the top 250 Hollywood films (Lauzen).

Ideologies of gender that adversely affect women's participation in the film industry also inform the kind of stories told in Hollywood films. Feminist critics Margery Rosen, who wrote *Popcorn Venus* (1973), and Molly Haskell, who wrote film reviews for *The Village Voice* and published *From Reverence to Rape* (1974), criticized the stereotyped depiction of women onscreen. At about the same time, Laura Mulvey broke the ground for feminist film theory in scholarly circles, arguing that Hollywood films offered narratives centering on male protagonists whose primary activities involved investigating and punishing women, whose difference from men threatened male spectators as well as screen characters. Mulvey's work gave rise to the field of feminist film theory—an area whose practitioners continue to forward a critique of the representations of women in mainstream films, to explore forgotten or unacknowledged work by women filmmakers, and to develop theories of gendered spectatorship.

A basic premise that serves as a good starting point for studying feminist film criticism is the argument that the vast majority of films invite audiences to identify with male characters. In classical movies, men do the action and propel the plot forward. Women are passive. They are objects of desire, looked at and pursued by male protagonists. They motivate

10.11 Two machines: two clearly defined genders in *Wall-E*.

action in men (for example, they land themselves in dire situations and need to be rescued), but rarely undertake action themselves. Classical films typically paint women who *are* active agents, such as the *femme fatale* in *film noir*, as threatening and destructive.

The foundational work in feminist criticism may have developed during the 1970s, but ideologies of gender remain an important subject within film studies. Recent accounts by scholars such as Peter Lehman, David Gerstner, and Yvonne Tasker examine and critique the way films characterize (and enforce) ideologies of masculinity.

A brief discussion of *Wall-E* demonstrates how studying any film from a feminist perspective can open it up to new and thought-provoking interpretations. At first glance *Wall-E* might seem an inappropriate choice for the feminist critic, since it is an animated children's film that isn't explicitly about gender roles, but rather develops as a humorous critique of human consumption. But, in fact, it is precisely because *Wall-E* is a popular entertainment, which most audiences watch with an uncritical eye, that makes it a ripe subject for a feminist scholar interested in contemplating how films facilitate the socialization of gender roles.

To begin, despite the fact that the two central characters are robots, they are clearly coded as male and female. The film begins on a desolate planet Earth, years after humans have abandoned the planet because it can no longer sustain life. The lone Wall-E wanders empty streets collecting the odd knick-knacks humanity has left behind: clothing, videos, machinery. One day, a mysterious spaceship leaves behind another robot, Eve, who becomes the object of Wall-E's persistent affection. Initially stand-offish, eventually Eve warms up and the two fall in love. Crucially, the two central characters speak only a few words, yet audiences immediately recognize their genders, which are constructed around visual and behavioral cues that trade on shared assumptions about masculinity and femininity. He is rugged and ragged: dirty, square, and mechanically oriented. She is dainty: clean, sleekly curvaceous, and maternal (fig. **10.11**). As her name implies, her sole purpose is to find and collect the first sign of new life on Earth, and when she discovers a small seedling, she stores it in her midsection. She is literally destined to nurture life in the electronic equivalent of a womb.

Furthermore, the interplay between Wall-E and Eve still exhibits the familiar gender dynamics that feminist critics in the 1970s and 1980s singled out as being integral to the Hollywood style. Wall-E is the audience's point of identification (i.e., he is the main character), and plays the active role in shaping the plot. Eve, on the other hand, is the mysterious object of desire who motivates the male lead, but who remains essentially passive herself: she is literally deposited on the planet and proceeds to cover the terrain involuntarily. Wall-E finds himself entranced by this sexy—but cold and mysteriously unavailable—"woman," and thus the remainder of the film revolves around his efforts to woo her and, later, to rescue her when the space ship that deposited her returns once again only to snatch her away. Eventually the two play more of a cooperative role protecting one another and ensuring that life returns to Earth, but Wall-E instigates this action. And while both Wall-E and Eve must rescue one another at different points in the story, the manner in which they do so only reinforces the male = active/female = passive dynamic. Wall-E risks his life, so to speak, for

Eve. On the other hand, when Wall-E's memory and personality get erased, she need only give him an erotically charged nuzzle to restore his identity. He acts, and she is acted upon. Wall-E is, to be blunt, Eve's knight in shining armor for the post-Apocalyptic age.

These observations point to larger, unanswered questions for the feminist film scholar. To what degree does repeating these familiar representations of male and female encourage audiences to accept essentialist arguments about gender roles? Does the film offer audience members any opportunities for broadening their concept of gendered behavior? For example, does the fact that Wall-E is a connoisseur of classic Hollywood musicals complicate traditional notions about masculine taste? Or does the film simply reinforce age-old stereotypes?

One of the central agendas behind the rise of feminist film criticism was, quite simply, to establish an intellectual movement that would generate more demand for a wider array of roles and professional opportunities for women of all ages, shapes, and sizes in the industry. Katherine Heigl's comments about her role in *Knocked Up* point to ways in which the mainstream has absorbed the once radical feminist scholarship of the 1970s. Heigl complained that the movie is "a little sexist. It paints the women as shrews, as humorless and uptight, and it paints the men as lovable, goofy, fun-loving guys. ... I had a hard time with it, on some days. I'm playing such a bitch; why is she being such a killjoy?" (qtd. in O'Rourke). The fact that the star of a popular film could express her concerns is some measure of how feminist criticism has moved beyond the corridors of academia and has indeed inspired a more broadly realized consciousness about the lingering stereotypes used to portray women onscreen.

Another development that accompanied the feminist critique of mainstream films—and which grew out of the women's liberation movement more generally—was the feminist filmmaking movement. In 1971, thirty-six feminist films were produced; by the end of the decade, more than 250 were made every year (Rosenberg, p. 17). Documentary films were prized as offering antidotes to the unreal women manufactured by Hollywood. Film scholar Julia LeSage argued that feminist documentaries incorporate the practice of consciousness-raising in their formal organization and politicize the personal experiences of the women subjects they document. (The work of many independent women filmmakers is available through Women Make Movies [www.wmm.com], a multicultural non-profit organization that supports women's filmmaking and distributes films.) During the 1980s, several women directors began their careers in feature films as well, including Jane Campion (*Sweetie* 1989), Amy Heckerling (*Fast Times at Ridgemont High* 1982), Kathryn Bigelow (*Near Dark* 1987), Penelope Spheeris (*The Decline of Western Civilization* 1981), and Alison

10.12 In *Orlando*, the title character refuses to adhere to society's gender roles.

Anders (*Border Radio* 1987). Even singer and actress Barbra Streisand tried her hand at directing (*Yentl* 1983).

One important international director to emerge from the feminist film movement is the writer, director, dancer, and performance artist Sally Potter. Her formally challenging works include her debut film, *Thriller* (1979) a contemporary revision of Puccini's opera *La Bohème* that adopts the style of *film noir* to examine the victimization of women in fiction. Potter's best-known work is *Orlando* (1992), a film based on Virginia Woolf's novel about a character who refuses to conform to the ordinary rules of existence, particularly those of gender. In the film, as in the book, Orlando begins life as a man but is transformed into a woman (fig. **10.12**). Potter has written: "it is Orlando's unwillingness to conform to what is expected of him as a man that leads—within the logic of the film—to his change of sex. Later, of course, as a woman, Orlando finds that she cannot conform to what is expected of her as a female either." (Potter, "Notes") Like the work of many feminist filmmakers, Potter's film moves beyond a focus on gender to critique the British class system as well. Echoing the ideas of feminist film theorists such as Laura Mulvey regarding the question of visual "pleasure" for feminist filmmakers and spectators, Potter makes a distinction between the intellectual and aesthetic pleasures that cinema is rightly able to provide—"hard earned by hard work"—versus "the kind of 'pleasing' that is dangerous [...] where we don't dare say what we really think, or don't make the work with courage, or don't go far enough or aim high enough. Sometimes it is important to accept not being liked, not pleasing with niceness, with conformity or even with modesty." (Potter, "Response")

Men direct most Hollywood films. However, women continue to be an increasingly visible presence in the director's chair. Scholars should appreciate that these women don't limit their work to dealing just with "women's issues." After directing Hilary Swank's breakout, Oscar-winning performance as a woman passing as a man in *Boys Don't Cry*, Kimberly Pierce tackled the subject of combat in Iraq from the male perspective in *Stop Loss* (2008), Indy wunderkind Kelly Reichardt has explored the intimacies of male bonding in *Old Joy* (2006) and the touching relationship between an out of work wanderer and her dog in *Wendy and Lucy* (2008; fig. **10.13**). Hit maker Nancy Meyers has made a career out of directing light-hearted romantic comedies such as *Something's Gotta Give* (2003) and *It's Complicated* (2008). By point of comparison, Kathryn Bigelow has spent nearly three decades carving out a niche as a purveyor of action films full of exciting, tightly choreographed sequences. Her film *The Hurt Locker* (fig. **10.14**), about a military company of bomb defusers, earned near universal acclaim as the best of the first

10.13 Loving companions—*Wendy and Lucy*.

10.14 The Oscar-winning male action film, *The Hurt Locker*.

wave of films dealing with the American involvement in Iraq. By combining eye-popping action with a thoughtful portrait of male codes of honor under pressure, Bigelow earned herself an Oscar for Best Director in 2010, becoming the first woman to be recognized in this way.

In short, thanks to the inroads made by the feminist movement in academia and filmmaking in the 1970s, women have gradually become a more visible presence behind the camera as in front of it. And while some might assume that women filmmakers would focus their attention on issues that solely relate to questions about gender, the all-too-brief list above should indicate that their approaches to filmmaking are as wide and varied as those of their male counterparts.

Sexuality and Cinema

Ideologies of sexuality attempt to make sense of, and implicitly to regulate, sexual choices and practices. For much of the twentieth century, only two sexual orientations were recognized—heterosexual (straight) and homosexual (gay or lesbian); the former was considered normal and the latter deviant. Being gay or lesbian was not only stigmatized, but also criminalized. Individuals have been, and continue to be, fired from their jobs, involuntarily institutionalized, jailed, physically assaulted, and even murdered because they are, or are perceived to be, gay or lesbian, bisexual or transgendered.

Historians such as Martin Duberman, Martha Vicinus, and George Chauncey argue that gay and lesbian culture has been hidden from history, and film scholar Vito Russo coined the term the "celluloid closet" to refer to the fact that Hollywood films rarely depict gay and lesbian protagonists. During Hollywood's heyday, the Production Code's section II.4 stated, "Sex perversion or any inference to it is forbidden" ("Production Code of 1930"). Throughout the era of studio Hollywood, gay and lesbian stars remained in the closet as well, sometimes dating or marrying members of the opposite sex in order to maintain for the public the illusion of heterosexuality.

Yet contemporary film scholarship by Richard Dyer, Patricia White, and Richard Barrios reveals that gay and lesbian characters make numerous appearances in cinema history, although mainstream films tend to treat characters and situations that depart from the heterosexual norm with subtle encoding. Gay and lesbian characters often function as plot devices that affirm the heterosexual coupling that occurs with great regularity at the conclusion of Hollywood films. Frequently, alternative sexualities and gender play are meant to provoke humor or pity. A case in point is the American Film Institute's list of the 100 greatest comedies. The first two titles are films whose plots involve male cross-dressing: *Some Like it Hot* (Billy Wilder 1959) and *Tootsie* (Sydney Pollack 1982).

Although the representation of gays and lesbians in early cinema probably seems more obvious to viewers in the twenty-first century than it did in the early twentieth century, the humor of many early film comedies depended on the audience's ability to recognize gay stereotypes (Gagne). The Edison film *The Gay Brothers* (1895), directed by Thomas Dickson, is considered by some to be the first representation of gay men in cinema: it is a short film that depicts two men waltzing. Other films, including those by German directors G.W. Pabst (*Pandora's Box* ["*Die Büchse der Pandora* "; 1929]) and Leontine Sagan (*Girls in Uniform* ["*Mädchen in Uniform*"; 1931]) unapologetically depict fully developed lesbian love stories. Readers (and film scholars) interested in the historical representation of gays and lesbians thus have a wide range of films to examine, including some that subtly encode gay and lesbian desires and some that depict them overtly. One consideration for readers pursuing historical research on sexual ideologies and practices and cinema is the shifting social understanding of sexual identities; as with racial and gender identities, concepts of sexuality differ across historical periods and cultural contexts. In the late nineteenth and early twentieth centuries in the U.S., for example, heterosexuality and homosexuality were not understood as defining an identity, as they tend to be understood today.

Because the Production Code strictly limited the depiction of alternative sexualities during the height of studio Hollywood (1930–60), it is far more common to find explicit references to gay and lesbian sexualities in independent and underground filmmaking. Kenneth Anger (discussed in Chapter 9), Gregory Markopolous, Jack Smith, and Paul Morrissey (who made a number of the films that were credited to Andy Warhol), among others, documented the dreams, fantasies, and lifestyles of people who were consigned to, or in many cases sought out, the margins of respectable culture. With the breakdown of the studio system by the mid-1960s, and the abandonment of the Production Code in favor of the ratings system in 1968, gay and lesbian subject matter slowly infiltrated mainstream cinema.

As with the civil rights and women's movements, the late 1960s period represented a watershed moment for gay rights. During a police raid on the Stonewall Inn bar in New York on June 28, 1969, the bar's patrons—largely drag queens—fought back. This rebellious show of community solidarity ignited the movement to assert the rights of gays and lesbians (and often is marked by Gay Pride parades during the month of June). The next decade in cinema witnessed a spate of feature films in which lesbian, gay, bisexual, and transgender characters occupy central positions—including *Midnight Cowboy* (John Schlesinger 1969),

10.15 *(left)* The romantic comedy *Go Fish*.

10.16 *(below)* *Far from Heaven* revisits the 1950s melodramas of Douglas Sirk.

Boys in the Band (William Friedkin 1970), *Dog Day Afternoon* (Sidney Lumet 1975), *Cruising* (William Friedkin 1980), *Personal Best* (Robert Towne 1982), and *Lianna* (John Sayles 1982). Critics have argued that these films may have upgraded gay and lesbian characters from mere supporting roles, but they also rely heavily on stereotypes. During 1980s, independent films such as *Parting Glances* (Bill Sherwood 1986) and *Longtime Companion* (Norman Rene 1990), which dealt with the effects of the AIDS epidemic on the gay male community, developed into a subgenre of AIDS cinema. One film that was hailed as a mainstream breakthrough was *Philadelphia* (Jonathan Demme 1993), a Hollywood film that starred Tom Hanks as a gay man dying of AIDS who sues his law firm for discrimination, with the assistance of his reluctant straight lawyer (Denzel Washington). Despite its critical and commercial success, some critics saw the film as perpetuating a stereotype of the tragic, helpless gay man.

By the early 1990s, following the explosion of independent filmmaking and the rise in the number of gay and lesbian film festivals, a new crop of films appeared that veteran film critic B. Ruby Rich dubbed New Queer Cinema. One result of political activism around AIDS and around gay civil rights was the reclamation of the formerly derisive term "queer," which became an umbrella term of pride designating a variety of non-normative genders and sexualities. Two early directors included Todd Haynes (*Poison* 1991) and Gregg Araki (*The Living End* 1992). New Queer Cinema films are often experimental in form and unapologetically assertive in attitude. They explicitly address queer audiences rather than seeking the approval of straight audiences for their characters' sexual and lifestyle choices, dreams, and fantasies. The unabashed style of New Queer Cinema inspired a host of less experimental, but no less risky, feature films dealing with gay and lesbian life. *Desert Hearts* (Donna Deitch 1985) offered a surprising twist to the lesbian coming-out story—a happy ending—and by 1994, the lesbian romantic comedy *Go Fish* (Rose Troche and Guinevere Turner 1994) moved beyond the issue of coming out to explore an urban, multicultural lesbian community (fig. **10.15**). In *Mala Noche* (1985) and *My Own Private Idaho* (1991), Gus Van Sant

10.17 *Milk*: the energy of New Queer Cinema goes mainstream.

focuses on gay male relationships. Todd Haynes's feature films, including *Safe* (1995) and *Velvet Goldmine* (1998), explore queer themes without necessarily focusing on gay communities. In *Far From Heaven* (2002), Haynes reconceptualizes the 1950s melodramas of Douglas Sirk (several of which starred Rock Hudson, a prominent movie star who revealed he was gay when he was dying of AIDS in the 1980s). In Haynes's tale of middle-class boredom and marital infidelity, the unauthorized desires that Sirk's films repressed are brought to the surface. Prominent corporate executive and family man, Frank Whittaker (Dennis Quaid) lives a double life because he desires men; ultimately, he chooses to leave his family (fig. **10.16**).

A number of film critics have observed that, during the first decade of the 2000s, the energy of New Queer Cinema went mainstream, as evidenced by the popularity of, and the Oscar nominations garnered by, films such as *Monster*, *Capote*, *Brokeback Mountain*, and *A Single Man* (Tom Ford 2009). The fact that Sean Penn won an Oscar for his performance in *Milk* (Van Sant 2008; fig. **10.17**) as the influential, openly gay politician Harvey Milk is certainly some indication that critics and general audiences are more and more willing to embrace stories about alternative sexualities.

Moreover, the accolades Penn, Heath Ledger, Charlize Theron, Philip Seymour Hoffman and others have earned playing gay roles makes it clear that such parts no longer carry the stigma they once did. But the fact that the actors above who earned praise for playing gay characters are all (presumably) straight points to another debate brewing in the critical community: are audiences as open to their favorite stars being "out of the closet" as they are to characters who are homosexual? Openly gay actor Rupert Everett caused waves recently when he advised actors *not* to come out of the closet: "[Being open] just doesn't work and you're going to hit a brick wall at some point. [You might] make it roll for a certain amount of time, but at the first sign of failure [the industry] will write you off" (quoted in "Coming Out"). Everett's comments might suggest that, while straight actors earn credibility for being able to "cross over" onscreen, gay actors still find themselves limited to playing only homosexual characters. Curiously, if this is the case, it means that audiences are willing to accept a discrepancy between a straight actor's offscreen persona and his onscreen character, but are less able to suspend their disbelief when watching a gay man playing a straight romantic hero.

Disability and Cinema

Following the civil rights struggles of the disabled, and the increased awareness of social issues related to disability brought about by the Americans with Disabilities Act of 1990, film studies has recently begun to address the ideologies implicit in cinematic representations of disability. Film history is rife with examples of popular movies in which the disabled are treated as abnormal deviants. In Tod Browning's infamous horror film *Freaks* (1932), a trapeze artist, Cleopatra (Olga Baclanava), and her strongman lover, Hercules (Henry Victor), try to kill Cleopatra's husband, Hans (Harry Earles)—a dwarf who is one of the circus sideshow acts. Their attempt fails, but when the rest of the "freaks" hear of the plot, they seek revenge against the "normal" lovers. Browning insisted on casting real circus performers in the central roles, including Siamese twins Violet and Daisy Hilton, torsoless Johnny Eck, and limbless Prince Randian. The decision lent the film remarkable authenticity—but Browning's studio, MGM, feared the general public would deem it too grotesque. MGM quickly pulled the film out of distribution and washed its hands of the project; the movie was banned in Great Britain until the 1960s. *Freaks'* subsequent cult following and scholarly appeal make it an evocative case study for exploring questions relevant to cinematic representations of the disabled: are disabled characters developed with depth and complexity, or are they two-dimensional "curios" that function only to provide atmosphere or to act as a convenient plot device? Is a character's disability her single defining trait? What assumptions does a film make about the impact a disability has on the quality of life? Does the industry provide access to disabled actors, and to what degree does this access affect the way disabilities are represented in film?

The fact that this discussion begins with a description of *Freaks* points to a common and misguided assumption that informs perceptions of disability: that a disability is necessarily accompanied by a pronounced physical marker of difference. Even films that portray "invisible" disabilities, such as mental illness or dyslexia, assign disabled characters physical traits or make them social deviants. Scholar Lisa Lopez Levers identifies more than thirty iconic images that equate mental disability with madness. Some of this imagery associates the mentally ill with starkly lit windows or doors, unkempt physical appearance, cages, hidden hands, and flailing limbs. Lopez's list details the various ways the visual arts—including the cinema—have stereotyped the disabled for centuries.

These ubiquitous visual markers of difference point to the broader tendency in the cinema to represent the disabled as strange, exotic specimens. *Freaks'* blunt title clearly identifies the disabled as something less than human and promises audiences the cinematic equivalent of a sideshow. MGM's exploitative

marketing strategy was equally apparent in taglines that boldly advertised the film's "half-human creatures" (fig. **10.18**).

But the story line in *Freaks* actually disturbs this tendency to identify the disabled as "others." In Browning's film, those with conventionally beautiful bodies—the strong man and the trapeze artist—are the unsympathetic figures whose behavior threatens social stability. Cleopatra agrees to marry (and plots to kill) the smitten dwarf Hans because an inheritance has made him wealthy. In one of the film's most famous scenes, Cleopatra and Hans throw a wedding party where the sideshow performers welcome the trapeze artist into their community by ritualistically chanting, "One of us, one of us." Their invitation rests on the assumption that, in their society, the able-bodied are in the minority and are outsiders.

The film challenges traditional representations of disability in another way. Cleopatra is clearly an unsympathetic character. On hearing the chant, she becomes visibly discomfited. Her fear of disability is clearly linked to her more obvious unseemly behavior: the fact that she is a gold digger and a potential killer. The chanting scene thus calls into question normative social attitudes, which brand the physically disabled as social pariahs. According to film scholar Sally Chivers:

> [A]udience members are explicitly physically aligned with Cleopatra and are, by implication, incited to become one of the group. Cleopatra's outright rejection, then, supposedly mirrors the reaction of an ableist viewership, except that to align oneself with her would be to identify with a murderess. (Chivers, p. 61)

Topics in Ideological Criticism

In other words, the film invites viewers to recognize and potentially repudiate their affinity with one of the film's two contemptible antagonists.

By emphasizing the communal orientation of the so-called "freaks" while simultaneously alluding to the social pathology of the able-bodied, the episode points to the film's challenge to the cinematic stereotype of the disabled. Paradoxically, however, the episode also illustrates how *Freaks* undercuts the humanity of the sideshow performers by trading on their "otherness" to generate the gothic atmosphere so critical to the horror genre. Disability comes to symbolize monstrosity itself. The ritualistic mantra "one of us" resonates with viewers because its delivery is certifiably creepy, and because it foreshadows the fate that is in store for the unfaithful Cleopatra: she is hunted down by the wrathful sideshow performers who mutilate her body and turn her into a circus spectacle named "The Feathered Hen." Cleopatra literally becomes "one of them," condemned to spend the rest of her days as a sideshow act. The film encourages the audience to interpret the *dénouement* as suitable retribution for Cleopatra's sins. But by encouraging this vantage point, the film reiterates dominant assumptions that equate disability with suffering and unhappiness. Thus, while on the one hand Browning attempts to render the physically disabled with humanity, on the other he "reinscribe[s] physical difference as a terrifying spectacle." (Cook, p. 48) In this way *Freaks* demonstrates how a single film can contain competing ideologies. One dominant theme (the idea that the circus performers are more human than those with conventional bodies) is subtly contradicted by opposing ideological undercurrents (the presentation of disability as monstrous and grotesque).

Despite its contradictions, *Freaks* is exceptional for its treatment of the disabled as main characters, worthy of their own storyline. Most depictions of disability in the first decades of American cinema cast disabled characters as disaffected and dangerous oddities. The most superficial characterizations relied on disabled minor characters to generate eerie atmosphere or comic relief. Films that did feature conflicts involving central disabled characters focused on their sociopathic inability to "fit in." According to film scholar Martin Norden, male characters in films such as *The Hunchback of Notre Dame* (Wallace Worsley 1923), *The Unknown* (Tod Browning 1927), and *Devil Doll* (Tod Browning 1936) are noteworthy for their destructive tendencies; like Captain Ahab and his suicidal obsession to kill the mighty whale that took his leg, these characters are irrational and angry about their lack. In their zeal to avenge their losses, they take aim at, or simply bring down, others around them. On the other hand, depictions of disabled women in films such as D.W. Griffith's *Orphans of the Storm* (1921) and Charlie Chaplin's *City Lights* (1931) emphasize the characters' complete passivity and their childlike innocence (Norden, "Hollywood," p. 22).

With the advent of World War II, the film industry's depiction of disability grew considerably more complex. Responding to the historical circumstance of an entire generation coping with the scars of combat, studios began to explore the emotional and physical challenges of disability. With a sensitivity and maturity virtually unheard of in studio films from previous decades, *Since You Went Away* (John Cromwell 1944), *The Enchanted Cottage* (John Cromwell 1945), *Pride of the Marines* (Delmer Davies 1945), and *Till the End of Time* (Edward

Dmytryk 1946) depict veterans struggling to adjust to a new life with disabilities. Undoubtedly, the most accomplished and memorable film during this era is William Wyler's *The Best Years of Our Lives* (1946), which explores the sense of displacement that a group of veterans experiences upon returning home from the war along with their fears of rejection (Norden, *Cinema*, pp. 145–83).

Though Hollywood trended toward greater sensitivity in its portrayals of disabilities after the war, this did not necessarily eradicate stereotypes. Rather, a new generation of standardized treatments arose. Film scholar Colin Barnes identifies victimization as a common narrative trope of disability. Disabled characters are often victims, reinforcing "the notion that disabled people are helpless, pitiable, and unable to function without protection." (Barnes, pp. 10–11) Supporting roles for disabled characters tend to focus on how they are burdens for the active, primary characters to shoulder. In *What's Eating Gilbert Grape* (Lasse Hallström 1993), Gilbert Grape (Johnny Depp) longs for the adventure of the open road, but is trapped in his hometown because of his obligation to care for his obese mother (Darlene Cates) and his autistic brother Arnie (Leonardo DiCaprio).

Yet another stereotype depicts the disabled as defeatists who wallow in self-pity, making themselves "their own worst enemies." (Levers) Movies such as *Born on the Fourth of July* (Oliver Stone 1989), *Passion Fish* (John Sayles 1992), and *Girl, Interrupted* (James Mangold 1999) all revolve around self-loathers who must learn to "rise to the challenge," often from others who are not disabled; this narrative strategy uses "disability as a metaphor for dependence and vulnerability." (Barnes, p. 14) Rather than addressing the legal, social, and architectural barriers that contribute to these characters' frustration and hostility, this narrative suggests that the most significant struggle the disabled face is their own lack of courage.

All of these cinematic stereotypes share the assumption that a disability is a defining trait. While other characters exhibit a range of complex emotions and reveal demonstrative emotional growth as they pursue their goals, disabled characters are frequently motivated *only* by their perceived physical or mental limitations. In *Million Dollar Baby*, Maggie (Hillary Swank) plays a tough-as-nails boxer—but when she is paralyzed in the ring, the film suggests her only legitimate option is to commit suicide. Some critics complain that Maggie's all-too-predictable decision to end her life perpetuates the ideological assumption that "the quality of life of individuals with disabilities is unquestionably not worth living" ("Million"). In fact, the plot goes out of its way to position Frankie (Clint Eastwood) as the central figure in the third act. *He* struggles with the decision whether to end her life, but his internal conflict is based on a "legal distortion," since "it would be perfectly legal for [Maggie] to request withdrawal of the life-sustaining treatment [...]" ("Million"). In short, even though Maggie is a dynamic character who shares equal billing with Frankie in the first two acts, once she becomes disabled she no longer invites audience identification but, instead, serves as a problem for the main character to solve.

Shortly after its release, *Avatar* was earning praise from many in the disabled community for its complex portrait of a paraplegic war veteran. According to J. Scott Richards, director of research at the University of Alabama's Physical

Medicine & Rehabilitation Center, *Avatar* succeeds precisely because the protagonist, Jake Sully, is neither idealized nor patronized: "people in wheelchairs might appreciate […] having a key character who is not a super achiever." Richards argues that *Avatar* avoids both of the extremes Hollywood relies on when depicting disability: "A physically achieving athlete in a wheelchair, or the opposite end of that—someone who is miserable and has a horrible life." (quoted in Cox) Unlike Maggie in *Million Dollar Baby*, Jake Sully doesn't give up on life when he's injured. Rather, he struggles through and enjoys life rather matter-of-factly.

Many stars have solidified their artistic reputation by playing disabled characters. Lon Chaney, Daniel Day-Lewis, Tom Cruise, and Angelina Jolie have had breakthrough performances playing disabled characters. But critics complain that casting able-bodied actors in such roles effectively excludes disabled actors from the industry—the equivalent of casting white actors in blackface to play African-American roles. Such casting choices contribute to the continuing proliferation of two-dimensional characterizations of people with disabilities. When an actor who is not disabled garners acclaim for portraying a disabled character, it can be a sign that disability is the character's defining trait. But, when a disabled actor plays a role that was not written with disability in mind, the casting choice confirms that disability is not the primary determinant of a character's experiences. Marlee Matlin and Peter Dinklage have become stars by playing some characters whose disabilities define them and others whose disabilities are secondary. Their stardom may provide them with more opportunities to play roles that are not based solely on disability.

The increased visibility of disabled actors in front of the camera is in part the by-product of advocacy groups and legal reforms that have encouraged a growing awareness of disability rights in the industry and among the general public. In 2004 Charles Kaplan articulated the charge of California's Access Media Office: to change the public's perception of disability by changing the film industry's hiring practices:

> We want the entertainment industry to reflect America's true diversity—that includes people with disabilities as well as people of color and various ethnicities. We want disabilities portrayed accurately and want people with disabilities to have a chance to perform in mainstream roles—not be restricted to roles where the disability itself figures into the plot. (quoted in Leotta)

Kaplan's quote reflects the growing understanding that discrimination against the disabled is a front in the ongoing civil rights struggle, and that gaining control of the representation of disability is of fundamental importance in this struggle.

This chapter has explored several ways that ideologies that pervade American society also influence the economics and cultural politics of the film industry (including who works in the industry and in what capacity) and shape the content of popular narrative cinema. Chapter 11 examines the relationship between social context and filmmaking not only in Hollywood cinema (arguably, the U.S. national cinema) but also in diverse national and transnational contexts.

Works Consulted

Barnes, Colin. "Disabling Imagery and the Media: An Exploration of the Principles for Media Representations of Disabled People." *The British Council of Organisations of Disabled People*. Ryburn Publishing. **http://studydisability.uoregon.edu/films.html**. October 2, 2006.

Barrios, Richard. *Screened Out: Playing Gay in Hollywood from Edison to Stonewall*. New York: Routledge, 2002.

Bogle, Donald. *Toms, Coons, Mulattoes, Mammies, and Bucks: An Interpretive History of Blacks in American Films*. New York: Continuum, 2001.

Chivers, Sally. "The Horror of Becoming 'One of Us': Tod Browning's *Freaks* and Disability." *Screening Disability: Essays on Cinema and Disability*. Eds. Christopher R. Smit and Anthony Enns. Lanham: University Press of America, 2001, pp. 57–64.

"'Coming Out as a Gay Actor Ruined My Career in Hollywood,' says Actor Rupert Everett." *Daily Mail Online*. Dec. 2, 2009. **http://www.dailymail.co.uk/tvshowbiz/article-1232588/Rupert-Everett-Coming-gay-actor-ruined-career-Hollywood.html**.

Cook, Méira. "None of Us: Ambiguity as Moral Discourse in Tod Browning's *Freaks*." *Screening Disability: Essays on Cinema and Disability*. Eds. Christopher R. Smit and Anthony Enns. Lanham: University Press of America, 2001.

Cox, Lauren. "*Avatar* Gets Mixed Praise from Paraplegics." *ABCNews.com*. Jan. 8, 2010. **http://abcnews.go.com/Health/WellnessNews/wheelchair-users-applaud-avatars-parapalegic-character/story?id=9505175&page=1**.

Dick, Kirby. "Rating the M.P.A.A." [Letter to the Editor]. *The New Yorker*. September 18, 2006. p. 5.

Donalson, Melvin. *Black Directors in Hollywood*. Austin, TX: University of Texas Press, 2003.

Douthat, Ross. *The New York Times*. "The Unfunny Truth" August 9, 2009.

Dyer, Richard. *White*. London and New York: Routledge, 1997.

Gagne, Nicole. "Gay and Lesbian." *Allmovie.com* **www.allmovie.com/cg/avg/dll?p=avg&sql=23:35** October 14, 2006.

Gerstner, David. *Manly Arts: Masculinity and Nation in Early American Cinema*. Durham, NC: Duke University Press, 2006.

Golus, Carrie. "Doc Films Screening Pre-1950s 'race films' that Students will be Discussing in Seminar." University of Chicago *Chronicle*. January 10, 2002. **http://chronicle.uchicago.edu/020110/racefilms.shtml** September 10, 2006.

Guerrero, Ed. *Framing Blackness: The African-American Image in Film*. Philadelphia: Temple University Press, 1993.

Hansen, Miriam. "The Mass Production of the Senses: Classical Cinema as Vernacular Modernism." *Modernism/Modernity*, 6/2 (1999), pp. 59–77.

"Hollywood Ten." Spartacus. **www.spartacus.schoolnet.co.uk/USAhollywood10.htm**. October 3, 2006.

Hopfensperger, Jean. "'Whiteness Studies' Researchers at University of Minnesota Look at Racial Identity." *Star Tribune.com*. September 11, 2006. **www.startribune.com/462/story/667886.html**. September 20, 2006.

Kellner, Douglas. "Hollywood Films and Society," in *American Cinema and Hollywood*, ed. John Hill and Pamela Church Gibson. Oxford and New York: Oxford University Press, 2000, pp. 128–38.

Kramer, Gary M. *Independent Queer Cinema: Reviews and Interviews*. Binghamton, NY; Haworth Press (Southern Tier Editions): 2006.

Lauzen, Martha. "The Celluloid Ceiling: Behind-the-Scenes Employment of Women in the Top 250 Films of 2005." *Movies Directed by Women*. 2006. **www.moviesbywomen.com/marthalauzenphd/stats2005.html** October 12, 2006.

Lehman, Peter. *Running Scared: Masculinity and the Representation of the Male Body*. 2d edn. Detroit, MI: Wayne State University Press, 2006.

Leotta, Joan. "Spotlight on the Silver Screen: California's Media Access Office." *Solutions Marketing Group*. **http://www.disability-marketing.com/profiles/ca-mao.php4**. October 19, 2006.

LeSage, Julia. "The Political Aesthetics of the Feminist Documentary Film." *Quarterly Review of Film Studies*, 3/4 (1978), pp. 507–23.

Lopez Levers, Lisa. "Representation of Psychiatric Disability in Fifty Years of Hollywood Film: An Ethnographic Content Analysis." *Theory and Science*. 2001. **http://www.theoryandscience.icaap.org/content/vol002.002/lopezlevers.html**.

Maltby, Richard. "Censorship and Self-Regulation," in *The Oxford History of World Cinema*, ed. Geoffrey Nowell-Smith. New York: Oxford University Press, 1996, pp. 235–48.

Massood, Paula J. "An Aesthetic Appropriate to Conditions: Killer of Sheep, (Neo)Realism, and the Documentary Impulse." *Wide Angle*, 21/4 (October 1999), pp. 20–41.

"McCarthyism." *Wikipedia: The Free Encyclopedia*. **en.wikipedia.org/wiki/Mccarthyism** September 22, 2006.

"Media Stereotyping—Introduction." *Media Awareness Network*. **http://www.media-awareness. ca/english/issues/stereotyping/** October 2, 2006.

"Million Dollar Baby Built on Prejudice about People with Disabilities." Disability *Rights Education and Defense Fund*. **http://www.dredf.org/mdb_statement.html**. October 1, 2006.

Morris, Gary. "A Brief History of Queer Cinema." *GreenCine*. **www.greencine.com/statis/ primers/queer.jsp**. October 14, 2006.

Naremore, James. *More Than Night: Film Noir in its Contexts*. Berkeley: University of California Press, 1998.

Negra, Diane. *Off White Hollywood: American Culture and Ethnic Female Stardom*. London and New York: Routledge, 2001.

Norden, Martin F. *The Cinema of Isolation*. New Brunswick, NJ: Rutgers University Press, 1994.
————. "The Hollywood Discourse on Disability." *Screening Disability: Essays on Cinema and Disability*, eds. Christopher Smit and Anthony Enns. Lanham, MD: University Press of America, 2001, pp. 19–32.

Norden, Martin, and Madeleine Cahill. "Violence, Women, and Disability in Tod Browning's Freaks and Devil Doll." *Journal of Popular Film and Television*. Summer 1998. **http://findarticles. com/p/ articles/mi_m0412/is_n2_v26/ai_21221638**. October 10, 2006.

O'Rourke, Meghan. "Katherine Heigl's *Knocked Up*: The Demise of the Female Slacker." *Slate.com*. December 11, 2007.

Potter, Sally. "Notes on the Adaptation of the Book *Orlando*." Virginia Woolf Seminar. **http:// www.uah.edu/woolf/Orlando_Potter.htm**. October 10, 2006.
————. "Response to Thought Fox." *Yes* Message Board. March 27, 2006. **www. yesthemovie.com/forum_thread.jsp?articleType=Content.TALK%20TO%20SALLY.Film-making&threadId=132**. October 10, 2006.

"Production Code of 1930." *The Production Code of the Motion Picture Industry, 1930–68*. **http://prodcode.davidhayes.net/** October 12, 2006.

Rosenbaum, Jonathan. "A Perversion of the Past," in *Movies as Politics*. Berkeley: University of California Press, 1997, pp. 118–24. Originally published in *Chicago Reader*, December 16, 1988.

Rosenberg, Jan. *Women's Reflections: The Feminist Film Movement*. Ann Arbor, MI: UMI Research Press, 1983.

Russo, Vito. *The Celluloid Closet: Homosexuality in the Movies*. New York: Harper and Rowe, 1987.

Shannon, Jeff. "Access Hollywood: Disability in Recent Film and Television." *New Mobility*. May 2003. **http://www.newmobility.com/review_article.cfm?id=690&action=browse**. October 10, 2003.

Stam, Robert. *Film Theory: An Introduction*. Malden, MA, and Oxford: Blackwell, 2000.

Tasker, Yvonne. *Spectacular Bodies: Gender, Genre, and the Action Cinema*. London and New York: Routledge, 1993.

Vertov, Dziga. "Provisional Instructions to Kino-Eye Groups." *The European Cinema Reader*, ed. Catherine Fowler. London and New York: Routledge, 2002.

"Waldorf Statement." *Wikipedia: the Free Encyclopedia*. **en.wikipedia.org/wiki/Waldorf_ Statement**. October 4, 2006.

Walker, Janet, and Diane Waldman. *Feminism and Documentary*. Minneapolis, MI: University of Minnesota Press, 1999.

Wood, Robin. "Ideology, Genre, Auteur: *Shadow of a Doubt*" in *Hitchcock's Film's Revisited*. New York: Columbia University Press, 1989, pp. 288–303.

Worrell, Joseph. "Oscar Micheaux." *Silent Era People*. **www.silentera.com/people/directors/ Micheaux-Oscar.html**. September 2, 2006.

Social Context and Film Style: National, International, and Transnational Cinema

///

Hollywood was the place where the United States perpetuated itself as a universal dream and put the dream into mass production

Angela Carter

///

At the turn of the twentieth century, New York City was the center of commercial filmmaking. But by 1910, filmmakers began to move west from New York to Hollywood, drawn to the area's climate, cheap real estate, and the opportunity to avoid paying equipment licensing fees to Thomas Edison's Motion Picture Patents Company. By the end of the decade, film production was a lucrative industry and Wall Street investors helped Hollywood dominate the international film market. Ever since the 1920s, many people have equated Hollywood with moviemaking.

But Hollywood is not the world's only major film industry, and its preference for larger-than-life, escapist fantasies represents only one approach to filmmaking. This chapter discusses several cultural contexts for filmmaking by looking at

11.1 Marlene Dietrich on set with Josef von Sternberg.

343

the Hollywood studio system, international art cinema, Italian Neorealism, Third Cinema, and Fourth Cinema. Each of these social contexts is associated with an economic, political, and cultural approach to the art and the business of film-making. The films that have emerged from these locations and traditions reflect these important differences.

This discussion also engages with ideas about national and transnational cinemas, in part because so many of these social contexts for filmmaking are organized by the idea of national identity and by the economic and social practices of nation states. Cinema has operated as an international art form and commercial endeavor since its inception, with the traveling exhibitions and exotic views of foreign lands the Lumière brothers provided. As such, it has played an important role in sometimes defining, and sometimes blurring the geographical and psychological borders of nationality.

Hollywood's Industrial Context: The Studio System as Dream Factory

American film production and reception were at their height during what has become known as the Hollywood studio era. Though film historians debate the exact dates, many pinpoint 1915 as its beginning. This was the year that D.W. Griffith released *The Birth of a Nation*, one of the first feature-length narrative films to demonstrate the medium's artistic and commercial potential. The end of the Hollywood studio era, though hard to define precisely, was signaled by a 1948 Supreme Court decision. That decision, called the Paramount Consent Decree, ordered the major Hollywood studios to cease their monopolistic business practices.

Between 1915 and 1948, five **major studios** (Metro-Goldwyn-Mayer [MGM], Paramount, Warner Brothers, Twentieth Century Fox, and RKO) and several **minor studios** (Universal, Columbia, and United Artists) perfected a mode of filmmaking that, in turn, generated a standardized film style. Hollywood's efficient mode of production, distribution, and exhibition, known as the **studio system**, gave rise to an instantly recognizable type of film. The next section briefly describes the classical Hollywood style before examining the economic and social practices that gave rise to it.

Classical Style

Classical Hollywood narratives exhibit four important traits, as discussed in Chapter 4. Those traits include clarity (viewers should not be confused about space, time, or events), unity (cause and effect connections are direct and complete), goal-oriented characters (they are active and invite identification), and closure (loose ends are tied up, often through romantic union). All other components of a classical Hollywood film are subservient to narrative. In fact, the classical Hollywood style is often called "the invisible style," because it relies on "unobtrusive craftsmanship," (Thompson 1999, p. 11) ensuring that viewers will become absorbed in the narrative without paying attention to the filmmaking process.

More specifically, in this style of filmmaking, the *mise en scène* depicts an external world that adheres to the norms of "realism" determined by the conditions of the story. The *mise en scène* offers spectators a seemingly objective presentation of the story space, as opposed to the subjectivity of Expressionism or the self-consciousness of formalism. Similarly, the cinematography eschews exaggerated angles or flamboyant techniques.

On those occasions when a film does employ obvious visual distortions, there is almost always a narrative justification. In *Notorious*, when Alicia realizes that Alex knows she is a spy, he and his mother suddenly appear as undulating silhouettes (fig. 11.2). This brief moment threatens to remind viewers they are looking through a lens. However, the distortion is motivated by the narrative: Alicia is hallucinating because she has been poisoned, and this is her point of view.

11.2 This rare moment of visual distortion (from *Notorious*) has narrative justification.

Classical editing follows the rules of continuity editing, as outlined in Chapter 7. It functions primarily to excise events that aren't immediately relevant to the plot, to create a unified sense of space and time, and to punctuate the emotional content of a scene by drawing attention to characters and their actions.

Finally, a classical Hollywood film privileges dialogue over other sounds because it expresses character traits and motivations and helps to explain cause-and-effect logic. Because dialogue is the sound most responsible for conveying this information, it tends to be audible above everything else.

In short, the classical Hollywood style attempts to guarantee that "at any moment in a movie, the audience [is] to be given the optimum vantage point on what [is] occurring on screen." (Ray, p. 33) The perspective it creates is so ideal that audiences forget they are watching a carefully orchestrated fictional representation. Indeed, some critics call the classical style escapist because it creates the illusion of stories unfolding in real space and time and takes audiences away from their own lives.

It might appear that the classical Hollywood style is the only logical way to approach narrative filmmaking. But as the following sections illustrate, the invisible style was as much a product of economic and political circumstances as it was a set of conscious aesthetic choices.

Economic Practice and Hollywood Convention

The profit-driven studio system was designed to deliver products to consumers as quickly as possible. Its mode of production was, to a large degree, the assembly line of the modern factory system. Studios relied on a division of labor to generate products rapidly and cheaply. At the beginning of the process, producers conferred with studio heads to generate ideas and to determine which projects to pursue. Once they had decided on a project, a team of writers would draft and revise the screenplay while the art director designed the sets, the costume designer fashioned the wardrobe for the cast, and the casting office selected actors.

The project's producer and assistant director oversaw much of this pre-production process, and when it was completed, the director took over, handling most of the decisions during shooting. After shooting was complete, the editor assembled the shots, working to ensure continuity. Sometimes the director was involved in this process, but often he was not. After the final cut was assembled, the score was composed. This is a simplified description of the process, which evolved and became more complex as the industry grew, but it offers some indication of how compartmentalized film production was.

This compartmentalization contributed to the standardization of Hollywood's style. For example, producers used the same production teams again and again to facilitate the process of turning out a standardized product. At Paramount, for example, Marlene Dietrich, director Josef von Sternberg (fig. **11.1**), screenwriter Jules Furthman, and cinematographer Lee Garmes collaborated on a series of four successful romantic melodramas in the early 1930s: *Morocco* (1930), *Dishonored* (1931), *Blonde Venus* (1932), and *Shanghai Express* (1932). Costumes and sets could be reused as well, saving the studios both money and time. Relying on stories and production practices that had succeeded before led to relatively consistent quality and style.

The classical Hollywood conventions for continuity and camera placement do not constitute an inherently superior method of conveying narrative information, but they became Hollywood's standard partly because they too contributed to production efficiency. The "rules" provided directors with a predetermined shot set-up for each scene. In other words, Hollywood's visual style was largely shaped by a powerful determinant: the logic of industrial capitalism. The ultimate goal was studio profitability; every decision that was made, from the choice of writers, directors, and cast to the look of the sets and costumes, was in some way affected by the studio's fiscal bottom line. Within these constraints, individuals who wrote, shot, directed, designed sets for, and acted in studio films adhered to aesthetic and professional standards.

The studios' reliance on stars also reflected the market logic of capitalism on several levels. Stars served as a marketing device, helping the studios to pre-sell a picture to fans. But the star system also facilitated the production and distribution of films. Once a star became associated with a particular type of character, that star could serve as an economical means of shorthand character development. Screenwriters wouldn't have to worry about how to establish important character traits since, theoretically, audiences would already have those traits in mind as soon as the actor walked on screen. Star personas also helped the studios distribute their products to the theaters, since theater owners would have a clear idea of what they were getting with a "Marlene Dietrich picture" or a "Lon Chaney movie." Put simply, in the name of efficiency, character development often depended upon typed, or standardized, performances.

Because Hollywood sold an ideal of technical perfection—the seamless reproduction of a larger than life "reality"—technological innovations became part of the economic and aesthetic enterprise of studio filmmaking as well. The conversion to sound offers an example of the way that the incorporation of new technologies for the production or exhibition of films relates to a larger social and economic context. Hollywood studios undertook enormous investments in the 1920s and 1930s to re-tool their production methods and exhibition venues to make and project films with synchronized soundtracks. Media scholar Steve Wurtzler links this activity, which forced many studios to become dependent on Wall Street finance, to developments in sound that cut across media forms. Innovations in "electrical acoustics" were taking place in radio, film, and the phonograph at the same time. "Hollywood's conversion to sound and cinema audiences' enthusiasm," he writes, "were merely components of the larger pervasiveness and reaction to a new technological mediation of sound." (Wurtzler, p. 1) In other words, Hollywood adopted sound technologies in part because they were becoming part of the daily experiences of Americans. These innovations contributed to a profit-oriented industry, as corporations such as AT&T, General Electric, Westinghouse, and United Fruit Company and others had formed a patent-holders cartel in 1920 that maximized their profits and limited competition (Wurtzler, p. 5). Major investments in technological innovation remain an important feature of Hollywood cinema to this day. As digital technologies have become part of everyday life, our expectations about the way images and sounds can be experienced in movies have changed as well, in a mutually determining relationship.

Finally, the hierarchical structure of the industry itself and its profit-driven *modus operandi* played a key role in determining a film's narrative structure. Some producers and studio heads would test screen movies and then re-edit, or sometimes reshoot, the films, according to audience response. The practice helped guarantee a crowd-pleasing product—but it also led to the desecration of some profound works of art. Thomas Schatz describes how, on seeing a test screening of *Tess of the D'Urbervilles* (1924), MGM studio head Louis B. Mayer was disappointed because the film concluded with the heroine being hanged for killing the man who had raped her. He demanded a new, happy ending. Director Marshall Neilan protested and sought out the novel's author Thomas Hardy for support, but MGM owned the rights to the novel and Mayer prevailed (Schatz, p. 32).

In short, Hollywood during the studio era (and still today) was a profit-driven industry whose financial considerations played a significant role in shaping its products' aesthetic characteristics.

American Values and Hollywood Style

While economic concerns have always been of paramount importance to Hollywood's profit-oriented studios, they are not the only cultural influences on Hollywood and its classical style.

The Hollywood Production Code illustrates the way that art and commerce can be shaped by non-economic factors that limit the choices screenwriters, directors, and producers are able to make. (An explication of the Production

Code, in terms of the ideologies it embodied, appears in Chapter 10, pp. 314–16). The Production Code was established in 1930—and began to be enforced in 1934 by the Production Code Administration (PCA)—with the sole purpose of regulating the content of Hollywood films. All films had to obtain a certificate of approval from the PCA: as film scholar Thomas Doherty writes, "the visible mark of quality control would be a quite literal Production Code Seal of Approval, an oval logo encircling the MPPDA initials, printed on the credits of every Code-worthy film." (Doherty)

The Code delineated what could and could not be shown on movie screens. As such, it served as a blueprint for American morality, as articulated and interpreted by those who administered the PCA. In doing so, it defined the values that Hollywood films were forced to adhere to, and thus had an effect on the stories that could be told and the way they were presented. The Code, Doherty writes, "sought to yoke Catholic doctrine to Hollywood formula: The guilty are punished, the virtuous are rewarded, the authority of church and state is legitimate, and the bonds of matrimony are sacred." (Doherty 2006) This statement reflects the moral premises of the Code itself, but it does not necessarily characterize all of the films that were made during its heyday. Producers, screenwriters, and directors negotiated directly with the PCA regarding potentially unacceptable content and they sometimes flouted the rules. Most often, however, they developed a stylistic shorthand to suggest plot events or scenarios that could not be represented directly. "The Code regulated the spoken word and the visible image," Doherty notes, "but the unsaid and the unseen lurk under the lilt of the dialogue and beyond the edge of the frame: the spectator has only to fill in the blanks." (2007 p. 98) The fact that state-imposed and self-imposed censorship alike can produce stylistic repercussions is a topic that has inspired a number of film scholars studying the film cultures of Spain (see Works Consulted for D'Lugo, Higginbotham, Kinder, Mira), Britain (Robertson), Germany (Hake, Welch), China (Chow, Lu, Zhang), and many other countries.

Crucially, the PCA's enforcement of the Code was, like the studios' stylistic choices, largely motivated by financial interest. While the Code may be most famous for the way it suppressed sexuality of all kinds and demanded that those who break the law be punished, it also influenced the political issues that could be represented and the way they could be depicted. The script for the Warner Brothers film *Black Fury* (Michael Curtiz 1935) depicted life in American coal mines as a struggle between greedy mine owners and workers who are forced to strike because of appalling working conditions. After the script was submitted to PCA head Joseph Breen, he demanded the elimination of "the critique of the mine owners and the idea of class struggle in the coalfields," which resulted in a film that failed to criticize either management or labor (Black, p. 185). According to Black, Breen's goal was to eliminate all controversial content so as to "maximize the worldwide appeal of Hollywood films." (Black, p. 168) In fact, as Black explains, by 1930 every European nation and many nations in Asia and Latin America had established censorship boards of their own. To protect their domestic film industries against the commercial threat of Hollywood cinema, they established quotas and censored Hollywood films (especially gangster pictures) because of inappropriate or offensive content (Black, p. 169). The PCA worked in part to ensure that these markets remained open to Hollywood's products.

An important thread that emerges here, but which is often overlooked, is the fact that the Production Code Administration was a uniquely American institution whose operations were aimed at both the domestic market and at potential viewers who lived outside the United States. The Code was the Hollywood film industry's instrument for presenting itself as a responsible guardian of American moral virtues as initially defined by a small but powerful segment of society. Yet it also played an important role in promoting Hollywood products for consumption in international markets. This double function points to the way that Hollywood both reflects the national culture from which it has emerged, but also responds to the commercial reality that film is an international art form and commercial product. Put another way, the Production Code stands as one more example of how Hollywood's uniformity of style benefited the industry economically.

Hollywood Conquers the World?

When we consider Hollywood cinema as an industry aiming its products at a global audience, two concerns emerge: the drive for profits inherent to the capitalist mode of production and the costly nature of cinema's dependence upon technology. These economic matters are, in fact, relevant to the type of films made in the U.S. and in every national context. "The capital intensive nature of film production," writes Paul Willeman, "requires a fairly large market in which to amortize costs [...] any film industry must address an international market or a very large domestic one." (Willeman, p. 35) The United States boasts a large domestic market for film consumption, yet the Hollywood industry has sought to dominate international cinema since the 1920s. It has proven extremely successful at doing so, beginning in the 1910s, and, some would say, with the advent of the narrative feature length film. In 1914, 90 percent of films shown worldwide were French; by 1928, 85 percent were American (Moussinac, p. 238; Crofts, p. 44). A recent statistic illustrates Hollywood's continued hegemony: in 2009, Hollywood films accounted for more than 50 percent of box office revenues in France, and 60–85 percent of revenues in Germany, Italy, Spain, and the United Kingdom (Scott, p. 160). People everywhere in the world see Hollywood films. "The American national cinema," according to film scholar Tom O'Regan, is "the most international of national cinemas." (O'Regan, p. 46)

One implication of Hollywood's long-term dominance of international cinema is that its aesthetic conventions became something like default scenarios: the paradigms that filmmakers around the world have chosen to imitate or to resist, or both. Hollywood's textual norms have informed the expectations and viewing experiences of filmgoers around the world for decades. Film scholar Shohini Chaudhuri explains, "due to its economic and culturally dominant position, Hollywood has defined the choices available to other cinemas, which have frequently reshaped or countered its models." (Chaudhuri, p. 2) The next section of this chapter examines several cinemas that have departed in some ways from the style and the production mode of the classical Hollywood studio system: International Art Cinema, Italian Neorealism, Third Cinema, and Fourth Cinema.

International Art Cinema

Not all cinema traditions value Hollywood's industrial efficiency and emphasis on narrative. During the 1950s and 1960s, a wave of European and Asian films garnered international attention because they departed from Hollywood's commercialism, uncomplicated characters, and invisible style. At the height of this era, filmgoers around the world were drawn to films from Sweden, Japan, India, Italy, and France. Many cinephiles referred to these films collectively as the art cinema movement.

The moniker assumes a marked distinction between Hollywood film and art film. Whereas the former is assumed to be escapist entertainment, the latter is seen to have a more serious intellectual purpose and a more sophisticated approach. Indeed, the films produced in this era addressed a number of weighty issues, including the discrepancy between memory and lived experience (*Hiroshima, mon amour* [Alain Resnais 1959]), the plight of the financially, but not spiritually, impoverished (*Pather Panchali* [Satyajit Ray 1955]), the relationship between art and life (*Breathless*), and spiritual doubt in the face of death (*The Seventh Seal*).

These films abandon goal-oriented characters, preferring instead to explore the psychology of complex characters who often have no sense of what they want out of life, much less how to achieve it. Rather than dedicating screen time to action, these films often dwell on scenes in which little or nothing (physical) happens. Stylistically, they flout Hollywood conventions in bold attempts to depict subjectivity or to draw the audience's attention to film's status as art. By no means is there a consistent narrative or stylistic model to which international art films adhere. The single trait they have in common is their contrast from the Hollywood studio model.

Jean-Luc Godard's *Breathless* exemplifies the way art cinema differs from classical Hollywood films. At first glance, the film promises to be a gangster film about Michel Poiccard (Jean-Paul Belmondo), a car thief who somewhat impulsively shoots a policeman (fig. **11.3**). But Michel is far from the conventional outlaw on the lam. Rather than setting to work on a plan to evade the police, he fritters his time away in Paris, alternately trying to seduce his American girlfriend Patricia (Jean Seberg) and take her to the movies. In one extended scene, Michel and Patricia playfully romp half-clothed in bed together, and their dialogue is full of sexual innuendo (fig. **11.4**). This frank depiction of sexuality was in sharp contrast to Hollywood's sanitized

11.3 *(above)* Michel gazes at a poster of Humphrey Bogart in *Breathless*.

11.4 *(below)* Michel and Patricia romp under the bedcovers in *Breathless*.

bedrooms of the same era, where even married couples slept in separate beds. In fact, one reason for the popularity of art films in the U.S. is that audiences, used to the rigid moral standards imposed by the Production Code, were intrigued and titillated by art cinema's open display of sexuality, occasional nudity, and its characters' youthful insouciance.

By conventional standards, Michel and Patricia's actions are indecipherable and often self-contradictory. At one point Michel inexplicably follows a stranger into a building and up several flights on an elevator. He gets off the elevator and proceeds to steal the man's car, but the film makes no attempt to explain why he follows the man in the first place. Patricia is a college student, but, despite her intellectual bent, she is drawn to the pointedly vulgar Michel. She confesses that she loves him only after discovering that he's a wanted man—and then proceeds to alert the police as to his whereabouts.

In keeping with the disjointed narrative and quirky characters, the film's style is playfully fragmented. Most noticeable is its use of jump cuts throughout, which excise chunks of time. Frequently the editing and the soundtrack conceptualize time differently. For example, as Michel drives toward Paris, jump cuts visually interrupt the narrative flow and condense the amount of time spent on the road, even while Michel's singing runs fluidly. In other words, chronological time is removed from the image, but not from the soundtrack.

The film's cinematography resembles that of a documentary, complementing the film's spontaneous feel. Cinematographer Raoul Coutard relied extensively on handheld cameras (then a relatively unheard of approach in fiction films), natural lighting, and an unusual film stock: rolls of fast film made exclusively for still photography spliced together for the 35 mm camera. According to Coutard, Godard's goal was to "escape from convention and even run counter to the rules of 'cinematographic grammar'." (quoted in Neupert, p. 210)

In short, rather than making style subservient to a tightly structured narrative, *Breathless* draws attention to the expressive and aesthetic vitality of cinema: the director "wanted to give the feeling that the techniques of filmmaking had just been discovered or experienced for the first time." (Godard, quoted in Marie, p. 162) Again, by no means does *Breathless* define a common sensibility among all art films. Whereas it revels in playful spontaneity, other films, such as Alain Resnais's *Last Year at Marienbad* or Federico Fellini's *8½*, adopt a highly stylized, formalist approach (fig. **11.5**). Still others, such as *Pather Panchali*, strive for a heightened and poetic sense of realism.

11.5 Surreal poetry marks the final circus scene from *8½*.

The Industry and Ideology of "Art"

To refer to these films as "art cinema" may imply that there were no commercial concerns associated with their production and distribution, which is not the case. Historians attribute the expansion of art cinema in part to the public financing of national cinemas after World War II, as government policy in many countries financed productions that would stand as visible and marketable documents of national culture (Nowell-Smith, p. 567). While these filmmakers did not work in a highly regimented industrial structure, funding still depended on a project's potential marketability. Art films were produced in the hopes of generating a profit, and many successfully competed against the Hollywood juggernaut because their self-conscious artistry helped to distinguish them from Hollywood's more immediate accessibility.

While many cinephiles appreciate these films as examples of high culture—sophisticated and highly intellectual art—and Hollywood films as mass culture—commercial art appealing to unrefined tastes—the distinction between the two is an oversimplification. Such rote categorization reveals a class-based ideological precept implicit in the art cinema movement: the assumption that popular film is too plebeian, crude, and unsophisticated to be considered worthy of serious consideration.

The case of India's film industry illustrates how privileging high art dictates that most international audiences overlook indigenous popular cinemas. India's film industry is the largest film industry in the world in terms of the number of films produced. The Hindi film industry has been dubbed "Bollywood" because of its Bombay location and prodigious size, rivaling Hollywood. Yet many in the West were introduced to Indian cinema in 1956, when the jury at the Cannes Film Festival voted *Pather Panchali*, "Best Human Document." Bengali director Satyajit Ray achieved international fame for his work, and for many Western enthusiasts, Ray's films are the face of Indian cinema. However, Ray's work is a departure from the norm in that country.

> Popular Indian films are typically an eclectic hodgepodge of styles: comic interludes, musical sequences, religion, adventure, fights, socio-political considerations—all get mixed up together in commercial (pan-Indian mainstream) cinema, often characterized by the epithet *masala* (spicy). (Thoraval, p. 118)

One of the most popular Indian films ever made, the "curry" Western *Embers* ("*Sholay*"; Ramesh Sippy 1975), exemplifies how Hindi films distinguish themselves by fusing competing narrative strategies and visual styles. The film includes episodes of extreme brutality: one man throws glowing coals on a thief; outlaws cut the arms off a policeman. But it also contains absurdly comic sequences, as when two men flip a coin—which stands on its side instead of falling on heads or tails. Bollywood films also rely on elaborate sets and ornate costuming to create a kaleidoscopic visual appeal.

In contrast, *Pather Panchali* follows the hardships of a poor Bengali family, focusing on the young children, Apu (Subir Bannerjee) and his older sister, Durga (Uma Das Gapta). Ray's film consists of loosely linked episodes that portray the daily routines of an impoverished family: Apu and Durga see a train for the first time; Apu asks his father for money to buy candy; Apu watches his sister dance in the first rains of the monsoon. When the father leaves home for an extended period of time to find work, a series of tragic events besets the family, culminating in Durga's death from pneumonia. While popular Indian films don't shy away from depicting social problems, their aesthetic approach favors escapist fantasy over the melancholic and provocative realism of Ray's work.

Pather Panchali's visual style also stands in sharp contrast to India's popular cinema. It abandons studio shooting in favor of locations. Ray uses the Indian landscape to capture the family's fleeting pleasures and mounting hardships. Animals and insects wander in and out of the frame to suggest how precariously situated is the family's crumbling homestead (fig. **11.6**).

11.6 *Pather Panchali* was shot on location, to capture the aura of rural India.

Following the international success of *Pather Panchali*, the Indian government founded the Indian Film Finance Corporation to improve the quality and heighten the international reputation of the country's films. The Indian government hoped to capitalize on Ray's critical success by subsidizing films that might bring more international prestige to the country's film industry.

In effect, Ray's international popularity and the government's subsequent decision to fund "serious" movies established a two-tier system in which international acclaim is lavished on directors whose films meet certain criteria associated with high art. Those criteria may include a bias toward Western art: Ray's most obvious influences were not other Indian film directors, but Americans and Europeans, including David Lean, Frank Capra, John Ford, Sergei Eisenstein, Jean Renoir, and Vittorio De Sica (Thoraval, p. 243). Perhaps a film that was less Western might not have received such lavish praise from American critics. Tellingly, the world premiere of *Pather Panchali* was not in India, but in New York.

While a remarkable cinematic achievement, Ray's film does not reflect the everyday Indian movie-going experience. The international acclaim for his work, which recently has been eclipsed by the global embrace of Bollywood, demonstrates how art films are seen as more legitimate cultural expressions than mainstream films.

In short, the art cinema movement of the 1950s and 1960s provided audiences with a wide range of cinematic experiences that differed dramatically from classical Hollywood's standard fare. Still, the production and reception of these films were profoundly shaped by cultural, historical, and economic circumstances.

11.7 Directness and immediacy were the main characteristics of *Rome, Open City*.

11.8 The depiction of minute detail is a stylistic feature of *Umberto D*, a film about an impoverished pensioner.

Fig. **11.13** at the end of this chapter offers a brief schematic of these two filmmaking contexts, as well as others that are discussed below: Italian Neorealism, Third Cinema, and Fourth Cinema.

Italian Neorealism

Italian Neorealism was an influential postwar cinema whose social and economic context defined its style in crucial ways. In Italy after World War II, Roberto Rossellini, Vittorio De Sica, and Luchino Visconti, actors and directors who had trained and worked in the commercial Italian film industry before the war, produced startling and distinctive films that seemed to capture the reality of the physical devastation, the moral degradation, and the human suffering of the war years. In the words of De Sica, "the experience of the war was decisive for us all. Each felt the mad desire to throw away the old stories of the Italian cinema, to plant the camera in the midst of real life." (quoted in Marcus, pp. xiii–xiv)

Neorealism pre-dated (and in many ways influenced) the international art cinema discussed above. Its principles and visual style were even further removed from Hollywood than those of art cinema.

Neorealist filmmaking grew from real-life events—yet the films were fictionalized accounts of experiences during the war and of the hardships of postwar Italy. Although Rossellini's *Rome, Open City* ("*Roma, città aperta*"; 1945) and De Sica's *Bicycle Thieves* were scripted, they convincingly relayed the harsh realities of wartime and its aftermath with a directness and immediacy that seemed to be missing from the escapist Italian and Hollywood films of the 1930s (fig. **11.7**).

According to the theorist and screenwriter Cesare Zavattini, Neorealism presented everyday life through stories involving working-class or poor protagonists, the use of location shooting, long takes, natural lighting, non-professional actors, vernacular dialogue, grainy black-and-white film stock, and unobtrusive editing (Marcus, p. 22). These distinctive characteristics derived partly from the economic circumstances of post-war filmmaking—a lack of equipment, film stock, and studio soundstages—and partly from the directors' commitment to filmmaking with a social purpose.

Neorealist cinema was concerned with telling the stories of ordinary Italian people struggling to survive. Films such as *Bicycle Thieves*—the story of a poor man and his son who attempt to recover their stolen bicycle because it represents the family's economic future—convey the breakdown of traditional social institutions. In terms of narrative form, Neorealist films depict people going about their daily lives. They devote screen time to the depiction of the mundane and favor a digressive storytelling style. Peter Lehman and William Luhr describe the difference between De Sica's *Umberto D* (1952; fig. **11.8**) and a Hollywood film in terms of the organization of the action:

> De Sica seeks to give a wholeness to the reality he represents. He
> does not break it down into parts, decide what is important and
> unimportant and then only show us the important part. He shows
> us everything in the belief that we can decide what is important [...]
> The [Classical Hollywood] style [...] uses a continuity system based
> on eliding unimportant parts of an action. (Lehman and Luhr, p. 215)

Italian Neorealism had a significant influence on many postwar cinemas, including Hollywood's *film noir* and social problem films of the 1940s and 1950s, the British New Wave of the 1960s, and Third Cinema movements such as Cinema Novo in Brazil and post-revolutionary Cuban cinema. Its social vision and conventions were taken up by politically committed filmmakers in Africa, Latin America, and Asia during the revolutionary fervor of the 1960s.

Third Cinema

In 1969 Argentine filmmakers Fernando Solanas and Octavio Getino relabeled cinema movements emerging from Europe's newly independent former colonies in Africa, Asia, and Latin America as Third Cinema. Third Cinema as a concept announced its opposition to the First Cinema (commercial and industrial Hollywood) and Second Cinema (the international, author-driven art cinema). Rather than designating a specific geographical or cultural location, Third Cinema championed a political stance that favored liberation and cultural decolonization.

One extremely important film in the Third Cinema tradition is *The Battle of Algiers* ("*La battaglia di Algeri* "; Gillo Pontecorvo 1966), a film that depicts events of the late 1950s, when Algerians began forcefully to resist French colonial rule. The filmmakers wanted to present an experience of political struggle that "seemed to embody for so many Third World nations a model for the course of liberation from colonialism." (Bignardi, p. 16) In aesthetic terms, that model emphasized collective social experience: "historical struggle is not narrated through idealized star actors and heroic characters but through the mass movement

11.9 An Algerian woman dons Western dress in *The Battle of Algiers*.

of peoples." (Shohat and Stam, p. 252) Except for one role—the French General Mathieu (Jean Martin)—Pontecorvo used non-professional actors.

In undertaking this historic and historical project, Pontecorvo adopted Italian Neorealism's newsreel aesthetic to achieve the "tone of truth." (Bignardi, p. 20) He and cameraman Marcello Gatti were so adept at achieving this tone (using hand-held cameras, location shooting, and fast film stock) that several American directors who screened the film suggested that Pontecorvo put a disclaimer at the beginning of the film assuring audiences that "not one foot" of newsreel or documentary film was included (Kruidenier, p. 3).

The film exposes the reality that both the Algerian insurgents and the French colonizers perpetrated inhumane violence. Yet it ultimately sympathizes with the revolutionaries, led for a time by former petty criminal Ali La Pointe (Brahim Haggiag). *The Battle of Algiers* depicts the way Algerians used their knowledge of Western ideology against the French authorities. In one scene, Algerian women don Western clothing and dye their hair: they look as if they have assimilated Western culture in order to move past checkpoints and plant bombs in the French area of the city (fig. **11.9**). In the concluding moments of the film, the French round up and defeat the revolutionary group's leadership, but this is a tenuous and temporary victory. Closing shots show the streets crowded with people celebrating Algerian independence in 1962.

Third Cinema encompasses a variety of cinema practices, not all of them influenced by Italian Neorealism. According to scholar Paul Schroeder, seminal Cuban directors in the 1960s learned how to produce films with limited resources from the example set by the French New Wave (Schroeder, p. 3). Works by Julio García Espinoza, Tomás Gutiérrez Alea, and Hernando Solas embrace art cinema's formalist experimentation instead of remaining steadfastly committed to the rhythms of real life.

In Brazil's *Cinema Novo* movement, Glauber Rocha and Neorealist Nelson Pereira Dos Santos examined the material realities of poverty among the country's minorities, indigenous peoples, and the disenfranchised. Rocha's *Black God White Devil* (*"Deus e o diablo na Terra do Sol"*; 1963) and Dos Santos's *Barren Lives* (*"Vidas Secas"*; 1963) paint unsentimental portraits of oppressed peasants, reflecting what Rocha called an "aesthetics of hunger" (fig. **11.10**). After a 1964 military coup in Brazil curtailed the movement, the Brazilian directors remaining in the country transformed the "aesthetics of hunger" into Tropicalism, an approach that rejected the opposition between indigenous authenticity and Hollywood commercialism (Sklar, p. 355). Rather than choose between colonial power and indigenous authenticity, Tropicalism "aggressively juxtaposed the folkloric and the industrial, the native and the foreign." (Shohat and Stam, p. 310)

As these few brief examples suggest, Third Cinema encompassed a wide variety of cinematic practices that were concerned with film as both a political and an aesthetic medium. Borrowing from both Neorealism and the international art cinema of the 1960s, Third Cinema directors used cinema to examine the complex relationship between colonial power and indigenous culture during a time of revolution. While the overriding concern with cultural decolonization drove the theory and practice of Third Cinemas, local economic, political, and cultural contexts also informed the unique films produced.

Fourth Cinema

Fourth Cinema is a term coined by Maori filmmaker and theorist Barry Barclay to describe the filmmaking practices of indigenous people, also called aboriginal people or First Nations. Aboriginal people are "outside the national outlook *by definition*, for Indigenous cultures are ancient remnant cultures persisting within the modern nation state." (Barclay) First, Second, and Third Cinemas are "cinemas of the Modern Nation State," according to Barclay: "from the Indigenous place of standing, these are all invader Cinemas." Barclay describes a cinema that exists outside the orthodoxy of the nation state. Film scholar Corinn Columpar writes that the Fourth World "does not refer to a geographical terrain [...] but to the absence of such a terrain [...] members of the Fourth World must hold in tension competing national allegiances and negotiate

11.10 (*above*) Peasant life is presented in unsentimental fashion in *Black God White Devil*.

11.11 (*below*) A new chief takes the helm in *Whale Rider*.

11.12 *Smoke Signals* deconstructs Hollywood's stereotype of the stoic Native American.

cultural influences that are frequently in conflict." (p. 466)

In the last two decades, Fourth World filmmakers have been committing their experiences to film, garnering an international audience in the process. In addition to Barclay's *Ngati* (1989), two other notable films have come from the indigenous Maori culture of New Zealand. *Once Were Warriors* (Lee Tamahori 1994) and *Whale Rider* (Niki Caro 2002) depict the struggles of Maori women within the context of both the *Pakeha* (the colonial British settler culture) and the Maori community itself. *Whale Rider*, adapted from a novel by Witi Ihimaera, traces the story of Paikea (Keisha Castle-Hughes), a girl who is the descendant of tribal leaders of the Ngato Konihi people. Pai is destined to become the chief of her people, but must convince her stubborn grandfather that a girl can handle the responsibilities (fig. **11.11**). Ironically, the notion of Maori opposition to a dominant British settler culture may give way to a celebration of the indigenous *as* the national culture. The international popularity of *Once Were Warriors* and *Whale Rider* illustrates how Maori culture seems to be "celebrated as [New Zealand's] distinctive 'brand' (along with the landscape and environmental 'purity'), in the global trade, culture, and tourist markets." (Prentice, p. 253) In this view, films transform indigenous identities into global commodities and tourist attractions that, oddly enough, symbolize a nation that has long treated the indigenous population as non-citizens.

Smoke Signals (1998), a film directed by Chris Eyre, a member of the Cheyenne and Arapaho tribes, was based on short stories by Sherman Alexie, a Spokane/ Coeur d'Alene Indian. In shaping the odyssey of Victor (Adam Beach) and the talkative Thomas Builds-the-Fire (Evan Adams) as they travel from the Coeur d'Alene reservation in Idaho to Phoenix on a mission to collect Victor's father's ashes, Eyre reclaims and re-conceives the road movie genre from an indigenous perspective. The two men travel by bus, an unexpected mode of transport across a landscape typically traversed by thundering horses or screeching trains in the Western (fig. **11.12**). Victor and Thomas are highly conscious of the differential treatment they receive as Native Americans, and they humorously discuss stereotypes born of a century of cinematic depictions of Indians in the Wild West. For example, Thomas dons a shirt that announces "Fry Bread Power," a comic nod to his rejection of the stereotype of the stoic Indian warrior that Victor embraces. The film was highly acclaimed for its delicacy in handling the myriad issues that affect indigenous people living in reservations (that is, in sovereign nations) within the United States.

National and Transnational Cinemas

The example of these Fourth Cinema films raises important concerns that also animate a good deal of recent scholarship. That concern is the question of cinema's tenuous relationship to nation.

As Valentina Vitali and Paul Willemen point out, in the earliest years of cinema, the national origin of films was inconsequential: reels were shipped from production companies directly to exhibitors who "screened them as novelty objects without paying much attention to their national provenance [origin]." (Vitali and Willemen, p. 1) Many early film companies operated in more than one country (as they do today). In 1905 Pathé was the leading supplier of films to the American market (Vitali and Willeman, p. 1; Abel p. xi). This situation would change by the mid-1910s. As Richard Abel writes, as part of their fierce struggle for industry dominance, American filmmakers and critics began to denounce the "foreignness" of French films and to champion a new American genre: the Western. Abel argues that, despite the continued habit of categorizing films according to national boundaries—often used by government and private industry to brand a product—filmmakers influence one another regardless of their nationality, and audiences are capable of being moved by films from many different cultural and national locations. Abel points in particular to the fact that French cinema shaped the films produced within the fledgling American industry, which in turn had a tremendous impact on French films after World War I.

In our discussion of international art cinema and Italian Neorealism, films are categorized and discussed according to the nation in which they were produced. The theories and practices surrounding Third and Fourth cinemas also are predicated on the fact that there is some relationship between filmmaking and nation, even if that nation is a postcolonial entity, or if an indigenous individual's multiple national and cultural allegiances are difficult to define.

Film enthusiasts are fairly comfortable with the idea of grouping films according to the nation that produced them. We routinely speak of Hong Kong cinema, and we may also accept the argument that Hollywood films, for better and for worse, embody and promote American values of individualism and competition. But assuming there is a connection between a group of films and a national culture without asking about the nature of that connection would be unwise. Our premises require further exploration. Can films "from" a particular national cinema be distinguished from those of other national cinemas because of the stories they tell, the languages and locations they use, by a recognizable visual style, or by a common approach to genre?

What determines the "nationality" of a film: the nation of origin of the screenwriter or director? It's useful to remember that many Hollywood studio films were made by European émigrés. Does the fact that an American production company shot a film mean it is an American film? How should we take account of co-productions: films that are made with funding, crew, and cast from different countries? Does the location where the film was shot, or where the story is set, or the language(s) used, figure in the discussion? Was the *Lord of the Rings* trilogy a New Zealand film? (The IMDb lists the country of origin as "New Zealand/United States".)

Is it possible to identify a "national style" that applies to many films from the same country? And over what period of time? Are we perhaps depending upon genre, like Hong Kong Action cinema, or a director, like Spain's Pedro Almodóvar, to define a national cinema? That would certainly be understandable, since national film industries that seek to compete with Hollywood often depend upon a marketable trait to distinguish their products from those of Hollywood.

How do propaganda films function in relation to a country's national cinema? Or, put another way, what is the relationship between national cinema and nationalism? If a director makes a film that criticizes the beliefs or actions of her government or compatriots, does that also represent part of that country's national cinema?

In the midst of the many unanswerable questions raised by the national cinema model, scholars such as Susan Hayward remain committed to exploring the way that films articulate ideologies about the nation in obvious and subtle ways, addressing audience members as part of a national culture, and in so doing, helping to construct them as citizens. Films become a means by which a nation represents itself to itself (Hayward, p. 93). At one end of the spectrum, propaganda films, such as those commissioned by government-owned film industries in Italy, Germany, and Japan in World War II, seek to convince spectators of the unchanging, clearly defined idea of national identity by presenting a heroic and unified vision of the national body politic pitched in battle against the forces of evil. In the U.S., Hollywood studios contributed to the Allied war effort by making propaganda films as well as commercial releases, all coordinated through the newly created Bureau of Motion Pictures. Less obviously promoting the idea of national invincibility than these propaganda films are heritage films. Famous for their nostalgic reminiscence over a past golden age, these films, associated primarily with Britain, work to create a national narrative by projecting simpler, innocent, halcyon days onto a past era, when the British empire spanned the globe.

The ongoing economic battle between Hollywood and many national film industries suggests that a great deal is at stake in the survival of national cinemas. To preserve the possibility of a local film industry, many nations adopt economic policies such as quotas and tariffs designed to protect domestic filmmaking. In Europe today, filmmaking is subsidized by regional and supranational entities such as Eurimages, a Council of Europe fund that supports co-productions among its thirty-four member states. No industrial rubric (these films are made in the same way, in the same nation or region) and no textual one (these films look the same) can fully explain the seeming self-fulfilling prophecy that is the national cinema. What is certain, however, is that while some might treasure national cinema industries as cultural institutions, like Hollywood, these industries are commercial as well as aesthetic enterprises.

If Third and Fourth Cinemas offer a "decisive refutation of the easy Western assumption of the coincidence of ethnic background and home," (Crofts, p. 49) then the concept of the transnational in cinema goes one step further, to question the notion of home altogether. In the past thirty years, partly in response to globalization, to the restructuring of nation states in many regions of the world, and to continuing violence that has produced millions of refugees and exiles, scholars in a number of fields, from political science, geography, and philosophy to cultural studies and film studies have begun to look more closely at the complexity, and changing nature, of nation and national identity. Certainly many film cultures have incorporated transnational elements—even the émigré directors of the studio system (Lubitsch, Murnau, Wilder, Sirk, Von Sternberg) can be said to complicate nationality. In contemporary international cinema, filmmakers whose national identities are complicated by war, conflict, migration, or diaspora, tap into experiences of dislocation and connection common to those for whom

11.13 Cinema styles and contexts.

	Classical Hollywood (1920s–1960s)	Art Cinema (1950s–1960s)	Neorealism (1943–52)	Third Cinema (1960s–1970s)	Fourth Cinema (1980s–present)
Characters	One or two active, goal-oriented characters	One or two psychologically complex characters with unclear goals	Everyday individuals who struggle to survive and become heroic in the process	Focus is on collective experience, whether represented through an individual or group	Indigenous people, as individuals and within clans or tribal communities, living uneasily within a modern nation state
Narrative	Cause-and-effect logic; three-act or four-part structure; closure	Loose cause–effect relations; episodic structure; open-ended	Tales of average people struggling in postwar Italy; open-ended	Revolutionary stories that resonate at personal and social levels	Explore multiple, conflicting identities: struggle between tradition and contemporary values without necessarily rejecting either one completely; raising questions of colonial practices and transnational experiences
Visual Style and Sound	Studio and location shooting; continuity editing; visual and sound techniques enhance storytelling	Studio and location shooting; emphasis on expression and artistry rather than storytelling; self-reflexivity	Location shooting, non-professional actors, and direct sound contribute to documentary immediacy	Location shooting; non-professional actors; many adopt documentary techniques, others use indigenous art traditions	Variable: may be lower budget but not necessarily guerrilla filmmaking practices of Third Cinema; also can become part of a national cinema project (e.g., New Zealand and Maori film)
Mode of Production	Industrial studio system	*Auteur*-driven studio and government-supported filmmaking	Studio-trained directors worked outside industrial system	Government-supported, independent, and artisanal productions; many varied national contexts	May be independent, artisanal, and government supported

no definitive site exists that can be called home. Palestinian filmmakers, for example, have difficulty presenting their work as part of a national enterprise in the traditional sense of the nation state. Hamid Naficy argues for the existence of an independent transnational genre by identifying a common thread in the depiction of claustrophobic spaces in Turkish exile and Iranian films.

Hong Kong auteur Wong Kar Wai's *Chungking Express* (1994) rejects the possibility of a simple notion of national identity through his musical motifs. The soundtrack includes a hefty selection of music of various national origins: reggae, Indian raga, and American pop music all become sound motifs. The music pours out of jukeboxes and portable radios, suggesting the eclectic mix of ethnicities in Hong Kong. At the time of filming, Hong Kong was a bustling hub for international trade destined to be re-integrated with China when Britain relinquished control on July 1, 1997. Residents greeted this change with skepticism, since Hong Kong had been a British colony for over 150 years. The assortment of music underscores the territory's fluid cultural makeup and its pronounced diversity. Even the non-diegetic music evokes Hong Kong's troubled concept of nationhood. Faye Wong's adaptation of the Cranberries' song "Dreams" plays twice on the soundtrack and it resonates on a number of levels. The Cranberries are an Irish rock band, so the song alludes to Hong Kong and Ireland's shared history as British colonies. Yet Wong Kar Wai uses an adaptation of this song, not the original, which undercuts the idea of a fixed national identity. Is the song British? Irish? Cantonese? The music explores the way Hong Kong's identity is no longer legible in the terms of traditional ideas about the nation state. In short, filmmakers creating transnational cinemas, and scholars who study this work, contemplate the notion that people may have multiple modes of identification, or possibly none at all, when it comes to national identity.

This discussion of social context and style broadly considers how economic and political factors can influence filmmaking. Fig. **11.13** establishes the rough historical timeframes for classical Hollywood, art cinema, Neorealism, Third Cinema, and Fourth Cinema, and charts the different characteristics of each movement with regard to character, narrative, visual style, and mode of production. The next chapter focuses on stardom, and how this specific facet of Hollywood and other commercial cinemas affects the way audiences consume and interpret films.

Works Consulted

Abel, Richard. *The Red Rooster Scare: Making Cinema American, 1900–1910*. Berkeley: University of California Press, 1999.

Barclay, Barry. "Celebrating Fourth Cinema." *Illusions Magazine*. July 2003.

Betz, Mark. "The Name above the (Sub)Title: Internationalism, Coproduction, and Polyglot European Art Cinema." *Camera Obscura*, 16/1 (2001). March 8, 2002. **http://muse.jhu.edu/journals/camera_obscura/v016/16.1betz.htm**.

Bignardi, Irene. "The Making of *The Battle of Algiers*." *Cineaste*, Spring 2000, pp. 14–22.

Black, Gregory D. "Hollywood Censored: The Production Code Administration and the Hollywood Film Industry, 1930–1940." *Film History* 3.3 (1989): pp. 167–89.

Bordwell, David. "Story Causality and Motivation," in *The Classical Hollywood Cinema: Film Style and Mode of Production to 1960*, ed. David Bordwell *et al.* New York: Columbia University Press, 1985, pp. 12–23.

Carter, Angela. *Expletives Deleted*. London: Chatto and Windus, 1992.

Chanan, Michael. "Tomás Gutiérrez Alea," in *The Oxford History of World Cinema*, ed. Geoffrey Nowell-Smith. Oxford: Oxford University Press, 1996, p. 744.

Chaudhuri, Shohini. *Contemporary World Cinema: Europe, The Middle East, East Asia and South Asia*. Edinburgh: Edinburgh University Press, 2005.

Chow, Rey. *Sentimental Fabulations, Contemporary Chinese Films: Attachment in the Age of Global Visibility*. New York: Columbia University Press, 2007.

Columpar, Corinn. *Unsettling Sights: The Fourth World on Film*. Southern Illinois University Press, 2010.

——————. "'Taking Care of Her Green Stone Wall": The Experience of Space in *Once Were Warriors*. *Quarterly Review of Film and Video* 24.5 (2007): pp. 463–74.

Cook, David. *A History of Narrative Film*, 3rd edn. New York: Norton, 1996.

——————. "'We're in the Money': A Brief History of Market Power Concentration and Risk Aversion in the American Film Industry from the Edison Trust to the Rise of Transnational Media Conglomerates," in *Theorising National Cinema*, ed. Valentina Vitali and Paul Willeman. London: British Film Institute Publishing, 2006, pp. 158–71.

Crofts, Stephen. "Reconceptualizing National Cinemas." in *Theorising National Cinema*, ed. Valentina Vitali and Paul Willeman. London: British Film Institute Publishing, 2006, pp. 44–57.

D'Lugo, Marvin. "Recent Spanish Cinema in Global Context," in *Post-Scripts: Essays in Film and the Humanities* 21.2 (Winter/Spring, 2002).

Doherty, Thomas. *Hollywood's Censor: Joseph I. Breen and the Production Code Administration*. New York: Columbia University Press, 2007.

——————. "Church's reach diminished—at least when it comes to films." *The Washington Post*. May 20, 2006; A23. **my.brandeis.edu/news/**.

Elsaesser, Thomas. *European Cinema: Face to Face with Hollywood*. Amsterdam: Amsterdam University Press, 2005.

——————. *New German Cinema*. New Brunswick, NJ: Rutgers University Press, 1989.

Galt, Rosalind and Karl Schoonover, ed. *Global Art Cinema: New Theories and Histories*. London and New York: Oxford University Press, 2010.

Guerrero, Ed. *Framing Blackness: The African American Image in Film*. Philadelphia: Temple University Press, 1993.

Hake, Sabine. *German National Cinema*. London: Routledge, 2008.

Hay, James. *Popular Film Culture in Fascist Italy*. Bloomington: Indiana University Press, 1987.

Hayward, Susan. "Framing National Cinemas," in *Cinema and Nation*, ed. Mette Hjort and Scott Mackenzie. London: Routledge, 2000, pp. 88–101.

Heines, Marjorie. *Sex, Sin, and Blasphemy. A Guide to American's Censorship Wars*. New York: The New York Press, 1998.

Higginbotham, Virginia. *Spanish Film under Franco*. Austin: University of Texas Press, 1988.

"John Ford's *Young Mr. Lincoln*." Collective text by the editors of *Cahiers du Cinéma*. *Film Theory and Criticism: Introductory Readings*, 3rd edn., ed. Gerald Mast and Marshall Cohen. New York: Oxford University Press, 1985, pp. 695–740.

Kinder, Marsha (ed). *Refiguring Spain: Cinema/Media/Representation*. Durham: Duke University Press, 1997.

Kruidenier, David. "Postcolonialism and Feminism in *The Battle of Algiers*." Unpublished paper. February 2004.

Lane, Anthony. "Borderlines." *The New Yorker*. August 28, 2006. pp. 82–3.

Lastra, James. *Sound Technology and the American Cinema*. New York: Columbia University Press.

Lehman, Peter, and William Luhr. *Thinking about Movies: Watching, Questioning, Enjoying*. Fort Worth: Harcourt, 1999.

Lewis, Jon. *Hollywood versus Hardcore: How the Struggle over Censorship Saved the Modern Film Industry*. New York: New York University Press, 2000.

Lu Sheldon H. *Transnational Chinese Cinemas: Identity, Nationhood, Gender*. Honolulu: University of Hawaii Press, 1997.

Maltby, Richard. "Censorship and Self-Regulation," in *The Oxford History of World Cinema*, ed. Geoffrey Nowell-Smith. New York: Oxford University Press, 1996, pp. 235–48.

Marcus, Millicent. *Italian Film in the Light of Neorealism*. Princeton: Princeton University Press, 1986.

Marie, Michel. "It Really Makes You Sick," in *French Film: Texts and Contexts*, 2nd edn., ed. Susan Hayward and Ginette Vincendeau. London: Routledge, 2000, pp. 158–73.

Miller, Toby. "Screening the Nation: Rethinking Options." *Cinema Journal* 38.4 (Summer 1999): pp. 93–7.

Mira, Alberto. *The A to Z of Spanish Cinema*. London: Scarecrow Press, 2010.

Moussinac, Leon. *L'Age Ingrat du Cinema*. Paris: EFR, 1967.

Murray, Stewart. *Images of Dignity: Barry Barclay and Fourth Cinema*. Wellington, New Zealand: Huia, 2008.

Naficy, Hamid. "Phobic Spaces and Liminal Places: Independent Transnational Film Genre." In *Multiculturalism, Postcoloniality, and Transnational Cinema*, eds. Ella Shohat and Robert Stam. New Brunswick, NJ: Rutgers University Press 2003. pp. 203–26.

Naremore, James. *More than Night: Film Noir in its Contexts*. Berkeley: University of California Press, 1998.

Neupert, Richard. *A History of the French New Wave*. Madison: University of Wisconsin Press, 2002.

Nowell-Smith, Geoffrey. "Art Cinema," in *The Oxford History of World Cinema*, ed. Geoffrey Nowell-Smith. New York: Oxford University Press, 1996, pp. 567–75.

O'Regan, Tom. *Australian National Cinema*. New York and London: Routledge, 1996.

Prentice, Chris. *"Riding the Whale? Postcolonialism and Globalism in Whale Rider."* In *Global Fissures: Postcolonial Fusions*, eds. Clara A.B. Joseph and Janet Wilson. Amsterdam and New York: Rodopi, 2006. pp. 247–68.

Rajadhyaksha, Ashish. "Realism, Modernism, and Post-colonial Theory," in *The Oxford Guide to Film Studies*, ed. John Hill and Pamela Church Gibson. Oxford: Oxford University Press, 1998, pp. 413–25.

Ray, Robert. *A Certain Tendency of the Hollywood Cinema, 1930–1980*. Princeton: Princeton University Press, 1985.

Robertson, J.C. *The Hidden Cinema: British Film Censorship in Action, 1913–1972*. London: Routledge, 1993.

Schatz, Thomas. *The Genius of the System: Hollywood Filmmaking in the Studio Era*. New York: Pantheon, 1988.

Schroeder, Paul A. *Tomás Gutiérrez Alea: The Dialectics of a Filmmaker*. New York and London: Routledge, 2002.

Scott, Allen John. *Hollywood: The Place, The Industry*. Princeton NJ: Princeton University Press, 2005.

Shohat, Ella, and Robert Stam. *Unthinking Eurocentrism: Multiculturalism and the Media*. London and New York: Routledge, 1994.

Sklar, Robert. *Film: An International History of the Medium*, 2nd edn. Saddle River, NJ: Prentice-Hall and Harry N. Abrams, 2002.

Sontag, Susan. "The Imagination of Disaster," in *Movies*, ed. Gilbert Adair. London: Penguin, 1999, pp. 170–85.

Staiger, Janet. "Standardization and Differentiation: The Reinforcement and Dispersion of Hollywood's Practices," in *The Classical Hollywood Cinema: Film Style and Mode of Production to 1960*, ed. David Bordwell *et al.* New York: Columbia University Press, 1985, pp. 96–112.

Thoraval, Yves. *The Cinemas of India*. New Delhi: Macmillan India, 2000.

Vir, Parminder. "The Mother of All Battles." *The New Statesman*. July 8, 2002, pp. 40–2.

Vitali, Valentina and Paul Willeman. "Introduction." *Theorising National Cinema*. London: British Film Institute Publishing, 2006, pp. 1–14.

Welch D. *Propaganda and the German Cinema, 1933–1945*. London: I.B. Tauris, 2001.

Willeman, Paul. "The National Revisited," in *Theorising National Cinema*, ed. Valentina Vitali and Paul Willeman. London: British Film Institute Publishing, 2006, pp. 29–43.

Wood, Robin. "Ideology, Genre, Auteur: *Shadow of a Doubt*," in *Hitchcock's Films Revisited*. New York: Columbia University Press, 1989, pp. 288–303.

Wurtzler, Steve J. *Electric Sounds: Technological Change and the Rise of the Corporate Mass Media*. New York: Columbia University Press, 2007.

Zhang, Yingjin. *Chinese National Cinema*. London: Routledge, 2004.

CHAPTER TWELVE

Film Stardom as a Cultural Phenomenon

Among the strange characteristics of the tribes who populate this continent, North America, is the one by which its inhabitants choose specific stars for themselves and live their lives in worship of them.

Sergei Eisenstein

Throughout the United States, images of James Dean and Marilyn Monroe (fig. **12.1**) are still ubiquitous half a century after their deaths. For audiences of all ages, Dean's name is synonymous with modern angst and youthful rebellion. Although he starred in only three feature films, Dean is such a pervasive

12.1 Marilyn Monroe: still an icon of beauty and glamor.

component of American popular culture that, without a doubt, many who have not seen one of his movies have some sense of Dean's magnetic persona (see fig. 5.17).

America's lingering obsession with figures such as Monroe and Dean exemplifies the star culture that is central to the economic success of Hollywood and other film industries. As anyone who owns a poster for Dean's *Rebel Without a Cause* can attest, audiences do not just appreciate a star's performance onscreen; they also consume the public image that a star gradually acquires over the course of a career. Fans are so drawn to these larger-than-life figures that they imitate the attire and mannerisms of their favorite stars, they scour gossip magazines looking for them, and they even vote them into political office. Stars represent ideals of beauty, dreams of wealth, and models of masculinity and femininity.

To state the obvious, "actor" is not synonymous with "star." In film, actors play characters onscreen, and good actors can create complex characters. But a star's presence transcends the performance; a star doesn't just make her character believable—a star also possesses a publicly acknowledged magnetism that lures audiences to the film and lingers in viewers' memories after they leave the theater. While stars may come by this charisma naturally, in most cases studio heads, talent agencies, publicity outlets, and the stars themselves carefully cultivate the public's admiration.

Stars are an integral part of every major film industry and play a pivotal role in production and marketing. For producers, a star is raw material. Occasionally writers, directors, and producers design a project specifically with a particular star in mind, hoping to capitalize on audience expectations. Such projects are called "star vehicles," because they showcase that star's persona—a vehicle to be driven by the star, so to speak. Some consider *Talladega Nights* (Adam McKay 2006) a star vehicle for Will Ferrell, or *Dreamgirls* (Bill Condon 2006; fig. **12.2**) a vehicle for Beyoncé Knowles.

Of course, Hollywood isn't the only film industry to rely on stars. Hong Kong's film industry, for example, has had a number of internationally recognized stars, including Bruce Lee, Jackie Chan, Chow Yun-Fat, and Maggie Cheung. Britain has made stars out of Sean Connery, Hugh Grant, and Julie Christie, among others. France's art cinema turned Brigitte Bardot, Jeanne Moreau, Jean-Paul Belmondo, and Jean Reno into world-renowned stars.

From its early days the film industry has recognized the importance of the star. A bizarre promotional campaign for silent movie "starlet" Florence Lawrence (fig. **12.3**) served as an early attempt to

12.2 *Dreamgirls*—a star vehicle for Beyoncé Knowles.

draw audiences to a film by marketing the biographical details of its key player. According to film historian Richard DeCordova, in 1910 the *St. Louis Post-Dispatch* supposedly reported that Lawrence had been killed by a New York streetcar (although no one has ever produced a copy of this original article). On March 5, Lawrence's studio, Independent Motion Picture Company (IMP), purchased an ad in *Moving Picture World*, decrying that "the blackest and at the same time the silliest lie yet circulated by enemies of 'Imp' was the story foisted on the public of St. Louis last week to the effect that Miss Lawrence … had been killed by a street car." (quoted in DeCordova, p. 58) DeCordova hypothesizes that IMP itself intentionally began circulating the story of Lawrence's death. More importantly, IMP's subsequent denial of the rumor demonstrates a two-tiered strategy to generate public interest in Lawrence's films. By dispelling the rumor, IMP drew public attention to the star. And, by painting its competitors as mendacious perpetrators of an outrageous lie, IMP sought to generate public sympathy for the primary victims of the deception: IMP Studios and, of course, Florence Lawrence.

This often cited episode in the rise of Hollywood's star culture underscores how the film industry relies on stardom to lure audiences into the theater by marketing an actor's biography (fictionalized or not).

12.3 Florence Lawrence: one of the first movie stars.

Star studies explores how stardom attracts audiences and affects what audiences respond to onscreen. The appeal of celebrity is an integral part of music, sports, television, and politics in many cultures. Some of the earliest, best, and most systematic analyses of celebrity come out of film studies approaches. This chapter will introduce five basic approaches scholars use to analyze the star system: stars and the movie industry; the dynamics of performance; the star persona; stardom and ideology; and stars and subcultures.

Stars and the Movie Industry

Stars are so instrumental that they influence the economic viability of not just individual films but entire film industries. Some film scholars explore topics such as the economic impact of studio contracts versus the "free agency" stars now enjoy, and how these trends affect overall industry output and profitability.

For example, the abolition of lengthy studio contracts following the disintegration of the Hollywood studio system in the 1950s helped facilitate a growth in independent productions. Producers were now able to arrange star contracts for a single film or for a small cluster of films (as opposed to the old system, where stars were bound to a particular studio for years). This arrangement—called the package-unit approach to production, since stars were "packaged" with individual projects—led to the subsequent proliferation of talent agents responsible for managing star careers (Thompson and Bordwell, p. 336).

Tom Cruise's lengthy and lucrative relationship with Paramount demonstrates the fact that individual stars play a central role within the economic structure of the Hollywood film industry. In 2005, Cruise's appeal secured him a broad sphere of influence. He wielded so much power that, according to press reports, in the spring of 2006 Cruise threatened to boycott his own publicity appearances for the upcoming release of *Mission: Impossible III* if the TV network Comedy Central broadcast an episode of *South Park* that ridiculed the Church of Scientology, an organization whose tenets Cruise has vociferously advocated. Because Comedy Central's parent company, Viacom, owned Paramount Pictures—the company that produced Cruise's film—the network flinched, at least temporarily. (They initially pulled the episode but later broadcast it). The conflict points to how Hollywood's biggest stars cast a wide and sometimes tangled web of influence across the entertainment industry.

Subsequent events undermined Cruise's clout in the industry. His crusade against *South Park* was one of a string of unusual public outbursts: Cruise ridiculed actress Brooke Shields's bout with post-partum depression and dismissed the entire psychiatric profession to boot; during an interview with talk show host Oprah Winfrey he leapt up on a sofa to proclaim his love for actress Katie Holmes; and he purportedly refused to allow Holmes, pregnant with his child, to talk during childbirth. By the fall of 2006, Viacom Chairman Sumner Redstone stated that Cruise's "recent conduct has not been acceptable," and Viacom subsidiary Paramount Pictures severed its fourteen-year ties with the volatile actor's production company ("Paramount").

Instantly, entertainment reporters nationwide erupted into a frenzied chorus. Some argued that the actor's outrageous offscreen antics affected the way audiences responded to him onscreen:

> The essence of Mr. Cruise's appeal going all the way back to *Risky Business* [...] was a fresh-faced, unpretentious exuberance [...]. But in the last year his life has become a public relations debacle as he has gone into full Scientology mode, and he has come to seem self-righteous and intolerant. (James)

Others couched the discussion in terms of the industry's narrower economic interests:

> Redstone said such displays cost the studio up to $150 million in lost ticket sales for Cruise's last film, *Mission: Impossible III*. [...] Studios, seeing profits shrink, are trying to dump the long-held economic system in Hollywood that led to stars earning paychecks upwards of $20 million. (Gentile)

And still others pondered both the aesthetic and economic impact of Paramount's decision:

The fear in Hollywood is that Mr. Redstone may be smashing the star-driven model without putting anything in its place but financial responsibility, and audiences don't line up to see financial responsibility. (Gabler)

Viacom/Paramount banked on Cruise to attract an audience; when his behavior jeopardized his star image, it also affected the studio's financial stability. While Cruise's public persona stabilized, the question of economic viability and star power became an issue in 2010 with the publicity surrounding Mel Gibson, a bankable star with a career spanning decades, and his alleged physical abuse of his girlfriend.

Film scholars (and economists) question the economic logic of a star system that pays figures like Cruise $20 million or more for a single performance. Recent studies have suggested that, contrary to commonly held assumptions, stars are not the thing that lures audiences to the theaters. After studying the box office receipts of nearly 200 films released in the early 1990s, economist S. Abraham Ravid discerned virtually no correlation between a star's presence and a film's box office gross: "Stars help to launch a film. They are meant as signals to create a big opening. But they can't make a film have legs." (Porter and Fabrikant, p. 5) This may partly explain the rise of reality TV programming: the participants are paid much less than movie stars.

The Dynamics of Performance

One aspect of a star's appeal is, quite obviously, her performance on screen. Why are audiences still mesmerized by Audrey Hepburn (and not, one might add, George Peppard) in *Breakfast at Tiffany's* (Blake Edwards 1961)? Why did fans suddenly scour the internet for pictures of Orlando Bloom after seeing his performance in *The Return of the King* (Peter Jackson 2003)? Rather than attributing a star's appeal to an enigmatic, indefinable talent, film scholars are interested in trying to explain what makes a particular performance memorable.

Stars create a following by developing a memorable and recognizable persona (fig. **12.4**). Two elements of that persona are the roles a star plays and the techniques he uses to create these roles. While character actors play a variety of different roles and experiment with various acting techniques depending on the type of characters they play, many stars often play one type of character and perfect one style of performance.

Charlie Chaplin is one of the few silent film stars still recognized by mainstream audiences today, because his signature character, the Little Tramp, still appeals to viewers. One of Chaplin's best-loved scenes comes in *The Gold Rush* (Charles Chaplin 1925), when, stuck in the dead of winter in the middle of the Yukon with nothing to eat, the Little Tramp dresses a boot to eat. James Naremore considers this scene indicative of Chaplin's work, and, in this excerpt from his analysis of Chaplin's acting, he argues that Chaplin's performance not only evokes both laughter and sympathy from the audience, but also resonates for audiences who recognize the down-and-out Tramp as a victim of capitalism.

12.4 *FoxTrot* pokes fun at the star system. FoxTrot © 2009 Bill Amend. Reprinted with permission of Universal Uclick. All rights reserved.

Naremore argues that the humor in the scene arises from the Tramp's meticulous attention to formality; even though he is serving a boot for dinner, he maintains "extravagant table manners."

And yet even though this famous scene can be used as a definition of comedy, it has another quality as well. The situation is pitched near to real horror, and the camera watches Chaplin from a relatively close vantage, framing his spot at the table and bringing us near to the character's suffering. His makeup is a visible, chalky pancake with heavy black circles beneath the eyes, but there is an authentically glassy, hallucinated look on his face. [...]

The mixed effect is basic to Chaplin's work. Although he seldom invites the audience to identify with his character in the same way they would with the protagonists of realistic drama, he involves them in a more complex way than the other silent comics. *The Gold Rush* can be read not only as a slapstick comedy but also as an allegory of Capital, full of symbolic implications about Greed, Fate, and the *condition humaine*; hence, the Tramp is designed to elicit the audience's sympathy more directly than the typical clown. (Naremore, pp. 124–6)

12.5 Charlie Chaplin's performance in *The Gold Rush* earned plaudits.

Naremore's analysis draws attention to particular aspects of the performance—his exaggerated mimicry, his facial expression—to explain why this is such a powerful performance (fig. **12.5**). (In contrast, audiences called Chaplin's contemporary Buster Keaton the "Great Stoneface" for his supposed lack of expression (fig. **12.6**). At first glance, Keaton's immobile face appears to be devoid of emotion, but it actually betrays a determined stoicism.) When Naremore argues that the mixture of comedy and horror "is basic to Chaplin's work," he suggests that this approach is an integral part of Chaplin's persona. It is a recognizable characteristic of Chaplin's career on screen. Naremore's discussion does not just consider Chaplin's performance; it also pays careful attention to other elements of *mise en scène* (the boot, Chaplin's makeup) and cinematography (the close-up) that complement the actor's physical presence.

This approach to star studies synthesizes much of the material covered in Part Two of this book. But rather than analyzing how a film's narrative, visual, and sound systems develop themes, this approach emphasizes how these cinematic elements help create the screen persona that audiences come to recognize as the star's signature.

The Star Persona

Richard Dyer argues, "the star phenomenon depends upon collapsing the distinction between the star-as-person and the star-as-performer" (1991, p. 216). Jennifer Aniston's and Vince Vaughn's film *The Break-Up* (Peyton Reed 2006; fig. **12.7**) is an obvious example of this collapse. This romantic comedy explores the increasingly bitter disintegration of a serious relationship. Prior to the production of the film, Aniston herself suffered a humiliating and very public breakup with her Hollywood-hottie husband, Brad Pitt. So when audiences flocked to see *The Break-Up*, many viewers read the film in terms of Aniston's own romantic woes. Aniston's comments at the height of its publicity onslaught fueled such speculation: "Laughter is a real necessity in healing," she said. "And to go and make […] a story that's real, and these arguments that are real, […] we get to sort of have fun winking at them, and then […] kind of just work through it" (quoted in "Aniston"). Conveniently, Aniston's "confessional" interviews in popular magazines like *Vanity Fair* helped lure fans to the theaters presumably to see her "real" life played out on screen. Intentional or not, these interviews targeted fans who would attend the film not to see the character Brooke, but to watch Aniston "play" herself.

Dyer argues that a star's image is constructed across four different public arenas: films, promotion, publicity, and commentary. During the studio era, studios kept stars under contract for years at a time. This allowed the studios to craft each star's image carefully by developing appropriate movies for them and controlling (in most cases) how audiences perceived each star's life offscreen. Today stars are free agents. They make deals with studios to make individual films, or a cluster of films, but they are not bound to a single studio for any length of time. Nevertheless, stars, agents,

12.6 Buster Keaton, the "Great Stoneface," is famous for his deadpan expression.

12.7 *The Break-Up* plays on audience knowledge of stars' "real life" romances.

12.8 Jodie Foster's role in *Inside Man* capitalized on her star persona as a confident, shrewd woman.

and studios still manipulate the star's appearances in film, promotion, publicity, and commentary to finesse public perception. The image constructed across these outlets makes up what critics call the **star persona**.

This persona is most obviously shaped by a canon of films: Jodie Foster's star persona is that of a rugged, independent woman, in part because of her past performances as a tomboy, a teenage prostitute, an FBI agent, an astronomer, and a single mother trying to protect her daughter from violent criminals (fig. **12.8**). In contrast, Scarlett Johansson tends to play romantic roles that fuse braininess with traditional femininity and glamor (*Lost in Translation* [Sofia Coppola 2003], *Girl With the Pearl Earring* [Peter Webber 2003], *Match Point* [Woody Allen 2005]). Halle Barry won an Oscar for her performance as a widow who has an affair with the prison guard who executed her husband in Marc Forster's drama *Monster's Ball* (2001). But since then, she has consistently played stoic but physically resourceful heroines in thrillers, including *Die Another Day* (Lee Tamahori 2002), and comic book action films such as *Catwoman* (Pitof 2004) and the *X-Men* franchise (fig. **12.9**).

Some stars will occasionally expand their range. Tom Cruise shed his hair and his trim physique (thanks to makeup and prostheses) to play hot-headed movie studio executive Les Grossman in *Tropic Thunder* (Ben Stiller 2008). In 2010, Paramount announced that a film was being developed for this campy, crude character.

12.9 Action star Halle Berry in *X-Men*.

Promotion refers to those materials intentionally released by a studio in order to market a particular film, but which often construct a star's image in the process. These materials include press packets distributed to theaters and film critics, ads in the press and on billboards, organized public appearances such as interviews, and website promotions. In the 1930s, Fox Studios promoted child star Shirley Temple by licensing her image for use in dolls, comics, coloring books, and even sheet music (McDonald 2000, p. 60).

Whereas promotion is carefully planned and disseminated, publicity is not (or does not appear to be) intentional. Gossip columnists, *paparazzi* (photographers who follow celebrities to capture their candid moments), entertainment magazines, and websites like YouTube grant fans apparent intimate access to celebrities' lives by capturing stars at their most spontaneous—although, as Dyer implies, even these spontaneous moments are often staged. In doing so, this publicity industry may blur the distinction between a star's roles and his off-screen behavior.

The recent resurgence of Mickey Rourke's career serves as an especially poignant example of how the star phenomenon blurs the boundary between performance and star personality. In the 1980s, Rourke became one of Hollywood's hottest sex symbols, thanks to his leading roles in erotically charged dramas such as *Rumble Fish* (Francis Ford Coppola 1983), *9½ Weeks* (Adrian Lynne 1986), and *Angel Heart* (Alan Parker 1987) (fig. **12.10**). Rourke sabotaged his career, partly through his hard partying lifestyle and the disagreeable temperament he brought to the set. In the 1990s Rourke took a stab at professional boxing, destroying his pretty-boy looks in the process; for all intents and purposes, his career as a hunky leading man was shot. But his performance in Darren Aronofsky's *The Wrestler* (2008) brought fans back in droves and earned Rourke a Golden Globe award and an Oscar nomination. In the film Rourke plays Randy "The Ram" Robinson, a down-and-out professional wrestler trying to recapture the glory days of his career in the 1980s while facing dwindling crowds, financial troubles, a battered body, and a potentially fatal heart disease. Roger Ebert (along with nearly every critic who reviewed the film) singled out the striking parallels between Rourke and his character:

> Like many great performances, it has an element of truth. Rourke himself was once young and glorious and made the big bucks. [...] He fell from grace and stardom, but kept working, because he was an actor and that was what he did. Now here is his comeback role, playing Randy the Ram's comeback. (fig. **12.11**)

Ebert's comments point to how many audiences watched *The Wrestler* on two levels simultaneously: on the level of the diegesis and also in the context of the star's personal history.

12.10 *(left)* Mickey Rourke in his glamorous heyday: *9½ Weeks*.

12.11 *(right)* Mickey Rourke as the unglamorous "Ram" in *The Wrestler*.

Finally, star discourse circulates through criticism and commentaries. Critics evaluate and study a star's work, either contemporaneously or posthumously in popular reviews in magazines, newspapers, television, radio, fan websites and blogs, and academic research. Film criticism can play a crucial role in determining a star's persona, either by reflecting public sentiment or by shaping public opinion.

The immense popularity of reality television has had an impact on contemporary stardom and stardom studies. Reality television, for some, represents the true democratization of stardom because it promotes the idea that anyone can become a celebrity. For others, it rewards bad behavior and reinforces class-based notions of taste and propriety. Reality stars are not celebrated for possessing a talent, but, rather, are famous for being recognizable and for having a personality (partly a construct based on the needs of a particular television program for dramatic conflict).

Academic scholarship in this area typically defines the specific dimensions of a star's image and explores how her films, promotional materials, publicity, and criticism all converge to create this persona. Film scholar Maria LaPlace's analysis of Bette Davis's star persona as a strong, assertive woman (fig. **12.12**) serves as an effective example of how film criticism can study the way a star's persona is constructed via multiple intersecting sources of public information:

> In cinema the Independent Woman falls into two categories: one is the "good" strong woman, noble, generous, sympathetic; the other is "evil," aggressive, domineering, sexual, "neurotic." Both convey strength and take action.

> Davis's film roles are almost all one or the other Independent Woman. Some of her famous early roles are the latter type—"bitches" Dyer calls them: *Of Human Bondage* (1934), *Dangerous* (1935, Oscar for Davis), *Jezebel* (1938, Oscar for Davis) and *Little Foxes* (1941). In the years just preceding *Now, Voyager*, there were a growing number of "good" women [...]: *Marked Woman* (1937, which actually combined both roles), *The Sisters* (1939), *Dark Victory* (1939), and *All This and Heaven, Too* (1941).

> What links these roles is Davis's performance style. Characterized by a high level of intensity, energy, and charged emotionality, it conveys a specific "personality" that interacts with each film role. The Davis style consists in a deliberate, clipped vocal inflection; darting eye movements and penetrating stares; a swinging, striding walk; gestures such as clenching fists and sudden, intense drags on cigarettes; and quick shifts in mood and register. These connote assertiveness, intelligence, internal emotional conflict and strength. (LaPlace, pp. 135–6)

12.12 In *Jezebel*, Bette Davis plays one of her characteristically "bitchy" roles.

LaPlace also illustrates how Davis's promotional materials and publicity emphasize these same qualities in her private life. Notice how LaPlace cites original publicity materials (specifically, biographical information) to show how Bette Davis was presented to the general public:

> [T]he Davis "story" is of a plucky, resourceful, "self-made" woman whose success is due not to beauty, but to personal qualities of talent, determination, and down-to-earth self-awareness. The product of a fatherless, mother-supported, lower-middle-class family, Davis [...] meets and surmounts adversity because she knows who she is and what she wants [...]. Thus, [her] image is strongly marked by attributes of strength and independence, constructed in another way through the depiction of Davis as anti-glamor and anti-consumerism, eschewing all the trappings of stardom:
>
>> Davis dislikes equally the stuffed shirts and glamor girls of Hollywood and makes no effort to please them ... Her social circle is made up of non-professionals, including her sister; her closest approach to a hobby is her interest in dogs. Informality is her keynote ... she no longer dyes her hair and she never diets. ("Bette Davis," *Life*, January 8, 1939)
>
> Work is the privileged aspect of the Davis image; she is portrayed as completely dedicated to her career. (LaPlace, p. 136; *excerpts reprinted courtesy of BFI*)

LaPlace begins by describing the common characteristics of Davis's characters and identifying the acting techniques that help Davis portray each of these similar characters (her stride and clipped voice). She then shows how contemporary publicity painted a picture of Davis's personality that is remarkably similar to that of her typical character.

This approach to star studies does not assume that actors play themselves on screen; nor does it posit the idea that a star's persona is defined solely by the roles she plays. Rather, a star's persona—the image that lures audiences to theaters, that attracts their attention in fan magazines, that sells products in endorsement campaigns—is created by the interplay between the screen, media coverage, and the (selective) biographical details to which audiences gain access. In effect, the real Bette Davis is supplanted by a public image.

Stardom and Ideology

Chapter 10 argued that films inevitably bear some relationship to the political and social values of the culture that produces and consumes them. Mainstream narrative films tend to express popular sentiment and often reflect the dominant ideological assumptions of their culture. Scholars in star studies frequently explore how stars function as cultural barometers, embodying the political, moral, and cultural assumptions of those fans who consume their images.

At the most obvious level, the idealized star's body—the visible image that fixates and arouses spectators—may reinforce dominant ideas about sex and gender. Film scholar Heather Addison argues that film culture in the 1920s helped to transform national ideals of sexual attractiveness. During the late 1800s, "abundant flesh" in both men and women was desirable because it symbolized a life of middle-class ease. But in the 1920s, America's first fitness craze took hold, suddenly popularizing slenderness and visible musculature. Addison links this craze to the advance of the Machine Age (as the culture began to value the sleek efficiency of machinery) and a backlash against the feminist movement (as the media countered images of women voting and working outside the home by idealizing waifish feminine figures) (Addison, pp. 18–20).

The film industry reinforced this new ideal. To attract the audiences who now held slenderness as the key physical standard of beauty, filmmakers cast slim actors and actresses in lead roles. Actresses in particular were bound by clauses in their studio contracts, which required them to maintain a particular weight and size. Fan magazines frequently published the weight clauses of particular stars, publicizing the importance the new visual culture placed on maintaining the "proper" weight. By implication, if a woman wanted to be a star, she needed to be slender.

This escalating spiral of media coverage equating fitness with thinness points to how the star phenomenon and the film industry in general compounded popular trends. Addison doesn't argue that the star system created the new standard of beauty. Rather, she illustrates how the star system responded to these trends; in doing so, it helped to market slenderness as the physical ideal for men and women by effectively excluding any alternatives to the slender look. Assembling a broad array of biographical details, fan magazine articles, and industry documents, Addison shows how Clara Bow's career—which rose and fell inversely with her body weight—exemplifies Hollywood's emphasis on replicating the culture's feminine ideal:

> At Paramount, where Bow remained for over five years, keeping her figure under control became a constant duty, especially at those times when she packed on additional pounds. In 1926, *Motion Picture Classic* noted that Bow exercised regularly to keep her figure in check: "She hikes over the hills [...]. She rides, too. Exercise keeps her slim—for her ambition." Bow's weight ballooned in 1929. [...]. [W]hen her second talkie, *The Saturday Night Kid*, was released, '[m]ost critics paid more attention to Clara's girth than her performance. Their verdict: The "It" girl had more "It" than ever, especially around her midsection. (Addison, p. 31)

While Addison's analysis focuses on stardom's relationship to cultural ideals of femininity, scholars also explore how stars reveal cultural attitudes toward race, class, religion, politics, and culture. For example, one of India's most recognized stars, Lata Mangeshkar, never appears on screen. The nature of her phenomenal success can in part be attributed to Hindu spiritual beliefs. As Chapter 11 points out, most mainstream Indian films include several musical numbers, yet the actors never actually perform the musical numbers—all of the songs are lip-synched (fig. **12.13**). Lata Mangeshkar is one of a handful of "playback singers" who records female vocals on these songs. Even though she remains unseen, she is a cultural icon.

Neepa Majumdar argues that Mangeshkar's star persona as the unseen, disembodied voice represents for Hindu spectators the feminine ideal, unspoiled by secular Western culture. In contrast to Mangeshkar, the stars who appear onscreen embody Western values. As with Hollywood stars, Indian fan magazines help shape each actress's star image, and frequently this coverage focuses on their decadent lifestyles and tawdry exploits. Thus, when these actresses lip-synch Mangeshkar's vocals, the musical numbers effectively combine two star personas into one multifaceted performance. This dual performance allows Hindu audiences to bridge the gap between competing traditional and Western value systems: "The attempt [...] of Hindi films to negotiate the contradictory values of material consumption (associated with the West) and austerity (associated with traditional Indian values) can be seen as the general principle behind the dual star text in the voice–body split in female song sequences." (Majumdar, p. 174)

12.13 In lavish Bollywood musicals like *Devdas*, actors rarely sing their own musical numbers.

As the cases of Clara Bow and Lata Mangeshkar demonstrate, star personas can embody a culture's social, political, and religious ideals. Because the star's body serves as the site of an entire culture's fantasies, it reveals what that culture values.

Stars and Subcultures

Generally speaking, a star's appeal reaches across a broad spectrum of fans, garnering iconic status in mainstream culture. Riding the wave of the enormous popularity of *Titanic*, Leonardo DiCaprio became America's hunk *du jour*. Though his fan base consisted primarily of swooning teenage girls, he was, at the close of the twentieth century, generally understood by everyone—even those who didn't consider themselves fans—to be America's heartthrob. For many male viewers, Marilyn Monroe is still the quintessential fantasy of feminine sexuality. Clint Eastwood, Brad Pitt, Russell Crowe, and Will Smith have all laid claim to representing a masculine ideal.

On occasion, however, a star can appeal to a discrete subculture, a group of fans that defines itself through its position outside of mainstream society. Al Pacino's performance as Tony Montana in *Scarface* (Brian De Palma 1983) is still heralded as iconic in gangster rap circles more than twenty-five years after its release (fig. **12.14**). While Pacino is certainly a mainstream star, rappers latch onto his performance in *Scarface* (and not, say, his role as a television news

12.14 Al Pacino as Tony Montana in *Scarface*, a gangster-rap prototype.

producer in Michael Mann's *The Insider*), reading his character as a forerunner of the gangster rapper. Rather than adopting the mainstream interpretation of the film as a cautionary tale about organized crime, rappers identify with Tony Montana's status as an outsider who accumulates a considerable amount of wealth and prestige despite the odds stacked against him. In fact, the 2004 DVD release of the film includes a documentary in which Sean "Puffy" Combs, Andre 3000, Big Boi, Snoop Dogg, and Method Man, among others, discuss the influence the film has had on their own stage personas. At one point in the documentary, Kevin Liles, president of Def Jam Music Group, explains, "I look at *Scarface* … as a ghetto tale. I don't look at *Scarface* as a drug movie." (*Origins*)

As Liles's quote illustrates, when a subculture appropriates a star's image, it often goes "against the grain," drawing a significance from that image that may be overlooked by mainstream audiences. As Paul McDonald points out, subcultures define themselves through a common value system that sets them apart from the mainstream, and some star images come to embody this value system.

To mainstream audiences, singer/actress Judy Garland—star of *Meet Me in St. Louis* (Vincent Minnelli 1944), *Broadway Melody of 1938* (Roy Del Ruth 1937), and *The Wizard of Oz*—represents virtue and innocence. But gay audiences, aware of the discrepancy between Garland's innocent onscreen image and her personal battles with drug and alcohol addiction, consider her an icon partly because she represents the artificiality of "all-American wholesomeness." (McDonald 1998, p. 192)

Scholars explore why a subculture reveres a star's image in ways that defy mainstream expectations by evaluating the sometimes contradictory details that make up a star's persona, examining historical context (of both the period of image production and the period of public consumption of that image), and cataloging viewer responses to a star's persona.

Fan Culture

One important element of star system economics is fan culture. In order for stars to function as commercial products, a loyal fan base must be cultivated that will consume the films, products, and magazines that relay information about their favorite stars. Film scholars have studied the behavior of fans and theorized about the emotional investment of fans in film stars and other celebrities.

Fan cultures create communities; they also create further opportunities for profit-making, as is the case with a community of fans devoted to the *Lord of the Rings* trilogy organized through TheOneRing.net (TORn). The site, owned by four fans, sponsored parties for the Academy Awards in 2002, 2003, and 2004, inviting fans and stars to attend, and using proceeds to maintain the website. In 2004 a competing party was held by the official *Lord of the Rings* fan club, which was licensed by New Line Cinema (the distributor of the films) and run by a private corporation.

Such fan communities underscore how stars help advertise films and may make it easier for studios to do so. Marketing campaigns rely on star images to differentiate one film from the next. Stars serve as a kind of shorthand for a film's content and style. Audiences will generally assume that a Lindsay Lohan vehicle (*Freaky Friday* [Mark Waters 2003], *Mean Girls* [Mark Waters 2004], *Herbie: Fully Loaded* [Angela Robinson 2005]) will differ from a film that features Indie icon Catherine Keener (*Being John Malkovich* [Spike Jonze 1999], *The 40 Year Old Virgin, Capote, Synecdoche, New York*). Film studios seek out a film's target audience with publicity campaigns designed to address the star's fan base, selectively advertising in magazines, on television, and on the web. Trailers can be tailored to play up the significance of one star over another: the campaign for Nicole Holofcener's ensemble film *Friends With Money* (2006) prominently featured Jennifer Aniston, downplaying Frances McDormand and Catherine Keener, who played equally significant roles.

This chapter has focused on what is, to many viewers, the most immediately visible and emotionally compelling element of a film: its stars. It has emphasized that when audiences pay attention to a star, they watch more than a performance—they see acting technique, an accumulation of onscreen and offscreen roles that the actor has played, and the market force of that star's persona. Stars' ability to hold audiences in their sway underscores the power of celebrity as a cultural and economic institution.

Works Consulted

Adair, Gilbert. "Eistenstein on Disney," in *Movies*. London: Penguin, 1999.

Addison, Heather. "Capitalizing their Charms: Cinema Stars and Physical Culture in the 1920s." *The Velvet Light Trap*, 50 (Fall 2002), pp. 15–34.

"Aniston: *Break-Up* Was Therapeutic." CBS News.com, June 1, 2006. **http://www.cbsnews.com/ stories/2006/06/01/earlyshow/leisure/celebspot/main1673655shtml**. August 28, 2006.

Collins, Nancy. "Lust and Trust." *Rolling Stone*, July 8, 1999. *Academic Search Elite*. Online. Ebsco. January 9, 2004.

DeCordova, Richard. *Picture Personalities: The Emergence of the Star System in America*. Urbana: University of Illinois Press, 1990.

Dyer, Richard. "Four Films of Lana Turner," in *Star Texts: Image and Performance in Film and Television*, ed. Jeremy G. Butler. Detroit: Wayne State University Press, 1991, pp. 214–39.

————. *Heavenly Bodies: Film Stars and Society*. New York: St. Martins, 1986.

————. *Stars*. 2nd edn, London: British Film Institute Publishing, 1998.

Ebert, Roger. "*The Wrestler*." *The Chicago Sun-Times*. December 23, 2009. **rogerebert.suntimes. com**.

Gabler, Neal. "Risky Business." *The New York Times*, August 25, 2006. **http://www.nytimes.com/ 2006/08/25/opinion/25gabler.html**. August 25, 2006.

Gentile, Gary. "Split Not Likely to Kill Cruise's Career." Associated Press. *Lexington Herald-Leader*, August 24, 2006. *Kentucky.com* August 25, 2006.

Holmes, Su. "'Reality Goes Pop!' Reality TV, Popular Music, and Narratives of Stardom in Pop Idol." *Television and New Media* 5.2 (May 2004): pp. 147–72.

Holmlund, Chris. *Impossible Bodies: Femininity and Masculinity at the Movies*. London: Routledge, 2002.

James, Caryn. "Mission Imperative for a Star: Be Likable." *New York Times*, August 24, 2006. **http://www.nytimes.com/2006/08/24/movies/24cele.html**. August 25, 2006. **http://www.Kentucky.com/mld/Kentucky/15346746.htm**.

LaPlace, Maria. "Stars and the Star System: The Case of Bette Davis," in *The Film Studies Reader*, ed. Joanne Hollows *et al*. New York: Oxford University Press, 2000, pp. 134–9. Originally published in Christine Gledhill (ed.), *Home is Where the Heart Is*. London: British Film Institute Publishing, 1987.

Majumdar, Neepa. "The Embodied Voice," in *Soundtrack Available: Essays on Film and Popular Music*, ed. Pamela Robertson Wojcik and Arthur Knight. Durham, NC: Duke University Press, 2001, pp. 161–81.

McDonald, Paul. Afterword ("Reconceptualising Stardom"), in *Stars*, 2nd edn. London: BFI, 1998, pp. 177–211.

————. *The Star System: Hollywood's Production of Popular Identities*. London: Wallflower, 2000.

Naremore, James. *Acting in the Cinema*. Berkeley: University of California Press, 1988.

Origins of a Hip Hop Classic. Dir. Benny Boom. *Scarface*. DVD Supplementary Material. Universal. 2003.

"Paramount: Cruise is Risky Business." *CNN Money.com*. August 23, 2006. **money.cnn.com/ 2006/08/22/news/newsmakers/cruise_paramount/index.htm**. September 27, 2006.

Porter, Eduardo, and Geraldine Fabrikant. "A Big Star May Not a Profitable Movie Make." *The New York Times*, August 28, 2006, C, pp. 1, 5.

Scott, A.O. "The New Golden Age of Acting," *The New York Times*, February 15, 2004, 2A: pp. 1, 25.

Thompson, Kristin and David Bordwell. *Film History: An Introduction*, 2nd edn. Boston: McGraw-Hill, 2003.

Genre

///

CHAPTER THIRTEEN

Critics have ignored genre films because of their
prejudice for the unique.

Leo Braudy

///

Most filmgoers choose movies they would prefer to see (and others they would
like to avoid) without reading any reviews. They do so because films can be categorized according to **genre**, and audiences have grown so accustomed to what
these categories represent that genres play a significant role in shaping audience
expectations. A musical will feature romance and songs; a Western will involve
horses and shootouts; a thriller will contain fast-paced action set in big cities; a
screwball comedy will depict characters who get into a tight situation because of
a misunderstanding. Each of these can be seen as a distinct genre.

13.1 Will Kane in *High Noon*—a typical Western hero.

The origin of genre (derived from the Latin word for "kind") can be traced back to the Greek philosopher Aristotle, who in the fourth century BC defined drama according to three types: epic poetry, tragedy, and comedy. Subsequently, genre became a useful tool for classifying works of art. Yet the process of classification, also called taxonomy, is not as simple as it may seem. First, the criteria used to create or identify genres can be ill defined or inconsistent. For example, in literature, genres are defined primarily by their formal attributes: rules that govern structure and expression. The most basic literary genres are poetry, prose, and drama. Yet we also commonly speak of literary genres whose subject matter establishes the type of work it is, such as mystery novels or detective fiction. For other genres, the audience addressed by the work is of paramount importance, such as young adult fiction.

Film scholar Rick Altman has argued that genre categories in film are a continuation of literary classification methods (*Film/Genre*, p. 13). Thus, it may come as no surprise that the problem of irregular category distinctions haunts film studies as well: for example, do documentary films constitute a genre in the same way that horror films make up a genre? Andrew Tutor notes that the Western is defined by "certain themes, certain typical actions, certain characteristic mannerisms," yet the horror film is defined by those elements and the "*intention* to horrify." (Tutor, p. 120)

Similarly perplexing questions arise that relate to the origin of film genres. Do filmmakers create genres when they make films? Do film critics retrospectively create these categories? Do viewers and devoted fans play any role in the shaping of genres? Some scholars have argued that genres possess a deep connection to history and cultural mythologies: the Western genre, for example, is tied to the history of the American west. Genre labels function as a marketing tool within a commercial film industry, so it becomes important to distinguish between these various definitions of genre when using the term. And, finally, how do genres change? How and when have certain genres arisen, and how have they changed and evolved over time?

This chapter explores these questions about genre by first looking at the way genres have been defined within film culture—in familiar and sometimes imprecise ways—and then by examining several key ideas that may help us to understand both the usefulness and the limitations of genre. The chapter then describes several major film genres: the Western, *film noir*, the action film, science fiction, and the musical. The final section looks at some issues related to genre that have formed the basis for academic research and popular criticism.

What Makes a Genre?

In film studies, a genre refers to a group of films that share a set of narrative, stylistic, and thematic characteristics or conventions. While not every film in a given genre will exhibit all of the genre's conventions, every film in a given genre will exhibit at least some of them. This allows for a certain amount of ambivalence when critics try to establish the parameters of a genre, and such ambivalence often leads to spirited debates. Despite the slipperiness of genre categories, film industry personnel, scholars, critics, and audiences inevitably begin any discussion of genre by considering conventions.

Dark, rainy nights. Bloody knives. Teenagers in peril. A monster. For many readers these dreadful images may provoke fond memories of cringing in fear at the movie theater. As one of the most important and beloved genres in American cinema, the horror film exemplifies how conventions define a group of films.

Film scholar Thomas Schatz postulates that narrative conventions are among the most important criteria for defining a genre. Films that belong to the same genre share character types and plot events. Without a doubt, the most crucial character type in a horror film is the monster, a figure that elicits the revulsion and fear that make the genre so compelling. In some films the source of terror is supernatural. Protagonists find themselves haunted by ghosts from beyond the grave or by demon spirits. Some monsters are ghouls, beings that are suspended between two biological states: human and animal, living and dead: werewolves, zombies, vampires, mummies, and aliens. Monsters can even be human, ranging from truly deranged psychotics driven to murderous rampages by inexplicable emotions (*Psycho*, *Halloween*) to sadistic teenagers pulling a sick prank (*Scream* [Wes Craven 2002]), to people who torture and kill others for fun and profit (*Funny Games* [Michael Haneke 1997 and 2007], *Hostel* [Eli Roth 2005; sequel 2007]) or for supposedly moral reasons (*Saw* series 2004 09).

If monsters represent one specific character type, their victims represent another. Classical horror films of the 1930s often featured respectable members of society, such as detectives or doctors, struggling to contain the violence and vanquish the monster's threat to the social order. Since the 1970s it has become commonplace for the monster to terrorize teenagers or young adults. Those who behave recklessly—often those who are sexually active—are the first to die. Those who survive are frequently the ordinary kids or social misfits who prove to be both cautious and resourceful. After studying the wave of "slasher films" in the 1970s and 1980s (*The Texas Chainsaw Massacre* [Tobe Hooper 1974], *Halloween*), film scholar Carol Clover identified a remarkably consistent victim/survivor, whom she deemed "the final girl." This sole survivor is often an unassuming young woman who eventually proves herself capable of tapping into a primal brutality that allows her to defend herself against the monster and to survive.

Beyond character types, another important narrative convention of any genre is its predictable set of plot events. The first act in a horror film focuses on central characters beginning a venture into a strange and ultimately threatening setting. In F.W. Murnau's *Nosferatu*, Jonathan Harker (Alexander Granach) goes into the Carpathian Mountains to make a business deal with the mysterious Count Orlock (who, unbeknownst to Jonathan, is a vampire). Three college students trudge through a mysterious forest in search of a local legend in *The Blair Witch Project* (Daniel Myrick and Eduardo Sanchez 1999). Spelunkers investigate an inhospitable cavern in *The Descent* (Neil Marshall 2005). Stumbling into a forbidding, and often forbidden, setting unleashes a wave of violence that leaves many (if not most) of the protagonists dead. As those who survive the initial onslaught begin to fight back, fear and fatigue provoke dissention within the group, putting them at a greater risk. Those who have come in contact with the monster may try to warn the larger community, or they go to the authorities to muster up support, only to be met with disbelief and derision. The climax of the film generally involves a dramatic, sometimes apocalyptic, showdown between the main characters and the monster, with varying results. In contemporary horror films the resolution of the plot often leaves open the possibility of the monster's return.

In addition to sharing similar narrative characteristics, films from the same genre exhibit the same visual and sound techniques. Horror films borrow from the visual rhetoric of German Expressionism: low-key lighting, chiaroscuro, extreme camera angles, and distorted lines function as a visual signature for the genre (fig. **13.2**). These devices serve as narrative shorthand for indicating danger. Because horror film narratives thrust their characters into unfamiliar territory, settings are often barren and isolated—emphasizing the hostility of the environment—and may also be labyrinthine—underscoring the difficulty of escaping this distorted landscape.

Moreover, sound often draws attention to the terrifying possibilities that neither the characters nor the audience can see: in *Psycho*, Marion Crane listens to Mother berate her son in the distance; the would-be filmmakers in *The Blair Witch Project* hear mysterious rustling outside their tent at night; in *Paranormal Activity*, the evil spirit that haunts Katie (Katie Featherston) is never shown on camera, although terrible sounds are heard on the soundtrack. Such examples demonstrate the way horror films evoke fear indirectly—by suggesting that danger lurks nearby while withholding its specific location.

Wes Craven's *Scream* openly satirizes the predictability of the genre's conventions. Teenagers at a party—knowing that a killer is on the loose—discuss famous horror movie scenarios as they jokingly debate how they should behave if they want to survive the night. The film is funny precisely because it plays on the audience's foreknowledge of horror conventions: who will get killed first? How will they die? Who will survive? But situating a film within a genre is not as simple as *Scream* suggests. Craven's film parodies a particular type of horror film—the slasher movie—but does a movie about a maniacal case of blood lust belong in the same category as *Rosemary's Baby*, a horror classic in which the audience never even sees a monster? Does *The Others* (Alejandro Almenábar 2001), a period drama that provides more atmosphere than shocks, deserve to be lumped together with a bloody gore-fest like *Saw* (James Wan 2004) or a monster film like *Jeepers Creepers* (Victor Salva 2001)? The standard conventions of the horror film, iden-

13.2 *Frankenstein* exhibits the influence of German Expressionism.

tified above, cannot fully account for every single film within the genre.

Paradoxically, genres rely as much on variation as they do on repetition. Genres produce pleasure in part by meeting audience expectations. After all, who would be satisfied with a horror film if it did not depict characters who quake in fear? Would audiences pay to see a Western if it didn't have horses, six-shooters, and panoramic vistas of wide-open spaces? Yet filmmakers also understand that relying on repetition without "changing the pitch," so to speak, produces boredom. A genre film that has no surprises becomes a cliché. Consequently, film genres are always in a state of flux.

The horror film, for example, has evolved dramatically since its infancy. Early entries delved into the realm of the fantastic. During this era, mon-

13.3 An early monster in *King Kong*.

sters were, by and large, clearly not human: vampires, werewolves, mutants, aliens, ghosts, and enormous apes (fig. **13.3**). Michael Powell's *Peeping Tom* (1960) and *Psycho* introduced the human monster in the form of the mad killer. With these films the realm of the horrific wasn't so clearly distinguishable from the audience's everyday world. Knife-wielding maniacs look like us. In fact, *Psycho* was based on the exploits of Ed Gein, an actual serial killer who lived in the plains of Wisconsin during the 1950s. A shift in settings accompanied this humanization of the monster: subsequent horror films make so-called "normal" spaces alienating and terrifying: in *The Exorcist* (William Friedkin 1972), Satan torments a little girl in a posh Georgetown neighborhood; in *Dawn of the Dead* (George Romero 1978), zombies wander the corridors of a Pittsburgh shopping mall; in *Halloween* and *Scream*, knife-wielding killers wander bland suburban streets (fig. **13.4**).

Because genres change and evolve—often in response to wider cultural concerns—it is possible to identify **subgenres**, smaller clusters of films in which additional conventions come in play. For example, early horror films with a paranormal bent tend to focus on inexplicable, ethereal hauntings. The slasher films that became prominent in the 1970s are more likely to depict a knife-wielding maniac, which distinguishes them from these earlier monster movies. Likewise, zombie movies, which span both the classical and the modern horror cinema, are clearly horror films, yet they share conventions that distinguish them from their counterparts.

Further compounding the difficulty of defining a genre is that some films fuse the conventions of two or more genres into one **hybrid**. *Alien*, for example, uses the narrative conventions of a horror film—a small group is trapped in a confined

13.4 The site of modern horror: suburbia in *Halloween*.

environment and terrorized by a vicious monster—but employs the visual iconography of science fiction: the characters are crew members of a space ship that has inadvertently picked an alien life form. *Near Dark* (Kathryn Bigelow 1987) fuses the Western with the vampire tale: an innocent cowpoke is inadvertently drawn into a band of outlaws/vampires and must go on the lam across the American West.

The fact that such disparate titles can all be called horror films illustrates why some critics rely on more than visual and narrative characteristics to categorize films. Some critics argue that horror is defined not by its conventions, but by the emotional response it elicits from the audience. As its name implies, the horror film is designed to make the audience feel fear, revulsion, and disgust. This is why most viewers would definitively label *Solaris* (Andrei Tarkovsky 1972; Steven Soderbergh 2002) a science fiction film, even though it shares the same basic premise as *Alien*: astronauts threatened by an alien presence while they are holed up in a remote outpost. But *Alien* provokes shock and surprise, whereas both versions of *Solaris* are slowly paced, philosophical meditations on the nature of memory, life, and death. (Even this distinction can be murky, as audiences' propensity for shock has evolved since the earliest days of the genre. Whereas viewers in 1931 may have been frightened by Frankenstein's monster, contemporary audiences probably respond more to the pathos of Boris Karloff's performance than to the monster's grotesqueness.)

Some critics argue that the most effective means of defining a genre is to articulate the common themes within a group of films. For example, film scholars Richard Dyer and Robin Wood maintain that the monster has always represented the repressed desires of its potential victims … and the audience. The monster's appearance in horror films, therefore, represents the struggle to contain unspoken—and socially destructive—impulses. Vampires tend to be linked with unbridled sexual desire: Count Dracula comes out at night and preys on vulnerable women. Those who encounter him find him simultaneously revolting and captivating. Contemporary slasher movies often equate murder with voyeurism; the point-of-view shot that puts the viewer in the killer's perspective as he stalks his victim draws a parallel between the killer and the audience. After all, one reason why horror films are so popular is the twisted pleasure audiences derive from seeing victims sliced and diced. *Peeping Tom* makes this connection explicit, as the main character kills with a blade attached to a camera so he can film each victim's expression at the moment of her death (fig. **13.5**). In the documentary film *The American Nightmare* (Adam Simon 2000) scholars such as Adam Lowenstein, Tom Gunning, and Carol Clover, along with filmmaker Wes Craven, point to ground-breaking films like *Night of the Living Dead* (George Romero 1968) to suggest that contemporary horror films portray evil as an integral part of American society and the American psyche.

This discussion of the horror film suggests that, while we may feel we know our favorite genres quite well, these categories leave many questions open to debate. In fact, film scholar Janet Staiger repudiates the very idea of clear genre categories, arguing that, while patterns exist, in fact, "Hollywood genres have never been pure instances of genres." (Staiger, p. 6) In attempting to classify films, sometimes narrative patterns are more important to defining a genre (the Western or the Musical), and sometimes elements of style are pre-eminent (*film noir*). Finally, although the film industry, including film critics, seem to manufacture genres as a marketing strategy, genres cannot exist or thrive without a community of viewers who engage with, understand, and enjoy the repetition of familiar conventions as well as the transgressions or modifications of those rules.

Rick Altman proposes one way genre critics can account for the various, and sometimes contradictory, methods for defining genre: embrace them all. For Altman, recognizing the context in which a genre is studied is what's imperative. He presents four approaches to defining genre, each linked to a specific rhetorical purpose. The first approach considers how genre functions as a "model" to be used as a formula or template in film production. The second sees genre as a "structure," which refers to the film's textual system, which may be analyzed by critics and scholars. Altman designates the third definition of genre as an "etiquette," which refers to the names distributors and exhibitors create to help categorize and market films. The fourth is the "contract"—the implicit agreement between a film and its audience that governs the way fans enjoy it. Altman argues that genre operates differently in each of these contexts and that each mode offers insight into the way films relate to other films, to filmmakers, and to audiences.

The next section of this chapter explores five major American film genres: the Western, *film noir*, the action film, the science fiction film, and the musical. As a survey of American film genres, this list is far from exhaustive. Several of Hollywood's most noteworthy genres, including the gangster film, the screwball comedy, and the family melodrama, are not analyzed here. But the discussions below offer models for studying the conventions and themes that genres share.

13.5 A human monster in *Peeping Tom*.

Major American Genres

The Western

For many, the Western is the quintessential Hollywood genre. Even while younger audiences today see few Westerns, most recognize the genre's narrative and visual conventions because the mythology and iconography of the Western form an integral part of the way the United States defines its character. The staying power of the Western is even evident in the nation's political realm: President George W. Bush was applauded in some quarters and pilloried in others because he borrowed phrases and imagery from Westerns to describe the country's struggle against international terrorists.

Westerns tend to fall in one of two categories. In the first, a male hero helps restore law and order to a community by killing a band of notorious outlaws, as in *High Noon* (Fred Zinneman 1953; fig. **13.1**), *A Fistful of Dollars* (Sergio Leone 1964), and *Unforgiven* (Clint Eastwood 1992). The second group, which includes *Distant Drums* (Raoul Walsh 1951), *The Unforgiven* (John Huston 1959), and *The Searchers*, portrays the bloody struggle between Native Americans and settlers for control of the land. John Ford's classic Western *Stagecoach* incorporates both of these plotlines.

Perhaps more than any other genre, the Western is defined by its visual conventions. It relies on the spacious, post-Civil War, American frontier setting to emphasize the struggle to survive in an inhospitable environment. The white settlers who brave the frontier carry with them the promise (and perils) of U.S. territorial expansion and modern industrial society. To this end, props (six-shooters, horses, whiskey glasses), costumes (cowboy hats, jangly spurs, dusty work-wear), and location (the arid desert of the American Southwest) play an integral role in defining the characters' rugged independence. Appropriately, the cinematography relies on extreme long shots, offering audiences a panoramic perspective of solitary wanderers navigating the craggy terrain. Even sound effects evoke the feel of an inhospitable environment: a bullet's ping, a buzzard's caw, and the wind itself, invariably echo across vast empty expanses. That the cowboy at the center of the Western survives in this environment is what makes his character so admirable to fans of the genre: he is resourceful and bound to no one, fully capable of roaming the frontier on his own without having to rely on the securities of civilization. Yet he also has a code of honor; though he is ruggedly independent, the cowboy respects the rules of society and is unwilling to exploit others or to condone the careless disregard for human life exhibited by outlaws and Indians (in classical Westerns, Indians are stereotyped Native American figures who embody the savage forces of nature that the settlers are attempting to tame).

Audiences recognize that not every movie that features horses is a Western. Rather, the genre is concerned with the tension between the contradictory impulses of individual liberty and communal responsibility. Whether the Western hero wards off a gang of violent criminals or a tribe of hostile Native Americans, he does so by getting involved and tempering his desire to remain free from entanglements. As most critics have noted, the cowboy acts out of a reluctant sense of obligation. In *Stagecoach*, Ringo helps the passengers survive a band of marauding Apaches and, in an act of revenge, kills the Plummer brothers, making the sinful town of Lordsburg just a little less seedy in the process. But the film makes it clear that Ringo's commitment to the other passengers is temporary: he could never be contained by the social order depicted in the towns of Tonto and Lordsburg. In the resolution he rides into the sunrise with Dallas by his side, headed for the Mexican border, where they'll be, in Doc Boone's words, "safe from the blessings of civilization."

This tension between the longing for the unencumbered freedom of the wilderness and the physical security promised by civilization forms the thematic core of the genre. Consequently, critics are prone to call some films Westerns even when they don't exhibit all the standard visual conventions.

Critics routinely discussed *Brokeback Mountain* as a Western, even though the film depicts a romance that spans the late twentieth century. Once again, the remote Western landscape represents unbridled freedom: it is the only environment where two men can express their love for one another. They spend the summer tending sheep in the idyllic clutches of Brokeback Mountain. When summer comes to a close, they part company. Eventually, both start families and get traditional hourly jobs. Though they routinely meet up on Brokeback to rekindle their affair, Ennis (Heath Ledger) is unable to commit to a non-traditional relationship but, instead, leads an unfulfilling life that adheres to conventional social norms. He doesn't ride off into the sunset with his lover. He realizes the emotional cost of not doing so only after discovering that Jack (Jake Gyllenhaal) has been killed. The film concludes with the poignant scene of Ennis alone in his claustrophobic trailer, looking at a postcard of Brokeback Mountain and clutching Jack's empty shirt (fig. **13.6**). The dingy and cramped pre-fab abode epitomizes the loss of the frontier spirit and stands in stark contrast to the liberating expanse of Brokeback. As in more conventional Westerns, the setting clearly reflects the sense of lost opportunity and the stifling of a dream.

An important point to consider in relation to film genres is their cultural specificity and their global address. The Western seems to be the quintessential American film and it is recognized as such around the world.

As a point of comparison, consider one of the Japanese film industry's

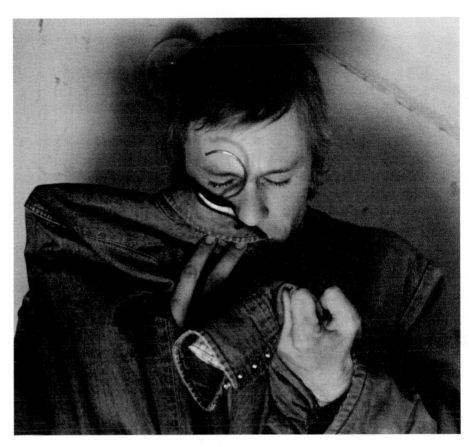

13.6 Ennis loses the promise of the frontier forever in *Brokeback Mountain*.

THE INTERDISCIPLINARY ROOTS OF GENRE THEORY

During the 1970s, the burgeoning field of cinema studies struggled to earn respect as a legitimate academic discipline. Scholars expanded their field by drawing on concepts from other disciplines, adapting models from structural linguistics, political theory, and psychoanalysis in order to account for the perceptual, aesthetic, and social effects of the medium, "dignifying cinema studies as a discipline" in the process (Wexman, p. 144). In particular, models that used language as a sign system were seen as helpful for understanding the way film, a different sort of sign system, produces meaning.

Rick Altman adapted concepts from semiotics to help analyze the relationship between individual films and genre categories. To Altman, genres are formed through, and transmit meaning by, a combination of the **syntactic** and the **semantic**. In **semiotics**, syntax defines the grammatical rules for arranging words that determine whether sentences produce meaning. (For example, the subject comes before the verb in English.) Semantics refers to the more nebulous process of connotation whereby some combinations of words work together, while others don't. For example, the following sentence is syntactically correct because it follows the rules of English grammar (subject/verb/object), yet it makes no sense semantically: "The loud hair fell to my hand." The sentence may be structurally sound, yet it produces nonsense because the adjective "loud" can't be used to modify the noun "hair."

In Altman's genre theory, semantics refers to the building blocks: the clusters of film elements that form a vocabulary that coheres. Just as readers understand that certain words function logically in a sentence, viewers know that certain conventions belong together in a genre, while others don't. For example, audiences wouldn't expect to see a cowboy ride upon a menacing castle on a dark stormy night; those two images don't work together semantically because viewers have been taught to cluster the cowboy with the open range and the monster with the castle.

But semantics alone can't explain how genres are produced and understood. Just as a reader looks for the proper arrangement of words to grasp the meaning of a sentence, viewers respond to the structural arrangement of a film's syntax. Genre films organize semantic details within recognizable narrative and thematic patterns. For example, one common syntactical arrangement in the Western is as follows: a lonesome cowboy stumbles onto a group of desperate strangers; despite some reluctance, he helps them ward off danger before he rides off into the sunset. This familiar arrangement of details establishes the Western's central theme: the individual's quest to balance his desire for independence with his moral sense of social obligation. Crucially, the cowboy riding into the sunset is the *last* image in a Western; the syntactic arrangement of plot events confirms that the hero can contribute to human society while continuing to live his life unencumbered.

But Altman argues that this relationship between syntax and semantics is never fixed. Some films might display semantic elements without using the syntax typically associated with the same genre. Altman writes, "it is simply not possible to describe Hollywood cinema accurately without the ability to account for the numerous films that innovate by combining the syntax of one genre with the semantics of another." (Altman, *Film/Genre*, p. 12)

This fluid relationship between syntax and semantics can account for genre hybridity, or, what Altman called "differing levels of 'genericity'." ("Semantic," p. 636) This theory from the 1970s can help contemporary viewers explain why *Avatar* has been described as a science fiction–Western. Even though *Avatar* has the semantics of science fiction (the story is set on a distant planet occupied by towering blue warriors, and its plot revolves around space travel, computer technology, and genetic engineering), numerous critics have compared it to literature about the European conquest of the American continent, like James Fenimore Cooper's *Last of the Mohicans*, and to Western films like *Dances With Wolves*. This apparent contradiction can be explained if one considers how the film fuses its sci-fi semantics with a familiar syntax belonging to a long tradition of narratives of European colonialism. These narratives inevitably revolve around the opposition between insiders and outsiders: a person from a more industrially advanced society ventures into a seemingly primitive "new world" and becomes personally involved with the native people he encounters. They eventually adopt him (officially or unofficially) and he is romantically linked to a member of the group. When the time comes to choose sides between the powerful empire that seeks to destroy the indigenous population, the hero pledges his allegiance to the indigenous population and uses the skills and wisdom he takes from both cultures to battle the imperial army.

In at least one interview, Cameron admitted to being influenced by *Dances With Wolves*. His description of the creative process reveals an intuitive understanding of the way semantics and syntax work: "I just gathered all this stuff and [...] looked at it through the lens of science fiction and it [came] out looking very different but [was] still recognizable in a universal story way. It's almost comfortable for the audience—'I know what kind of tale this is.'" (quoted in

Boucher) Astute viewers might recognize that Cameron incorporates some of the semantics of the Western into his science fiction tale as well: the Na'vi's attire resembles the costumes created for Native Americans in classic Westerns, and the Na'vi ride flying creatures that resemble horses.

With these conceptual tools in hand, it's possible to move a discussion of genre from an argument over whether a film is or is not a member of a genre, to a consideration of the ways a film utilizes elements from several genres in its syntax and semantics, and, perhaps, to whether such hybrids reflect the development of a new generic form.

important genres. *Jidai-geki* (jee-dye gecky), "stories of the old times," are historical costume dramas, usually set just before or during the collapse of the Japanese feudal system during the late 1800s. (By contrast, *gendai-geki* (gen-dye gecky) feature contemporary stories, from comedies to *yakuza* gangster films.) *Jidai-geki* depict stories of feudal warlords and wandering swordsmen, or *ronin*. One might assume that the slashing samurai is the equivalent of the gunslinger of American Westerns, but an examination of the two character types highlights the differences between American and Japanese film cultures. The *jidai-geki* focuses on the warrior's struggle to live up to his code, or *Bushido*—which demands honor, loyalty, and self-sacrifice—even when this loyalty conflicts with other obligations or desires. For example, in *The Hidden Fortress* (Akira Kurosawa 1958), General Rokurota (Toshiro Mifune) sacrifices his sister and risks his own life to guarantee his princess's survival. The samurai's commitment to familial and community obligation contrasts sharply with the cowboy's spontaneity and individuality. While the cowboy ultimately is swayed by a sense of communal obligation, he accepts this commitment begrudgingly, and with the tacit agreement that the commitment is temporary. The cowboy hero rides off into the sunset alone; Rokurota stays with the princess, a loyal servant for the rest of his life.

The cultural resonance of genres such as the Western or the samurai film, however, does not limit their appeal in terms of audience. If Westerns seem to define something important about American culture for American viewers, they may also define American-ness—for better and for worse—for international audiences. Furthermore, genres are adapted across national contexts, generating fruitful cross-pollination. The John Sturges Western *The Magnificent Seven* (1960) remade Akira Kurosawa's *Seven Samurai* ("*Shichinin no samurai*"; 1954); in turn, Kurosawa's later film *High and Low* ("*Tengoku to jigoku*"; 1963) borrowed from an American detective novel by Ed McBain, *King's Ransom*. The Western genre has served as an inspiration for Italian and German directors, who made so-called "spaghetti" and "sauerkraut" Westerns in the 1960s. In fact,

Sergio Leone's Italian Westerns revitalized the genre for American audiences, and transformed television actor Clint Eastwood into a film icon.

Film Noir and the Hard-boiled Detective Film

Thanks in part to the popularity of *Sin City* and, before it, *Pulp Fiction*, the loosely defined genre of *film noir* has experienced a resurgence. Most film historians link *film noir*'s initial popularity to a specific historical circumstance: the suppressed cynicism that followed America's involvement in World War II. Having witnessed the industrialized slaughter of the war, audiences embraced films whose dark moodiness marked a dramatic departure from the lavish spectacle and optimism characteristic of Hollywood films in the 1930s.

Appropriately, the genre focused on characters who are down and out: a walking corpse who has twenty-four hours to discover who poisoned him before he dies (*D.O.A.* [Rudolph Maté 1949]), a woebegone hitchhiker biding his time before the cops arrive to arrest him for murder (*Detour* [Edgar G. Ulmer 1945]), and a second-rate boxer waiting for a match he's supposed to throw (*The Set-Up* [Robert Wise 1948]). These characters face grim circumstances beyond their control. Unlike the Western hero, these protagonists don't always triumph over adversity; many wind up dead or imprisoned. Furthermore, these protagonists wander crowded urban streets, not expansive Western plains; rather than romanticizing a distant historical past, *film noir* taps into anxieties about contemporary moral blight.

Whereas horror films personify evil through the monster, and the Western casts some outlaws and most Indians as vicious savages, *film noir* embodies amorality through the *femme fatale*, a sexually provocative and dangerous woman willing to lie and to use her seductive wiles to exploit others to her advantage. Frequently, her sexual advances trap the protagonist in a web of deceit where he must compromise his values to remain with her. Duped by the *femme fatale*, who wields power through sexual manipulation, he loses his moral compass and must struggle to retain his ethical principles.

The hard-boiled detective film is the most recognizable and consistently popular approach to *film noir*. It differs dramatically from its more genteel precursors, mysteries featuring investigators such as Sherlock Holmes and Charlie Chan. Whereas Holmes and Chan project an aura of rigorous, intellectual sophistication, hard-boiled detectives such as Philip Marlowe and Sam Spade are streetwise and brash. Holmes and Chan work through mysteries as if they were games of cat and mouse between two foes trying to outwit one another, while Marlowe and Spade solve mysteries by relying on physical stamina. Their investigative prowess relies as much on legwork and street smarts as it does on cognitive skills (Cawelti 1977, p. 185).

In contrast to the rational optimism of Chan and Holmes, the hard-boiled detective embodies the loneliness and alienation of the modern human condition. He has few friends, and he works alone. Above all, the hard-boiled detective works apart from the law. In some cases he has worked as a police officer in the past, but inevitably he has quit the force, either out of self-interest or disgust. In short, the hard-boiled detective is a figure of isolation who can trust no one.

Given his asocial lifestyle and business practices, very little distinguishes the detective from the outlaws he pursues, save for an abstract (and at times, questionable) moral code.

The criminals he encounters exacerbate the detective's feelings of distrust. These characters tend to be the powerful elite rather than mere criminal thugs; often they carry clout in the political or legal system. The conflict between detective and criminal reflects an unspoken class dichotomy between the honorable (though imperfect) working class and the maliciously deceitful upper class.

Hard-boiled detective narratives are notoriously convoluted. Just as the detective is confused by a web of deceit, so is the audience. Often the film begins with the detective accepting a simple case, following a series of false leads, then realizing that the crime is far more complex than he suspected. The plot of Howard Hawks's *The Big Sleep* (1946) is so convoluted that, when asked whether or not one of the corpses was murdered or committed suicide, the director reportedly confessed that he didn't know! (Mellen, p. 139).

While neo-*noirs* such as *Devil in a Blue Dress* (Carl Franklin 1996) and *The Black Dahlia* (Brian De Palma 2006) set their stories in the 1940s and 1950s, others adapt *film noir* to contemporary settings. The Coen Brothers' *Fargo* (1996) situates the genre in the empty, frozen plains of Minnesota, while *Brick* (Rian Johnson 2005) transposes a 1940s-era hard-boiled detective plot by resituating it within a contemporary Los Angeles high school, where the students' *patois* is an odd amalgamation of classic *noir* banter and skateboarder slang.

The Action Film

As its name implies, the action film provides audiences with a visceral thrill. Whereas the horror film depicts the trauma of violence, the action film revels in the excitement produced by mayhem and carnage. The genre encompasses a wide variety of approaches, from the super-heroic triumphs in *Superman* and *Batman* films, to the ramped-up adventures of renegade cops in the *Lethal Weapon* series, *Speed*, *Face/Off* and *Miami Vice*. But action films are united by two defining characteristics: an emphasis on masculine heroics and over-the-top violence.

Like the Western and the detective film, the action film is predominantly about male heroes facing a potent villain who threatens to rupture social stability. While the action hero is typically male, entries such as *La Femme Nikita* (Luc Besson 1990) and *Salt* (Phillip Noyce 2010) have proffered female leads. The popular *X-Men* series takes the generic evolution of

13.7 Wolverine in the *X-Men* series is a subtle variation on the male action hero.

action films a step further by featuring a diverse group of social misfits, though some might argue that the films still foreground the youthful and rebellious man in the group, Wolverine (Hugh Jackman), as the most compelling character (fig. **13.7**).

Action film plots place the hero (or a small group of heroes) in increasingly thorny, and violent, confrontations. Consequently, action sequences become the central organizing feature of the genre and violent spectacle becomes the vehicle for expressing character development: "The [action] film pares down its story and the interactions between characters to the absolute minimum required to suture viewers into the rhythm of the action." (Gallagher, p. 207) In fact, the exposition of action films typically employs a brief action sequence to introduce characters and central conflicts. Crucially, while the depiction of violent action has become increasingly graphic (reflecting, in part, a desire to exploit the latest digital technologies), the audience reads these sequences as merely "cartoonish." Because of the generic context, "viewers learn to enjoy displays of violence as displays rather than as violence." (Gallagher, p. 205) In other words, whereas some viewers might read the elaborate battle sequences in a combat drama like *Saving Private Ryan* as painful reminders that war is hell, most audiences respond to the fights and car chases in an action film like *Inception* as choreographed spectacle.

One of most distinctive subgenres of the action film is the paranoid conspiracy film. In Alfred Hitchcock's *North by Northwest*, ad exec Roger Thornhill (Cary Grant) raises his hand to call for a waiter in a crowded bar in the middle of the afternoon. His request for a phone is ill-timed, as two goons consequently mistake him for an American Secret Service agent they are supposed to eradicate. The turn of events leads Thornhill into an existential nightmare in which he loses his identity, is framed for murdering a U.N. ambassador (fig. **13.8**), and ends up dangling off the face of Mt. Rushmore. Such is the logic of the paranoid conspiracy film: in this world of Cold War espionage and urban anonymity, subtle nuances of everyday behavior may unleash a wave of chaotic and life-threatening repercussions.

13.8 Framed for murder at the U.N.: *North by Northwest*.

The paranoid conspiracy film focuses exclusively on innocent individuals who stumble on a devious plot. These films typically begin by depicting the daily routine of a blissfully ignorant citizen. Through an arbitrary act, he stumbles upon the conspiracy: a young woman befriends a kindly old lady in *The Lady Vanishes* (Alfred Hitchcock 1938); a teenager parks his scooter in the wrong place at the wrong time in *Diva* (Jean-Jacques Beineix 1982); a lawyer buys lingerie for his wife in *Enemy of the State* (Tony Scott 1998). The hero of the paranoid thriller differs dramatically from professional spies in other categories of the action movie (the Bourne films; *Salt*). Unlike Jason Bourne, he is an unwilling participant in violent spy games. He is motivated by self-preservation, not by any sense of obligation toward his country.

The genre's narrative then unfolds, following a fairly regular pattern. Although the protagonist is initially ignorant of what he has witnessed, he finds himself pursued by the conspirators. He runs for his life in a state of befuddlement, failing to comprehend why others are trying to kill him (fig. **13.9**). When he finally does ascertain the truth, he cannot convince the authorities to help him. The police either refuse to believe the elaborate conspiracy theory, or are actually involved in the plan.

13.9 Jules rides for his life in *Diva*, though he doesn't know why he's being pursued.

The film builds to its climax when the hero stops passively fleeing danger and begins proactively dismantling the conspiracy, utilizing his unique skills or behavioral idiosyncrasy. Just as Thornhill employs his ad man's adeptness at lying to help him manipulate scenarios to his advantage, singer Jo MacKenna (Doris Day) uses her voice to prevent a political assassination and to locate her kidnapped son in *The Man Who Knew Too Much* (Alfred Hitchcock 1956).

The genre's primary visual characteristic is an urban setting, which is crucial for underscoring the protagonist's justified paranoia: she is surrounded by people, any of whom might be trying to murder her. Complementing the urban setting is the genre's reliance on rapid transportation systems: cars, trains, subways, even scooters. The fact that characters move from place to place so rapidly underscores the all-encompassing nature of the scheme. The further and faster the protagonist runs, the more it becomes apparent that options for escape are nil.

From the 1930s to the early 1960s, paranoid thrillers reflected a preoccupation with the threat to established order posed by external forces, such as the Nazis in *The 39 Steps* (Hitchcock 1935) and *Ministry of Fear* (Fritz Lang 1944), or Communists in *North by Northwest* and *Man Hunt* (Fritz Lang 1941). During the politically turbulent 1960s, the genre began to depict evil emanating from within the U.S. government or the corporate world. Paranoid conspiracy films have implicated big business in *The Conversation* and *The Parallax View* (Alan J. Pakula 1974); the medical industry in *Coma* (Michael Crichton 1978), the political process in *Blow Out* and *Bullworth* (Warren Beatty 1994); the secret service in *Enemy of the State* and *The Bourne Identity* (Doug Liman 2002); and the international recording industry in *Diva*. Roman Polanski's *The Ghost Writer* (2009) implicates the publishing industry and news corporations as potential co-conspirators with CIA covert operations, revealing how they market political intrigue as crowd-pleasing narratives.

The Science Fiction Film

Of the many popular film genres, science fiction is perhaps the most difficult to define through a set of conventions. It's possible to associate science fiction with stories about space travel or futuristic societies—stories that take place in settings where technology plays a dominant role in the characters' lives. Yet, such a definition excludes films such as *Back to the Future* (Robert Zemeckis 1985), a comedy in which Marty McFly (Michael J. Fox) travels back in time to 1955 in a mad scientist's sports car.

How can a single genre accommodate *Frankenstein* (James Whale 1931), *The Fly* (Kurt Neumann 1958), *The Thing from Another World* (Christian Nyby and Howard Hawks 1951), and *Star Wars*? The genre does not have the visual and narrative conventions so readily locatable in the Western. Instead, what links the wide array of science fiction films is a thematic interest in the relationship between technology and humanity (fig. **13.10**). Science fiction films explore the potential of human ingenuity and ponder the spiritual, intellectual, and/or physical costs of technological development. They suggest that technology alone is impotent, or worse, destructive, unless its development coincides with an expansion in the human capacity for creativity, empathy, and/or humility.

In the most general terms, science fiction films begin with protagonists confronting a problem associated with their over-reliance on rational thought. In some cases the conflict is literally the product of scientific inquiry, such as Frankenstein's monster or Dr. Jekyll's alter ego Mr. Hyde in *Dr. Jekyll and Mr. Hyde* (Rouben Mamoulian 1932). Sometimes the protagonists are less directly responsible for the source of conflict, as in alien invasion films such as *Invasion of the Body Snatchers* (Don Siegel 1956) and *The Thing from Another World*. Nevertheless, the arrival of these alien creatures is often associated with society's increasing preference for the rational (and often secular) over an instinctive, ruminative, and spiritual imagination.

The conflict is resolved only when protagonists learn to balance the scientific approach with a more humanistic one. Dr. Frankenstein (Colin Clive) defeats the monster (and his will to power) by joining a community mob and confronting his creation face to face. In *Star Wars*, Luke Skywalker (Mark Hamill) blows up the evil Empire's "Death Star" only after he ignores his computer monitor and follows his own inner "force." Often the solution doesn't necessitate completely abandoning scientific thought. Rather, the protagonist must

13.10 The horror of scientific exploration in *The Thing from Another World*.

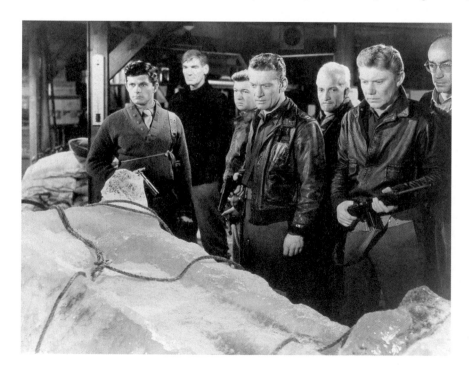

adopt a balanced approach that utilizes rationality alongside spontaneity, emotions, spirituality, and creativity.

Science fiction can be subdivided into four subgenres, each of which is distinguishable by narrative and visual conventions. Perhaps the most familiar subgenre is the exploration film, which involves a group of travelers exploring different worlds. These travelers are driven by their thirst for knowledge.

The paradigmatic film in this category is Georges Méliès's *A Trip to the Moon*. Others include *Forbidden Planet* (Fred M. Wilcox 1956), *2001: A Space Odyssey*, the *Star Trek* series, and *Pitch Black* (David Twohy 2000). By no means is the subgenre limited to films about travel in outer space. The travelers might find themselves hurtling through time—as in *The Time Machine* (George Pal 1960) and *La Jetée* (Chris Marker 1962)—or venturing into other-earthly environments in the present. In *The Fantastic Voyage* (Richard Fleischer 1966), scientists shrink themselves and explore the inside of a human body, and in *Tron* (Steven Lisberger 1982), a computer programmer is sucked into a video game, literally becoming one of the digital combatants. In most cases, these adventurers discover more about themselves than they learn about the world they visit.

Another strain of science fiction is more concerned with invaders encroaching on supposedly safe territory. On occasion the invaders turn out to be benevolent, as in *The Day the Earth Stood Still* (Robert Wise 1951), *E.T.*, and *District 9*. But more often the invaders pose a threat to humanity.

These invaders do not necessarily have to be extraterrestrial, as a wave of monster movies in the 1950s suggested, including *Them!* (Gordon Douglas 1954) and *Tarantula* (Jack Arnold 1955). These films depict humanity threatened by earthly creatures. Typically the monsters demonstrate the destructive folly of human ambition. They are the by-products of scientific inquisitiveness and/or technological development, as in the *Godzilla* series, in which the monster's rampage is linked to radioactivity lingering from the atomic bombs the U.S. dropped on Hiroshima and Nagasaki.

Since invaders, whether alien or not, are physically superior, they can only be conquered by luck or ingenuity. In *The War of the Worlds* (Byron Haskin 1953), bacteria ultimately undo the Martian attack. In many cases it is the everyday citizen (or people banding together), not the brilliant scientist, who succeeds in driving off the foes. In *The Terminator*, a working-class woman defeats a robot from the future, and in *Independence Day*, a hodgepodge assortment of outcasts launches a counter-offensive on attacking aliens. Invasion films value cooperation, ingenuity, and sheer tenacity over advanced technology and firepower.

The third subgenre explicitly criticizes unbridled scientific inquiry. This subgenre grows out of the legendary Faust myth, in which an

13.11 Technology trumps humanity in *Metropolis*.

alchemist trades his soul to Mephistopheles for knowledge. After he sacrifices his eternal soul for fleeting, earthly knowledge, Faust learns that knowledge divorced from wisdom is destructive. In science fiction, this premise is reformulated in stories of reclusive, often mad, scientists who are so fixated on their quests for scientific discovery that they fail to recognize the self-destructive ramifications of their behavior. Notable examples include *The Invisible Man* (James Whale 1933) and both versions of *The Fly* (Kurt Neumann 1958; David Cronenberg 1986). In these films, brilliant scientists are threatened or destroyed by their audacious experiments.

The fourth subgenre, films about dystopias, suggests how an entire society can be corrupted if "progress" goes unchecked. In Fritz Lang's seminal film *Metropolis* (1926; fig. **13.11**), industrial technology has run amok and workers are reduced to mere drones, ceaselessly providing for the towering factory machinery. In *Fahrenheit 451* (François Truffaut 1966), books are outlawed (fig. **13.12**). In *Minority Report* (Steven Spielberg 2002), the legal system places so much stock in a procedure for predicting crime that people are arrested before they have committed any offense. These societies assume that human emotions are flawed because they are irrational and impossible to control. But these films question the benefits of technological progress by suggesting that societies devoid of emotions are devoid of humanity.

In short, science fiction is a diverse genre unified by a central conceit—to explore the possibilities and potential dangers of technological advancement.

13.12 Books are ceremonially burned in *Fahrenheit 451*.

The Musical

For some, the Hollywood musical is the most cinematic of genres. The musical is the perfect showcase for cinema's magic, thanks to its uncanny ability to integrate character-driven romances with visual and aural sensation. The genre's highly choreographed dance routines exploit the medium's visual technology to produce kaleidoscopic spectacles, and its songs make use of the soundtrack's ability to provide lushly orchestrated musical interludes that transcend the mundane spoken word.

Yet the musical's requisite song-and-dance numbers present an inherent problem to Hollywood's standard narrative model: how can a filmmaker include a lot of singing and dancing without diverting attention away from the story? Early musicals dispensed with narrative logic altogether. During the nascent years of the genre, the sheer joy and novelty of sound justified the emphasis on musical numbers at the expense of a coherent narrative. Showcase films such as *Hollywood Revue of 1929* (Charles Reisner 1929) and *Paramount on Parade* (Dorothy Arzner et al. 1930) are simply musical reviews, which abandon narrative altogether. Other filmmakers simply plunked musical interludes into the middle of genre films, from science fiction (*Just Imagine* [David Butler 1930]) to comedies (*The Cocoanuts* [Robert Florey and Joseph Santley 1929]), with little concern for the consequent narrative disruption (Altman, "Musical," p. 295).

But the most important musicals during the Hollywood studio era fused story and song by making the struggle to produce music central to the story. In the groundbreaking scene from Alan Crosland's *The Jazz Singer*, Jakie Rabinowitz (Al Jolson) performs "Blue Skies" on the piano for his mother. In between verses he stops singing and defends his decision to follow his musical calling. The scene fuses narrative conflict and music by making performance itself the source of narrative tension.

Many musicals follow *The Jazz Singer*'s lead and depict performers struggling to stage a musical show. These so-called "backstage musicals" consistently incorporate two plotlines: the romantic and the professional. In "**backstage musicals**" such as *Show Boat* (Harry Pollard 1929/James Whale 1936/George Sidney 1951), *Gold Diggers of 1933* (Mervyn LeRoy 1933; fig. **13.13**), and *Easter Parade* (Charles Walters 1948), the eruption of musical numbers is narratively justified by the theatrical plotline. The characters burst into song because they are performers, and they deliver their performances on stage or to an attentive private audience.

13.13 *Gold Diggers of 1933*: a lavish backstage musical.

Although the musical numbers are usually performed on a stage within the diegesis, the lyrics reflect the emotional undercurrents circulating offstage. Typically, a performer struggles to express his romantic longing for a woman while simultaneously working to attain success and fame in the theater. While these musicals focus on the conflict between professional ambition and romance, the climactic numbers often bridge the gap between emotional and professional desires. The closing numbers offer proof that love can provide artistic inspiration, which pays off both romantically and professionally.

In contrast, **integrated musicals** show characters who do not need an audience—or a visible orchestra for that matter—to make music. *Singin' in the Rain* (Stanley Donen and Gene Kelly 1952), *The Sound of Music* (Robert Wise 1952), and *Cabaret* (Robert Fosse 1972) all include characters who spontaneously break out in song. Although these three films are not backstage musicals, they maintain the link to the theater by foregrounding characters who are connected to the performing arts, thereby rationalizing their propensity to sing at the drop of a hat. Other integrated musicals abandon the theatrical plotline altogether. The Hollywood musical is rife with characters who have no professional connection to the stage but who nevertheless feel compelled to express their joy, heartache, and desire through melody: Dorothy in *The Wizard of Oz*, or the juvenile delinquents in *West Side Story* (Robert Wise and Jerome Robbins 1961), who simultaneously rumble and harmonize, or the odd assortment of young lovers and activists who bring the Beatles' music to life in *Across the Universe* (Taymor

13.14 An integrated musical about murder and meatpies: *Sweeney Todd*.

2007). Even the famously macabre Tim Burton turned out an integrated musical with his adaptation of the Broadway play about murder and revenge in Victorian London, *Sweeney Todd* (2007, fig. **13.14**).

Since 1927 the popularity of the musical has come and gone, with the genre reaching its creative and economic zenith in the late 1940s and early 1950s. Over the course of that decade MGM alone produced over thirty musicals (Cook p. 486). Though still a formidable presence, musicals in the latter half of the 1950s and through the 1960s were less common and less consistently well received, both critically and financially. As the major Hollywood studios crumbled in the 1960s, for every successful musical, there were several box-office stinkers.

Despite its lapses in popularity in the United States, the musical has shown remarkable resilience. Just when critics deliver the genre's obituary, new musicals prove to be surprisingly popular and revitalize the genre. In the late 1970s the one-two punch of *Saturday Night Fever* (John Badham 1977) and *Grease* (Randal Klieser 1978) attracted audiences in droves, as did *Fame* (Alan Parker 1980), *Footloose* (Herbert Ross 1984), *A Chorus Line* (Richard Attenborough

13.15 *A Chorus Line* exemplifies the realism of the backstage musicals popular in the 1980s.

1985; fig. **13.15**), and *Dirty Dancing* (Emile Ardolino 1987) in the following decade. The revival of the backstage musical in the 1980s attracted new fans in part by abandoning the glitzy spectacle of Hollywood in favor of capturing a sparer, more realistic depiction of life on the stage. Again, the genre lay dormant for a decade until another wave of films—*Dancer in the Dark* (Lars von Trier 2000), *Moulin Rouge*, *Chicago* (Rob Marshall 2002), *Idlewild* (Bryan Barber 2006), and *Dreamgirls*—proved that the musical remains economically, intellectually, and aesthetically viable.

Using Genre to Interpret Films

The proliferation of genres in Hollywood's studio era can be explained, at least in part, by the major studios' industrial filmmaking strategies, described in Chapter 11. Genre films allowed the studios to conceptualize, produce, market, and distribute their products efficiently and rapidly. For any given genre film, a studio might be able to reformulate popular storylines and reuse sets, costumes, and even production units. In turn, genre films lured audiences into theaters by offering them familiar pleasures. Thus, repetition was, and still is, a crucial component of any genre, from both the industry's and the audience's perspective.

Because genre films depend on repetition and are so closely linked to Hollywood's industrial practices, critics overlooked their aesthetic and intellectual potential until the 1960s. Until then, genre automatically connoted mindless, homogeneous entertainment. Now genre films inspire a wide array of provocative academic analysis and popular criticism. The remainder of the chapter will explore four approaches that critics employ when they contemplate genre films: the use of repeated formulae; the social implications of adhering to convention; the way genres themselves are prone to change; and the relation of the individual filmmaker to the established conventions of the genre.

Genre Film and Aesthetic Appeal: Cliché or Strategic Repetition?

Popular film critics regularly measure the degree to which a given film relies on conventional plot devices and visual details. While following convention is an integral part of any genre film, good genre films rely on more than sheer repetition. Any film that merely rehashes tried and true strategies quickly lapses into cliché. Genres thrive when filmmakers find ways to modify the conventions. So, while audiences carry a set of expectations with them whenever they attend a genre film, for most audiences, one of these expectations is that the film will surprise them by *upsetting* some of their expectations.

For most critics, the most pronounced criterion for evaluating a film is how much originality it injects into the formula without totally abandoning the conventions of the genre. Genre films shouldn't sacrifice the pleasures of familiarity for obtuseness; nor should they mindlessly repeat every property of films past.

Altering the conventions of a genre may entertain viewers with a new combination of familiarity and novelty. But it can also provoke ideas. Scott Foundas's review of *District 9* (see pp. 59–61) makes just this point. Foundas begins by emphasizing how the film makes one bold departure from science fiction's conventions and thus initiates an interrogation of xenophobia and immigration. According to Foundas, science fiction, from H.G. Wells's 1898 novel *The War of the Worlds* to *Cloverfield,* repeatedly structures narrative conflict around the terrifying experience of alien invasion. But *District 9* sidesteps this convention by beginning the *syuzhet* well after the aliens have landed and established a home on Earth. This adjustment to convention provokes the film's novel central idea: how would humans treat alien visitors who are just "worker bees," with neither the inclination nor the technology to conquer Earth?

As his review demonstrates, meaning in a genre comes in part from measuring one film against its antecedents. Films converse with other films in the same genre. Scholars and fans can't fully appreciate the aesthetic worth and intellectual depth of a genre film unless they recognize how it is adding to and departing from what other films have already contributed to the genre.

Typically, genre films develop their ideas by making minor adjustments to convention. But sometimes a film might boldly reject the basic patterns of a genre. When films such as *Psycho* and *Peeping Tom* radically modify conventions (in this case, by transforming the monster from a repulsive other to the boy next door), critics refer to it as **revisionist**. As the name implies, by upending firmly established conventions, a revisionist film has the effect of changing a genre…it expands our sense of what a genre can do and may send the genre off in a new direction entirely.

Genre and the Status Quo

Another approach to genre criticism considers the social implications of a reliance on repetition. By repeatedly telling the same types of stories over and over again, these tales begin to inform the way audiences interpret the world around them. Genre films capture, and at the same time reinforce, cultural values. Adopting this perspective assumes that, because genre films are a popular, mass-produced form of entertainment, they are the modern equivalent of a cultural mythology—a set of narrative formulas told and retold as a way of transmitting basic social lessons.

Robert Warshow, for example, argues that the characteristics of the Western hero—his solitude, his commitment to unfettered movement across the plains, his reluctant but morally clarified use of violence—make him "the last gentleman." Inevitably, the cowboy is presented as brave, independent, and considerate, and the reappearance of these qualities in film after film suggests how the cowboy functions as a symbol of a (real or imagined) national heritage (Warshow, p. 457).

Often a more critical perspective informs this approach. Marxist film scholar Judith Hess Wright, for example, argues that genre films lull audiences into complacency by their promise to be nothing more than mere entertainment. As a result, viewers are little more than passive receptacles, mindlessly absorbing a reassuring cultural mythology that celebrates the status quo: "Genre films produce satisfaction rather than action, pity, and fear rather than revolt. [… T]hey throw a sop to oppressed groups who [...] eagerly accept the genre film's absurd solutions to economic and social conflicts." (Wright, p. 41)

In the Western, she argues, such a conflict arises over the issue of whether violence is justifiable. The genre naïvely solves this conflict by boiling its characters down into two simplistic types: guilty and innocent. Violence is always justified when it is inflicted on the guilty in the name of justice. The result is a genre that justifies vigilantism, ignoring questions regarding the environmental causes of antisocial behavior (Wright, pp. 42–3).

In a comment that reflects Wright's theory about genre, filmmaker Paul Haggis (*Crash*, *In the Valley of Elah* [2007]) critiques the most recent wave of action films in light of the United States' wars in Afghanistan and Iraq. He argues that, by turning violence into exciting spectacle, action films stir up wartime fervor by allowing the audience to imagine the triumph of battle without experiencing its bloody consequences: "The pro-war films aren't actually about the war. A few months ago all the coming attractions were about vengeance, violence, and kicking someone's ass. We're living in a fantasy where the message is that if we can't win over there, we can win at home on our screens. To make a movie like *Transformers* at a time of war is a political act." (quoted in Jaafar) In other words, Haggis feels these films, which appear to be "just entertainment," are pro-war precisely because they foment a desire to take violent action and provide a fantasy of limitless conquest to audiences frustrated by wars that seem never to end.

These perspectives share the assumption that, at their core, genre films contain certain unchanging elements. What makes a genre potent, in other words, is its consistency. By analyzing this consistency one can measure its aesthetic and social impact. But this assumes that viewers' responses are standardized—that audiences are only capable of reading a film according to dominant cultural values.

However, making such assumptions about how audiences respond to what they see is too reductive because it discounts the fact that a film like *Hostel* (Eli Roth 2005) might provoke contradictory responses. Some viewers might see the gruesome horror film as a critique of the United States' overbearing presence overseas (its plot depicts a group of brash students traveling abroad who find themselves in a heap of trouble after obnoxiously throwing their money around in bars). But others read the film as a twisted revenge fantasy in which primitive and opportunistic cultural others get their comeuppance after picking on Americans.

Genres as Culturally Responsive Artifacts

Another mode of criticism measures how genres gradually change, or evolve. While on one level genres retain their basic conventions, over time certain conventions will give way to others.

Some critics try to account for and evaluate such shifts in convention by exploring how a popular genre at a given point in time reflects the *immediate*, albeit unacknowledged, concerns of its audience. This approach is predicated on the assumption that genre films attract audiences because they appeal to popular sentiment, whether or not viewers are aware of their concerns and anxieties.

Consequently, the subtext of a genre at any point in time may grant critics and filmgoers alike access to a culture's approach to complex social issues. Genre films are akin to a mass-produced ritual, wherein cultures see their fantasies acted out on screen. When a culture's fantasies evolve, so do its generic conventions.

For example, the hard-boiled detective film came of age during and just after World War II, when Americans grappled with the war's industrialized genocide and the frustrating return to the postwar status quo. The 1970s saw a new wave of detective films reinvigorate the formula: *The Long Goodbye* (Robert Altman 1973), *Chinatown*, and *Farewell, My Lovely* (Dick Richards 1975). Thomas Schatz links the nostalgic flair apparent in this revitalization to America's longing for the bygone days of the 1940s and 1950s. But the nostalgia of these films was accompanied by an unremitting pessimism even more pronounced than that of their predecessors. This pessimism has been cited as evidence of the emotional and psychological by-products of the Vietnam War—urban blight, political corruption, and racial strife:

> [T]he detective-hero necessarily reflected the change in values. As did his '40s prototype, the screen detective of the 1970s accepted social corruption as a given and tried to remain isolated from it, still the naïve idealist beneath the cynical surface. *But the new* detective of the '70s inhabited a milieu he was unable to understand or to control [...]. (Schatz, p. 149, emphasis added)

More recently, a spate of horror films that seem to reflect national anxieties followed the terrorist attacks in the United States on September 11, 2001. Some of these films recycle familiar monstrous characters as thinly disguised metaphors for the terrorist assault on American soil: zombies in *I Am Legend*, alien invaders in *Cloverfield*, and vampires in *30 Days of Night*.

Instead of assuming that genres remain static, this approach focuses on the way the flexibility of a genre's conventions ensures its adaptability for popular culture's shifting interests.

Genre and Film Authorship

In his interviews with François Truffaut, Alfred Hitchcock explains how he developed the idea for the famous crop-dusting sequence in *North by Northwest*, where Roger Thornhill finds himself nearly gunned down in a cornfield by a crop-dusting plane:

> I found I was faced with the old cliché situation: the man who is put on the spot, probably to be shot. Now, how is this usually done? A dark night at a narrow intersection. The waiting victim standing in a pool of light under the street lamp. ... The slow approach of a black limousine, et cetera, et cetera. Now, what was the antithesis of a scene like this? No darkness, no pool of light, no mysterious figures in windows. Just nothing. Just bright sunshine and a blank, open countryside with barely a house or tree in which lurking menaces could hide. (quoted in Truffaut, p. 256)

Hitchcock's quote suggests how a filmmaker can operate within a genre while at the same time self-consciously working against its conventions, upsetting audience expectations and providing a richer cinematic experience in the process.

A fourth approach to genre criticism looks at how notable directors or *auteurs* work with **genre conventions** to assert a personal vision. This approach assumes that good genre films distinguish themselves from the rest, and that a director may be responsible for a particular genre film's originality.

In his review of Martin Scorsese's musical *New York, New York* (1977), the critic Richard Combs argues that the director brings a unique set of ideas to the musical genre. At first glance, Scorsese's decision to film a musical seems like a radical departure from his usual interest in gangster films and male violence. But, as Combs points out, *New York, New York* is informed by the director's interest in self-destructive male psychology.

> Situated in fantasy, Jimmy Doyle (Robert De Niro) … becomes uniquely blessed among Scorsese heroes—he is allowed to achieve his ambition, the fulfillment of what he calls the "major chord," when you have everything in life that you want. But Scorsese plays the figure not as fantasy but as a character streaked by the same self-destructive fanaticism, unwavering drive and crippling ambivalence as any of his street punks on the make—and compresses the psychology of the character not into the predictable narrative of breakdown and break-up, but most tightly into the scenes where one most expects relaxation, i.e., the musical numbers. (Combs, p. 252)

Combs finds consistency in the way Scorsese's films evoke masculine emotional and psychological intensity, and this intensity is evident even in a musical. His analysis demonstrates how some critics value some genre films over others because a director created a unique vision while working with a genre's conventions.

The work of the *auteur* underscores the complexities of genre criticism. On the one hand, definitions of genres require stasis and consistency. On the other hand, economic, cultural, and artistic forces inevitably undermine such assumptions. The next chapter explores in more detail the theoretical underpinnings (and the fallacies) of the *auteur* theory—the argument that some directors have the ability to inscribe their own personal signature on the films they direct.

Works Consulted

Altman, Rick. *Film/Genre*, British Film Institute Publishing, London, 1999.

——————. "A Semantic/Syntactic Approach to Film Genres." *Film Theory and Criticism*. 5th ed. Eds. Leo Braudy and Marshall Cohen. New York: Oxford University Press, 1999, pp. 630–41.

——————. "The Musical." *The Oxford History of World Cinema*. Ed. Geoffrey Nowell-Smith. New York: Oxford University Press, 1996, pp. 294–303.

Boucher, Geoff. "James Cameron: Yes, *Avatar is Dances With Wolves* in Space...Sorta" Part II of the Hero Complex Blog Interview. *L.A. Times*. August 10, 2000. **http://latimesblogs.latimes.com/ herocomplex/2009/08/james-cameron-the-new-trek-rocks-but-transformers-is-gimcrackery.html**.

Brandy, Leo. "Genre: The Conventions of Connection," in *Film Theory and Criticism*, 4th edn. New York: Oxford University Press, 1992.

Cavell, Stanley. *Pursuits of Happiness: The Hollywood Comedy of Remarriage*. Cambridge, MA: Harvard University Press, 1981.

Cawelti, John G. *Adventure, Mystery and Romance: Formula Stories in Art and Popular Culture*. Chicago: University of Chicago Press, 1977.

——————. "*Chinatown* and Generic Transformation in Recent American Films," in *Film Genre Reader*, ed. Barry Keith Grant. Austin: University of Texas Press, 1986, pp. 183–201.

——————. *The Six Gun Mystique Sequel*. Madison: Popular Press/University of Wisconsin Press, 1999.

Clover, Carol. *Men, Women, and Chainsaws: Gender in the Modern Horror Film*. Princeton, NJ: Princeton University Press, 1992.

Combs, Richard. "New York, New York." *Sight and Sound*, Fall, 1977, pp. 252–3.

Cook, David. *A History of Narrative Film*, 3rd edn. New York: Norton, 1996.

Corrigan, Timothy. *A Cinema without Walls: Movies and Culture After Vietnam*. New Brunswick: Rutgers University Press, 1991.

Gallagher, Mark. "I Married Rambo." *Mythologies of Violence in Postmodern Media*. Ed. Christopher Sharrett. Detroit, MI: Wayne State University Press, 1999, pp. 199–226.

Guerrero, Ed. *Framing Blackness*. Philadelphia, PA: Temple University Press, 1993.

Gunning, Tom. "'Those Drawn with a Very Fine Camel's Hair Brush': The Origins of Film Genres." *Iris* 20 (Fall 1995): pp. 49–61.

Hutchings, Peter. "Genre Theory and Criticism." *Approaches to Popular Film*, ed. Joanne Hollows and Mark Jancovich. Manchester and New York: Manchester University Press, 1995, pp. 59–77.

Jafaar, Ali. "Casualties of War." *Sight and Sound*, 18 (February 08), pp. 16–22.

Kawin, Bruce. "Children of the Light," in *Film Genre Reader*, ed. Barry Keith Grant. Austin: University of Texas Press, 1986, pp. 236–57.

Lent, Tina Olsin. "Romantic Love and Friendship: The Redefinition of Gender Relations in Screwball Comedy," in *Classical Hollywood Comedy*, ed. Krisine Brunovska Karnick and Henry Jenkins. London: Routledge, 1995, pp. 314–31.

Lowenstein, Adam. *Shocking Representation: Historical Trauma, National Cinema, and the Modern Horror Film*. New York: Columbia University Press, 2005.

Mellen, Joan. "Film Noir," in *The Political Companion to American Film*, ed. Gary Crowdus. Chicago: Lakeview Press, 1994, pp. 137–44.

Neale, Steve. *Genre and Hollywood*. London: Routledge, 2000.

O'Hehir, Andrew. "Beyond the Multiplex" salon.com. **salon.com/ent/movies/review/2006/08/03/btm/**. September 22, 2006.

Prince, Stephen, ed. *The Horror Film*. New Brunswick, NJ: Rutgers University Press, 2004.

Richie, Donald. *Japanese Cinema: An Introduction*. New York: Oxford University Press, 1990.

Ryall, Tom. "Genre and Hollywood," in *The Oxford Guide to Film Studies*, ed. John Hill and Pamela Church Gibson. London: Oxford University Press, 1998, pp. 327–37.

Schatz, Thomas. *Hollywood Genres: Formulas, Filmmaking, and the Studio System*. Philadelphia: Temple University Press, 1981.

Solomon, Stanley J. *Beyond Formula: American Film Genres*. San Diego: Harcourt Brace, 1976.

Sontag, Susan. "The Imagination of Disaster," in *Film Theory and Criticism*. 3rd edn., ed. Gerald Mast and Marshall Cohen. New York: Oxford University Press, 1985, pp. 451–65.

Stack, Peter. "Satirical *Scream* is Out for Blood—And Lots of It." *San Francisco Chronicle*. December 26, 1996. *SFGate.com*. February 13, 2003.

Staiger, Janet. "Hybrid or Inbred: The Purity Hypothesis and Hollywood Genre History." *Film Criticism* 22.1 (Fall 1997): pp. 5–20.

Truffaut, François. *Hitchcock*, rev. edn. New York: Touchstone, 1984.

Tutor, Andrew. *Theories of Film*. London: Martin Seeker and Warburg, 1973. Rpt. as "Genre and Critical Methodology." *Movies and Methods*. Ed. Bill Nichols. Berkeley: University of California Press, 1976, pp. 118–126.

Warshow, Robert. "Movie Chronicle: The Westerner," in *Film Theory and Criticism*. 4th edn., ed. Gerald Mast, Marshall Cohen, and Leo Braudy. New York: Oxford University Press, 1992, pp. 453–66.

Wexman, Virginia Wright. "Media Studies and the Academy: A Tangled Tale." *Cinema Journal* 49.1 (Fall 2009): pp. 140–6.

Wood, Robin. *Hollywood from Vietnam to Reagan*. New York: Columbia University Press, 1986.

——————. "Introduction," in *The American Nightmare: Essays on the Horror Film*, ed. Andrew Britton, Richard Lippe, Tony Williams, and Robin Wood. Toronto, Canada: Festival of Festivals, 1979, pp. 7–28.

Wright, Judith Hess. "Genre Films and the Status Quo," in *Film Genre Reader*, ed. Barry Keith Grant. Austin: University of Texas Press, 1986, pp. 236–57.

Film Authorship

> The studio had expected this to be a nice little murder mystery, an ordinary kind of picture. Well, you don't have Orson Welles and have an ordinary anything. He could only make it extraordinary.
>
> **Janet Leigh on** *Touch of Evil*

How do people decide which films to see? They read film reviews in newspapers, magazines, and journals, and on websites. They listen to their friends. Many fans flock to see movies featuring their favorite star; others line up for a film by a director whose work they enjoy. These viewers use their knowledge of a director's *oeuvre* as well as historical and biographical information to analyze, interpret, and evaluate her latest film.

14.1 One of John Ford's famous frame within a frame compositions in *Shenandoah*.

The common practice of using a film's director as an organizing principle is based on the *auteur* theory, developed by French cinephiles in the 1940s and 1950s. At its most basic, the theory proposes that a director is the author of the film: *auteur* translates as "author." The term implies that the director is the primary creative source and his films express his distinctive vision of the world. John Ford was an important Hollywood director who is rightly associated with the Western genre: as the director of more than sixty Westerns during a career that spanned six decades, Ford established many of the genre's now familiar conventions. In visual terms he made the Old West synonymous with the desert terrain of Monument Valley on the border of Utah and Arizona. He worked with the same actors again and again, including John Wayne, Victor McLaglen, and Ward Churchill. Wayne became a Western icon thanks to Ford's films. Ford's best-known visual technique is probably the frame within a frame composition (fig. **14.1**). In terms of theme, Ford's films focus on outsiders who find it difficult to fit into a community. Just as "Dickensian" might be used to describe Charles Dickens's literary style, so "Fordian" would be used to describe a film exhibiting these characteristics and "Wellesian" would be applied to a film using Orson Welles's signature devices of deep-focus cinematography and fluid camera movement.

The French critics who argued on behalf of the *auteur* did not just extol the work of recognized French writer–directors. Instead, they argued for the artistry of Hollywood directors. Their theory claimed that even commercial Hollywood directors (whose films others disparaged as mass entertainment, made in an assembly-line fashion) could be viewed as artists.

More than fifty years after the *auteur* theory emerged, it seems unremarkable to assume that the director is the primary creative force behind a film. Directors, studios, and film critics all encourage this notion. But the customary use of the *auteur* approach to film should be tempered by an understanding of its full implications. This chapter examines the idea of film authorship as it developed in France and, later, in the U.S., and the way the *auteur* can be used as a marketing tool. Then it looks at the application of this approach when writing about film and provides examples of four contemporary international *auteurs* in the context of research questions raised by *auteur* theory. This chapter explores both the value and limitations of the *auteur* approach.

The Idea of the *Auteur*: From *Cahiers du Cinéma* to the Sarris–Kael Debate

The *auteur* theory emerged from a specific cultural milieu: postwar France. During the 1940s and 1950s in Paris, intellectuals who loved cinema used it to explore aesthetic and philosophical questions. Many of these cinephiles—including François Truffaut, Eric Rohmer, Jean-Luc Godard, and Claude Chabrol—also made important films. Others, including André Bazin and Alexandre Astruc, contributed to film theory. Their early arguments in favor of the *auteur* approach to film criticism were published in the influential film journal *Cahiers du Cinéma*.

Alexandre Astruc looked at film as a medium of personal expression, like literature. He elaborated this idea in a 1948 essay, where he used the phrase "*caméra-stylo*," which literally means "camera pen." In 1954 Truffaut published "A Certain Tendency of French Cinema," a *Cahiers* essay that endorsed Astruc's ideas by advocating the *auteur* approach. In the essay, Truffaut argued that the average, unremarkable film director merely translates a pre-existing work onto film, but an *auteur* transforms the material. In the process, he makes it his own (an especially remarkable feat when accomplished by directors working within the commercial Hollywood studio system). Writer–directors *and* directors who shape pre-existing material according to a distinctive, creative sensibility are *auteurs*.

Truffaut favorably compared Hollywood films with the French cinema's "tradition of quality." To him, Hollywood provided models for daring cinematic creativity whereas the latter produced dull translations of literary works. Truffaut and Bazin elevated Hollywood studio filmmakers who they thought had been neglected, though Bazin also warned against making the director a cult hero.

The *auteur* theory challenged the prevailing view of the aesthetic superiority of European cinema over American. As Robert Stam notes:

> Filmmakers like Eisenstein, Renoir and Welles had always been regarded as *auteurs* [...] The novelty of *auteur* theory was to suggest that studio directors like Hawks and Minnelli were also *auteurs*.
> (Stam, p. 87)

The theory not only reconsidered popular films as potential works of art; it also spurred debates about which directors deserved to be called *auteurs*. In the United States the discussion of authorship appeared in the journal *Film Culture* and *The New Yorker* magazine, in a well-known debate between film critics Andrew Sarris and Pauline Kael.

In "Notes on the Auteur Theory in 1962," Andrew Sarris created a version of the *auteur* approach designed to evaluate directors. Sarris's criteria are meant to determine: (1) whether or not an individual director is an *auteur*; and (2) where a director ranks among all *auteurs*. A necessary (but not sufficient) criterion for an *auteur* is technical competence; a director must be capable of creating a well-made film. Second, the director must demonstrate a distinguishable personality. Finally, Sarris argued that the films in an *auteur*'s body of work share an interior meaning, defined as an underlying tension between the director's vision and the subject matter.

Sarris did not define this last criterion to the satisfaction of many critics, but it can be thought of as the continuing elaboration of a director's perspective on the world through the treatment of themes. An example of interior meaning would be Stanley Kubrick's ironic view of imperfect human beings and the flawed technologies they create in their own image. Many of his films satirize the desire for control and transcendence through technology, but they also reveal a grudging respect for the creative potential of human beings.

New Yorker critic Pauline Kael challenged Sarris. She argued that technical competence was a weak criterion: it failed to acknowledge the true masters of technique, such as Antonioni. She also pointed out that the distinguishable personality criterion penalized directors who risked venturing beyond a familiar genre or style, and she found the "interior meaning" criterion impossibly vague. She pointed out that the *auteur* approach might lead critics to overvalue trivial films, elevating them simply because they had been made by a recognized *auteur*.

Kael also criticized the *auteur* approach for refusing to take into account the collaborative nature of filmmaking. The theory ignores the fact that many people's creative decisions are part of the process of making films. Kael claimed that in many cases the director was not the driving creative force. Although she argued incorrectly that screenwriter Herman Mankiewicz, not Orson Welles, was responsible for the final version of the *Citizen Kane* script (and therefore should be considered its *auteur*), most film historians agree with her point that, like most films, that project was a collaboration. The innovative visual elements of *Citizen Kane* resulted from Welles's collaboration with cinematographer Gregg Toland. A number of film scholars have argued that it is appropriate in certain cases to label producers (Val Lewton, Christine Vachon), actors (Clint Eastwood), and screenwriters (Dudley Nichols) as *auteurs*.

One additional limitation of the approach should be considered. *Auteur* criticism implies that the director possesses conscious intentions and, perhaps, unacknowledged ideas, all of which combine to produce a film, and, eventually, a body of work. The approach views the director as the primary source of meaning. But film theorists such as Peter Wollen argue that the meaning of any text, whether it is a film, novel, short story, television show, or a billboard, exceeds the intentions of the person or people who created it. Wollen questions whether anyone—even the author—can fix any film's meaning definitively for all time. To him, a strict *auteurist* approach may ignore the complexity inherent in any text by insisting that the only authorized readings be linked to some notion of what a director meant to convey.

A simple example illuminates Wollen's concerns. It is well known that Orson Welles was intrigued by the idea of making a film based on the life of newspaper magnate William Randolph Hearst. Although pursuing this avenue of research may prove fruitful for analyzing *Citizen Kane*, to constrain an interpretation to this single aspect would exclude the many ideas the film generates about American culture, aging, and the nature of human relationships, as well as other themes that Welles may or may not have intended to address.

Despite many shortcomings, the *auteur* approach remains central to film scholarship and criticism. Moreover, the powerful notion of film authorship exerts an influence on filmmaking as an economic practice, as the next section will show.

Auteur as Marketing Strategy: Old and New Hollywood

The potential commercial appeal of the *auteur* drives many marketing campaigns. In 2006 Paul Greengrass became the first director to address the fraught subject matter of the terrorist attacks of September 11, 2001, in a mainstream feature film, *United 93* (fig. **14.2**). One strategy within Universal Studios' marketing campaign was to characterize Greengrass as a "compassionate and socially aware writer/director of films that study the impact of terrorism in Northern Ireland in *Bloody Sunday* and *Omagh*" ("Production Notes"). Two points illustrate the way auteurism is used to market the film: first, the films mentioned deal with the subject of terrorism and adopt a near-documentary visual style (fig. **14.3**). Thus they establish Greengrass's legitimacy as a director of thought-provoking films who is able to depict political violence in a sensitive, rather than an exploitative, manner. Second, the promotional materials overlooked a popular film that, ironically, helped establish the director's reputation in the United States: *The Bourne Supremacy* (2004). One reason for this omission may be that the latter film is a spy thriller that trades on the excitement generated by violence. To appeal to potential viewers concerned that a film about September 11 would exploit the events for entertainment, the studio touted only the films that helped to solidify Greengrass's reputation as a compassionate and conscientious director.

Other examples point to the ubiquity of using a director to market a film. DVD box sets are packaged by director: Hitchcock, Kubrick, Scorsese, Kurosawa, and Tarantino. As film theorist André Bazin predicted, the film director has become something of a cult celebrity.

But in fact, commerce has always informed the idea of film authorship. The next section looks at the careers of Orson Welles and Alfred Hitchcock to examine the way the *auteur* has been used by the commercial film industry during the studio era and in post-studio Hollywood.

14.2 *(above)* *United 93* adopts the style of documentary filmmaking.

14.3 *(below)* *Sunday Bloody Sunday* also demonstrates the director's knack for realism.

Studio-era *Auteurs*: Welles and Hitchcock

Orson Welles personified the creativity and fierce independence of the *auteur*. When he began making films in the 1940s, the U.S. film industry was in its heyday. Although the hierarchical organization of the major studios positioned directors as mere studio employees, a unit production system that had emerged in the 1930s offered some latitude to certain directors and producers. The demand for features was so great that studios also hired independent producers and directors, as RKO did when they hired Welles in 1939.

Welles was well known because of his successful Mercury Theater productions (including the legendary radio broadcast of

14.4 Alfred Hitchcock in a publicity still for *Psycho*.

H.G. Wells's *The War of the Worlds*). Because of Welles's reputation, RKO studios granted him unprecedented creative control to make three films. His first, *Citizen Kane*, did not achieve box office success. During the editing of his second film, *The Magnificent Ambersons* (1942), Welles was filming a documentary in Brazil. In his absence, studio executives excised forty minutes of footage and appended a happy ending. The film was not commercially successful; nor was Welles's third film, *Journey into Fear* (1943), and the director was unceremoniously fired by RKO. Over the course of the next three decades, Welles rejected the notion that studio executives knew how to make good films, but periodically he submitted to studio discipline (as an actor and director) in order to make his own films.

Because his work was formally audacious and challenging, and because he clashed with executives who sought to exert control, Welles became notorious as an outsider reviled by the Hollywood power structure. No other American director before or since has so epitomized the genius who flouted the profit-oriented commercial system. He directed films at B studios and in Europe, before returning to Hollywood to make *Touch of Evil* for Universal in 1958, yet another production that generated conflict between Welles and studio executives.

One example of Welles's importance as a marketing tool is the 1998 re-release of *Touch of Evil*. As was the case with most of his studio films, Welles clashed with Universal over its decisions regarding editing and sound. He wrote a detailed memo urging the studio to make a number of changes before releasing the film. Welles's fifty-eight-page memo to Universal studio head Edward Muhl formed the basis for the film's restoration in 1998. Film critic Jonathan Rosenbaum (who participated in the restoration) explained the process:

> Rick Schmidlin concocted a wild scheme: to follow all of the memo's instructions for the first time and put together the *Touch of Evil* Welles had had in mind. After Schmidlin showed Universal an edited sample of one of Welles's suggestions, the studio saw a way to get more value out of an old chestnut. (Rosenbaum, *Touch of Evil* pp. 134–5)

The impetus for the project was financial gain: Universal would "get more value out of an old chestnut." Thus, Universal used Welles's reputation as a fiercely independent artist to entice viewers to see the restored film, one that promised to be superior to the original because it hewed more closely to the *auteur*'s intentions. The "revamping" project would be a worthwhile endeavor in any case, but the Welles name made it feasible to a profit-driven corporation. A lesser director's work might not receive the same commitment.

Like Orson Welles, Alfred Hitchcock is a celebrated *auteur*. Edward R. O'Neill notes that Hitchcock's very image is famous and that his name "has passed into the vernacular in the word 'Hitchcockian'" (O'Neill, p. 310). Like Welles, Hitchcock clashed with producers and corporate executives in Hollywood, and particularly the independent producer David O. Selznick.

Unlike Welles, however, Hitchcock earned a reputation as a popular and prolific director. His steady output—fifty-three features between 1925 and 1976—seemed to confirm his persona as a craftsman rather than a tortured genius. This reputation was so entrenched that influential critics such as Claude Chabrol, Eric

Rohmer, François Truffaut, and Robin Wood had to argue forcefully in order for Hitchcock's work to be taken seriously.

Hitchcock's authorial persona was used to market his films at the time they were released. A lengthy trailer advertising his 1960 film *Psycho* follows the director around the set, as he mugs for the camera and exaggerates his dour personality by hinting at the shocking events that take place in the hotel, in the shower, and in the gothic mansion where Norman Bates lives (fig. **14.4**). In this trailer, Hitchcock performs his "Master of Suspense" persona to entice viewers to see the film. In the trailer, Paramount used the audience's idea of Hitchcock— and not the stars, genre, or plot line—as the hook. In other words, even during the studio era, some directors were celebrities used as fodder for the studio marketing machine.

Blockbuster *Auteurs*: Spielberg and Lucas

The shift to a corporate entertainment environment in the 1980s and 1990s did not eradicate the idea of the *auteur*, but modified its profile. Jon Lewis cites Steven Spielberg and George Lucas as examples of the successful blockbuster *auteur* (2007; p. 64). This is the director who is savvy about exploiting the economic potential of vertically and horizontally integrated film corporations in post studio Hollywood, including product tie-ins and DVD sales.

The *auteur* is alive and well and "bound up with the celebrity industry of Hollywood" according to Tim Corrigan (Corrigan, p. 39). The director functions as a brand name to signify a consistent product. Corrigan claims that the *auteur* assures blockbuster profits by doing interviews and television appearances.

Another economic and technological development that exploits the *auteur* as brand name is the marketing of DVDs and Blu-ray. The director's cut solidifies the director as *auteur*, particularly on commentary tracks where he describes the film in detail. Without disputing the value of a director's insight, this practice speaks to entertainment conglomerates' ability continually to reap the financial benefits of the *auteur* as celebrity and brand name (figs. **14.5**, **14.6**).

Thus far, this chapter has concentrated on the origins and implications of film authorship. The remainder of the chapter examines methods of incorporating the *auteurist* approach into research and writing and presents examples of the *auteur* approach by analyzing the careers of several established and up-and-coming *auteurs*.

14.5 *(above)* George Lucas.

14.6 *(below)* As this *Star Wars* figurine demonstrates, director George Lucas is a cult figure: eager fans consume his image.

Using the *Auteur* Approach to Interpret and Evaluate Films

The concept of the film *auteur* functions in practical terms as an organizing principle, helping scholars and fans to explore and evaluate films by categorizing them according to their director. Other concepts that can be used to classify films according to aesthetic and historical characteristics include genre (Western, screwball comedy), studio (Warner Brothers, Disney, or Miramax), national contexts (Bollywood, Hong Kong), production or industrial contexts (studio, independent, avant-garde) and historical eras (silent, sound, studio-era Hollywood, post-studio Hollywood). Choosing one of these systems to group films is not a neutral decision: each of these frameworks contains implicit assumptions about the aspects of cinema that the scholar believes are most important to study.

This last section of the chapter explores specific models for using *auteur* theory as the basis for film interpretation. The first reading, which focuses on Japanese director Akira Kurosawa, demonstrates how one can try to locate consistency across a director's films.

The *Auteur* and the Consistency Thesis

The idea that an individual film director possesses a stylistic sensibility that makes his or her films recognizable and distinct from those of other filmmakers should be treated as a hypothesis that we posit whenever we utilize *auteur* theory. One goal of analyzing many films by a single director is to prove or disprove this hypothesis, and thus, film scholars routinely investigate this research question: is there a marked consistency across all the films made by a director, whether in subject matter, visual style, and overall sensibility (or worldview)? There is an implicit belief that true *auteurs* possess a compelling vision for their work that emerges from all their films, despite often challenging circumstances of collaboration in industrial filmmaking contexts, including intervention on the part of studio executives, clashes with writers and actors, and so on.

The career of Japanese director Akira Kurosawa (1910–98) offers an instructive case study of a director whose filmmaking approach and visual style remains discernible across a substantial number of films (fig. **14.7**). A discussion of Kurosawa (or any director) that forwards a claim of consistency should present a precise descriptive rubric that identifies the key components of a director's style and that encompasses the vast majority of her or his films. It may also seek to identify certain influences on those components of style, possibly in historical events and the director's biography. Finally, this type of analysis may trace the way a director's visual or narrative concerns develop over time. In fact, some

14.7 Akira Kurosawa.

writers discuss an *auteur*'s early style versus their late style (the latter assumed to embody a confrontation with mortality), recognizing that a director's entire catalog will incorporate both consistency and change.

Akira Kurosawa directed thirty-one films in a fifty-year career spanning the second half of the twentieth century. Kurosawa began making films in Japan in 1943, after a period of apprenticeship with Kajiro Yamamoto at PCL studios (which later merged with JO to form Toho). His importance as a major international filmmaker became undeniable when his 1950 film *Rashômon* "burst forth with the force of a new discovery," (Berhnardt p. 39) winning the Golden Lion at the Venice Film Festival and earning best film and director honors from the National Board of Review in the U.S. Kurosawa was the first Japanese director to garner such international acclaim.

Kurosawa earned screenwriting credits on all the films he directed, often adapting screenplays from literary works and collaborating with one or two other writers. His adaptations draw from diverse sources and include works of classical literature. Shakespeare's *Macbeth* and *King Lear* inspired *Kumonosu-jô* ("*Throne of Blood*"; 1957) and *Ran* (1985) and Tolstoy's *The Death of Ivan Ilyich* influenced *Ikiru* ("*Doomed*"; 1952). He drew from the work of Fyodor Dostoyevsky (*The Idiot*) and Maxim Gorky (*Donzoko* [*The Lower Depths*], 1957) as well as popular writers. *Rashômon* (1950) was based on two stories by Ryunosuke Akutagawa, and American pulp fiction writer Ed McBain's *King's Ransom* formed the narrative basis for *Tengoku to jigoku* ("*High and Low*"; 1963). Kurosawa's frequent use of literary source material from Russia and the West gave him a reputation for blending the values and aesthetics of East and West. Because his *Shichinin no Samurai* (*Seven Samurai*, 1954) was widely admired and re-made as *The Magnificent Seven* (John Sturges 1960), Kurosawa is often credited with reinventing the American Western.

Kurosawa's films influenced international directors for many decades. Martin Scorsese writes, "For me and for many others, he instantly became our master. Our sensei. You can see his visual mastery in [his] drawings [...] and, of course, in his films, which taken together add up to one of the greatest bodies of work in cinema." (Scorsese) The drawings Scorsese refers to are the sketches, storyboards, and paintings that Kurosawa made throughout his life, many of which have been exhibited in museums around the world since his death in 1998.

These art works are an important clue to Kurosawa's distinctive visual style: the director trained as a painter at the Doshusha School of Western Painting prior to becoming a filmmaker. In fact, he exhibited his work when he was only eighteen years old, before he decided to pursue a career in film. Kurosawa overtly expresses his love for painting in his penultimate film, *Yume* ("*Dreams*"; 1990), where a young twentieth-century Japanese man pursues Vincent Van Gogh (played by Scorsese) by literally walking through his canvases on screen.

The significance of Kurosawa's artistry as a painter is that it helps to explain the way he approaches the film frame as a two-dimensional canvas. His distinctive style is defined by his frequent use of widescreen compositions; Kurosawa quickly adopted the new technology of CinemaScope, beginning with *Donzoko* (*The Lower Depths*), and the action adventure film *The Hidden Fortress* (1958), which exerted a strong influence on George Lucas and *Star Wars*. In terms of the look of his images, Kurosawa often used telephoto lenses, whose optical properties tend to flatten the frame, compressing the distance between foreground and background, recreating the two dimensional effects of looking at a canvas. Describing his use of extremely long lenses (up to 750 mm) for *Akahige* ("*Red Beard*"; 1965), Kurosawa stated "I wanted to get that crowded, two-dimensional, slightly smoky effect that only a long distance lens can give you." (quoted in Richie, p. 182)

Moreover, Kurosawa typically situates his actors so that they fill the screen horizontally and orchestrates movement across the screen. Film scholar Stephen Prince observes "lateral motion across the frame is one of the visual signatures of his cinema," (Prince, p. 18) while critic J. Hoberman emphasizes Kurosawa's influence on other filmmakers including "Sam Peckinpah, Sergio Leone, George Lucas, Walter Hill, John Woo, and just about anyone who has ever used the widescreen format with a modicum of pizzazz." (Hoberman) The use of wipes as transitions contributes to the emphasis on the horizontal dimension of the film frame in Kurosawa's films.

14.8 Mottled leaves in a painterly shot from *Rashômon*.

This emphasis can be seen as early as *Rashômon*, even though that film was shot in the 1.33:1 aspect ratio. In this film, Kurosawa choreographs the movement of his central characters in a linear fashion rather than emphasizing the depth of the frame: one notable example is the scene early in the film when the woodcutter runs through the forest: because of his rapid movement, the leaves behind him are transformed into a flattened, abstract background (fig. **14.8**). This scene also depends upon a highly mobile camera—a technique of Kurosawa's that is most apparent in his samurai action films.

One additional visual signature of Kurosawa's—the use of multiple cameras to shoot a single scene—is also evident in *Rashômon*. This technique allows for rapid cuts on action and introduces fragmentation, mobility, and kinetic energy, all of which contribute to dramatic action scenes in *Seven Samurai* and *Ran*. This technique does far more than simply jolt the audience viscerally; it also speaks to one of Kurosawa's signature themes: the idea that individuals hold radically different perspectives on the world around them. In fact, the title of *Rashômon* has become synonymous with this philosophical conundrum: when several people remember a real life event they have witnessed or participated in, there may well be several different versions of the truth. This theme reappears in *High and Low* with a slight variation; in this film, Kurosawa looks at the way the rich and the poor experience the world differently.

Moving from visual style to issues related to theme and genre also reveals Kurosawa's consistency. He is best remembered for his sweeping, epic samurai action films, made in the tradition of the Japanese *jidai-geki*, or historical drama, including *Seven Samurai, Yojimbo* (1961), and *Ran*, although he also made films of contemporary Japanese life, the *gendai-geki*, including *Ikiru* and *High and Low*. Whether orchestrating grand battle scenes, or observing the subtle warfare his characters engage in as they navigate modern life, Kurosawa always focuses on the difficult moral choices individuals make. One early film review of *Ikiru* made a point that came to define the director's *oeuvre*: "Kurosawa has endowed the film with compassion and understanding, with an ironic awareness of human weakness and a knowledge of the dignity of the individual." (Bernhardt p. 41) A scholar and admirer of Kurosawa's work, Donald Richie, emphasizes the psychological and social dimension of Kurosawa's work by pointing out that his heroes refuse to be defeated. Many of those heroes were played by Toshiro Mifune, who starred in sixteen of Kurosawa's films. "In Kurosawa's hands" writes Ed Park in *The Village Voice*, "[Mifune] was grandly human: not just vanquishing bandits but grappling with the dictates of fear and the maddening logic of responsibility." (Park)

In a career that spanned decades, Akira Kurosawa made films that remain instantly recognizable, due in large part to his consistent visual style, which is rooted in his wide screen compositions and use of the telephoto lens, and his repeated engagement with questions of morality, choice, and individual responsibility.

The Life and Work of an *Auteur*: Studying Biographical Influence

A second approach to using this theory of authorship as a method of interpretation is to consider how biographical experiences have shaped a director's career. Typically, scholars who pursue this line of interrogation analyze a director whose reputation as an *auteur* has already been established. In this mode, explaining what influenced a director's sensibility is as important as spelling out recurring themes and stylistic techniques. In the discussion below of Ousmane Sembene (1923–2007), the author explores how the director's experiences growing up in Senegal, a French colony in Africa, which attained independence in 1960, influenced his work.

In 1963, novelist and essayist Sembene (fig. **14.9**) turned to filmmaking, partly because he realized that most of his fellow Senegalese were illiterate. He trained at Moscow's Gorky film school. Sembene made his first African feature, *Black Girl* ("*Le Noire de...*"), in 1966 and he continued making films until his death in 2007. His style was influenced by both Italian Neorealism and indigenous Senegalese traditions, evident in the way his films often critically examine French colonialism as well as post-independence Senegal.

Sembene's career was shaped by the historical context of his childhood and his experiences in Senegal and in France as a young man. Caryn James identifies a common theme in the director's *oeuvre*: the depiction of Sengalese and African histories through a central character. Sembene's *Camp Thiaroye* ("*Camp de Thiaroye*"; 1988), concerns the experiences of African troops who fought for France in World War II but are detained at a transit camp on their return home to Dakar. France repays the soldiers' service by making them suffer the indignity of being forced to live in what amounts to a P.O.W. camp. Sergeant Diatta (Sidiki Bakaba)—the protagonist who fiercely defends his fellow soldiers' right to return home, but who is also married to a French woman and is a connoisseur of Western music and literature—embodies the complex struggles associated with postcolonial and globalizing African identities.

John Pym argues that Diatta gives voice to Sembene's concerns as a postcolonial subject. But Pym draws an even more direct link between the character and the director by referencing Sembene's specific biographical details:

> It's not reading too much into this character [Diatta] to see in him [...] a portrait of the principled young Sembene, the one-time union organizer of the Marseille waterfront who went on to write, among other books in French, *Les bouts de bois de Dieu*, a novel set against the 1947–48 French railway strike. (Pym, p. 280)

Embracing the biographical approach to *auteur* criticism, Pym educates the audience about Sembene's youth, arguing that Sembene's pursuits as a political activist and author are relevant details for interpreting his cinema.

Bérénice Reynaud's reading of Sembene's *Moolaadé* (2004) takes this approach one step further, demonstrating the possibilities of reading a film in light of a director's professional experiences within a film industry. *Moolaadé*, which won the *Prix Un Certain Regard* at the Cannes film festival, explores the

14.9 Ousmane Sembene.

topic of female genital mutilation in Burkina Faso. In the film, villagers struggle to negotiate the tension between modern values, which have made their way into the community (as a motif involving portable radios makes clear), and traditional customs. The heated debate over whether or not a group of young girls should undergo the age-old ritual makes explicit this conflict between competing value systems. One woman, Colle, refuses to force her daughter to undergo the painful procedure, but her husband Amsatou, an elderly village patriarch, obeys tradition and publicly whips Colle for defying the elders.

Reynaud argues that the complexly drawn Amsatou and his struggle to choose between tradition and modernity mirrors the director's own professional tribulations. Sembene, she explains, used his status as Senegal's foremost director to make films that give voice to women in his culture. Because he was a man, Sembene had the power and privilege to champion women's rights. At the same time, Sembene's status as a colonized African subject laboring to finance his films diminished his capacity to fully articulate a progressive vision. Sembene relied on French subsidies for his early films, putting his need to finance his career at odds with his interest in exploring anti-colonialist themes. As Sembene's work became more radical, he found it more difficult to secure funding.

Reynaud argues that this dilemma is strikingly apparent in one dramatic close-up of Amsatou's face as he weighs whether to support his wife in her effort to change tribal customs, or to yield to tradition: "*Moolaadé* is a paean to the strength, the determination of women; it is about Colle's fight. Yet it is a man, entangled in his own contradictions, who chose to tell the story. [...] Sembene represented his dilemma, on the margin on the filmic discourse, where it could move us subliminally." (Reynaud)

James, Pym, and Reynaud all interpret Sembene's work in light of the director's life experiences. Film scholars interested in pursuing this approach inevitably conduct research, scouring libraries and archives for any information that might be relevant for understanding the director's outlook. Family life, biographical anecdotes, education, and cultural and economic conditions are but a few of the many possible fruitful areas of inquiry.

Auteurs and Anomalies: Studying Aberrational Films

Accounting for and exploring the differences between films that epitomize a director's creative signature and those that seem anomalous is another way scholars and critics approach *auteur* theory. Writers who adopt this approach might begin by asking questions: in what ways does one film appear to differ from the director's other work? Do production circumstances or historical eras account for these differences? Do any components of the director's established signature show up in the film, albeit in a modified fashion?

Starting with these broad questions might lead to some intriguing new ways of interpreting a film or reconsidering the gist of a director's *oeuvre*. Sometimes writers discover that a film that appears incongruous at first glance is actually in step with a director's other work. The process of attempting to uncover similarities between the anomalous film and the director's established films may or may not yield this conclusion. A scholar might meditate on how obvious shifts in a director's approach signal that he's taken his work in a new direction—perhaps the changes noted in a particular film mark the beginning of a new stage in his career, or perhaps they represent a one-time experiment.

Wes Anderson's animated *Fantastic Mr. Fox* (2009) serves as a useful example of how an apparent departure can actually be understood to cohere with a director's earlier work. Before the release of *Mr. Fox*, Anderson had earned a reputation as one of American cinema's most distinctive *auteurs* after having made just five features—*Bottle Rocket* (1996), *Rushmore* (1998), *The Royal Tenenbaums* (2001), *The Life Aquatic With Steve Zissou* (2004) and *The Darjeeling Limited* (2007)—each of which he made with a dependably idiosyncratic voice (fig. **14.10**). The fact that Anderson wrote or co-wrote all of his screenplays and repeatedly returned to a stalwart cast of loveable misfits (including Owen and Luke Wilson, and Bill Murray) helped shape his authorial signature.

But *Fantastic Mr. Fox* marked a dramatic departure for Anderson. For the first time, he adapted someone else's work, developing his film from British novelist Roald Dahl's children's novel. This fact invited questions about whether or not Anderson could maintain his cinematic identity while working with material someone else had composed. Furthermore, Anderson was venturing into animated film for the first time; for a director famous for his meticulously studied costumes and sets, and his string of familiar cast members, the decision to use

14.10 Wes Anderson shares Mr. Fox's sartorial taste.

stop motion animation seemed like a complete abandonment of the style that had made him famous. With Dahl's *Mr. Fox*, however, Anderson selected source material that allowed him to elaborate the same characters and themes he had tackled in his earlier work: in all of his films, he portrays iconoclastic individuals whose egotistical and misguided need to micromanage the world around them leaves them unhappy and isolated from people they care about. In order to maintain their relationships with others, these characters must learn to cultivate a more mature outlook on life and embrace the choices others make.

What unites Anderson's most endearing characters is their immature vanity, which reveals itself in the controlling and condescending manner with which they treat others. In *Rushmore*, prep-school underachiever Max Fischer (Jason Schwartzman) falls in love with teacher Rosemary Cross (Olivia Williams) and blithely assumes they are intellectual and emotional equals. She tries to befriend Max, but when she pursues other romantic interests, Max insists on insulting her suitors and sabotaging her relationships. While Royal Tenenbaum (Gene Hackman) in Anderson's next film is considerably older than Max, he's as emotionally stunted as the teenager. Royal longs to return home to the family he abandoned. To win his way back into the fold, Royal pretends to be dying from a terminal disease. Inevitably, what Max, Royal, and nearly all of Anderson's ne'er-do-wells come to realize is that their stubborn attempts to exert control over others is always self-defeating; it only drives the objects of their affection further away.

Although "Foxy" Fox, an animated *Canis rufus*, might initially appear to be a very different type of character for Anderson, in reality he is a four-legged, furry combination of Max and Royal. The film begins with Fox (voiced by George Clooney) and his wife (Meryl Streep) successfully knocking off a chicken coop. During the getaway, however, he winds up ensnared in a trap because he ignores his wife's pleas not to tug on a mysterious rope dangling above him. His stubborn curiosity gets the best of him…and it lands the two of them inside a cage. The episode defines their relationship: she is cautious and concerned about keeping the family safe, while he is drawn to adventure and often fails to consider how his impetuous behavior threatens the family's stability. More to the point, Mr. Fox is convinced that he is crafty enough to always "outfox" the farmers, and that Mrs. Fox wants to "change his nature" by meddling with his wily schemes.

As with Royal Tenenbaum, Mr. Fox's self-centeredness plays out in his relationship with his son Ash (Jason Schwartzman). Although Ash actively seeks his father's approval, Mr. Fox lavishes his attention on his athletic, alternative cousin Kristofferson (Eric Anderson). Perhaps Mr. Fox loves his escapades so much that he's bored by his own son, or he's so vain that he would rather associate with his accomplished nephew because it makes him look better, or he may simply be more comfortable around others who are adventurous like he is, or whom he sees as gifted. In keeping with Anderson's entire coterie of misguided male characters, Mr. Fox is bent on "winning"—on making himself look good by outwitting his friends and foes—even if his plans hurt those he cares for the most.

With *Fantastic Mr. Fox,* Anderson maintains several other key ingredients of his distinctive style. Two are particularly relevant: Anderson's scrupulous attention to costuming and his emphasis on literary, theatrical, and cinematic talent and invention. Anderson's characters tend to maintain a trademark look: Max Fischer rarely takes off his prep-school blazer; Chas Tenenbaum (Ben Stiller) and his sons never remove their red tracksuits and his brother Ritchie (Luke Wilson) wears tennis-pro sweatbands even though his career on the court has collapsed. The fact that Anderson hired couturiers Fendi and Lacoste to design costumes for *The Royal Tenenbaums* is some indication of how crucial wardrobe is to the director's vision (Mayshark p. 128). Apparel becomes one of the most important ways his characters express their identities. Max Fischer isn't a model student ("He's the worst student we have," bemoans the school's headmaster) but he dresses like one; his blazer defines not who he is, but what he wants to project. Mr. Fox likewise lives by the motto "the clothes make the man." He's a petty criminal who dresses the part of a suave cosmopolitan. Anderson hired seamstresses to create a rust colored corduroy suit and tie for Mr. Fox, transforming the furry critter into a double-breasted dandy.

Anderson repeatedly fashions characters who are creative artists: Max directs school plays; Margot Tenenbaum (Gwyneth Paltrow) is a playwright; and Steve Zissou is a documentary filmmaker. Their involvment in creative endeavors complements Anderson's interest in characters who want to take creative control over their lives; Max, for example, directs the people in his life as if they were cast members of the elaborate plays he stages. This interest in characters who literally see all the world as a stage resonates with the stylized and synthetic quality of Anderson's costumes and sets. The most dramatic example of this pronounced artificiality may be Steve Zissou's ship in *The Life Aquatic*, a dioramic set constructed and filmed in long shots so that it looks like the cross section of a dollhouse. Expressionist set design is one way Anderson's visual style underscores the fact that his characters abandon authentic, messy emotions, and instead try to live out perfectly crafted storybook lives.

Mr. Fox doesn't direct plays or make movies; for him, creativity lies in planning and executing his capers. And, as film critic Nathan Gelgud observes, the animals who involve themselves in Foxy's schemes are drawn to the possibility of reinventing themselves:

> The self-aware, kid-fitted references to action-movie tropes—bandit hats, poison dog bait, "this time it's personal"—work incredibly well because the characters themselves, especially Fox and his son Ash, are self-conscious about defining their roles: Fox [...] describes his habit of whistling and clicking his teeth as his trademark. ("Masterpiece")

When his master plan doesn't unfold according to script, though, Mr. Fox realizes that his vanity has life or death consequences. Ultimately, Max Fischer, Steve Zissou, and Mr. Fox don't abandon their creative urges to assert control over their lives. But for these controlling characters to mature in Wes Anderson's world, they must learn to accept creative input from others. In *Mr. Fox*, each critter—even Ash—gets to help write his or her own part and helps to save the entire animal community from the farmer's destructive rage.

As this brief reading of *Fantastic Mr. Fox* demonstrates, explaining why a text that appears to be uncharacteristic actually adheres to a director's usual mode can be a useful way to employ *auteur* theory. Locating similarities across a director's work, and making a special attempt to include seemingly eccentric texts, can help the fan, student, or scholar recognize themes at work and more fully appreciate a director's visual and narrative choices in every film.

Auteurs and Ancestors: The Question of Influence

A fourth way to develop a scholarly understanding of a director's body of work using *auteur* theory is to explore the influence of another director. Many *auteurs* are recognized as such because their distinctive style endures in the work of subsequent generations of filmmakers who borrow ideas from them. Critics and fans are usually delighted to recognize an *hommage* to a beloved *auteur*. Some influences can be overt, appearing in obvious references, while others may become apparent only with careful, close analysis.

Adopting this approach requires the writer to first identify the stylistic profile of the director whose status as an *auteur* is well-established, and then to argue that these traits re-appear in another director's films. The purpose behind this exercise isn't necessarily to argue that the latter filmmaker is a lesser artist whose work is derivative, though film critics may pursue this line of logic. Rather, exploring the role of artistic influence can provide a useful framework for interpreting new films by comparing and contrasting them with older works. This approach can also lead to a re-evaluation of an older director by demonstrating how his artistic vision continues to have relevance for new filmmakers. It may also help to identify important questions regarding cultural and historical factors that may be involved when one director invokes the work of another. Have historical events, for example, or a mood or zeitgeist suddenly thrust the concerns and vision of the original *auteur* into relief in new ways? And finally, what are the tangible pieces of evidence that link the work of the original *auteur* to the director under consideration: can the writer/researcher be certain that he saw and took note of the earlier figure? Interviews with filmmakers are often critical to establishing a conscious borrowing from another director's work.

Whereas many critics have focused their analysis of Kathryn Bigelow's much-admired *The Hurt Locker* (2008) on the question of whether or not the film is pro- or anti-war, careful consideration of the director's artistic influences helps draw attention to her central theme. Bigelow (fig. **14.11**) is more interested in exploring the psychological impact of combat on individual soldiers than she is in debating ideological questions regarding the ethics of the U.S. war in Iraq. As this analysis will demonstrate, understanding how Bigelow's film incorporates the visual strategies and thematic ideas associated with the directors that influenced her opens the door to a new and compelling angle for interpretation.

One of the most obvious influences on Bigelow's films is the work of Sam Peckinpah, famous for gracefully choreographed and violently bloody Westerns like *Ride the High Country* (1963), *The Wild Bunch* (1969), and *Pat Garrett and Billy the Kid* (1973). Film critic Amy Taubin has called Bigelow Peckinpah's artistic "daughter" because of her films' "double-faced critique of—and infatuation with—the codes of masculinity." (quoted in Dargis) Bigelow herself explicitly acknowledged her connection to "Bloody Sam" in January 2010 when she introduced *The Wild Bunch* for the "Films That Inspired Me" film series at the Hammer Museum in Los Angeles.

The comparison with Peckinpah is an apt one, since the bomb defusers in *The Hurt Locker* look and act like modern day cowboys. Renegade Sergeant William James (Jeremy Renner) flaunts his unhesitating stride as he walks down arid boulevards toward unexploded ordnance: he certainly wouldn't look out of place in the climactic scene in *The Wild Bunch,* sauntering into the middle of a heavily armed Mexican villa to rescue an abducted *compadre* (fig. 15.3). James's near suicidal obsession with dismantling bombs arises from the same impulses that drive Peckinpah's ragtag anti-heroes. Addiction to the adrenaline rush and an existential ambivalence toward the meaning of life propel these men as much as any sense of loyalty or obligation. Like Peckinpah, Bigelow works in the arena of the taut male action film, which, in her case, also coincided historically with the hardbody action flick, analyzed by scholars Susan Jeffords and Yvonne Tasker. Bigelow's films include *K-19: The Widowmaker* (2002), a Cold War nuclear submarine saga; *Point Break* (1991), about an FBI agent who is in deep cover with a gang of thieves; and *Blue Steel* (1989), a neo-*noir* cop thriller. Bigelow orchestrates tension and explosive violence in these films, unveiling "the hysteria beneath [men's] seeming rationality." (Taubin, quoted in Dargis)

Just a casual glance at Bigelow's use of cinematography reveals Peckinpah's influence. In *The Hurt Locker* and in *The Wild Bunch*, both directors carefully frame their male protagonists in wide shots, often with telephoto lenses. This technique situates the men in unfriendly settings while also emphasizing their singular composure under pressure. Put another way, Bigelow and Peckinpah amp up the tension in long, languid moments when men wait for something to happen: they are vulnerable but poised in a hostile environment. Rapid zooms to random details—onlookers, animals, and enemies—suggest in a very kinetic way the pressure of having to maintain the appearance of calm while constantly surveying one's surroundings. The camera's unrelenting surveillance in these moments evokes the men's mental agility and stamina, adjuncts to the physical prowess typically associated with strong masculinity. The rapid camera movement also implies their distrust of the world around them and a frenetic quality of being very near the edge of sanity.

When action does erupt, Peckinpah and Bigelow dissect and multiply the violence; they cut quickly to capture from multiple points of view the surreal choreography of bodies under assault. But they also punctuate rapid barrages of imagery with slow-motion shots, which transform the rituals of violence into a bloody ballet.

Earlier in her career, Bigelow identified another influence on her style, which is less obvious than the Peckinpah connection, but potentially more provocative, given that Bigelow makes action films. She noted her indebtedness to Douglas Sirk. Sirk is known for directing melodramatic Hollywood "weepies" in the 1950s, particularly *Magnificent Obsession* (1955), *All that Heaven Allows* (1955), *Written on the Wind* (1956), and *Imitation of Life* (1959). Claiming Peckinpah and Sirk as one's lineage might appear contradictory, since these directors are a study in contrasts: the former is associated with male-oriented action spectacles, whereas the latter specialized in stylized family dramas centering on women facing tragic romantic and familial dilemmas. Nevertheless, Sirk's work has been an influence on Bigelow since her first feature, *The Loveless* (1982), which pays tribute via overt references to *Written on the Wind* (*Beyond Melodrama*). What makes this connection so compelling is the fact that the relationship between Sirk and Bigelow is underneath the surface. The fan or critic may have to dig to see how so-called "women's films" might influence a war movie, but the process of discovery can be a rewarding intellectual experience that prompts the viewer to rethink the apparent simplicity of the testosterone-driven action film.

Peckinpah's and Sirk's competing aesthetics run throughout *The Hurt Locker*, revealing the way Bigelow's film grapples not just with the physical mechanics of defusing bombs, but also with the emotions at the heart of Sergeant James's motivations. Thomas Elsaesser argues in his seminal essay on melodrama that in action films the characters' inner dilemmas get translated into physical quests: "A jail-break, a bank-robbery, a Western chase or cavalry charge, and even a criminal investigation lend themselves to psychologized, thematized representations of the hero's inner dilemmas […]." (Elsaesser, p. 55) By contrast, family melodramas in the vein of Douglas Sirk "more often [record] the failure of the protagonist to act in a way that could shape the events and influence the

14.11 Kathryn Bigelow.

emotional environment, let alone change the stifling social milieu." (p. 55) In other words, action heroes express their emotions through actions that change the external environment; in melodrama, "the world is closed, and the characters are acted upon." (p. 55)

In *The Hurt Locker* Bigelow treats these conflicting impulses of Peckinpah and Sirk—action and melodrama—as a structuring device. The first half of the film focuses on bomb defusing set pieces rife with heart stopping action. Bigelow depicts James's attempt to change and control his environment by defying both his commanding officer and his odds of survival. He takes unnecessary risks in the field merely for the sake of adding another neutralized detonation device to his collection, which he stores in a box under his bed. The second half of the film moves squarely into Sirkian territory: it illuminates James's desire to have some kind of intimate connection to another person, explains his most reckless behavior, and exposes his vulnerability.

The connection between James's self-destructive behavior and his emotional longing becomes explicit when, over the course of a night of heavy drinking, we witness James's desire to bond with other men, and his simultaneous impulse to deny any intimacy. The three men drink to celebrate having survived a tense sniper attack. But after James opens up about his family life, he begins to spar with squad leader Sergeant J.T. Sanborn (Anthony Mackie): "As if to deny the comradeship they felt, they throw punches that are meant to hurt." (Taubin, p. 35) Eventually, the playful roughhousing spirals out of control and real anger erupts, culminating with Sanborn pulling a knife on James. These men clearly crave some kind of friendship, but the masculine code prohibits close homosocial bonds and so their actions defuse any sign of emotional connection.

James also tries to nurture a bond with Beckham, the local boy who works on the base and who becomes James's surrogate son. But when James finds that this relationship makes him emotionally vulnerable, he must once again deny his feelings and resort to action instead. On one mission, James's team discovers a corpse stuffed with a "body bomb." James thinks the body is Beckham. Thereafter, James becomes consumed with avenging Beckham's death, threatening the vendor who hired the boy and sneaking out in the middle of the night to interrogate the boy's family to punish them for sacrificing their son to the insurgency. These scenes make it clear that, despite James's attempt to avoid emotional entanglements, his feelings still intrude. His only mechanism for addressing these feelings is to resort to violent, male bluster.

Rather than accomplishing anything productive, much less avenging Beckham's death, James's efforts prove to be ineffectual: the vendor whom he threatens apparently has no clue as to Beckham's whereabouts (or even why James is so agitated). To make matters worse, the couple he interrogates are not involved with the insurgency, nor are they Beckham's parents. Later, when his team responds to a bombing, James is so frustrated by feelings of impotence that he leads his men on a dangerous wild-goose chase through Baghdad's alleyways in the middle of the night—an exercise in futility that gets a soldier seriously injured. In short, James tries to be a super action hero in his effort to address his feelings of loss, sadness, and helplessness, but his efforts are in vain.

This portrait of masculinity as self-defeating posturing has more in common with Sirk's brand of melodrama than Peckinpah's outlaw heroes. The notion that the war and its social context are too complex for James to understand, much less have an impact on, hits home when Beckham reappears on the base. James had been mistaken. Whereas a more heroic protagonist would have succeeded in either saving the boy's life or avenging his death, James realizes he has completely misinterpreted the situation around him and utterly overestimated his own importance. "[Melodrama's protagonists] emerge as lesser human beings for having become wise and acquiescent to the world." (Elsaesser, p. 55)

Sirk's films are justifiably famous for the stunning beauty of his imagery. While his characters lead lives of desperate misery, they at least manage to do so in immaculate houses stuffed with ornate objects. Indeed, it is this tension between visual beauty and tragic circumstance that fascinates Bigelow, who is drawn to the "interesting juxtaposition between [the character's] nihilistic interior and this lush, almost exotic exterior." (*Beyond Melodrama*) Put another way, Sirk surrounds characters with the material goods that replace the emotional connections missing in their lives. His characters value their homes as symbols of middle class success, but these spaces also come to represent the characters'

14.12 (*above*) The technological trappings of consumer culture in *All That Heaven Allows*.

14.13 (*below*) The gastronomical trappings of consumer culture in *The Hurt Locker*.

inner emptiness. In *All That Heaven Allows*, for example, Cary Scott's (Jane Wyman) children buy her a new television set to fill the void left by their absence. In 1950s America, the television was the quintessential symbol of status and prestige. Cary's children fill her living room with the most fashionable items, but they don't encourage her to fulfill her emotional needs by marrying the working class man she loves (in fact, they prohibit it). One especially dramatic shot reveals Cary's blankly melancholic gaze reflected off the set's screen, making her sadness and sense of entrapment within a world of electronic gadgetry palpable (fig. **14.12**).

A similar moment of tragedy befalls Sergeant James when he returns home from his tour of duty. The first scene stateside finds him not at home with his family, but shopping for groceries. He leaves Baghdad's dangerous, war-torn landscape behind and finds himself embedded in consumer culture. Rather then feeling comforted, James clearly feels at odds with this environment. When he goes to fetch a box of cereal, Bigelow uses a wide-angle lens

and positions the camera at a low angle slightly behind James as he surveys the shelves (fig. **14.13**). Like Cary Scott staring at the soul-deadening television before her, James gazes at "the endless possibility of what's available," overwhelmed (Bigelow, Commentary). The second half of the film has been leading to this emotional dead end. In typical melodramatic fashion, the film depicts a vicious cycle in which James goes on one self-defeating mission after another as a substitute for emotional connection, only to find that when he returns home he is completely alienated from the society and family he has fought to defend.

The tragedy of melodrama is that its characters are imprisoned by social factors beyond their control (Elsaesser, p. 55), and Sergeant James's decision to re-enlist should be interpreted in such terms. This choice is not an action film gesture in which the hero takes one last stand to correct what's wrong; James returns simply out of disillusionment and resignation—there's simply no other place for him to go. Indeed, Mark Boal and Kathryn Bigelow view James, dressed in his bomb disposal gear in the final image of the film, as a man walking to his death, facing the "futility and the inexorable tide of violence" awaiting him (Commentary).

As this discussion of Kathryn Bigelow demonstrates, studying an *auteur*'s artistic ancestry involves careful consideration of how the interior meaning and cinematic techniques running throughout one director's canon of films appear in another director's work. Students should appreciate how this approach doesn't require an exact correspondence from one director to the next. Rather, the most thoughtful analysis will typically explore how a director pays respect to her influences while also updating or adapting the approach. Bigelow doesn't just ape Peckinpah's portrait of male violence; she transforms his vision into something new, in part by also drawing on Sirk's legacy of melodrama. When a director pays tribute to those who influenced her, in a sense she is engaging in a dialogue: acknowledging, elaborating on, and sometimes even challenging or contradicting another's powerful artistic statements.

Works Consulted

Ansen, David, and Jeff Giles. "The New Visionaries," *Newsweek*, 143/6 (September 2, 2004). Online. Academic Search Elite. February 26, 2004.

Appelo, Tim. "Chasing the Chador," *The Nation*, 272/17 (April 30, 2001). Online. Academic Search Elite. February 25, 2004.

Bernhardt, William. "*Ikiru*." *Film Quarterly* 13.4 (Summer 1960): pp. 39–41.

Beyond Melodrama. Dir. Robert Fischer. Included on *Magnificent Obsession* DVD (Criterion), 2008.

Brown, Georgia. "Heart of Darkness," *Village Voice*, 35 (September 11, 1990), p. 64.

Cineaste. Editorial, 28/1 (Winter 2002). Online. Academic Search Elite. February 25, 2004.

Cinema Journal, 43/4 (Summer 2004) [articles on *Crouching Tiger* by Kenneth Chan, Christina Klein, and James Schamus].

Commentary Track Featuring Katherine Bigelow. *The Hurt Locker*, Summit Entertainment DVD, 2010.

Cook, David. *A History of Narrative Film*, 3rd edn. New York and London: W.W. Norton, 1996.

Corliss, Richard. "Gay and Gaudy," *Time*, 150/17 (October 27, 1997), p. 111.

Corrigan, Timothy. "*Auteurs* and the New Hollywood," in *The New American Cinema*, ed. Jon Lewis. Durham, NC: Duke University Press, 1998, pp. 38–63.

Cousins, Mark. *Scene by Scene*. London: Laurence King, 2002.

Dargis, Manhola. "The Work of War, at a Fever Pitch." *The New York Times*. January 7, 2010. **http://www.nytimes.com**.

Desser, David. *The Samurai Films of Akira Kurosawa*. Ann Arbor: UMI Research Press, 1983.

Economist, The. "On screen it's Iran's Shout," 336/7921 (January 7, 1995). Online. Academic Search Elite. February 25, 2004.

Elsaesser, Thomas. "Tales of Sound and Fury: Observations on the Family Melodrama" in *Home is Where the Heart Is: Studies in Melodrama and the Women's Film*, ed. Christine Gledhill. London: BFI, 1987, pp. 43–69.

Franklin, Garth. "Interview with Ang Lee." December 7, 2005. **www.darkhorizons.com/news05/ brokeback2.php**. August 16, 2006.

Fuller, Graham. "Death and the Maidens," *Sight and Sound*, new series, 10/4 (April 2000). Online. Humanities Art Database. February 26, 2004.

Galbraith, Stuart, IV. *The Emperor and the Wolf: The Lives and Films of Akira Kurosawa and Toshiro Mifune*. New York: Faber and Faber, 2002.

Gargan, Edward. "Hong Kong's Master of Internal Pyrotechnics," *New York Times*, October 12, 1997, Section 2, pp. 13, 29.

Gelgud, Nathan. "Wes Anderson's Stop-Motion Masterpiece, *Fantastic Mr. Fox*." *The independent Weekly*. Nov. 25, 2009. **http://www.indyweek.com/gyrobase/Content?oid=oid%3A406182**.

Goldberg, Michelle "Where are the Female Directors" *Salon.com*. August 27, 2002. **archive.salon. com/ent/movies/feature/2002/08/27/women_directors/index.html** September 20, 2006.

Goodwin, James (ed). *Perspectives on Akira Kurosawa*. New York: G.K. Hll, 1994.

————. *Akira Kurosawa and Intertextual Cinema*. Baltimore: Johns Hopkins University Press, 1993.

Hoberman, J. "Akira Kurosawa." *Village Voice* September 22, 1998:137. Lexis Nexis.

"Hollywood's Women Directors Hit Celluloid Ceiling," Buzzle.com. July 4, 2002. **www.buzzle. com/ editorials/7-4-2002-21795.asp**. September 20, 2006.

Hultkrans, Andrew. "Reality Bytes—Interview with Hollywood Director Kathryn Bigelow." *ArtForum*, November 1995. **www.findarticles.com/p/articles/mi_m0268/is_n3_v34/ ai_17865932** September 18, 2006.

"Interview with Ang Lee and James Schamus." *The Guardian*. November 7, 2000. **http://film. guardian.co.uk/interview/interviewpages/0,,394676,00.html**. July 20, 2006.

Iwasaki, Akira. "Kurosawa and his Work," in *Focus on Rashômon*, ed. Donald Richie. Englewood Cliffs: Prentice Hall, 1972, pp. 21–31.

James, Caryn. "Loyalties Scalded by Humiliation," *The New York Times*, September 5, 1990, p. C16.

Jeffords, Susan. *Hard Bodies: Hollywood Masculinity in the Reagan Era*. New Brunswick, NJ; Rutgers University Press, 1994.

Jermyn, Deborah and Sean Redmond, eds. *The Cinema of Kathryn Bigelow: Hollywood Transgressor*. London: Wallflower Press, 2003.

Jermyn, Deborah, and Sean Redmond. "Introduction" to *Hollywood Transgressor: the Cinema of Kathryn Bigelow*. Ed. Deborah Jermyn and Sean Redmond. London and New York: Wallflower Press, 2003, pp. 1–19.

Johnson, William. "The Circle," *Film Quarterly*, 54/3 (Spring 2001). Online. Communication and Mass Media Complete. February 25, 2004.

Johnston, Sheila. "The Author as Public Institution," in *The European Cinema Reader*, ed. Catherine Fowler. London and New York: Routledge, 2002, pp. 121–31.

Jones, Kent. "Animal Planet." *Film Comment*. November–December 2009, pp. 22–5.

Kaes, Anton. "The New German Cinema," in *Oxford History of World Cinema*, ed. Geoffrey Nowell-Smith. Oxford and New York: Oxford University Press, 1996, pp. 614–27.

Kurosawa, Akira. *Something Like an Autobiography*. New York; Vintage Books, 1983.

Lane, Anthony. "Mondo Bond." *The New Yorker*, 78/33 (November 4, 2002), pp. 78–82.

Lewis, Jon. "The Perfect Money Machine(s): George Lucas, Steven Spielberg, and Auteurism in the New Hollywood," in *Looking Past the Screen: Case Studies in American Film History and Method*, eds. Jon Lewis and Eric Loren Smoodin. Durham: Duke University Press, 2007, pp. 61–86.

Magombe, P. Vincent. "Ousmane Sembene," in *Oxford History of World Cinema*, ed. Geoffrey Nowell-Smith. Oxford and New York: Oxford University Press, 1996, pp. 668–9.

Mayshark, Jesse Fox. *Post-Pop Cinema: The Search for Meaning in New American Film*. Westport CT: Praeger, 2007.

Minh-ha T Pham, "The Asian Invasion (of Multiculturalism) in Hollywood." *Journal of Popular Film and Television*, 32/3 (Fall 2004), pp. 121–31.

Murphy, David. *Sembene*. Oxford and Trenton, NJ: Africa World Press, 2001.

"The Oberhausen Manifesto," in *The European Cinema Reader*, ed. Catherine Fowler. London and New York: Routledge, 2002, p. 73.

O'Neill, Edward R. "Alfred Hitchcock," in *Oxford History of World Cinema*, ed Geoffrey Nowell-Smith. Oxford and New York: Oxford University Press, 1996, pp. 310–11.

Park, Ed. "Last Man Standing." *The Village Voice*. July 23, 2002. **www.villagevoice.com/2002-07-23/film/last-men-standing/1**.

Prince, Stephen. *The Warrior's Camera*. Princeton, NJ: Princeton University Press, 1999.

"Production Notes: *United 93*." Universal Studios. **www.militaryspot.com/resources/item/united_93_movie**.

Pym, John. "Soldier's Pay," *Sight and Sound*, 58/4 (Autumn 1989), p. 280.

Reynaud, Bérénice. "Cinema For/Against the Lure of Images." *Senses of Cinema*. December 2004. **http://www.sensesofcinema.com**.

Richie, Donald. *The Films of Akira Kurosawa*, 3rd ed. Berkeley: University of California Press, 1999.

Rosenbaum, Jonathan. "*Touch of Evil* Retouched," in *The Best American Movie Writing 1999*, ed. Peter Bogdanovich. New York: St Martin's Griffin, 1999, pp. 133–6.

————. "The Problem with Poetry," in *Movies as Politics*. Berkeley: University of California Press, 1997, pp. 183–94.

————. "Cult Confusion," *The Chicago Reader*, January 9, 1998. February 25, 2004. **http://www.chireader.com/movies/archives/1998/0198/01238.html**.

San Filippo, Maria. "Lost in Translation," *Cineaste*, 29/1 (Winter 2003). Online. Academic Search Elite. February 25, 2004.

Sato, Tadao. "The Films of Akira Kurosawa and the Japanese People," *Film International*, 6/2 (1998), pp. 61–4.

Scorsese, Martin. "Akira Kurosawa." *Architectural Digest* Vol. 65 Issue 11 (Nov 2008): pp. 72–6. *Academic Search Premier*, EBSCO*host* (accessed March 1, 2010).

Sheng-mei Ma, "Ang Lee's Domestic Tragicomedy," *Journal of Popular Culture*, 30/1 (Summer 1996), pp. 191–201.

Stam, Robert. *Film Theory: An Introduction*. Malden, MA, and Oxford: Blackwell Publishers, 2000.

Tasker, Yvonne. *Spectacular Bodies: Gender, Genre and the Action Cinema*. New York: Routledge, 1993.

Taubin, Amy. "Hard Wired." *Film Comment*. May/June 2009, pp. 30–5.

Taylor, Charles. "Hong Kong Tango," Salon.com. October 31, 1997. September 10, 2002. **http://www.salon.com/ent/movies/1997/10/31happy.html?CP=SAL&DN=110**.

Webb, Veronica. "Big Bad Bigelow." *Interview*, November 1995. **www.findarticles.com/p/articles/ mi_m1285/is_n11_v25/ai_17632982**. October 1, 2006.

Wollen, Peter. "From *Signs and Meaning in Cinema*: The Auteur Theory," in *Film Theory and Criticism,* 5th edn, ed. Leo Braudy and Marshall Cohen. Oxford: Oxford University Press, 1999, pp. 519–35.

Yoshimoto, Mitsuhiro. *Kurosawa: Film Studies and Japanese Cinema*. Durham, NC: Duke University Press, 2000.

Zhang, Ziyi. "Ang Lee: The Cross Cultural Cowboy of Film." *Time*. May 8, 2006.

Cinema as Industry: Economics and Technology

CHAPTER FIFTEEN

The movie business is macabre. Grotesque. It is
a combination of a football game and a brothel.

Federico Fellini

Well before *Avatar* (James Cameron 2009) hit screens, headlines trumpeted the film's pioneering and costly special effects, focusing on Cameron's innovations in performance capture technology and the decision to release the film in 3-D and IMAX 3-D as well as a traditional theatrical format (termed a "flattie" by Bernard Mendiburu). Publicity materials suggesting that viewers were witnessing major technological advances helped to lure customers into theaters. The film, whose pre-publicity budget was estimated at $237 million, became the highest grossing film of all time, earning $2.7 billion worldwide. By contrast, when writer-director Oren Peli's *Paranormal Activity* (2007) was released in 2009, the press repeatedly pointed out that Peli made the film for less than $15,000 by shooting it in his own home on digital video (fig. **15.2**). Paramount had purchased the distribution rights to the film and any sequels for a modest $300,000. Surprisingly, *Paranormal Activity* made more than $9 million in its first weekend, and its reputation began to build. *Los Angeles Times* critic Betsy Sharkey predicted, "with midnight screenings selling out, even with marketing costs, this film will soon be wallowing in gravy." (Sharkey) Ultimately the film

15.1 *Easy Rider* engaged a new generation of filmgoers.

15.2 Low budget chills: *Paranormal Activity*.

went on to gross more than $109 million and Paramount announced in 2010 that a sequel would be made.

Paranormal Activity became a potent symbol of how low budget, do-it-yourself filmmaking was still possible in the age of technology-driven, special effects extravaganzas like *Avatar, Iron Man 2* (Jon Favreau 2010), and *Transformers: Revenge of the Fallen* (Michael Bay 2009). Even Neill Blomkamp's well-regarded science fiction film *District 9* (2009), with a budget of $30 million, and Michel Gondry's *Be Kind Rewind* (2008), made for $20 million, seemed like "small" productions, considering that the average cost to make and market a Hollywood film topped $100 million in 2007, according to the Motion Picture Association of America (MPAA).

Though *Avatar* and *Paranormal Activity* seem to be polar opposites in many ways, the media coverage surrounding each film's release was remarkably consistent. The press focused attention on production costs and box office receipts; in one case, the director (Cameron) was called upon to justify his extravagance and in the other, the filmmaker (Peli) was expected to transcend the limitations of guerilla filmmaking, an approach first associated with Robert Rodriguez's *El Mariachi* (1992), which was made for $10,000 and went on to gross $2 million. In other words, critical and journalistic discourses surrounding both *Avatar* and *Paranormal Activity* emphasized the fact that filmmaking is a business: while fans and critics may be drawn to the creative aspects of the film enterprise, there is no denying the fact that money matters in this multi-billion dollar industry. And plenty of journalists, critics, and film scholars have made it their business to investigate and write about the economics of the film industry.

Although economic practices have always shaped the film industry, increasingly, the business side of filmmaking determines the way fans think and talk about movies. Magazines such as *Vanity Fair* and *Entertainment Weekly* routinely publish articles on the powerful players in Hollywood, many of whom are not movie stars, but producers and executives. Newspapers, television news, entertainment magazines, and blogs publicize statistics on box office receipts, ensuring that a film's financial success or failure gets as much public scrutiny as aesthetic considerations.

In terms of popular and scholarly research and writing, journalists and academics have begun to focus more and more on the way the film industry functions *as* an industry. While authors Dade Hayes and Jonathan Bing, editors for the trade paper *Variety*, identified a growing interest among the general public in box office figures in *Wide Open: How Hollywood Box Office Became a National Obsession* (Miramax 2004), at least two scholarly collections confirm this trend in academia as well: *An Economic History of Film* (ed. John Sedgwick and Michael Pokorny 2005) and *The Contemporary Hollywood Film Industry* (Paul McDonald and Janet Wasko 2008). Both emphasize the global dimensions of the film industry and discuss the industry's responses to the proliferation of digital media forms, including DVD and Blu-ray, cable, satellite, and internet delivery of films. This type of research does not involve deciphering motifs, themes, or structural attributes of individual films; instead, this body of scholarship examines the business practices—including topics such as labor relations, intellectual property rights, changes in the star system, product licensing, profit margins on theatrical releases versus DVDs, and so on—of film studios and the international conglomerates that own them.

Whereas Part Two of this book focused on films as texts to be watched, studied, and thoughtfully interpreted and Part Three has looked at film and culture, this final chapter considers films from a strictly economic perspective, as products to be consumed. It looks at films as commodities whose quality, appeal, and profitability are shaped by the structure of the industry, by methods of production, distribution, and marketing, and by technological developments. More specifically, the discussion focuses on important changes in the structure of the film industry and in business practices—notably industry consolidation—that have shaped film and culture in the post-studio era. It concludes by examining a major technological development that has complemented industry consolidation—digital technology—and considers its impact on the way viewers experience films.

The Changing Structure of the Film Industry

From Oligopolies to Conglomerates

During Hollywood's golden age, from the 1920s through the 1940s, five major studios dominated the industry. **Vertical integration**—where a few powerful companies controlled the industry from the top down by making, distributing, and exhibiting films in their own theaters—helped the studios guarantee stable box office receipts through practices such as **block booking** (forcing exhibitors to rent a studio's less lucrative films along with the sure box office successes). But the Supreme Court's 1948 Paramount Decree declared that the five majors and three minors had been engaged in monopolistic practices, colluding to keep independent producers out of their theaters. This decision forced Paramount, Warner Brothers, Loew's/MGM, Twentieth Century Fox, and RKO to divest themselves of their theater holdings. But although the majors relinquished their theater chains, they maintained their hold over distribution and began to seek methods for increasing profits through distribution.

The majors began investing in and distributing smaller, independent films rather than producing their own. This defensive economic practice had implications for film style and culture more generally. Studios used this strategy because it reduced risk; independent productions with small budgets didn't have to rely on huge audiences to turn a profit. At the same time, independent directors were emboldened to explore challenging subject matter and to experiment with style. During the late 1960s and 1970s, American films became more adventurous. Films such as *Easy Rider*, *The Wild Bunch* (Sam Peckinpah 1969), *Medium Cool*, and *Woodstock* shook up the industry and engaged younger audiences (figs. **15.1**, **15.3**). "Hollywood Renaissance" filmmakers addressed social and political issues head-on and rejected the classical style in favor of more daring approaches borrowed from international art cinema directors.

By the early 1970s, Hollywood studios had made significant headway in reviv-

15.3 Outlaw heroes in *The Wild Bunch*.

ing themselves commercially through the work of independent directors. This revival was solidified in 1972, when audiences swarmed to Paramount's *The Godfather*. Director Francis Ford Coppola was, like many of his peers, an independent committed to making personal films. Coppola accepted Paramount Studio's offer to direct a screen adaptation of Mario Puzo's bestselling novel *The Godfather* in order to finance his production studio, Zoetrope, and his next personal project, *The Conversation*. Paramount's gamble paid off, and the film surpassed *Gone with the Wind* as the top box office grossing film of all time, taking in $86.2 million (Biskind, p. 163).

That film marked the studios' re-emergence and renewed an emphasis on production rather than distribution. That interest was facilitated by conglomeration, which began in 1966, when Gulf and Western bought Paramount. Since then, all of the major studios and several minors—including Paramount, Warner Brothers, MGM/UA, Twentieth Century Fox, Universal, and Columbia—have been absorbed into larger media corporations. Under the *laissez-faire* economic policies of the Reagan administration in the 1980s, studios were allowed to merge with conglomerates that also owned theater chains, thus reintroducing vertical integration.

Media conglomeration effectively re-established vertical integration because mergers provided studios with distribution and exhibition outlets, including cable and satellite television, video and DVD rental chains, and internet service providers. For example, Rupert Murdoch, who owns News Corporation, CBS/Fox video distribution, and Deluxe film labs, purchased Twentieth Century Fox. In 1993, Viacom added Paramount to its list of holdings, which included MTV, Nickelodeon, Showtime, and various television stations. Viacom went on to buy Blockbuster, "creating for itself an automatic distribution outlet for its product." (Allen, p. 37) Pro-business government policies effectively rendered the Paramount Decree irrelevant and encouraged virtual monopolies on production and distribution, only now on a global scale.

Horizontal Integration: Merchandise and Games

The corporate mergers that began in 1966 and continued unabated through the 1980s and 1990s not only revived vertical integration; they also produced **horizontal integration**, aligning complementary businesses and allowing companies to expand "across" the entertainment industry. This industrial shift has influenced the way films function as cultural experiences: for one thing, movies are rarely seen as discrete aesthetic experiences but, rather, are part and parcel of large-scale acts of consumption.

The reason for this is that studios take advantage of market synergy: they use movie releases to make money in many venues simultaneously. Film scholar Jon Lewis describes how Time-Warner earned massive profits from *Batman* (Tim

Burton 1989) by licensing the DC comic character; taking a share of profits from shirts, toys, and other merchandise sold at Warner Brothers outlet stores and elsewhere; showing the film on Time-Warner's cable companies throughout the country; selling the soundtrack album through Time-Warner record labels; and selling videos, DVDs, and laser discs through a Time-Warner label. All of these profits were over and above the film's $250 million gross from theatrical exhibition. Not only did this merchandising add to profits—it also marketed the film. Of course, the film also received free promotional coverage via Time-Warner's news magazines: *Time*, *Life*, and *Entertainment Weekly* (Lewis, p. 103).

An allied industry that has grown dramatically in importance in the twenty-first century is gaming. In 2010, more than fifty video games had been created based on theatrically released feature films, and the number is sure to grow. In 2008, Steven Spielberg was credited as lead designer on a Wii game called Boom Blox (Chatfield).

The relationship between film and gaming is not a one-way street, however. Film scholar Will Brooker has analyzed the influence of video games on film style. "On a broad aesthetic level," he writes "the term 'video game' is used to connote spectacular, showy displays of effects at the expense of subtext and character [...] More directly, critics and fans have identified specific video game memes in films, such as the progression through levels, power-ups, and signature moves." (Brooker, p. 123) Scholars have remarked upon the fact that a generation of people raised on Playstation has contributed to the development of numerous interactive media forms, including games, websites, and interactive CD-ROMs, which, in turn, may affect narratives in feature films. Films such as *Run Lola Run*, the *Matrix* trilogy (1999–2003), *Syriana* (Stephen Gaghan 2005), and *Inception* are replete with feedback loops, multiple perspectives, repetition, and other modes of non-linearity that Brooker defines as the video game's "cycles of character death and reset." (Brooker, p. 124) While narrative circularity is not brand new to cinema, director Christopher Nolan attributes the more frequent use of non-linearity to the contemporary era, arguing "people's ability to absorb a fractured *mise en scène* is extraordinary compared to forty years ago" (quoted in Harkin). Nolan's comment points to developments in cinematic storytelling over the past forty years, as the classical model of a linear narrative has been modified by narratives influenced by postmodern concepts of fracture and irrationality, and non-linear story structures from the world of gaming.

Globalization

Another effect of the wave of mergers has been the globalization of the Hollywood film industry. Universal Studios is part of NBC Universal (formed by a merger of G.E. and Vivendi, a French media company); Columbia Pictures is owned by Japan's Sony corporation; and Twentieth Century Fox is part of News Corporation, Australian Rupert Murdoch's empire. Though still based within the United States, the other three major studios—Warner Brothers, Disney, and Paramount—are part of international conglomerates. The nature of corporate structure is transitory. In 2005, Paramount (a subsidiary of Viacom) acquired DreamWorks. In 2008, DreamWorks made a deal with Indian investment firm Reliance for capital and in 2009 signed a distribution deal with Disney in order to maintain its independence.

Corporate conglomeration has bolstered Hollywood's ability to compete in the domestic and foreign markets; its position of dominance is unrivaled. According to the MPAA, domestic (U.S. and Canada) receipts for the Hollywood film industry were $10.6 billion in 2009, whereas foreign box office revenues reached $19.3 billion; the record breaking $29.9 billion total represented an 8 percent increase over 2008, and a 30 percent increase over 2005. The continuing growth in the importance of international markets was reflected in the percentage of box office receipts from international releases, which accounted for 65 percent of revenues, up from 40 percent just five years earlier. In other words, the film industry prospered during the global economic downturn in 2008–10, repeating a historical trend often attributed to people's desire for escapism during hard times.

Hollywood films dominate international screens. They account for more than 50 percent of box office receipts (and in some cases, far more than that) in Australia, France, Germany, Italy, Spain, and the United Kingdom (Scott, p. 160). In 2010, *Avatar* became the biggest-grossing film of all time in China, Spain, Russia, Hong Kong, and Chile. But Hollywood does not plan to rely solely on big-budget spectacles to entice audiences outside the U.S.; studios such as Warner Brothers and Sony have invested in international production units to finance local productions in several European countries, Mexico, and India. Warner Brothers International planned forty of these "local" productions in 2011. According to the chief executive of Focus Features, which includes the international division of Universal Pictures, "For a studio to thrive they are going to have to keep delivering blockbusters, but will also have to operate with a tremendous amount of cultural expertise in markets around the world." (quoted in Pfanner)

Industry Labor Practices

As in any industry, the film industry's labor force, its location, and its wages all play critical roles in determining the quality and profitability of the product. In the contemporary Hollywood industry, four trends have emerged with respect to labor practices: the **outsourcing** of labor, restructured contracts with stars, **runaway productions**, and the concentration of creative control.

Outsourcing

In the studio era, major studios kept production within the confines of studio back lots, which contained the sets, equipment, costumes, and personnel needed to complete a project. If a scene required location shooting, cohesive units traveled together to complete the work. Under the unit production system, an effective team of technicians would work together on project after project. Today, studios outsource much of the labor involved in shooting a picture. On a given production, one independent firm might handle lighting, while another might construct the required sets. The motivation for sub-contracting the work is financial. For example, Asian inkers and colorists do much of Disney's animation work at a fraction of the wages American workers would demand (Thompson and Bordwell, p. 707).

Star Compensation

Historically, the highest proportion of labor costs is paid to movie stars in the form of huge fees and percentages of profits. Popular stars cannot be replaced or outsourced, and their involvement can make or break a movie at the box office. During the economic downturn that began in 2008, however, film studios began revising the way they compensated stars. Michael Cieply noted the increased frequency of deals that limit the salaries that major stars earn in advance and, instead, base financial compensation on an agreed-upon percentage of the profits earned after the studio breaks even. These agreements are called "cash-break zero" deals and represent a major departure from contracts that paid stars a percentage of first dollar gross receipts—that is, revenues earned before the studio breaks even. Cieply gives one example of the CB zero deal: Sandra Bullock earned half her usual fee of $10 million for *The Blind Side* (John Lee Hancock 2009) but stood to earn an estimated $20 million from the film because it was a hit (Cieply).

As part of a larger concern over compensation, actors and their agents are also worried about the performance capture technology James Cameron employed in *Avatar*, arguing that it might allow directors to replace human actors with their captured performances. Zoe Saldana played a lead character in Cameron's film entirely through performance capture, whereas the other lead actors (Sigourney Weaver and Sam Worthington) appeared as themselves and their Na'vi doubles. Some felt Saldana did not earn the same recognition for her work, in terms of pay or her star persona. In 2010, the Screen Actors Guild announced that it plans to examine compensation and recognition issues for actors in performance capture roles and in video games.

Pessimistically imagining the limitless possibilities of this new technology, Jeff Bridges, winner of the Best Actor Academy Award in 2010, speculated, "Actors will kind of be a thing of the past. We'll be turned into combinations. A director will be able to say, 'I want 60 percent Clooney; give me 10 percent Bridges; and throw some Charles Bronson in there.' They'll come up with a new guy who will look like nobody who has ever lived and that person or thing will be huge." (Abramovitz) In the same article, Steven Spielberg, who used performance capture on *The Adventures of Tintin*, reaffirmed the importance of actors by calling it "digital makeup, not augmented animation." Spielberg also touted the fact that performance capture allowed him to cut his shooting time in half because he avoided the time consuming set-ups typical of live action scenes. Here again, financial concerns motivate decisions about technology's role in the creative process.

Runaway Productions

In the 1990s and 2000s, rising costs, coupled with tax and other financial incentives offered by state governments in the U.S. and by foreign governments have lured productions out of Southern California and, in many cases, out of the U.S. altogether. Spending on films shot in the U.S. declined 14 percent between 1998 and 2005, and on-location feature filmmaking in Los Angeles declined by 30 percent in 2009; it was down a full 60 percent from its peak in 1996. For studio executives, so-called runaway productions—films shot outside the U.S.—make economic sense because it can be less expensive to move a production overseas

15.4 New Zealand has provided exotic locations for many runaway productions.

and use local technicians than it is to pay the location costs and requisite union wages in the United States.

A Canadian production incentive program initiated in 1998 was responsible for a significant increase in the number of runaway productions, and this program encouraged many other countries to follow suit. In 2002, Canada earned $1.7 billion through foreign-financed productions, more than any other country (Seguin).

Runaway productions cost an estimated 47,000 jobs in the U.S. between 2000 and 2006 and untold billions of dollars in economic benefits (McNary). Recently, New Zealand's lower costs and sophisticated post-production facilities have made it a popular location for films and commercials (fig. **15.4**). In 2009, even a commercial advertising campaign promoting California's happy cows was shot in New Zealand—with New Zealand cows, of course—which aroused much consternation.

The fierce competition to attract major film productions is not merely a high stakes international game: states and localities within the U.S. engage in the same tactics. It seemed to be adding insult to injury when the alien invasion film *Battle: Los Angeles* (Jonathan Liebesman 2011), which is set in Santa Monica, was filmed in Louisiana, a state that has one of the most aggressive incentives program for filmmaking, along with Michigan and New Mexico (Cieply). Expenditures on filmmaking in Louisiana grew from $12 million in 2002 to $330 million in 2004 after tax incentives were put in place.

Runaway productions may be more important to the industry, for economic reasons, than they are to film audiences. Even locations selected because of favorable tax incentives will be scouted beforehand; that is, a pre-production team will choose sites that look appropriate for the film.

Creative Centralization

Although the film industry's labor force is now decentralized via the practice of outsourcing, the production of ideas has become more centralized, owing to the horizontal organization of the industry. Unless screenwriters work for one of the massive media conglomerates, there are fewer and fewer markets for their ideas. The expenditures of six media companies account for three-quarters of the total spending on screenwriting in the U.S. ("Tangled Webs"). Fearing the intellectual consequences of the conglomerates' increasing control of content production, The Writers Guild of America recently argued that the current marketplace stifles creativity, either by absorbing new, creative talent into impersonal conglomerates that churn out standardized product, or by ignoring this talent altogether.

As outsourcing, contract negotiation, runaway productions, and creative consolidation illustrate, film industry practices that may at first glance seem to have little to do with social or aesthetic issues do in fact have a significant impact on film and culture.

Films as Products

To illustrate the way industrial practices shape viewers' experiences of film, this section discusses how film industry practices of the 1970s and 1980s created the **blockbuster** and the **high concept film**. Those industrial products, and the saturation marketing used to promote them, in turn prompted a backlash: the independent film culture of the late 1980s.

The Blockbuster

The Godfather taught the studios the importance of the blockbuster: a film that swamps all competition, in part by the sheer number of prints in circulation at once.

The Godfather, *Jaws*, and *Star Wars* transformed the way Hollywood distributed and marketed its product to the public. During the 1950s and 1960s, studios commonly used a tactic called **roadshowing**. A film would have a lengthy run in a few premier theaters to generate word-of-mouth publicity before being distributed more broadly. With *The Godfather*, studios began booking prints in as many theaters as possible, saturating the market with a single film to make a film's opening weekend an event. Studios realized that they could count on the press to cover a film's opening weekend, luring audiences into the theater with peer pressure: "Everyone else is seeing the film, so I guess I should too."

In fact, one of the economic justifications for the multiplex was not to offer patrons more diversity or convenience but, rather, to guarantee that major releases could open on many screens simultaneously. Universal opened *Jaws* in 495 theaters nationwide. By the year 2010, major releases like *Salt* typically opened on more than three thousand screens.

The goal of guaranteeing a blockbuster has had a tremendous impact on film style. Hollywood catered to general audiences by producing less risky material, often based on novels or television series that have a built in or "pre-sold" audience. *The Godfather* was based on Mario Puzo's already popular novel. *Jaws*, also a popular novel, appealed to an even wider audience, becoming a family event. In fact, a survey of several influential blockbusters of the 1970s reveals a steady trend away from intellectual and moral complexity and toward fantasy: *The Godfather* (1972; fig. **15.5**), *Jaws* (1975), *Star Wars* (1977), *Raiders of the Lost Ark* (1981), and *E.T.* (1982; fig. **15.6**). That trend has continued in the late 1990s, with *Titanic*, and in 2001–3 with the *Lord of the Rings* trilogy.

The High Concept Film

Hollywood's movement away from complexity and ambiguity and toward simple entertainment coalesced in the high concept film, which fuses star power, genre appeal, and a basic scenario into a bankable package. High concept appropriates and combines the most identifiable traits from other films, stars, and

15.5 *The Godfather* was one of many films to target an adult audience.

15.6 (above) *E.T.* was part of a trend toward fantasy in the 1980s and targeted children.

15.7 (below) *Jurassic Park* took market synergy to new levels.

popular trends into a twenty-five-word marketable pitch that appeals to financially minded studio executives. The pitch for *Snakes on a Plane* (David R. Ellis 2006) was "Take two of the biggest fears people have—fear of flying and fear of snakes—and throw then together at 30,000 feet and see what happens." (Jensen, p. 27) According to screenwriter Howard Rodman, pitching a screenplay has become tantamount to "writing a prospectus for a stock offering." (quoted in Maltby, p. 38)

The practice allows studios to combine already established and successful ingredients into one enticing morsel that the domestic and international markets will find easy to digest. The appeal of the high concept film is that audiences, both domestic and foreign, can readily understand its basic premise and admire its stars, thus improving its chances of profitability.

New Modes of Marketing

The rise of the blockbuster film coincided with the rise of national marketing campaigns. Studios launched nationwide marketing blitzes, which bombarded the public with ads in newspapers, magazines, television, and radio.

The winning synergetic strategy for marketing a blockbuster, according to MCA/Universal marketing executive Elizabeth Gelfand, is to make merchandising deals in three venues: toys, fast food, and video games (Seagrave, p. 242). Steven Spielberg's *Jurassic Park* still stands tall as one of the monsters of market synergy (fig. **15.7**). By the time MCA/Universal released the film in 1993, the studio had made licensing deals with toy company Kenner Products, McDonald's, Sega games, Nintendo games, K-Mart, Weetabix, Pepsi, Coca-Cola, and Nisson foods; "sales of licensed merchandising passing $1 billion nine months after the film's release." (Seagrave, p. 242) As film historian Peter Bart puts it, movie releases are highly orchestrated events: "Today a movie is unveiled, not with a quietly orchestrated build, but with a cosmic paroxysm, a global spasm of hype involving giant marketing partners like McDonald's and a profligate network on the Super Bowl or the Olympics." (quoted in Allen, p. 55)

Saturation marketing led to the expansion of advertising budgets for most Hollywood productions: the advertising budget for *Austin Powers: The Spy Who Shagged Me* (Jay Roach 1999), for example, outweighed its production budget (Thompson and Bordwell, p. 684).

By 2009, however, movie studios began to implement cost-saving measures to reduce the size of their advertising budgets, partly in response to shrinking sales of DVDs. DVDs proved to be a more lucrative revenue stream than theatrical releases in the 2000s, but even DVD sales began to slide after 2007, dropping a full 25 percent in 2009. Other new sources of revenue, including iTunes and video on demand had not generated significant profits. In 2009, Lionsgate cut its marketing costs by 66 percent over the previous year and Disney slashed its marketing staff by about a dozen people (Barnes).

To compensate for reductions in traditional advertising, and to take advantage of new opportunities to advertise created by the proliferation of digital media, studios have come to depend more and more on "earned media": free spots on television, magazines, newspapers, and the internet. Interviews with stars on popular television talk shows also provide advertising for upcoming film releases; in many cases the fact that movie studios and television networks are owned by the same parent company, such as Disney and ABC, makes this a seamless process. Blogs, and social networking sites such as Facebook and Twitter have changed the landscape of advertising as well. Film actors and reality TV celebrities routinely communicate with fans through these formats, and studios have begun to create interactive Facebook pages for their characters and films in addition to constructing official sites. In March 2010, the Facebook page for the new release, *Alice in Wonderland* (Tim Burton 2010), boasted more than 1.2 million fans. This trend may offer critics and scholars a way to examine the changing nature of stardom, as these technologies purport to provide fans greater access to and interactivity with their favorite stars.

15.8 *Killer of Sheep*: a groundbreaking American independent film.

Independent Film Culture

Independent filmmaking has always been a part of American film culture, but in the 1980s, audiences began to identify, and identify with, a movement opposed to corporate filmmaking. A number of independent filmmakers who debuted low-budget, idiosyncratic films in the 1980s garnered larger audiences and international reputations for their work, including Charles Burnett, Joel and Ethan Coen, Todd Haynes, Jim Jarmusch, David Lynch, and John Sayles. Burnett's *Killer of Sheep* (1977) is internationally admired for its neorealist portrayal of an

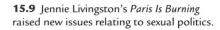

15.9 Jennie Livingston's *Paris Is Burning* raised new issues relating to sexual politics.

average African-American man in an inhospitable, yet everyday, environment (fig. **15.8**). Steven Soderbergh's *Sex, Lies, and Videotape* (1989) was a breakthrough film for contemporary independent production. The spirit of experimentation evident in the American independent films of the late 1980s and the early 1990s lives on in the films of Sofia Coppola (*Marie Antoinette* [2006]), and French film and music video director Michel Gondry (*Eternal Sunshine of the Spotless Mind* [2004] and *The Science of Sleep* [2006]).

In the most literal sense, an independent film is not financed by a major Hollywood studio. Independent filmmakers secure funds by seeking out sponsors, drumming up investors, or borrowing money from friends and relatives. They often present an alternative sensibility, in terms of both their low production values and their autonomy from large-scale corporate interests.

Independent filmmakers are freer to explore complex topics and social issues that may be off-limits to major studios afraid of offending their general audience. The New Queer Cinema of the early 1990s offered complex representations of gay and lesbian culture in

Haynes's *Poison* (1990), *Paris Is Burning* (Jennie Livingston 1990; fig. **15.9**), and *My Own Private Idaho* (Gus Van Sant 1991). Jim Jarmusch's portrayals of foreigners adrift in American culture (*Down by Law* [1986], *Mystery Train* [1989]), John Sayles's exploration of race relations and labor politics (*Matewan* [1987]), and Mary Harron's feminist re-evaluation of the cult of Andy Warhol (*I Shot Andy Warhol* [1996]) are far more critical of American culture than mainstream films are. Smaller independent films can earn a modest gross but still make a profit. For example, *Little Miss Sunshine* (Jonathan Dayton and Valerie Faris 2006) grossed more than $41 million against a budget of $8 million.

The box office success of blockbusters like *Avatar* and *Transformers: Revenge of the Fallen* (Michael Bay 2009), together with changes in the industry's distribution practices, have had a significant adverse impact on art house films and art house theaters in recent years. Film critic Zack Smith reports that a number of small film distributors and art house divisions of larger studios retrenched significantly or closed down altogether between 2000 and 2010. One result is that films such as *Up In The Air* (Jason Reitman 2008), originally planned as a limited release for art house audiences, was released widely in multiplexes instead, because Paramount had closed down the specialty division responsible for the film's release, Paramount Vantage (Smith, p. 15).

This shift from limited to wide releases, along with the rush to release films to more quickly reap the benefits of DVD sales, has hurt small art theaters and undermined the thriving independent film culture that blossomed in the 1990s. Single-screen art house cinemas, which represent about 4 percent of screens in the U.S., have a difficult time competing directly with the multiplexes (which total 46 percent of screens) on big budget effects-driven action films in part because many cannot afford the expensive conversion to digital projection, and thus they depend on character-driven comedies and dramas. *Precious* (Lee Daniels 2009) was initially released in a limited number of smaller theaters in four cities, in part because its devastating story of the abuse of a young African-American woman was deemed challenging and controversial. Producers operated on the assumption that word of mouth publicity would precede its widespread release. After the film broke box office records for limited release films, it was eventually accorded a general release and played in both multiplexes and art house cinemas. The demarcation between multiplex and art house fare is less strict than in the past (partly because multiplexes can devote one screen to *Precious* and three or four to *Avatar*), offering a further challenge to art house film culture.

Two Independent Institutions: Sundance and Miramax

In 1981 actor and director Robert Redford founded the Sundance Institute, a non-profit organization providing training and financial support for emerging screenwriters and directors. The institute was long associated with the Sundance Film Festival in Park City, Utah, a showcase for independent filmmaking. The independent movement gained momentum in the early 1990s, when a string of small films became box office hits—most notably *The Crying Game* (Neil Jordan 1992), *Pulp Fiction*, *Clerks* (Kevin Smith 1994), and *Sling Blade* (Billy Bob Thornton 1996).

Audiences in the 1990s gained greater access to independent films, thanks to an increasing number of film festivals as well as more opportunities to see independent films on cable and satellite TV. By the end of the decade, independent film was a household phrase, familiar even to those with the most conventional tastes.

Some critics argue that the popularity of the movement has made independent cinema just another part of the mainstream, threatening the idiosyncratic approach to filmmaking that attracted audiences in the first place. Large conglomerates now seek to maximize profits by distributing lower-budget independent films. This phenomenon played itself out in the case of *The Blair Witch Project*. Made for $20,000, the film was picked up by Artisan entertainment for $1 million at the 1999 Sundance Film Festival and became one of the most successful independent films ever, grossing more than $200 million.

Connections between Sundance and studio conglomerates have created a perception (accurate or not) that the festival showcases only directors with potentially profitable films or those who are interested in making conventional industry films. The philosophy that such corporate connections compromise creativity inspired the Slamdance Festival, an alternative to the alternative, whose name suggests its derisive attitude toward Sundance.

The history of Miramax pictures contributes to the perception that truly independent cinema is difficult to sustain. Disney acquired Miramax, a pioneer in independent film, in the mid-1990s, and many critics allege that the parent company's need to promote "family values" soon overshadowed alternative perspectives. Moreover, Miramax became infamous for mounting lavish campaigns designed to promote its Academy Award-nominated films. In 2004, the relationship between parent company (Disney) and subsidiary (Miramax) had frayed to the point of unraveling. At issue was the decision by Disney head Michael Eisner not to release Michael Moore's controversial documentary *Fahrenheit 9/11* and Harvey and Bob Weinstein's desire to distribute the film, which they finally did through another company. In the fall of 2005, the Weinstein brothers left Disney (a public statement suggested the break was by mutual agreement), which retained Miramax. Bob and Harvey Weinstein took the Dimension film label with them and went on to form the Weinstein Company.

In early 2010, Disney put Miramax up for auction, following the trend of larger studios to close down or reduce the size of their independent film divisions in the 2000s. It would seem that studios are betting on big budget digital-effects driven and 3D features, as well as their investment in local filmmaking in foreign markets, to shore up their fiscal balance sheets in the near future.

In short, the industry's horizontal and vertical integration has filmmakers, film lovers, and film scholars alike wondering whether alternative forms of filmmaking can continue to challenge Hollywood hegemony in any meaningful way. In the early 2000s, a group of young American filmmakers, working on shoestring budgets and shooting primarily on digital cameras, managed to carry the low budget, non-commercial film aesthetic into the new millennium. This collection of films was termed **Mumblecore**, although many of the filmmakers associated with this type of filmmaking might resist the idea that these films represent a coherent or organized movement.

THE DREAM PALACES

The earliest venues for watching a program of short one-reelers were vaudeville theaters, lecture halls, and churches. Around 1905, permanent storefront theaters called nickelodeons emerged. Then, after the popular success of Italian spectacles such as *Quo Vadis?* (Enrico Guazzoni 1913) and *Cabiria* (Giovanni Pastrone 1914), the industry turned to feature-length films.

As comic shorts gave way to these dramatic feature-length epics, exhibitors built monumental movie theaters to attract and accommodate middle-class audiences (fig. **15.10**). The Regent and Strand theaters in New York City, which opened in the 1910s, were the first such "dream palaces." With more than 3,000 seats and a thirty-piece orchestra, the Strand's lavish interior was appointed with a marble foyer and crystal chandelier (Cook, p. 39). By the late 1920s, most movie theaters were air-conditioned and summertime became the peak season for film going (Gomery, p. 51).

15.10 A publicity still of a typical early movie palace.

Film and New Technology

As with any business, the film industry relies on technological advances to facilitate production and distribution of the product. Digital technologies and the convergence of communication and information technologies promise to play important roles in marketing and exhibition. Digital technology is literally changing films themselves, as well as the circumstances of their consumption.

From an economic perspective, films are just one among many entertainment commodities in the marketplace. Whereas early film exhibitors created beautiful movie palaces for audiences to watch movies in high style, contemporary studios, eager to sell the movies as both an experience and a product, have embraced old, new, and "old made new again" technologies of exhibition, from the resurgence of 3D and IMAX in digital formats, to DVDs and Blu-ray, to cable television and streaming video on broadband. They maximize profits by selling a film many times over. However, in the process, they are changing the way the medium is perceived as an aesthetic and cultural institution.

Until the advent of television in the 1950s and the VHS tape in the 1970s, movie theaters were the primary venues for seeing Hollywood films. In 1946, the average American filmgoer saw twenty-nine films in the theater every year; in 2007, that number had dropped to eight. Although the industry has initially feared that every new development in viewing technology will undermine profitability, these fears repeatedly prove to be unfounded. Audiences haven't stopped going to the movies. More importantly, the studios have learned how to diversify and capitalize on each new development, for example by selling network broadcast rights to their films and repackaging different versions of the same film on DVDs and Blu-ray. In 2009, the DVD market accounted for 65 percent of the major film corporations' revenues worldwide; theatrical releases accounted for 35 percent.

INVENTIVE VOICES: MUMBLECORE AND DIGITAL INDEPENDENCE

Mumblecore refers to a collection of extremely low budget independent films, usually (but not always) shot on digital video formats, which focus on the lives of educated and somewhat aimless young people, who are often played by the filmmaker's friends, family, and acquaintances. Central narrative conflicts revolve around relationships and sexuality. The first film to be considered Mumblecore was the 16 mm feature film *Funny Ha Ha*, directed by Andrew Bujalski, which premiered at the South By Southwest Film Festival (SXSW) in Austin, Texas in 2002 (fig. **15.11**). The term Mumblecore, which was somewhat jokingly coined in 2005 by Eric Masunaga, a member of Bujalski's crew on *Funny Ha Ha*, suggests a quality of slightly confused inarticulateness, and this tends to be an attribute of most characters in these films. *The New York Times* critic Dennis Lim claims that Mumblecore captures a "true twenty-first-century sensibility," with its aesthetic of "low-key naturalism, low-fi production values and a stream of low-volume chatter." (Lim)

Whereas Lim is hesitant to describe Mumblecore as a movement, other critics compare this do-it-yourself

15.11 *Funny Ha Ha*—quintessential Mumblecore.

approach to other twentieth-century new wave cinemas, including the *Nouvelle Vague*/French New Wave (and especially Eric Rohmer's films of romantic entanglement); the New American Cinema Group (and particularly John Cassavetes's improvisational aesthetic); and the New Talkie sensibility of Richard Linklater. What unites the often idiosyncratic directors associated with these diverse new waves is their approach to filmmaking rather than a common subject matter or set of aesthetic principles. Filmmakers such as Truffaut and Godard, Cassavetes and Linklater challenged conventional cinema by embracing new production technologies (including 16 mm film, video, and digital video) that made it possible to reject the model of industrial filmmaking and its attendant financial and creative pressures. They also sought out or established new avenues for distribution: Linklater founded the Austin Film Society, for example, which premiered his film *Slacker* in 1991. Aaron Katz, who directed the Mumblecore films *Dance Party USA* (2006) and *Quiet City* (2007), puts it this way: "This is the first time, mostly because of technology, that someone like me can go out and make a film with no money and no connections." (quoted in Lim) Several of the directors are able to make films because they share the use of a DVX100 camera that they ship back and forth to one another (Debruge).

While Katz may be overstating the case for the pioneering aspects of Mumblecore, he does identify one key aspect of Mumblecore that distinguishes it from the cinemas that came before. Digital production, editing, and distribution has made filmmaking viable for millions of people who would otherwise have no access to this art form. These directors are able to take advantage of twenty-first century distribution channels. They may distribute their films and DVDs on the web, promote their work through film festivals like SXSW and rely on word of mouth advertising, or social networking, to drum up an audience for their work in the absence of theatrical distribution by a major studio. By

2007, Mumblecore had sparked enough interest that New York's Independent Film Center (IFC), mounted a ten-film retrospective, which featured work by Bujalski, Joe Swanberg, and Jay and Mark Duplass.

In response to the IFC's retrospective, film critic Amy Taubin invited readers of *Film Comment* to bid farewell to "the indie movement that never was more than a flurry of festival hype and blogosphere branding." (Taubin) She suggested that the designation of Mumblecore as a movement was mostly an advertising strategy, arguing that the work of these directors attracted attention because the films were considered part of a new movement—or a new brand—rather than simply being interesting work by new filmmakers. Taubin raises interesting questions here about the relationship between genre and *auteur*. For example, are unknown filmmakers more likely to gain attention if they can be linked to an emerging genre? Does the same hold true if he or she works within an established genre? *Humpday* director Lynn Shelton accepts the label of Mumblecore "begrudgingly" (fig. **15.12**). Shelton admits "we all recognize that being labeled under any kind of "movement" moniker is likely to get our smaller than average films more attention than they might otherwise garner on an individual basis." (Yamato)

Taubin also laments the way that the politics of defining a new movement can involve the imposition of a strict, and unproductive, uniformity on directors and subject matter. In this case, she criticizes the narrowly American and overtly male perspective that seems to define Mumblecore films. "So Yong Kim's lovely *In Between Days* (2006)," Taubin writes, "would seem to fit the Mumblecore parameters (DIY production, a protagonist whose problems with language and communication frustrate her desire for a romantic

relationship), but because the filmmaker is a Korean–American woman and her heroine is a Korean immigrant, no one thought to invite the movie to the party." (Taubin)

New York Times critic Lynn Hirschfield has heralded the emergence of a second generation of Mumblecore directors, namely Eric Kutner, Alex Holdridge, Barry Jenkins, and Adam Goldstein, and writes that several first generation directors have moved into mainstream projects: the Duplass brothers made *Cyrus* (2010) with Marisa Tomei, and Greta Gerwig starred in Noah Baumbach's *Greenberg* (2010). In 2010, Paramount announced the creation of Insurge Pictures, a unit designed to distribute micro-budget films, with an initial slate of ten films budgeted at $100,000. Although the moment for Mumblecore as an oppositional movement may have passed, it's clear that the digital technologies that enable cheaper and faster shooting, editing, and distribution of films are here to stay. In other words, this is the age of the digital *auteur*.

Selected Mumblecore directors and films:

Andrew Bujalski: *Funny Ha Ha* (2002), *Mutual Appreciation* (2005), *Beeswax* (2009)

Jay and Mark Duplass: *Cyrus* (2010), *Baghead* (2007), *The Puffy Chair* (2005)

Greta Gerwig: *Nights and Weekends* (2008)

Aaron Katz: *Cold Weather* (2010), *Let's Get Down to Brass Tacks* (2008), *Quiet City* (2007), *Dance Party, USA* (2006)

Lynne Shelton: *Humpday* (2009), *My Effortless Brilliance* (2008)

Joe Swanberg: *Alexander the Last* (2009), *Nights and Weekends* (2008), *Swedish Blueballs* (2008), *Hannah Takes the Stairs* (2007), *LOL* (2006)

15.12 Director Lynn Shelton makes an appearance in *Humpday*.

The Rise of the DVD and Blu-ray

Home-viewing technology entered the digital age in the 1990s. DVDs allow studios to sell films multiple times: at the theater, with the initial DVD release, and with any subsequent releases of "Collector's Editions" that include new bonus features.

Not everyone considers technological change neutral in its impact on the film medium. James Morrison suggests that the DVD has adversely affected film culture. The DVD's ability to store vast amounts of information, including a "director's cut," may ultimately compromise a director's vision. Directors must sign contracts that restrict the content of their films when they are screened in theaters, because studios expect to "put back in the DVD what was banned in the theatrical release, and use it as a selling point." (Morrison, p. 52) Morrison also questions the value of the supplementary material on DVDs:

> If the advent of DVD has contributed a greater awareness to many filmgoers' experience of movies, it's of a very specific kind, a cultish type of knowledge, in which localized background detail used to sell the disc, or production tidbits commemorated in the filmmakers' commentaries on DVDs, turn into a new form of mythology. (Morrison, p. 52)

In his view, the DVD encourages commodity fetishism (endowing consumer goods with mystical qualities), enabling viewers to think of films as collectable items prized only for their connection to celebrated personalities.

A case in point might be Fox Studios' 2003 release of *The Alien Quadrilogy*, a collector's set of nine discs containing fifty-eight hours of *Alien*. Such an overwhelming amount of deleted scenes and "making of" documentaries doesn't attract casual fans as much as *Alien* "completists," bent on owning the latest—and longest—version of the films. Much like an "all you can eat buffet," such DVDs attract consumers by selling quantity of material, not quality.

Many of these issues also apply to Blu-ray, the latest home viewing technology, officially designated the successor to DVD by Disney, Fox, Warner, Paramount, Sony, Lionsgate, and MGM. Blu-ray uses a blue-violet rather than a red laser to record data (hence the name). The blue laser's shorter wavelength offers more precise focus, allowing the data to be packed more tightly. Blu-ray discs can hold up to six times the data that DVDs hold. Blu-ray has been touted as delivering better image and sound quality than DVDs and HD DVDs; it delivers higher resolution images and sound because it uses a more efficient system for data compression that limits the information lost in converting studio originals. While most of the improvements can be attributed to the larger storage capacity of Blu-ray discs, Blu-ray also offers greater possibilities for interactivity. For example, the 2007 Blu-ray release of *Cars* (John Lasseter and Joe Ranft 2006) allows viewers to play a game called "Car Finder" where players spot various makes and models of cars that appear throughout the movie. In 2009, Universal announced that upcoming releases will allow viewers to use an iPhone as a remote control and keyboard to send Facebook and Twitter updates from their Blu-ray players. Film spectatorship on Blu-ray promises to become a far more interactive, integrated, and networked activity than ever before.

Film and Digital Technologies

Digital technologies have transformed the film business, from production to distribution to exhibition. In 2010, *Slumdog Millionaire* became the first film shot predominantly on a digital format to win the Academy Award for Best Cinematography. Moreover, digital formats have driven the recent resurgence of 3D as well: twenty films were released in 3D in 2009, more than double that of 2008. Because 3D was still something of a novelty, and proved to be extremely popular, exhibitors increased ticket prices for 3D movies in 2009 by as much as 25 percent. (McClintock and Stewart). These price increases benefit both exhibitors and distributors.

In terms of theatrical exhibition, the shift to digital projection is well underway, with the fastest growth occurring in Europe. At the end of 2009, there were more than 16,000 digital cinema screens worldwide (out of a total of 150,000 screens), representing an 86 percent increase from 2008. Digital screens increased 196 percent in Europe in 2009, with 3D installations increasing 506 percent. Digital 3D now represents 55 percent of all digital screens in the world ("MPAA Theatrical Market Statistics 2009" pp. 13–15).

In terms of home exhibition, DVD players, Blu-ray players, and televisions are no longer the only hardware for viewing films. Personal computers provide an array of viewing experiences. Beyond playing DVDs, computers grant access to trailers and full-length films on the internet. This is one reason why cinephiles and critics widely tout the internet's ability to democratize film culture.

Initially, the web was used primarily as a marketing vehicle for films, but its role in film culture continues to evolve. Film scholar J.P. Telotte chronicles the way that the internet marketing campaign for *The Blair Witch Project* (fig. **15.13**) blurred the distinction between fact and fiction (a theme that the film itself addresses) and between watching films and surfing the internet. The website subordinated the film—presumably the product at the center of the project—to the marketing campaign by offering links to sites that helped to perpetuate the fictional notion that the film was composed of found footage shot by three college students who got lost in the Maryland woods. The website "point[ed] in various ways away from the film's privileged status as a product of the entertainment industry," (Telotte) while, at the same time, the film acquired some of the characteristics of the internet. This process is a portent of the future: the internet "threatens, much as television did, to supplant the film industry, in part by offering its own pleasures to a young audience that has grown up with electronic narratives." (Telotte)

The web continues to be an important venue for marketing films, but its inherent ability to promote interactivity (such as video games that allow viewers to determine the ending of a story) gives the web a new role to play in filmmaking. A website created for the action thriller *Snakes on a Plane* included a blog for fans to contribute ideas that the filmmakers included in the finished product.

Websites also provide an alternative to traditional venues for film distribution. Atomfilms.com and YouTube permit amateur filmmakers to upload their own videos for others to watch for free. The fact that broadband allows users to download feature films as digital

15.13 *The Blair Witch Project*—a film for the internet age.

files makes executives who helm entertainment conglomerates uneasy. Digital copies are perfect copies: there is no degradation of image or sound quality with each subsequent generation.

Film corporations have responded to the threat of digital piracy by raising the technological barriers against duplication (including regional coding on DVDs) and by pursuing legal action against unauthorized downloading. In 2010, the MPAA and seven Indian film studios formed an alliance to fight piracy—in large part by cracking down on the policing of camcorders that are brought into movie theaters. Some estimate that Indian consumers buy 700 million pirated DVDs a year. The MPAA has similar alliances with movie studios in Europe and Hong Kong (Kinetz).

A further development in distribution is the shortening of the theatrical window—the length of time between the theatrical release of a film and the date on which it becomes available on DVD or on broadcast on cable channels—so that audiences will obtain authorized access to a major release rather than pirating it. Steven Soderbergh experimented with the complete elimination of the theatrical window (which is called "the bubble" in the industry) by releasing *Bubble* (2005) in theaters, on cable television, and on DVD on the same day. Industry trends had already been slowly moving in that direction and should continue to do so: the theatrical window shrank by about two weeks between 2003 and 2005.

In 2010, the standard theatrical window was four months and thirteen days (Smith, p. 15). But a dispute arose between the Odeon cinema chain and Walt Disney Pictures over *Alice In Wonderland* because Disney planned to release the DVD only twelve weeks after its theatrical debut in Britain, Ireland, and Italy, rather than the usual seventeen weeks. Odeon threatened to boycott the film, complaining that the shorter window meant the company was less likely to recoup its investment in the digital projection equipment that could show the 3D film ("UK movie chain").

The digital era has transformed many aspects of film culture. Hollywood had one of its most profitable years ever in 2009, but it's clear that the tension surrounding theatrical exhibition versus Blu-ray and DVD releases, not to mention new opportunities for streaming media, will remain, as the industry determines how best to protect the profitability of each of these modes of exhibition.

In terms of exhibition, the digital era has its costs as well as benefits. Two contemporary filmmakers who have embraced the technological advances that digital media offers on the production side have nevertheless expressed their resistance, on aesthetic grounds, to the migration of films from cinemas to small screens. David Lynch, whose psychological drama films tend toward the gothically strange, and James Cameron, who makes pull-out-all-the-stops action films, have both gone on record lamenting the practice of watching films on mobile phones. At the press conference announcing the Blu-ray release of *Avatar*, Cameron stated: "If someone wants to watch it on an iPhone, I'm not going to stop them, especially if they're paying for it, but I don't recommend it. I think it's dumb." (Chacksfield) On the DVD release of *Inland Empire* (2006), a film Lynch shot using a low-resolution digital camera, the director provides an interview that includes his thoughts on the subject: "if you're playing the movie on a telephone," he states, "you will never in a trillion years experience the film. You will think you have experienced it, but you'll be cheated."

Given the substantial growth of investment in digital and 3D screens around the world, it's clear that the exhibitor chains are betting that their multiplexes will remain a viable choice as a venue for watching movies. Home cinemas, now enhanced with large format, high definition televisions and the internet streaming possibilities of Blu-ray, may be the movie theater's biggest competitor, rather than handheld devices such as mobile phones. But one aspect of the cinema's future is clear: a plethora of opportunities exist for viewing amateur films on YouTube and Vimeo; for watching avant-garde films by recognized artists on Ubu; for catching trailers on mobile phones; and for seeing lengthy Hollywood spectacles in movie theaters equipped with the latest, most sophisticated projection equipment.

There seem to be no limits to the possibilities afforded to film culture by digital technologies. Yet, the fundamental questions in film studies remain the same ones that fans, critics, and scholars have been tackling for decades: does technological change drive film style or does it work the other way around? Will greater access to filmmaking tools help individuals to create new forms of film art, and new methods for creating that art? Will new institutions arise, in the form of new business models or cultural movements, to accompany the digital revolution in film culture? In addition to technological change, what other historical and cultural circumstances are relevant to the changing patterns within film production and consumption?

Questions specific to this historical moment relate to the transition from film to digital media: How will traditional modes of filmmaking on 16 mm or 35 mm film fare in the next decade? What will happen to the library of existing films, which some may deem obsolete—what will be preserved, and who will be able to see them? What, if any, are the implications of losing the celluloid object—the film reel—that has been the focus of film study and theorizing for more than a century?

We would suggest that cinema as an art form and social practice is not dependent upon any single type of technology. We consider film studies in the broadest sense to be a field that examines, from a variety of methods and perspectives, the way people interact with the imaginary worlds created by people they may know, and people they will never meet. They may interact with screens individually, using technologies such as the kinetoscope or cell phone, or as part of a group, in front of a home theater or at a movie theater. The aesthetic challenges and social character of cinema will continue to inspire admiration and disapproval, awe, wonder, and curiosity, across all of these modes of engagement.

Works Consulted

Abramovitz, Rachel. "Avatar's Animated Acting." *L.A. Times*. February 18, 2010. **www.latimes.com**.

Allen, Michael. *Contemporary US Cinema*. Edinburgh Gate: Longman/Pearson, 2003.

Barnes, Brooks. "Ad Budget Tight? Call the P.R. Machine." *The New York Times*. November 21, 2009. **www.nytimes.com**.

Belton, John. "Digital Cinema: A False Revolution," *October*, 100 (2002). Academic Search Elite. Online. Ebscohost. January 21, 2004.

Biskind, Peter. *Easy Riders, Raging Bulls: How the Sex-Drugs-and Rock 'n' Roll Generation Saved Hollywood*. New York: Simon and Schuster, 1998.

Brooker, Will. "Camera-Eye, CG-Eye: Videogames and the 'Cinematic.'" *Cinema Journal* 48.3 (Spring 2009): pp. 122–8.

Captain, Seán. "Will Digital Cinema Can Pirates?" *Wired News*. January 3, 2006. **www.wired. com/ news/technology/0,69922-0.html**. October 1, 2006.

Carvell, Tim. "Hello, Mr. Chips (Goodbye, Mr. Film)," *Fortune*, 140 (1999). Academic Search Elite. Online. Ebscohost. January 21, 2004.

Chacksfield, Marc. "James Cameron: Watching *Avatar* on an iPhone is Dumb." Techradar.com. **www.techradar.com**.

Chatfield, Tom. "Videogames now Outperform Hollywood Movies." *The Observer*. September 27, 2009. **www.guardian.co.uk**.

Cieply, Michael. "For Movie Stars, the Big Money is now Deferred." *The New York Times*. March 4, 2010. **www.nytimes.com**.

——————. "For Hollywood, Stand-Ins Play California's Part." *The New York Times*. February 5, 2010. A1; A3.

Cohen, Tyler. "Cinema: Ticket for One?" *Forbes*, April 28, 2003: n. page. Online. Safari. February 6, 2004.

Cook, David. "Auteur Cinema and the 'Film Generation' in 1970s Hollywood," in *The New American Cinema*, ed. Jon Lewis. Durham, NC: Duke University Press, 1998, pp. 11-37.

——————. *A History of Narrative Film*. New York: Norton, 1996.

Cowie, Peter. *Coppola: A Biography*. New York: Da Capo, 1994.

Culkin, Nigel, and Keith Randle. "Digital Cinema: Opportunities and Challenges." *Convergence*, 9/4 (2003), pp. 79-98.

Debruge, Peter. "Mumblecore goes mainstream." *Variety*. February 29, 2008. **www.variety.com/**.

Denby, David. "Disasters." *The New Yorker*. September 4, 2006, pp. 139-41.

——————. "The Moviegoers: Why Don't People Love the Right Movies Anymore?" in *The Best American Movie Writing 1999*, ed. Peter Bogdanovich. New York: St. Martin's, 1999, pp. 6-19.

——————. "Youthquake: mumblecore movies." *The New Yorker*. March 16, 2009. **www. newyorker.com**.

Doherty, Thomas. "DVD, PDQ," *The Chronicle of Higher Education*, April 26, 2002: n. page. Online. Safari. May 1, 2002.

Ebert, Roger. "Start the Revolution Without Digital," *volksmovie.com*. **http://www.volksmovie.com/ rants/archive/rogerebert.html**.

Ellis, Jack, and Virginia Wright Wexman. *A History of Film*, 5th edn. Boston: Allyn and Bacon, 2002.

Fellini, Federico. *Fellini on Fellini*. Trans. Isabel Quigley. Cambridge and New York: Da Capo Press, 1996.

Gilbert, Sarah. "It's udderly silly: California's 'happy cow' ads will be filmed in New Zealand." *Daily Finance*. November 15, 2009. **Daily Finance.com**.

Goldstein, Patrick. "Hollywood Gets Tough on the Talent: $20 million Movie Salaries Go Down the Tubes." *Los Angeles Times*. August 3, 2009. **www.latimes.com**.

Gomery, Douglas. "The Hollywood Studio System," in *The Oxford History of World Cinema*, ed. Geoffrey Nowell-Smith. Oxford and New York: Oxford University Press, 1996, pp. 43-53.

Harkin, James. "Losing the Plot." *The Observer*. March 22, 2009. **www.guardian.co.uk**.

Hayes, Dade and Jonathan Bing. *Open Wide: How Hollywood Box Office became a National Obsession*. New York: Miramax, 2004.

Hill, John. "British Film Policy," in *Film Policy: International, National, and Regional Perspectives*, ed. Albert Moran. London: Routledge, 1996, pp. 101-13.

Hirschberg, Lynn. "Core Values." *The New York Times*. December 31, 2009. **www.nytimes.com**.

Hopewell, John and Emilio Mayorga. "Europe Leads in Digital Screens." *Variety*. March 12, 2010. **www. variety.com**.

"InDigEnt: Independent Digital Entertainment." **www.indigent.net**. October 1, 2006.

Itzkoff, Dave. "You Saw What in *Avatar*? Pass Those Glasses!" *The New York Times*. January 20, 2010. **www.nytimes.com**.

Jensen, Jeff. "Slithering Heights," *Entertainment Weekly*. August 4, 2006, p. 27.

Kinetz, Erika. "Hollywood and Bollywood Join Arms to Fight Piracy." Associated Press, March 19, 2010. **news.yahoo.com**.

Klosterman, Chuck. "The *Snakes on a Plane* Problem." *Esquire*. 146/2 (August 2006), pp. 60-2.

Kramer, Peter. "Post-Classical Hollywood," in *American Cinema and Hollywood*, ed. John Hill and Pamela Church Gibson. New York: Oxford University Press, 2000, pp. 63-83.

Lewis, Jon. "Money Matters: Hollywood in the Corporate Era," in *New American Cinema*, ed. Jon Lewis. Durham, NC: Duke University Press, 1998, pp. 87-121.

Lim, Dennis. "A Generation Finds its Mumble." *The New York Times*. August 19, 2007. **www.nytimes.com/2007/08/19/movies/19lim.html?8dpc**.

Maltby, Richard. "'Nobody Knows Everything': Post-Classical Historiographies and Consolidated Entertainment," in *Contemporary Hollywood Cinema*, ed. Steve Neale and Murray Smith. London: Routledge, 1998, pp. 21–57.

McClintock, Pamela and Andrew Stewart. "Big Ticket Price Increase for 3D Pics." *Variety*. March 24, 2010. **www.variety.com**.

McDonald, Paul and Janet Wasko. *The Contemporary Hollywood Film Industry*. London: Wiley-Blackwell, 2008.

McNary, Dave. "LA Shoots down 30% in 2009; overall offlot filming slid 19%" *Variety*. January 14, 2010. **www.variety.com**.

————. "Runaway Drain?" *Variety*. July 31, 2006. **www.variety.com**.

Mendiburu, Bernard. *3D Movie Making: Stereoscopic Digital Cinema from Script to Screen*. Focal Press: Burlington, MA, 2006.

Morrison, James. "Buzz Factor: The DVD Release of Todd Solondz's *Storytelling* itself Tells a Story about Contemporary Film Culture," *The Independent Weekly*, 19/30 (July 17–23, 2002), p. 52.

"MPAA Theatrical Market Statistics 2009." Motion Picture Association of America. **www.mpaa.org**.

Pfanner, Eric. "Foreign Films Get a Hand from Hollywood." *The New York Times*. May 17, 2009. **www.nytimes.com**.

Riambau, Esteve. "Public Money and Private Business (Or, How to Survive Hollywood's Imperialism): Film Production in Spain (1984–2002)," *Cineaste*, 29/1 (2004), pp. 56–61.

Riding, Alan. "Filmmakers Seek Protection from U.S. Dominance," *New York Times*, February 5, 2003, p. B3.

Rosenbaum, Jonathan. *Movies as Politics*. Berkeley: University of California Press, 1997.

Ross, Matthew. "Industry Spotlight" DV Approaches the Mainstream." *Indiewire People*. July 31, 2002. **www.indiewire.com/people/int_Winick_Gary_020731.html**. October 1, 2006.

Schamus, James. "A Rant," *The End of Cinema As We Know It: American Film in the Nineties*, ed. Jon Lewis. New York: New York University Press, 2001.

Schatz, Thomas. *The Genius of the System: Hollywood Filmmaking in the Studio Era*. New York: Pantheon, 1988.

Scott, Allen John. *On Hollywood: The Place, The Industry*. Princeton, NJ: Princeton University Press, 2005.

Seagrave, Kerry. *American Films Abroad: Hollywood's Domination of the World's Movie Screens from the 1890s to the Present*. Jefferson: McFarland, 1997.

Seguin, Denis. "The Battle for Hollywood North." *Canadian Business*, 76 (2003). Academic Search Elite. Online. Ebscohost. January 21, 2004.

Sharkey, Betsy. 'Paranormal Activity': Somewhere Hitchcock is smiling." *Los Angeles Times: The Guide*. October 3, 2009. **www.calendarlive.com**.

Sklar, Robert. *Film: An International History of the Medium*, 2nd edn. Upper Saddle River, NJ: Prentice-Hall, 2002.

Smith, Zack. "A Decade of Wonder and Tumult." *Independent Weekly* 27.1. January 6, 2010. pp. 15–16.

"Tangled Webs." *The Economist*, 363 (2002). Academic Search Elite. Online. Ebscohost. January 21, 2004.

Taubin, Amy. "All Talk? Supposedly the voice of its generation, the indie film movement known as Mumblecore has had its 15 minutes." *Film Comment*. Nov/Dec 2007. **www.filmlinc.com**.

Telotte, J.P. "*The Blair Witch Project* Project," *Film Quarterly*, 54 (2001). Academic Search Elite. Online. Ebscohost. January 21, 2004.

Thompson, Kristin, and David Bordwell. *Film History: An Introduction*, 2nd edn. Boston: McGraw-Hill, 2003.

"UK movie chain boycotts *Alice* in DVD dispute." Associated Press. February 23, 2010.

"UK Pioneers Digital Film Network." *BBC News*. 26 February 2005. **News.bbc.co.uk/2/hi/technology/4297865.stm**. October 1, 2006.

Van Couvering, Alicia. "What I meant to Say." *Filmmaker Magazine*. Spring 2007. **www.filmmakermagazine.com/spring2007/features/mumblecore.php**.

Vasey, Ruth. "The Worldwide Spread of Cinema," *The Oxford History of World Cinema*, ed. Geoffrey Nowell-Smith. Oxford: Oxford University Press, 1996, pp. 53–62.

"Worldwide Box Office Continues to Soar; U.S. Admissions on the Rise." MPAA Press Release. March 10, 2010. **www.mpaa.org**.

Wyatt, Justin. "From Roadshow to Saturation Release: Majors, Independents, and Marketing/Distribution Innovations," in *New American Cinema*, ed. Jon Lewis. Durham, NC: Duke University Press, 1998, pp. 64–86.

Yamato, Jen. "Is Mumblecore a Dirty Word?" *Cinematical.com*. December 19, 2009. **www.cinematical.com/**.

Glossary

180-degree rule A continuity editing rule for positioning the camera in order to maintain consistent screen direction. The camera does not move across an imagined line drawn between two characters, for example, because to do so would reverse their positions in the frame.

3D The exploitation of stereoscopic vision to produce the illusion of depth. Human beings perceive depth because they view the world with two eyes; in cinema, various film and digital technologies attempt to recreate this phenomenon.

30-degree rule The convention that the camera should move at least 30 degrees any time there is a cut within a scene.

Academy ratio The aspect ratio of 1.33:1, standardized by the Academy of Motion Picture Art and Sciences until the development of widescreen formats in the 1950s. See also **Aspect ratio**.

Acousmetre A disembodied voice. Michel Chion theorizes that delaying or withholding the source of the voice endows the voice with mysterious powers.

Actualités Early films that documented everyday events, such as workers leaving a factory.

ADR (Automatic dialogue replacement) A technique for recording synchronized dialogue in post-production, using a machine that runs forward and backward. Also called "looping," because it is achieved by cutting several identical lengths of developed film and having actors record the dialogue repeatedly.

Aerial shot A shot filmed from an airplane or helicopter.

Analog video A videotape system that records images onto magnetic tape, using electronic signals.

Anamorphic lens A technique for creating a widescreen aspect ratio using regular 35 mm cameras and film. During shooting, an anamorphic lens squeezes the image at a ratio of 2:1 horizontally onto a standard film frame. During projection, an anamorphic lens on the projector unsqueezes the image, creating a widescreen aspect ratio during presentation. See also **Aspect ratio**.

Animation Creating the appearance of movement by drawing a series of frames that are projected sequentially, rather than photographing a series of still images.

Anime A style of Japanese animation, distinguished primarily by the fact that it is not all geared for young audiences.

Antagonist A character who in some way opposes the protagonist, leading to protracted conflict.

Aperture A small, variable opening on a camera lens that regulates the amount of light entering the camera and striking the surface of the film.

Apparatus theory A body of thought initiated by the French theorist Jean-Louis Baudry, which argues that the film medium's technological apparatus—including lenses, cameras, and projectors—and not only the content of films, is inherently ideological.

Aspect ratio The shape of the image onscreen as determined by the width (horizontal dimension) of the frame relative to its height (vertical dimension). An image with an aspect ratio of 1.33:1 (Academy ratio) will be thirty-three percent wider than it is high. See also **Academy ratio**.

Assistant editor A member of a film crew who assists the editor with various tasks, including taking footage to the lab, checking the condition of the negative, cataloging footage, and supervising optical effects, often produced by an outside company.

Aural object The term French film theorist Christian Metz used to describe film sound, which, he argued, is often wrongly treated as an attribute of the image rather than as an entity in and of itself, with its own aesthetic characteristics.

Auteur Translates as "author." A term for film directors that was popularized by French film critics and refers to film directors with their own distinctive style.

Available light Also called "natural light," the process of using sunlight rather than artificial studio lights when filming.

Avant-garde film Also called "experimental film" or "underground cinema." The goal of avant-garde filmmakers is not commercial success, but artistic invention. Avant-garde films are generally made by one person or a small group, distributed in very limited ways, and exhibited at specialized venues such as universities, museums, and cinema clubs.

Average shot length The average length in seconds of a series of shots, covering a portion of a film or an entire film. A measure of pace within a scene or in the film as a whole.

Backstage musical A musical film in which each song and dance number is narratively motivated by a plot that situates characters in performance contexts.

Backstory The details of a character's past that emerge as the film unfolds, and which often play a role in character motivation.

Base A flexible celluloid strip that, along with the emulsion layer, comprises 35 mm film stock.

Best boy A crew member who assists the gaffer in managing lighting and electrical crews.

Blaxploitation An action film cycle of the late 1960s and early 1970s that featured bold, rebellious African-American characters.

Bleach bypass A process of film development that involves leaving the silver grains in the emulsion rather than bleaching them out. This produces desaturated color.

Block booking An outlawed studio era practice, where studios forced exhibitors to book groups of films at once, thus ensuring a market for their failures along with their successes.

Blockbuster A large-budget film whose strategy is to swamp the competition through market saturation.

Blocking A production term referring to coordinating actors' movements with lines of dialogue.

Blue screen A technique used during production to create traveling mattes for special visual effects. Live action is filmed in front of a blue screen and a matte (black mask) created for use when filming a separate background. The live-action footage is joined with the background footage (which essentially has a black hole that the live action fills). See also **Green screen**.

Brechtian distanciation Drawing attention to the process of representation (including narrative and characterization) to break the theatrical illusion and elicit a distanced, intellectual response in the audience.

B-roll Secondary footage that is interspersed with master shots, sometimes in the form of footage shot for another production or archival footage.

Cameo A short screen appearance by a celebrity, playing himself or herself.

Camera distance The space between the camera and the subject it is filming. The effect of camera distance depends on other visual, narrative, and sound details and patterns. While, for example, long shots (with a large distance between camera and subject) may evoke a sense of a character's powerlessness, the specific effect must be considered in relation to a film's overall ideas and themes.

Canted angle Also called a "Dutch angle," a shot resulting from a static camera that is tilted to the right or left, so that the subject in the frame appears at a diagonal.

Cel A transparent sheet on which animation artists draw images. The sheet is laid over an unchanging background, allowing animation artists to draw only the elements that change from frame to frame.

Character actor An actor whose career rests on playing minor or secondary quirky characters rather than leading roles.

Charge coupled device The chip in a video camera that converts the incoming light to an electronic signal.

Chiaroscuro The artful use of light and dark areas in the composition in black and white filmmaking.

Cinerama A widescreen process that uses three cameras, three projectors, and a wide, curved screen.

City symphony A type of short film that blends elements of documentary and avant-garde film to document and often to celebrate the wonder of the modern city.

Classical style A style associated with Hollywood filmmaking of the studio and post-studio eras, in which efficient storytelling, rather than gritty realism or aesthetic innovation, is of paramount importance.

Close-up A shot taken when the camera is so close to a subject that it fills the frame. It is most commonly used for a shot that isolates and encompasses a single actor's face, to emphasize the expression of emotion.

Closure A characteristic of conventional narrative form, where the conclusion of the film wraps up all loose ends in a form of resolution, though not necessarily with a happy ending.

Color consultant A specialist who monitors the processing of color on the set and in the film lab.

Color filter A type of filter that absorbs certain wavelengths but leave others unaffected. On black and white film, color filters lighten or darken tones. On color film, they can produce a range of effects.

Color timing Because film stock is sensitive to the color of light, directors work with film labs in post-production to monitor the color scheme of each scene in a film, making adjustments for consistency and aesthetic effect.

Compilation film A film composed entirely of footage from other films.

Compositing Creating images during post-production by joining together photographic or CGI material shot or created at different times and places.

Composition The visual arrangement of objects, actors, and space within the frame.

Composition in depth A technique of arranging the actors on the set to take advantage of deep-focus cinematography, which allows for many planes of depth in the film frame to remain in focus.

Computer-generated imagery (CGI) Images that originate from computer graphics technology, rather than photography.

Continuity editing Also called "invisible editing," a system devised to minimize the audience's awareness of shot transitions, especially cuts, in order to improve the flow of the story and avoid interrupting the viewer's immersion in it.

Continuity editor A crew member whose job is to maintain consistency in visual details from one shot to the next.

Continuity error Any noticeable but unintended discrepancy from one shot to the next in costume, props, hairstyle, posture, etc.

Crab dolly A wheeled platform with wheels that rotate, so the dolly can change direction.

Crane shot A shot taken from a camera mounted on a crane that moves three-dimensionally in space.

Cut An abrupt shot transition that occurs when Shot A is instantaneously replaced by Shot B. A cut joins two non-consecutive frames of film.

Cutaway A shot that focuses audience attention on precise details that may or may not be the focus of characters.

Dailies Also called "rushes," footage exposed and developed quickly so that the director can assess the day's work.

Day for night The practice of shooting during the day but using filters and under-exposure to create the illusion of nighttime.

Deep-focus cinematography A cinematography technique that produces an image with many planes of depth in focus. It can be accomplished by using a small aperture ("stopping down the lens"), a large distance between camera and subject, and/or a lens of short focal length (wide-angle lens).

Dénouement The falling or unraveling action after the climax of a narrative that leads to resolution.

Depth of field The distance that appears in focus in front of and behind the subject. It is determined by the aperture, distance, and focal length of lens.

Desaturated Muted, washed-out color that contains more white than a saturated color.

Descriptive claim A neutral account of the basic plot and style of a film, a part of a film, or a group of films.

Diegesis The imagined world of the story.

Diffusion filters These filters bend the light coming into the lens, softening and blurring the image.

Digital cinema Also called "d-cinema." Not to be confused with digital cinematography (shooting movies on digital video), this term refers to using digital technologies for exhibition.

Digital compositing Creating an image by combining several elements created separately using computer graphics rather than photographic means.

Digital set extension Using computer graphics to "build" structures connected to the actual architecture on set or location.

Digital video A system for recording images on magnetic tape using a digital signal, that is, an electronic signal comprised of 0s and 1s.

Direct address Sound and visual technique that presents one or more characters speaking into the camera as if talking to the film audience.

Direct cinema Also called *cinéma vérité*, a documentary style in which the filmmaker attempts to remain as unobtrusive as possible, recording without obvious editorial comment.

Direct sound Sound recorded on a set, on location or, for documentary film, at an actual real-world event, as opposed to dubbed in post-production through ADR or looping.

Director The person in charge of planning the style and look of the film with the production designer and director of photography, working with actors during principal photography, and collaborating with the editor on the final version.

Dissolve A shot transition that involves the gradual disappearance of the image at the same time that a new image gradually comes into view.

Dolly A platform on wheels, used for mobile camera shots.

Double exposure A technique of exposing film frames, then rewinding the film and exposing it again, which results in an image that combines two shots in a single frame.

Dutch angle See **Canted angle**.

Dye coupler A chemical embedded in the emulsion layer of film stock that, when developed after exposure, releases a particular color dye (red, green, or blue).

Editor A person responsible for putting a film together from a mass of developed footage, making decisions regarding pace, shot transitions, and which scenes and shots will be used.

Emulsion A chemical coating on film stock containing light-sensitive grains.

Episodic A non-standard narrative organization that assumes a "day in the life" quality rather than the highly structured three-act or four part narrative, and that features loose or indirect cause–effect relationships.

Establishing shot In a standard shot sequence, the establishing shot is the first shot. Its purpose is to provide a clear representation of the location of the action.

Ethnographic film A type of documentary film whose purpose is to present the way of life of a culture or subculture.

Evaluative claim A statement that asserts a judgment that a given film or group of films is good or bad, based on specific criteria, which may or may not be stated.

Exposition Dense accumulation of detail conveyed in the opening moments of a film.

Exposure Light striking the emulsion layer of the film, activating light-sensitive grains.

Exposure latitude The measurement of how "forgiving" a film stock is. It determines whether an acceptable image will be produced when the film stock is exposed to too little or too much light.

Extra An uncredited actor, usually hired for crowd scenes.

Extradiegetic Also called "non-diegetic," any element in the film that is not a part of the imagined story world.

Extreme close-up A shot taken from a vantage point so close that only a part of the subject is visible. An extreme close-up of an actor might show only an eye or a portion of the face.

Extreme long shot A shot that makes the human subject very small in relation to his or her environment. The entire figure from head to toe is onscreen and dwarfed by the surroundings.

Extreme wide-angle lens Also called a "fish-eye lens." With a focal length of 15 mm or less, this lens presents an extremely distorted image, where objects in the center of the frame appear to bulge toward the camera.

Eye-level shot A shot taken from a level camera located approximately 5 to 6 feet from the ground, simulating the perspective of a person standing before the action presented.

Eyeline match A continuity editing technique that preserves spatial continuity by using a character's line of vision as motivation for a cut.

Fabula A chronological and complete account of all the events in a narrative. Also referred to as the "story." See also **Syuzhet**.

Fade-out A shot transition where shot A slowly disappears as the screen becomes black before shot B appears. A fade-in is the reverse of this process.

Fast A description of film stock that is highly sensitive to light.

Fast motion Recording images at a slower speed than the speed of projection (24 frames per second). Before cameras were motorized, this was called undercranking. Fewer frames are exposed in one minute, so, when projected at 24 fps, that action takes less than a minute on screen and appears unnaturally rapid.

Figure placement and movement The arrangement of actors on screen as a compositional element that suggests themes, character development, emotional content, and visual motifs.

Film stock Thin, flexible material comprised of base and emulsion layers, onto which light rays are focused and which is processed in chemicals to produce film images.

Filter A device used to manipulate the amount and/or color of light entering the lens.

First-person narration A story narrated by one of the characters within the story, using the "I" voice.

Fish-eye lens See **Extreme wide-angle lens**.

Flashback The non-chronological insertion of events from the past into the present day of the story world.

Flashing Also called "prefogging," a cinematographic technique that exposes raw film stock to light before, during, or after shooting, resulting in an image with reduced contrast. This effect can also be created using digital post-production techniques.

Flashforward The non-chronological insertion of scenes of events yet to happen into the present day of the story world.

Focal length The distance in millimeters from the optical center of a lens to the plane where the sharpest image is formed while focusing on a distant object.

Focus puller A crew member whose job is to measure the distance between the subject and the camera lens, marking the ring on the camera lens, and ensuring that the ring is turned precisely so that the image is in focus.

Fog filter Glass filters whose surface is etched with spots that refract light, so they create the appearance of water droplets in the air.

Foley artist A crew member who works in post-production in a specially equipped studio to create the sounds of the story world, such as the shuffling of shoes on various surfaces for footsteps.

Forced development A technique of "pushing" the film (overdeveloping it) to correct problems of underexposure (resulting from insufficient light during shooting) by increasing image contrast.

Forced perspective A system of constructing and arranging buildings and objects on the set so that they diminish in size dramatically from foreground to background, which creates the illusion of depth.

Formalist style An alternative to classical and realist styles, formalism is a self-consciously interventionist approach that explores ideas, abstraction, and aesthetics rather than focusing on storytelling (as in classical films) or everyday life (as in realist films).

Four-part structure A contemporary modification of the standard three-act structure that identifies a critical turning point at the halfway mark of most narrative films.

Frame narration The plotline that surrounds an embedded tale. The frame narration may or may not be as fully developed as the embedded tale.

Freeze frame Projecting a series of frames of film with the same image, which appears to stop the action.

Front projection A technique to join live action with pre-recorded background images. A projector is aimed at a half-silvered mirror that reflects the background, which the camera records as being located behind the actors.

Frozen time moment A visual effect achieved through the use of photography and digital techniques that appears to stop time and allow the viewer to travel around the subject and view it from a multitude of vantage points.

Gaffer A crew member who reports to the Director of Photography (DP) and is in charge of tasks involving lighting and electrical needs.

Gauge The gauge of the film stock is its width, measured across the frame. Typical sizes are 8 mm, 16 mm, 35 mm and 70 mm.

Genre A class or type of film, such as the Western or the horror movie. Films belonging to a particular genre share narrative, visual, and/or sound conventions.

Genre conventions The rules of character, setting, and narrative that films belonging to a genre—such as Westerns, horror films, and screwball comedies—generally obey.

German Expressionism A film style that emerged in the 1910s in Germany. It was heavily indebted to the Expressionist art movement of the time and influenced subsequent horror films and *film noir*.

Glass shot A type of matte shot, created by positioning a pane of optically flawless glass with a painting on it between the camera and scene to be photographed. This combines the painting on the glass with the set or location—seen through the glass—behind it.

Go-motion A digital technique developed by Industrial Light and Magic, which builds movement sequences from single frames of film.

Grain Suspended particles of silver in the film's emulsion, which may become visible in the final image as dots.

Graphic match A shot transition that emphasizes the visual similarities between two consecutive shots.

Green screen A compositing method that allows cinematographers to combine live action and settings that are filmed or created separately. Actors are filmed against a green or blue background. During post-production, this background is filled in with an image through the use of a traveling matte. See also **Blue screen**.

Handheld shot A shot taken by a camera that is held manually rather than supported by a tripod, crane, or Steadicam. Generally, such shots are shaky, owing to the motion of the camera operator.

Hard light Light emitted from a relatively small source positioned close to the subject. It tends to be unflattering because it creates deep shadows and emphasizes surface imperfections.

High-angle shot A shot taken from a camera positioned above the subject, looking down at it.

High concept film A post-studio era Hollywood film designed to appeal to the broadest possible audience by fusing a simple story line with major movie stars and mounting a lavish marketing campaign.

High-key lighting Lighting design that provides an even illumination of the subject, with many facial details washed out. High-key lighting tends to create a hopeful mood, in contrast to low-key lighting.

Hollywood blacklist Individuals who were prevented from working in the film industry because of their suspected involvement with Communist interests.

Hollywood Ten Ten Hollywood writers and directors cited for Contempt of Congress for refusing to cooperate with the House Committee on Un-American Activities' attempts to root out Communists in the film industry.

Horizontal integration A term that refers to the organization of an industry wherein one type of corporation also owns corporations in allied industries, for example, film production and video games.

Hue Color. The strength of a hue is measured by its saturation or desaturation.

Hybrid A film that fuses the conventions of two or more genres.

Insert A shot that interrupts a scene's master shot and may include character reactions or cutaways.

Integrated musical A musical in which some or all musical numbers are not motivated by the narrative; for example, characters sing and dance throughout the film but at least some performances are not staged for an onscreen audience. Examples include *Oklahoma*, *The Umbrellas of Cherbourg*, *Grease*, and *Chicago*.

Interlaced scanning A property of older television monitors, where each frame was scanned as two fields: one consisting of all the odd numbered lines, the other all the even lines. If slowed down, the television image would appear to sweep down the screen one line at a time.

Interpellation Louis Althusser's term for the way in which a society creates its subjects/citizens through ideological (as opposed to repressive) state apparatuses, which include education, media, religion, and the family.

Interpretive claim A statement that presents an argument about a film's meaning and significance.

Intertextual reference A narrative, visual, or sound element that refers viewers to other films or works of art.

Iris in A form of shot transition, generally concluding a scene, where a circular mask constricts around the image until the entire frame is black.

Iris out The reverse of iris in: an iris expands outward until the next shot takes up the entire screen.

Jump cut An abrupt, inexplicable shift in time and place of an action not signaled by an appropriate shot transition.

Kuleshov effect A mental phenomenon by which viewers derive more meaning from the interaction of two sequential shots than from a single shot in isolation.

Lens A glass element on a camera that focuses light rays so that the image of the object appears on the surface of the film.

Letterboxing A process of transferring film to video tapes or DVDs so that the original aspect ratio of the film is preserved.

Lightning mix A sound editing technique that links several scenes through parallel and overlapping sounds. Each sound is associated with one scene, unlike a sound bridge, where a sound from one scene bleeds into that of another.

Line of action The narrative path of the main or supporting characters, also called a plotline. Complex films may have several lines of action.

Line reading The way an actor delivers a line of dialogue, including pauses, inflection, and emotion.

Long shot A camera shot taken at a large distance from the subject. Using the human body as the subject, a long shot captures the entire human form.

Long take A relatively long, uninterrupted shot, generally of a minute or more.

Looping See **ADR**.

Loose framing A technique of leaving empty space around the subject in the frame, in order to convey openness and continuity of visible space and to imply off-screen space.

Low-angle shot A shot taken from a camera positioned below the subject.

Low-key lighting Lighting design in which the greater intensity of the key light makes it impossible for the fill to eliminate shadows, producing a high-contrast image (with many grades of light and dark), a number of shadows, and a somber mood.

Major studios The five vertically integrated corporations that exerted the greatest control over film production, distribution, and exhibition in the studio era: MGM, Warner Brothers, RKO, Twentieth Century Fox, and Paramount.

Masking A method for producing a widescreen image without special lenses or equipment, using standard film stock and blocking out the top and bottom of the frame to achieve an aspect ratio of 1.85:1.

Master positive The first print made from a film negative.

Master shot A single take that contains an entire scene.

Match on action A rule in continuity editing, which dictates that if a cut occurs while a character is in the midst of an action, the subsequent shot must begin so that audiences see the completion of that action.

Matte A black masking device used to block out a portion of the frame, usually for the insertion of other images. See also **Blue screen** and **Traveling matte**.

Matte painting A painting used on the set as a portion of the background.

Medium close-up A shot that includes a human figure from the shoulders up.

Medium long shot A shot that depicts a human body from the feet up.

Medium shot A shot depicting the human body from the waist up.

Method acting A style of stage acting developed from the teachings of Constantin Stanislavsky, which trains actors to get into character through the use of emotional memory.

Minor studios Smaller corporations that did not own distribution and/or exhibition companies in the studio era, including Universal, Columbia, and United Artists.

Mixing A process of blending the three elements of the sound track (dialogue, music, and effects) in post-production.

Mockumentary A fiction film (often a comedy) that uses documentary conventions on fictional rather than real-world subject matter.

Montage sequence A series of related scenes joined through elliptical editing that indicates the passage of time.

Morphing An animation technique that uses a computer program to interpolate frames to produce the effect of an object or creature changing gradually into something different. The program calculates the way the image must change in order for the first image to become the second over a series of frames.

Motif Any narrative, visual, or sound element that is repeated and thereby acquires and reflects its significance to the story, characters, or themes of the film.

Motivation The central cause(s) behind a character's actions.

Mumblecore Extremely low budget, DIY American independent filmmaking, beginning in the early 2000s. Often compared to the French New Wave because of its improvisational style and personal subject matter.

Narrative A story; a chain of events linked by cause-and-effect logic.

Narrative sequencing The arrangement of images to depict a unified story time.

Natural-key lighting Lighting design where the key light is somewhat more intense than the fill light, so the fill does not eliminate every shadow. The effect is generally less cheerful than high-key lighting, but not as gloomy as low-key lighting.

Natural light See **Available light**.

Negative Exposed and developed film stock from which the master positive is struck. If projected, the negative would produce a reverse of the image, with dark areas appearing white and vice versa or, if color film, areas of color appearing as their complementary hue.

Negative cutter A technician responsible for splicing and assembling the film negative to the editor's specifications.

Neutral-density filter A filter that simply reduces the amount of light entering the lens, without affecting the color characteristics.

Newsreel A short documentary on current events, shown in movie theaters along with cartoons and feature films beginning in the 1930s.

Non-diegetic A term used for any narrative, sound, or visual element not contained in the story world. Also called "extradiegetic."

Normal lens Any lens with a focal length approximately equal to the diagonal of the frame. For 35 mm filmmaking, a 35–50 mm lens does not distort the angle of vision or depth. See also **Wide-angle lens** and **Telephoto lens**.

Oeuvre A director's, or another artist's, entire body of work.

Offscreen space A part of the story world implied by visual or sound techniques rather than being revealed by the camera.

Omniscient narration The technique of telling the story from an all-knowing viewpoint rather than that of one individual character. Films that use restricted narration limit the audience's perception to what one particular character knows, but may insert moments of omniscience.

On-the-nose dialogue Dialogue that re-states what is already obvious from images or action.

Open-ended A term describing a conclusion that does not answer all the questions raised regarding characters or storylines, nor tie up all loose ends.

Optical printer A machine used to create optical effects such as fades, dissolves, and superimpositions. Most are now created digitally.

Orthochromatic A term for film stock used in early cinema that was insensitive to red hues.

Outsourcing The practice of Hollywood studios contracting out post-production work to individuals or firms outside the U.S.

Out-take A scene filmed and processed but not selected to appear in the final version of the film.

Overexposure An effect created when more light than is required to produce an image strikes the film stock, so that the resulting image exhibits high contrast, glaring light, and washed out shadows. This effect may or may not be intentional on the filmmaker's part.

Overhead shot A shot taken from a position directly above the action, also called a "bird's eye shot."

Overlapping dialogue Sound design that blends the speech of several characters talking simultaneously, used to create spontaneity, although it may also confuse the audience.

Pan The horizontal turning movement of an otherwise immobile camera across a scene from left to right or vice versa.

Panchromatic A type of film stock that is sensitive to (in other words, registers) all tones in the color spectrum.

Panning and scanning Also called "full screen," the technique of re-shooting a widescreen film in order to convert it to the original television aspect ratio of 1.33 to 1. Rather than reproduce the original aspect ratio, as a letterboxed version does, a panned and scanned copy eliminates some of the visual information and introduces camera movement and editing that are not in the original.

Parallel A similarity established between two characters or situations that invites the audience to compare the two. It may involve visual, narrative, and/or sound elements.

Parallel editing A technique of cutting back and forth between action occurring in two different locations, which often creates the illusion that they are happening simultaneously. Also called "cross cutting."

Performance capture A production process that allows filmmakers to record the physical details of an actor's performance, using special costumes with reflective markers or LEDs, and turn it into digital code to create a complex animated version of that performance. It differs from motion capture in that it is achieved in real time.

Persistence of vision An optical effect whereby the eye continues to register a visual stimulus in the brain for a brief period after that stimulus has been removed.

Phenomenology A field within philosophy that attempts to study conscious experience objectively.

Phi phenomenon An optical effect whereby the human eye fills in gaps between closely spaced objects, so that two light bulbs flashing on and off are understood as one light moving back and forth.

Pixel A picture element, a measure of image density. There are approximately 18 million pixels in a frame of 35 mm film and 300,000–400,000 in a video image.

Pixilation Also called "stop motion photography." A technique of photographing a scene one frame at a time and moving the model between each shot.

Plot summary A brief chronological description of the basic events and characters in a film. It does not include interpretive or evaluative claims.

Plotline See **Line of action**.

Point-of-view shot A technique in which the audience temporarily shares the visual perspective of a character or a group of characters. The camera points in the direction that the character looks, simulating the character's field of vision.

Polarizing filters Filters that increase color saturation and contrast in outdoor shots.

Post-production The period after principal photography during which editing and looping take place, and special visual effects are added to the film.

Pre-fogging See **Flashing**.

Pre-production The period of time before principal photography during which actors are signed, sets and costumes designed, and locations scouted.

Product placement An agreement made between filmmakers and those who license the use of commercial products to feature those products in films, generally as props used by characters.

Production values A measure of the visual and sound quality of a film. Low-budget films tend to have lower production values because they lack the resources to devote to expensive pre- and post-production activities.

Progressive scanning An attribute of newer television monitors, where each frame is scanned by the electron beam as a single field. If slowed down, each frame would appear on the monitor in its entirety on the screen, rather than line by line, as is the case with interlaced scanning.

Promotion Materials intentionally released by studios to attract public attention to films and their stars. Promotion differs from publicity, which is information that is not (or does not appear to be) intentionally disseminated by studios.

Propaganda film A documentary or occasionally a narrative film that presents only one side of an argument or one approach to a subject.

Prostheses Devices that attach to actors' faces and/or bodies to change their appearance.

Protagonist A film's main character, one whose conflicts and motives drive the story forward.

Pulling A technique of underdeveloping exposed film stock (leaving it in a chemical bath a shorter amount of time than usual) in order to achieve the visual effect of reducing contrast.

Pushing A technique of overdeveloping exposed film stock (leaving it in the chemical bath longer than indicated) in order to increase density and contrast in the image.

Rack focus A change of focus from one plane of depth to another. As the in-focus subject goes out of focus, another object, which has been blurry, comes into focus in either the background or the foreground.

Realist style A film style that, in contrast to the classical and formalist styles, focuses on characters, place, and the spontaneity and digressiveness of life, rather than on highly structured stories or aesthetic abstraction.

Rear projection A technique used to join live action with a pre-recorded background image. A projector is placed behind a screen and projects an image onto it. Actors stand in front of the screen and the camera records them in front of the projected background.

Recursive action A technique of shooting a scene at a very high speed (96 frames per second), then adding and subtracting frames in post-production, "fanning out" the action through the overlapping images.

Re-establishing shot A shot that appears during or near the end of a scene and re-orients viewers to the setting.

Reframing A technique of shifting the camera angle, height or distance to take into account the motion of actors or objects within the frame.

Release prints Reels of film that are shipped to movie theaters for exhibition. Digital cinema, which can be distributed via satellite, broadband, or on media such as DVDs, may soon replace film prints because the latter are expensive to create, copy, and distribute.

Restricted narration A narrative approach that limits the audience's view of events to that of the main character(s) in the film. Occasional moments of omniscient narration may give viewers more information than the characters have at specific points in the narrative.

Reverse shot A shot in a sequence that is taken from the reverse angle of the shot previous to it.

Revisionist A genre film that radically modifies accepted genre conventions for dramatic effect.

Roadshowing A marketing strategy of screening a blockbuster prior to general release only in premier theaters.

Rotoscope A device that projects photographs or footage onto glass so that images can be traced by hand to create animated images.

Runaway production Film productions shot outside the U.S. for economic reasons.

Running time The length in minutes for a film to play in its entirety (for example, 120 minutes). Also referred to as "screen time."

Saturation The measure of intensity or purity of a color. Saturated color is purer than desaturated color, which has more white in it and thus offers a washed-out, less intense version of a color.

Scanning See **Panning and scanning**.

Scene A complete narrative unit within a film, with its own beginning, middle, and end. Often scenes are unified, and distinguished from one another, by time and setting.

Score A musical accompaniment written specifically for a film.

Scratching A technique of intentionally adding scratches in a film's emulsion layer for aesthetic purposes, such as to simulate home movie footage.

Screen time See **Running time**.

Screenplay The written blueprint for a film, composed of three elements: dialogue, sluglines (setting the place and time of each scene), and description. Feature-length screenplays typically run 90–130 pages.

Script supervisor A crew member responsible for logging the details of each take on the set so as to ensure continuity.

Second unit A production crew responsible not for shooting the primary footage but, instead, for remote location shooting and B-roll. See also **B-roll**.

Selective focus A technique of manipulating focus to direct the viewer's attention.

Semantics In grammar, the way certain words produce meaning in combination. Simply placing a verb after a noun—that is, using proper syntax (structure)—will not necessarily produce a meaningful sentence. An appropriate semantic relationship is required as well. In Rick Altman's genre theory, this term refers to clusters of attributes that define a genre on the surface level: for instance, horses, cowboy hats, tumbleweeds, and guns help to form the semantics of the Western.

Semiotics A science that explores sign systems (including, but not limited to, language) to determine how they create meaning in readers, listeners, and observers.

Set-up The individual arrangement of lighting and camera placement used for each shot.

Shooting script The annotated script, containing information about set-ups used during shooting.

Shot The building block of a scene; an uninterrupted sequence of frames that viewers experience as they watch a film, ending with a cut, fade, dissolve, etc. See also **Take**.

Shot/reverse shot A standard shot pattern that dictates that a shot of one character will be followed by a shot of another character, taken from the reverse angle of the first shot.

Shot transition The use of editing techniques, such as a fade or dissolve, to indicate the end of one scene and the beginning of another.

Shutter A camera device that opens and closes to regulate the length of time the film is exposed to light.

Slow A term applied to film stock that is relatively insensitive to light. This stock will not yield acceptable images unless the amount of light can be carefully controlled.

Slow motion A technique that involves filming at a speed faster than the speed of projection (24 frames per second), then projecting the footage at normal speed.

Because more frames are recorded per second, the action appears to slow down when projected. For example, if 36 frames are recorded in one second, capturing an action, when the footage is projected at 24 fps, it will take 1.5 seconds for that action to unfold.

Soft light Light emitted from a larger source that is scattered over a bigger area or reflected off a surface before it strikes the subject. Soft light minimizes facial details, including wrinkles.

Sound bridge A scene transition wherein sound from one scene bleeds over into the next scene, often resulting in a contrast between sound and image.

Soundtrack Everything audiences hear when they watch a sound film. The soundtrack is the composite of all three elements of film sound: dialogue, music, and sound effects.

Soviet montage An alternative to continuity editing, this style of editing was developed in silent Soviet cinema, based on the theory that editing should exploit the difference between shots to generate intellectual and emotional responses in the audience.

Spec script A screenplay written and submitted to a studio or production company without a prior contract or agreement.

Special visual effects Optical illusions created during production, including the use of matte paintings, glass shots, models, and prostheses.

Speed A measure of a film stock's sensitivity to light. "Fast" refers to sensitive film stock, while "slow" film is relatively insensitive.

Split screen An optical technique that divides the screen into two or more frames.

Standard shot pattern A sequence of shots designed to maintain spatial continuity. Scenes begin with an establishing shot, then move to a series of individual shots depicting characters and action, before re-establishing shots re-orient viewers to the setting.

Star filter A filter that creates points of light that streak outward from a light source.

Star persona Public identity created by marketing a film actor's performances, press coverage, and "personal" information to fans as the star's personality.

Star system A system initially developed for marketing films by creating and promoting stars as objects of admiration. The promotion of stars has now become an end in itself.

Steadicam A device worn by a camera operator that holds the motion picture camera, allowing it to glide smoothly through spaces unreachable by cameras mounted on a crane or other apparatus.

Stop motion photography See **Pixilation**.

Storyboard A series of individual drawings that provides a blueprint for the shooting of a scene.

Studio system A model of industrial organization in the film industry from about 1915 to 1946, characterized by the development of major and minor studios that produced, distributed and exhibited films, and held film actors, directors, art directors, and other technical crew under contract.

Subgenre A group of films within a given genre that share their own specific set of conventions that differentiate them from other films in the genre. For example, the slasher film is a subgenre of the horror genre.

Subtext An unstated meaning that underlies and is implied by spoken dialogue.

Superimposition A technique of depicting two layered images simultaneously. Images from one frame or several frames of film are added to pre-existing images, using an optical printer, to produce the same effect as a double exposure.

Swish pan A pan executed so quickly that it produces a blurred image, indicating rapid activity or, sometimes, the passage of time.

Syntax In linguistics, syntax refers to the rules of structure that produce meaningful sentences (see also **Semantics**). In film genre theory, the term refers to an underlying structure that organizes the semantic elements of a genre.

Syuzhet The selection and ordering of narrative events presented in a film, as distinct from the *fabula*, which is the chronological accounting of all events presented and suggested.

Tableau shot A long shot in which the film frame resembles the proscenium arch of the stage, distancing the audience.

Take A production term denoting a single uninterrupted series of frames exposed by a motion picture or video camera between the time it is turned on and the time it is turned off. Filmmakers shoot several takes of any scene and the film editor selects the most appropriate one to use. See also **Shot**.

Telecine A machine that converts film prints to videotape format.

Telephoto lens A lens with a focal length greater than 50 mm (usually between 80 mm and 200 mm), which provides a larger image of the subject than a normal or wide-angle lens but which narrows the angle of vision and flattens the depth of the image relative to normal and wide-angle lenses.

Text The term for a film's spoken dialogue, as opposed to the underlying meaning contained in the subtext.

Third-person narration Literary narration from a viewpoint beyond that of any one individual character.

Three-act structure The classical model of narrative form. The first act introduces characters and conflicts; the second act offers complication leading to a climax; the third act contains the *dénouement* and resolution.

Three-point lighting An efficient system developed for film lighting. In a standard lighting set-up, the key light illuminates the subject, the fill light eliminates shadows cast by the key light, and the back light separates the subject from the background.

Tight framing A visual effect created when the subject in the frame is restricted by the objects or the physical properties of the set.

Tilt A vertical, up-and-down, motion of an otherwise stationary camera.

Time-lapse photography A technique of recording very few images over a long period of time—say, one frame per minute or per day.

Tinting An early color process, involving bathing lengths of processed film in dye one scene at a time.

Toning An early color process that replaced silver halide grains with colored salts.

Tracking shot A technique of moving the camera, on a dolly, along a specially built track. Such shots often trace character movement laterally across the frame or in and out of the depth of the frame.

Trailer A short segment of film used to promote an upcoming release.

Traveling matte A system for combining two separately filmed images in the same frame that involves creating a matte (a black mask that covers portion of the image) for a live action sequence and using it to block out a portion of the frame when filming the background images. See also **Blue screen**.

Trombone shot A shot combining two kinds of movement: the camera tracks in toward the subject while the lens zooms out.

Turning point A narrative moment that signals an important shift of some kind in character or situation.

Two-shot A shot that contains two characters within the frame.

Typecasting The practice of repeatedly casting actors in similar roles across different films.

Undercranking A technique of running the motion picture camera at a speed slower than projection speed (24 frames per second), in order to produce a fast motion sequence when projected at normal speed. The term derives from early film cameras, which were cranked by hand.

Underexposure An effect created when too little light strikes the film during shooting. As a result the image will contain dark areas that appear very dense and dark (including shadows) and the overall contrast will be less than with a properly exposed image.

Vertical integration A business model adopted by the major studios during the Hollywood studio era, in which studios controlled all aspects of the film business, from production to distribution to exhibition.

Video assist A device attached to the film camera that records videotape of what has been filmed, allowing the director immediate access to video footage.

Vista Vision A film process that uses 35 mm film stock but changes the orientation of the film so that the film moves through the camera horizontally instead of vertically. The larger image is of higher quality than standard 35 mm processes.

Visual effects Optical illusions created during post-production.

Voice-over A direct vocal address to the audience, which may emanate from a character or from a narrating voice apparently unrelated to the diegesis.

Wide-angle lens A lens with a shorter focal length than a normal or telephoto lens (usually between 15 mm and 35 mm). The subject appears smaller as a result, but the angle of vision is wider and an illusion is created of greater depth in the frame.

Wide film A format that uses a larger film stock than standard 35 mm. IMAX, Omnimax, and Showscan are shot on 70 mm film. See also **Gauge**.

Widescreen Processes such as Cinemascope and Cinerama, developed during the 1950s to enhance film's size advantage over the smaller television image.

Wipe A scene transition in which the first frame of the incoming scene appears to push the last frame of the previous scene off the screen horizontally.

Wireframe The first step in the process of creating CGI. The wireframe is a three-dimensional computer model of an object, which is then rendered (producing the finished image) and animated (using simulated camera movement frame by frame).

Zoom in A technique of moving a zoom lens from a wide-angle position to a telephoto position, which results in a magnification of the subject within the frame, and keeps the subject in focus.

Zoom lens A lens with a variable focal length that allows changes of focal length while keeping the subject in focus.

Zoom out A technique of moving from the telephoto position to the wide-angle position of a zoom lens, which results in the subject appearing to become smaller within the frame, while remaining in focus.

Bibliography

Adair, Gilbert. "Eistenstein on Disney," in *Movies*. London: Penguin, 1999.

Addison, Heather. "Capitalizing their Charms: Cinema Stars and Physical Culture in the 1920s," *The Velvet Light Trap*, 50 (Fall 2002), pp. 15–34.

Allen, Michael. *Contemporary US Cinema*. Harlow, UK, and NY: Longman/Pearson, 2003.

American Cinematographer's Manual. Hollywood, CA: ASC Press, 1993.

Anderson, Barbara and Joseph. "The Myth of Persistence of Vision Revisited," *Journal of Film and Video*, 45/1 (Spring 1993), pp. 3–12.

"Aniston: *Break-Up* Was Therapeutic." CBS News.com, June 1, 2006. http://www.cbsnews.com/stories/2006/06/01/earlyshow/leisure/celebspot/main1673655shtml. August 28, 2006.

Ansen, David, and Jeff Giles. "The New Visionaries," *Newsweek*, 143/6 (September 2, 2004). Online. Academic Search Elite. February 26, 2004.

Appelo, Tim. "Chasing the Chador," *The Nation*, 272/17 (April 30, 2001). Online. Academic Search Elite. February 25, 2004.

Arden, Darlene. "The Magic of ILM." www.darlenearden.com/articleILM.htm. 6/22/04.

Ascher, Steven, and Edward Pincus. *The Filmmaker's Handbook: A Comprehensive Guide for the Digital Age*. New York: Plume, 1999.

Barbarow, George. "*Rashômon* and the Fifth Witness," in *"Rashômon": Akira Kurosawa, Director*. New Brunswick and London: Rutgers University Press, 1987, pp. 145–48.

Barclay, Steven. *The Motion Picture Image: From Film to Digital*. Boston: Focal Press, 2000.

Barnes, Colin. "Disabling Imagery and the Media: An Exploration of the Principles for Media Representations of Disabled People." *The British Council of Organisations of Disabled People*. Ryburn Publishing. http://studydisability.uoregon.edu/films.html. October 2, 2006.

Bazin, André. *Jean Renoir*. New York: Simon and Schuster, 1971. Trans. 1973.

Bazin, André. "The Evolution of the Language of Cinema," in *Film Theory and Criticism*, ed. Gerald Mast *et al.*, 4th edn. New York: Oxford University Press, 1992, pp. 155–67.

Belton, John. "Digital Cinema: A False Revolution," *October*, 100 (2002). Academic Search Elite. Online. Ebscohost. January 21, 2004.

Betz, Mark. "The Name above the (Sub)Title: Internationalism, Coproduction, and Polyglot European Art Cinema," *Camera Obscura*, 16/1 (2001). March 8, 2002. http://muse.jhu.edu/journals/camera_obscura/v016/16.1betz.htm.

Bignardi, Irene. "The Making of *The Battle of Algiers*," *Cineaste* (Spring 2000), pp. 14–22.

Biskind, Peter. *Easy Riders, Raging Bulls: How the Sex-Drugs-and Rock 'n' Roll Generation Saved Hollywood*. New York: Simon and Schuster, 1998.

Bizony, Piers. "Shipbuilding," in *The Making of "2001: A Space Odyssey."* New York: Random House, 2000, pp. 43–54.

Bogle, Donald. *Toms, Coons, Mulattoes, Mammies, and Bucks: An Interpretive History of Blacks in American Films*. New York: Continuum, 2001.

Bordwell, David. *On the History of Film Style*. Cambridge, MA: Harvard University Press, 1997.

Bordwell, David. "Story Causality and Motivation," in *The Classical Hollywood Cinema: Film Style and Mode of Production to 1960*, ed. David Bordwell *et al.* New York: Columbia University Press, 1985, pp. 12–23.

"Brad Pitt goes to extremes in *Troy*." Reuters. May 13, 2004. http://msnbc.msn.com/id/4953083. 6/20/2004.

Brakhage, Stan. "Remarks." *By Brakhage: An Anthology*. Criterion Collection DVD, 2003.

Brakhage, Stan. *Film at Wit's End: Eight Avant-garde Filmmakers*. New York: McPherson, 1989.

Brandt, Michael. "Traditional Film Editing vs. Electronic Nonlinear Film Editing: A Comparison of Feature Films," *Nonlinear 4: The Website of Digital Video and Film Editing*. http://www.nonlinear4.com/brandt.htm. May 16, 2002.

Brandy, Leo. "Genre: The Conventions of Connection," in *Film Theory and Criticism*, 4th edn. New York: Oxford University Press, 1992.

Brown, Georgia. "Heart of Darkness," *Village Voice*, 35 (September 11, 1990), p. 64.

Buscombe, Edward. *Stagecoach*. London: British Film Institute, 1992.

Carlsson, Sven. "Sound Design of *Star Wars*." Film Sound.org. http://www.filmsound.org/starwars/. August 13, 2006.

Carter, Angela. *Expletives Deleted*. London: Chatto and Windus, 1992.

Carvell, Tim. "Hello, Mr. Chips (Goodbye, Mr. Film)," *Fortune*, 140 (1999). Academic Search Elite. Online. Ebscohost. January 21, 2004.

Cavell, Stanley. *Pursuits of Happiness: The Hollywood Comedy of Remarriage*. Cambridge, MA: Harvard University Press, 1981.

Cawelti, John G. "*Chinatown* and Generic Transformation in Recent American Films," in *Film Genre Reader*, ed. Barry Keith Grant. Austin, TX: University of Texas Press, 1986, pp. 183–201.

Cellini, Joe. "An Interview with Walter Murch." http://www.apple.com/pro/film/murch/index.html. June 16, 2004.

Chanan, Michael. "Tomás Gutiérrez Alea," in *The Oxford History of World Cinema*, ed. Geoffrey Nowell-Smith. Oxford: Oxford University Press, 1996, p. 744.

Chion, Michel. *Audio-Vision: Sound on Screen*. New York: Columbia University Press, 1994.

Chivers, Sally. "The Horror of Becoming 'One of Us': Tod Browning's Freaks and Disability." *Screening Disability: Essays on Cinema and Disability*. Eds. Christopher R. Smit and Anthony Enns. Lanham: University Press of America, 2001, pp. 57–64.

Cineaste. Editorial, 28/1 (Winter 2002). Online. Academic Search Elite. February 25, 2004.

Clair, René. "The Art of Sound." *Film Sound. org*. http://lavender.fortunecity.com/hawkslane/575/art-of-sound.htm. August 11, 2006.

Clark, VeVe, Millicent Hodson, and Catrina Neiman (ed.) *The Legend of Maya Deren*, vol. 1, part 2. New York: Anthology Film Archives/Film Culture, 1984.

Cocks, Jay, and Martin Scorsese. *"The Age of Innocence": The Shooting Script*. New York: Newmarket Press, 1995.

Cohen, Tyler. "Cinema: Ticket for One?" *Forbes* (April 28, 2003): n. page. Online. Safari. February 6, 2004.

Collins, Nancy. "Lust and Trust," *Rolling Stone*, (July 8, 1999). *Academic Search Elite*. Online. Ebsco. January 9, 2004.

Combs, Richard. "New York, New York," *Sight and Sound* (Fall 1977), pp. 252–3.

Cook, David. "Auteur Cinema and the 'Film Generation' in 1970s Hollywood," in *The New American Cinema*, ed. Jon Lewis. Durham, NC: Duke University Press, 1998, pp. 11–37.

Cook, David. *A History of Narrative Film*, 3rd edn. New York: Norton, 1996.

Cook, Méira. "None of Us: Ambiguity as Moral Discourse in Tod Browning's *Freaks*." *Screening Disability: Essays on Cinema and Disability*. Eds. Christopher R. Smit and Anthony Enns. Lanham: University Press of America, 2001.

Corliss, Richard. "Gay and Gaudy," *Time*, 150/17 (October 27, 1997), p. 111.

Corner, John. *The Art of Record: A Critical Introduction to Documentary*. Manchester and NY: Manchester University Press, 1996.

Corrigan, Timothy. *A Cinema without Walls: Movies and Culture After Vietnam*. New Brunswick: Rutgers University Press, 1991.

Corrigan, Timothy. "*Auteurs* and the New Hollywood," in *The New American Cinema*, ed. Jon Lewis. Durham, NC: Duke University Press, 1998, pp. 38–63.

Cousins, Mark. *Scene by Scene*. London: Laurence King, 2002.

Crafton, Donald. "Tricks and Animation," in *The Oxford History of World Cinema*, ed. Geoffrey Nowell-Smith. Oxford and New York: Oxford University Press, 1997, pp. 71–8.

Creed, Barbara. "Horror and the Monstrous Feminine: An Imaginary Abjection," in *Feminist Film Theory*, ed. Sue Thornham. New York: New York University Press, 1999, pp. 251–66.

Culkin, Nigel, and Keith Randle. "Digital Cinema: Opportunities and Challenges," *Convergence*, 9/4 (2003), pp. 79–98.

Curtis, David. *Experimental Cinema: A Fifty Year Evolution*. New York: Dell, 1971.

DeCordova, Richard. *Picture Personalities: The Emergence of the Star System in America*. Urbana: University of Illinois Press, 1990.

Denby, David. "Killer: Two Views of Aileen Wuornos," *The New Yorker* (January 26, 2004), pp. 84–6.

Denby, David. "The Moviegoers: Why Don't People Love the Right Movies Anymore?" in *The Best American Movie Writing 1999*, ed. Peter Bogdanovich. New York: St. Martin's, 1999, pp. 6–19.

Denby, David. Review of *Ali*. *The New Yorker* (January 28, 2002), p. 27.

Digital Cinema Initiatives, LLC. "Digital Cinema System Specification." July 20, 2005. DCI_Digital_Cinema_System_Spec_v1.pdf: 1–176. October 1, 2006.

Dobbs, Lem. Commentary track. *The Limey* (DVD), dir. Steven Soderbergh. Artisan, 1999.

Doherty, Thomas. "DVD, PDQ," *The Chronicle of Higher Education* (April 26, 2002): n. page. Online. Safari. May 1, 2002.

Donalson, Melvin. *Black Directors in Hollywood*. Austin, TX: University of Texas Press, 2003.

Dyer, Richard. "Four Films of Lana Turner," in *Star Texts: Image and Performance in Film and Television*, ed. Jeremy G. Butler. Detroit: Wayne State University Press, 1991, pp. 214–39.

Dyer, Richard. *Heavenly Bodies: Film Stars and Society*. New York: St. Martins, 1986.

Dyer, Richard. *Stars*, 2nd edn. London: British Film Institute, 1998.

Dyer, Richard. *White*. London and New York: Routledge, 1997.

Ebert, Roger. "Start the Revolution Without Digital," volksmovie.com. http://www.volksmovie.com/rants/archive/rogerebert.html.

Economist, The. "On screen it's Iran's Shout," 336/7921 (January 7, 1995). Online. Academic Search Elite. February 25, 2004.

Eisenstein, Sergei. "A Dialectic Approach to Film Form." *Film Form*. San Diego, New York, and London: Harcourt Brace Jovanovich, 1949, pp. 45–63.

Eisenstein, S.M., V.I. Pudovkin, G.V. Alexandrov. "A Statement." *Film Sound.org*. http://lavender.fortunecity.com/hawkslane/575/statement.htm. August 11, 2006.

Eisner, Lotte. *The Haunted Screen*. Berkeley, CA: University of California Press, 1952. Trans. 1969.

Ellis, Jack C., and Virginia Wright Wexman. *A History of Film*, 5th edn. Boston: Allyn and Bacon, 2002.

Elsaesser, Thomas. *Weimar Cinema and After: Germany's Historical Imaginary*. New York: Routledge, 2000.

Fellini, Federico. *Fellini on Fellini*, trans. Isabel Quigley. Cambridge and New York: Da Capo Press, 1996.

Festinger, Rob, and Todd Field. *In the Bedroom*. New York: Hyperion, 2002.

Figes, Orlando. *A People's Tragedy*. New York: Viking, 1997.

"Focus on Jim Jarmusch" interview with Elvis Mitchell. Independent Film Channel, January 18, 2004.

Franklin, Garth. "Interview with Ang Lee." December 7, 2005. www.darkhorizons.com/news05/brokeback2.php. August 16, 2006.

Frayling, Christopher. *Sergio Leone: Something to Do with Death*. London: Faber, 2000.

Fuller, Graham. "Death and the Maidens," *Sight and Sound*, new series, 10/4 (April 2000). Online. Humanities Art Database. February 26, 2004.

Gabler, Neal. "Risky Business." *The New York Times*, August 25, 2006. http://www.nytimes.com/2006/08/25/opinion/25gabler.html. August 25, 2006.

Gagne, Nicole. "Gay and Lesbian." Allmovie.com www.allmovie.com/cg/avg/dll?p=avg&sql=23:35 October 14, 2006."

Gallagher, Mark. "I Married Rambo." *Mythologies of Violence in Postmodern Media*. Ed. Christopher Sharrett. Detroit, MI: Wayne State University Press, 1999, pp. 199–226.

Gargan, Edward. "Hong Kong's Master of Internal Pyrotechnics," *New York Times*, Sunday October 12, 1997, Section 2, pp. 13, 29.

Gerstner, David. *Manly Arts: Masculinity and Nation in Early American Cinema*. Durham, NC: Duke University Press, 2006.

Gibson, Pamela Church. "Film Costume," in *The Oxford Guide to Film Studies*, ed. John Hill and Pamela Church Gibson. Oxford and New York: Oxford University Press, 1998, pp. 36–42.

Gidal, Peter. *Materialist Film*. London: Routledge, 1989.

Goldberg, Michelle "Where are the Female Directors" *Salon.com*. August 27, 2002. archive.salon.com/ent/movies/feature/2002/08/27/women_directors/index.html September 20, 2006.

Gomery, Douglas. "The Coming of Sound; Technological Change in the American Film Industry," in *Film Sound*, ed. Elizabeth Weis and John Belton. New York: Columbia University Press, 1985, pp. 5–24.

Gomery, Douglas. "The Hollywood Studio System," in *The Oxford History of World Cinema*, ed. Geoffrey Nowell-Smith. Oxford and New York: Oxford University Press, 1996, pp. 43–53.

Gorbman, Claudia. *Unheard Melodies: Narrative Film Music*. Bloomington: Indiana University Press, 1987.

Gorky, Maxim. "The Kingdom of Shadows," in Gilbert Adair, *Movies*, pp. 10–13. London and New York: Penguin, 1999.

Gras, Vernon and Marguerite (ed.). *Interviews: Peter Greenaway*. Jackson, MI: University of Mississippi Press, 2000.

Guerrero, Ed. *Framing Blackness: The African American Image in Film*. Philadelphia: Temple University Press, 1993.

Haines, Richard W. *Technicolor Movies: The History of Dye Transfer Printing*. Jefferson, NC: McFarland, 1993.

Haller, Robert. "Kenneth Anger." Harvard Independent Film Group. February 1980. www.geocities.com/Hollywood/Lot/1162/HCAngerBio_html.html August 20, 2006.

Handy, Bruce. "This is Cinerama." *Vanity Fair*, 488 (April 2001), pp. 258–74.

Hansen, Miriam. "The Mass Production of the Senses: Classical Cinema as Vernacular Modernism." *Modernism/Modernity*, 6/2 (1999), pp. 59–77.

Hay, James. *Popular Film Culture in Fascist Italy*. Bloomington: Indiana University Press, 1987.

Heines, Marjorie. *Sex, Sin, and Blasphemy. A Guide to America's Censorship Wars*. New York: The New Press, 1998.

Hill, John. "British Film Policy," in *Film Policy: International, National, and Regional Perspectives*, ed. Albert Moran. London: Routledge, 1996, pp. 101–13.

Hiltzik, Michael. "Digital Cinema Take 2." *Technology Review*, September 2002, pp. 36–44.

"Hollywood's Women Directors Hit Celluloid Ceiling," Buzzle.com. July 4, 2002. www.buzzle.com/editorials/7-4-2002-21795.asp. September 20, 2006.

"Hollywood Ten." Spartacus. www.spartacus.schoolnet.co.uk/USAhollywood10.htm. October 3, 2006.

Holmlund, Chris. *Impossible Bodies: Femininity and Masculinity at the Movies*. London: Routledge, 2002.

Hopfensperger, Jean. "'Whiteness Studies' Researchers at University of Minnesota Look at Racial Identity." *Star Tribune.com*. September 11, 2006. www.startribune.com/462/story/667886.html. September 20, 2006.

Horak, Jan-Christopher. "The First American Avant-Garde, 1919–1945," in *Lovers of Cinema: The First American Film Avant-Garde 1919–45*, ed. Jan-Christopher Horak. Madison: University of Wisconsin Press, 1995, pp. 14–66.

Horn, John. "Producers Pursue a *Potter* with Pizzazz." *Raleigh News and Observer* (January 25, 2004), p. 3G.

Hultkrans, Andrew. "Reality Bytes—Interview with Hollywood Director Kathryn Bigelow." *ArtForum*, November 1995. www.findarticles.com/p/articles/mi_m0268/is_n3_v34/ai_17865932 September 18, 2006.

Hutchings, Peter. "Genre Theory and Criticism." *Approaches to Popular Film*, ed. Joanne Hollows and Mark Jancovich. Manchester and New York: Manchester University Press, 1995, pp. 59–77.

"Interview with Ang Lee and James Schamus." *The Guardian*. November 7, 2000. http://film.guardian.co.uk/interview/interviewpages/0,,394676,00.html. July 20, 2006.

Iwasaki, Akira. "Kurosawa and his Work," in *Focus on Rashômon*, ed. Donald Richie. Englewood Cliffs: Prentice Hall, 1972, pp. 21–31.

James, Caryn. "Loyalties Scalded by Humiliation," *The New York Times* (September 5, 1990), p. C16.

James, Caryn. "Mission Imperative for a Star: Be Likable." *New York Times*, August 24, 2006. http://www.nytimes.com/2006/08/24/movies/24cele.html. August 25, 2006. http://www.Kentucky.com/mld/Kentucky/15346746.htm.

James, David. *Allegories of Cinema: American Film in the 1960s*. Princeton: Princeton University Press, 1989.

"John Ford's *Young Mr. Lincoln*." Collective text by the editors of *Cahiers du Cinéma*. *Film Theory and Criticism: Introductory Readings*, 3rd edn., ed. Gerald Mast and Marshall Cohen. New York: Oxford University Press, 1985, pp. 695–740.

Johnson, William. "The Circle," *Film Quarterly*, 54/3 (spring 2001). Online. Communication and Mass Media Complete. February 25, 2004.

Johnston, Sheila. "The Author as Public Institution," in *The European Cinema Reader*, ed. Catherine Fowler. London and New York: Routledge, 2002, pp. 121–31.

Kaes, Anton. "The New German Cinema," in *Oxford History of World Cinema*, ed. Geoffrey

Nowell-Smith. Oxford and New York: Oxford University Press, 1996, pp. 614–27.

Kawin, Bruce. "Children of the Light," in *Film Genre Reader*, ed. Barry Keith Grant. Austin: University of Texas Press, 1986, pp. 236–57.

Keller, James R. *Queer (Un)friendly Film and Television*. London and Jefferson, NC: McFarland, 2002.

Kellner, Douglas. "Hollywood Film and Society," in *American Cinema and Hollywood*, ed. John Hill and Pamela Church Gibson. Oxford and New York: Oxford University Press, 2000, pp. 128–38.

Kelly, Mary Pat. *Martin Scorsese: A Journey*. New York: Thunder's Mouth Press, 1991.

Kenez, Peter. *Cinema and Soviet Society: From the Revolution to the Death of Stalin*. New York: I.B. Tauris, 2001.

Kinder, Marsha, and Beverle Houston. *Close-Up: A Critical Perspective on Film*. New York: Harcourt, Brace, Jovanovich, 1972.

King, Barry. "Articulating Stardom," *Screen*, 26/5 (1985), pp. 27–50.

Klosterman, Chuck. *"The Snakes on a Plane Problem." Esquire*. 146/2 (August 2006), pp. 60–2.

Kracauer, Siegfried. *From "Caligari" to Hitler: A Psychological History of the German Film*. Princeton, NJ: Princeton University Press, 1971.

Kramer, Gary M. *Independent Queer Cinema: Reviews and Interviews*. Binghamton, NY; Haworth Press (Southern Tier Editions): 2006.

Kramer, Peter. "Post-Classical Hollywood," in *American Cinema and Hollywood*, ed. John Hill and Pamela Church Gibson. New York: Oxford University Press, 2000, pp. 63–83.

Kruidenier, David. "Postcolonialism and Feminism in *The Battle of Algiers*." Unpublished paper. February 2004.

Lane, Anthony. "Mondo Bond." *The New Yorker*, 78/33 (November 4, 2002), pp. 78–82.

LaPlace, Maria. "Stars and the Star System: The Case of Bette Davis," in *The Film Studies Reader*, ed. Joanne Hollows *et al*. New York: Oxford University Press, 2000, pp. 134–39. Originally published in Christine Gledhill (ed.), *Home is Where the Heart Is*. London: British Film Institute, 1987.

Lauzen, Martha. "The Celluloid Ceiling: Behind-the-Scenes Employment of Women in the Top 250 Films of 2005." *Movies Directed by Women*. 2006. www.moviesbywomen.com/ martha lauzenphd/stats2005.html October 12, 2006.

Le Cain, Maximilian. "Kenneth Anger." Senses of Cinema. January 2003. http://www. sensesof cinema.com/contents/directors/03/ anger.html September 15, 2006.

Lee, Joanna. "The Music of *In the Mood for Love*." *In the Mood for Love*. Dir. Wong Kar-Wai. DVD. USA/Criterion, 2002.

Leeper, Jill. "Crossing Borders: The Soundtrack for *Touch of Evil*," in *Soundtrack Available: Essays on Film and Popular Music*, ed. Pamela Robertson Wojcik and Arthur Knight. Durham, NC: Duke University Press, 2001, pp. 226–43.

Lehman, Peter. *Running Scared: Masculinity and the Representation of the Male Body*. 2d edn. Detroit, MI: Wayne State University Press, 2006.

Lehman, Peter, and William Luhr. *Thinking about Movies: Watching, Questioning, Enjoying*. Fort Worth: Harcourt, 1999.

Lent, Tina Olsin. "Romantic Love and Friendship: The Redefinition of Gender Relations in Screwball Comedy," in *Classical Hollywood Comedy*, ed. Krisine Brunovska Karnick and Henry Jenkins. London: Routledge, 1995, pp. 314–31.

Leotta, Joan. "Spotlight on the Silver Screen: California's Media Access Office." *Solutions Marketing Group*. http://www.disability-marketing.com/profiles/ca-mao.php4. October 19, 2006.

LeSage, Julia. "The Political Aesthetics of the Feminist Documentary Film." *Quarterly Review of Film Studies*, 3/4 (1978), pp. 507–23.

Lewis, Jon. *Hollywood versus Hardcore: How the Struggle over Censorship Saved the Modern Film Industry*. New York: New York University Press, 2000.

Lewis, Jon. "Money Matters: Hollywood in the Corporate Era," in *New American Cinema*, ed. Jon Lewis. Durham, NC: Duke University Press, 1998, pp. 87–121.

Lewis, Jon. "The Perfect Money Machine(s): George Lucas, Steven Spielberg, and Auteurism in the New Hollywood," in *Looking Past the Screen: Case Studies in American Film History and Method*, eds. Jon Lewis and Eric Loren Smoodin. Durham: Duke University Press, 2007, pp. 61–86.

Leyda, Jay. *Kino: A History of the Russian and Soviet Film*. Princeton: Princeton University Press, 1960.

Lipton, Lenny. *Independent Filmmaking*. New York: Simon and Schuster, 1983.

LoBrutto, Vincent. *Principal Photography: Interviews with Feature Film Cinematographers*. London and Westport, CT: Praeger, 1999.

LoBrutto, Vincent. *Sound on Film: Interviews with Creators of Film Sound*. Westport, CT: Praeger, 1994.

Lopez Levers, Lisa. "Representation of Psychiatric Disability in Fifty Years of Hollywood Film: An Ethnographic Content Analysis." *Theory and Science*. 2001. http://www.theoryandscience.icaap.org/ content/vol002.002/lopezlevers.html.

Lowenstein, Adam. *Shocking Representation: Historical Trauma, National Cinema, and the Modern Horror Film*. New York: Columbia University Press, 2005.

McDonald, Paul. Afterword ("Reconceptualising Stardom"), in *Stars*, 2nd edn. London: BFI, 1998, pp. 177–211.

McDonald, Paul. "Film Acting," in *The Oxford Guide to Film Studies*, ed. John Hill and Pamela Church Gibson. Oxford and New York: Oxford University Press, 1998, pp. 30–6.

McDonald, Paul. *The Star System: Hollywood's Production of Popular Identities*. London: Wallflower, 2000.

MacDonald, Scott. *Avant Garde Film: Motion Studies*. Cambridge: Cambridge University Press, 1993.

Magid, Ron. "Vision Crew Unlimited's Artisans Lay Scale-model Keels for *Titanic*," *American Cinematographer*, 78/12 (December 1997), pp. 81–5.

Magombe, P. Vincent. "Ousmane Sembene," in *Oxford History of World Cinema*, ed. Geoffrey Nowell-Smith. Oxford and New York: Oxford University Press, 1996, pp. 668–69.

Majumdar, Neepa. "The Embodied Voice," in *Soundtrack Available: Essays on Film and Popular Music*, ed. Pamela Robertson Wojcik and Arthur Knight. Durham, NC: Duke University Press, 2001, pp. 161–81.

Maltby, Richard. "Censorship and Self-Regulation," in *The Oxford History of World Cinema*, ed. Geoffrey Nowell-Smith. New York: Oxford University Press, 1996, pp. 235–48.

Maltby, Richard. "'Nobody Knows Everything': Post-Classical Historiographies and Consolidated Entertainment," in *Contemporary Hollywood Cinema*, ed. Steve Neale and Murray Smith. London: Routledge, 1998, pp. 21–57.

Marcus, Millicent. *Italian Film in the Light of Neorealism*. Princeton: Princeton University Press, 1986.

Marie, Michel. "It Really Makes You Sick," in *French Film: Texts and Contexts*, 2nd edn., ed. Susan Hayward and Ginette Vincendeau. London: Routledge, 2000, pp. 158–73.

Martin, Kevin H. "Jacking into the Matrix," *Cinefex*, 79 (October 1999), pp. 66–89.

Massood, Paula J. "An Aesthetic Appropriate to Conditions: Killer of Sheep, (Neo)Realism, and the Documentary Impulse." *Wide Angle*, 21/4 (October 1999), pp. 20–41.

Mast, Gerald, and Bruce Kawin. *A Short History of the Movies*, 6th edn. Boston and London: Allyn and Bacon, 1996.

"McCarthyism." *Wikipedia: The Free Encyclopedia*. en.wikipedia.org/wiki/ Mccarthyism September 22, 2006.

"Media Stereotyping—Introduction." *Media Awareness* Network. http://www.media-awareness.ca/english/issues/stereotyping/ October 2, 2006.

Mellen, Joan. "Film Noir," in *The Political Companion to American Film*, ed. Gary Crowdus. Chicago: Lakeview Press, 1994, pp. 137–44.

"Million Dollar Baby Built on Prejudice about People with Disabilities." Disability *Rights Education and Defense Fund*. http://www. dredf.org/mdb_statement.html. October 1, 2006.

Minh-ha T Pham, "The Asian Invasion (of Multiculturalism) in Hollywood." *Journal of Popular Film and Television, 32/3* (Fall 2004), pp. 121–31.

Modleski, Tania. *The Women Who Knew Too Much: Hitchcock and Feminist Theory*. London and New York: Routledge, 1988.

Monaco, James. *How to Read a Film: Movies, Media, Multimedia*, 3rd edn. Oxford and New York: Oxford University Press, 2000.

Moritz, William. "Americans in Paris," in *Lovers of Cinema: The First American Film Avant-Garde 1919–45*, ed. Jan-Christopher Horak. Madison: University of Wisconsin Press, 1995, pp. 118–36.

Morris, Gary. "A Brief History of Queer Cinema." *GreenCine*. www.greencine.com/ statis/ primers/queer.jsp. October 14, 2006.

Morris, Gary. "Behind the Mask: Sadie Benning's Pixel Pleasures." *Bright Lights Film Journal*, 24 (April 1999). http://www.bright lightsfilm.com/24/benning.html. 2/17/04.

Morrison, James. "Buzz Factor: The DVD Release of Todd Solondz's *Storytelling* itself Tells a Story about Contemporary Film

Culture," *The Independent Weekly*, 19/30 (July 17–23, 2002), p. 52.

Mottram, James. *The Making of "Memento."* London: Faber and Faber, 2002.

Murphy, David. *Sembene*. Oxford and Trenton, NJ: Africa World Press, 2001.

Naremore, James. *Acting in the Cinema*. Berkeley, CA: University of California Press, 1990.

Naremore, James. *More than Night: Film Noir in its Contexts*. Berkeley: University of California Press, 1998.

Neale, Steve. *Genre and Hollywood*. London: Routledge, 2000.

Negra, Diane. *Off White Hollywood: American Culture and Ethnic Female Stardom*. London and New York: Routledge, 2001.

Neupert, Richard. *A History of the French New Wave*. Madison: University of Wisconsin Press, 2002.

Nichols, Bill. *Introduction to Documentary*. Bloomington and Indianapolis: Indiana University Press, 2001.

Nichols, Bill. *Representing Reality*. Bloomington and Indianapolis: Indiana University Press, 1991.

Norden, Martin F. *The Cinema of Isolation*. New Brunswick, NJ: Rutgers University Press, 1994.

Norden, Martin F. "The Hollywood Discourse on Disability." *Screening Disability: Essays on Cinema and Disability*. Eds. Christopher Smit and Anthony Enns. Lanham, MD: University Press of America, 2001, pp. 19–32.

Norden, Martin, and Madeleine Cahill. "Violence, Women, and Disability in Tod Browning's Freaks and Devil Doll." *Journal of Popular Film and Television*. Summer 1998. http://findarticles.com/p/articles/mi_m0412/is_n2_v26/ai_21221638. October 10, 2006.

Nowell-Smith, Geoffrey. "Art Cinema," in *The Oxford History of World Cinema*, ed. Geoffrey Nowell-Smith. New York: Oxford University Press, 1996, pp. 567–75.

Nowell-Smith, Geoffrey. *The Oxford History of World Cinema*. Oxford and New York: Oxford University Press, 1997.

"The Oberhausen Manifesto," in *The European Cinema Reader*, ed. Catherine Fowler. London and New York: Routledge, 2002, p. 73.

O'Hehir, Andrew. "Beyond the Multiplex," Salon.com. salon.com/ent/movies/review/2006/08/03/btm/. September 22, 2006.

O'Hehir, Andrew. "Fog of War," Salon.com. salon.com/ent/movies/review/2001/12/28/black_hawk_down/index.html.

O'Neill, Edward R. "Alfred Hitchcock," in *Oxford History of World Cinema*, ed Geoffrey Nowell-Smith. Oxford and New York: Oxford University Press, 1996, pp. 310–11.

Origins of a Hip Hop Classic. Dir. Benny Boom. *Scarface*. DVD Supplementary Material. Universal. 2003.

Orr, John. *Cinema and Modernity*. Cambridge: Polity Press, 1993.

Otto, Jeff, and Spence D. "Howard Shore Interview." ign.com. http://music.ign.com/articles/446/446567p1.html.

"Paramount: Cruise is Risky Business." CNN *Money.com*. August 23, 2006. money.cnn.com/2006/08/22/news/newsmakers/cruise_paramount/index.htm. September 27, 2006.

Perisic, Zoran. *Visual Effects Cinematography*. Boston: Focal Press, 2000.

Peterson, James. *Dreams of Chaos, Visions of Order: Understanding the American Avant-Garde Cinema*. Detroit: Wayne State University Press, 1994.

Pierson, Michele. *Special Effects: Still in Search of Wonder*. New York: Columbia University Press, 2002.

Porter, Eduardo, and Geraldine Fabrikant. "A Big Star May Not a Profitable Movie Make." *The New York Times*, August 28, 2006, C, pp. 1, 5.

Potter, Sally. "Notes on the Adaptation of the Book *Orlando*." Virginia Woolf Seminar. http://www.uah.edu/woolf/Orlando_Potter.htm. October 10, 2006.

Potter, Sally. "Response to Thought Fox." *Yes* Message Board. March 27, 2006. www.yesthemovie.com/forum_thread.jsp?articleType=Content.TALK%20TO%20SALLY.Film-making&threadId=132. October 10, 2006.

Prendergast, Roy M. *Film Music: A Neglected Art*, 2nd edn. New York: Norton, 1992.

Prince, Stephen, ed. *The Horror Film*. New Brunswick, NJ: Rutgers University Press, 2004.

"Production Code of 1930." *The Production Code of the Motion Picture Industry*, 1930–68. http://prodcode.davidhayes.net/October 12, 2006.

Pudovkin, V.I. *Film Technique and Film Acting*. New York: Grove Press, 1970.

Pym, John. "Soldier's Pay," *Sight and Sound*, 58/4 (Autumn 1989), p. 280.

Rajadhyaksha, Ashish. "Realism, Modernism, and Post-colonial Theory," in *The Oxford Guide to Film Studies*, ed. John Hill and Pamela Church Gibson. Oxford: Oxford University Press, 1998, pp. 413–25.

Ray, Robert. *A Certain Tendency of the Hollywood Cinema, 1930–1980*. Princeton: Princeton University Press, 1985.

Rees, A.L. *A History of Experimental Film and Video*. London: British Film Institute, 1999.

Rhines, Jesse Algernon. *Black Films/White Money*. New Brunswick, NJ: Rutgers University Press, 1996.

Riambau, Esteve "Public Money and Private Business (Or, How to Survive Hollywood's Imperialism): Film Production in Spain (1984–2002)," *Cineaste*, 29/1 (2004), pp. 56–61.

Richie, Donald. *Japanese Cinema: An Introduction*. New York: Oxford University Press, 1990.

Richie, Donald, ed. *"Rashômon": Akira Kurosawa, Director*. New Brunswick and London: Rutgers University Press, 1987.

Richie, Donald, ed. *Focus on "Rashômon"*. Englewood Cliffs, NJ: Prentice-Hall, 1972.

Rickitt, Richard. *Special Effects: The History and Technique*. London: Virgin Publishing, 2000.

Riding, Alan. "Filmmakers Seek Protection from U.S. Dominance," *New York Times* (February 5, 2003), p. B3.

Rigney, Melissa. "Sadie Benning," *Senses of Cinema. Great Directors: A Critical Database*. www.sensesofcinema.com/contents/directors/03/benning.html. 2/17/04.

Rogers, Pauline. *Contemporary*

Cinematographers on Their Art. Boston: Focal Press, 1998.

Rosenbaum, Jonathan. "Cult Confusion," *The Chicago Reader* (January 9, 1998). February 25, 2004. http://www.chireader.com/movies/archives/1998/0198/01238.html.

Rosenbaum, Jonathan. *Movies as Politics*. Berkeley, CA: University of California Press, 1997.

Rosenbaum, Jonathan. "A Perversion of the Past," in *Movies as Politics*. Berkeley, CA: University of California Press, 1997, pp. 118–24. Originally published in *Chicago Reader*, December 16, 1988.

Rosenbaum, Jonathan. "The Problem with Poetry," in *Movies as Politics*. Berkeley CA: University of California Press, 1997, pp. 183–94.

Rosenbaum, Jonathan. "*Touch of Evil* Retouched," in *The Best American Movie Writing 1999*, ed. Peter Bogdanovich. New York: St Martin's Griffin, 1999, pp. 133–36.

Rosenbaum, Jonathan. "The World According to Harvey and Bob," in *Movies as Politics*, pp. 159–65. Berkeley and Los Angeles, CA: University of California Press, 1997.

Rosenberg, Jan. *Women's Reflections: The Feminist Film Movement*. Ann Arbor, MI: UMI Research Press, 1983.

Ross, Matthew. "Industry Spotlight" DV Approaches the Mainstream." *Indiewire People*. July 31, 2002. www.indiewire.com/people/int_Winick_Gary_020731.html. October 1, 2006.

Rudolph, Eric. "This is your Life," *American Cinematographer*, 79/6 (June 1998), pp. 74–85.

Russell, Catherine. *Experimental Ethnography*. Durham, NC, and London: Duke University Press, 1999.

Russo, Vito. *The Celluloid Closet: Homosexuality in the Movies*. New York: Harper and Rowe, 1987.

Ryall, Tom. "Genre and Hollywood," in *The Oxford Guide to Film Studies*, ed. John Hill and Pamela Church Gibson. London: Oxford University Press, 1998, pp. 327–37.

Ryan, Michael, and Douglas Kellner. *Camera Politica: The Politics and Ideology of Contemporary Hollywood Film*. Bloomington: Indiana University Press: 1988.

Salt, Barry. *Film Style and Technology: History and Analysis*, 2nd edn. London: Starword, 1992.

Salt, Barry. "Film Style and Technology in the Thirties: Sound," in *Film Sound*, ed. Elizabeth Weis and John Belton. New York: Columbia University Press, 1985, pp. 37–43.

San Filippo, Maria. "Lost in Translation," *Cineaste*, 29/1 (Winter 2003). Online. Academic Search Elite. February 25, 2004.

Sarris, Andrew. *The Primal Screen*. New York: Simon and Schuster, 1973.

Sato, Tadao. "The Films of Akira Kurosawa and the Japanese People," *Film International*, 6/2 (1998), pp. 61–4.

Schaefer, Dennis, and Larry Salvato. *Masters of Light: Conversations with Contemporary Cinematographers*. Berkeley, CA: University of California Press, 1984.

Schamus, James. "A Rant," in *The End of Cinema As We Know It: American Film in the Nineties*, ed. Jon Lewis. New York: New York University Press, 2001.

Schatz, Thomas. *Hollywood Genres: Formulas, Filmmaking, and the Studio System.* Philadelphia: Temple University Press, 1981.

Schatz, Thomas. *The Genius of the System: Hollywood Filmmaking in the Studio Era.* New York: Pantheon, 1988.

Schroeder, Paul A. *Tomás Gutiérrez Alea: The Dialectics of a Filmmaker.* New York and London: Routledge, 2002.

Scott, A.O. "The New Golden Age of Acting," *The New York Times* (February 15, 2004), 2A: pp. 1, 25.

Scott, Walter. "Personality Parade," *Parade Magazine* (June 13, 2004), p. 1.

Segrave, Kerry. *American Films Abroad: Hollywood's Domination of the World's Movie Screens from the 1890s to the Present.* Jefferson: McFarland, 1997.

Seguin, Denis. "The Battle for Hollywood North," *Canadian Business,* 76 (2003). Academic Search Elite. Online. Ebscohost. January 21, 2004.

Shannon, Jeff. "Access Hollywood: Disability in Recent Film and Television." *New Mobility.* May 2003. http://www.newmobility.com/review_article.cfm?id = 690&action = browse. October 10, 2003.

Sheng-mei Ma, "Ang Lee's Domestic Tragicomedy," *Journal of Popular Culture,* 30/1 (Summer 1996), pp. 191–201.

Shohat, Ella, and Robert Stam. *Unthinking Eurocentrism: Multiculturalism and the Media.* London and New York: Routledge, 1994.

Shreger, Charles. "Altman, Dolby, and the Second Sound Revolution," in *Film Sound,* ed. Elizabeth Weis and John Belton. New York: Columbia University Press, 1985, pp. 348–55.

Sitney, P. Adams. *Visionary Film: The American Avant-Garde, 1943–1978,* 3rd edn. Oxford and New York: Oxford University Press, 2002.

Sklar, Robert. *Film: An International History of the Medium,* 2nd edn. Upper Saddle River, NJ: Prentice Hall and Harry N. Abrams, 2002.

Smith, Jeff. *The Sound of Commerce.* New York: Columbia University Press, 1998.

Smith, Steven. "A Chorus of Isolation," *Taxi Driver.* Dir. Martin Scorsese. Laser Disc. Criterion/Voyager Co. 1990.

Solomon, Stanley J. *Beyond Formula: American Film Genres.* San Diego: Harcourt Brace, 1976.

Sontag, Susan. "The Imagination of Disaster," in *Film Theory and Criticism,* 3rd edn., ed. Gerald Mast and Marshall Cohen. New York: Oxford University Press, 1985, pp. 451–65.

Sontag, Susan. "The Imagination of Disaster," in *Movies,* ed. Gilbert Adair. London: Penguin, 1999, pp. 170–85.

Spoto, Donald. *The Art of Alfred Hitchcock: Fifty Years of His Motion Pictures.* New York: Doubleday, 1979.

Stack, Peter. "Satirical *Scream* is Out for Blood—And Lots of It," *San Francisco Chronicle* (December 26, 1996). SFGate.com. February 13, 2003.

Staiger, Janet. "Standardization and Differentiation: The Reinforcement and Dispersion of Hollywood's Practices," in *The Classical Hollywood Cinema: Film Style and Mode of Production to 1960,* ed. David Bordwell *et al.* New York: Columbia University Press, 1985, pp. 96–112.

Stam, Robert. *Film Theory: An Introduction.* Malden, MA, and Oxford: Blackwell, 2000.

Street, Rita. *Computer Animation: A Whole New World.* Gloucester, MA: Rockport Publishers, 1998.

Sussex, Elizabeth. *The Rise and Fall of British Documentary.* Berkeley and Los Angeles, CA: University of California Press, 1975.

Swann, Paul. *The British Documentary Film Movement, 1926–46.* Cambridge: Cambridge University Press, 1989.

"Tangled Webs," *The Economist,* 363 (2002). Academic Search Elite. Online. Ebscohost. January 21, 2004.

Tasker, Yvonne. *Spectacular Bodies: Gender, Genre, and the Action Cinema.* London and New York: Routledge, 1993.

Taylor, Charles. "Hong Kong Tango," Salon. com. October 31, 1997. September 10, 2002. http://www.salon.com/ent/movies/1997/10/31happy.html?CP = SAL&DN = 110.

Telotte, J.P. "*The Blair Witch Project* Project," *Film Quarterly,* 54 (2001). Academic Search Elite. Online. Ebscohost. January 21, 2004.

Thompson, Kristin. *Storytelling in Film and Television.* Cambridge: Harvard University Press, 2003.

Thompson, Kristin. *Storytelling in the New Hollywood.* Cambridge: Harvard University Press, 1999.

Thompson, Kristin, and David Bordwell. *Film History: An Introduction,* 2nd edn. Boston: McGraw-Hill, 2003.

Thoraval, Yves. *The Cinemas of India.* New Delhi: Macmillan India, 2000.

Triggs, Jeffery Alan. "The Legacy of Babel: Language in Jean Renoir's *Grand Illusion,*" *The New Orleans Review,* 15/2 (1988), pp. 70–4.

Truffaut, François. *Hitchcock,* rev. edn. New York: Touchstone, 1993.

Tsivian, Yuri. "Dziga Vertov," in *The Oxford History of World Cinema,* ed. Geoffrey Nowell-Smith. Oxford and New York: Oxford University Press, 1996, pp. 92–3.

Usai, Paolo Chechi. "The Early Years," in *The Oxford History of World Cinema.* Oxford and New York: Oxford University Press, 1997, pp. 6–13.

Vasey, Ruth. "The Worldwide Spread of Cinema," *The Oxford History of World Cinema,* ed. Geoffrey Nowell-Smith. Oxford: Oxford University Press, 1996, pp. 53–62.

Vertov, Dziga. "Provisional Instructions to Kino-Eye Groups," in *The European Cinema Reader,* ed. Catherine Fowler. London and New York: Routledge, 2002.

Vir, Parminder. "The Mother of All Battles," *The New Statesman* (July 8, 2002), pp. 40–2.

Von Sternberg, Josef. *Fun in a Chinese Laundry.* New York: Macmillan, 1965.

"Waldorf Statement." *Wikipedia: the Free Encyclopedia.* en.wikipedia.org/wiki/Waldorf_ Statement. October 4, 2006.

Walker, Janet, and Diane Waldman. *Feminism and Documentary.* Minneapolis, MI: University of Minnesota Press, 1999.

Warshow, Robert. "Movie Chronicle: The Westerner," in *Film Theory and Criticism,* 4th edn., ed. Gerald Mast, Marshall Cohen, and Leo Braudy. New York: Oxford University Press, 1992, pp. 453–66.

Webb, Veronica. "Big Bad Bigelow." *Interview,* November 1995. www.findarticles.com/p/articles/ mi_m1285/is_n11_v25/ai_17632982. October 1, 2006.

Wheeler, Paul. *High Definition and 24p Cinematography.* Oxford: Focal Press, 2003.

Wollen, Peter. "From *Signs and Meaning in Cinema: The* Auteur *Theory,*" in *Film Theory and Criticism,* 5th edn, ed. Leo Braudy and Marshall Cohen. Oxford: Oxford University Press, 1999, pp. 519–35.

Wood, Robin. *Hollywood from Vietnam to Reagan.* New York: Columbia University Press, 1986.

Wood, Robin. "Ideology, Genre, *Auteur: Shadow of a Doubt,*" in *Hitchcock's Films Revisited.* New York: Columbia University Press, 1989, pp. 288–303.

Wood, Robin. "Introduction," in *The American Nightmare: Essays on the Horror Film,* ed. Andrew Britton, Richard Lippe, Tony Williams, and Robin Wood. Toronto, Canada: Festival of Festivals, 1979, pp. 7–28.

Worrell, Joseph. "Oscar Micheaux." *Silent Era People.* www.silentera.com/people/directors/Micheaux-Oscar.html. September 2, 2006.

Wright, Judith Hess. "Genre Films and the Status Quo," in *Film Genre Reader,* ed. Barry Keith Grant. Austin: University of Texas Press, 1986, pp. 236–57.

Wyatt, Justin. "From Roadshow to Saturation Release: Majors, Independents, and Marketing/Distribution Innovations," in *New American Cinema,* ed. Jon Lewis. Durham, NC: Duke University Press, 1998, pp. 64–86.

Zettl, Herbert. *Sight, Sound, Motion: Applied Media Aesthetics,* 3rd edn. Belmont, CA: Wadsworth Publishing Co., 1999.

Zhang, Ziyi. "Ang Lee: The Cross Cultural Cowboy of Film." *Time.* May 8, 2006.

Zunser, Jesse. Review of *Rashômon,* in *Focus on "Rashômon."* Englewood Cliffs: Prentice-Hall, 1972, pp. 37–8.

Index

Picture Credits

Grateful acknowledgement is extended for use of the following images. Every effort has been made to trace and contact all film studios and copyright holders. The publishers apologize for any unintentional omissions or errors and will be pleased to insert the appropriate acknowledgement in any subsequent edition of this book.

Page xii © Magnolia / Everett / Rex Features; 1.5 © 2009 Twentieth Century Fox. Game Software excluding Twentieth Century Fox Film Corporation elements: ©2009 Ubisoft Entertainment. All Rights Reserved; 2.1 © 2008 Celador Films; 2.2 © 1963, renewed 1991 Columbia Pictures Industries, Inc. All Rights Reserved. Courtesy of Columbia Pictures; 2.4 © 2006 Bórd Scannán na hÉireann; 2.5 © 2006. Universal Pictures. Courtesy of Universal Studios Licensing LLLP; 2.6 Courtesy of Castle Hill Productions, Inc.; 2.7 © 1941 RKO Pictures Inc. All Rights Reserved; 2.13 Universal, Apatow Productions / The Kobal Collection / Hanover, Suzanne; 2.14, 2.15 © 2008 Herzliya Films; 2.16 © 2009 Universal Pictures; 2.17 © Paramount Pictures Corporation. All Rights Reserved; 2.18 © Warner Bros., Inc. All Rights Reserved; 2.19 © 1958 Universal City Studios Inc. for Samuel Taylor & Patricia Hitchcock O'Connell as trustees. Courtesy of Universal Studios Licensing LLLP; 2.18, 2.19 © Bavaria Media GmbH; 2.21 © 1952 Amato Film; 2.22 © 2008 Likely Story; 2.23 © Bavaria Media GmbH; 2.24 © 1963, renewed 1991. Columbia Pictures Industries, Inc. All Rights Reserved. Courtesy of Columbia Pictures; 2.25 Paramount Pictures Corporation. All Rights Reserved; 2.26 © 2009 Universal Studios 2.27–2.30 © 2006 Tequila Gang. 3.1 © 2008 EFTI; 3.3 © 1953, renewed 1981. Columbia Pictures Industries, Inc. All Rights Reserved. Courtesy of Columbia Pictures; 3.6 © 2000 Am Psycho Productions, Inc.; 3.7, 3.8 © 2008 EFTI; 3.9 © Sony Pics / Everett / Rex Features; p. 58 © 1971 Warner Bros., Inc. All Rights Reserved. Page 62 © Photos 12 / Alamy; 4.1 © 2003 Disney Enterprises, Inc. / Pixar. All Rights Reserved; 4.2 © 2001 Touchstone Pictures. All Rights Reserved; 4.3 © 1988 Metro-Goldwyn-Mayer Studios Inc. All Rights Reserved; 4.4 © 2005 Warner Bros., Inc. All Rights Reserved; 4.5 Courtesy of MK2 S.A; 4.6 United Artists / The Kobal Collection; 4.7–4.8 Courtesy of Castle Hill Productions Inc; 4.9 © 2008 Bad Robo; 4.10, 4.11 © ABC, Inc. All Rights Reserved; 4.12, 4.13 D.W. Griffith Productions; 4.14–4.17 © 1960 Shamley Productions, Inc., & Universal Studios Licensing LLLP; 4.18 © 1992 Courtesy of Miramax Films; 4.20–4.22 © 2008 Celador Films. 5.1, 5.2 © Paramount Pictures Corporation. All Rights Reserved; 5.4 © 1968 Twentieth Century Fox; 5.5 Courtesy of Sony Pictures Classics Inc.; 5.6 © 2000 Tiger Aspect Pictures (Billy Boy) Limited & Universal Studios Licensing LLP.; 5.7 © 1927 Fox Film Corporation 5.8–5.10 © 1987 Warner Bros., Inc. All Rights Reserved; 5.11, 5.12 Courtesy of Miramax Films & TF1 International; 5.13 Courtesy of ITN Archive / Channel 4 Films; 5.14 Courtesy of MK2 S.A.; 5.18 Everett Collection / Rex Features; 5.19 © 2001 Universal Studios & Le Studio Canal. Courtesy of Universal Studios Licensing LLLP; 5.20 © 1941 RKO Pictures, Inc. All Rights Reserved; 5.21 © Paramount Pictures Corporation. All Rights Reserved; 5.23, 5.24 Paramount / Miramax / The Kobal Collection / Coote, Clive; 5.26, 5.27 © MCMXCVII New Line Productions. All Rights Reserved; 5.28 © 1931 Universal Pictures Company, Inc. Courtesy of Universal Studios Licensing LLLP; 5.29 Cineriz; 5.30 Apatow Productions; 5.31 © Paramount Pictures Corporation. All Rights Reserved; 5.33 Mosfilm; 5.34 © 2005 Warner Bros., Inc. All Rights Reserved; 5.35 Warner Bros / D.C. Comics / The Kobal Collection / James, David; 5.38 © 1965 Twentieth Century Fox; 5.39 Focus Features; 5.41 © 2009 Warner Bros. All Rights Reserved; 5.40 Warner Bros / The Kobal Collection / Wallace, Merie W; 5.42 © 1938, renewed 1966 Columbia Pictures Industries, Inc. All Rights Reserved. Courtesy of Columbia Pictures; 5.43 © 2002 R.P. Productions S.A., Studio Babalsberg Gmbh, Heritage Films Sp., Runteam Limited. Courtesy of Universal Studios Licensing LLLP; 5.44 Cino Del Duca / Pce / Lyre / The Kobal Collection; 5.45 © 1955 Warner Bros., Inc. All Rights Reserved; 5.47 © 2005 Patalex III Productions Limited. Licensed by Warner Bros. Entertainment Inc. All Rights Reserved; 5.48, 5.49 Courtesy of Contemporary Films Limited; 5.50, 5.51 Ghoulardi Film Company; 5.52 © ABC, Inc. All Rights Reserved; 5.53 Courtesy of Canal + Image UK Limited; 5.54 © 1955 Warner Bros., Inc. All Rights Reserved; 5.55 © 1989 Universal City Studios, Inc. Courtesy of Universal Studios Licensing LLLP; 5.56 © MM New Line Productions. All Rights Reserved; 5.57 Courtesy of Fortissimo Films; 5.58 © Paramount Pictures Corporation. All Rights Reserved; 5.59 © Bundesarchiv, Filmarchiv / Transit Film GmbH; 5.60 Geffen Pictures / The Kobal Collection / Redmond, Pat; 5.61 © 2005 Warner Bros., Inc. All Rights Reserved; 5.62 Courtesy of Grands Films Classiques; 5.64–5.67, © 1991 Metro-Goldwyn-Mayer Studios Inc. All Rights Reserved. 6.1, 6.2 © 2006 Tequila Gang; All Rights Reserved; 6.6 © 2000 DreamWorks LLC & Universal Studios Licensing LLLP; 6.7 © Universal Pictures Company, Inc.; 6.8 © 2000 Warner Bros; 6.10 © Disney Enterprises; 6.11 Detour /

Independent Film / Line Research / The Kobal Collection; 6.12 © 1940 Turner Entertainment Co. A Warner Bros. Entertainment Inc. Company. All Rights Reserved; 6.13 Courtesy of Shochiku Co. Ltd. © ABC, Inc. All Rights Reserved; 6.14 © 2005 Focus Features & Universal Studios Licensing LLLP; 6.16 Walter Wanger Productions; 6.17–6.19 © 1965 Alberto Grimaldi Productions S.A. All Rights Reserved; 6.20 Lions Gate / The Kobal Collection; 6.21 © 1976 Columbia Pictures 6.22 © 1963 Alfred J. Hitchcock Productions, Inc. Courtesy of Universal Studios Licensing LLLP; 6.23 Courtesy of CineTamaris; 6.24 Egg Films; 6.25 © 2004 Twentieth Century Fox & Paramount Pictures Corporation. All Rights Reserved; 6.26 Frameline / Northern Film Company; 6.27 Société Générale des Films / The Kobal Collection; 6.29 © 2005 IMF International Medin Unfo Film Gmbh & Co3 Produktions Kg. Licensed by Warner Bros. Entertainment Inc. & Miramax Films. All Rights Reserved; 6.27 Courtesy of Studio Canal Image; 6.28 Courtesy of Svensk Filminstittut; 6.29 © 1968 Turner Entertainment Co. A Warner Bros. Entertainment Inc. Company. All Rights Reserved; 6.31 © 1989 Universal City Studios, Inc. Courtesy of Universal Studios Licensing LLLP; 6.32 EFTI; 6.34, 6.35 © 2000 Touchstone Pictures & Universal Pictures. All Rights Reserved; 6.36 Courtesy of Lions Gate Entertainment; 6.37 Eagle Film SS; 6.38, 6.39 Courtesy of HBO; 6.43, 6.44 © 1998 Universal City Studios, Inc. Courtesy of Universal Studios Licensing LLP; 6.45–6.47 © 1989 Universal City Studios, Inc. Courtesy of Universal Studios Licensing LLLP; 6.48 Courtesy of Lions Gate Entertainment; 6.49, 6.50 © Bavaria Media/Film; 6.51, 6.52 Pathé Pictures International; 6.53 © 1970 Wadleigh-Maurice; 6.54 © 2009 Focus Features; 6.56–6.58 Courtesy of American Zoetrope. All Rights Reserved; 6.58, 6.59 © 1958 Universal City Studios Inc. for Samuel Taylor & Patricia Hitchcock O'Connell as trustees. Courtesy of Universal Studios Licensing LLLP; 6.60 Robert Wise Productions; 6.61 Courtesy of London Features International Ltd.; 6.62 © Philadelphia Museum of Art / Corbis; 6.63 Mercury Productions; 6.64–6.66 © 1957 Harris Pictures Corp. All Rights Reserved; 6.67 Twentieth Century Fox / Aspen / The Kobal Collection; 6.69 Courtesy of Norsk Filmstudio AS.; 6.70 © 1960 Shamley Productions, Inc., & Universal Studios Licensing LLLP; 6.71–6.73 © Carlton International Media Ltd & London Features International Ltd.; 6.74 © Bundesarchiv, Filmarchiv / Transit Film GmbH; 6.75 © 1934 Turner Entertainment Co. A Warner Bros. Entertainment Inc. Company. All Rights Reserved; 6.76 © 1931 Twentieth Century Fox; 6.77 © Paramount Pictures Corporation. All Rights Reserved; 6.78 Courtesy of ITN Archive / Channel 4 Films; 6.79 © 2007 Mandate Pictures; 6.80 © Warner Bros., Inc. All Rights Reserved; 6.81 Courtesy of Cine-Tamaris; 6.82 © 2004 Twentieth Century Fox & Miramax Films; 6.86 Dreamworks Llc / The Kobal Collection / James, David; 6.87 Courtesy of ADC Holdings Corp. "Cinescape" and "Cinefex" covers courtesy of the publishers; 6.88 © 1956, renewed 1984 Columbia Pictures Industries, Inc. All Rights Reserved. Courtesy of Columbia Pictures; 6.89 © 1997 Twentieth Century Fox & Paramount Pictures Corporation; 6.91 Universal / The Kobal Collection; 6.92 © 1968 Turner Entertainment Co. A Warner Bros. Entertainment Inc. Company. All Rights Reserved; 6.94 © 1960 Shamley Productions, Inc., & Universal Studios Licensing LLLP; 6.96 © 2009 Twentieth Century Fox; 6.97 © 1989 Twentieth Century Fox; 6.98 New Line / The Kobal Collection / Talamon, Bruce; 6.99, 6.100 © 2000 Touchstone Pictures & Universal Pictures. All Rights Reserved; 6.101 © 1971 Warner Bros., Inc. All Rights Reserved; 6.102–6.106 Pathé Pictures International. 7.1 © Bundesarchiv, Filmarchiv / Transit Film GmbH; 7.2, 7.3 © 1932 Paramount Publix Corporation & Universal Studios Licensing LLLP; 7.4, 7.5 © 1960 Shamley Productions, Inc. & Universal Studios Licensing LLLP; 7.6, 7.7 © MMII New Line Productions, Inc. The Saul Zaentz Company d/b/a/ Tolkein Enterprises under license to New Line Productions, Inc. All Rights reserved; 7.8, 7.9 © Bavaria Media GmbH; 7.10 Toho Company; 7.11, 7.12 © ABC, Inc. All Rights Reserved 7.11–7.13 © 1976 Metro-Goldwyn-Mayer Studios Inc. All Rights Reserved; 7.14–7.16 Courtesy of MK2 S.A.; 7.17, 7.18 © 1967 Warner Bros., Seven Arts & Tatira-Hiller Productions. All Rights Reserved; 7.19 Courtesy of Svensk Filminstittut; 7.20 Courtesy of MK2 S.A.; 7.21, 7.22 Courtesy of Euro London Films Ltd.; 7.23 Star Films; 7.28–7.30 © 1960 Shamley Productions, Inc., & Universal Studios Licensing LLLP; 7.31, 7.32 © 1947 Twentieth Century Fox; 7.33, 7.34 Courtesy of Castle Hill Productions, Inc.; 7.35–7.38 © Paramount Pictures Corporation. All Rights Reserved; 7.39–7.40 © MMII New Line Productions, Inc. All Rights Reserved. Photo by David Lee. Courtesy of New Line Productions, Inc.; 7.41, 7.42 © Paramount Pictures Corporation. All Rights Reserved; 7.43, 7.44 Courtesy of Pathé Pictures; 7.45–7.51 Courtesy of Contemporary Films Limited; 7.55, 7.56 © Paramount Pictures Corporation. All Rights Reserved; 7.57–7.60 © ABC, Inc. All Rights Reserved. 8.1 © Paramount Pictures Corporation. All Rights Reserved; 8.2 Courtesy of Python Monty Pictures Limited; 8.7 © 1960 Shamley Productions, Inc., & Universal Studios Licensing LLLP; 8.8 American

ican Zoetrope; 8.9 Ghoulardi Film Company; 8.10 © 1931 Universal Pictures Company, Inc., Courtesy of Universal Studios Licensing LLLP; 8.11 Courtesy of Lucasfilm Ltd. © "Star Wars: Episode IV—A New Hope," 1997. All Rights Reserved. Used under authorization; 8.12, 8.13 Les Films Galaxie; 8.14 Metro-Goldwyn-Mayer (MGM); 8.15 © 2002 Les Armateurs / Production Champion / Vivi Film / France 3 Cinema / RGP France; 8.16, 8.17 © Paramount Pictures Corporation. All Rights Reserved; 8.18 Courtesy of American Zoetrope; 8.20 © 1999 Twentieth Century Fox; 8.21 © 2001 Touchstone Pictures. All Rights Reserved; 8.22 © 1967, renewed 2004 Columbia Pictures Industries, Inc. All Rights Reserved. Courtesy of Columbia Pictures; 8.23, 8.24 Paramount Vantage. 9.1 Bonne Pioche / Buena Vista / APC / The Kobal Collection / Maison, Jerome; 9.5 Cabin Creek / The Kobal Collection; 9.6 Discovery Films; 9.7 Courtesy of Magical Elves, Inc. (ph: Ian McIlgorm); 9.9 Courtesy of Chicago Historical Society; 9.10, 9.11 Courtesy of Fourth Floor Productions, Inc.; 9.13 Courtesy of Fortissimo Films & The Con; 9.14 Courtesy of Maysles Films, Inc.; 9.15, 9.16 Courtesy of Zipporah Films, Inc.; 9.17 Courtesy of Lions Gate Entertainment; 9.18 Palm Pictures / Umvd; 9.28 Vufku / The Kobal Collection; 9.29–9.31 Courtesy of Kino International Corporation; 9.32 Vufku / The Kobal Collection; 9.34 Courtesy of Olivo Barbieri & Brancoli Grimaldi Arte Contemporanea; 9.35 Courtesy of Anthology Films; 9.36, 9.37 Courtesy of Bruce Conner. Page 306 © Photos 12 / Alamy; 10.1 © 1939 Turner Entertainment Co. A Warner Bros. Entertainment Inc. Company. All Rights Reserved; 10.2 © 2007 Universal Pictures; 10.3 © Paramount Pictures Corporation. All Rights Reserved; 10.4 © 1944 Paramount Pictures, Inc. & Universal Studios Licensing LLLP; 10.5 Paramount Pictures, Inc.; 10.7, 10.8 Courtesy of Studio Canal Image; 10.9 Columbia / The Kobal Collection; 10.10 © Warner Bros., Inc. & MGM Home Entertainment LLC. All Rights Reserved; 10.11 Pixar Animation Studios; 10.12 Liam Longman © Adventure Pictures Ltd; 10.13 Field Guide Films; 10.14 © 2008 Voltage Pictures; 10.15 © 1994 Orion Pictures Corporation. All Rights Reserved; 10.16 © Universal City Studios Productions LLLP & Vulcan Productions, Inc.; 10.17 Focus Features/Kobal; 10.18 © 1932 Turner Entertainment Co. A Warner Bros. Entertainment Inc. Company. All Rights Reserved. 11.1 Paramount / The Kobal Collection; 11.2 © ABC, Inc. All Rights Reserved; 11.3, 11.4 Courtesy of Studio Canal Image; 11.5 © 1953 Columbia Pictures Industries, Inc. & Corinth Films, Inc. All Rights Reserved; 11.6 Courtesy of Contemporary Films Limited; 11.11 ShadowCatcher Entertainment; 11.12 South Pacific Pictures. 12.2 © 2006 Paramount Pictures Corporation. All Rights Reserved; 12.7, 12.8 © 2006 Universal Pictures. Courtesy of Universal Studios Licensing LLLP; 12.9 Twentieth Century Fox Film Corporation; 12.10 Galactic Films; 12.11 © 2008 Wild Bunch; 12.12 © 1938 Turner Entertainment Co. A Warner Bros. Entertainment Inc. Company. All Rights Reserved; 12.8 Universal / The Kobal Collection / Lee, David; 12.13 Damfx / The Kobal Collection; 12.14 © 1983 Universal City Studios, Inc. Courtesy of Universal Studios Licensing LLLP. 13.1 Stanley Kramer / United Artists / The Kobal Collection; 13.2 © 1931 Universal Pictures Company, Inc. Courtesy of Universal Studios Licensing LLLP; 13.3 © 1933 RKO Pictures, Inc. All Rights Reserved; 13.4 © 1978 Falcon International Productions. All Rights Reserved; 13.5 Courtesy of Canal + Image UK Limited; 13.6 © 2005 Focus Features & Universal Studios Licensing LLLP; 13.7 © Twentieth Century Fox. All Rights Reserved; 13.8 © 1959 Turner Entertainment Co. A Warner Bros. Entertainment Inc. Company. All Rights Reserved; 13.9 Courtesy of Studio Canal Image; 13.10 © 1951 RKO Pictures, Inc. All Rights Reserved; 13.12 © 1967 Universal City Studios, Inc. Courtesy of Universal Studios Licensing LLLP; 13.13 © 1933 Turner Entertainment Co. A Warner Bros. Entertainment Inc. Company. All Rights Reserved; 13.14 © Everett Collection / Rex Features; 13.15 © MGM Home Entertainment LLC & Studio Canal Image. All Rights Reserved. 14.1 RKO / The Kobal Collection / Kahle, Alex; 14.2 © 2006 Universal Pictures. Courtesy of Universal Studios Licensing LLLP; 14.3 © Paramount Pictures Corporation. All Rights Reserved; 14.4 © 1960 Shamley Productions, Inc. / Universal Studios LLLP & Alfred Hitchcock Estate; 14.6 © 2006 Lucasfilm Ltd. All Rights Reserved. Used under authorization; 14.7 Arnold Newman/Getty; 14.8 © 1950 Daiei Motion Picture Company; 14.10 © Ernesto Ruscio / Getty; 14.11 The Kobal Collection / Fefer, Stephane; 14.12 © 1955 Universal Pictures Company, Inc. Courtesy of Universal Studios Licensing LLLP; 14.13 © 2008 Voltage Pictures. 15.1 © 1969 Columbia Pictures Industries, Inc. All Rights Reserved; 15.2 © 2007 Blumhouse Productions; 15.3 © 1969 Warner Brothers / Seven Arts. 15.4 Frans Lemmens / Getty; 15.5 © Paramount Pictures Corporation. All Rights Reserved; 15.6 © 1982 Universal City Studios, Inc. Courtesy of Universal Studios Licensing LLLP; 15.7 © 1993 Universal City Studios, Inc. & Amblin Entertainment, Inc. Courtesy of Universal Studios Licensing LLLP; 15.8 © 1977 Oscilloscope Pictures; 15.9 Off White Prod. / The Kobal Collection; 15.11 © 2007 Diffusion Pictures; 15.12 © 2009 Momentum Pictures; 15.13 Courtesy of Lions Gate Entertainment.